# Building Websites

## ALL-IN-ONE

by Paul McFedries

for dummies®
A Wiley Brand

## Building Websites All-in-One For Dummies®

Published by: **John Wiley & Sons, Inc.,** 111 River Street, Hoboken, NJ 07030-5774, www.wiley.com



For general information on our other products and services, please contact our Customer Care Department within the U.S. at 877-762-2974, outside the U.S. at 317-572-3993, or fax 317-572-4002. For technical support, please visit https://hub.wiley.com/community/support/dummies.

Wiley publishes in a variety of print and electronic formats and by print-on-demand. Some material included with standard print versions of this book may not be included in e-books or in print-on-demand. If this book refers to media that is not included in the version you purchased, you may download this material at http://booksupport.wiley.com. For more information about Wiley products, visit www.wiley.com.

Library of Congress Control Number: 2026952066

ISBN 978-1-394-43153-3 (pbk); ISBN 978-1-394-43155-7 (ebk); ISBN 978-1-394-43154-0 (ebk)

SKY10169159_092226

# Contents at a Glance

# Table of Contents

## BOOK 2: DESIGNING YOUR WEBSITE

# Introduction

Here's a question I hear all the time, usually from someone wearing a slightly panicked expression: "I have to build a website. Where on earth do I even start?" It's a fair question. Maybe you run a small business and your web presence is three years out of date and looks it. Maybe you're the person at your company who got "voluntold" to handle the website because you're the one who's good with computers. Or maybe you're a manager who needs to understand what your web people do all day. Whatever brought you here, welcome.

Now let me let you in on a secret. Building a modern website is not the dark art that some people make it out to be. Sure, if you eavesdrop on professional web developers, you'll hear a lot of intimidating talk about frameworks and pipelines and something ominously called the *stack.* It's enough to make you want to close your laptop and take up a nice, quiet hobby, such as competitive napping.

But here's the thing: you don't need to know any of that to build a great website. Not today. The tools have become dramatically better, the shortcuts are plentiful, and there's a spectrum of ways to get the job done. At one end, you have point-and-click builders, where you never see a line of code. At the other, you have hand-crafted HTML and JavaScript for folks who want total control. Most people land somewhere in between. The trick is figuring out where on that spectrum *you* belong and then learning just enough to build something you're proud of. That's what this book is for.

So, take a breath. You've got this. And I'll be right here the whole way, pointing out the potholes so you don't have to discover them the hard way.

## About This Book

Welcome to *Building Websites All-in-One For Dummies.* My goal is simple: to take you from "I have no idea what I'm doing" to "I have a professional-looking website that gets results, that people can find, and that I understand." That's a big journey, which is why I've split this book into ten minibooks, each one covering a major piece of the website puzzle.

Along the way, you learn how to plan a site that meets your goals, design pages that look good on any device, write the HTML, CSS, and JavaScript that power the web (or how to skip most of that with a no-code tool, if that's more your speed), fill your site with content that both search engines and humans love, sell things online, and keep the whole operation running smoothly after it goes live.

I wrote this book with two readers in mind, and you're almost certainly one of them:

- **The webmaster:** The person (quite possibly the only person) who's been handed the job of building and running an organization's web presence and has to do most of the work solo. If that's you, consider this book your toolkit and your safety net.
- **The manager:** The person who needs a clear, jargon-free overview of how modern websites get built, so you can make smart decisions, ask the right questions, and tell when someone's blowing smoke. If you're that manager, consider this book your map of the territory.

Either way, you don't have to read every page in order. Think of this book less as a novel and more as a well-stocked toolbox: open the drawer you need, grab the right tool, and get to work.

# Foolish Assumptions

They say that assuming makes an, well, you know how the rest of that saying goes. But writing a book without making a few assumptions about you, dear reader, is impossible. So, here's what I'm taking for granted:

- **You can operate a computer.** You know how to launch programs, open and save files, and find your way around your operating system, whether that's Windows, macOS, or something more exotic.
- **You have internet access.** This one's non-negotiable for a book about building websites. (The nerve of me, I know.)
- **You know how to use a web browser.** You can type a web address, click a link, and juggle a few tabs without breaking into a cold sweat.
- **You have a reason to build a site.** Maybe you need a site for a business, a club, a portfolio, or a passion project. You don't need a fully formed plan (I help you build one in Book 1), but a rough idea of what you want helps a lot.

Note what's *not* on that list: any experience with coding, design, or web anything. I assume you're smart and curious, not that you're already an expert. If you were an expert, you wouldn't need me, and I'd have to go find another line of work.

## Icons Used in This Book

Like every *Dummies* book, this one parks little icons in the margins to flag certain kinds of information. Here's what each one means.

TIP

Tips point out shortcuts, timesavers, and clever little tricks that make your web-building life easier. When you see this icon, I'm handing you something worth tucking away for later.

WARNING

Heads up! This icon flags the kind of mistake that can cost you time, money, or dignity. When I mark something with a warning, it's usually because I (or someone I know) learned that particular lesson the hard way.

REMEMBER

This icon marks the important stuff: the key ideas and facts that keep coming up again and again. If you forget everything else on a page, try to hang on to whatever sits next to this icon.

## Beyond the Book

A lot of extra content that you won't find in this book is available at `www.dummies.com`. Go online to find the following:

- **The example files:** All the example files from this book — every snippet, page, and project, organized by book and chapter — are on GitHub at `github.com/paulmcfe/building-websites-aio-for-dummies`. You can view the code, copy it, and adapt it for your own site.
- **The book's cheat sheet:** Like all *Dummies* books, this one comes with a free online cheat sheet full of quick references. Just head to `www.dummies.com` and search for this book's title.

## Where to Go from Here

Well, that depends on you. (Told you this wasn't a novel.)

If you're new to all this, start at the beginning. Book 1 gives you the planning foundation and the big-picture understanding that makes everything else click into place. From there, work through the minibooks in order, and by the last page you'll have both a finished website and a real feel for how it all fits together.

If you already know your way around some of this, jump straight to what you need. Comfortable with HTML and CSS? Skip ahead to JavaScript in Book 4, or to SEO in Book 7. Just need to get a store online in a hurry? Book 8 is waiting for you. The minibooks are built to stand on their own, and whenever one topic leans on another, I point you to where to look.

If you're a manager who wants the lay of the land without getting your hands dirty, read the first chapter or two of each minibook. You'll come away fluent in what your team does and why, without having to hand-code a single thing.

Wherever you start, hang on to this thought: every professional web developer was once sitting exactly where you are now, staring at a blank page and quietly wondering if they were in over their head. They weren't, and neither are you.

Let's go build something.

# 1

# Getting Started with Your Website

# Contents at a Glance

IN THIS CHAPTER

» Figuring out what you want your website to accomplish

» Getting to know today's web

» Finding your niche in a crowded online world

» Creating a realistic budget and timeline

» Steering clear of common planning mistakes

# Chapter 1 Planning Your Web Presence

*A goal without a plan is just a wish.*

—ANTOINE DE SAINT-EXUPÉRY

Here's a secret that might surprise you: the biggest mistakes in website building happen *before* you write a single line of code or click a single "Add Page" button. They happen during planning or, really, during the *lack* of planning.

You've probably heard the carpenter's adage "Measure twice, cut once." In website building, it's more like "Plan twice, build once, and avoid rebuilding three times because you didn't think things through." Okay, that's not quite as catchy, but it's a lot more accurate.

This chapter helps you avoid those expensive do-overs by walking you through the essential planning steps that set up successful websites. You discover how to define clear goals, understand your audience, figure out your budget, and create a realistic timeline. To help things along, we're going to be building a project together throughout this book: Orbital Donuts, a space-themed donut shop that wants to take its confectionery game intergalactic. Grab a coffee (and maybe a donut), and let's get planning.

# Defining Your Goals and Target Audience

I know, I know: You're itching to get started picking colors, choosing fonts, or deciding between WordPress and Wix. But before you get to all that fun stuff, you need to answer two fundamental questions:

- What do I want this website to accomplish?
- Who am I trying to reach?

These questions might seem obvious, but you'd be amazed how many website projects skip right past them. Without answering these questions, you risk building something that's about as useful (and as visited) as a billboard in the middle of a desert.

## Setting clear goals

Your website goals should be specific, measurable, and realistic. Sorry, but "I want a website" isn't a goal; it's a statement of intent. Here are some examples of actual goals:

- **Generate leads.** Collect 50 qualified email addresses per month from potential customers.
- **Sell products.** Process $10,000 in monthly sales through an online store.
- **Provide information.** Reduce customer service calls by 30 percent by answering common questions online.
- **Build credibility.** Establish a professional presence that helps win three new business-to-business (B2B) clients per quarter.
- **Create community.** Build an engaged audience of 1,000 email subscribers within six months.

Note how each goal includes a number or a specific outcome. That's not by accident. Vague goals such as "increase brand awareness" are impossible to measure and even harder to achieve. You need to know what success looks like so you can tell whether you're getting there.

TIP

Write down your top three goals and put them somewhere visible during the building process. When you're deciding whether to add a feature or an element to your site, ask yourself: "Does this help achieve one of my three goals?" If the answer is no, you probably don't need it.

The owners of Orbital Donuts have three specific goals:

- **Drive foot traffic.** They want locals to see the menu and store hours to entice them to come into the shop. They believe their web presence can increase foot traffic by 20 percent within six months.
- **Sell merch online.** They have cool t-shirts ("I Need Space . . . and Donuts"), mugs, and other merchandise that they want to ship nationwide. Their goal is to eventually sell $5,000 of merch per month.
- **Catering inquiries.** They want a form where companies can order 500 Meteor Munchkins for office parties. The goal is to build up a catering client base of 50 companies within a year.

## Understanding your target audience

Once you know what you want to accomplish, you need to figure out who you're trying to reach. If you try to speak to everyone, you end up speaking to no one. You need to define your target audience, which will shape everything from your site's design to its functionality to the words you use. Some things to consider:

- **Demographics:** What are their age, location, job title, and so on?
- **Tech savviness:** Are they on mobile phones while walking the dog or on desktop computers in a corporate office?
- **Pain points:** What problem are you solving for them?

For the donut shop website, the target audience might include:

- **Local breakfast crowd:** People within 5 miles looking for quick morning food (ages 25–55).
- **Families:** Parents looking for treats for kids' birthdays or weekend outings.
- **Office managers:** People ordering donuts for workplace events.
- **Social media enthusiasts:** Younger customers (18–35) interested in a unique, Instagrammable food experience.

Each of these groups has different needs. The breakfast crowd cares about speed and location. Families want to see kid-friendly options and pricing. Office managers need bulk ordering capabilities. Social media folks want to take swoon-worthy photos of your galaxy-glazed masterpieces.

You can't be everything to everyone (that's how you end up with a confusing website that serves no one well), but you can identify your primary and secondary audiences. Orbital Donuts might decide that their primary audience is the local breakfast crowd, with families as a strong secondary focus.

## Creating simple audience personas

A *persona* is a semifictional representation of your ideal customer based on real data and educated guesses. Don't overthink this; you're not writing a novel! Some simple personas for Orbital Donuts might look like this:

**Morning Mike**

- **Age:** 32
- **Job:** Office worker
- **Needs:** A quick breakfast before his morning commute
- **Tech comfort:** Uses his phone for everything
- **Main concern:** "Is it open now? Where exactly is it?"

**Party-Planning Paula**

- **Age:** 39
- **Job:** Marketing manager, also a mom
- **Needs:** Order for daughter's birthday party
- **Tech comfort:** Shops online regularly
- **Main concern:** "Can I see all the options? Can I order ahead?"

You might create two or three such personas, but you don't need more than that. (If you think you *do* need more, that's a sign that your business model needs more focus.) The key is to keep these personas in mind as you make decisions. When you're designing your home page, ask yourself questions such as "Could Morning Mike find what he needs in 10 seconds?"

# Touring the Modern Web Landscape

The web has changed dramatically over the past few years, and understanding these changes will help you make better decisions about your own site. Let's look at what matters today.

## Mobile is no longer optional

Here's a fact that might shock you: more than 60 percent of web traffic now comes from mobile devices. For some industries, it's closer to 70–80 percent. This means that more people will see your website on a phone than on a desktop computer.

Creating a mobile-friendly website doesn't just mean you have to make things smaller. Mobile users have different behaviors. They:

- » Are often on the go (literally)
- » Have shorter attention spans
- » Are frequently multitasking
- » Expect instant loading
- » Are probably using their thumbs to navigate

Your website needs to work beautifully on phones, not just be a shrunk-down version of your desktop site. This concept — called *responsive design* — is so important that I dedicate an entire chapter to it later (Book 2, Chapter 3). For now, just know that mobile-friendliness isn't a nice-to-have feature anymore. It's the foundation.

## Speed matters more than ever

You know that feeling when you click a link and nothing happens for three seconds? That little voice in your head says "Did I click it? Should I click again? Is this site broken?" That's the voice of someone about to hit the back button.

Studies show that 53 percent of mobile users abandon sites that take longer than three seconds to load. Three seconds! Google now uses page speed as a ranking factor, which means slow sites get buried in search results.

The good news? You don't need expensive servers or advanced engineering to have a fast site. Most speed problems come from bloated images, unnecessary features, or poor hosting choices, all of which are things you learn how to control in this book.

### Accessibility is both right and required

Web accessibility means making your site usable by people with disabilities, including those who use screen readers, can't use a mouse, or have difficulty seeing certain color combinations. Creating an accessible website is not just the right thing to do (though it definitely is); in many cases, it's legally required.

The Americans with Disabilities Act (ADA) applies to websites, and businesses have faced lawsuits for inaccessible sites. The Web Content Accessibility Guidelines (WCAG) document provides the standards, and I cover accessibility in detail in Book 2, Chapter 4.

For now, remember that accessibility isn't a separate feature you add later. It needs to be baked into your planning from day one.

## Website versus Web Presence: The Full Picture

Here's where many people go wrong: they think building a website means creating a few pages with their address and phone number, clicking Publish, and calling it done. But your web presence consists of quite a few pieces:

- **Your main website:** The home base you control completely
- **Social media profiles:** Facebook, Instagram, LinkedIn, TikTok (depending on your audience)
- **Google Business Profile:** The information box that appears in Google search and maps
- **Review sites:** Yelp, TripAdvisor, industry-specific sites
- **Email marketing:** Newsletters, promotions, updates
- **Online directories:** Industry listings, local business directories

Think of your website as your house and everything else as the neighborhood. Your house is important, but people also encounter you through neighborhood signs, word-of-mouth, and seeing you around town.

## Why your website is still the centerpiece

Despite all these other platforms, your website remains your most important digital asset because:

- **You own it completely.** Facebook can change its algorithm tomorrow and tank your organic reach (it's happened before). Instagram can ban certain types of content. But your website? *You* control every pixel.
- **It's platform-independent.** When someone asks, "Where can I learn more about your business?" you can always give them one answer: your website URL. It works for everyone, regardless of whether they use Facebook, Instagram, or no social media at all.
- **It builds credibility.** A professional website signals that you're a real business. Try applying for a business loan or seeking a partnership with just an Instagram page!
- **You can do anything.** Want to add ecommerce? A blog? A booking system? Custom tools? You can do all that on your own site. Social platforms limit you to their features.

For Orbital Donuts, the website might be where customers discover the full menu, place catering orders, and learn the story behind those Orbital creations. Instagram is great for mouth-watering photos and daily specials, but when someone's planning a party or looking for the store's address and hours, they're heading to the website.

## Integrating everything into a cohesive strategy

The key is making all these pieces work together. Your Google Business Profile should link to your website. Your social media posts should drive traffic to specific pages. Your email newsletter should promote new website content.

A simple integration strategy for Orbital Donuts might look like this:

- **Instagram:** Daily donut photos with a link in bio directing now-hungry folks to the website menu
- **Google Business Profile:** Accurate hours, address, and website link

» **Website:** Clear links to Instagram, easy-to-find contact info, online ordering, a newsletter sign-up form

» **Email:** Weekly newsletter featuring new flavors with an Order Online button

Note how each piece feeds the others. That's the goal.

# Creating a Niche Strategy

The web is crowded. *Really* crowded. Nearly two billion websites are out there with more launching every day. So how do you stand out? The answer isn't to be everything to everyone; it's to be the perfect solution for someone specific. This is your niche.

Your niche is the intersection of what you offer and who needs it most. For a donut shop, "We sell donuts" isn't a niche; that's just a business description. But "We sell artisanal, space-themed donuts to customers who want Instagram-worthy treats" starts to carve out a specific identity.

Here's a simple exercise. Fill in these blanks:

> We help [specific audience] achieve [specific outcome] through [your unique approach].

For Orbital Donuts, it might be:

> We help adventurous food lovers celebrate special moments through unique, space-themed donuts that taste as good as they look.

Notice how this is more specific than "We make good donuts." That specificity helps you stand out and gives people a reason to choose you over the generic donut chain.

# Planning Your Website Budget

Let's talk money. Building a website can cost anywhere from $0 (DIY with free tools) to $50,000+ (custom design and development). That's not a typo — the range really is that wide. Happily, most small businesses can launch an excellent website for somewhere between $500 and $5,000, depending on their needs and how much they do themselves.

When planning your budget for the year, break it down into two buckets: the one-time costs associated with setting up the site, and the recurring costs associated with running the site.

| Item | Type | Estimated Cost | Notes |
|---|---|---|---|
| Theme and design | Setup | $0–$500+ | The look and feel of your site. Many great themes are free, but premium ones cost extra. Prepare to pay also for stock photos and a custom logo. |
| Content | Setup | $500–$2,000; or just your time | What appears on your site, including text and images. Getting others to write text and take photos is pricey. The DIY route is cheap but time-consuming. |
| Domain name | Recurring | $10–$50 per year | Your website address (for example, `orbitaldonuts.com`). A standard `.com` address is the cheapest. |
| Web hosting | Recurring | $5–$50 per month | The online space you rent to store and serve your website. Shared hosting is the least expensive; managed WordPress hosting costs more. |
| Plugins and apps | Recurring | $0–$100 per month | Extra site features such as fancy forms, email marketing, and backups. |

For Orbital Donuts, a realistic first-year budget might look like this:

- Domain name: $12
- Web hosting: $5/month × 12 = $60
- Stock photos: $120
- Logo design: $100
- Professional food photography: $500
- Total first year: Just under $800

Costs in years two and beyond would drop to around $100 (just hosting and domain renewal) unless the business owners add new features.

The biggest budget mistake? Underestimating the time investment. If you're doing this yourself, block out real time in your calendar. "I'll work on it when I'm free" usually means "I'll finish it in 18 months."

# Building a Realistic Project Timeline

Hofstadter's law: it always takes longer than you expect, even when you take into account Hofstadter's law.

Building a website is no exception. It *will* take longer than you think. Always. If you're certain you can get it done in four weeks, know for a fact that it will probably take eight.

Here's a realistic timeline for a DIY small business site (such as Orbital Donuts):

1. Planning (1 week): Goals, audience, and gathering content.
2. Design and setup (1–2 weeks): Picking a theme and colors, and setting up the hosting.
3. Content creation (2 weeks): Writing the About Us page, taking photos of the donuts, and writing menu descriptions. Note: this step is where most projects stall.
4. Building (1 week): Putting the text and photos onto the pages.
5. Testing (1 week): Clicking every link to make sure they work on mobile and desktop devices.

The total is about 6 to 7 weeks, which is typical. Can you do it faster? Sure. Should you plan on it? No.

# Avoiding Common Planning Pitfalls

I wrap up this chapter by looking at the mistakes that trip up even experienced website builders. Learn from their pain!

## Pitfall #1: Feature creep

Feature creep is the slow, insidious addition of just one more thing to your website. It starts innocently: "You know what would be cool? A customer forum!" Then it's "We should add a recipe section!" Then "How about some games?"

Before you know it, your simple business site has morphed into a complex project that never launches because you keep adding features.

**The solution:** stick to your three main goals (remember those?). Launch with what programmers call the *minimum viable product* (*MVP*), that is, the simplest version that accomplishes your goals. You can always add features later.

For Orbital Donuts, the MVP might be:

- Home page with hours and location
- Menu page with photos and descriptions
- Simple contact page
- Online ordering through a third-party service

The fancy custom ordering system, blog, and membership program? Those can wait for version 2.0.

## Pitfall #2: Perfectionism paralysis

In design circles, there's an old saying: the perfect is the enemy of the good. Yes, sure, you want to get things right, but if you spend months agonizing over whether the logo should be 2 pixels bigger or debating the pros and cons of 17 shades of blue, your website never gets built.

**The solution:** remember that websites aren't carved in stone. They're digital and endlessly changeable. Go ahead and launch a good-enough site and then improve it over time. Real user feedback is worth more than your internal debates anyway.

## Pitfall #3: Copying your competitors

Looking at competitor sites for inspiration? Smart. Copying them wholesale? That's a recipe for looking like a generic knockoff.

**The solution**: study your competitors to see what works and what doesn't but then find your own voice and your own design. Orbital Donuts shouldn't read and look like every other donut shop website. It should be Orbital Donuts through and through, with its unique space theme and personality.

## Pitfall #4: Ignoring mobile until the end

Designing your entire site on a big desktop monitor and then trying to make it work on phones is like building a model ship and then trying to get it inside the bottle: things are going to break.

**The solution:** think mobile from day one. Many designers now start with mobile designs and *then* expand to the desktop. This approach is called *mobile-first* design and is the practice you learn in this book.

## Pitfall #5: Forgetting about maintenance

Building a website isn't like building a shed. You can't just construct it once and walk away. Websites need updates, security patches, content refreshes, and ongoing attention.

**The solution:** budget time and money for maintenance. Plan to spend 2–4 hours per month on updates and maintenance. Schedule it on your calendar like any other business task.

## Pitfall #6: Skipping the testing phase

Launching without testing is like opening a restaurant (or a donut shop) without tasting the food first. You might get lucky, but probably not.

**The solution:** test everything. Click every link. Fill out every form. View it on your phone, your friend's tablet, your mom's old laptop. Get other people to test it too, because chances are they'll find issues that you've become accustomed to.

Remember that good planning doesn't guarantee a perfect website, but it dramatically increases your odds of success. Take the time to define clear goals, understand your audience, set a realistic budget and timeline, and avoid the common pitfalls that derail projects.

Now that you have your plan in place, the next chapter helps you choose the right approach for building your site. Should you use a website builder? WordPress? Code it yourself? Let's find out.

**IN THIS CHAPTER**

» **Figuring out your best approach**

» **Exploring visual tools and custom code**

» **Understanding the trade-offs**

# Chapter 2
# Choosing Your Web-Building Approach

*When you come to a fork in the road, take it.*

—YOGI BERRA

You've planned your web presence, defined your goals, and identified your audience. That's the hard work done, right? Hah, if only! Now you're faced with a decision that'll shape everything that follows: *how* are you actually going to build this thing?

The good news? You've got more options than ever before! The bad news? You've got more options than ever before! It's a bit like standing in the cereal aisle, staring at 47 varieties of granola. Having such a wide variety to choose from is great in theory, but the sheer abundance makes choosing nearly impossible.

This chapter's goal is to reduce all that paradox-of-choice anxiety by helping you pick the website-building approach that makes sense for your situation. Don't worry: this is a judgment-free zone. True, this book is geared toward those who want to code from scratch, but it's fine if you prefer to click your way through a no-code website builder. The only important thing is to find what works for *you*.

## Understanding What's Available

When it comes to building a website, I talk about four main approaches in this chapter. Here are quick descriptions of them:

- **Website builder:** An all-in-one service where you log in to a website, pick a template, and customize it using drag-and-drop tools. No coding is required. Everything you need (hosting, templates, tools) comes from one company as a complete package.
- **Page builder:** A visual design tool that works within an existing system (usually WordPress). Instead of writing code or editing text files, you drag elements onto a page and arrange them like you're working in PowerPoint or a desktop publishing program. The key difference from a website builder is that you're installing software on your website rather than using someone else's all-in-one service.
- **Visual tool:** A sophisticated design application that enables you to create professional websites visually, while the tool builds HTML, CSS, and JavaScript code behind the scenes. You're designing at a code level of precision without writing code. This type of tool sits somewhere between a website builder (very simple, limited control) and custom coding (complete control, very complex). Visual tools are powerful and produce high-quality results but have a steeper learning curve than a basic website builder.
- **Custom coding:** Building your website from scratch by writing HTML, CSS, and JavaScript files in a text editor. You create every page, style every element, and program every interaction by using code. Spoiler alert: This book offers a ton of guidance for custom coding, so in a sense I assume that custom coding will be your choice.

Okay, now that you know your choices, you can start weighing the pros and cons.

## The DIY Decision Tree: What's Right for You?

Before diving head-first into comparing all the different tools and platforms out there, it helps to start with the most important question: what's your situation?

That question is foremost because, surprisingly, choosing a web-building approach isn't about finding the best option. It's about finding the best option *for you right now.* Think of it like choosing a vehicle. A sedan, a minivan, a pickup truck, and a bicycle are all perfectly good ways to get from here to there, but which one makes sense depends on what you need to haul, how far you're going, how much you want to spend, and what you're comfortable driving.

For the four main website-building approaches that I define in the preceding section, here's a quick self-assessment to (I hope!) point you in the right direction:

Consider a website builder if

- You want to get online quickly (days instead of months).
- You're not particularly technical and don't want to become so.
- You need something that just works without much maintenance.
- You're working with a limited budget and can't hire developers.
- Your website needs are straightforward.

Consider WordPress with a page builder if

- You want a balance between ease of use and flexibility.
- You're comfortable learning new tools (but not necessarily coding).
- You like the idea of thousands of plugins to extend functionality.
- You want to own your content and have more control over your site.
- You don't mind a slightly steeper learning curve.

Consider visual tools if

- You have some design sensibility or experience.
- You want pixel-perfect control over how things look.
- You're willing to invest time learning a more sophisticated tool.
- You care deeply about performance and modern web standards.
- You want code-level control without having to write code.

Consider custom coding if

- You already know HTML, CSS, and JavaScript (or want to learn).
- You need something specific that no platform can provide.
- You want control over every aspect of your site.

- You have the time to build everything from scratch.
- You enjoy problem-solving and troubleshooting technical issues.

# Comparing Your Options

Now that you have a rough idea of what approach might be best for you, it's time to take a closer look at each approach. Think of what follows as your field guide to the website-creation ecosystem.

## Website builders

Website builders are the plug-and-play option of the web-building world. You sign up, pick a template, customize it with drag-and-drop tools, and boom — you've got a website. The process is like assembling furniture from IKEA, except the furniture assembles itself and you just decide where to put it.

### What's good

Website builders such as Shopify, Squarespace, and Wix handle the technical heavy lifting for you. Hosting? Included. Security updates? Automatic. Mobile responsiveness? Built in. You're essentially renting a complete solution rather than building and maintaining one yourself.

Most website builders offer

- Hundreds of professionally designed templates
- Drag-and-drop editors that work like visual design tools
- Built-in features such as contact forms, galleries, and blogs
- E-commerce capabilities (though Shopify specializes in this)
- Automatic mobile optimization
- Hosting and security

### What's not so good

The trade-off for all this convenience? Loss of control and flexibility. You're working within the boundaries the platform sets. It's a bit like renting an apartment versus owning a house: everything works and someone else handles maintenance, but you can't knock down walls or rewire the electrical system.

Common limitations of website builders include:

- Templates all tend to have a similar feel.
- Customization options end where the platform decides they end.
- You can't export your site and move it elsewhere easily.
- Monthly costs add up over time.
- You have only a limited ability to add custom functionality.
- Performance can be slower than custom-built sites.

### When to choose this option

Website builders shine when speed and simplicity matter more than complete control. They're perfect for small businesses, portfolios, basic online stores, and any situation where you need to be online now rather than eventually.

### Cost reality check

Plans typically run $12–$40 per month for basic sites, jumping to $25–$70 per month for e-commerce features. That's roughly $300–$800 per year, which seems reasonable until you realize that's an ongoing cost forever.

## Page builders and WordPress

WordPress deserves its own section because it's a bit of a chameleon. It can be as simple or as complex as you need it to be. Originally a blogging platform, it now powers over 40 percent of all websites on the internet, from personal blogs to major media outlets.

Think of WordPress as a foundation and framework rolled into one. You start with a solid base, and then add features through *themes* (which control how your site looks) and *plugins* (which add functionality). But here's something that confuses newcomers: there are *two* WordPress options. `WordPress.com` is a hosted service (similar to Squarespace), while `WordPress.org` is the free, installed-on-your-own-server software that most people mean when they say "WordPress." I'm talking about `WordPress.org` here, the one where you have full control.

While you *can* build WordPress sites by editing template files and writing code, most people use page builders instead. Tools like Elementor, Beaver Builder, or `WordPress.org`'s built-in Gutenberg editor enable you to design pages visually.

## What's good

Here's a list of the main advantages of going the WordPress route:

- Thousands of free and premium themes to start from.
- Over 60,000 plugins for almost any feature imaginable.
- Active community and abundant learning resources.
- You own your content and can move your site anywhere.
- Scales from simple blogs to complex e-commerce sites.
- Since so many sites use WordPress, there's lots of help available should you get stuck.
- Generally more affordable than website builders over time.

## What's not so good

Here are a few disadvantages of choosing WordPress:

- More moving parts means more things that can break.
- You're responsible for updates, backups, and security.
- Plugin quality varies wildly — some are great but others are disasters.
- Performance depends on your hosting and how well you optimize.
- The learning curve is steeper than with website builders.
- Your site can become bloated and slow if you're not careful.

## When to choose this option

WordPress makes sense when you want flexibility without custom coding, need specific features through plugins, or expect your site to grow and evolve over time. It's particularly strong for content-heavy sites, blogs, and businesses that need room to expand.

## Cost reality check

WordPress itself is free, but you'll pay for hosting ($5–$50 per month), a premium theme ($30–$100 one-time fee), and possibly premium plugins ($50–$200 per year). Figure $150–$800 for year one, then $100–$600 annually after that. The more complex your site, the higher the costs.

# Modern visual tools

The visual tools category represents the new generation of web-building tools — sophisticated visual designers that give you the power of code without requiring you to write it. If WordPress is like furnishing a house with premade furniture, these tools are like having a workshop where you can build custom furniture without knowing carpentry.



## Webflow: Visual design meets web standards

Webflow is essentially a visual interface for writing HTML and CSS. When you design something in Webflow, you're not just moving pictures around. You're building real web structure and styling.

Webflow produces clean, standards-compliant code; you're not locked into some proprietary system. You're building a website using web technologies, but with a visual interface instead of a text editor. And while you can't edit the main underlying HTML structure, you can add and edit custom HTML, CSS, and JavaScript directly inside the Webflow visual builder.

## Framer: Interactive design made visual

Framer started as a prototyping tool and evolved into a full website builder focused on interactive, animated experiences. It's particularly popular with designers who want their websites to feel more like polished applications.

Framer excels at creating smooth transitions, hover effects, and interactive elements without touching JavaScript. If your website needs to feel dynamic and app-like rather than just displaying information, Framer might be your tool.

## What's good

Here are some advantages you enjoy when using modern visual tools:

- Professional-grade design control without coding.
- Excellent performance because sites are optimized by default.

- Built-in content management system (CMS) for managing content.
- Modern web features such as animations and interactions.
- Clean, understandable code under the hood.
- Responsive design is intuitive and visual.

### What's not so good

Here are a few disadvantages that come with using modern visual tools:

- A steeper learning curve than website builders.
- More expensive than most alternatives.
- There's a smaller ecosystem of templates and extensions.
- You need some design sense to use these tools effectively.
- It's definitely overkill for simple websites.
- These tools are far less popular than WordPress, so there's correspondingly less help available.

### When to choose this option

A visual tool makes sense when design quality and performance matter deeply, you have the time to learn a sophisticated tool, and you need more control than website builders offer but don't want to code. Visual tools are popular with agencies, designers, and businesses that view their website as a key part of their brand experience.

### Cost reality check

Webflow runs $14–$39 per month for basic sites, up to $74 per month for e-commerce. Framer is similar at $5–$30 per month, and up to $100 monthly for premium features. You're paying for sophisticated tools and good performance. Add design time or hiring a designer if you're not confident in your own design skills.

## Custom coding

Building a website with HTML, CSS, and JavaScript means creating your site from the ground up using the core technologies that power the web. And here's the good news: that's exactly what a large portion of this book will teach you to do.

When you code a website from scratch, you:

- Write HTML to structure every page.
- Write CSS to style every element.
- Write JavaScript to add interactivity.
- Figure out how to make the code work on the most common devices and browsers.
- Implement your own solutions for common features.
- Handle security, performance, and accessibility yourself.
- Build any backend (that is, server-based) functionality you need.



Let's use our Orbital Donuts example. Sarah Keaton, the owner, needs to get her new space-themed donut shop online quickly. She's great at making donuts and creating fun, cosmic-themed flavors, but she's never built a website before. She needs:

- An attractive home page with her branding
- A menu showcasing her donut flavors
- Information about location and hours
- Eventually, online ordering capabilities

For Sarah, diving into custom coding herself would be like learning to forge her own donut cutters. Sure, it's technically possible, but probably not the best use of her time. A website builder or WordPress would get her online quickly so she can focus on what she does best: making stellar donuts. Ah, but here's the thing: Sarah has a niece named Sally who's trying to break into web development. Sally's an HTML, CSS, and JavaScript wiz and has offered to custom-code the Orbital Donuts website for free (and for the occasional on-the-house donut). Yay, Sally!

## What's good

Here are some advantages that come with choosing custom coding:

- Complete control over every aspect of your site.
- No monthly platform fees (just hosting).
- No limitations on what you can build.
- You get exactly the features you need and nothing you don't.

- The best possible performance when done well.
- A deep understanding of how websites work.
- Skills that transfer to any web project.
- The ability to customize any platform or tool later.

### What's not so good

Here are some custom coding disadvantages:

- Requires significant technical knowledge.
- Building even a simple site is time-consuming.
- You're responsible for everything, including security.
- No visual editor or preview; you code and then check.
- Maintenance and updates are all on you.
- It's easy to make mistakes that affect functionality or security.

### When to choose this option

Custom coding makes sense when you want to truly understand how websites work; have complete control over your web presence; build skills that'll serve you for years; create exactly what you envision without platform limitations; and avoid ongoing platform fees.

If you picked up this book wanting to learn how to build websites rather than just assemble them from templates, custom coding is your path. Books 3, 4, and 5 will teach you everything you need to know.

### Cost reality check

Your time investment is the main cost. Expect to spend several weeks learning the basics and months getting truly comfortable. But once you know HTML, CSS, and JavaScript, you can build anything. Hosting is inexpensive ($5–$30 per month), and you'll have skills that work on any platform or project.

## Hybrid approaches

Here's something the marketing materials for all these tools won't tell you: you don't have to choose just one approach for everything.

Many successful websites mix and match different tools based on what makes sense for each part. This is called a *hybrid approach*, and it's more common than you might think.

## Real-world hybrid examples

Someone might use Squarespace for their main website because it's quick and looks good but then use a specialized service such as Shopify for the e-commerce store because it handles payments and shipping better. They're linked seamlessly and customers barely notice that they're on two different platforms.

Another person might build their main site with WordPress, use a third-party booking system like Calendly for appointments, embed a Typeform for customer feedback, and integrate Mailchimp for an email newsletter. Each tool does one thing really well, and together they create a complete web presence.

Here are some common hybrid patterns:

- A website builder and a specialized e-commerce platform.
- WordPress for content and custom-coded components for specific features.
- A visual builder (Webflow) for marketing pages and a separate application for user accounts.
- A static site generator (for those with technical skills) and a headless (backend-only; refer to Book 1, Chapter 4) content management system for content.

## When hybrid makes sense

Consider mixing approaches when:

- One platform handles most of your needs but falls short in one area.
- You're growing and need to add capabilities gradually.
- Specialized tools exist for specific features (booking, payments, forms).
- You want to keep costs down by using free or cheaper tools where possible.
- Different parts of your web presence have different requirements.

## The trap to avoid

The danger with hybrid approaches is complexity. Every additional platform means another login, another set of features to learn, another potential point of failure. Don't use ten different services when three would do the job.

Start simple and add complexity only when you have a clear reason. Three well-chosen tools that work together smoothly beat seven mediocre ones that barely integrate.

# Making Your Decision

You've absorbed a lot of information in this chapter, so I'd like to bring it together with a practical framework for making your choice.

## Start with your constraints

What are your hard limits? Consider:

- **Budget:** How much can you spend upfront and monthly?
- **Time:** When do you need to be online?
- **Skills:** What do you know now and what are you willing to learn?
- **Growth:** How might your needs change in the next year? Three years?

For Orbital Donuts, Sarah's constraints are:

- **Budget:** $500 to start, $50 per month ongoing.
- **Time:** Go live in two months.
- **Skills:** She has an awesome niece with coding skills.
- **Growth:** She definitely wants to add online ordering sooner rather than later.

Those constraints point strongly toward the custom-coding option.

## Test before committing

Most platforms offer free trials. Use them! Spend a few hours building sample pages to get a feel for each tool. You'll quickly discover which interfaces make sense and which feel like wrestling with an octopus.

Build the same simple page on three different platforms. Include:

- A header with logo and navigation
- A hero (screen-filling) image with a headline

- A few paragraphs of text
- An image gallery
- A contact form

Whichever tool makes this easiest and most enjoyable is probably your best bet.

## Consider the whole picture

Don't optimize for just one factor. The best platform balances multiple needs:

- Ease of use versus flexibility
- Initial cost versus ongoing costs
- Speed to launch versus room to grow
- Platform control versus your control
- Features included versus features you need

Sarah doesn't need the most flexible platform (custom code) or the fastest to launch (website builder with zero customization). She needs the sweet spot that gets her online quickly while leaving room to add features as her business grows.

## Your decision framework

Here's a simple way to think about making a decision:

- Choose a website builder if getting online quickly matters more than having complete control, and your needs fit within standard templates.
- Choose WordPress if you want flexibility to grow and don't mind managing more complexity or you need specific features available through plugins.
- Choose a visual tool if design quality and performance matter deeply, you have time to learn, and your budget supports the investment.
- Choose custom coding if you're already technical, need something unique, or view learning to code as valuable in itself.
- Choose a hybrid approach if no single platform handles all your needs well, but be careful not to overcomplicate things.

## Moving Forward

The platform you choose today isn't necessarily the one you'll use forever. Many successful website owners have migrated between platforms as their needs evolved. What matters is choosing something that works for your current situation and doesn't make future growth unnecessarily difficult.

For our Orbital Donuts example, Sarah is going to use custom code because she wants complete control over the look and feel of the site and because she wants the flexibility to add features as needed.

Your choice might be different, and that's fine. There's no single right answer, only the right answer for your specific situation.

Remember: the best platform is the one you'll actually use to get your website online and maintained. Analysis paralysis helps no one. Make an informed choice, commit to it, and start building. You can always adjust course later if needed.

IN THIS CHAPTER

» Getting to know domain names

» Registering your very own domain

» Choosing a web host

» Getting yourself ready to get on the web

# Chapter 3

# Domain Names and Web Hosting

*The beginning of wisdom is to call things by their proper name.*

—CONFUCIUS

You've got your website plan, you've chosen your building approach, so now it's time to start creating, right? Hold on! Before you write your first HTML tag, it's a good idea to check two important items off your "Build a Website" to-do list: register a domain name (your website's address) and choose a web host (the digital plot of land where your site will live). Getting these two vital tasks done now will mean it will be easier down the road to test your site online and, eventually, to launch your site for all the world to marvel over.

The good news? Getting a domain name and setting up hosting is far easier than you might think. The not-so-good news? There are enough options, technical terms, and potential pitfalls to make your head spin if you're not prepared. That's where this chapter comes in. I walk you through everything you need to know about domain names and web hosting, from the basics of how they work to practical advice on choosing the right services for your needs.

# What's in a Domain Name?

Every website needs an address — a way for people to find it among the billions (literally!) of other sites on the internet. That address is known in the web trade as a *domain name,* and it's what people type into their browser to visit your site. For the Orbital Donuts website, the address will likely be a domain name along the lines of `orbitaldonuts.com`.

But here's the thing: domain names aren't how computers find websites. Behind the scenes, every website lives at a numeric address called an *IP (Internet Protocol) address,* which is something like 204.109.10.55. Ew. Imagine if you had to memorize number sequences like that for every website you wanted to visit! Domain names exist to spare us that nightmare. They're the human-friendly version that gets translated into computer-friendly numbers.

When you type a domain name in your browser, a technology called DNS (Domain Name System) springs into action, looking up the numeric IP address associated with that name. It's like having a massive phone book for the internet: look up a name and get back a number. The process happens way behind the scenes in milliseconds, which is why you barely notice it.

Domain names have a specific structure. Take `orbitaldonuts.com` as an example:

- The `.com` part is called the *top-level domain,* or *TLD*. Other common TLDs are `.edu` (educational institutions), `.org` (organizations, especially non-profits), and `.gov` (governments). There are also country-specific TLDs, such as `.ca` (Canada) and `.uk` (United Kingdom), and specialty TLDs, such as `.blog` (blogs, duh), `.website` (obvs), and `.me` (look at you!).
- The `orbitaldonuts` part is called the *second-level domain.*
- Together, they form your complete domain name, or what some nerds insist on calling your *root domain name.*

You'll also see domain names with additional parts, such as `shop.orbitaldonuts.com` or `blog.orbitaldonuts.com`. That first part (`shop` or `blog`) is called a `subdomain`, and you can create as many of those as you want once you own the root domain. Subdomains are useful for organizing different sections of your web presence. For example, the folks at Orbital Donuts might use `www.orbitaldonuts.com` for their main site, `shop.orbitaldonuts.com` for their online store, and `blog.orbitaldonuts.com` for their company blog.

REMEMBER

The www subdomain is so common that most people don't even think of it as a subdomain anymore. These days, it's optional because orbitaldonuts.com and www.orbitaldonuts.com can point to the same place, and most websites are set up that way.

# Domain Privacy and Protection

When you register a domain, you're required to provide contact information: your name, address, email, and phone number. This information gets added to the WHOIS (pronounced "who is") database, a public directory that anyone can search. Yes, that means by default, your personal information is available for the world to see.

This creates two problems. First, it's a privacy concern if you're registering a domain with your personal information. Second, it's a spam magnet — once your information is in WHOIS, expect an influx of spam emails and phone calls from people trying to sell you search engine optimization services, security certificates, and all manner of other things you probably don't need.

The solution is *domain privacy* (also called WHOIS privacy or privacy protection). This service, offered by most registrars, replaces your personal information in the WHOIS database with the registrar's contact information. Anyone searching for your domain's owner will see the registrar's details instead of yours. Your information is still on file with the registrar; it just isn't publicly visible. Whew!

Some registrars include domain privacy for free; others charge anywhere from $5 to $15 per year. It's worth every penny if you value your privacy and sanity. When comparing domain registrars, factor in whether privacy protection is included or costs extra.

TIP

Some TLDs such as .ca (Canada) and .uk (United Kingdom) include privacy by default or don't publicly display registrant details. If you're eligible to register one of these country-specific domains, you might get built-in privacy.

# Choosing and Registering Your Domain

Picking the right domain name is part art, part strategy, and part availability roulette. The perfect domain might already be taken (spoiler alert: it probably is), so you'll need to be creative while still staying true to your brand.

Here are the key principles for choosing a good domain name:

- **Keep it short and memorable.** Shorter is almost always better. orbitaldonuts.com beats orbitaldonutscoffeeshop.com every time. I wrote *almost* because a too-short domain — such as, say, ordo.com — can be hard to read, remember, and understand. People need to be able to remember your domain after hearing it once, and they definitely need to be able to type it without making errors.
- **Make it easy to spell.** Avoid unusual spellings or words that people commonly misspell. If your business name is "The Backwards Store," resist the temptation to get cute with the domain name sdrawkcab.com. Nobody wants to type that.
- **Avoid numbers and hyphens.** Both create confusion. If your shop is named *Tea for Two*, go with teafortwo.com. Yes, teafor2.com is shorter, but no one will get it right. And definitely don't go with tea-for-two.com just because now you can see the words easier. Save yourself (and your customers) the hassle.
- **Choose the right TLD.** The .com extension is still the gold standard: it's what people expect and what they'll try first. But with millions of .com domains already registered, you might need to consider alternatives like .net, .shop, .cafe, or even industry-specific options like .pizza or .space (hmmm, that just might be perfect for a space-themed donut shop!). Just be aware that anything other than .com requires a bit more customer education.
- **Consider your long-term plans.** Choosing a domain that reflects what you do or what your business does is perfectly fine. However, it pays to give some thought to where you or your business might be in five years. If Orbital Donuts might expand beyond donuts someday, maybe orbitalcafe.com would be a better, more flexible choice than orbitaldonuts.com.
- **Check availability everywhere.** Before you fall in love with a domain name, make sure the corresponding social media handles are available too. There's not much point in registering orbitaldonuts.whatever if @orbitaldonuts is already taken on Instagram, X, and Facebook. Tools like Namechecker (https://namechecker.org/) can help you verify availability across multiple platforms at once.

Once you've settled on a domain name (or, even better, have a short list of your preferred options), it's time to register it. You do this through a *domain registrar*, a company authorized to register domain names on your behalf. Popular registrars include:

- **Cloudflare (cloudflare.com):** At-cost domain pricing with excellent included features.

- **GoDaddy (`godaddy.com`):** The biggest registrar, though notorious for aggressive upselling.
- **Hover (`hover.com`):** A clean interface and no upselling pressure.
- **Namecheap (`namecheap.com`):** Great prices and a nice, intuitive interface.
- **Squarespace Domains (`domains.squarespace.com`):** Mid-level pricing that comes with lots of bells and whistles.

Domain registration costs vary by registrar and TLD, but expect to pay somewhere between $10 and $20 per year for a `.com` domain. Some hosting companies (which I get to shortly) throw in a free domain registration for the first year when you sign up for hosting.

WARNING

Watch out for registrars and hosts that advertise free or rock-bottom first-year prices like $2.99 but then jack up the renewal rate to $25 or more. Always check the renewal price before committing.

The registration process is straightforward: you search for your desired domain, add it to your cart if it's available, and provide your contact information. You'll typically register for one year at a time, though you can prepay for multiple years if you want to lock in the current price and ensure that you don't accidentally let the domain expire.

TIP

Set up auto-renewal for your domain. Losing a domain because you forgot to renew it is a nightmare. Someone else will snap it up immediately and getting it back can be expensive or impossible. Most registrars offer auto-renewal; turn it on and forget about it.



## DNS Basics: What You Need to Know

As mentioned, DNS is the system that translates domain names into IP addresses. Let's dig a bit deeper, because understanding DNS basics will help you troubleshoot issues and configure your domain correctly.

Think of DNS as a distributed phone book for the internet. When you type `orbitaldonuts.com` into your browser, here's what happens:

1. Your browser asks a nearby DNS server, "Yo, what's the IP address for `orbitaldonuts.com`?"
2. The DNS server says, "Hang on a second," looks up the domain, and returns the IP address.

3. Your browser says, "Why, thank you!," connects to that IP address, and loads the website.

This lookup happens automatically and almost instantly, which is why you rarely think about it. But behind the scenes, several types of DNS records make this magic happen:

- **A record:** Maps a domain name to an IPv4 address (such as 204.109.10.55). This is the most common and important DNS record.
- **AAAA record:** Maps a domain name to an IPv6 address (the newer, longer version of IP addresses, such as 2001:0db8:85a3:0000:0000:8a2e:0370:7334). Think of it as the A record's bigger sibling.
- **CNAME record:** Creates an alias that points one domain to another. For example, you'd use a CNAME (Canonical Name) record to make `www.orbitaldonuts.com` point to `orbitaldonuts.com`.
- **MX record:** Specifies which mail servers should receive email for your domain. You'll configure the MX (Mail eXchange) record when setting up email.
- **TXT record:** Stores text information, often used for verification or email authentication.

You don't need to memorize these, but knowing they exist helps when you're setting up your domain or troubleshooting. When you purchase hosting (up next), your hosting provider will give you the IP address or name servers you need to configure your DNS records.

WARNING

One more thing about DNS: changes take time to propagate. When you update a DNS record, it can take anywhere from a few minutes to 48 hours for the change to spread across all DNS servers worldwide. This process is called *DNS propagation*, and it's why you might see a change immediately while your friend across the country still sees the old configuration. Be patient — it'll sort itself out.

# Choosing Web Hosting Services

Your domain name is your website's address, but web hosting is where your website lives. Web-hosting companies provide space on *web servers*, which are specialized computers that stay connected to the internet 24/7. The web host sets you up with your own directory on the server, and that's where your website's files reside. When someone visits your domain, their browser requests the necessary files from your hosting server and then displays them as a website.

The web-hosting landscape is vast and sometimes confusing, with dozens of companies offering hundreds of different plans. The next three sections break down the main types of hosting you'll encounter.

## Shared versus managed hosting

*Shared hosting* is the most common starting point for small-business websites, and it's what you'll likely choose for your first site. With shared hosting, your website lives on a server alongside dozens (or even hundreds) of other websites. You're all sharing the server's resources, including its processing power, memory, and bandwidth. Think of it like living in an apartment building: you have your own unit, but you're sharing the building's infrastructure with your neighbors.

The advantages of shared hosting are clear: it's cheap (typically $3 to $10 per month), it's easy to set up, and the hosting company handles all the technical server maintenance. For a small business website that isn't expecting millions of visitors, shared hosting is perfectly adequate.

The disadvantages? Because you're sharing resources, a traffic spike on another website sharing your server could slow down your site. And if one of your neighboring websites gets hacked or does something shady, it could potentially affect your site too. Most reputable hosting companies have safeguards to prevent this.

Managed hosting takes things up a notch. With managed hosting, your hosting company not only provides the server space but also actively maintains your website software, handles updates, performs backups, and optimizes performance. It's like hiring a full-time website caretaker. Managed WordPress hosting is the most common type, optimized for WordPress sites.

Managed hosting costs more — typically $15 to $50+ per month — but it's worth it if you want someone else handling the technical maintenance while you focus on running your business. For sites built with page builders or custom code, managed hosting might be overkill. For WordPress sites, it's a game-changer.

Popular shared hosting providers include:

- **Bluehost (`bluehost.com`):** Officially recommended by WordPress
- **DreamHost (`dreamhost.com`):** Solid features, great for beginners
- **HostGator (`hostgator.com`):** Reliable with good uptime
- **SiteGround (`siteground.com`):** Excellent customer support and performance

Managed WordPress hosting specialists include:

- **Flywheel (`getflywheel.com`):** Designer-friendly with great features
- **Kinsta (`kinsta.com`):** Excellent performance and support
- **WP Engine (`wpengine.com`):** Premium managed WordPress hosting

## Cloud-hosting basics

Cloud hosting represents a different approach altogether. Instead of your website living on a single physical server, it's distributed across a network of connected servers — the *cloud. If* one server goes down, another picks up the slack automatically. Your website also draws resources from multiple servers, so you're not limited by a single machine's capabilities.

The main advantage of cloud hosting is scalability. If the Orbital Donuts website suddenly goes viral because a celebrity tweets about those galaxy-glazed donuts, cloud hosting can automatically allocate more resources to handle the traffic surge. With traditional hosting, that traffic spike might crash your site.

Cloud hosting is also more reliable because there's no single point of failure. And you typically pay only for the resources you use rather than a flat monthly fee.

The downside? Cloud hosting can be more complex to set up and manage, and the pricing can be unpredictable if you're not careful. For beginners, the complexity often outweighs the benefits until your site needs that level of scalability.

Popular cloud hosting providers include:

- **Amazon Web Services (`aws.amazon.com`):** The biggest, but complex.
- **Google Cloud Platform (`cloud.google.com`):** Robust but also complex.
- **DigitalOcean (`digitalocean.com`):** Developer-friendly with simple pricing.
- **Linode (`linode.com`):** Powerful and flexible.
- **Vultr (`vultr.com`):** Good performance at competitive prices.

For most small business websites, traditional shared or managed hosting is the better choice. Save cloud hosting for when you've outgrown traditional hosting or when you have specific technical requirements that demand it.

## WordPress-specific hosting

Since WordPress powers about 43 percent of all websites, it's worth mentioning WordPress-specific hosting separately. These are hosting plans optimized specifically for WordPress, with features like:

- One-click WordPress installation
- Automatic WordPress updates
- WordPress-specific security measures
- Caching configured specifically for WordPress
- Staging environments for testing changes
- Expert WordPress support

You'll find WordPress hosting in both shared and managed varieties. Shared WordPress hosting is basically shared hosting with WordPress preinstalled and some WordPress-specific optimizations. Managed WordPress hosting (which I mention earlier) takes it further by handling all the technical WordPress maintenance for you.

If you're building with WordPress, WordPress-specific hosting is worth considering but not absolutely necessary. Regular shared hosting can run WordPress just fine; you'll just need to handle the installation and maintenance yourself.



# Content Delivery Networks Explained

Here's a common scenario: you've built a beautiful website for your business or hobby and it's hosted on a server in, say, Virginia. Visitors from Virginia experience blazing-fast load times. But visitors from Tokyo? Not so much. Every image, every stylesheet, every JavaScript file has to travel halfway around the world before it reaches their browser.

That's where a Content Delivery Network (CDN) comes in. A CDN is a network of servers distributed around the globe, each storing a copy of your website's static files: images, CSS, JavaScript, and so on. When someone visits your site, the CDN serves those files from whichever server is closest to them geographically. Your Tokyo visitor gets files from a server in Asia rather than waiting for them to traverse the Pacific Ocean.

The benefits are tangible: faster page loads for visitors worldwide, reduced load on your hosting server, and better performance during traffic spikes. Many modern hosting plans include CDN service, or you can add one separately.

Popular CDN services include:

- **Amazon CloudFront (part of AWS, `aws.amazon.com`):** Powerful but complex
- **BunnyCDN (`bunny.net`):** Affordable with good performance
- **Cloudflare (`cloudflare.com`):** Excellent free plan, easy setup
- **Fastly (`fastly.com`):** Premium performance

For a small business website just starting out, Cloudflare's free plan is hard to beat. It's easy to set up (usually just changing a few DNS settings), provides meaningful performance improvements, and includes bonus security features.

TIP

Don't obsess over CDNs when you're just starting out. If your website is primarily serving a local audience — say, you're operating a physical shop in Chicago serving Chicago customers — a CDN provides minimal benefit. Focus on getting your site built first; you can always add a CDN later.

# Setting Up Email with Your Domain

Once you own `mydomain.com`, you probably want email addresses such as `info@mydomain.com` or `hello@mydomain.com`. Professional email addresses using your domain name look far more credible than using a free Gmail or Yahoo! address for your business.

You have several options for email hosting:

- **Email through your web hosting:** Lets you create email addresses using your domain name. Many hosting plans include email hosting. This feature is convenient because everything's in one place, but the email interfaces are often clunky and storage limits can be restrictive.
- **Google Workspace (`workspace.google.com`):** Formerly called G Suite, it gives you Gmail, Google Calendar, Google Docs, and other Google tools, all using your custom domain. Email addresses look like `yourname@yourdomain.com`, but they work through Gmail's familiar interface. Cost: $6 per user per month for the basic plan. This option is the gold standard for business email because it's reliable, professional, and packed with features.

- **Microsoft 365 (`microsoft.com/microsoft-365`):** Similar to Google Workspace but using Microsoft's tools — Outlook for email, Office for documents, OneDrive for storage. Cost: $6 per user per month for the basic plan. If you prefer Microsoft's ecosystem, this is the way to go.
- **Zoho Mail (`zoho.com/mail`):** A more affordable alternative with a limited free plan and paid plans starting at $1 per user per month. The interface isn't as polished as Google or Microsoft, but the price is right for budget-conscious businesses.
- **ProtonMail (`proton.me`):** A good choice if privacy is your top priority. ProtonMail offers encrypted email hosting with custom domains. Cost: $4.99 per user per month for the Mail Plus plan.

Setting up custom email typically involves configuring MX records (those DNS records I mention earlier) to point to your email provider's servers. Don't worry: every email hosting service provides step-by-step instructions, and most registrars and hosting companies have tools to simplify the process.

TIP

Start with Google Workspace or Microsoft 365 if you can afford it. The reliability, features, and professional interface are worth the cost. If your budget is tight, start with your hosting provider's included email and upgrade later.



# Pulling It All Together

Here's a recap of what you need to get your domain and hosting set up:

1. Choose and register your domain name through a reputable registrar ($10–$20 per year).
2. Add domain privacy protection if it's not included (free to $15 per year).
3. Select a hosting plan appropriate for your needs ($3–$50+ per month).
4. Configure your DNS records to point your domain to your hosting.
5. Set up email hosting with your custom domain ($0–$6+ per user per month).

For most sites, a realistic first-year budget might look like this:

- Domain registration: $15
- Domain privacy: Included or $10

- Shared hosting: $60 (averaging $5 per month)
- Google Workspace email (1 user): $72

Total for the first year: approximately $147 to $157. Subsequent years would be similar, though many hosting companies offer discounted first-year rates that increase upon renewal.

That's it! With your domain registered and hosting configured, you've laid the groundwork for your website. You've got an address people can visit and a place for your site to live. You're just about ready to begin the fun part: designing and building the thing. But first, the next chapter explains a bit more about how the modern web works.

**IN THIS CHAPTER**

- » **Understanding how browsers talk to servers**
- » **Getting to know HTML, CSS, and JavaScript**
- » **Learning about responsive and mobile-first design**
- » **Making sense of security and privacy**

Chapter **4**

# How Modern Websites Work

*People who are more than casually interested in computers should have at least some idea of what the underlying hardware is like. Otherwise, the programs they write will be pretty weird.*

—DONALD KNUTH

Before you start building your website, it helps to understand what's happening behind the scenes when someone visits your site. Don't worry, I'm not going to turn you into a computer science major here! But I am going to give you a Websites 101 course that I hope will demystify some aspects of the web's plumbing. Why? Because knowing the basics of how modern websites work will help you make better decisions about which technologies to use; it will be invaluable when you have to troubleshoot problems; and it will enable you to communicate more confidently and more effectively with developers or hosting support personnel when you need help. You won't turn into a nerd, but you will become nerd-adjacent (which is a good thing, believe me).

# The Client-Server Model Demystified

When you type a URL into your browser and press Enter, something interesting happens: within a second or two, you end up looking at a web page complete with images, styled text, and maybe even animations. Although navigating to a website seems ho-hum to most of us now, you can see that it's quite wonderful, even a little magical, if you step back a bit. But what really happened during those few seconds after you pressed Enter?

## Client, meet server

The answer involves what's called the *client-server model*, which is a complicated-sounding term for a process that's straightforward. Your web browser (Chrome, Firefox, Safari, or whatever you use) is the *client*. It's the thing asking for information. Somewhere out there on the internet, a computer called a *server* stores the website files. That server's job is to respond to requests by sending back the requested files.

Here's how the conversation goes:

1. Your browser (the client) sends a request: "Hey, I need the files for `orbitaldonuts.com`, please."
2. The request travels across the internet to the server where the website files for Orbital Donuts live.
3. The server receives the request, finds the files, and sends them back: "Here are those files you asked for."
4. Your browser receives the files and assembles them into the page you see.

This whole process is called a *request-response cycle*, and it happens every single time someone visits a web page. When you click a link? Another request. When you submit a form? Yep, another request. The client asks, the server responds, and the cycle continues.

What makes this model so powerful is its simplicity. The client doesn't need to know anything about how the server stores its files or what database it uses. The server doesn't need to know what kind of device the client is using or what browser they prefer. They just need to speak the same language, which brings us to HTTP.

## Understanding HTTP and HTTPS

The language that clients and servers use to communicate is called *HTTP*, which stands for Hypertext Transfer Protocol. (The *Hypertext* part is a bit of internet history. It refers to text that contains links to other text, which was revolutionary back in the late 1980s when the web was born.) HTTP is basically a set of rules that defines how requests should be formatted and how servers should respond.

When you see a URL that starts with `http://`, you're seeing HTTP in action. But these days, you're much more likely to see `https://` — note the extra *s* at the end. That *s* stands for *secure*, and it means the communication between your browser and the server is encrypted. *Encrypted* means the data is scrambled in a way that makes it unreadable to anyone who might intercept it along the way. HTTPS also verifies the identity of the server, which protects folks from being redirected to a fake site.

Why does encryption matter? If you're just reading a blog post about space donuts, encryption might not seem crucial. But if you're entering your credit card information to buy a dozen Cosmic Crullers, you definitely want that data encrypted. These days, pretty much all websites use HTTPS by default. It's become the standard, and browsers will warn visitors if your site doesn't use it and will usually prevent visitors from accessing the site.

REMEMBER

Every modern website should use HTTPS, not just sites that handle payments or sensitive data. Search engines like Google favor HTTPS sites in their rankings, and browsers display alarming warnings for HTTP sites, which will scare away your visitors.

# HTML, CSS, and JavaScript: The Foundation

When the server sends files back to your browser in response to a request, it's usually sending three types of files that work together to create the page you see. Think of building a website like building a house: you need structure (the framing and walls), style (the paint and decoration), and functionality (the plumbing and electrical). In web terms, that's HTML, CSS, and JavaScript, respectively. (For the moment I'm ignoring other common web page files, such as images and videos.)

REMEMBER

What follows is an overview of HTML, CSS, and JavaScript to get you oriented to how websites look under the hood. Don't worry if you don't understand some or even all of what's in the next few sections. I explain it all in glorious detail in Books 3, 4, and 5.

## HTML: The structure

*HTML* (HyperText Markup Language; look, there's that *hypertext* thing again) provides the structure and content of your web page. It's the foundation that holds everything else together. HTML uses *tags* — little bits of code wrapped in angle brackets — to define different parts of the page. For example, `<h1>` defines a top-level heading, `<p>` defines a paragraph, and `<img>` inserts an image.

Here's a simple example of HTML:

```
<h1>Welcome to Orbital Donuts</h1>
<p>Where every donut is out of this world!</p>
<img src="cosmic-cruller.jpg" alt="A glazed donut floating in space">
```

When a browser receives this HTML, it knows to display *Welcome to Orbital Donuts* as a large heading, show the tagline as a paragraph below, and then display the image. That's it. HTML just tells the browser what content exists and what type each piece of content is.

HTML doesn't care what the heading looks like. It doesn't specify the font, the color, or the size (beyond the general concept that `<h1>` headings are bigger than `<h2>` headings). That's where CSS comes in.

## CSS: The style

*CSS* (cascading style sheets) handles all the visual styling of your website: the colors, fonts, spacing, layouts, and basically anything that makes your site look like your site instead of a plain text document. CSS works by targeting HTML elements and applying styles to them.

Here's a simple CSS example:

```
h2 {
    color: orange;
    font-family: Arial;
    text-align: center;
}
```

This CSS rule says, "Find all `<h2>` elements and make their text orange, use the Arial font, and center them on the page." The beauty of CSS is that you can style multiple elements at once. If you have ten `<h2>` headings on your page, this one CSS rule styles all of them.

CSS is incredibly powerful. You can create complex layouts, add animations, make elements appear and disappear, and even make your site look different on mobile devices versus desktop computers. In fact, that last point is so important that it gets its own section in just a moment.

## JavaScript: The interactivity

If HTML is the structure and CSS is the style, JavaScript is the behavior. JavaScript is a full-fledged programming language that runs in the browser and makes web pages interactive and dynamic. Without JavaScript, the web would be a pretty boring place because every page would just sit there, static and unchanging, waiting for you to click a link to load another page.

JavaScript enables things like:

- Validating web form entries before submission
- Creating image carousels that automatically rotate through photos
- Updating parts of a page without reloading the entire page
- Creating interactive maps, games, or calculators
- Showing and hiding content based on user actions

Here's a simple JavaScript example that responds when someone clicks a button:

```
document.querySelector('#order-button').addEventListener('click', function() {
    alert('Thanks for clicking! Your donut order is on its way.');
});
```

This code locates a particular button on the page and listens for when someone clicks it. When they do, it pops up a message. That's a trivial example, but JavaScript can handle far more complex interactions, everything from real-time chat systems to full-featured web applications.

The key thing to understand is that JavaScript runs in the user's browser, not on your server. When someone visits your page, their browser downloads the JavaScript code and executes it right there on their device. This process is different from HTML and CSS, which the browser just interprets and displays.

REMEMBER

Although you can technically build websites without knowing how to code HTML, CSS, and JavaScript, understanding what these technologies do will help you make better decisions about tools, troubleshoot problems, and communicate effectively with developers or technical support.

# Understanding Responsive and Mobile-First Design

Pop quiz: what percentage of web traffic comes from mobile devices these days? If you guessed around 60 percent, you're right. (Depending on your industry, it might be even higher.) This means that most of your visitors aren't sitting at a desktop computer with a big monitor. Instead, they're looking at your site on a phone while standing in line at the post office or lying on the couch.

Here's the problem: a website designed for a 27-inch desktop monitor looks terrible when crammed onto a 6-inch phone screen. Text becomes too small to read, buttons become too tiny to tap, and horizontal scrolling — the ultimate user experience nightmare — becomes necessary to see the whole page. Yuck.

The solution is *responsive design*, which is a fancy way of saying your website automatically adapts to fit whatever screen size it's being viewed on. A responsive website might display content in three columns on a desktop, two columns on a tablet, and a single column on a phone. Navigation menus might be displayed as a horizontal bar on desktop but collapse into a hamburger menu (≡) on mobile.

## How responsive design works

Responsive design relies heavily on CSS features called media queries. A *media query* is a conditional statement that says, "If the screen is this wide (or this narrow), apply these styles instead." Here's a simple example:

```
.menu {
    display: flex;
    flex-direction: row;
}

@media (max-width: 768px) {
    .menu {
        flex-direction: column;
    }
}
```

This CSS says, "Normally, display the menu items in a row across the page. But if the screen is 768 pixels wide or narrower (roughly tablet size), switch to displaying them in a column instead." The browser automatically detects the screen size and applies the appropriate styles.

Responsive design also involves using flexible units instead of fixed pixel sizes. Instead of saying "Make this image exactly 800 pixels wide," you might say "Make this image 100 percent of its container's width." That way, the image scales appropriately regardless of screen size.

## The mobile-first approach

*Mobile-first design* is a philosophy that says you should design for mobile devices right from the get-go, and then add enhancements for larger screens. This might seem backwards. Shouldn't you start with the full desktop version and then simplify for mobile?

Actually, no. Here's why mobile-first makes sense: first, designing for mobile forces you to prioritize. With limited screen space, you have to figure out what's really important and what can be secondary or even hidden. This approach usually results in cleaner, more focused designs even on a desktop.

Second, it's generally much easier to add features than it is to remove them. Starting with a simple mobile layout and progressively enhancing it for larger screens is technically easier than starting with a complex desktop layout and progressively simplifying it for smaller screens.

Third, mobile-first aligns with how most people access the web these days. If 60 percent of your visitors are on mobile, doesn't it make sense to optimize for that experience first?

This section represents a mere taste of what it means to go mobile-first when designing your site. You get a deeper look a bit later, in Book 2, Chapter 1.

# What Are APIs?



Let's say you're building a website for a small retail chain, and you want to include a map showing your store locations. You could, in theory, build a map system from scratch, which means creating the map tiles, handling the zoom functionality, drawing the location markers, and so on. If that sounds like it would be hard, you're right. It would take months of work and require expertise in geographic information systems and other map-related esoterica.

Or you could use the Google Maps API and have a fully functional map up and running in an afternoon. That's the magic of APIs.

## Understanding APIs

An *API* (application programming interface) is a way for different software systems to talk to each other. Think of it as a menu at a restaurant. The menu lists what you can order (the available options), tells you what information you need to provide (your order), and explains what you'll get back (your food). You don't need to know how the kitchen works or what recipe they use — you just need to know how to order from the menu.

Web APIs work the same way. A company like Google provides an API that says, "If you send us a request in this specific format asking for map data about this location, we'll send back the information you need to display a map." Your website sends the request, Google's servers send back the data, and your website displays it. Simple.

APIs are everywhere in modern web development:

- **Payment processing:** Stripe and PayPal provide APIs so you can accept payments without building a payment system from scratch.
- **Weather data:** Various weather services provide APIs that let you display current conditions or forecasts on your site.
- **Social media:** Facebook, X, and Instagram offer APIs for displaying social feeds or allowing users to log in with their social media accounts.
- **Email:** Services like Mailchimp provide APIs for managing email lists and sending newsletters.
- **Shipping:** UPS and FedEx provide APIs for calculating shipping costs and tracking packages.

The key benefit of APIs is that they enable you to add sophisticated functionality to your site without reinventing the wheel. Someone else has already built the complex system; you just need to learn how to use their API to tap into it.

## RESTful APIs

Most modern web APIs follow a pattern called *REST* (REpresentational State Transfer). Don't let the jargon scare you. REST is just a set of conventions for how APIs should be designed. RESTful APIs use standard HTTP methods (remember those from earlier?) and organize information into logical URLs.

For example, a RESTful API for managing donut orders might work like this:

- **`GET /orders`:** Retrieve a list of all orders.
- **`GET /orders/123`:** Retrieve the details of order #123.
- **`POST /orders`:** Create a new order.
- **`DELETE /orders/123`:** Cancel order #123.

The beauty of REST is its consistency. Once you've worked with one RESTful API, you have a good sense of how others will work. They follow the same patterns and conventions.

WARNING

APIs often require authentication (proving you're authorized to use them) and may have usage limits. Make sure you understand the terms before integrating an API into your site. Some are free for small-scale use but charge fees once you exceed certain usage thresholds.

# Content Management Systems (CMS) Overview

Let me tell you a secret: most websites aren't built by writing HTML, CSS, and JavaScript by hand. Instead, they're built using a content management system, or CMS for short. A *CMS* is software that handles the technical complexities of running a website while letting you focus on your content.

## What a CMS does

Think of a CMS as the operating system for your website. Just like Windows or macOS provides a graphical interface so you don't have to type command-line instructions to use your computer, a CMS provides an interface so you don't have to write code to manage your website.

With a CMS, you typically:

- Create and edit pages using a visual editor (no code required).
- Upload images and documents through a friendly interface.
- Manage your site's navigation and structure.
- Install plugins or extensions to add new features.

- » Update your site's design by switching themes.
- » Manage user accounts if you have multiple people working on the site.

Behind the scenes, the CMS handles all the technical stuff — generating the HTML, managing the database, handling file storage, and serving pages to visitors. You just create content and make decisions about what you want your site to do.

## Popular CMS options

The CMS landscape is diverse, but a few major players dominate:

- » **WordPress (`wordpress.org`):** Powers over 40 percent of all websites. Free, open-source, and has a huge ecosystem of themes and plugins. Originally designed for blogs but now used for all types of sites.
- » **Shopify (`shopify.com`):** Focused specifically on e-commerce. Handles everything from product listings to payment processing to shipping. Monthly subscription.
- » **Wix (`wix.com`):** A visual website builder with an easy drag-and-drop interface. Great for beginners but less flexible for complex sites. Monthly subscription.
- » **Squarespace (`squarespace.com`):** Known for beautiful, design-focused templates. Popular with creative professionals and small businesses. Monthly subscription.

Each CMS has its strengths and trade-offs. WordPress offers the most flexibility and control but has a steeper learning curve. Wix and Squarespace are easier to use but more limited. Shopify is unbeatable for e-commerce but overkill if you're not selling products.

## Headless CMS: A modern twist

Recently, a new breed of CMS has emerged called headless CMS. Traditional CMS platforms handle both the back end (content management) and the front end (how the site looks and functions). A *headless CMS* handles only the back end. It stores and manages your content but doesn't dictate how it should be displayed.

This separation gives developers more flexibility. They can use the headless CMS as a content repository and then build custom front ends using modern web frameworks. The content can even be displayed in multiple places — on your website, in a mobile app, on digital signage, wherever — all pulling from the same content source.

For most small business websites, a traditional CMS is simpler and more practical. But if you're building something more complex or working with a development team, a headless CMS might be worth considering.

REMEMBER

Using a CMS doesn't mean you never need to think about HTML, CSS, or JavaScript. Even with a CMS, understanding these fundamentals helps you troubleshoot issues, customize your site, and make better decisions about themes and plugins.

# Web Security Fundamentals

It's time to talk about something that keeps website owners up at night: security. The internet is full of automated bots and malicious actors looking for vulnerable websites they can exploit. Before you panic, know that basic security isn't rocket science. You just need to understand the main threats and take reasonable precautions.

## Common security threats

Here are the main things you need to protect your site against:

- **Brute force attacks:** Attackers use automated tools to try thousands of username and password combinations, hoping to guess their way into your admin panel. The solution is simple: use strong passwords and limit login attempts.
- **SQL injection:** Attackers try to insert malicious database commands into your web forms. Sounds complicated, but modern web frameworks and CMS platforms automatically protect against this threat if you keep them updated.
- **Cross-site scripting (XSS):** Attackers try to inject malicious JavaScript code into your site that runs in your visitors' browsers. Again, modern platforms protect against this, but you need to be careful about allowing user-submitted content.
- **DDoS attacks:** Short for Distributed Denial of Service, this type of threat occurs when attackers flood your site with so much junk traffic that it becomes overwhelmed and crashes. Good hosting providers offer DDoS protection. Note that DDoS attacks are rare for small business sites.
- **Malware and hacking:** The ultimate nightmare — someone gains control of your site and uses it to spread malware, steal customer data, or redirect visitors to scam sites. You can prevent these threats by securing your site with a strong password.

## Essential security practices

The good news is that following a few basic practices protects you against most attacks. First, keep everything updated. Whether you're using WordPress, Shopify, or custom code, updates often include security patches. Putting off updates is like leaving your front door unlocked — eventually, someone will notice.

Second, use HTTPS (remember, the secure version of HTTP?), which encrypts data traveling between your server and your visitors' browsers. The encryption of HTTPS is handled by a cryptographic protocol named SSL (Secure Sockets Layer; these days it's actually TLS, short for Transport Layer Security, but everyone still calls it SSL). Most hosting providers now offer free SSL certificates through a service called Let's Encrypt, so there's no excuse not to use HTTPS.

Third, implement strong authentication. Use complex passwords (or better yet, a password manager), enable two-factor authentication when available, and limit the number of people who have admin access to your site.

Fourth, make regular backups. If disaster strikes and your site gets hacked or accidentally deleted, backups let you restore everything quickly. Many hosting providers offer automatic daily backups, but check whether the automatic option is available and back up manually if it's not. It's also a good idea to take a couple of minutes now to learn how to restore from a backup, because believe me you don't want to have to figure it out when you need it and are desperate to get your site back up and running.

Fifth, use security plugins or services. For WordPress sites, plugins like Wordfence or Sucuri provide additional protection. For custom sites, services like Cloudflare can filter traffic and block attacks before they reach your server.

WARNING

Never use *admin* as your username or *password123* as your password. These are the first combinations attackers try. Use unique usernames and strong passwords that mix uppercase, lowercase, numbers, and symbols.

# Privacy Compliance in Plain English

If you've visited websites recently, you've probably seen those annoying cookie consent banners: "This site uses cookies. Accept all? Reject all? Manage preferences?" Thank privacy laws for those.

## Understanding privacy laws

Two major privacy laws have reshaped how websites handle user data:

- » ***GDPR*** (General Data Protection Regulation) is a European law that went into effect in 2018. Despite being European, it affects any website that has visitors from the EU, which is potentially most websites. GDPR gives users control over their personal data and requires websites to be transparent about what data they collect and how they use it.
- » ***CCPA*** (California Consumer Privacy Act) is similar but applies to California residents. If you have visitors from California (and you probably do), CCPA gives them rights to know what data you're collecting, to request deletion of their data, and to opt out of data selling.

Other regions have their own privacy laws, and more are being enacted all the time. The trend is clear: user privacy is being taken increasingly seriously, and websites need to respect that.

## What these laws mean for you

Here's what privacy compliance typically requires:

- » **Cookie consent:** You need to tell visitors what cookies and tracking technologies your site uses and get their consent before setting most cookies. Those cookie banners aren't there just to annoy people (though they certainly do); they're legally required.
- » **Privacy policy:** You must have a clearly written privacy policy that explains what data you collect, why you collect it, how you use it, and how users can request deletion or opt out. No, you can't skip this.
- » **Data collection transparency:** If you're collecting email addresses, credit card information, or any personal data, you need to be upfront about it. Users have a right to know.
- » **User rights:** You need a process for handling requests when users want to see what data you have about them or request that you delete it.
- » **Breach notification:** If you experience a data breach, you may be required to notify affected users and authorities.

For small business websites, compliance usually isn't as overwhelming as it sounds. Major platforms like Shopify or WordPress have plugins and features that help with compliance. If you're working with a web developer, make privacy compliance part of the conversation from the start.

TIP

The easiest way to handle privacy laws is to minimize data collection. Only collect the information you need, don't share it with third parties unnecessarily, and delete it when you no longer need it. Less data means less responsibility and less risk.

## Cookie consent solutions

Setting up proper cookie consent used to be complicated, but now services can handle it for you. Tools like OneTrust, Cookiebot, or Termly can scan your site, identify all the cookies and trackers, and automatically generate compliant consent banners. Many are free for small sites.

The key is being honest about what you're tracking. If you're using Google Analytics, Facebook Pixel, or any advertising trackers, you need to disclose that and get consent. Users are generally okay with reasonable tracking — they just want to know about it and have a choice.

# 2 Designing Your Website

# Contents at a Glance

IN THIS CHAPTER

» Understanding user experience fundamentals

» Creating personas and information architecture

» Wireframing with modern design tools

» Designing mobile-first for today's web

# Chapter 1
# Modern Web Design Principles

*If you can't make something self-evident, you at least need to make it self-explanatory.*

—STEVE KRUG

Here's a fun fact: you could build a technically perfect website with clean code, blazing-fast load times, and bulletproof security, and *still* have nobody use it. Why? Because you skipped the design phase. And no, I'm not talking about making things pretty (though that helps!). I'm talking about thinking through how people will use your site, what they're looking for, and how to help them find it without frustration.

Think of web design as the architecture of your site, the blueprint that determines whether visitors feel welcomed and guided or confused and lost. Just as you wouldn't build a house without architectural plans (unless you *want* doors that open into walls), you shouldn't build a website without a solid design foundation. Fortunately, you don't need to be an artist or have a degree in design to create an effective, user-friendly website. You just need to understand some core principles and follow a proven process.

That's where this chapter comes in. Here you learn the fundamentals of modern web design in a way that makes sense even if you've never designed anything before. You won't become a design guru overnight, but you'll have the knowledge to make smart design decisions and avoid the most common pitfalls. And hey, that's a pretty good start!

# Learning Some User Experience Fundamentals

Before you dive into the nuts and bolts of web design, you need to know about *user experience*, or *UX* as the cool kids say. UX sounds highly technical, but it's just a way of thinking about *what it's like* for people to interact with your website. Do they find what they're looking for easily? Does the site make sense? Or do they feel like they've stumbled into a labyrinth designed by someone who really doesn't like people?

Good UX is invisible. When a website works well, users don't think about the design — they just accomplish their goals and move on with their day. Bad UX, on the other hand, is *very* visible. It's the "Where's the menu?" moment. It's the "How do I get back to the home page?" confusion. It's the "I give up. I'm going to their competitor's site" abandonment.

## The three-second rule

Here's a sobering reality: you have about three seconds to convince a visitor that your site is worth their time. In those three seconds, they're making snap judgments: Is this site trustworthy? Does it have what I need? Is it going to be easy to use? If the answer to any of these questions is *probably no*, they're gone. *Poof.* Back to the search results.

So, what makes someone stick around? A few key things:

- **Clarity:** They can tell immediately what your site is about and whether it can help them. For Orbital Donuts, a visitor should know within seconds that this is a donut shop (not a space museum) and that they can order donuts online.
- **Navigation:** They can see how to get to the main sections of your site. The menu should be obvious, not hidden behind some clever design trick that makes sense only to you.

- **Visual hierarchy:** The most important things on the page stand out. If everything is screaming for attention, nothing gets heard.
- **Trust signals:** The site looks professional and legitimate. This means no spelling errors, no missing images, no "under construction" pages from 2005.

Let's use Orbital Donuts as an example. Imagine two versions of the home page:

- **Version A:** A giant, screen-filling image (known in the trade as a *hero image*) of a beautiful glazed donut floating in space, with the headline "Out-of-This-World Donuts Delivered Daily" and two prominent buttons: "Order Now" and "View Menu." The navigation menu is clearly visible at the top.
- **Version B:** A cluttered page with five different font styles, multiple spinning animations, a pop-up asking you to subscribe to the newsletter before you've even seen the site, and a menu button hidden in the corner that uses an icon you've never seen before.

Which one passes the three-second test? Version A, obviously. It's clear, it guides you to action, and it doesn't assault your senses. Version B? That's a bounced visitor waiting to happen.

WARNING

Don't mistake activity for progress when designing your site. Just because you *can* add animations, parallax scrolling, auto-playing videos, and seventeen different fonts doesn't mean you *should*. Every element should serve a purpose, and that purpose should be helping your visitors, not impressing them with your technical abilities.

## The "don't make me think" principle

One of the most famous books about web usability is called *Don't Make Me Think* by Steve Krug, and the title pretty much says it all. Good UX means users don't have to puzzle out how your site works. They see a link, they know it's a link. They see a button, they know what will happen when they click it. They see a form, they understand what information you need and why.

Here's what "don't make me think" looks like in practice:

- **Use familiar patterns:** Put your logo in the top-left corner and make it clickable to return home. Put your main navigation at the top or side. Put your shopping cart icon in the top-right. These conventions exist for a reason: people have learned them, so why make them learn something new?

- **Use clear labels:** Don't call your "About Us" page "Our Story" or "The Journey" or "Who We Are" if the standard term works better. Don't be clever at the expense of clarity.
- **Provide feedback:** When someone clicks a button, something should happen immediately. A loading spinner, a confirmation message, *something*. A lack of response is confusing: Did it work? Should I click again? Did I break something?
- **Make links obvious:** Links should look like links — colored text, underlined, something that signals "click me." Sure, you might think it looks cleaner to have links that blend into the text, but you know what's cleaner? Links that visitors can find.

For Orbital Donuts, "don't make me think" means if you have a "Catering" section, don't hide it under "Special Services" or "Corporate Offerings" or some other vague term. Call it "Catering" or "Catering & Events" and be done with it. People searching for donut catering will look for the word *catering*, not your creative interpretation of it.

# Creating User Personas

Okay, pop quiz: who is your website for? If you answered "everyone," I have bad news: a website designed for everyone appeals to no one. You need to know specifically who you're designing for, and that's where user personas come in.

As I mention in Book 1, Chapter 1, a *user persona* is a fictional character who represents a segment of your target audience. It's like creating a composite sketch of your ideal user based on real data, research, and — let's be honest — some educated guessing. The goal is not to describe every possible visitor but to identify the main types of people who will use your site and what they need from it.

## Building your first persona

Let's build a persona for Orbital Donuts. Here's what you'd want to include:

- **Name and basic info:** Quinn, 34, Marketing Manager.
- **Goals:** Needs to order donuts for weekly team meetings, wants reliable delivery, cares about variety for different dietary needs.
- **Frustrations:** Tired of bakeries that require 48-hour notice, annoyed by confusing ordering systems, and frustrated when dietary options aren't clear.

- **Tech comfort level:** Uses smartphone for everything, comfortable with online ordering, and expects mobile apps to work smoothly.
- **What they need from your site:** Easy bulk ordering, clear allergen information, next-day delivery option, and the capability to save favorite orders.

Now, you'd probably want at least two or three personas. Maybe you also have "Dave, 19, College Student" who orders donuts at 11 p.m. for a study session and cares mainly about price and late-night availability. Or "Jennifer, 42, Event Planner" who needs to coordinate large orders for corporate events and cares about reliability and presentation.

Each persona helps you make design decisions. When you're deciding whether to add a feature, you can ask: "Would Quinn find this useful? Would Dave care? Would this solve Jennifer's problem?" If the answer is no across the board, maybe you don't need that feature. (Shocking, I know, but not every cool feature serves your users!)

TIP

Don't create personas in a vacuum. Talk to customers or potential customers. Ask them about their frustrations with similar websites. Watch them try to complete tasks on competitor sites. The insights you get from real people will be worth far more than anything you dream up in a conference room.

## Using personas to guide design

Once you have your personas, use them! Print them out and stick them on the wall where you work on your site. When you're making a design decision, pull out your personas and run through them:

> Decision: "Should we add a live chat feature?"
>
> Quinn's perspective: "That could be helpful for quick questions about allergens or delivery times."
>
> Dave's perspective: "At 11 p.m.? Nobody's going to be there to chat. I'd rather just have good FAQs."
>
> Jennifer's perspective: "I need responses to email inquiries within 24 hours, but chat seems like overkill for bulk orders."

Maybe the conclusion is to skip the 24/7 live chat, but make sure your FAQ section is comprehensive and your email response time is fast. See how that works? Personas help you see your site through your users' eyes, not just your own.

# Information Architecture and Sitemaps

Information architecture is where you start organizing all the stuff that's going to be on your website. *Information architecture* — or *IA* for short — is the practice of organizing and labeling your content in a way that makes sense to users. Think of it as creating the blueprint for how information flows through your site.

The goal of good IA is simple: help people find what they're looking for without making them think too hard or click too many times. If someone has to dig through five layers of menus to find your contact information, your IA needs work. If they can't tell the difference between Products, Services, and Solutions in your navigation, your IA needs work. (Seriously, what's the difference? Nobody knows, and nobody wants to guess.)

## Creating a content inventory

Before you can organize anything, you need to know what you're organizing. So, step one is to make a list of every piece of content your site needs. For Orbital Donuts, that might include:

- Home page
- Menu (with individual donut descriptions)
- General info about the company
- Store locations
- Online ordering
- Catering info
- FAQs
- Contact info
- Privacy policy
- Terms of service

Don't worry about organizing yet — just brain dump everything. You can always cut things later. In fact, you probably *should* cut things later. Most sites have too much content, not too little.

## Grouping and categorizing content

Now comes the fun part: organizing your content into logical groups. There are a few common approaches:

- **By topic:** Group related content together. Products, Information, Support.
- **By user task:** Organize around what people want to do. Order Now, Find a Location, Learn More, Get Help.
- **By audience:** Create sections for different user types, such as For Customers, For Partners, For Investors.

For most small business sites, a task-based organization works best because it matches how people will use your site. They're not thinking, "I wonder what's in the About section," they're thinking, "I need to order donuts."

So, for Orbital Donuts, you might organize the main navigation like this:

- **Menu:** Displays all donuts with filters for dietary needs.
- **Order Online:** Takes you straight to the ordering system.
- **Locations:** Store finder and hours.
- **Catering:** Everything about catering and events.
- **About:** Company story, values, contact info.

Notice what's *not* in the main navigation? Things like Privacy Policy, Terms of Service, and FAQ. Those go in the footer. Why? Because they're important but not primary tasks. People don't visit your site thinking "I can't wait to read their privacy policy!" (If they do, they might need a hobby.) But they might need to find that info someday, so the footer is perfect.

## Creating a sitemap

A *sitemap* is a visual representation of your site's structure — basically a family tree for web pages. It shows all your pages and how they relate to each other. Creating a sitemap forces you to think through your entire site structure before you start building.

You don't need fancy software to create a sitemap. A piece of paper works fine. Or use a free tool like FigJam, Whimsical, or even just Google Slides with boxes and arrows. The point isn't to create a masterpiece — it's to visualize your structure and spot problems before they become expensive to fix.

For Orbital Donuts, a simple sitemap might look like Figure 1-1.

```
Home Page
├── Menu
│   ├── Classic Donuts
│   ├── Specialty Donuts
│   └── Dietary Options
├── Order Online
├── Locations
│   └── Store Details
├── Catering
│   ├── Corporate Events
│   └── Weddings
└── About
    ├── Our Story
    └── Contact Us
```

**FIGURE 1-1:** A sitemap for Orbital Donuts.

See how that works? The indentation shows the hierarchy — which pages are subpages of which main sections. The hierarchy helps you ensure that nothing important is buried too deep and that your navigation makes logical sense.

# Wireframing with Modern Tools

Alright, I've talked about strategy and structure. Now it's time to start sketching out what your pages will *look* like. That's where wireframes come in.

A *wireframe* is like a blueprint for a web page. It shows the basic layout and structure without getting into colors, fonts, or images. A wireframe is all about placement: where does the header go, where's the navigation, what's in the main content area, where does the sidebar live? Think of it as the skeleton of your page before you add the flesh and clothes.

Figure 1-2 shows an example. (Yep, the text in Figure 1-2 is impossible to read, but the point is to demonstrate the layout, not the placeholder text.)

## The power of low-fidelity sketches

Here's a dirty little secret: the best wireframes are ugly. Really ugly. We're talking boxes, lines, and labels. No colors (except maybe gray). No images. No content. Just placeholders and layout.

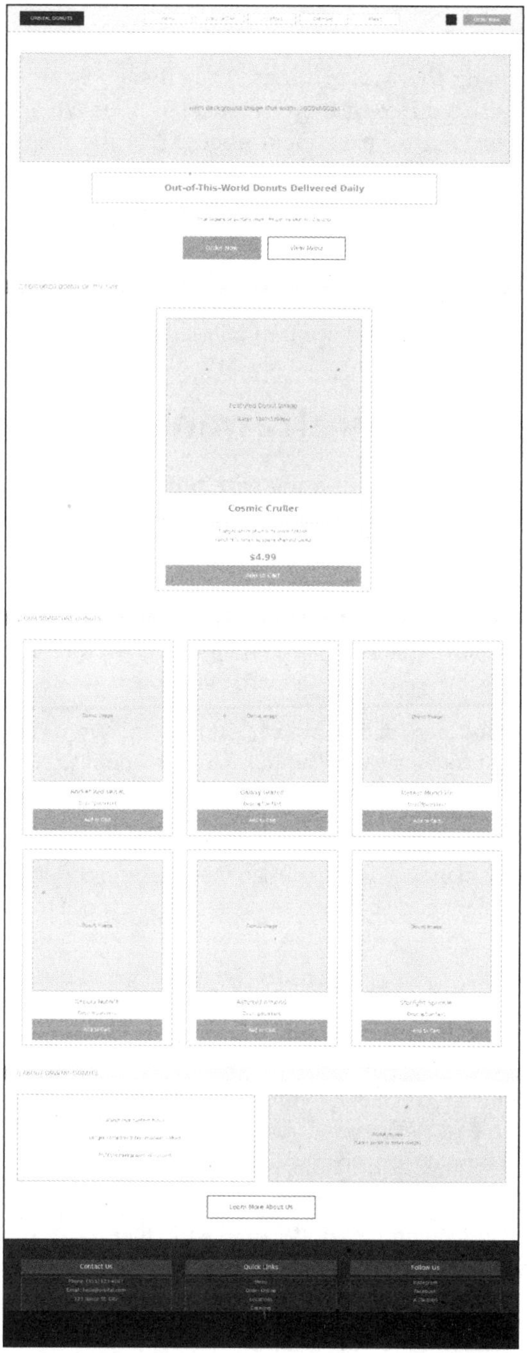


**FIGURE 1-2:** A wireframe for the desktop version of the Orbital Donuts home page.

Why deliberately make them ugly? Because when wireframes look too polished, people start critiquing the wrong things. They'll say "I don't like that shade of blue" or "Can we use a different font?" instead of "Does this layout make sense? Is the call-to-action button prominent enough? Is the navigation in the right place?"

Low-fidelity wireframes keep the conversation focused on structure and usability, not aesthetics. Save the pretty stuff for later — right now, you're just figuring out where things go. (And trust me, it's a lot easier to move a box in a wireframe than to redesign an entire page later because you realized the layout doesn't work.)

## Choosing your wireframing tool

You have plenty of options for creating wireframes, from dead simple to incredibly sophisticated:

- **Figma (`figma.com`):** Free for individuals, powerful for teams. Browser-based, so nothing to install. Great for collaboration — you can share a link and work together in real time. Has a bit of a learning curve, but tons of tutorials are available. Figma is the industry standard right now.
- **Adobe XD (`adobe.com/products/xd`):** Adobe's answer to Figma. Free starter plan available. If you're already comfortable with Adobe products, this tool might feel more natural. Integrates well with other Adobe tools.
- **FigJam (`figma.com/figjam`):** Think of it as Figma's casual cousin. More like a digital whiteboard than a precise design tool. Perfect for quick, collaborative sketching. Great for early brainstorming before you move to more detailed wireframes.
- **Balsamiq (`balsamiq.com`):** Intentionally sketchlike interface that forces low-fidelity wireframes. Good for people who might be tempted to make things too pretty, too soon. Has a free trial.
- **Paper and pencil:** Don't laugh — this is still a legitimate tool, especially for initial sketches. Fast, flexible, and you can't accidentally spend three hours perfecting a button design when you should be focusing on layout.

For most people, I'd recommend starting with Figma. It's free, it's powerful, and if you eventually work with a designer, there's a good chance they're already using it. Plus, the web-based nature means you can access your work from anywhere. (Which is either convenient or dangerous, depending on your ability to stop working.)

### What to include in your wireframes

A good wireframe shows the following:

- **Page structure:** Header, main content area, sidebar (if any), footer. The basic skeleton of the page.
- **Navigation elements:** Where's the menu? How do people get around? What about mobile navigation?
- **Content blocks:** Boxes that represent where text, images, forms, or other content will live. Use labels like Hero Image, Product Description, or Call to Action Button.
- **Interactive elements:** Buttons, form fields, dropdowns — anything users can click or interact with.
- **Hierarchy indicators:** Show what's most important through size and placement. The primary call-to-action should be more prominent than secondary actions.

What you *don't* need in your wireframes:

- Final colors
- Final fonts (just use a placeholder such as Arial)
- Images (use gray boxes with X's through them)
- Final copy (*Lorem ipsum* or *Headline Goes Here* is fine)
- Perfect pixel alignment

Remember, the wireframe stage is about answering questions like "Does this layout work? Is the flow logical? Are we showing users what they need to see?" not "Does this look good?" There'll be plenty of time to make it look good later.

## Mobile-First Design Strategy

Here's a stat that should change how you approach web design: more than half of all web traffic now comes from mobile devices. Not computers. Not tablets. Phones. Little screens that people hold in one hand while they're drinking coffee with the other or waiting for the bus or pretending to pay attention in meetings.

So, here's the thing: if you design for desktop first and then try to squeeze everything onto a phone screen, you're doing it backwards. That approach leads to awkward compromises, hidden content, and frustrated users who can't find what they need. The better approach? Start with mobile and work your way up. This approach is called *mobile-first design*, and it's not just a trendy buzzword — it's a fundamental shift in how you think about web design.

## Why start small

Designing for mobile first forces you to prioritize. When you have only a 360-pixel-wide screen to work with (that's a typical phone), you can't cram everything in. You have to make choices: What's truly essential? What can wait? What can we leave out entirely?

This constraint is a gift because it makes you focus on what matters most. For Orbital Donuts, that might mean the following:

- **On mobile:** Show the logo, a simple hamburger menu, and a prominent Order Now button. Below that, feature today's special and a few menu highlights. Make the phone number tap-to-call. Keep the page simple and scannable.
- **On desktop:** You can add a full navigation menu, a larger hero image, and maybe a newsletter signup, store hours, and upcoming events. The extra space lets you show more, but you're adding to a solid mobile foundation, not trying to shrink a cluttered desktop design.

See the difference? Starting mobile-first means you're enhancing the experience as screens get bigger, not compromising it as screens get smaller.

REMEMBER

Mobile-first doesn't mean mobile-only. It means you start with the most constrained scenario and then enhance the experience for larger screens. Everyone gets a good experience: mobile users get a site that works, and desktop users get extra features that take advantage of the larger space.

## Designing for thumbs

When people use their phones, they're usually holding them with one hand and navigating with their thumb. This means you need to think about what web designers call the *thumb zone:* the area of the screen that's easy to reach without repositioning your hand.

The middle and bottom of the screen? Easy to reach. The very top? Not so much. You need to stretch or use two hands, which is why so many mobile sites put their main navigation at the bottom instead of the top. It's not just a design trend; it's ergonomics.

Here's what taking the thumb zone into account means for your design:

- **Make buttons big enough.** Apple recommends at least 44 × 44 pixels for touch targets. Smaller than that, and people will mis-tap. A lot.
- **Add spacing.** Put some breathing room between interactive elements. Nobody likes accidentally hitting the wrong button because everything's crammed together.
- **Put important actions in the thumb zone.** Your Order Now button? Middle to bottom of the screen. Your logo? Fine at the top because it doesn't need to be interactive. (Though making it link to the home page is still a good idea.)
- **Consider a bottom navigation bar.** Use the bottom bar for key actions like Menu, Order, Locations, and Account. Easy to reach, always visible, and intuitive.

For Orbital Donuts, a bottom navigation might include Menu, Order, Locations, and Account. Tap any of these and you go straight to that section. No hunting through a hamburger menu, no multiple taps. Just one thumb-friendly tap and you're there. Figure 1-3 shows a wireframe for the mobile-first Orbital Donuts home page.

## Testing on real devices

Here's a critical point: don't just design for mobile by using Chrome's device simulator on your desktop computer. Yes, that's a useful tool for checking layouts, but it's not the same as *using* your site on a phone.

When you test on a real device:

- You discover that buttons you thought were big enough are too small.
- You notice that text you thought was readable is tiny.
- You find that things you thought were obvious are confusing.
- You realize that load times matter a lot more on mobile data than on your office Wi-Fi.

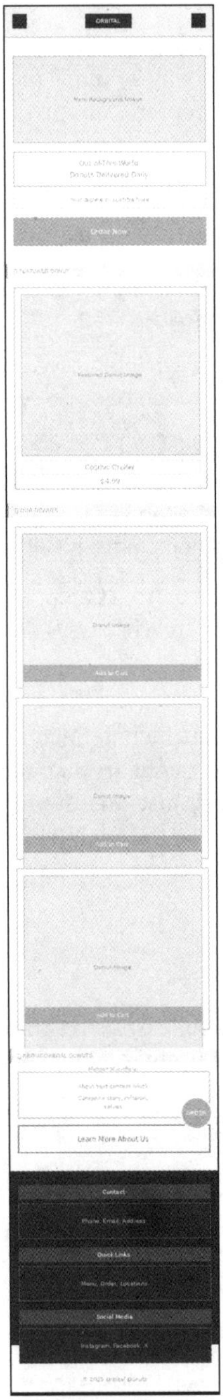


**FIGURE 1-3:** A wireframe for the mobile version of the Orbital Donuts home page.

Test on your own phone. Test on your friend's phone. Test on an older phone. Test while you're walking (carefully!). Test while you're standing on the bus. The real world is messier than your desk, and your site needs to work in the real world.

# Designing for Speed: Performance Considerations

Here's an uncomfortable truth: people are impatient. If your site takes more than three seconds to load, about half of your visitors will give up and leave. Three seconds! That's barely enough time to sneeze and say "excuse me."

Performance isn't just a technical concern — it's a design concern. Every image you add, every font you load, every animation you include adds weight to your page and increases load time. You need to make conscious choices about what's worth the performance cost and what's not.

## The performance budget concept

Think of performance like a budget. You have a certain amount of load time currency to spend, and you need to spend it wisely. A *performance budget* is a limit you set for your page — maybe you decide your home page can't exceed 1MB or must load in under 2 seconds on a 3G connection.

Having a budget forces you to make trade-offs:

> Trade-off 1: "We want that beautiful hero image, but it's 2MB. Can we optimize it to 200KB without losing too much quality?"
>
> Trade-off 2: "We want to use three custom fonts, but each font adds 100KB. Can we stick to one custom font and use system fonts for the rest?"
>
> Trade-off 3: "We want this fancy animation on scroll, but the JavaScript library is 50KB. Is the animation worth it, or can we achieve the same effect with CSS?"

For Orbital Donuts, you might decide that the home page hero image is crucial because donuts are visual, but you'll compress the image heavily. The menu page will use *lazy loading*, so images load only when you scroll to them. And you'll skip the parallax scrolling effect because it's not worth the performance hit.

## Design decisions that affect speed

Here are some design choices that have major performance implications:

- **Images:** Your biggest performance hog. Use modern formats like WebP that compress better than JPEG. Resize images to the exact dimensions needed — don't upload a 4000×3000 pixel image and then display it at 400×300. Use lazy loading for images below the fold.
- **Fonts:** Every custom font you load costs time and bandwidth. Stick to one or two fonts max. Consider using system fonts (fonts already on users' devices) for body text and save custom fonts for headlines.
- **Animation:** Subtle animations add personality, but heavy animations can bog down older devices. Prefer CSS animations over JavaScript when possible — they're much more efficient.
- **Third-party scripts:** Every Facebook widget, X feed, or Instagram integration adds external requests. Each one is a potential slowdown. Ask yourself: do we really need this?

The rule of thumb: every design element should earn its place. If it is not making the site significantly better and is costing performance, cut it. Your users won't miss what they never saw, but they *will* notice if your site is slow.

# Iterating on Your Design

Here's a secret that will save you a lot of frustration: your first design will not be perfect. It won't even be close. And that's okay! Good design is an iterative process: you create, you test, you learn, you improve, you test again. Lather, rinse, repeat.

The biggest mistake you can make is thinking you need to get everything perfect before launching. You don't. In fact, trying to achieve perfection before launch will likely mean you never launch at all. (Trust me, I've seen this happen many times.) Better to launch something good and improve it based on real feedback than to spend months perfecting something that might not even solve the right problem.

## Getting feedback early and often

Before you build anything, show your wireframes to other people: potential customers, your most critical friend, your tech-phobic aunt who still uses AOL. The more diverse your feedback pool, the better.

Ask specific questions:

- "What do you think this site is for?" (Tests if your purpose is clear.)
- "How would you order donuts from this site?" (Tests if your main task is obvious.)
- "What's confusing about this?" (Opens the door to honest criticism.)
- "What's missing?" (Catches things you overlooked.)

Don't ask "Do you like this?" That's too vague and people will try to be nice. Ask questions that uncover real usability issues. And when people point out problems, don't defend your design. Just listen and take notes. (Even if your inner voice is screaming "But that was intentional! They just don't get it!" Spoiler alert: if multiple people don't get it, it's probably not them.)

## The power of A/B testing

Once your site is live, you can use A/B testing to make data-driven design decisions. *A/B testing* means showing half your visitors version A of something and half your visitors version B, and then seeing which one performs better.

For example, Orbital Donuts might test the following:

- **Button color:** An orange Order Now button versus a blue Order Now button. Which gets more clicks?
- **Headline:** *Fresh Donuts Delivered Daily* versus *Out-of-This-World Donuts, Delivered.* Which resonates more?
- **Layout:** A hero image with text overlay versus a hero image with text beside it. Which performs better?

The beauty of A/B testing is that it removes guesswork. You don't have to argue about which design is better; you can see which one performed better with users. Just remember to test one thing at a time (so you know what made the difference) and run tests long enough to get meaningful data.

## Knowing when to stop

A fine line exists between iterating to improve and endlessly tinkering. At some point, you need to declare victory and move on to the next challenge. How do you know when you've reached that point?

Following are a few signs that it's time to stop iterating:

- Your changes are getting smaller and smaller (moving things 2 pixels left, adjusting colors by 3 percent, and so on).
- Users are accomplishing their goals successfully (high conversion rates, low bounce rates, positive feedback).
- You're iterating because you're bored, not because there's a real problem to solve.
- You catch yourself saying "just one more tweak" for the twentieth time.

Remember, perfect is the enemy of done. Your site doesn't have to be perfect — it just has to work well for your users. Once it does, move on to improving other parts of your web presence. (There's always something else that needs attention!) You can come back later if real problems emerge, but don't let perfection paralysis keep you from launching a perfectly good site.

IN THIS CHAPTER

» Building a strong visual identity

» Creating effective color schemes

» Matching fonts to your brand

» Working with modern image formats and optimization

» Creating style guides and design systems

# Chapter 2
# Visual Design and Branding

*Design is thinking made visual.*

—SAUL BASS

In the preceding chapter, I walk you through the foundational principles of web design, including understanding your users, creating information architecture, and wireframing your ideas. Now it's time for the fun part: making your website look good! (And I mean *really* good.)

Visual design is where your website transforms from a functional framework into a memorable experience. This chapter covers everything from choosing the right colors and fonts to optimizing images and creating design systems that keep your site looking cohesive. Whether you're building a site for your small business, your employer, or just yourself, the visual design decisions you make will have a huge impact on how visitors perceive you or your company. So, let's dive in and make something beautiful!

# Creating a Visual Identity

Before you start picking colors and fonts at random (tempting, I know), you need to think about your overall visual identity. Your visual identity is the distinctive look and feel that makes your brand recognizable across all touchpoints: your website, social media, business cards, everywhere.

Think about brands you recognize instantly. Apple's clean minimalism with its endless white space and simple typography. Nike's bold athleticism with that swoosh and strong, confident fonts. Target's cheerful red bullseye that feels friendly and approachable. Mailchimp's playful yellow and quirky illustrations. Patagonia's earthy, outdoorsy aesthetic with nature photography and rugged fonts.

These companies didn't achieve that recognition by accident. They developed cohesive visual identities and stuck with them, year after year, across every customer touchpoint. When you see that particular shade of Tiffany blue, you don't need to see the logo to know what company it is. That's the power of a strong visual identity.

Your visual identity should reflect your brand's personality. Are you playful or serious? Modern or traditional? Luxury or budget-friendly? Cutting-edge or time-tested? These aren't just abstract questions — the answers directly inform every design choice you make.

## Understanding brand personality

Let's say you're building the Orbital Donuts website. What personality should it have? Well, it's a donut shop with a space theme, so you want something fun and approachable, but not childish. You want to feel modern and fresh, since you're competing with established chains like Dunkin' and Krispy Kreme. And you want just a touch of whimsy because, well, space donuts!

Here's a useful exercise: pick three to five adjectives that describe your brand. For Orbital Donuts, I might choose: *playful*, *modern*, *cosmic*, and *delicious*. These adjectives become your north star when making design decisions.

Now test your ideas against these adjectives. If you're going for modern, would a script font from the 1950s fit? Probably not. If playful is key, should your color palette be all black and charcoal gray? Nope. If cosmic matters, would stock photos of generic coffee shops work? Definitely not. Your adjectives help you stay consistent and make decisions that all point in the same direction.

Let's look at how different brands express different personalities through design:

- **Luxury brands** (such as Rolex or Chanel) use lots of white space, serif fonts that feel classic and established, muted color palettes, and high-quality photography. Everything whispers rather than shouts.
- **Tech startups** (such as Stripe or Notion) often use bright, saturated colors, clean sans-serif fonts, bold geometric shapes, and illustrations over photos. Everything feels fresh and forward-thinking.
- **Eco-friendly brands** (such as Seventh Generation or Allbirds) lean into earth tones, natural textures, organic shapes, handwritten-style fonts, and imagery of nature. Everything feels grounded and authentic.
- **Kids' brands** (such as Crayola or LEGO) embrace primary colors, rounded fonts, playful illustrations, and energetic layouts. Everything feels fun and accessible.



Notice how each category makes consistent choices that reinforce the same message. That's what you're aiming for with your own visual identity.

## Creating a mood board

A *mood board* — a collection of images, colors, textures, and typography samples that capture the feeling you want to convey — is one of the best tools for developing your visual identity. Think of it as a visual brainstorming session where you gather inspiration without committing to a specific design yet.

You can create mood boards using tools such as Pinterest, Figma, or even just a folder of saved images on your computer. The key is to collect freely without overthinking it. If an image speaks to you and feels like it fits your brand personality, save it.

For Orbital Donuts, I might collect images of galaxies and nebulae in deep purples and blues, retro NASA posters with bold geometric type, modern coffee shops with clean minimalist interiors, close-up artisanal bakery photography showing the craftsmanship, and maybe some vintage sci-fi book covers. I'd look for examples where playful meets sophisticated — think NASA meets artisan bakery meets neighborhood coffee shop.

As you build your mood board, you'll start to notice patterns emerging naturally. Maybe most of your images feature deep blues and purples. Maybe you're drawn to sans-serif fonts with a bit of geometric flair. Maybe you keep saving images with lots of white space and one pop of bright color. These patterns reveal your instincts about the visual direction, even before you consciously articulate them.

Once you have 15–20 images, step back and look at them all together. What feelings do they evoke? What colors dominate? What styles of typography appear? What photography styles recur? This bird's-eye view helps you identify the common threads that will become your visual identity guidelines.

TIP

Don't just collect images of websites or designs. Include textures, patterns, architecture, nature, fashion, art — anything that captures the feeling you want. Sometimes a photo of weathered wood or a piece of mid-century furniture communicates more about your desired aesthetic than yet another website design.

# Understanding Color Psychology

Alright, let's talk about color. Color might seem like a purely aesthetic choice — you like purple, so you use purple, right? Well, not quite. Color is rooted in psychology and cultural associations, and different colors evoke different emotions and reactions in your visitors.

Understanding color psychology doesn't mean you need to become a color theorist, but knowing the basics helps you make intentional choices rather than random ones.

## The psychology of color

Different colors trigger different psychological responses. Here's what research and years of marketing experience have to say about common color associations:

- **Blue** suggests trust, stability, and calm. That's why you see it everywhere in banking (Chase, Capital One), tech (Facebook, the original Twitter, LinkedIn), and healthcare. It's the most universally liked color and feels safe and professional. But it can also feel cold or corporate if not balanced with warmer elements.
- **Red** creates urgency, excitement, and passion. It increases heart rate and grabs attention fast. You'll see it in food brands (Coca-Cola, KFC, McDonald's) because it stimulates appetite and in sale signs because it creates urgency. But too much red can feel aggressive or alarming.
- **Green** conveys growth, health, and nature. It's the go-to for organic brands, environmental companies, and health-focused businesses. It feels fresh, peaceful, and balanced. Whole Foods, Spotify, and Starbucks all use green to feel approachable and natural.

- **Yellow** radiates optimism, energy, and cheerfulness. It's attention-grabbing but in a friendly way. Snapchat and Best Buy use yellow to feel young and energetic. However, yellow can be hard to read and overwhelming in large doses.
- **Purple** suggests creativity, luxury, and wisdom. Historically associated with royalty (purple dye was expensive), it still carries an upscale, imaginative vibe. Twitch and Hallmark use purple to feel creative and distinctive.
- **Orange** combines red's energy with yellow's friendliness. It feels playful, confident, and adventurous. Nickelodeon and Home Depot use orange to feel approachable and fun without being childish.
- **Black** communicates sophistication, elegance, and power. Luxury brands love black because it feels exclusive and premium. Chanel, Prada, and Nike use lots of black for that sleek, high-end feel.
- **White** represents simplicity, cleanliness, and modernity. It creates space and lets other elements breathe. Apple's use of white space is legendary; it makes everything feel premium and uncluttered.



Here's the key insight: these aren't universal rules; they're cultural tendencies. In Western cultures, white suggests purity and cleanliness, which is why wedding dresses are white. In some Eastern cultures, white represents mourning. Red means good luck and prosperity in China but danger or stop in Western contexts. So, consider your audience and their cultural background.

For Orbital Donuts, the space theme suggests deep blues and purples (cosmic, mysterious, sophisticated), but you'd want to avoid making it feel cold or distant. Adding a warm orange or yellow as an accent color brings in that approachable, delicious feeling. The navy provides stability, the purple adds creativity and fun, and the orange makes it inviting.

## The 60-30-10 rule

Once you know which colors fit your brand personality, you need to figure out how to use them together. Professional designers often use the *60-30-10 rule* when creating color schemes. It's beautifully simple and works for everything from websites to interior design:

- **60 percent** is your dominant color, used for backgrounds and large sections. This color is usually a neutral or muted version of your main brand color. It sets the overall mood without overwhelming visitors.

- **30 percent** is your secondary color, used for content areas and supporting elements. This color adds visual interest and helps create hierarchy. It should complement your dominant color.
- **10 percent** is your accent color, used for calls-to-action, highlights, and interactive elements such as buttons and links. This color should pop and draw the eye to important actions.

For Orbital Donuts, I might use a dark navy blue for the dominant color (60 percent), creating a cosmic nighttime sky feeling for most backgrounds. A lighter cosmic purple becomes the secondary (30 percent), used for content sections and creating depth. And a vibrant orange, like a sunrise on Mars, serves as the accent (10 percent), making the Order Now button and important links impossible to miss.

This rule keeps your design balanced. Too many colors competing for attention creates chaos. Sticking to this proportion creates visual harmony while still allowing for personality and variety.

## Creating color harmony

Colors that work well together create *color harmony.* The color wheel — that circular diagram showing relationships between colors, shown in Figure 2-1 — gives us several tried-and-true approaches:

- **Complementary colors** sit opposite each other on the color wheel, like blue and orange or purple and yellow. They create high contrast and vibrant energy. They're attention-grabbing but can feel overwhelming if both colors are used at full saturation. The trick is to use one color as the dominant color and the other as an accent.
- **Analogous colors** sit next to each other on the wheel, like blue, blue-green, and green. These feel naturally harmonious and calm because they share similar undertones. This approach works great for creating a serene, cohesive look.
- **Triadic colors** are three colors equally spaced on the wheel, like red, yellow, and blue. These create vibrant, balanced schemes with lots of visual interest. Think of the Tide detergent logo — blue lettering on red and yellow concentric circles — hitting multiple, evenly spaced points on the wheel.
- **Monochromatic** uses different shades, tints, and tones of a single color. This approach creates a cohesive, sophisticated look that's nearly impossible to mess up. It's perfect for minimalist designs or when you want your images and content to be the focus.

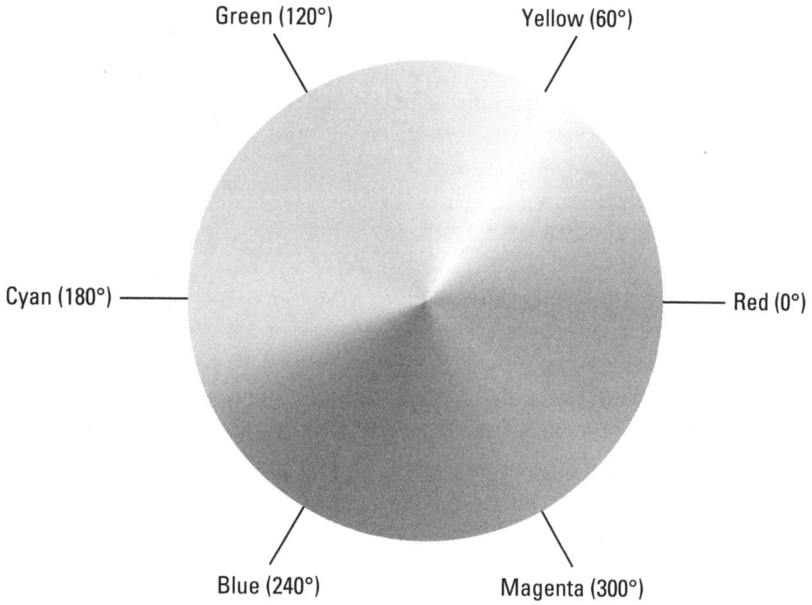


**FIGURE 2-1:** The color wheel with a few color values pointed out.



You don't need to memorize color theory or mix paints to create great color schemes. Tools like Adobe Color (`color.adobe.com`), Coolers (`coolers.co`), and Paletton (`paletton.com`) generate harmonious palettes automatically based on these principles. But understanding why certain combinations work helps you make intentional adjustments when a generated palette isn't quite right.

REMEMBER

Whatever colors you choose, they need to be accessible to everyone, including people with visual impairments. I go into this vital topic in detail in Book 2, Chapter 4.

# Making Text Sing: Typography for the Web

Typography is huge. I mean that literally, since text makes up the vast majority of web content, but also figuratively, because good typography can make or break your design. Great typography is invisible: it just works, enhancing your message without calling attention to itself. Bad typography screams amateur hour and sends visitors running.

The good news? Getting typography right on the web is easier than ever, thanks to thousands of free web fonts and modern browser capabilities. The challenge is choosing wisely from all those options.

## How fonts convey personality

Fonts have personalities just as distinct as colors. A font isn't just a way to display letters — it's a visual voice that communicates feeling and character before anyone reads a single word.

Consider these examples:

- **Serif fonts** (such as Times New Roman, Georgia, and Merriweather) have little decorative strokes at the ends of letters, as shown in Figure 2-1. They feel traditional, trustworthy, and established. Newspapers, law firms, and universities love serif fonts because they communicate authority and respectability. If you want to feel classic and credible, serif fonts deliver.
- **Sans-serif fonts** (such as Arial, Helvetica, and Open Sans) have clean, simple strokes without decorative elements (again, refer to Figure 2-2). They feel modern, clean, and straightforward. Tech companies and startups gravitate toward sans-serifs because they communicate innovation and simplicity. If you want to feel contemporary and accessible, sans-serif is your friend.

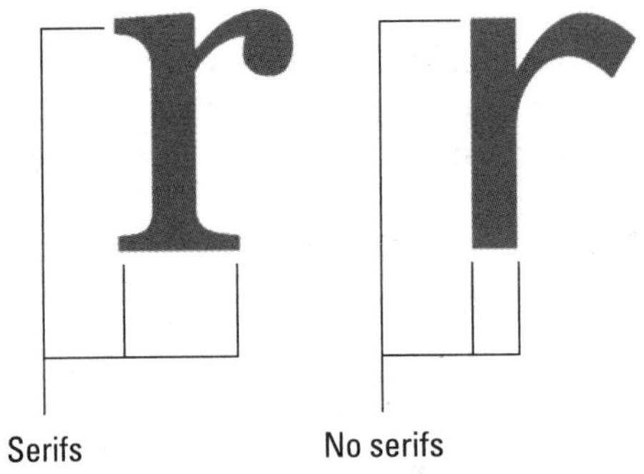


**FIGURE 2-2:** The letter on the left has serifs; the letter on the right does not.

- **Display fonts** are designed to be eye-catching and used for headlines, not body text. They can be geometric (such as Futura), handwritten-style (such as Pacifico), decorative (such as Lobster), or ultra-modern (such as Orbitron). They pack personality but should be used sparingly — a little goes a long way.
- **Script fonts** mimic handwriting or calligraphy. They feel elegant, personal, or fancy depending on the style. Wedding invitations love script fonts. But they're often hard to read, especially at small sizes or on screens, so use them very carefully and never for body text.

The same words in different fonts create different impressions. Imagine a law firm website with Comic Sans (yikes!), or a children's toy store with a stern, heavy serif (wrong vibe entirely). The font has to match the message.

For Orbital Donuts, a geometric sans-serif like Orbitron for headings captures that space-age, modern feeling. As shown by Orbitron's Google Fonts specimen page in Figure 2-3, it looks like something from a retro sci-fi movie poster. But you wouldn't want to read a full paragraph in Orbitron; it's too distinctive and tiring. So, pairing it with a highly readable sans-serif like Open Sans for body text gives you personality where it counts (headlines) and clarity where you need it (content).

**FIGURE 2-3:** The Orbitron specimen page on Google Fonts.

## The art of font pairing

Most websites use two fonts: one for headings and one for body text. This approach creates visual hierarchy and interest without overwhelming visitors with too many competing voices. But not every combination works well.

To help you create effective pairings, here are a few principles worth writing on your arm:

» **Create contrast.** If both fonts are too similar, they just look like a mistake. If both are wildly different, they fight each other. You want clear distinction with complementary personalities. A decorative heading font paired with a simple body font works beautifully — the heading grabs attention, the body text delivers the message clearly.

- **Serif + sans-serif is a classic for good reason.** This pairing creates natural contrast. You might use Merriweather (serif) for headings to feel established and trustworthy, with Lato (sans-serif) for body text to feel modern and readable. Or flip it: Montserrat (sans-serif) headings for a bold, contemporary feel with Lora (serif) body text for elegance.
- **Match the mood, not the style.** Your fonts don't have to be from the same era or style, but they should support the same personality. A playful, rounded sans-serif heading font pairs well with a clean, friendly body font. Both feel approachable even if they're technically different styles.
- **Readability comes first for body text.** Your body font appears in paragraphs, lists, and navigation, so it's doing the heavy lifting. It must be highly readable at small sizes and comfortable to read for extended periods. Save the personality for headings and accents where it won't tire readers.
- **Consider superfamilies.** Some font families include both serif and sans-serif versions designed to work together perfectly. Roboto and Roboto Slab are one example. These pairings are nearly foolproof because they share underlying proportions and structure.

If you're struggling with font pairings, sites such as FontPair (`https://www.fontpair.co`) and Typewolf (`typewolf.com`) show proven combinations used on real websites. You can also look at websites you admire and identify which fonts they're using: right-click the text, click Inspect, click Computed in the browser developer tools that show up, and then check out the `font-family` value, as shown in Figure 2-4.

TIP

Stick to two fonts maximum for most small websites. Three is acceptable if you need a special display font for your logo or a monospace font for code examples. More than three almost always creates visual clutter. Simplicity wins.

## Understanding web fonts

*Web fonts* are fonts that browsers download from a server so they can display them on your site. These are different from *system fonts*, such as Arial, Times New Roman, and Georgia, which are already installed on most computers.

For years, web designers were stuck with system fonts because browsers could display only fonts already on users' computers. That's why so many older websites look the same — everyone used Arial or Verdana. But web fonts changed everything, giving designers access to thousands of typefaces.

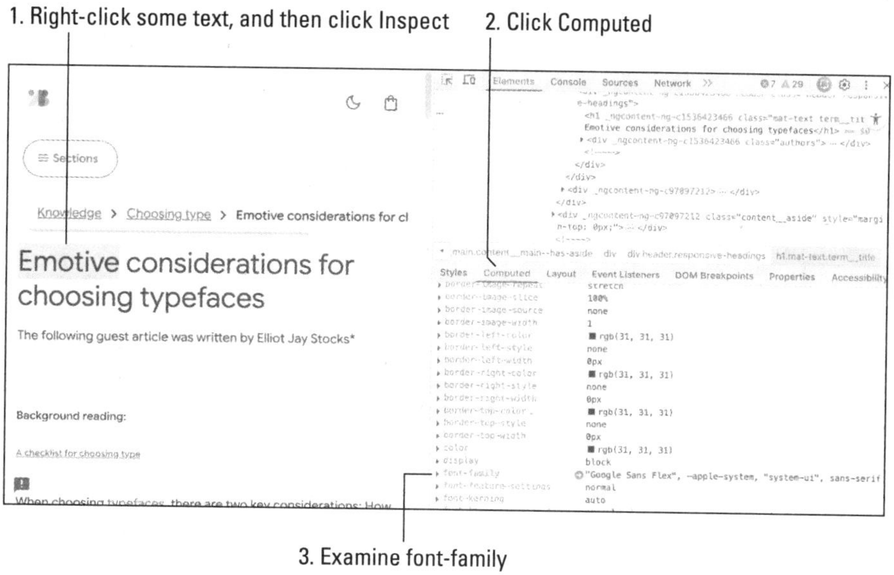


**FIGURE 2-4:** Using the browser developer tools to find out which fonts a site is using.

The most popular source for web fonts is Google Fonts (`fonts.google.com`), which offers hundreds of free, high-quality typefaces that work across all modern browsers. You just select the fonts you want, and Google provides the code to add them to your site. Other great options include Adobe Fonts (`fonts.adobe.com`), which is included with Creative Cloud subscriptions, and Font Squirrel (`fontsquirrel.com`), a free alternative.

Most website builders like Wix, Squarespace, and WordPress have web font libraries built right in. You just click to select a font from their collection, and they handle all the technical implementation. If you're coding your site from scratch, you'll add the fonts using Google Fonts or another service.

# Dealing with Images

Images make websites come alive. They provide visual interest, communicate information faster than text, break up walls of words, and reinforce your brand identity. A website without images feels stark and uninviting, like a newspaper from the 1800s.

But images also present challenges. They're often the biggest files on your site, which means they have the biggest impact on loading speed. A poorly optimized image gallery can turn a snappy website into a sluggish one. The key is finding the right balance: high-quality images that look great without dragging down performance.

# Modern image formats: WebP, AVIF, and SVG

For years, the web had three main image formats: JPEG for photos, PNG for graphics with transparency, and GIF for simple animations. Those formats still work perfectly fine, but modern formats offer much better compression and quality.

*WebP* is a modern format developed by Google that creates smaller file sizes than JPEG while maintaining the same visual quality, typically 25–35 percent smaller. That's a huge win for page load times, especially on mobile devices where data speed matters. WebP also supports transparency like PNG and animation like GIF, so it's incredibly versatile.

All modern browsers now support WebP, so it's safe to use. Many image-editing tools and online converters can save your photos as WebP. Tools like Squoosh (`squoosh.app`) let you upload a JPEG and export it as WebP with a visual comparison so you can see the quality difference (usually none) and the file size savings (usually substantial).

*AVIF* is even newer than WebP and offers even better compression — often 50 percent smaller than JPEG with the same quality. It's amazing for performance. The trade-off is that encoding images to AVIF is slower, and browser support, while growing rapidly, isn't quite universal yet. Major browsers like Chrome, Edge, Firefox, and Safari support it now.

For most small websites, WebP is the sweet spot: widely supported, easy to create, and significantly smaller than JPEG. AVIF is worth exploring if you're building an image-heavy site where every kilobyte matters.

*SVG* (Scalable Vector Graphics) is different from the others because it's vector-based rather than pixel-based. Instead of storing millions of colored dots, SVG stores mathematical instructions for drawing shapes. This means SVG files can scale infinitely without losing quality, making it perfect for logos, icons, and illustrations. But because SVG files don't use pixels, they're not suitable for photos.

The Orbital Donuts logo should definitely be SVG. That way, it will look crisp on everything from a tiny mobile screen to a giant 4K display. SVG files are also usually quite small (just a few kilobytes), and you can even change their colors or animate them using website code.

The rule of thumb: use SVG for logos, icons, and simple illustrations. Use WebP or AVIF for photos and complex graphics.

## Finding great stock photos

Not everyone has a professional photographer on speed dial or the budget to hire one for every website update. That's where stock photos come in — professional-quality images available for use on your website, often for free.

Here are excellent resources for finding stock photos:

- **Unsplash (`unsplash.com`)** offers high-quality, free photos from talented photographers worldwide. The quality is genuinely impressive, and the collection is massive. Great for modern, artistic shots with excellent composition.
- **Pexels (`pexels.com`)** is similar to Unsplash, with a large, curated collection of free photos and videos. The search functionality is excellent, making it easy to find exactly what you need.
- **Pixabay (`pixabay.com`)** provides lots of variety, including photos, illustrations, and vectors. The quality varies more than Unsplash, but the selection is huge.
- **Adobe Stock (`stock.adobe.com`)** is a premium option with professional-grade images. It requires payment but offers higher quality, a wider variety of unique content, and model releases for images featuring people.

When using stock photos, try to avoid the obviously generic shots that scream stock photo. You know the ones — overly enthusiastic business people high-fiving in an impossibly clean office or a diverse group of young professionals laughing at a laptop. These images feel fake because we've all seen them a thousand times.

Look for authentic, natural images that feel genuine; close-up shots of real products or processes; candid photos that capture real moments; and images with interesting composition or lighting that don't look staged. The goal is finding images that enhance your content without looking like obvious stock photos.

REMEMBER

Always check the license on stock photos. Most free stock photo sites use Creative Commons Zero (CC0) licenses, which allow commercial use without attribution. But some images require credit, and premium sites have different terms. Spending two minutes reading the license (or, better yet, have your favorite AI tool summarize the license for you) can save you legal headaches later.

# Creating Style Guides and Design Systems

Okay, you've chosen your colors, picked your fonts, and optimized your images. Now what? Now you need to document these decisions so you (and anyone else working on the site) can maintain consistency over time. That's where style guides and design systems come in.

## What's a style guide?

A *style guide* is a document that defines your visual design standards. Think of it as the rulebook for your brand's appearance. It tells you and your collaborators which colors, fonts, spacing, and design elements to use.

A typical style guide includes:

- **Color palette** with color values (refer to Book 4, Chapter 3) for primary, secondary, and accent colors. Often includes tints and shades of each color for different uses.
- **Typography** specifying font families, sizes, weights, and line heights for the text elements. What font for headings? What size for body text? How much space between lines?
- **Spacing** standards for margins, padding, and gaps between elements. Consistent spacing makes layouts feel organized and professional.
- **Component styles** showing how buttons, forms, cards, and other UI elements should look. What color are buttons? How much padding? What happens when you hover your cursor over them?
- **Logo usage rules** for how your logo should be displayed, including minimum sizes, clear space requirements, and which color variations to use on different backgrounds.
- **Image guidelines** describing the style of photography or illustrations you use. Bright and colorful or moody and dramatic? Candid or staged? These guidelines keep your visual style consistent.

For a small site like Orbital Donuts, the style guide might be just a simple document — even a one-page PDF or a well-organized Google Doc works fine. For larger organizations, it could be a comprehensive website with live examples, downloadable assets, and interactive demonstrations.

The key is writing down those style guidelines. Without documentation, those careful design decisions you made today will be forgotten in six months when you need to add a new page. You'll waste time trying to remember which exact shade of orange you used, or whether headings should be bold or regular weight.

## Moving to design systems

A *design system* takes the style guide concept further. It's not just documentation; it's a collection of reusable components, patterns, and principles that work together cohesively. Think of it as a LEGO set for your website: you have prebuilt, standardized pieces that you can combine in different ways to create consistent pages.

Major companies maintain extensive design systems, such as Google (Material Design), Apple (Human Interface Guidelines), IBM (Carbon Design System), and Salesforce (Lightning Design System). These design systems aren't just for their designers — they publish them publicly so anyone building products on their platforms can create a consistent experience.

But you don't need a team of 50 designers to benefit from design system thinking. For a site such as Orbital Donuts, a simple design system might include:

- **Button variations** showing the primary button (orange accent color for key actions like Order Now), secondary button (navy outline for less important actions), and text-only button for tertiary actions. Each has defined states for hover, active, and disabled.
- **Card components** for displaying individual donuts in the menu, each with an image, a name, a description, and a price formatted consistently.
- **Navigation patterns** specifying how the menu should look and behave on a desktop (horizontal navigation bar) versus mobile (hamburger menu that slides in from the side).
- **Form elements** with consistent styling for input fields, labels, error messages, and success states. When someone fills out the contact form, it should look and feel like the same website as the order form.

The beauty of a design system is efficiency. Instead of redesigning a button from scratch every time you need one, you just use your primary button component. Everything stays consistent, and you work faster.

## Documenting your design decisions

Finally, write down not just what you decided, but why. You don't have to be fancy; a simple text document or dedicated page on your site works fine. Include the following:

- **The reasoning behind your color choices.** Why orange for Orbital Donuts? Because it's energetic, friendly, and evokes a sunrise — the beginning of a new day and a perfect pairing with morning coffee.
- **Your font pairings and when to use each one**. For example, Orbitron for headings to capture that space theme, Open Sans for body text because it's highly readable.
- **Standard spacing values and when to apply them.** For example, 8px for tight spacing, 16px for normal, 32px for loose, 64px for section breaks.
- **Examples of how components should look in different states.** What happens when you hover your cursor over a button? What does an error message look like? How do disabled form fields appear?

Six months from now, when you're adding a new section to your site, you'll be grateful for this documentation. It helps you maintain consistency without having to reverse-engineer your own design decisions or rely on memory. And if your site grows and you bring on help — maybe a freelance designer or a new employee — that documentation becomes invaluable for getting them up to speed quickly.

## Iterating and refining your design

Here's something important: your visual design doesn't have to be perfect from day one. In fact, it probably won't be. Great design emerges through iteration — trying things, seeing what works, and refining based on real-world feedback.

Launch with a solid design that reflects your brand personality and meets your goals. Then pay attention to how people use your site. Do they struggle to read your body text? Maybe the font size is too small or the line spacing too tight. Do they miss important call-to-action buttons? Maybe your accent color doesn't provide enough contrast. Do they comment that your site feels cluttered? Maybe you need more white space.

Your style guide isn't carved in stone. It's a living document that evolves as your brand grows and you learn what works. Maybe you discover that your purple secondary color looks muddy on certain monitors. Update it. Maybe you find a better font that's more readable on mobile devices. Switch it. Maybe your business expands and you need new component types you didn't anticipate. Add them.

The key is making intentional changes, not random ones. When you update your design, update your documentation too. That way it always reflects your current decisions, and you maintain consistency even as things evolve.

Visual design and branding aren't just about making things pretty. They're about creating a cohesive, memorable experience that reflects your brand's personality and makes your visitors feel confident and engaged. Take the time to make intentional choices about colors, fonts, images, and components. Document those choices so you can maintain consistency. And remember that great design emerges through iteration and refinement based on real-world use.

With the principles and strategies from this chapter, you're equipped to create a visual identity that's not just beautiful, but effective — one that supports your goals and resonates with your audience.

IN THIS CHAPTER

» Understanding component-based design thinking

» Planning for multiple screen sizes

» Creating design systems for consistency

» Designing micro-interactions and feedback

# Chapter 3

# Responsive and Component-Based Design

*Favor elegance of simple things over flexibility of complex things.*

—NATHAN CURTIS

In Book 1, Chapter 4, I talk about how modern websites need to work across all kinds of devices, from tiny smartphones to giant desktop monitors. And in Book 2, Chapter 1, I explain how mobile-first design helps you prioritize what matters most.

But before you write a single line of code, you need to *design* for that responsive, multidevice world. You need to think in terms of flexible, reusable building blocks — what we call *components* — and plan how those components will adapt to different screen sizes. This chapter is all about the design thinking and planning that happens *before* you start coding. By the end of this chapter, you'll know how to break down a design into components, plan for multiple screen sizes, create a design system for consistency, and think about all those little interactive details that make a website feel polished, possibly even professional.

# Understanding Component-Based Design

With *component-based design*, instead of treating your website as a monolith, you break it down into smaller, reusable pieces that you can mix and match. Each piece (a button, a card, a navigation menu) is a *component*, and you build your website by combining these components in different ways.

When you design with components, you make your life easier in about a dozen ways. You create consistency across your site (because the same button looks the same everywhere). You save time (because you have to design that button only once). And you make future changes simpler (because when you update the button design, it updates everywhere automatically).

## What are design components?

A *component* is a self-contained piece of your user interface that does one job well. Think of it as a building block. Some components are tiny and simple (such as a button or an input field), while others are larger and more complex (such as a navigation bar or a product card).

Here are some common components you'll find on most websites:

- **Buttons:** Clickable elements that trigger actions
- **Input fields:** Places where users type information
- **Cards:** Contained blocks of information (such as product cards or blog post previews)
- **Navigation menus:** Lists of links that help users move around your site
- **Headers:** The top section of your pages, usually containing your logo and main navigation
- **Footers:** The bottom section with copyright info, links, and contact details
- **Forms:** Collections of input fields and buttons for collecting user information

Let me use Orbital Donuts (my ongoing example throughout this book) to make these general components more concrete. The Orbital Donuts website needs all of these components:

- **A header component:** Contains the Orbital Donuts logo, the main navigation (Menu, Order Online, Locations, Catering, About), and maybe a shopping cart icon.

- **A donut card component:** Shows an image of a donut, its name, description, and price, and an Add to Cart button
- **Button components:** Primary buttons (such as Order Now) and secondary buttons (such as Learn More)
- **A footer component:** Contains location information, social media links, and a copyright notice

Notice how I can describe each component independently? That's the key. Each component stands alone and does a specific job, whether it's displaying a donut or providing navigation.

## Thinking in components

When you look at a website, your first instinct might be to see it as one big page. But when you think in components, you start to see it differently: as a collection of smaller, independent pieces that fit together.

Here's a useful framework. Imagine breaking down a web page into three levels of components:

- **Small components (atoms):** Individual elements such as buttons, input fields, labels, or icons. These are the tiniest building blocks.
- **Medium components (molecules):** Groups of small components that work together, such as a search box (which combines an input field and a search button) or a donut card (which combines an image, text, and a button).
- **Large components (organisms):** Complete sections of a page, such as a header (containing logo, navigation, and a search box) or a product grid (containing multiple donut cards).

You don't need to obsess over whether something is an atom, a molecule, or an organism. This comparison is just a helpful (I hope!) way to think about how components nest inside each other. The point is to recognize that complex things are built from simpler things.

For Orbital Donuts, the home page might break down like this:

- **Header (large):** Contains the logo (small), navigation links (small), a search box (medium), and an Order Now button (small)
- **Hero section (large):** Features a background image, headline text (small), and a call-to-action button (small)

- **Featured donuts section (large):** Contains multiple donut cards (medium), each with an image, name, description, and button (all small)
- **Footer (large):** Contains location info, social links (small), and copyright text (small)

See how everything nests? Small components combine into medium components, and medium components combine into large components. It's components all the way down!

## Designing components for flexibility

Here's where component-based design gets really powerful: when you design a component, you're not just designing it for one specific use. You're designing it to work in multiple contexts and with different content.

Let's say you're designing that donut card for Orbital Donuts. You could design it for one specific donut (the Rocket Red Velvet), but that would be shortsighted. Instead, you need to design it to handle *any* donut. That means thinking about variations:

- **Content flexibility:** What if some donut names are short (Glazed) and others are long (Triple Chocolate Galaxy Explosion)? What if some descriptions are one sentence and others are three sentences? Your component design needs to handle the full range.
- **State variations:** The donut card needs to look good whether the donut is in stock, out of stock, or on sale. You might need variations like Out of Stock badges or Sale! ribbons.
- **Size variations:** The same donut card component might appear large on the home page but smaller in a sidebar. Can your design scale up and down gracefully?

The goal is to design a component that's flexible enough to handle real-world content variations while maintaining a consistent look and feel. This approach is harder than designing for one specific case, but it's what makes components truly reusable.

TIP

When designing components, test them with extreme content scenarios: the longest possible text, the shortest possible text, missing images, extra-long words that don't wrap nicely. If your component design survives these edge cases, it'll work great with normal content.

## Planning component variations

Most components need multiple variations. Your primary button might be blue and bold, but you also need a secondary button that's more subtle (maybe just an outline). For example, your donut card might have a default version and a compact version.

For Orbital Donuts, here are some component variations I'd plan:

- **Buttons:** Primary (bright red, bold), secondary (outlined, subtle), and text-only (just text, no background)
- **Donut cards:** Standard (for product grids), featured (larger, for highlighting), and compact (for sidebars)
- **Navigation:** Desktop version (horizontal, always visible) and mobile version (hamburger menu, collapsible)

When you plan these variations up front, you avoid the nightmare of designing everything from scratch for each new use case. You're building a toolkit of variations that covers most situations you'll encounter.



# Designing for Multiple Screen Sizes

As I mention in Book 1, Chapter 4, modern websites need to work on everything from a smartphone (maybe 375 pixels wide) to a giant desktop monitor (2000+ pixels wide). That's a huge range! But here's the good news: you don't need to design a completely different site for each screen size. You just need to think strategically about how your design *adapts* as the screen gets wider.

## The breakpoint strategy

A *breakpoint* is a specific screen width where your design changes. Maybe at 768 pixels wide (the width of a tablet in portrait orientation), your single-column layout becomes two columns. Or at 1024 pixels (the width of a tablet in landscape orientation), your sidebar appears. These transition points are your breakpoints.

Most designers work with three or four main breakpoints:

- **Mobile:** 0 – 767 pixels wide. Single column, simplified navigation, stacked content.

- **Tablet:** 768 – 1023 pixels wide. Two columns, expanded navigation, more breathing room.
- **Desktop:** 1024 – 1439 pixels wide. Multicolumn layouts, sidebars, full navigation.
- **Wide desktop:** 1440+ pixels wide. Wider layouts, more whitespace, maybe additional columns.

These numbers aren't magical; they're just common ranges based on typical device sizes. The important thing isn't hitting a particular number but rather choosing breakpoints that make sense for *your* content.

REMEMBER

Choose breakpoints based on when your design breaks, not based on specific devices. If your layout starts looking cramped at 650 pixels, that's where you need a breakpoint, even if it doesn't match a standard device size.

For Orbital Donuts, I'd sketch out the home page at three key sizes:

- **Mobile (375px):** Logo centered, hamburger menu, single column of content, donut cards stacked vertically, full-width buttons
- **Tablet (768px):** Logo left, expanded navigation menu, two-column donut grid, slightly wider layout
- **Desktop (1200px):** Logo left, full horizontal navigation, three-column donut grid, sidebar with filters, more whitespace

Note how I'm not just shrinking everything proportionally. The layout changes structure at each breakpoint: columns appear, navigation transforms, and content reorganizes.

## Content prioritization across screens

Here's a critical question: what's essential on a mobile screen?

On a tiny mobile screen, you don't have room for everything. You need to prioritize. This is where that mobile-first thinking from Book 2, Chapter 1 really pays off: by starting with the mobile version, you're forced to identify what truly matters.

For Orbital Donuts, the mobile home page must include the following:

- **Logo:** So people know where they are
- **Main navigation:** Menu, Order Online, Locations option (in a hamburger menu)

- **Hero message:** A compelling tagline and an Order Now button
- **Featured donuts:** A few (not all) donut cards showcasing popular items
- **Contact info:** Phone number and locations link in the footer

The following can wait until the screen is larger:

- **Detailed company story:** Nice to have on a desktop but not essential on a mobile device
- **Social media feed:** Fun, but not critical for ordering donuts
- **Newsletter signup:** Can be condensed on a mobile device and expanded on a desktop
- **Decorative elements:** Space-themed graphics that enhance the brand but aren't functional

This is *progressive enhancement:* you start with the essentials on mobile, and then add more features and content as screen size increases. Everyone gets a functional site, but desktop users get extra bells and whistles.



## Layout pattern planning

When designing for multiple screen sizes, you need to think about how your layout patterns transform. A grid that shows one column on a mobile device might become two columns on a tablet and three columns on a desktop. A sidebar that's below the main content on a mobile screen might move to the side on larger screens.

Here are some common responsive patterns:

- **Column dropping:** On a mobile device, everything stacks in a single column. As the screen widens, columns start appearing side by side. At full width, you might have three or four columns.
- **Layout shifter:** The entire layout structure changes at different breakpoints. Maybe content that's stacked on a mobile device appears in a sidebar on a desktop.
- **Off canvas:** Navigation or additional content that's hidden off-screen on a mobile device (and accessed via a menu button) but always visible on a desktop.

For the Orbital Donuts donut grid, I'd use the column dropping pattern:

- **Mobile:** Single column, cards stacked vertically
- **Tablet:** Two columns, cards side by side
- **Desktop:** Three columns, more cards visible at once

When you sketch these layouts (and yes, paper sketches work great for this!), you start to see how everything flows and transforms. This planning now will save you from nasty surprises when you start coding in Book 3.

# Designing Responsive Navigation

Navigation is one of the trickiest parts of responsive design. On a desktop, you have plenty of horizontal space for a navigation bar. On a mobile device, you have almost none. So, how do you solve this?

## Mobile navigation patterns

The most common solution is the *hamburger menu,* those three horizontal lines (≡) that people tap to reveal a menu. Love it or hate it, the hamburger menu has become a universal symbol for "menu here." But it's not your only option.

Here are three popular mobile navigation patterns:

- **Hamburger menu:** Hides all navigation links behind a menu icon. When tapped, the menu slides in from the side or drops down from the top. This method works when you have lots of menu items but not much screen space.
- **Bottom navigation bar:** Shows three to five of the most important navigation items as icons at the bottom of the screen (as in the Instagram or X apps). This approach keeps navigation always visible and thumb-friendly.
- **Priority+ pattern:** Shows as many menu items as will fit on screen, and then hides the rest behind a More button (sometimes rendered as an ellipsis, . . .). This technique works when you have a medium number of items and want to keep some visible.

For Orbital Donuts, I'd probably go with a hamburger menu on a mobile device. Here's why:

- **The site has several top-level pages.** Menu, Order Online, Locations, About, Contact.
- **The top-level pages are text-heavy.** They don't translate well to the icons that a bottom nav bar would require.
- **Users expect the hamburger menu.** For a business website (not an app), the hamburger menu is familiar and accepted.

The mobile navigation would look like this:

- **Header:** Hamburger icon (top left), Orbital Donuts logo (center), shopping cart icon (top right).
- **When tapped:** The hamburger icon triggers a full-screen menu overlay with all navigation links, large and tappable.
- **Close button:** A large X or back arrow to close the menu and return to the page.

WARNING

Don't hide important actions behind the hamburger menu! If Order Now is your most important call-to-action, keep it visible as a button in the header; don't bury it in the menu.

## Desktop navigation patterns

On a desktop, you have space to breathe. You can show all your navigation links horizontally across the top of the page. This classic horizontal navigation bar pattern works great for most sites.

For Orbital Donuts desktop navigation, I'd have the following:

- **Logo:** Top left, clickable to return home
- **Main navigation:** Horizontally in the center or right side (Menu, Order Online, Locations, About, Contact links)
- **Call to action (CTA):** Order Now button in bright red, far right, always visible
- **Shopping cart:** Icon with item count, far right next to the CTA button

If Orbital Donuts had more complex navigation (say, dozens of donut categories), I might consider a *mega menu*, a large dropdown panel that appears when you hover your cursor over Menu, showing all donut categories organized in columns. But for a small business with simple navigation, a basic horizontal nav bar is perfect.

### Sticky navigation

One design decision you'll need to make is whether your navigation should stay visible as users scroll down the page or scroll away with the rest of the header.

A *sticky navigation bar* stays pinned to the top of the screen even as the user scrolls. This approach is helpful for long pages, where users might want to navigate elsewhere without scrolling all the way back up.

For Orbital Donuts, I'd make the navigation sticky. Why?

- **The menu page is long.** Lots of donuts to scroll through! Users will appreciate having navigation always available.
- **The Order Now button is crucial.** Keeping the Order Now button visible at all times makes it easy to start ordering from anywhere on the page.
- **The shopping cart needs visibility.** Users want to see their cart count as they add items.

The trade-off? A sticky navigation bar takes up some vertical screen space, which is especially precious on a mobile device. So, you might make the mobile version of the sticky nav bar more compact (smaller logo, icons instead of text) than the desktop version.

## Design Systems and Consistency

Imagine building a website where every button looks slightly different. One button is blue, another is navy, a third is teal. Some buttons have rounded corners, others are sharp. Some are big, some are tiny. The result? Visual chaos. Your site looks unprofessional and confusing.

This is why you need a *design system*, a set of rules and components that ensures visual consistency across your entire website.

## Creating a design system

A design system is essentially your website's visual rulebook. It defines:

- **Colors:** Your primary color, secondary colors, neutral grays, and colors for specific purposes (such as error red and success green)
- **Typography:** Which fonts you use, what sizes for headings and body text, line heights, and font weights
- **Spacing:** Consistent spacing values for margins, padding, and gaps between elements
- **Components:** Reusable component designs (buttons, cards, forms) with defined styles and variations
- **Patterns:** Common layout patterns and interaction patterns you'll reuse throughout the site

For a small business website like Orbital Donuts, you don't need an elaborate 50-page design system document. A simple 1-page style guide covering the essentials works great. Here's what Orbital Donuts' mini design system might include:

- **Brand colors:** Rocket Red (primary), Galaxy Purple (accent), Cosmic Blue (secondary), Space Black, Moonlight White, and neutral grays
- **Typography:** Headings in Orbitron (bold, space-age feel), body text in Open Sans (clean and readable)
- **Spacing scale:** 4px, 8px, 16px, 24px, 32px, 48px, 64px (multiples of 8 for consistency)
- **Button styles:** Primary (Rocket Red), secondary (outlined), and text-only versions
- **Card component:** White background, subtle shadow, rounded corners (8px radius), image on top, content below

Once you define these rules, you follow them everywhere. Every button uses one of your button styles. Every heading uses your heading fonts. Every space between elements uses your spacing scale. This discipline creates that polished, professional look.

## Design tokens

Here's a fancy term that describes a simple concept: *design tokens* are named values for your design decisions. Instead of remembering "that shade of red is #E63946," you give it a name like Rocket Red or primary-color. Instead of remembering "16 pixels of space," you call it space-md (*md* for medium spacing).

Design tokens make your design system easier to remember and apply. Here are the main types:

- **Color tokens:** primary-color, secondary-color, text-color, background-color, error-color, success-color
- **Spacing tokens:** space-xs (4px), space-sm (8px), space-md (16px), space-lg (24px), space-xl (32px)
- **Typography tokens:** font-heading, font-body, text-xs, text-sm, text-base, text-lg, text-xl
- **Border radius tokens:** radius-sm (4px), radius-md (8px), radius-lg (12px), radius-full (for circles)
- **Shadow tokens:** shadow-sm (subtle), shadow-md (standard), shadow-lg (prominent)

For Orbital Donuts, here are some example tokens:

- **color-rocket-red:** #E63946 (used for primary buttons and important accents)
- **color-galaxy-purple:** #9C27B0 (used for special promotions and sale badges)
- **space-donut:** 24px (consistent spacing around donut cards)
- **radius-donut:** 8px (rounded corners on cards and images)

When you implement your design in code (coming up in Book 3!), these tokens become CSS variables that you can reuse everywhere. But right now, in the design phase, they're just names that help you stay consistent.

## Component states

Components aren't (or shouldn't be) static because they often need to respond to user interaction. A button isn't just a button; it has multiple states:

- **Default:** How the button looks when you're not interacting with it.
- **Hover:** How it looks when your mouse pointer is over it (usually slightly brighter or darker).
- **Active or pressed:** How it looks when you're clicking it (usually darker or slightly indented).

- **Focus:** How it looks when navigating with a keyboard (usually an outline or glow).
- **Disabled:** How it looks when it's not clickable (usually grayed out).

You need to design *all* these states for your interactive components. It sounds like a lot of work, but here's a shortcut: most states are just variations on the default. A hover state might be the default color but 10 percent darker. An active state might be the hover state but with a subtle shadow inset. Once you establish these patterns, they apply to all your buttons.

For the Orbital Donuts Order Now button, the design states are:

- **Default:** Rocket Red background, white text, subtle shadow
- **Hover:** Slightly darker red (10 percent darker), same shadow
- **Active:** Even darker red, shadow appears pressed inward
- **Focus:** Default appearance plus a blue outline (for keyboard users)
- **Disabled:** Gray background, gray text, no shadow, cursor displays *not allowed*

When you document all these states in your design system, you eliminate guesswork during implementation. You (or your developer, if you're working with one) know exactly how every component should behave.



# Designing for Dark Mode

Dark mode has become a standard feature in modern websites and apps. Some people prefer it for late-night browsing because it's easier on the eyes, while others just think it looks cool. Either way, if you're building a modern website, you should at least *consider* dark mode, even if you ultimately decide it's not right for your project.

## Dark mode design principles

Here's the thing about dark mode: it's not just inverting colors. You can't take your light theme, flip white to black and black to white, and call it done. Good dark mode design requires thoughtful color choices.

Here are the key principles (you learn how to implement these in code in Book 3, Chapter 5):

- **Don't use pure black.** Pure black (#000000) is too harsh. Use dark grays instead (such as #121212 or #1a1a1a) for your background.
- **Reduce contrast.** In light mode, you might use jet black text on white. In dark mode, use light gray text (not pure white) on dark gray backgrounds. The contrast should be adjusted to make it feel less harsh.
- **Adjust your colors.** Bright, saturated colors that look great on white backgrounds can be overwhelming on dark backgrounds. Desaturate them slightly for dark mode.
- **Communicate elevation subtly.** In light mode, you create depth with shadows. In dark mode, shadows don't show up well. Instead, use slightly lighter grays for elements that should appear elevated.
- **Think about images.** Photos and images designed for light backgrounds might need adjustments. Consider adding a subtle dark overlay or reducing brightness.

Not every website needs dark mode. It makes sense for:

- **Apps used for extended periods:** Social media, documentation sites, reading apps.
- **Technical and developer sites:** Developers often prefer dark mode.
- **Entertainment sites:** Gaming, streaming, and anything focusing on visual content.

It's less critical for:

- **E-commerce sites:** People shopping want to see products clearly in bright, accurate colors.
- **Heavily branded sites:** If your brand identity relies on specific colors and high contrast, dark mode might dilute that.
- **Photo-heavy sites:** Photography portfolios or art galleries usually showcase better on light backgrounds.

## Planning your color system for dark mode

If you decide to support dark mode, you need to plan your color system differently. Instead of choosing specific colors, you choose *semantic colors:* colors based on their purpose, not their appearance.

Here's how this works:

- **background:** White (#FFFFFF) in light mode and dark gray (#121212) in dark mode.
- **surface:** For cards and elevated elements. Light gray (#F5F5F5) in light mode and slightly lighter gray (#1E1E1E) in dark mode.
- **text-primary:** Near-black (#1A1A1A) in light mode and light gray (#E0E0E0) in dark mode.
- **text-secondary:** Medium gray (#666666) in light mode and medium-light gray (#AAAAAA) in dark mode.
- **primary-color:** Your brand color, adjusted for each mode. Orbital Donuts' Rocket Red might be #E63946 in light mode but #FF6B7A (slightly lighter, less saturated) in dark mode.

When you design components, you reference these semantic colors rather than specific hex values. Your button uses primary-color and text-on-primary colors. Your cards use surface and text-primary colors. Then when users toggle between light and dark mode, the system swaps in the appropriate color values.

For Orbital Donuts, I decided against dark mode. Why? It's an e-commerce site selling colorful donuts. The vibrant product photos and playful space theme work best on a light background. Dark mode would make those bright, delicious donuts look less appetizing. Not every design decision needs to follow every trend!



# Micro-Interactions and Feedback Design

When you click a button on a well-designed website, something happens *immediately.* The button changes color, maybe shifts slightly, gives you instant feedback that you clicked it. When you hover your cursor over a link, the cursor changes and the link color shifts. These tiny moments of interaction are called *micro-interactions,* and they're what separate great websites from merely good ones.

## What are micro-interactions?

Micro-interactions are small, focused moments where the user and the interface communicate. They answer questions such as: "Did my click register?" "Is this clickable?" "Is something loading?" "Did my action succeed?"

Following are examples of micro-interactions:

- **Button hover effect:** Button brightens or darkens when you move your mouse over it.
- **Form validation:** A green checkmark appears next to your email address when you type it correctly.
- **Loading spinner:** A spinning circle appears when you submit a form, showing you that the site is working.
- **Add to cart animation:** The product image shrinks and flies into the cart icon when you add an item.
- **Notification toast:** A small message slides in from the corner: *Item added to cart!*

These moments might seem trivial, but they make a huge difference in how your site *feels.* Without them, users feel disconnected and uncertain. With them, the site feels responsive and alive.

The key is subtlety. Good micro-interactions guide and delight without distracting. Bad ones are obnoxious and slow down the experience. (Nobody wants a three-second animation every time they click a button!)

## Designing interaction feedback

Every interactive element needs feedback. Here's how to think about designing that feedback:

- **Hover states show affordance.** When your cursor changes or an element highlights on hover, it signals "This is clickable." Plan what happens on hover for links, buttons, cards, anything interactive.
- **Active or pressed states confirm action.** When you click, the element should respond *immediately.* A button might darken or appear to press down slightly. This tells users "Yes, I received your click."
- **Loading states manage expectations.** If something takes time to load, show a spinner or progress indicator. Users are patient when they know something is happening, but anxious when they don't.
- **Success and error states complete the loop.** After an action completes, tell users what happened. A green checkmark for success, a red X for errors, and a helpful message explaining the outcome.

For Orbital Donuts' Add to Cart button, I'd design:

- **Default:** Rocket Red button with Add to Cart text.
- **Hover:** Button darkens slightly, and cursor becomes a pointer.
- **Click or active:** Button darkens more, and appears to press inward.
- **Loading:** Button text changes to *Adding. . .* with a small spinner.
- **Success:** Button briefly shows a checkmark and *Added!* before returning to the default. Cart icon in the header bounces and updates count.
- **Error:** Button shows *Error* and turns red, with a message below: *Sorry, this item is out of stock.*

All of these states need to be designed. You can't leave them to chance!

## Animation and transition planning

Animations make interactions feel smooth and natural. But there's a fine line between helpful animation and annoying animation.

Here are guidelines for planning animations (refer to Book 3, Chapter 5):

- **Fast is better than slow.** Most animations should complete in 200 – 300 milliseconds. Anything longer feels sluggish. Anything shorter might be jarring or might pass unnoticed.
- **Easing makes it natural.** Real-world objects don't move at a constant speed; they accelerate and decelerate. Your animations should too. Ease-out (start fast, end slow) works for most transitions.
- **Choose purpose over decoration.** Every animation should serve a purpose — guide attention, show relationships, or provide feedback. Don't animate just because you can.
- **Respect user preferences.** Some users get motion sickness from animations. Plan for a reduced-motion mode where animations are minimized or eliminated.

For Orbital Donuts, I have the following animations to plan:

- **Mobile menu:** Slide in from the side over 250ms with ease-out timing.
- **Donut cards:** Gently lift up (move up 4px) on hover, with a subtle shadow increase.

» **Cart icon:** Bounce when items are added (scale up to 1.1×, back to 1× over 200ms).

» **Success messages:** Fade in at the top of the screen, stay visible for 3 seconds, and then fade out.

REMEMBER

Not everything needs animation! Static designs are often clearer than animated ones. Use animation strategically for key interactions, not everywhere.

# Creating a Component Library

All this design thinking — components, responsive layouts, design systems, micro-interactions — needs to be documented somewhere. That's where a component library comes in.

## Documenting your component designs

A *component library* is a visual inventory of all your components, showing how they look, how they behave, and when to use them. For big companies, the library might be a fancy interactive website (such as Google's Material Design or Apple's Human Interface Guidelines). For a small business, a component library can be as simple as a Figma file or even a PDF with screenshots and annotations.

Your component library should show:

» **What each component looks like:** Visual examples of all variations (primary button, secondary button, and so on)

» **All states:** Default, hover, active, focus, and disabled states for interactive components

» **Responsive behavior:** How components adapt at different screen sizes

» **Usage guidelines:** When to use each component, and when not to

» **Specifications:** Measurements, colors, fonts, and basically everything needed for implementation

For Orbital Donuts, a simple component library page might include:

» **Color palette:** Swatches showing Rocket Red, Galaxy Purple, and all other brand colors with hex codes

- **Typography:** Examples of all heading sizes and body text styles
- **Buttons:** All three button variations in all their states (15 total combinations)
- **Donut card:** Standard, featured, and compact versions with annotations showing padding, image sizes, and text styles
- **Navigation:** Desktop and mobile versions with notes on behavior
- **Form elements:** Text inputs, dropdowns, checkboxes in all states

Creating this documentation might feel like busy work, but trust me: the payoff is huge when you start implementing in Book 3. Instead of making dozens of design decisions on the fly while coding, you reference your component library and build exactly what you planned.

## From design to implementation

Here's the beautiful thing about this design-first approach: when you're ready to start coding in Book 3, you're not guessing. You have a complete design system to follow. You know exactly what colors to use (they're in your design tokens). You know how buttons should look and behave (it's in your component library). You know how layouts should respond (you've sketched the breakpoints).

The transition from design to code becomes straightforward:

- **Your design tokens become CSS variables.** That primary-color token becomes `--primary-color` in your stylesheet.
- **Your components become reusable code.** That button design becomes a CSS class you apply everywhere.
- **Your breakpoints become media queries.** Those 768px and 1024px breakpoints become exact CSS breakpoints.
- **Your state designs become CSS pseudo-classes.** Hover states become `:hover` rules.

This is why I insisted that you do all this design work *before* you learn to code. When you jump straight into coding without planning, you end up making design decisions on the fly, leading to inconsistency and rework. But with a solid design system and component library, coding becomes implementing what you've already carefully planned.

IN THIS CHAPTER

- » Getting to know WCAG guidelines and accessibility principles
- » Designing with accessible colors, contrast, and typography
- » Making your site work for keyboard users and screen readers
- » Testing your website for accessibility issues

# Chapter 4
# Designing for Accessibility

*The one argument for accessibility that doesn't get made nearly often enough is how extraordinarily better it makes some people's lives. How many opportunities do we have to dramatically improve people's lives just by doing our job a little better?*

—STEVE KRUG

Here's a statistic that might surprise you: according to the World Health Organization, over 1.3 billion people worldwide — that's about 16 percent of the global population — experience some form of disability. And here's the thing: when you're designing websites, accessibility isn't just about helping people with permanent disabilities. It's also about helping people with temporary disabilities (like a broken arm), situational disabilities (like trying to use a phone in bright sunlight), and age-related changes (like declining vision). In other words, accessibility helps *everyone*, and that makes it one of the smartest design decisions you can make.

# Why Accessibility Matters

When I write about why folks should implement accessibility features, I almost always start with the business case because it gets people's attention: accessible websites reach more people, rank better in search engines, and face fewer legal risks. That's all great, but honestly, the real reason to care about accessibility goes *way* deeper.

## The human side of accessibility

Imagine trying to navigate a website when you can't see the screen. Or trying to fill out a form when you can't use a mouse. Or trying to understand a video when you can't hear the audio. For millions of people, this isn't a thought experiment — it's their daily reality on the web.

When you design an accessible website, you're essentially saying "everyone is welcome here." You're making sure that someone using a screen reader can navigate your menu just as easily as someone using a mouse. You're ensuring that someone with color blindness can still tell which fields in your form have errors. You're guaranteeing that someone who can't use a mouse can still interact with every feature on your site.

## The business benefits

Okay, so accessibility is the right thing to do. But it's also smart business:

- **Larger audience:** By making your site accessible, you're not excluding 16 percent of potential customers. That's a significant market segment you'd be leaving on the table.
- **Better search results:** Many accessibility practices (like proper heading structure, alt text for images, and semantic HTML) also happen to be what search engines love. Accessible sites often rank better than non-accessible ones.
- **Improved usability for everyone:** When you design for accessibility, you often make the site better for everyone. Clear navigation helps all users. Good color contrast is easier on everyone's eyes. Keyboard shortcuts benefit power users.
- **Future-proofing:** As we all age, we're likely to experience vision changes, hearing loss, or reduced dexterity. An accessible website serves users across their entire lifespan.

## The legal reality

In many countries, web accessibility isn't just a nice-to-have — it's legally required. In the United States, the Americans with Disabilities Act (ADA) has been interpreted to apply to websites, and companies have faced lawsuits over inaccessible sites. The European Union has the European Accessibility Act. Canada has the Accessible Canada Act. The list goes on.

Even if you're a small business, you're not necessarily exempt. The good news? Many of the basic accessibility improvements I cover in this chapter will put you in a much better position, legally and ethically.

TIP

If you're worried about legal compliance, consulting with a lawyer who specializes in digital accessibility is never a bad idea. But don't let legal concerns paralyze you. Start making improvements now and document your ongoing efforts to improve accessibility.

# Understanding the WCAG Guidelines

The Web Content Accessibility Guidelines, known as WCAG (pronounced "double-u-kag" or "wuh-kag" in case you're wondering), are the international standard for web accessibility. They're published by the World Wide Web Consortium (W3C), the same folks who standardize HTML and CSS. Your starting point is the overview page at `www.w3.org/WAI/standards-guidelines/wcag/`.

Now, I'll be honest: the full WCAG documentation is dense and technical. But don't worry about that because thankfully you don't need to memorize every guideline. What you need is to understand the core principles and know where to look when you have questions.

## The four POUR principles

WCAG is built on four principles, handily organized into the *POUR* acronym:

- **Perceivable:** Users must be able to perceive the information being presented. Provide text alternatives for images and captions for videos, and ensure sufficient color contrast. If someone can't see or hear your content, you need to provide it in an alternative format they can perceive.
- **Operable:** Users must be able to operate the interface. Your site should work with a keyboard alone (no mouse required), give users enough time to read

and use content, not cause seizures (yep, that's a real concern with flashing content), and provide ways to help users navigate and find content.

- **Understandable:** Users must be able to understand the information and how to use the interface. Use clear language, provide helpful error messages, and make your interface predictable and consistent.
- **Robust:** Content must be robust enough to work with current and future technologies, including assistive technologies such as screen readers. Use clean, standards-compliant HTML and follow web standards.

These four principles form the foundation of accessible design. If you're ever unsure whether something is accessible, ask yourself: Can everyone perceive it? Can everyone operate it? Will everyone understand it? Will it work with assistive technologies?

## WCAG conformance levels

WCAG has three levels of conformance:

- **Level A:** The minimum level. If you don't meet Level A, some groups will find it impossible to access your content.
- **Level AA:** The standard target for most websites. This is what most laws and regulations require, and it removes most barriers for most users.
- **Level AAA:** The highest level. This isn't always achievable for all content, but it represents the gold standard.

For most small business websites, I recommend aiming for WCAG 2.1 Level AA conformance. It is achievable, is what most regulations require, and covers the vast majority of accessibility needs.

REMEMBER

WCAG is currently on version 2.2, with version 3.0 in development. When you're looking up WCAG guidelines, make sure you're reading WCAG 2.1 or 2.2 (they're very similar). WCAG 1.0 is outdated.

# Accessible Color Contrast and Typography

Let's get into some practical stuff. As I discuss in Book 2, Chapter 2, color and typography are fundamental to your visual design. They're also critical for accessibility.

## Color contrast ratios

Here's a number you need to know: 4.5:1. That's the minimum *contrast ratio* between text and background colors for normal text to meet WCAG Level AA. For large text (24px and larger, or 18.66px bold and larger), the minimum is 3:1.

What's a contrast ratio? It's a measurement of the difference in brightness between two colors, ranging from 1:1 (no contrast, like white text on white background) to 21:1 (maximum contrast, like black text on white background). The higher the ratio, the easier the text is to read.

For example:

- Black text on white background is 21:1 (perfect!)
- Dark gray (#333) on white is 12.6:1 (excellent)
- Medium gray (#777) on white is 4.5:1 (just barely meets AA)
- Light gray (#999) on white is 2.8:1 (fails!)

(If font sizes such as 24px and colors such as #333 have you scratching your head, you learn all about these and other CSS units in Book 4.)

The good news is you don't need to calculate these ratios by hand. As shown in Figure 4-1, WebAIM (web accessibility in mind) Contrast Checker (`webaim.org/resources/contrastchecker/`) enables you to plug in your foreground and background colors and instantly see if they pass WCAG standards.

## Don't rely on color alone

Here's a common mistake: using only color to convey information. For example, let's say you have a form and highlight invalid fields in red. That's fine for people who can see red, but what about people with color blindness?

Instead, use multiple indicators:

- Color change (the field turns red)
- Icon (a warning icon appears next to the field)
- Text message (*This field is required* appears)

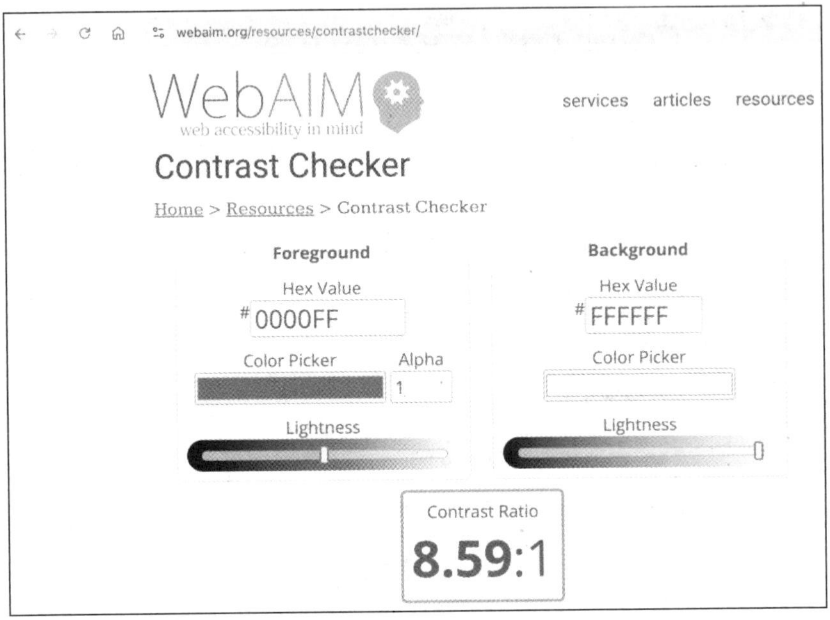


**FIGURE 4-1:** Use WebAIM's Contrast Checker to see if your foreground and background colors pass muster.

This principle applies to all information conveyed by color. If you're using green for success and red for error, add checkmarks and X marks. If you're color-coding a chart, also use patterns or labels.

## Typography choices that help accessibility

Some typeface choices are more accessible than others. Here's what I recommend:

- **Sans-serif fonts for body text:** Fonts like Arial, Verdana, and Helvetica are generally easier to read on screens than serif fonts, especially at smaller sizes.
- **Adequate font size:** Body text should be at least 20px. Many designers default to 14px or even 12px, but these sizes are hard to read, especially for people with vision impairments.
- **Comfortable line height:** Use a line height of at least 1.4 times the font size. So, if your font size is 20px, your line height should be at least 28px. This white space makes text much easier to read.
- **Reasonable line length:** Lines of text shouldn't be too long. Aim for 50 – 75 characters per line. Much longer and eyes have trouble finding the next line. Much shorter and reading becomes choppy.

- **Avoid all caps for long text:** ALL CAPS TEXT IS HARDER TO READ because we recognize words by their shape, and all caps text has a uniform rectangular shape. Use all caps sparingly, if at all.

WARNING

Never disable the user's ability to zoom or resize text. Some developers add viewport meta tags that prevent zooming. Don't do this: it creates a major accessibility barrier.

# Keyboard Navigation and Focus Management

Here's a quick test you can do right now: Try navigating a favorite website using only your keyboard. No mouse, no trackpad, just the Tab key, Enter key, and arrow keys. Can you access every interactive element? Can you tell where you are on the page?

For many users — including people with motor disabilities, power users who prefer keyboards, and people using screen readers — the keyboard is their primary or only way to navigate the web.

## Keyboard navigation basics

When someone navigates with a keyboard, they typically use these keys:

- **Tab:** Moves forward through interactive elements (links, buttons, form fields).
- **Shift+Tab:** Moves backward through interactive elements.
- **Enter:** Activates links and buttons.
- **Space:** Clicks buttons, toggles checkboxes, and scrolls down the page.
- **Arrow keys:** Navigate within certain elements, such as dropdown menus or radio button groups.

For keyboard navigation to work well, you need to ensure that:

- All interactive elements can receive keyboard focus.
- The tab order is logical and intuitive.
- The keyboard focus is clearly visible.

## The focus indicator problem

By default, browsers show a *focus indicator* — usually a blue or black outline — around the element that currently has keyboard focus. This is crucial for keyboard users to know where they are on the page.

Unfortunately, many designers find the default focus indicator ugly and remove it with CSS. Please, please don't do this. Or if you must customize it, replace it with something equally visible. A focus indicator might look like a design flaw, but it's an essential accessibility feature.

If you want to customize your focus indicators, make sure they meet WCAG requirements:

- The focus indicator should have a contrast ratio of at least 3:1 against the background.
- It should be visible on all interactive elements.
- It should be clearly distinguishable from the unfocused state.

## Logical tab order

The tab order — the sequence in which elements receive focus when someone presses the Tab key — should follow a logical, predictable pattern. For languages that read left-to-right, this usually means top-to-bottom, left-to-right.

In most cases, you don't need to do anything special to get a logical tab order. If you use semantic HTML and structure your content in a logical order in the HTML source code, the tab order will naturally be correct.

Where you can run into trouble is when you use CSS to visually rearrange content. For example, if you use CSS Grid or Flexbox to change the visual order of elements but don't update the HTML source order to match, the tab order will seem random and confusing.

## Skip links for navigation

Imagine having to tab through a navigation menu with 20 links every single time you want to get to the main content. That's the reality for keyboard users on many websites.

A *skip link* is a link placed at the beginning of your page that allows keyboard users to jump straight to the main content, bypassing repetitive navigation. It's typically hidden visually (so sighted users don't see it) but becomes visible — and its link text is read aloud by a screen reader — when it receives keyboard focus.

For the Orbital Donuts site, you might have a skip link that says Skip to Main Content, which, when activated, jumps the focus down to the start of the donut menu or main content area. This simple feature can dramatically improve the experience for keyboard users.

# Screen Reader Considerations

A *screen reader* is software that reads web page content aloud to users who are blind or have low vision. Popular screen readers include JAWS, NVDA (both for Windows), VoiceOver (for macOS and iOS), and TalkBack (for Android).

Screen readers don't just read text from top to bottom. They interpret the structure and semantics of your HTML to help users navigate efficiently. This means your choice of HTML elements is important.

## Semantic HTML is your friend

When I talk about *semantic HTML,* I mean using HTML elements for their intended purpose. Use heading elements (`h1`, `h2`, `h3`) for headings, not just to make text big and bold. Use `button` elements for buttons, not `div` elements with JavaScript click handlers. Use lists (`ul`, `ol`) for lists of items.

(If you have no idea what things like `h1`, `div`, and `ul` represent, don't worry about them for now. These and other HTML elements in this chapter get explained in full in Book 3.)

Why does semantic HTML matter? Because screen readers use these semantic elements to help users navigate. Many screen reader users navigate by headings, jumping from one `h2` to the next to find the section they want. They can pull up a list of all links on the page. They can navigate by landmarks like navigation, main content, and footer.

When you use generic `div` elements for everything and rely on CSS classes to style them, you strip away all this semantic meaning, making your site much harder to navigate with a screen reader.

## Heading structure and hierarchy

Your headings should follow a logical hierarchy:

- One h1 per page (usually the page title)
- h2 elements for main sections
- h3 elements for subsections within h2 sections
- And so on, without skipping heading levels

Don't skip heading levels (such as jumping from h1 to h3) because this creates confusion for screen reader users who are trying to understand your page structure.

## Alternative text for images

As I mention in Book 3, Chapter 3, every meaningful image on your site should have *alt text* — a text description that screen readers can read aloud. This accessibility requirement is one of the most basic, but it's often done poorly.

Good alt text is:

- **Descriptive:** It describes what's in the image. "Two chocolate donuts with sprinkles" not just "donuts."
- **Concise:** It's usually one or two sentences at most. You don't need to describe every detail.
- **Contextual:** It considers why the image is there. A photo of the owner needs different alt text on an About page ("Sarah Keaton, Orbital Donuts owner") than in a blog post about opening a new store location ("Sarah cutting the ribbon at our latest store").
- **Omitted for decorative images:** If an image is purely decorative and doesn't convey information, use empty alt text (`alt=""`) so screen readers skip it.

## ARIA: The escape hatch

ARIA stands for Accessible Rich Internet Applications, and it's a set of attributes you can add to HTML elements to make them more accessible, especially for complex interactive widgets.

For example, you might use ARIA to indicate that a `div` is actually a button (`role="button"`), or to label a form field (`aria-label="Search"`), or to indicate that content has been updated (`aria-live="polite"`).

Here's the thing about ARIA: if you're using semantic HTML correctly, you often don't need it. A proper button element doesn't need `role="button"` because it's already a button. But for more complex components — such as custom dropdowns or tabs — ARIA can be essential.

The golden rule of ARIA: don't use it if you don't have to, and if you do use it, test it with screen readers to make sure it works as expected.

# Accessible Forms and Interactive Elements

Forms are where accessibility often breaks down. A contact form, newsletter signup, or e-commerce checkout might work perfectly with a mouse but be unusable with a keyboard or screen reader.

## Labels and form fields

Every form field needs a *label,* and that label needs to be properly associated with the field using the HTML label element. Screen readers use these associations to tell users what each field is for.

As I discuss in Book 3, Chapter 4, labels should be visible on screen (not just placeholders, which disappear when you start typing) and should be positioned consistently: usually above or to the left of the field.

## Clear error messages and validation

When someone makes a mistake filling out a form, you need to tell them:

- **What went wrong:** Not just *Error in form* but *Email address is required* or *Password must be at least 8 characters.*
- **Where the problem is:** The error message should be near the problematic field, and that field should be easy to locate. (Don't just rely on color — add an icon or move focus to the field.)

» **How to fix it:** When possible, tell users how to correct the error. *Please enter a valid email address* is better than *Invalid input.*

For screen reader users, error messages should be announced automatically when they occur. You can use ARIA live regions for this, but test to make sure they work with the screen readers your users are likely to use.

## Required fields and instructions

Make it clear which form fields are required. The standard convention is to mark required fields with an asterisk (*), but you should also:

» Explain the asterisk convention at the top of the form

» Use the HTML `required` attribute on required fields

» Consider also including the word *required* in the label

If a field has specific requirements (such as *password must include at least one number*), state those requirements before the field, not just when someone makes a mistake.

## Interactive widgets

Custom dropdown menus, date pickers, sliders, and other interactive widgets can be accessibility nightmares if they're not implemented carefully. The problem is that these elements are often built from scratch using `div` elements and JavaScript, with no consideration for keyboard users or screen readers.

My advice: whenever possible, use native HTML elements (such as the `select` element for dropdowns or the `date` input type for date pickers) or well-tested accessible component libraries. Building custom accessible widgets from scratch is hard and requires expertise.

If you do need custom widgets, make sure they:

» Work completely with the keyboard.

» Announce their role and state to screen readers.

» Follow established keyboard interaction patterns.

» Maintain visible focus indicators.

# Common Accessibility Mistakes and How to Avoid Them

Let me walk you through some of the most common accessibility mistakes I see, so you can avoid them in your own work.

## The "click here" problem

Link text that says *click here* or *read more* is terrible for accessibility. Why? Because many screen reader users navigate by pulling up a list of all links on the page. When they do that, they just see

Click here

Click here

Click here

Not helpful at all. Instead, make your link text descriptive:

Read our privacy policy

View the full donut menu

Learn about our space-themed ingredients

Now each link makes sense on its own, out of context.

## Placeholder text instead of labels

Using *placeholder text* (the light gray text inside a form field) instead of a proper label is a common design trend, but it's bad for accessibility:

- Placeholder text disappears when you start typing, so you can't remember what the field was for.
- It usually has low contrast (light gray on white) that doesn't meet accessibility standards.
- Screen readers may not read placeholder text as a label.

Use real labels that stay visible even when the field is filled in. You can still use placeholder text for examples or hints, but don't rely on it as the primary label.

## Auto-playing content

Videos or audio that start playing automatically are annoying for everyone, but they're especially problematic for people using screen readers (autoplaying audio interferes with the screen reader's audio) and people with cognitive disabilities (unexpected motion or sound can be disorienting).

Give users control. Don't autoplay. If you absolutely must use autoplay, provide prominent controls to pause or stop the content, and keep it muted by default.

## Tiny click targets

For people with motor disabilities, small buttons or links can be difficult or impossible to click. WCAG recommends that interactive elements be at least 24 by 24 pixels, but should be at least 44 by 44 if you're targeting touchscreen users (and you are).

This doesn't mean your button has to look huge — you can use padding to make the clickable area larger while keeping the visual design compact. The important thing is that the area that responds to clicks is adequately sized.

## Ignoring motion preferences

Some people experience dizziness, nausea, or even seizures from motion on screen — things like parallax scrolling effects, animated backgrounds, or auto-playing carousels. Modern browsers support a prefers-reduced-motion setting that users can enable.

You should respect this setting. When someone has indicated they prefer reduced motion, tone down or eliminate animations, parallax effects, and other motion. The content should still work; it just won't be as visually dynamic.

## PDF accessibility

If your site provides PDF documents (such as a menu, a brochure, or an application form), those PDFs need to be accessible too. An image-based PDF — basically just a picture of a document — is inaccessible to screen readers.

Accessible PDFs should have:

- Actual text (not images of text)
- A proper heading structure
- Tagged content (this is like semantic HTML for PDFs)
- Alt text for images
- A logical reading order

Creating accessible PDFs is its own specialized topic, but if you're creating PDFs from Word documents, most of the accessibility you build into the Word doc will carry over to the PDF if you export it using Word (be sure to select the option that optimizes accessibility) or import it using Adobe Acrobat.

# Testing for Accessibility

You can't know if your site is accessible unless you test it. Here's the good news: accessibility testing doesn't have to be complicated or expensive. You can catch most problems with free tools and manual testing.

## Automated testing tools

Automated testing tools can catch a lot of common accessibility issues: missing alt text, insufficient color contrast, improper heading structure, and more. They can't catch everything (more on that in a moment), but they're a great first step.

Two tools I recommend:

- **WAVE (Web Accessibility Evaluation Tool):** Available as a browser extension or web service at `wave.webaim.org`. WAVE is visual and easy to understand, showing you exactly where problems are on your page.
- **axe DevTools:** A browser extension that integrates with your browser's developer tools. axe DevTools is thorough and provides detailed explanations of issues and how to fix them.

I use both. WAVE is great for a quick overview, while axe DevTools is better for detailed testing and debugging.

## Manual keyboard testing

The following is a simple but crucial aspect of testing: unplug your mouse and try to use your website with just the keyboard. Can you:

- Navigate through all the links and buttons?
- Submit all the forms?
- Open and close all the menus and modals?
- See where you are at all times (thanks to the focus indicator)?

If the answer to any of these is no, you've found an accessibility problem. Fix it.

## Screen reader testing

Testing with a screen reader is more advanced, but it's the best way to understand how blind users experience your site. Every major operating system includes a free screen reader:

- **Windows:** NVDA (free, download from `nvaccess.org`) or Narrator (built-in)
- **macOS:** VoiceOver (built-in, activate with Command+F5)
- **iOS:** VoiceOver (in Settings⇨Accessibility)
- **Android:** TalkBack (in Settings⇨Accessibility)

Learning to use a screen reader takes some time — the keyboard shortcuts alone can be overwhelming. Start by learning the basics: how to navigate by headings, how to navigate links, how to interact with forms. WebAIM has excellent tutorials for all the major screen readers at `webaim.org`.

## Color contrast checkers

As I mention earlier in this chapter, you need adequate color contrast between text and backgrounds. The easiest way to check this is with a contrast checker tool.

I like the WebAIM Contrast Checker (`webaim.org/resources/contrastchecker/`) because it's simple and tells you immediately whether your colors pass or fail for normal text, large text, and at different WCAG levels. You just plug in your foreground and background colors and it does the math.

Both WAVE and axe DevTools also check contrast automatically, which is handy for checking your entire page at once.

## What automated tools miss

Here's the thing about automated testing: it can only catch about 30 – 40 percent of accessibility issues. The rest require human judgment. For example:

- » A tool can check that an image has alt text but can't tell you if the alt text is good or descriptive.
- » A tool can verify that your headings are hierarchical but can't tell you if the heading text is clear and descriptive.
- » A tool can detect that a custom widget has ARIA attributes but can't tell you if those attributes are used correctly or if the widget works with a keyboard.

This is why manual testing is essential. Use automated tools to catch the low-hanging fruit, and then do manual keyboard and screen reader testing to catch the rest.

## User testing with people with disabilities

The absolute best way to know if your site is accessible? Have people with disabilities test it. No amount of automated testing or simulated screen reader use can replace the insight of someone who relies on these technologies every day.

If you have the budget, you can hire accessibility consultants or testing services. If not, you can reach out to local disability organizations or put out a call on social media for volunteers. Many people with disabilities are happy to provide feedback, especially if you're genuinely committed to making your site more accessible.

## Making accessibility part of your workflow

The best approach to accessibility is to build it in from the start rather than trying to bolt it on later. Make accessibility testing a regular part of your development process:

- » Run automated accessibility tests on every page before considering it complete.
- » Do keyboard testing before launching any interactive feature.
- » Check color contrast when choosing your color scheme.
- » Test with a screen reader periodically as you build.

It's much easier to fix accessibility issues as you go than to try to retrofit an entire website after it's built.

TIP

Create an accessibility testing checklist for yourself. Include things like "Keyboard navigation works," "All images have alt text," and "Color contrast meets WCAG AA." Run through this checklist before launching any new page or feature.

Here's the bottom line: accessibility is not a one-time checkbox to tick. It's an ongoing commitment to making sure your website works for everyone. Start with the basics I've covered in this chapter — good color contrast, keyboard navigation, semantic HTML, proper labels — and build from there. Use automated tools to catch common issues, and then supplement with manual testing. Most importantly, keep learning. Accessibility guidelines evolve, your understanding will deepen, and you'll get better at designing accessible experiences from the start.

And remember: when you design for accessibility, you're not just checking a legal box or following guidelines. You're making a statement about who's welcome on your website. And the answer should always be: everyone.

# 3

# HTML and CSS Essentials

# Contents at a Glance

IN THIS CHAPTER

» Learning modern page structure

» Adding semantic tags

» Creating effective links

» Adding images and multimedia

» Optimizing your site for search

# Chapter 1 HTML Fundamentals

*First learn computer science and all the theory. Next develop a programming style. Then forget all that and just hack.*

—GEORGE CARRETTE

Okay, you learned the theory (Book 1), you learned about design (Book 2), now it's finally time to start building! And I mean *actually* building: writing the HTML code that forms the foundation of every web page.

HTML might seem intimidating at first. After all, it's code, which is something that super-smart computer science types write, right? Well, here's the thing: HTML isn't programming in the traditional sense. You're not writing algorithms or debugging logic errors. You're simply describing the structure and content of your pages using a straightforward markup language that's designed to be read by humans. If you can write an email and follow basic instructions, you can write HTML.

In this chapter, you learn the fundamentals of HTML. I show you how to structure your documents properly, use semantic tags that give meaning to your content, create links that connect your pages, and add images and multimedia. By the end, you'll have the foundation you need to build web pages, not just read about them. How exciting is *that*?

# Figuring Out HTML Elements and Tags

At its most basic, HTML is nothing more than a collection of markup codes — called *elements* — that specify the structure of your web page. In HTML, *structure* is a rubbery concept that can refer to anything from the overall layout of the page all the way down to a single word or even just a character or two.

For most of your HTML chores, you create a kind of container. What types of things can reside in this container? Mostly text but often entire chunks of the web page and even other elements.

Most HTML containers use the following generic format:

```
<element>content</element>
```

What you have here are a couple of codes that define the container for a particular HTML element. Many elements are one- or two-letter abbreviations, but sometimes they're entire words. You always surround these elements with angle brackets `<>`; the brackets tell the web browser that it's dealing with a chunk of HTML and not just random text. An element surrounded by angle brackets is called a *tag.*

The first of these codes — `<element>` — is called the *start tag* and marks the opening of the container; the second code — `</element>` — is called the *end tag* and marks the closing of the container. (Note the extra slash (`/`) that appears in the end tag.)

In between the start and end tags, you have `content` which refers to whatever is contained in the tag. For example (refer to `bk03ch01/example01.html` in this book's example files):

```
This is a web page with something <em>important</em> to say.
```

Notice how I've surrounded the word `important` with `<em>` and `</em>`? The first `<em>` is the start tag, and it says to the browser, "Yo, Browser Boy! You know the text that comes after this? Be a good fellow and treat it as emphasized text." The browser continues to treat text this way until it reaches the end tag `</em>`, which lets the browser know that it's supposed to stop what it's doing. So the `</em>` tells the browser, "Okay, okay. That's enough with the emphasis already!"

All web browsers display emphasized text in italics, so that's how the word now appears, as shown in Figure 1-1.

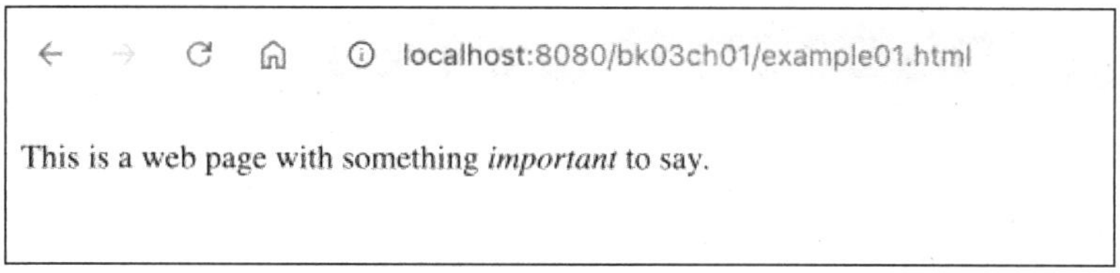


**FIGURE 1-1:** A sentence that italicizes the word `important`.

There are tags for lots of other structures, including important text, paragraphs, headings, page titles, links, and lists. HTML is just the collection of all these tags.

**WARNING**

One of the most common mistakes rookie web weavers make is to forget the slash (/) that identifies an end tag. If your page looks wrong when you view it in a browser, look for a missing slash. Also look for a backslash (\) instead of a slash, which is another common error.

# Understanding Modern HTML Document Structure

Every HTML document follows a specific structure, kind of like how every business letter has a letterhead, date, greeting, body, and signature. This structure isn't arbitrary, though. Browsers expect it, search engines rely on it, and accessibility tools need it. Get the structure right, and everything else becomes much easier.

Here's the basic skeleton of every HTML document (refer to `bk03ch01/example02.html` in this book's example files):

```
<!DOCTYPE html>
<html lang="en">
<head>
    <meta charset="UTF-8">
    <meta name="viewport" content="width=device-width, initial-scale=1.0">
    <title>Your Page Title</title>
</head>
<body>
    <!-- Your visible content goes here -->
</body>
</html>
```

Don't worry if this looks like gibberish right now. I'm going to break down every piece of this structure so it makes perfect sense.

## The DOCTYPE declaration

That first line — <!DOCTYPE html> — might seem weird, but it's incredibly important. It tells the browser, "Hey, this is an HTML5 document, so please render it using modern standards."

Older versions of HTML had insanely long DOCTYPE declarations that were impossible to remember. (I mean, who could memorize something like <!DOCTYPE HTML PUBLIC "-//W3C//DTD HTML 4.01 Transitional//EN" "http://www.w3.org/TR/html4/loose.dtd">? Not me, that's for sure.) HTML5 (the current version of HTML) simplified this to just <!DOCTYPE html>, which is mercifully short and easy to remember.

WARNING

Always include the DOCTYPE declaration as the very first line of your HTML document. Without it, browsers might fall into *quirks mode*, where they intentionally ignore your HTML and CSS in favor of older (and quirky, hence the name) code used to support legacy websites built prior to modern web development standards. Quirks mode will almost certainly render your page incorrectly, leading to weird layout issues that are hard to debug.

## The html element

Right after DOCTYPE, you have the <html> tag. This is your *root element*, which means that everything else in your document lives inside this tag. Notice how it has lang="en"? That's telling browsers and assistive technologies that your content is in English.

Why specify the language? Screen readers use the lang attribute to pronounce text correctly. Search engines use it to understand what language your content is in. And browsers can use it to offer translation options. So, if your Orbital Donuts website is in English, use lang="en". If it's in French, use lang="fr". If it's in Spanish, use lang="es". You get the idea.

## The head section: Invisible but essential

The <head> section contains information *about* your page, not content that visitors will see. Think of it as the metadata (data about data). It's like the title page and copyright information in a book: you don't read those for the story, but they're important for cataloging and distribution.

Here's what goes in the <head> section:

- **Character encoding:** The <meta charset="UTF-8"> tag tells the browser how to interpret the text in your file. UTF-8 is the standard encoding that supports basically every language and symbol you'll ever need. Always include this tag.

- **Viewport settings:** The `<meta name="viewport">` tag is crucial for responsive design (as I mention in Book 2, Chapter 3). It tells mobile browsers not to zoom out and show a tiny desktop version of your page. Instead, it makes your page display at the device's width.
- **Page title:** The `<title>` tag shows up in browser tabs and search engine results. For the Orbital Donuts home page, you might use `<title>Orbital Donuts – Out-of-This-World Donuts Delivered Daily</title>`.
- **Links to CSS files:** This is where you connect your HTML to your stylesheets (which I cover in Book 3, Chapter 3).
- **Links to JavaScript files:** You can link to JavaScript files here as well, though sometimes it's better to put them at the bottom of the `<body>` section. Refer to Book 4.
- **Metadata for search engines:** Information that helps search engines understand and rank your content.

## The body section: Where content lives

Everything visitors see on your page goes inside the `<body>` section. Text, images, videos, buttons, forms, all of it lives in the body. If it appears on screen, it's in the body.

Here's a simple example for the Orbital Donuts homepage (`bk03ch01/example03.html`):

```
<!DOCTYPE html>
<html lang="en">
<head>
    <meta charset="UTF-8">
    <meta name="viewport" content="width=device-width, initial-scale=1.0">
    <title>Orbital Donuts - Out-of-This-World Donuts</title>
</head>
<body>
    <h1>Welcome to Orbital Donuts</h1>
    <p>Where every donut is out of this world!</p>
</body>
</html>
```

That's it! That's a complete, valid HTML5 document. It's simple, but it works. When you save this as a `.html` file and open it in a browser, you'll see a heading and a paragraph. (Go ahead, try it! Create a file called `test.html`, paste in that code, and open it in your browser.)

TIP

Use descriptive filenames for your HTML files: `about.html` instead of `page2.html`, `menu.html` instead of `items.html`. Your site will be easier to organize and maintain, and they're better for search engines too.

# Semantic HTML Elements: Why They Matter

You could, technically, build an entire website using only the tags `<div>` (a generic container for text that automatically adds a line separating it from the text that follows) and `<span>` (a generic container for text that remains on the same line as surrounding text), styled with CSS to look however you want. But that would be like building a house where every room is a generic box with no indication whether it's a kitchen, bedroom, or bathroom. Sure, you could make it work, but it would be confusing and impractical.

*Semantic HTML* means using tags that describe their content, not just tags that hold content. Instead of a generic `<div>`, you use `<article>` for an article, `<nav>` for navigation, or `<aside>` for sidebar content. The element name — `article`, `nav`, `aside` — tells you (and browsers and search engines) its purpose.

## Why semantic HTML matters

There are three huge reasons to use semantic HTML:

- **Accessibility:** Screen readers for people who are blind or have low vision use semantic elements to help users navigate. A screen reader can jump straight to the `<main>` content or list all the `<nav>` tags on the page. But if everything's a `<div>`, the screen reader has no idea what anything is.
- **SEO:** Search engines allocate the weight of content appropriately in semantic elements. For example, content in an `<article>` tag is understood as main content, while content in an `<aside>` is understood as supplementary. This approach helps search engines understand what's important on your page.

- **Maintainability:** When you come back to your code six months later, <header> and <footer> immediately tell you what those sections are. But <div class="top-section"> and <div class="bottom-section"> require you to remember what those class names mean.

## The essential semantic tags

HTML5 introduced a bunch of semantic tags that replace the generic <div> tags. Here are the most important ones:

- **<header>:** The header of your page or section, which typically contains your logo, site title, and main navigation. For Orbital Donuts, the header would include the logo and the navigation menu.
- **<nav>:** Navigation links, which are links that help users navigate your site, such as your main navigation menu, a sidebar menu, or footer links.
- **<main>:** The main content of your page. Each page should have exactly one <main> tag containing the primary content. For the Orbital Donuts menu page, the <main> tag would wrap all the donut listings.
- **<article>:** A self-contained piece of content that could be distributed independently. A blog post, a news article, or even a donut listing could be an <article> tag.
- **<section>:** A thematic grouping of content, typically with a heading. You might have a <section> for "Featured Donuts" and another <section> for "Customer Testimonials."
- **<aside>:** Content tangentially related to the main content, such as a sidebar with related links, a callout box with additional information, or a widget showing social media feeds.
- **<footer>:** The footer of your page or section. This tag typically contains copyright information, contact details, and secondary navigation links.

Here's how these tags might structure the Orbital Donuts home page (bk03ch01/example04.html):

```
<!DOCTYPE html>
<html lang="en">
<head>
    <meta charset="UTF-8">
    <meta name="viewport" content="width=device-width, initial-scale=1.0">
```

```
    <title>Orbital Donuts - Out-of-This-World Donuts</title>
</head>
<body>
    <header>
        <h1>Orbital Donuts</h1>
        <nav>
            <a href="menu.html">Menu</a>
            <a href="order.html">Order Online</a>
            <a href="locations.html">Locations</a>
            <a href="catering.html">Catering</a>
            <a href="about.html">About</a>
        </nav>
    </header>
    <main>

<section>
            <h2>Featured Donut of the Day</h2>
            <article>
                <h3>Cosmic Cruller</h3>
                <p>A twisted masterpiece glazed with stardust and dreams.</p>
            </article>
        </section>

<section>
            <h2>Our Signature Donuts</h2>
            <article>
                <h3>Rocket Red Velvet</h3>
                <p>Classic red velvet with cream cheese frosting.</p>
            </article>
            <article>
                <h3>Galaxy Glazed</h3>
                <p>Our signature glaze with edible glitter.</p>
            </article>
        </section>
    </main>
    <footer>
        <p>© Orbital Donuts. All rights reserved.</p>
    </footer>
</body>
</html>
```

Notice how you can immediately understand the structure just by reading the element names? That's the power of semantic HTML. Figure 1-2 shows how things look in the browser.

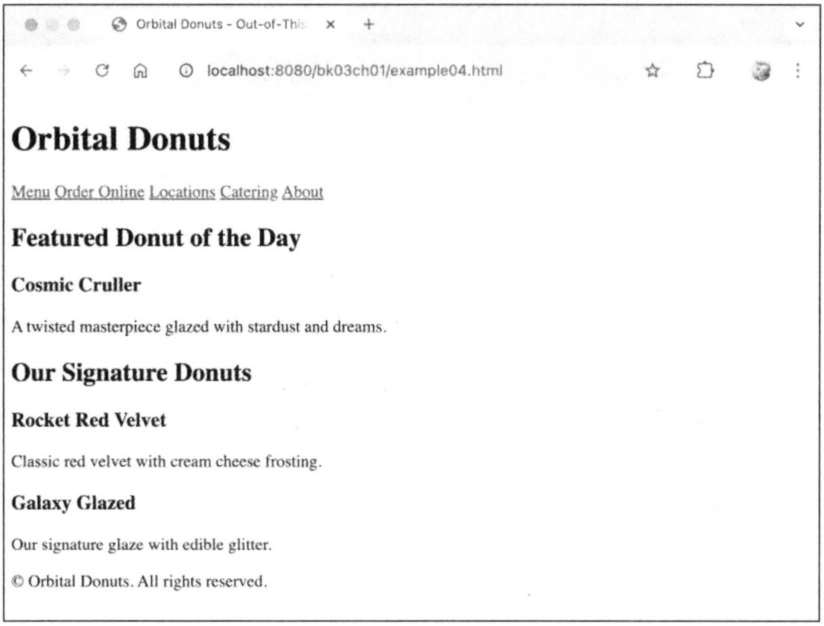


**FIGURE 1-2:** The Orbital Donuts home page so far.

## Headings: Creating document hierarchy

Headings (<h1> through <h6>) are some of the most important semantic tags because they create the outline of your document. They're a lot like chapter titles and section headings in a book because they tell readers (and search engines) how your content is organized.

Here's the rule: every page should have exactly one <h1> tag, which is typically your page title or main heading. Then use <h2> for main sections, <h3> for sub-sections within those, and so on. Don't skip levels. For example, don't jump from <h2> to <h4> without an <h3> tag in between.

For the Orbital Donuts menu page, the heading structure might look like this:

```
<h1>Our Menu</h1>
    <h2>Classic Donuts</h2>
        <h3>Rocket Red Velvet</h3>
        <h3>Galaxy Glazed</h3>
    <h2>Specialty Donuts</h2>
        <h3>Cosmic Cruller</h3>
        <h3>Nebula Nutella</h3>
    <h2>Dietary Options</h2>
        <h3>Vegan Donuts</h3>
        <h3>Gluten-Free Donuts</h3>
```

This creates a clear hierarchy (which I've exaggerated a bit by indenting): under the main heading (<h1>), the menu has three main categories (<h2>), and each category has specific donuts (<h3>). A screen reader user could navigate this structure easily, jumping from one <h2> to the next to browse categories.

REMEMBER

Never choose a heading level based on how it looks. Use heading levels to reflect the structure of your content. If you want a heading to look different, use CSS to style it. The heading level itself should be determined by where it fits in your content hierarchy.

## Paragraphs and text formatting

For body text, you use the <p> tag to create paragraphs. Each paragraph gets its own <p> tag:

```
<p>Welcome to Orbital Donuts, where we've been making out-of-this-world donuts
since 2020. Our space-themed shop combines artisanal baking techniques with
cosmic creativity.</p>
<p>Every donut is handmade fresh daily using locally sourced ingredients and
topped with our signature space-inspired glazes and decorations.</p>
```

HTML also provides several tags for emphasizing text:

- **<strong>:** For important text that should stand out from the rest of the text. Browsers typically render this as bold text, for example, `<strong>All donuts must be consumed within 24 hours for peak freshness.</strong>`.
- **<em>:** For text that should be emphasized. Browsers typically render this as italic text, for example, `We <em>really</em> recommend trying the Cosmic Cruller.`
- **<mark>:** For highlighted text, such as `<mark>Now on sale!</mark>`.
- **<small>:** For fine print or legal disclaimers, such as `<small>Some restrictions apply.</small>`.

REMEMBER

Here's an important point: use <strong> and <em> when you want to add semantic emphasis; that is, when the words are more important or stressed. Don't use these tags just to make text bold or italic for visual purposes. For purely visual styling, use CSS (as I explain in Book 3, Chapter 3).

# Working with Links and Navigation

Links are what make the web, well, a web. Without links, you'd just have isolated pages with no way to connect them. Learning to create effective links is fundamental to building any website.

## Creating basic links

You forge a link with the <a> (anchor) tag. The destination is specified with the href attribute:

```
<a href="menu.html">View our menu</a>
```

When someone clicks the View our menu link, their browser loads menu.html.

But here's something crucial about link text: it should be descriptive. *Click here* is terrible link text because it doesn't tell users (or search engines) what they're clicking to. *View our menu* is much better because it's clear and specific.

Here are examples of good versus bad link text:

- To order donuts:
  - *Bad:* <a href="order.html">click here</a>
  - *Good:* <a href="order.html">Order donuts online</a>
- To learn more about the company:
  - *Bad:* <a href="about.html">Click</a>
  - *Good:* <a href="about.html">Learn more about Orbital Donuts</a>
- To view the menu:
  - *Bad:* <a href="menu.html">Read more</a>
  - *Good:* <a href="menu.html">View the full donut menu</a>

As I mention in Book 2, Chapter 4, descriptive link text is also crucial for accessibility. Screen reader users often navigate by pulling up a list of all links on the page. If your links all say *Click here* or *Read more,* that list is useless.

# Absolute versus relative links

There are two ways to specify link destinations: using absolute URLs and relative URLs.

An *absolute URL* includes the full address, including the protocol (the https:// part) and domain name:

```
<a href="https://orbitaldonuts.com/menu.html">View menu</a>
```

This link works from anywhere on the web. Use absolute URLs when linking to external websites or when you want to be explicit about the full path.

A *relative URL* is relative to the current page's location. If you're on https://orbitaldonuts.com/index.html and link to menu.html, the browser looks for the menu page in the same directory:

```
<a href="menu.html">View menu</a>
```

Relative links are shorter and more flexible. If you move your entire site to a new domain, all your relative links still work. But they can be tricky if your site has a complex directory structure.

Here's how relative links work with different directory structures:

- **Same directory:** <a href="menu.html">Menu</a> links to a file in the same directory.
- **Subdirectory:** <a href="pages/menu.html">Menu</a> links to a file in the pages subdirectory.
- **Parent directory:** <a href="../menu.html">Menu</a> links to a file one level up.
- **Root directory:** <a href="/menu.html">Menu</a> links to a file at the site root.

For most simple sites, keep all your HTML files in the same directory and use simple relative links like menu.html. As your site grows, you might organize files into subdirectories, but start simple.

TIP

Use relative links for internal pages on your site and absolute links for external websites. This approach makes your site more portable and easier to test locally before uploading to your web server.

## Creating navigation menus

Navigation menus are just lists of links, but you wrap them in the semantic `<nav>` tag to indicate their purpose. Here's a simple navigation menu for Orbital Donuts:

```
<nav>
    <a href="index.html">Home</a>
    <a href="menu.html">Menu</a>
    <a href="order.html">Order Online</a>
    <a href="locations.html">Locations</a>
    <a href="catering.html">Catering</a>
    <a href="about.html">About</a>
</nav>
```

This menu works, but it's often better to structure navigation as an unordered list (`<ul>`; refer to the next section) because it's more semantic and easier to style with CSS:

```
<nav>
    <ul>
        <li><a href="index.html">Home</a></li>
        <li><a href="menu.html">Menu</a></li>
        <li><a href="order.html">Order Online</a></li>
        <li><a href="locations.html">Locations</a></li>
        <li><a href="catering.html">Catering</a></li>
        <li><a href="about.html">About</a></li>
    </ul>
</nav>
```

By default, this code renders as a bulleted list. But with CSS (which you learn in Book 3, Chapter 3), you can style it to appear as a horizontal navigation bar, vertical sidebar menu, or dropdown menu — whatever your design requires.

# Building Bulleted and Numbered Lists

When your page requires a list of things, HTML has a few tags that are designed to ease your list-building chores. For example, you can create a bulleted list that has those little bullets out front of each item. Nice! Want a top ten list, instead? HTML has your back by offering special tags for numbered lists, too.

## Making your point with bulleted lists

Bulleted lists use two types of tags:

- The entire list is surrounded by the `<ul>` and `</ul>` tags. Why `ul`? Well, what the rest of the world calls a bulleted list, the HTML poohbahs call an *unordered list.*
- Each item in the list is preceded by the `<li>` (list item) tag and is closed with the `</li>` end tag. (Technically, the `</li>` end tag is optional as long as the next item is another `<li>` tag or the `</ul>` end tag.)

The general setup looks like this:

```
<ul>
    <li>Bullet text goes here</li>
    <li>And here</li>
    <li>And here</li>
    <li>You get the idea...</li>
</ul>
```

Note that I've indented the list items by four spaces, which makes it easier to see that they're part of a `<ul></ul>` container. Here's an example to chew on (`bk03ch01/example05.html`):

```
<h3>My All-Time Favorite Oxymorons</h3>
<ul>
    <li>Pretty ugly</li>
    <li>Military intelligence</li>
    <li>Jumbo shrimp</li>
    <li>Original copy</li>
    <li>Random order</li>
    <li>Act naturally</li>
    <li>Tight slacks</li>
    <li>Freezer burn</li>
    <li>Sight unseen</li>
    <li>Microsoft Works</li>
</ul>
```

Figure 1-3 shows how the browser renders this code, cute bullets and all.

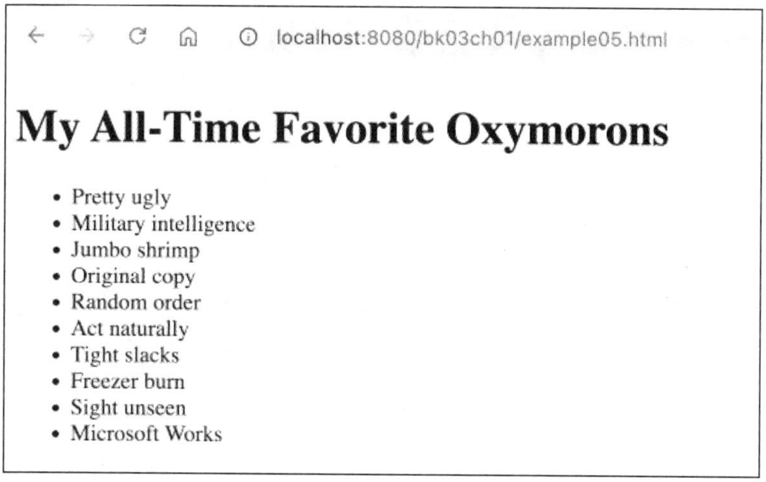


**FIGURE 1-3:** A typical bulleted list.

## Numbered lists: Easy as one, two, three

As do bulleted lists, numbered lists use two types of tags:

- The entire list is surrounded by the <ol> and </ol> tags. The ol here is short for *ordered list,* because those HTML nerds just have to be different, don't they?
- Each item in the list is surrounded by <li> and </li>.

Here's the general structure to use:

```
<ol>
    <li>First item</li>
    <li>Second item</li>
    <li>Third item</li>
    <li>You got this...</li>
</ol>
```

I've indented the list items by four spaces to make it easier to notice that they're inside an <ol></ol> container. Here's an example (bk03ch01/example06.html):

```
<h3>My Ten Favorite U.S. College Nicknames</h3>
<ol>
    <li>U.C. Santa Cruz Banana Slugs</li>
    <li>Delta State Fighting Okra</li>
    <li>Kent State Golden Flashes</li>
    <li>Evergreen State College Geoducks</li>
```

```
    <li>New Mexico Tech Pygmies</li>
    <li>South Carolina Fighting Gamecocks</li>
    <li>Southern Illinois Salukis</li>
    <li>Whittier Poets</li>
    <li>Western Illinois Leathernecks</li>
    <li>Delaware Fightin' Blue Hens</li>
</ol>
```

Notice that I didn't include any numbers before each list item? However, when I display this document in a browser (check out Figure 1-4), the numbers are automatically inserted. Pretty slick, huh?

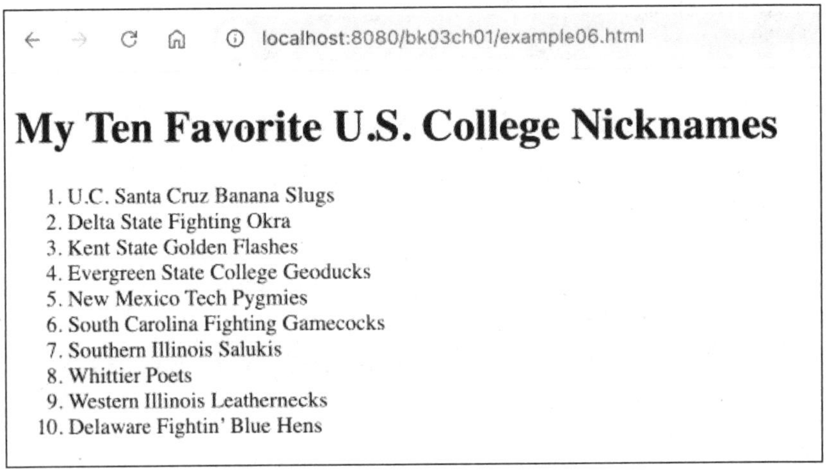


**FIGURE 1-4:** When the web browser renders the ordered list, it's kind enough to add the numbers for you.

# Adding Images and Multimedia

Text-only websites are boring. Images, videos, and other multimedia make your site engaging, help communicate your message, and — in the case of a donut shop — make people hungry!

## The img element

You add images with the `<img>` tag. Unlike most HTML tags, `<img>` doesn't have a closing tag. It's what HTML nerds called a *self-closing tag* or *void tag.*

Here's a simple image:

```
<img src="cosmic-cruller.webp" alt="Twisted cruller with purple and blue
galaxy glaze and edible stars">
```

Two attributes are essential:

- **`src`:** The source file, which specifies the name and location of the image. This attribute can be a relative or absolute URL, just like links.
- **`alt`:** Alternative text that describes the image. Alternative text is crucial for accessibility (screen readers read this text aloud) and SEO (search engines can't see images, so they rely on alt text to understand them).

For the Orbital Donuts featured donut section, you might have the following code (`bk03ch01/orbital-donuts/index.html`):

```
<section>
    <h2>Featured Donut of the Day</h2>
    <article>
        <h3>Cosmic Cruller</h3>
        <img src="/images/cosmic-cruller.webp"
            alt="Twisted cruller with purple and blue galaxy glaze and edible
                 stars"
            height="256" width="256">
        <p>A twisted masterpiece glazed with stardust and dreams.</p>
        <p><strong>$4.99</strong></p>
        <p><em>[Add to Cart button will go here]</em></p>
    </article>
</section>
```

Note that I also specified the `height` and `width` attributes, which helps the web browser allot the correct amount of space for the image. Figure 1-5 shows how things turned out in the browser. (Yep, I know: this isn't a great-looking page! But *great-looking* requires CSS, so we'll get there in Book 3, Chapter 3.)

## Writing effective alt text

Alt text is one of those things that's easy to do badly and crucial to do well. As I discuss in Book 2, Chapter 4, good alt text is:

- **Descriptive:** Describe what's in the image. *Cosmic Cruller donut* is better than just *donut.*

**FIGURE 1-5:** An image added to the Orbital Donuts web page.

- **Concise:** Usually one or two sentences at most. You're describing the image, not writing a novel about it.
- **Contextual:** Consider why the image is there. An image of the owner needs different alt text on an About page ("Owner Sarah Keaton in the Orbital Donuts kitchen") than in a blog post about a new location ("Sarah cutting the ribbon at our newest store").
- **Omitted for decorative images:** If an image is purely decorative and doesn't add information, use empty alt text (`alt=""`) so screen readers skip it.

Here are some examples of alt text for Orbital Donuts:

- **Product image:** `alt="Rocket Red Velvet donut with cream cheese frosting"`
- **Hero image:** `alt="Assorted Orbital Donuts arranged on a dark blue background with glittering stars"`
- **Owner photo:** `alt="Sarah Keaton, Orbital Donuts owner, holding a tray of fresh donuts"`
- **Decorative star graphic:** `alt=""`

REMEMBER

Never skip the `alt` attribute. Even if the image is decorative, use `alt=""` so screen readers know to skip it. Missing `alt` attributes are accessibility errors and hurt your SEO.

## Responsive images

As I mention in Book 2, Chapter 3, your images need to work across different screen sizes. One way to handle this requirement is with responsive image syntax, which lets you provide different image files for different devices:

```
<img src="cosmic-cruller-800.webp"
     srcset="cosmic-cruller-400.webp 400w,
             cosmic-cruller-800.webp 800w,
             cosmic-cruller-1200.webp 1200w"
     sizes="(max-width: 600px) 400px,
            (max-width: 1200px) 800px,
            1200px"
     alt="Cosmic Cruller donut with purple galaxy glaze">
```

This solution looks complicated, but here's what it does:

- **`src`:** The default image (for older browsers that don't support responsive images)
- **`srcset`:** A list of available images with their widths
- **`sizes`:** Instructions about which image to use at different viewport widths

The browser picks the most appropriate image based on the device's screen size and resolution. On a small phone, it downloads the 400px version. On a large desktop monitor, it uses the 1200px version. This approach saves bandwidth and improves loading times for mobile users.

For most small business sites, this level of optimization might be overkill initially. Start with good-quality images at a reasonable size (800–1200px wide) and add responsive image syntax later if page speed becomes an issue.

## Adding videos

Videos are added with the `<video>` tag:

```
<video src="donut-making.mp4" controls width="640" height="360">
    Your browser doesn't support video playback.
</video>
```

The `controls` attribute adds play, pause, and volume controls. The text between the opening and closing tags is displayed only if the browser doesn't support video.

For better browser compatibility, provide multiple video formats:

```
<video controls width="640" height="360">
    <source src="donut-making.mp4" type="video/mp4">
    <source src="donut-making.webm" type="video/webm">
    Your browser doesn't support video playback.
</video>
```

The browser uses the first format it supports. MP4 has the widest support, while WebM offers better compression.

However, here's a reality check: hosting video files on your own website can be problematic. Video files are large, which means slow page loads and expensive bandwidth bills. For most small businesses, it's better to host videos on YouTube or Vimeo and embed them using an `<iframe>` tag:

```
<iframe width="560" height="315"
        src="https://www.youtube.com/embed/VIDEO_ID"
        title="How We Make Our Cosmic Donuts"
        frameborder="0"
        allow="accelerometer; autoplay; clipboard-write; encrypted-media;
              gyroscope; picture-in-picture"
        allowfullscreen>
</iframe>
```

YouTube and Vimeo handle all the technical complexities of video delivery, including adaptive bitrates, different formats, and content delivery networks. They also provide convenient embedding codes so you don't have to write the `<iframe>` tag yourself. And, as a bonus, anyone browsing YouTube or Vimeo for space-themed donuts might happen upon your videos and learn about Orbital Donuts!

IN THIS CHAPTER

» Understanding forms

» Exploring essential form elements

» Validating user input

» Making forms accessible to everyone

» Keeping spam at bay

# Chapter 2
# HTML Forms and User Input

*Form and function should be one, joined in a spiritual union.*

—FRANK LLOYD WRIGHT

Forms are where your website stops being a one-way broadcast and becomes a two-way conversation. They're how visitors contact you, how customers place orders, how people sign up for your newsletter.

Forms are also where most websites completely blow it. You've experienced this: a contact form that asks for way too much information, a signup form where you can't tell which fields are required, an order form that throws cryptic errors without telling you what you did wrong. Bad forms frustrate users and cost you conversions, plain and simple.

The good news? Creating good forms isn't rocket science. You just need to understand the basic HTML form elements, follow some user experience principles, and think about accessibility from the start. That's what this chapter covers. You learn how to build forms that work — forms that are easy to fill out, clear about what they need, and accessible to everyone.

# Understanding What Makes Forms Work

Before you start adding input fields and buttons, you need to understand what a form *is* at the HTML level. Your garden-variety form consists of four bits and pieces:

- **The `<form>` and `</form>` tags:** A container for the rest of the form elements that also defines what happens when someone submits the form
- **One or more input elements:** Fields that are used to enter or select the form data
- **One or more labels:** Elements — `label` elements, to be precise — that each name or describe a particular input element
- **One or more buttons:** Elements — usually `button` elements — that do something to the form, such as submit the form data for processing

Figure 2-1 shows an example of a contact form.

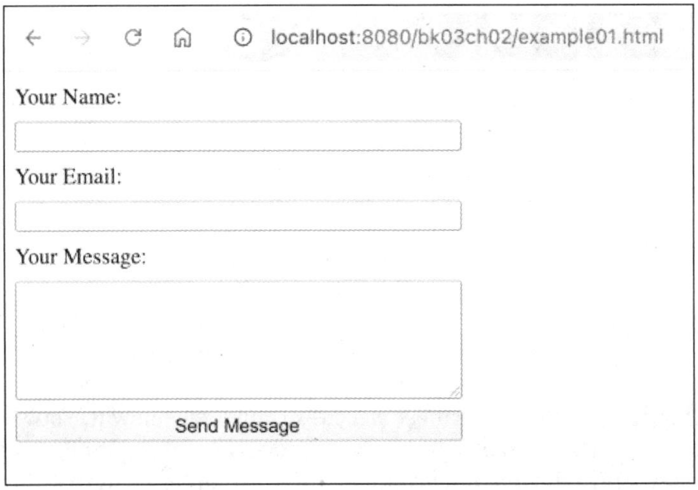


**FIGURE 2-1:** A typical contact form.

Here's the HTML that's behind the form shown in Figure 2-1 (refer to `bk03ch02/example01.html` in this book's example files):

```
<form action="/submit-contact" method="POST">
    <label for="name">Your Name:</label>
    <input type="text" id="name" name="name" required>
```

```
    <label for="email">Your Email:</label>
    <input type="email" id="email" name="email" required>

    <label for="message">Your Message:</label>
    <textarea id="message" name="message" rows="5" required></textarea>

    <button type="submit">Send Message</button>
</form>
```

I explain elements such as `label`, `input`, and `textarea` a bit later (check out the "Learning the Essential Form Input Types" section), but for now you should know that the `form` element has two key attributes:

- **`action`:** The URL where the form data gets sent when someone clicks Submit. This URL could be a server script, a third-party service like Formspree, a page on your own site that processes the data, or even some JavaScript code on the form page.
- **`method`:** How the data gets sent. The two options are `POST` (send data in the request body, good for most forms) and `GET` (append data to the URL, used mainly for search forms). For contact forms, order forms, and basically any form that submits information, use POST.

That's really all you need at the structural level. The form wraps everything and defines where and how to send the data, and the browser handles the rest of the plumbing.

## Keep it short

Here's one of the most important principles of form design: every field you add increases the chances that someone will abandon the form. Think about it from the user's perspective. They came to your site to accomplish something (order donuts, send you a message, whatever), and now you're asking them to fill out a form. Each additional field feels like more work.

So, be ruthless about eliminating unnecessary fields. For a simple contact form, do you really need their phone number, company name, job title, and mailing address? Or do you just need their name, email, and message? If you need more information for some reason, you can always ask for it later via email.

This doesn't mean you can never have long forms. If someone's ordering custom donut catering for 200 people, you legitimately need details about dietary restrictions, delivery address, and preferred delivery time. But even then, only ask for what you need. Don't request information just in case or for your records. If you can't explain why you need a piece of information, you probably don't need it.

TIP

A great exercise is to print your form and circle every field. Then go through and ask "Why do I need this?" for each one. If you can't come up with a good answer, delete the field. You'll probably end up cutting at least a third of your fields, and your conversion rate will thank you.

## Group related fields

When you do have multiple fields, group related ones. This technique helps users understand the structure of your form and makes it easier to fill out. For a catering form, you might have these groups:

- **Contact information:** Name, email, phone
- **Event details:** Date, time, number of guests
- **Donut selection:** Which donuts, dietary restrictions
- **Delivery:** Address, special instructions

You can use visual grouping (spacing, borders, background colors) and semantic HTML elements such as `fieldset` and `legend` to make these groups clear. I cover these elements in detail later in this chapter in the "Making Forms Accessible" section.

## Label everything clearly

Every single form field needs a clear label that tells users what to enter. This requirement seems obvious, but you'd be surprised how many forms use placeholder text instead of real labels (for example `<input type="email" placeholder="you@example.com">`) or use vague labels such as Input or Field 1.

Good labels are:

- **Specific:** Name a label using descriptive text, such as Email Address not just Email, or Event Date not just Date.
- **Visible:** Make sure the labels are always displayed, not hidden inside the field as placeholder text.
- **Positioned consistently:** Position the labels usually above or to the left of the field.

» **Properly associated:** Connect the label to the field using the `for` attribute (refer to the previous contact form example; I explain more in the "Making Forms Accessible" section).

# Learning the Essential Form Input Types

HTML provides a rich set of form elements, each designed for specific types of input. Over the next few sections, you explore the essential ones you'll use most often, starting with the workhorse of forms: the text input.

HTML Forms and User Input

## Text inputs: The workhorse

The basic text input is the most common form element you'll use:

```
<input type="text" id="name" name="name" required>
```

Simple and straightforward. Let's break down the attributes:

» **`type="text"`:** Specifies that this is a text input field.

» **`id`:** A unique identifier for this field. The identifier connects the field to its label (via the label's `for` attribute) and can be used in CSS and JavaScript.

» ***`name`*:** The name of this piece of data when the form is submitted. The name is what your server or email service will use to identify this field's value.

» **`required`:** Makes this field mandatory. The browser won't let the user submit the form until this field is filled in. Omit this attribute if the field is optional.

You can also add other attributes to control the input:

```
<input type="text"
    id="full-name"
    name="full-name"
    placeholder="Enter your full name"
    maxlength="100"
    required>
```

The `placeholder` attribute provides hint text (but remember, this is *not* a replacement for a proper label!), and `maxlength` limits how many characters can be entered.

## Specialized input types

HTML5 introduced specialized input types that provide better user experiences, especially on mobile devices. These types trigger appropriate mobile keyboards and provide built-in validation. Let's look at the most useful ones:

- **`email`:** For email addresses. Mobile devices show a keyboard with the @ and . keys easily accessible.

  ```
  <input type="email" id="email" name="email" required>
  ```

  The browser automatically validates that the entered text looks like an email address (has text followed by an @ symbol, plus a domain). The `email` input type is perfect for a contact form or a newsletter signup.

- **`tel`:** For phone numbers. Mobile devices show the numeric keypad.

  ```
  <input type="tel" id="phone" name="phone" placeholder="555-123-4567">
  ```

  Phone numbers don't have a universal format, so browsers don't validate them automatically. But showing the numeric keyboard makes it much easier for mobile users to enter phone numbers.

- **`number`:** For numeric values. You can specify minimum, maximum, and step values.

  ```
  <input type="number"
      id="guest-count"
      name="guests"
      min="1"
      max="500"
      step="1"
      required>
  ```

  The `number` input type is perfect for the Orbital Donuts catering form where you need to know how many guests to plan for. Thanks to the `min` and `max` attributes, the browser ensures that users can enter only numbers between 1 and 500.

- **`date`:** For date selection. Browsers provide a calendar picker.

  ```
  <input type="date" id="event-date" name="event-date" required>
  ```

  Presenting a calendar is much better than asking users to type a date manually! The calendar picker ensures that the date is in the correct format and makes it easy to select dates that are weeks or months away.

- **`url`:** For website addresses. Mobile keyboards show a .com key and make other domain extensions easily accessible.

```
<input
    type="url"
    id="website"
    name="website"
    placeholder="https://example.com">
```

The browser validates that the entered text looks like a valid URL (starts with http:// or https://).

Here's a complete catering inquiry form for Orbital Donuts that uses several specialized input types (`bk03ch02/example02.html`):

```
<form action="/catering" method="POST">
    <h3>Contact Information</h3>

    <label for="contact-name">Your Name:</label>
    <input type="text" id="contact-name" name="name" required>

    <label for="contact-email">Email:</label>
    <input type="email" id="contact-email" name="email" required>

    <label for="contact-phone">Phone:</label>
    <input type="tel" id="contact-phone" name="phone"
           placeholder="555-123-4567">

    <h3>Event Details</h3>

    <label for="event-date">Event Date:</label>
    <input type="date" id="event-date" name="date" required>

    <label for="guest-count">Number of Guests:</label>
    <input type="number" id="guest-count" name="guests"
           min="10" max="500" required>

    <button type="submit">Request Quote</button>
</form>
```

These specialized input types are a huge improvement over plain text inputs. They make forms easier to fill out on mobile devices, provide built-in validation, and communicate intent clearly. Use them whenever they fit the type of data you're collecting!

## Textareas for longer input

When you need users to enter more than a sentence or two, use a `textarea` element instead of a `text` input:

```
<label for="message">Your Message:</label>
<textarea id="message" name="message" rows="5" cols="40"
          required></textarea>
```

The `rows` attribute controls how tall the `textarea` element appears, and the `cols` attribute controls width (though width is better controlled with CSS, which I cover in Book 3, Chapter 3). Users can type as much as they want (although you can include the `maxlength` attribute to set the maximum number of characters allowed in the text; refer to the "Validating Forms" section), and the `textarea` automatically shows a scroll bar if needed.

For the Orbital Donuts contact form, `textarea` is perfect for the message field. For the catering form, you might use `textarea` for special instructions or dietary restriction details.

## Checkboxes and radio buttons

When you need users to select from a set of options, checkboxes and radio buttons are your friends. Checkboxes allow multiple selections, while radio buttons allow only one selection from a group.

- **Checkboxes** are for options where users can select zero, one, or multiple items (`bk03ch02/example03.html`):

```
<fieldset>
    <legend>Dietary Restrictions:</legend>

    <input type="checkbox" id="vegan" name="dietary" value="vegan">
    <label for="vegan">Vegan Options Needed</label>

    <input type="checkbox" id="gluten-free" name="dietary"
           value="gluten-free">
    <label for="gluten-free">Gluten-Free Options Needed</label>

    <input type="checkbox" id="nut-free" name="dietary"
           value="nut-free">
    <label for="nut-free">Nut-Free Options Needed</label>
</fieldset>
```

Notice the `fieldset` and `legend` elements wrapping the checkboxes? These group related checkboxes and provide a label for the group, as shown in Figure 2-2. The label is important for accessibility (which I cover in detail later in the “Making Forms Accessible” section).

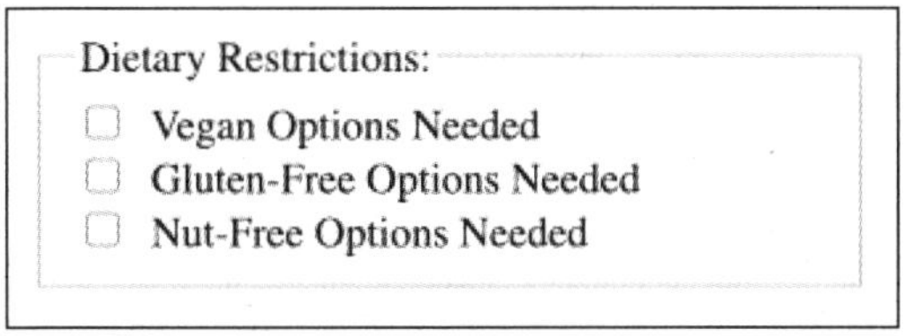


**FIGURE 2-2:** Some checkboxes arranged with a `fieldset` and `legend`.



- **Radio buttons** are for options where users must select exactly one item from a group (`bk03ch02/example04.html`):

```
<fieldset>
    <legend>Delivery or Pickup?</legend>

    <input type=”radio” id=”courier-delivery” name=”fulfillment”
           value=”courier” checked>
    <label for=”courier-delivery”>Courier delivery</label>

    <input type=”radio” id=”drone-delivery” name=”fulfillment”
   value=”drone”>
    <label for=”drone-delivery”>Drone delivery</label>

    <input type=”radio” id=”pickup” name=”fulfillment” value=”pickup”>
    <label for=”pickup”>In-store pickup</label>
</fieldset>
```

- The key with radio buttons is that all buttons in a group must have the same name attribute. This attribute tells the browser that they’re part of the same group, so selecting one automatically deselects the others. Note the checked attribute on the first radio button, which selects that button by default, as shown in Figure 2-3.

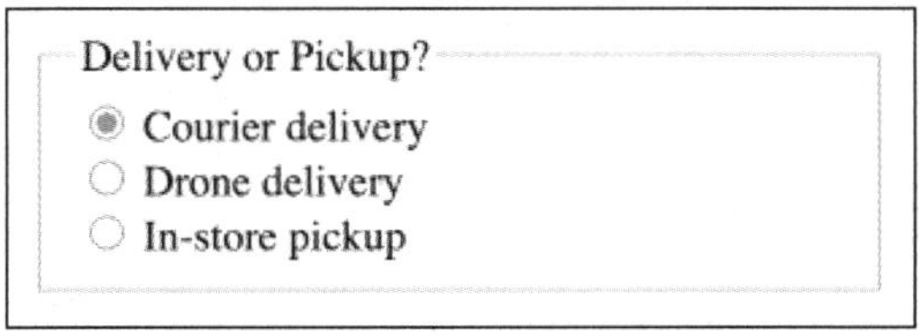


**FIGURE 2-3:** A group of three radio buttons, with the first one selected.

## Select dropdowns

When you have many options and limited space, dropdown menus created with the `select` element are a good choice (`bk03ch02/example05.html`):

```
<label for="donut-choice">Choose a Donut:</label>
<select id="donut-choice" name="donut" required>
    <option value="">-- Please choose --</option>
    <option value="cosmic-cruller">Cosmic Cruller</option>
    <option value="rocket-red-velvet">Rocket Red Velvet</option>
    <option value="galaxy-glazed">Galaxy Glazed</option>
    <option value="meteor-munchkin">Meteor Munchkin</option>
    <option value="nebula-nutella">Nebula Nutella</option>
</select>
```

Each `option` element represents one choice in the dropdown, as shown in Figure 2-4. The `value` attribute gets submitted to your server, and the text between the opening and closing tags is what users see.

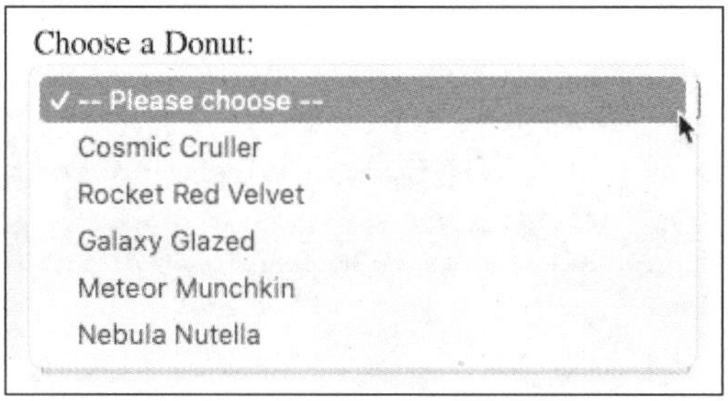


**FIGURE 2-4:** A select dropdown list in action.

Notice the first `option` with an empty value and `-- Please choose --` text? This common pattern forces users to make an active selection rather than accidentally submitting the first option. Using `option` and the `required` attribute on the `select` element ensures that users choose something.

# Validating Forms

Validation ensures that users provide the right kind of information before submitting the form. Nothing's more frustrating than filling out a form, clicking Submit, and then getting cryptic error messages. Good validation catches problems early and provides helpful guidance.

HTML5 provides built-in validation that works without JavaScript, which is great for both simplicity and accessibility. Let's explore how validation works.

I've already talked about the `required` attribute, which is the simplest form of validation. But HTML5 provides several other validation attributes:

- **`minlength`:** Minimum number of characters
- **`maxlength`:** Maximum number of characters
- **`min`:** Minimum value for numbers and dates
- **`max`:** Maximum value for numbers and dates
- **`pattern`:** A regular expression the value must match

Here's an example using several of these attributes (`bk03ch02/example06.html`):

```
<form>
    <label for="username">Username (3-15 characters):</label>
    <input type="text" id="username" name="username"
           minlength="3" maxlength="15" required>

    <label for="age">Age (must be 13 or older):</label>
    <input type="number" id="age" name="age"
           min="13" max="120" required>

    <label for="phone">Phone (format: 555-123-4567):</label>
    <input type="tel" id="phone" name="phone"
           pattern="[0-9]{3}-[0-9]{3}-[0-9]{4}"
           placeholder="555-123-4567" required>

    <button type="submit">Submit</button>
</form>
```

The `pattern` attribute uses regular expressions, which are a powerful (but admittedly cryptic) way to specify text patterns. The pattern `[0-9]{3}-[0-9]{3}-[0-9]{4}` means "three digits, a hyphen, three digits, another hyphen, and four digits" — the format for a US phone number.

When someone tries to submit the form and validation fails, the browser prevents submission and displays an error message, as shown in Figure 2-5. The exact appearance of the error message varies by browser, but they all clearly indicate which field has a problem.

REMEMBER

HTML5 validation happens in the browser, which means it's fast and doesn't require a server request. But it's not a security feature — malicious users can bypass it. HTML5 validation is about user experience, not security. Always validate on your server too.

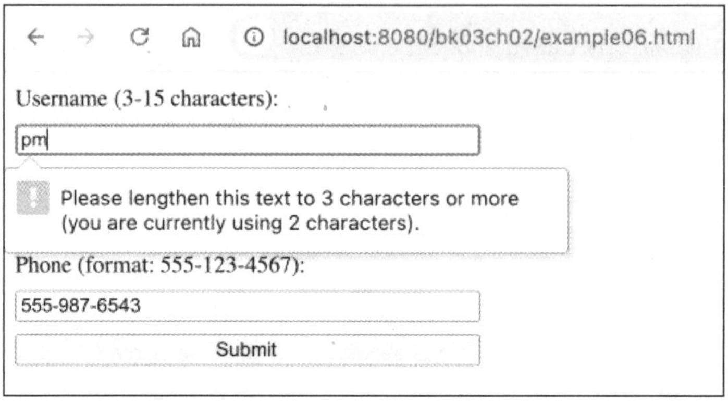


**FIGURE 2-5:** The browser displays an error message when form validation fails.

# Making Forms Accessible

As I mention in Book 2, Chapter 4, accessibility isn't optional; it's essential. Every form must be usable by everyone, including people who use screen readers, keyboard navigation, or other assistive technologies. The good news? Most accessibility features for forms are built right into HTML. You just need to use them correctly.

## Always use label elements

Every form field needs a `label` element properly connected to it. A `label` element is the single most important accessibility feature for forms. Here's the correct way to connect a `label` element to a form field:

```
<label for="email-address">Email Address:</label>
<input type="email" id="email-address" name="email" required>
```

The `for` attribute on `label` matches the `id` attribute on `input`, creating a programmatic connection that screen readers use to announce the purpose of each field. When a screen reader user focuses on the input, the screen reader says "Email Address, required, edit text" (or similar phrasing depending on the screen reader).

This connection also provides a usability bonus: clicking the label focuses the input field, which makes it easier for users (especially on mobile) to activate small form controls.

WARNING

Never use placeholder text as a substitute for a label. Placeholder text disappears when users start typing, it usually has poor contrast, and screen readers may not announce it consistently. Always use visible label elements.

## Fieldsets and legends for groups

When you have related form fields, group them with a `fieldset` element and give the group a label with a `legend` element:

```
<fieldset>
    <legend>Contact Information</legend>

    <label for="contact-name">Name:</label>
    <input type="text" id="contact-name" name="name" required>

    <label for="contact-email">Email:</label>
    <input type="email" id="contact-email" name="email" required>

    <label for="contact-phone">Phone:</label>
    <input type="tel" id="contact-phone" name="phone">
</fieldset>
```

This code creates both a visual grouping (most browsers add a border around `fieldsets`) and a programmatic grouping. Screen readers announce the `legend` when users enter the `fieldset` element, providing context for all the fields in it.

## ARIA labels when labels won't work

Sometimes a visible label doesn't make sense visually, but you still need to provide a text label for screen readers. That's when ARIA attributes come in handy.

For example, if you have a search field with a search button next to it, the button's icon or text might make the field's purpose obvious visually, but screen reader users still need a label:

```
<input type="search"
       name="search"
       aria-label="Search for donuts"
       placeholder="Search...">
<button type="submit">Search</button>
```

The `aria-label` attribute provides a text label that screen readers announce, even though there's no visible `label` element. This technique keeps the visual design clean while maintaining accessibility.

TIP

Visible labels are almost always better than `aria-label`. Use `aria-label` only when adding a visible label would genuinely hurt the design or user experience. When in doubt, use a visible `label` element.

### Keyboard accessibility

Many people navigate forms using only a keyboard: pressing Tab to move between fields, Space or Enter to activate buttons, and arrow keys to navigate radio buttons or select dropdowns. Your forms must work perfectly with keyboard-only navigation.

The good news is that HTML forms are keyboard accessible by default, as long as you use proper form elements. Text inputs, buttons, selects, and text areas all work with keyboard navigation out of the box.

Here's what keyboard users expect:

- **Tab:** Move forward to the next form field.
- **Shift+Tab:** Move backward to the previous field.
- **Enter:** Submit the form or activate a button.
- **Space:** Toggle checkboxes and activate buttons.
- **Arrow keys:** Navigate radio buttons in a group, and navigate options in a select dropdown.

To ensure good keyboard accessibility:

- Use semantic HTML form elements (`input`, `button`, `select`, and so on) rather than `div` elements with JavaScript.
- Make sure the tab order is logical (forms naturally tab in source order).
- Ensure that focus indicators are visible (browsers show an outline by default, so don't remove it with CSS unless you replace it with something equally visible).
- Test your form with keyboard-only navigation before launching.

The last point is crucial: test your forms using only a keyboard. Unplug your mouse and try to fill out and submit the form using just Tab, Enter, Space, and the arrow keys. If you run into any problems or confusion, your keyboard users will, too.

## Connecting Forms to Email and Services

Okay, you've built a beautiful form with proper validation and accessibility. Now what? How do you get the submitted data to where it needs to go? For most small-business websites, the answer is surprisingly simple: use a form-handling service.

# The simple solution: Formspree

Formspree (`https://formspree.io/`) is a service that receives form submissions and forwards them to your email address. It's incredibly simple to set up:

- Sign up for a free Formspree account at `formspree.io`.
- Create a new form and get your unique form endpoint URL.
- Use that URL as your form's `action` attribute value.

That's it! Form submissions now arrive in your email inbox. Here's what a form set up to use Formspree looks like in practice (`bk03ch02/example07.html`):

```
<form action="https://formspree.io/f/YOUR_FORM_ID" method="POST">
    <label for="name">Name:</label>
    <input type="text" id="name" name="name" required>

    <label for="email">Email:</label>
    <input type="email" id="email" name="email" required>

    <label for="message">Message:</label>
    <textarea id="message" name="message" rows="5" required></textarea>

    <button type="submit">Send</button>
</form>
```

Replace `YOUR_FORM_ID` with the form ID that Formspree gives you. When someone fills out and submits this form, Formspree receives the submission and sends you an email with all the form data.

Formspree's free plan allows 50 submissions per month, which is plenty for most small business contact forms. If you need more submissions, their paid plans start at $10/month (for annual billing; $15/month for monthly billing), which gets you up to 200 form submissions.

# Other form-handling services

Formspree isn't the only form-handling option. Here are other services worth considering:

- **Netlify Forms:** If you're hosting your site on Netlify, their form handling is built right in. Just add a `Netlify` attribute to your form tag and Netlify handles everything. Their free tier includes 100 submissions per month. Go to `https://docs.netlify.com/manage/forms/setup/`.

- **Google Forms:** Free and unlimited submissions, but you have to use Google's form interface. You can embed a Google Form on your site, but you don't have full control over the design. Visit `https://workspace.google.com/products/forms/`.
- **Typeform:** Beautiful, conversational forms that show one question at a time. Great user experience but more expensive than the alternatives. Their free plan is limited. Go to `www.typeform.com`.
- **Jotform:** Powerful form builder with templates for every use case. Handles payments, file uploads, and electronic signatures. The free plan includes 100 submissions per month. Visit `www.jotform.com`.

Which service should you choose? Here are my recommendations:

- For simple contact forms: Formspree or Netlify Forms (if you're on Netlify)
- For surveys or feedback forms: Google Forms or Typeform
- For complex forms with payments: Jotform
- For maximum control and customization: Formspree

# Preventing Spam

Here's an unfortunate reality: as soon as you put a form on the internet, spam bots will find it and try to submit garbage data. You need spam prevention, but you don't want to make life harder for legitimate users. Let's explore strategies that block bots without annoying humans.

## The honeypot technique

The honeypot technique is brilliant in its simplicity: add a field to your form that humans can't see but bots will fill in. If that hidden field has a value when the form is submitted, you know it's a bot.

To implement the honeypot technique (`bk03ch02/example08.html`):

```
<form action="/submit" method="POST">
    <!-- Regular visible fields -->
    <label for="name">Name:</label>
    <input type="text" id="name" name="name" required>
```

```
    <label for="email">Email:</label>
    <input type="email" id="email" name="email" required>

    <!-- Honeypot field: hidden from humans, visible to bots -->
    <input type="text"
           name="website"
           style="display:none"
           tabindex="-1"
           autocomplete="off">

    <button type="submit">Send</button>
</form>
```



The honeypot field is hidden with `display:none`, removed from the tab order with `tabindex="-1"`, and has autocomplete turned off so browsers don't accidentally fill it in. Humans never see this field and never fill it in. But bots that automatically fill in every field they find will populate it.

On your server (or in your form handling service), check if the honeypot field has a value. If it does, reject the submission as spam. Most services like Formspree have honeypot functionality built in — you just need to add the hidden field.

The honeypot technique is surprisingly effective against unsophisticated bots. It won't stop all spam, but it'll catch a lot of it with zero impact on legitimate users.

# reCAPTCHA

Google's reCAPTCHA is the heavy artillery of spam prevention. You've probably seen it: the "I'm not a robot" checkbox, or more recently, the invisible version that works in the background without user interaction.

The latest version, reCAPTCHA v3, is completely invisible. It scores each form submission based on how likely it is to be spam (based on user behavior, mouse movements, timing, and lots of other signals), and you can decide what to do with submissions that get low scores.

To use reCAPTCHA:

1. **Sign up for reCAPTCHA at** `google.com/recaptcha`.
2. **Get your site key and secret key.**
3. **Add Google's reCAPTCHA script to your page.**
4. **Add a small code snippet to your form.**

Here's what the code looks like:

```
<!-- Add this script to your page -->
<script src="https://www.google.com/recaptcha/api.js"></script>

<!-- Add this to your form -->
<form action="/submit" method="POST">
    <!-- Your form fields -->

    <div class="g-recaptcha" data-sitekey="YOUR_SITE_KEY"></div>
    <button type="submit">Submit</button>
</form>
```

Replace `YOUR_SITE_KEY` with your site key from Google. The reCAPTCHA widget will appear in the form, and Google will verify each submission on their servers.

The downside of reCAPTCHA is that it's an external dependency (you're relying on Google's service), it adds a slight delay to form submissions, and some users have privacy concerns about Google tracking. But it's extremely effective at blocking spam.

## Which spam prevention to use

The following are my recommendations for most small business forms:

- Start with a honeypot field (simple, invisible to users, catches basic bots).
- Check if your form service has built-in spam filtering (Formspree, Netlify Forms, and others do).
- Add reCAPTCHA only if you're still getting significant spam after trying the preceding two recommendations.

For Orbital Donuts, I'd implement the honeypot technique on both the contact form and catering form. If spam becomes a problem, I'd add the built-in spam-filtering features of Formspree. And I'd keep reCAPTCHA in my back pocket as a last resort.

IN THIS CHAPTER

» Understanding how CSS works

» Mastering selectors

» Learning the box model

» Styling colors, backgrounds, and fonts

» Using CSS custom properties

Chapter 3

# CSS Fundamentals

*CSS is awesome.*

—HÅKON WIUM LIE (INVENTOR OF CSS)

CSS (Cascading Style Sheets) is the language that transforms your plain HTML into something beautiful. It's the difference between a house with bare drywall and exposed wiring versus one with paint, moldings, and carefully chosen fixtures. HTML gives you the structure; CSS gives you the style.

In this chapter, I walk you through the fundamentals of CSS. You learn how CSS rules work, how to target specific elements on your page, how the box model affects layout, and how to style colors, backgrounds, text, and fonts. By the end of this chapter, you'll have the skills to take those plain HTML pages and make them look great. (Finally!)

## Getting to Know CSS Syntax

Before you can style anything, you need to understand how CSS is written. The good news? CSS syntax is remarkably straightforward. Once you learn the basic pattern, you can apply it to style virtually anything on your page.

## The anatomy of a CSS rule

Every CSS instruction follows the same basic structure, called a *rule* (or sometimes a *rule set*). Here's what it looks like:

```
selector {
    property1: value1;
    property2: value2;
    etc.
}
```

Let's break this down piece by piece:

- **`selector`**: This tells the browser which HTML elements you want to style. It could be an element name like `h1`, a class name like `.highlight`, or an ID like `#main-nav`.
- **Curly braces**: The opening { and closing } braces wrap all the styling instructions for that selector. Everything between these braces applies to the selected elements.
- **`property1, property2`**: These are the aspects of the element you want to change, things like `color`, `font-size`, `margin`, or `text-align`.
- **`value1, value2`**: These are the values you're assigning to each property, such as `red`, `2rem`, or `center`.
- **Semicolon**: Each property-value pair ends with a semicolon.

Here's an example that styles all the second-level headings on a page:

```
h2 {
    color: navy;
    font-size: 2rem;
    text-align: center;
}
```

This rule asks the web browser to do the following: "For all `h2` elements on the page make their text navy blue, set their font size to `2rem`, and center the text."

REMEMBER

`1rem` is equal to the browser's default font size, which is usually `16px`. Why not just use `16px`, instead? Because some users, especially users with vision difficulties, modify their browser's default font size, usually by making it larger. Instead of overriding this change with `px` values, you can respect the user's change by using `rem` values.

## Adding CSS to your HTML

You can add CSS to your HTML documents in three ways. Each has its place, though one is clearly the best for most situations:

- **Inline styles:** CSS rules applied directly to a single HTML element using the `style` attribute (refer to `bk03ch03/example01.html` in this book's example files):

  ```
  <h2 style="color: navy; font-size: 2rem; text-align: center;">Out-of-This-World Donuts Delivered Daily</h2>
  <h2 style="color: navy; font-size: 2rem; text-align: center;">Featured Donut of the Day</h2>
  <h2 style="color: navy; font-size: 2rem; text-align: center;">Our Signature Donuts</h2>
  ```

  Inline styles work, but maintaining them is tedious. If you want to change all your headings to purple, you'd have to edit every single `h2` tag. Ugh.

- **Internal stylesheet:** CSS rules grouped inside a `<style>` tag in the document's `<head>` section (`bk03ch03/example02.html`):

  ```
  <!DOCTYPE html>
  <html lang="en">
  <head>
      <meta charset="UTF-8">
      <title>Orbital Donuts</title>
      <style>
          h2 {
              color: navy;
              font-size: 2rem;
              text-align: center;
          }
      </style>
  </head>
  <body>
      <h2>Out-of-This-World Donuts Delivered Daily</h2>
      <h2>Featured Donut of the Day</h2>
      <h2>Our Signature Donuts</h2>
  </body>
  </html>
  ```

  Internal stylesheets are better than inline styles because you can style multiple elements using a single rule. But the CSS applies to only that single HTML file.

- **External stylesheet:** A separate `.css` file that you link to from your HTML (`bk03ch03/example03.html`):

```
<!DOCTYPE html>
<html lang="en">
<head>
    <meta charset="UTF-8">
    <title>Orbital Donuts</title>
    <link rel="stylesheet" href="example03.css">
</head>
<body>
    <h2>Featured Donut</h2>
</body>
</html>
```

  And then in a separate file called `example03.css` (in this case), you add your CSS rules (`bk03ch03/example03.css`):

```
h2 {
    color: navy;
    font-size: 2rem;
}
```

  External stylesheets are the gold standard because one CSS file can style multiple HTML pages. Change the CSS once, and every page that links to it updates automatically. That's the power of cascading style sheets!

TIP

Create a subdirectory named `css` in your project and put all your stylesheets there. Then link to them with `href="css/styles.css"`. Using subdirectories in this way keeps your project organized as it grows.

## Selecting elements by type

The simplest CSS selector is the *element selector* (also called a *type selector*). You use the HTML element's name as the selector, and your styles apply to every instance of that element on the page (`bk03ch03/example04.html`):

```
p {
    font-size: 1.25rem;
    line-height: 1.5;
}
a {
```

```
    color: darkblue;
}
section {
    max-width: 50rem;
}
```

These rules style, respectively, all paragraphs, all links, and all sections on the page. This approach is great for setting baseline styles that you want to apply consistently across your entire site.

## Selecting elements by class

What if you want to style only *some* paragraphs differently? That's where *class selectors* come in. First, you add a `class` attribute to the HTML elements you want to target (`bk03ch03/example05.html`):

```
<p>This is a regular paragraph.</p>
<p class="featured">This paragraph is featured!</p>
<p class="featured">So is this one.</p>
```

Then in your CSS, you select that class by putting a period (`.`) before the class name:

```
.featured {
    background-color: lightyellow;
    padding: 1rem;
    border-left: 4px solid orange;
}
```

Now only the paragraphs with `class="featured"` get that special styling. The regular paragraph remains unchanged. Classes are incredibly useful because you can apply the same class to any number of elements, and you can apply multiple classes to a single element.

For example, you might have both a `.featured` class and a `.warning` class:

```
<p class="featured warning">Watch out! This is important.</p>
```

This paragraph gets the styles from both classes. You can use as many classes as you need. Just be sure to separate each class name with a space in the tag's `class` value.

## Selecting elements by ID

Sometimes you need to style one specific element that appears only once on the page. That's the job of *ID selectors.* In HTML, you give the element a unique `id` attribute (`bk03ch03/example06.html`):

```
<header id="main-header">
    <h1>Orbital Donuts</h1>
    <nav>...</nav>
</header>
```

In your CSS, select it with a hash symbol (#) before the ID name:

```
#main-header {
    background-color: darkblue;
    color: white;
    padding: 20px;
}
```

WARNING

Each ID can be used only once per page. If you have two elements with `id="main-header"`, your HTML is invalid. For reusable styles, always use classes instead.

## Combining selectors

CSS lets you get more specific by combining selectors in various ways. Here are the most useful combinations:

- **Descendant selectors** target elements nested inside other elements. Separate them with a space (`bk03ch03/example07.html`):

  ```
  nav a {
      color: white;
      text-decoration: none;
  }
  ```

  This code styles the links inside only a nav element. Links elsewhere on the page aren't affected. (The `text-decoration: none` declaration removes the link underline.)

- **Class selectors** of the form *`element.class`* target a specific element that contains a specific class (`bk03ch03/example08.html`):

  ```
  p.intro {
      font-size: 1.25rem;
      font-weight: bold;
  }
  ```

This styles only paragraphs that have the `intro` class; not `div`s or `span`s with that class, just paragraphs.

- **Multiple selectors** let you apply the same styles to several selectors at once. Put each selector on its own line and separate them with commas (`bk03ch03/example09.html`):

```
h1,
h2,
h3 {
    font-family: Georgia, serif;
    color: darkslategray;
}
```

This code applies the same font and color to all three heading levels. This approach is much more efficient than writing three separate rules!

## Understanding the cascade and specificity

Remember how CSS stands for Cascading Style Sheets? The *cascading* part refers to how the browser determines which styles to apply when multiple rules target the same element.

Here's the basic principle: when two rules conflict, the more specific one wins. And if they're equally specific, the one that comes later in the CSS file wins.

Specificity follows a hierarchy:

- Inline styles (in the HTML element) have the highest specificity.
- ID selectors (`#main-header`) beat class selectors.
- Class selectors (`.featured`) beat element selectors.
- Element selectors (`p`, `h1`, `div`) have the lowest specificity.

Here's an example that demonstrates specificity (`bk03ch03/example10.html`):

```
p { color: black; }
.highlight { color: blue; }
#special { color: red; }
```

Here's the HTML:

```
<p>I'm black.</p>
<p class="highlight">I'm blue.</p>
<p class="highlight" id="special">I'm red!</p>
```

The third paragraph has both a class and an ID applied, but the ID selector wins because it's more specific. Understanding specificity helps you debug situations where your styles don't seem to be working. Often, a more specific rule is overriding your changes.

# Learning Box Model and Layout Basics

Every HTML element on your page is essentially a rectangular box. It doesn't matter if it's a short run of text or a round image; underneath, it's a box. Understanding how these boxes work is fundamental to controlling layout in CSS.

## Understanding the box model

The *CSS box model* describes how these rectangular boxes are structured. Each box has four areas, working from the inside out:

» **Content:** The stuff inside the element: text, an image, whatever. Content is the innermost area.

» **Padding:** Transparent space between the content and the border. Padding pushes the border away from the content.

» **Border:** A line (visible or invisible) that surrounds the padding. You can use CSS to mess around with its width, color, and style.

» **Margin:** More transparent space, this time outside the border. The margin creates distance between this element and neighboring elements.

Figure 3-1 shows how these four areas fit together.

## Setting width and height

The `width` and `height` properties set the size of an element's content area (`bk03ch03/example11.html`):

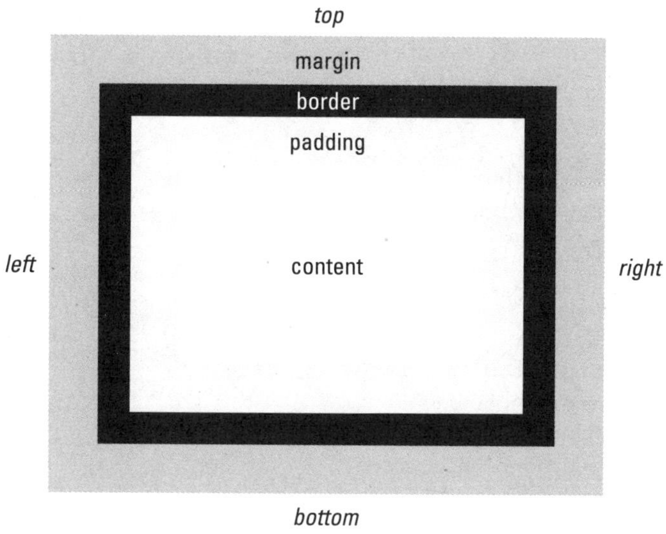


**FIGURE 3-1:** The CSS box model showing content, padding, border, and margin.

```
.sidebar {
    width: 250px;
    height: 400px;
}
```

REMEMBER

Note, however, that you'll only rarely set an element's `height` property. Why? Because given potentially changeable factors such as font size, line height, and vertical padding and margins, it's basically impossible to get the height right. It's best to just let the browser set the height based on the element's content and styling.

## Working with padding and margins

Padding and margins both create space, but in different places. The padding is inside the border (pushing the edge away from the content), while the margins are outside the border (pushing other elements away).

You can set all four sides at once or each side individually:

```
.example1 {
    /* Top, right, bottom, left (clockwise) */
    margin: 0px 10px 20px 10px;
    padding: 10px 20px 15px 25px;
}
.example2 {
    /* Top/bottom and left/right */
```

```
    margin: 10px 20px;
    padding: 5px 10px;
}
.example3 {
    /* All four sides the same */
    margin: 1rem;
    padding: 1.25rem;
}
.example4 {
    /* Individual sides */
    margin-top: 2.5rem;
    margin-bottom: .75rem;
    padding-left: 1rem;
    padding-right: .5rem;
}
```

The shorthand versions in the first example follow a clockwise pattern starting at the top: top, right, bottom, left. You can remember it with the word *TRouBLe* (T-R-B-L).

REMEMBER

One quirk to know about: vertical margins can collapse. If you have one element with `margin-bottom: 30px` followed by another with `margin-top: 20px`, the space between them won't be 50 pixels; it'll be 30 pixels (the larger of the two). This is called *margin collapse*, and it prevents excessive spacing between elements.

Here's another quirk (CSS has *so* many quirks): by default, `width` and `height` set only the content area size. The `padding` and `border` values are added on top of that! So if you set `width: 300px` but also have `padding: 20px` on both sides and `border: 2px` on both sides, the total width is 300 + 20 + 20 + 2 + 2 = 344 pixels!

This can make laying out your page frustrating. Fortunately, there's a fix.

## The box-sizing property

The `box-sizing` property changes how width and height are calculated. The magic value is `border-box`:

```
.card {
    box-sizing: border-box;
    width: 300px;
    padding: 20px;
    border: 2px solid gray;
}
```

With `box-sizing: border-box`, the width you set *includes* the padding and border. So `width: 300px` means the whole box is 300 pixels wide, period. The browser automatically adjusts the content area to fit.

Most developers apply `border-box` to everything on their page right at the top of their stylesheet:

```
* {
    box-sizing: border-box;
}
```

The asterisk (`*`) is the *universal selector*, which means it matches every element on the page. This one line makes layout math so much easier!

# The display property

The `display` property controls how an element behaves in the layout. The three most common values are:

- **`block`:** The element takes up the full width available and starts on a new line. Paragraphs, headings, and divs are block-level by default.
- **`inline`:** The element takes up only as much width as needed and doesn't start a new line. Links, spans, and emphasis tags are inline by default.
- **`inline-block`:** A hybrid that flows inline but can have width, height, padding, and margins like a block element.

Here's a practical example. The Orbital Donuts `nav` links reside in an unordered list:

```
<nav>
    <ul>
        <li><a href="index.html">Home</a></li>
        <li><a href="menu.html">Menu</a></li>
        <li><a href="order.html">Your Order</a></li>
        <li><a href="location.html">Location</a></li>
        <li><a href="catering.html">Catering</a></li>
        <li><a href="about.html">About</a></li>
    </ul>
</nav>
```

By default, each `li` element is a block, and so it appears on a new line, which is what you want for a regular bulleted list. However, for the navigation, it would be better if the links appeared on a single line, which you can do by setting their `display` property to `inline` (`bk03ch03/example12.html`):

```
nav li {
    display: inline;
    margin-right: 0.5rem;
}
```

By setting `display: inline` and adding a bit of a right margin, the links now appear on a single line, as shown in Figure 3-2.

**FIGURE 3-2:** Style the nav list items with `display: inline` to get them to line up neatly in a row.

# Sprucing Up Your Pages with Colors, Backgrounds, and Borders

Now we're getting to the fun stuff! Colors and backgrounds are where your website's personality starts to shine. Let's explore the many ways CSS lets you add visual flair to your pages.

## Color values in CSS

CSS gives you several ways to specify colors. Each has its place:

- **Named colors** are the simplest. CSS recognizes over 160 color names, from basics such as `red`, `blue`, and `green` to fancier options such as `coral`, `steelblue`, and `papayawhip` (yes, really). You can see the full list at `https://developer.mozilla.org/en-US/docs/Web/CSS/Reference/Values/named-color`. Here are some examples (`bk03ch03/example13.html`):

```
h3 { color: darkslategray; }
.highlight { background-color: yellow; }
.warning { border: 3px double tomato; }
```

» **Hexadecimal (hex) colors** give you access to millions of colors using a six-character code of the form `#rrggbb`. The six characters represent red, green, and blue hexadecimal values in pairs (`bk03ch03/example14.html`):

```
h2 { color: #0a1128; }         /* Space Navy */
.accent { color: #e63946; }   /* Rocket Red */
.subtle { color: #6b7280; }   /* Asteroid Gray */
```

(Note that the color names in the comments come from the Orbital Donuts design specs; they're not official names.) Each pair can range from `00` (none) to `ff` (full intensity). So `#ff0000` is pure red, `#00ff00` is pure green, and `#0000ff` is pure blue. Mix them to create any color you need.

» **RGB colors** use the `rgb(`*`red green blue`*`)` function with values from 0 to 255 for *`red`*, *`green`*, and *`blue`* (`bk03ch03/example15.html`):

```
h2 { color: rgb(10 17 40); }          /* Space Navy */
.accent { color: rgb(230 57 70); }   /* Rocket Red */
.subtle { color: rgb(107 114 128); } /* Asteroid Gray */
```

» **HSL colors** use the `hsl(`*`hue saturation lightness`*`)` function with the following values:

- *hue*: Between 0 and 359, which represents an angle on the color wheel, with red at 0, green at 120, and blue at 240
- *`saturation`*: Between `0%` and `100%`, which is the intensity or purity of the color (`0%` makes the color a shade of gray, while `100%` represents the most vivid version of the hue)
- *`lightness`*: Between `0%` and `100%`, which determines how light or dark the color appears (0% being completely black, 100% being completely white, and 50% representing the pure color).

Here's an example (`bk03ch03/example16.html`):

```
h2 { color: hsl(226 60% 10%); }         /* Space Navy */
.accent { color: hsl(355 78% 56%); }   /* Rocket Red */
.subtle { color: hsl(220 9% 46%); }    /* Asteroid Gray */
```

» **Alpha channel colors** add a fourth value (separated by a slash) for transparency (also called the *alpha channel*), ranging from `0` (fully transparent) to `1` (fully opaque). Here's an example (`bk03ch03/example17.html`):

```
.shadowed {
    border: 1px solid hsl(220 9% 46%);
    box-shadow: 8px 8px 5px hsl(220 9% 46% / 0.5); /* 50% opaque */
}
```

Transparency is incredibly useful for overlays, shadows, and any situation where you want to see through an element to what's behind it.

## Background properties

Backgrounds aren't limited to solid colors. CSS gives you extensive control over how backgrounds appear.

The `background-color` property sets a solid background color (`bk03ch03/example18.html`):

```
header {
    background-color: navy;
    color: white;
    padding: 1rem;
}
```

The `background-image` property adds an image as the background (`bk03ch03/example19.html`):

```
.hero {
    background-image: url('images/stars.webp');
    color: white;
    min-height: 100vh;
    padding: 1rem;
}
```

By default, background images tile (repeat) to fill the element. You can control this behavior with additional properties (`bk03ch03/example20.html`):

```
.hero {
    background-image: url('images/stars.webp');
    background-size: cover;
    background-position: center;
    background-repeat: no-repeat;
    color: white;
    min-height: 100vh;
    padding: 1rem;
}
```

where:

- **background-size: cover**: Scales the image to cover the entire element, cropping if necessary. This declaration is perfect for hero images.
- **background-position: center**: Centers the image within the element.
- **background-repeat: no-repeat**: Prevents the image from tiling.

You can combine these properties into a shorthand:

```
.hero {
    background: url('images/stars.webp') center/cover no-repeat;
}
```

## Border properties

Borders wrap around an element's padding. The `border` shorthand property sets width, style, and color all at once (`bk03ch03/example21.html`):

```
.card {
    border: 2px solid gray;
}
```

The style (middle) value determines how the border looks. Common options include:

- **solid**: A single solid line (most common)
- **dashed**: A series of dashes
- **dotted**: A series of dots
- **double**: Two parallel solid lines
- **none**: No border (the default)

You can set borders on individual sides (`bk03ch03/example22.html`):

```
.callout {
    border-left: 4px solid orange;
    padding-left: 1rem;
}
```

TIP

A left border with some left padding is a classic way to highlight important content.

## Rounded corners with border-radius

The `border-radius` property rounds the corners of an element's border (and background). This simple property makes a huge difference in how modern your site looks (`bk03ch03/example23.html`):

```
.button {
    border-radius: 4px;    /* Slightly rounded */
}
.card {
    border-radius: 8px;    /* More rounded */
}
.pill {
    border-radius: 50px;   /* Very rounded, pill shape */
}
.circle {
    width: 50px;
    height: 50px;
    border-radius: 50%;    /* Perfect circle */
}
```

For the Orbital Donuts website, I use 8 pixels for the `border-radius` on cards. It's rounded enough to feel friendly but not so rounded that it looks childish.

# Adding Text Styling and Web Fonts

As I mention in Book 2, Chapter 2, typography can make or break a design. On the "make" side of the equation, CSS gives you fine-grained control over how text appears, from basic font choices to spacing and decoration.

## Font properties

The `font-family` property specifies which typeface to use (`bk03ch03/example24.html`):

```
body {
    font-family: Arial, Helvetica, sans-serif;
}
```

Notice the list of fonts? This list is a *font stack.* The browser tries the first font (Arial); if it's not available, it tries Helvetica; if that's not available either, it falls back to any available sans-serif font. Always include a generic family (sans-serif, serif, or monospace) as your last resort.

The font-size property sets how large the text appears (bk03ch03/example25.html):

```
h1 { font-size: 2rem; }
p { font-size: 1.25rem; }
.small { font-size: 0.875rem; }
```

The font-weight property controls boldness (bk03ch03/example26.html):

```
.normal { font-weight: normal; }   /* or 400 */
.bold { font-weight: bold; }       /* or 700 */
.light { font-weight: 300; }
.heavy { font-weight: 900; }
```

The font-style property handles italics (bk03ch03/example27.html):

```
.italic { font-style: italic; }
.not-italic { font-style: normal; }
```



# Text properties

The color property sets the text color; the generic name is confusing, I know, but believe me that this property affects only text. Refer to the earlier section "Color values in CSS" for some examples.

The text-align property controls horizontal alignment (bk03ch03/example28.html):

```
.left { text-align: left; }
.center { text-align: center; }
.right { text-align: right; }
```

The text-decoration property adds or removes decorations such as underlines (bk03ch03/example29.html):

```
a { text-decoration: underline; }
a:hover { text-decoration: none; }
.strikethrough { text-decoration: line-through; }
```

The `line-height` property sets the spacing between lines of text. Use a *unitless number* (that is, a numeric value without an accompanying unit such as `px` or `rem`) that multiplies the font size (`bk03ch03/example30.html`):

```
p {
    font-size: 1.25rem;
    line-height: 1.4;  /* 1.4 × 1.25rem = 1.75rem line height */
}
```

A `line-height` of 1.4 to 1.6 is typically ideal for body text. It gives lines enough breathing room without looking too spaced out.

## Using web fonts

The fonts I've shown so far are *system fonts*, meaning fonts that are installed on most computers. But what if you want something more distinctive? That's where *web fonts* come in: they're fonts available online. For example, Google Fonts (`fonts.google.com`) offers hundreds of free fonts you can use on any website.

To use them, first, visit Google Fonts and find some fonts you like. Let's say you want to use Open Sans for body text and Orbitron for headings (a great combo for a space-themed donut shop!).

On Google Fonts, select the font weights you need, and then copy the `<link>` code they provide. Add it to your HTML's `<head>` section (`bk03ch03/example31.html`):

```
<head>
     <link rel="preconnect" href="https://fonts.googleapis.com">
     <link rel="preconnect" href="https://fonts.gstatic.com" crossorigin>
     <link href="https://fonts.googleapis.com/css2?family=Open+Sans:wght@
400;600&family=Orbitron:wght@500;700&display=swap" rel="stylesheet">
</head>
```

Now you can use these fonts in your CSS:

```
body {
    font-family: 'Open Sans', sans-serif;
}
h1,
h2,
h3 {
    font-family: 'Orbitron', sans-serif;
}
```

TIP

Load only the font weights you will use. Each weight adds to your page load time. If you need only regular (400) and bold (700), don't load all nine weights.

# Using CSS Custom Properties

Imagine you're building the Orbital Donuts website and you're using a particular shade of navy — `hsl(226 60% 10%)` — everywhere: in the header, the footer, button borders, and card shadows. Now imagine the owner decides they want to try a slightly different shade. You'd have to find and replace that `hsl()` function in dozens of places. Groan!

*CSS custom properties* (also called *CSS variables*) solve this problem by letting you define values once and reuse them throughout your stylesheet.

## Defining custom properties

Custom properties are defined using a special syntax: the property name starts with two dashes (`--`). They're typically defined in the `:root` selector so they're available everywhere (`bk03ch03/example32.html`):

```
:root {
    --color-primary: hsl(226 60% 10%);
    --color-accent: hsl(355 78% 56%);
    --color-text: hsl(220 9% 46%);
    --spacing-small: 0.5rem;
    --spacing-medium: 1rem;
    --spacing-large: 2rem;
    --border-radius: 8px;
}
```

## Using custom properties

To use a custom property, wrap its name in the `var()` function:

```
header {
    background-color: var(--color-primary);
    padding: var(--spacing-medium);
    margin-bottom: var(--spacing-medium);
}
```

```
.card {
    border: 2px solid var(--color-primary);
    border-radius: var(--border-radius);
    padding: var(--spacing-medium);
}
.button {
    background-color: var(--color-accent);
    border-radius: var(--border-radius);
}
```

Now if you want to change the primary color, you change it in only one place: the `:root` definition. Every element using that variable updates automatically. That's powerful!

### Fallback values

You can provide a fallback value in case the variable isn't defined. Add a second parameter to `var()`:

```
.card {
    border-radius: var(--border-radius, 8px);
}
```

If `--border-radius` isn't defined anywhere, the element uses `8px` instead. This makes your CSS more resilient.

## Browser Developer Tools for CSS

Here's a secret that professional web developers rely on every single day: browser developer tools (most often referred to as *dev tools* by the cognoscenti). These built-in tools enable you to inspect any element on a page, see what CSS is being applied, and even make live changes to test ideas before committing them to your code.

### Opening the developer tools

Every modern browser has developer tools baked in. Here's how to open them:

- **Chrome and Edge:** Press F12, Ctrl+Shift+I (Windows), or ⌘+Option+I (Mac), or right-click any page element and then click Inspect.

» **Firefox:** Press F12, Ctrl+Shift+I (Windows), or ⌘+Option+I (Mac), or right-click an element and then click Inspect Element.

» **Safari:** First enable the dev tools. In Safari, choose Settings⇨Advanced⇨Show Features for Web Developers. Then press ⌘+Option+I or right-click an element and then click Inspect Element.

The developer tools panel appears, usually at the bottom or right side of your browser window. Don't be intimidated by all the tabs and options because you'll mostly use just a few features.

## Inspecting elements

The Elements tab (or Inspector in Firefox) shows your page's HTML structure. Click the element selector icon (the arrow in a box) in the top-left corner of the dev tools, and then hover your cursor over elements on your page. You'll see them highlighted; click one to select it.

When you select an element, the Styles panel shows all the CSS rules affecting that element. You'll see:

» **The CSS rules:** Listed from most specific at the top down to least specific, showing you which rules are being applied

» **Crossed-out properties:** Styles that were overridden by more specific rules

» **The box model diagram:** A visual representation of the element's content, padding, border, and margin

Figure 3-3 shows the developer tools with an element selected and its styles displayed.

## Modifying CSS in real time

Where the dev tools really help you level up your CSS skills is with real-time editing. You can modify CSS values right in the developer tools and see changes immediately on the page. Click any value in the Styles panel and type a new value, press Tab, Enter, or Return to apply it, and the page updates instantly. Sweet!

This is incredibly helpful for:

» Experimenting with different colors, sizes, or spacing

» Figuring out why a layout isn't working as expected

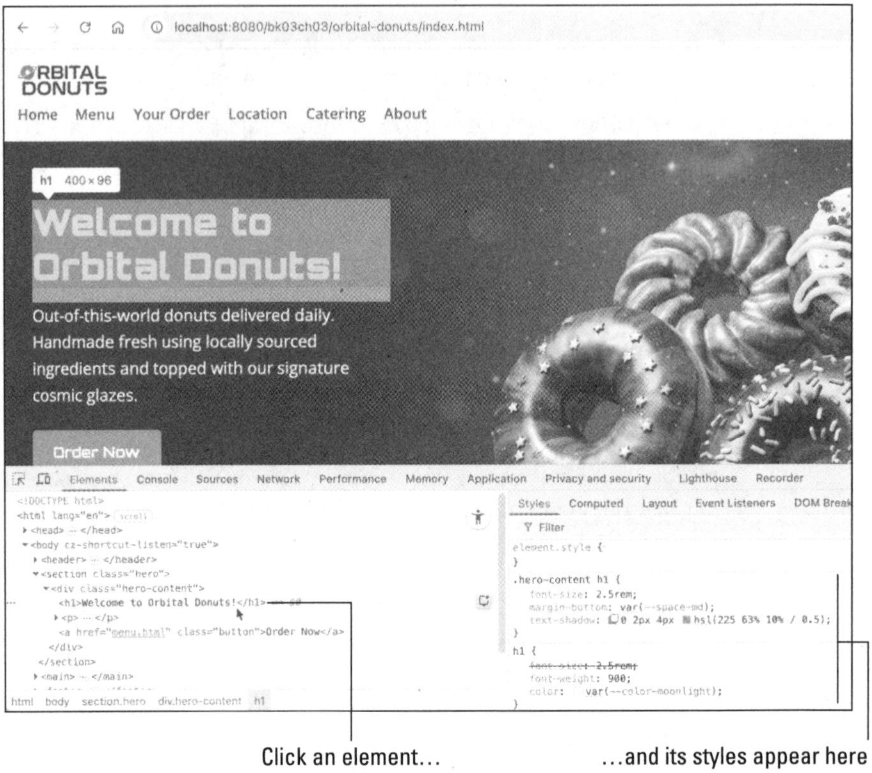


FIGURE 3-3: Chrome's developer tools showing an element's computed styles.

- Testing fixes before editing your CSS file
- Learning how CSS properties work by playing with values

REMEMBER

Any changes you make in the developer tools are temporary and will vanish the next time you reload the page. Once you find values you like, be sure to copy them to your stylesheet.

## Debugging CSS problems

When your styles don't work as expected, the dev tools can help you figure out why. Here's a troubleshooting workflow:

1. Inspect the problematic element to see what CSS is being applied.
2. Check for crossed-out styles, which tell you that another rule is overriding your style. Look at what's overriding it and why.

3. Check the Computed tab to see the final, calculated values for every property. These values show you what the browser is using, even if multiple rules contribute to it.
4. Look for typos. A misspelled property name or an invalid value simply gets ignored. If you don't see your property in the Styles panel at all, you probably have a typo in your CSS file.
5. Check the cascade. If your style is being overridden, you might need to make your selector more specific or move your rule later in the stylesheet.

Developer tools are your best friend when debugging CSS. You'll find yourself using them constantly as you build websites, so get comfortable using them as soon as you can.

IN THIS CHAPTER

- » Building flexible layouts with Flexbox
- » Creating complex grids with CSS Grid
- » Making your site responsive with media and container queries
- » Crafting practical layouts for navigation, cards, and columns

# Chapter 4
# CSS Layout Techniques

*The Web does not just connect machines, it connects people.*

—TIM BERNERS-LEE

When browsers lay out a web page, they do it in the most boring way imaginable: inline elements run across the page and block elements are stacked one on top of the other all the way down the page. *Yawn.* This way of laying out HTML is called *page flow,* and the main goal of the rather large topic called *CSS layout* is to break out of page flow.

In this chapter, you explore the most powerful layout tools that CSS has to offer: Flexbox and CSS Grid. You learn when to use each one (spoiler alert: you'll often use both on the same page), how to make your layouts adapt to different screen sizes by using media queries, and how to build the practical layout patterns that power modern websites. By the time you finish this chapter, you'll be able to build layouts that look great whether your visitor is sitting in front of a 27-inch monitor or checking your site while waiting for coffee.

## Flexbox for Flexible Layouts

*Flexbox* (short for Flexible Box Layout) is CSS's solution to a problem that plagued web designers for years: how do you arrange elements in a row or column and have them automatically adjust their size to fill the available space? Before Flexbox, developers resorted to all sorts of hacks involving floats and tables. Now, automatic adjustment is beautifully straightforward.

## Understanding the Flexbox model

Flexbox works with two types of elements: a *flex container* (the parent) and *flex items* (the children). Think of it like organizing books on a shelf: the shelf is the container, and the books are the items. You tell the shelf (container) how to arrange the books (items), and Flexbox handles the details.

Here's the most basic Flexbox setup:

```
.flex-container {
    display: flex;
}
```

That single line — `display: flex` — transforms any container into a flex container. All its direct children automatically become flex items and line up in a row. Just like that! (It's one of those rare moments in coding where something works exactly as you'd expect on the first try.)

## Controlling flex direction

By default, flex items line up in a row (horizontally). But you can change this with the `flex-direction` property. Here are your options:

- **`row`:** Items line up left to right (the default).
- **`row-reverse`:** Items line up right to left.
- **`column`:** Items stack top to bottom.
- **`column-reverse`:** Items stack bottom to top.

If you have a collection of `nav` items in a bulleted list (`ul` element), as in the Orbital Donuts header, here's some CSS that converts those items into a horizontal menu using Flexbox (refer to `bk03ch04/example01.html` in this book's example files):

```
header nav ul {
    display: flex;
    flex-direction: row;
    gap: 1rem;
    list-style: none;
    padding: 0;
}
```

This code creates a horizontal navigation menu with consistent spacing between items. The `gap` property adds `1rem` space between flex items without needing margins. That's pretty handy!

## Aligning items with justify-content and align-items

Once you have arranged flex items, you'll want to control how they're positioned. Flexbox gives you two main alignment properties:

- **`justify-content`**: Align items along the main axis (horizontally for rows, vertically for columns).
- **`align-items`**: Align items along the cross axis (vertically for rows, horizontally for columns).

The `justify-content` property has several useful values:

- **`flex-start`**: Items bunch up at the start (default).
- **`flex-end`**: Items bunch up at the end.
- **`center`**: Items cluster in the middle.
- **`space-between`**: Items spread out with space between them.
- **`space-around`**: Items have equal space around them.
- **`space-evenly`**: All spaces (including edges) are equal.

Here's some code that centers content vertically in a hero section (`bk03ch04/example02.html`):

```
.hero-content {
    display: flex;
    flex-direction: column;
    justify-content: center;
    align-items: flex-start;
    min-height: 400px;
}
```

As shown in Figure 4-1, this rule vertically centers the content (using `justify-content: center`) while keeping it aligned to the left (using `align-items: flex-start`). The trick is understanding which property controls which direction, which trips up *everyone* at first, so don't worry if you need to experiment a bit.

CSS Layout Techniques

**FIGURE 4-1:** Using Flexbox to center some text vertically in a hero section.

## Controlling flex item sizing

Individual flex items have three properties that control how they grow and shrink:

- **`flex-grow`**: How much the item should grow relative to other items when the flex container has extra space. The default is `0`, which means that items don't expand to fill the flex container by default.
- **`flex-shrink`**: How much the item should shrink relative to other items when the flex container doesn't have enough room. The default is `1`, which means that items always shrink to fit into the flex container by default.
- **`flex-basis`**: The initial size of the item before growing or shrinking.

You'll often see these properties combined using the `flex` shorthand property. Here's a common pattern:

```
.donut-card {
    flex: 1 1 300px;
}
```

This code tells the browser that you want the item to grow to fill the available space (the first `1`), shrink if needed (the second `1`), but start at `300px`. It's a flexible card that adapts to the available space while maintaining a minimum width. Behold the power of Flexbox!

## Allowing items to wrap

By default, flex items try to squeeze into one line, even if it means shrinking below their ideal size. The `flex-wrap` property changes this behavior (`bk03ch04/example03.html`):

```
header {
    display: flex;
    flex-wrap: wrap;
    align-items: center;
    justify-content: space-between;
    gap: 1rem;
}
```

With `flex-wrap: wrap`, header items automatically flow to the next line when they run out of space. It's like having a responsive grid without needing media queries. (You'll still use media queries for other things, but this saves you some work.)

TIP

When learning Flexbox, open your browser's developer tools (refer to Book 3, Chapter 3) and try adjusting the flex properties in real time. It's the fastest way to develop an intuition for how `flex-grow`, `flex-shrink`, and `flex-basis interact`.

# CSS Grid for Complex Designs

Flexbox is good for one-dimensional layouts (rows or columns), and CSS Grid excels at two-dimensional layouts (rows and columns). Grid lets you define a template of rows and columns, and then place items precisely where you want them. It's the layout system web designers dreamed about for years.

## Creating your first grid

Like Flexbox, Grid works with a container and items. Here's a simple three-column grid (`bk03ch04/example04.html`):

```
.grid-container {
    display: grid;
    grid-template-columns: 1fr 1fr 1fr;
    gap: 1.5rem;
}
```

You always start with the `display: grid` declaration, which sets up the element as a grid container. Then you use either `grid-template-columns` or `grid-template-rows` or both to carve up the grid container into the number of columns or rows (or both) that you want. Note: If you specify only, say, `grid-template-columns`, as in the preceding example, the browser will automatically create as many rows as needed to display all the items, as shown in Figure 4-2. The `1fr` unit represents one fraction of the available space in the grid container. So `1fr 1fr 1fr` creates three equal-width columns. (The `fr` unit is Grid's secret weapon; it's like Flexbox's `flex-grow` but for grids.)

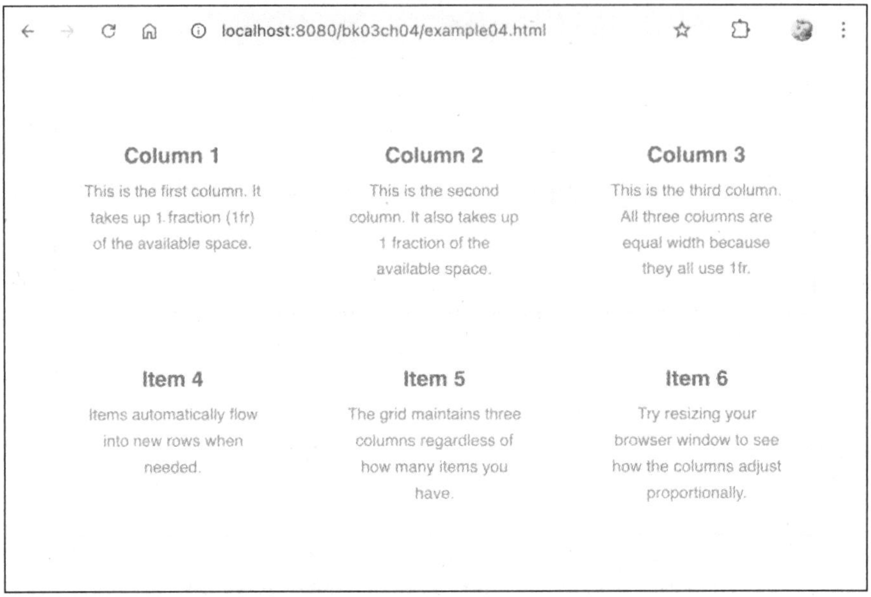


**FIGURE 4-2:** A basic three-column grid built using CSS Grid.

You can mix units too (`bk03ch04/example05.html`):

```
.layout-grid {
    display: grid;
    grid-template-columns: 250px 1fr 250px;
    gap: 2rem;
}
```

This example creates a classic three-column layout with fixed-width sidebars and a flexible center column. Simple and elegant.

## Using the repeat() function

Typing `1fr 1fr 1fr 1fr 1fr` gets tedious. The `repeat()` function saves you the trouble (`bk03ch04/example06.html`):

```
.donut-menu-grid {
    display: grid;
```

```
    grid-template-columns: repeat(5, 1fr);
    gap: 2rem
}
```

This code creates five equal columns, just like `1fr 1fr 1fr 1fr 1fr` does, but with less typing. The `repeat()` function takes two arguments: how many times to repeat and what to repeat.

## Creating responsive grids with auto-fit

You learn a few responsive design techniques a bit later (in the "Responsive Design with Media Queries" section), but CSS Grid has responsiveness baked in. For example, you can create a responsive grid that automatically adjusts the number of columns based on the available space (`bk03ch04/example07.html`):

```
.responsive-donut-grid {
    display: grid;
    grid-template-columns: repeat(auto-fit, minmax(300px, 1fr));
    gap: 2rem;
}
```

Let me break down what's happening with the `grid-template-columns` value: `auto-fit` tells Grid to fit as many columns as possible into the available horizontal space; `minmax(300px, 1fr)` tells Grid that each column should be at least `300px` wide but can grow to fill the available space, supplying each column with `1fr` of that space. The result? Your grid automatically adjusts from one column on phones to three or more columns on wide screens, all without media queries. Pretty slick!

## Defining grid areas for layouts

Grid areas let you name sections of your layout and assign items to them. It's intuitive once you see it in action (`bk03ch04/example08.html`):

```
.page-layout {
    display: grid;
    grid-template-areas:
        "header header header"
        "sidebar main main"
        "footer footer footer";
    grid-template-columns: 250px 1fr 1fr;
    grid-template-rows: auto 1fr auto;
```

```
    gap: 1rem
}
header {
    grid-area: header;
}
aside {
    grid-area: sidebar;
}
main {
    grid-area: main;
}
footer {
    grid-area: footer;
}
```

The `grid-template-areas` property defines your layout's structure, which is shown in Figure 4-3. Each quoted string represents a row, and each word represents a cell. Items span multiple cells when you repeat their name. Using `grid-template-areas` is visual, it's readable, and it makes reorganizing layouts a breeze.

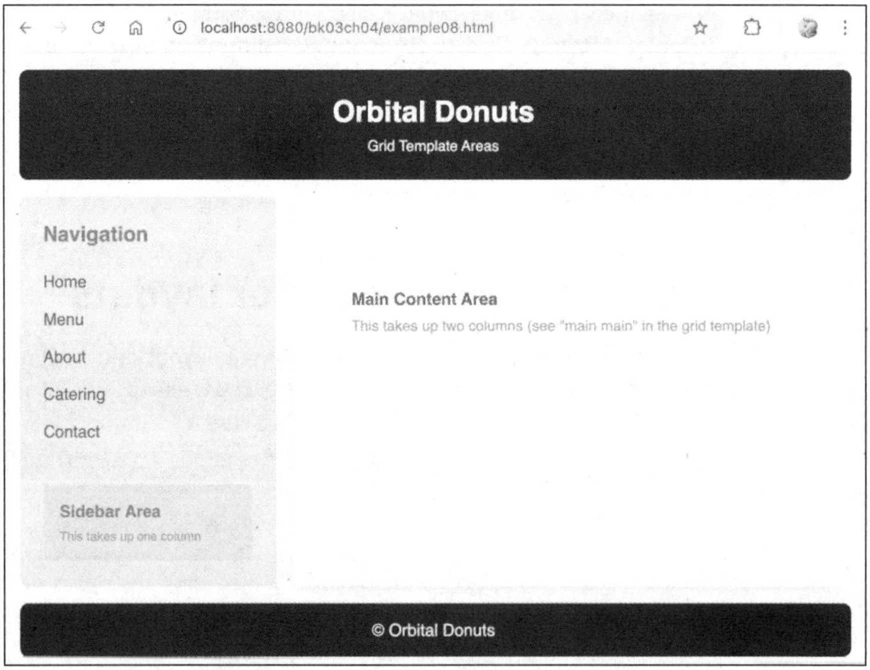


**FIGURE 4-3:** A layout built using grid areas.

REMEMBER

CSS Grid and Flexbox aren't competing technologies — they're complementary. Use Grid for the overall page layout and Flexbox for arranging elements within grid items. Many modern websites use both extensively.

# Responsive Design with Media Queries

Media queries are CSS's way of asking what kind of device is viewing this page. Based on the answer, media queries enable you to apply different styles based on screen size, orientation, or other device characteristics. Think of them as conditional statements for your CSS: if the screen is this wide, apply these styles; otherwise, apply those styles.

## Understanding media query syntax

A media query looks like this:

```
@media (min-width: 768px) {
    /* Styles for screens 768px and wider */
    .container {
        max-width: 1200px;
        margin: 0 auto;
    }
}
```

The `@media` rule wraps regular CSS. The condition in parentheses — `(min-width: 768px)`, in this example — tells the browser to "apply these styles when the viewport is at least 768 pixels wide." Simple as that.

## Choosing breakpoints

Media queries almost always use screen width, but one key is that your layout will stay the same over relatively large screen-width ranges. For example, your desktop layout will not change on the largest width screens all the way down to, say, screens that are 1024px wide. Below that width, you might change your design, say by setting a maximum content width.

A *breakpoint* is a screen width (such as 1024px) where your design changes. Here are a few common breakpoints:

- **Mobile:** Default styles (no media query needed)
- **Tablet:** 48em (768px) and up

» **Desktop:** 64em (1024px) and up

» **Wide:** 90em (1440px) and up

Note that we use `em` units instead of `px`. That's because `em` units in media queries respect the user's browser zoom level. If someone zooms in, your breakpoints adjust accordingly. It's a small accessibility win that costs you nothing.

In practice, you won't use many breakpoints. The Orbital Donuts site, for example, uses just one:

```
@media (min-width: 48em) {
    /* Styles for larger screens */
}
```

TIP

Don't pick breakpoints based on common device sizes. Instead, resize your browser window and add breakpoints wherever your layout starts looking awkward. Design for the content, not for the device.

## Mobile-first approach

As I discuss in Book 2, Chapter 1, the mobile-first approach means you write your base styles for mobile devices, and then use media queries to enhance the experience on larger screens. By starting with mobile devices, you ensure that the basic experience works everywhere, and then progressively enhance for devices that can handle more.

Here's how Orbital Donuts structures their footer using mobile-first (`bk03ch04/orbital-donuts/css/styles.css`):

```
/* Mobile: Single column */
.footer-grid {
    display: grid;
    grid-template-columns: 1fr;
    gap: var(--space-xl);
}

/* Tablet and up: Three-column grid, maximum width, centered */
@media (min-width: 48em) {
    .footer-grid {
        grid-template-columns: repeat(3, 1fr);
        max-width: 60rem;
        margin: 0 auto;
    }
}
```

Mobile users get a stacked footer that's easy to tap. Tablet and desktop users get a horizontal footer that makes better use of screen width. Everyone's happy!

## Common media query patterns

Beyond just screen width, media queries can test for other conditions:

```
/* Landscape orientation */
@media (orientation: landscape) {
    .hero {
        min-height: 300px;
    }
}
/* High-resolution displays */
@media (-webkit-min-device-pixel-ratio: 2),
       (min-resolution: 192dpi) {
    .logo {
        background-image: url('logo@2x.webp');
    }
}
/* Prefers reduced motion (accessibility) */
@media (prefers-reduced-motion: reduce) {
    * {
        animation: none !important;
        transition: none !important;
    }
}
```

The `prefers-reduced-motion: reduce` media query is particularly important. Some users experience motion sickness from animations, and they can set a preference in their operating system to reduce motion. Respecting this preference is basic accessibility courtesy.

CSS Layout Techniques

# Container Queries: The New Responsive Superpower

Media queries have a limitation: they know about only the viewport size, not the size of individual containers. Imagine you have a card component that looks great at `400px` wide. With media queries, you can check only if the entire browser window is `400px` wide, not if the card itself has `400px` of space available. Container queries solve this problem by letting you style elements based on the *container's* size, not the viewport's.

## Why container queries matter

Let's say you build a donut card for the Orbital Donuts site. This card might appear in a wide main content area, in a narrow sidebar, or in a grid with other cards. With media queries, you'd need to write CSS for every possible context. With container queries, the card adapts based on how much space it has, regardless of where it appears on the page. Write the component once, and it works everywhere.

This feature is particularly powerful for component-based designs. Each component becomes truly reusable because it can adapt to its context without knowing anything about the overall page layout. Nice.

## Setting up a container query

Container queries require two steps. First, you define an element as a container using the `container-type` property. Second, you write queries based on that container's size.

Here's a basic example (`bk03ch04/example09.html`):

```
.card-container {
    container-type: inline-size;
}
.donut-card {
    display: flex;
    flex-direction: column;
    gap: 0.75rem;
}
@container (min-width: 400px) {
    .donut-card {
        flex-direction: row;
        gap: 1rem;
    }
}
```

The `container-type: inline-size` declaration tells the browser that this element is a container and that you want to query its width. (`inline-size` is CSS-speak for width in left-to-right languages.) Then the `@container` rule works just like a media query, but it checks the container's width instead of the viewport's.

When the container is less than 400px wide, the card is displayed in a vertical layout (image on top, text below). When the container reaches 400px, it switches to a horizontal layout (image on the left, text on the right). The card doesn't care if it's in a 300px sidebar or a 1200px main area; it just responds to the space it has.

## Naming containers for clarity

When you have multiple containers on a page, it's helpful to name them so your container queries know which container they're querying (bk03ch04/example10.html):

```
.sidebar {
    container-type: inline-size;
    container-name: sidebar;
}
.main-content {
    container-type: inline-size;
    container-name: main;
}
@container sidebar (min-width: 250px) {
    .donut-card {
        font-size: 0.875rem;
    }
}
@container main (min-width: 600px) {
    .donut-card {
        font-size: 1.125rem;
    }
}
```

Now you can write different rules for cards in the sidebar versus cards in the main content area. The same component adapts differently based on its context. This kind of flexibility would have required JavaScript or complicated class names in the past.

## A complete Orbital Donuts example

Let's create a responsive donut card that adapts to its container. This card will work whether it's placed in a narrow sidebar, a medium-width column, or stretched across the full page (bk03ch04/example11.html):

```
/* Make any wrapper a container */
.donut-card-wrapper {
```

```
    container-type: inline-size;
}
/* Small container: Vertical layout */
.donut-card {
    display: flex;
    flex-direction: column;
    background-color: hsl(0 0% 100%);
    border-radius: 0.5rem;
    padding: 1rem;
    gap: 1rem;
}
.donut-card img {
    width: 100%;
    border-radius: 0.5rem;
}
/* Medium container: Horizontal layout */
@container (min-width: 400px) {
    .donut-card {
        flex-direction: row;
        align-items: center;
    }
    .donut-card img {
        width: 150px;
        flex-shrink: 0;
    }
}
/* Large container: Enhanced spacing and typography */
@container (min-width: 600px) {
    .donut-card {
        padding: 1.5rem;
        gap: 1.5rem;
    }
    .donut-card img {
        width: 200px;
    }
    .donut-card h3 {
        font-size: 1.75rem;
    }
}
```

This single component automatically adapts to three layouts based on the available space. In a 300px sidebar, the component is vertical and compact. In a 500px column, it goes horizontal. In an 800px featured area, it gets more generous spacing and larger text. One component, three presentations, zero duplication.

## Using container query units

Container queries come with their own set of units that are relative to the container's size:

- **cqw:** 1 percent of the container's width
- **cqh:** 1 percent of the container's height
- **cqi:** 1 percent of the container's inline size (usually width)
- **cqb:** 1 percent of the container's block size (usually height)
- **cqmin:** The smaller of `cqi` or `cqb`
- **cqmax:** The larger of `cqi` or `cqb`

These units let you size elements proportionally to their container:

```
.donut-card h3 {
    font-size: 5cqi;
}
```

### SETTING BOUNDS WITH CLAMP()

One common web design conundrum is figuring out a way to prevent a dynamic measurement from getting too large or too small. For example, setting the `font-size` property to `5cqi` means the text size reduces to a too-small 10px in a 200px-width container, and a too-large 50px in a 1000px-width container. It would be nice to have a way to prevent the `font-size` value from becoming either too small or too large.

Allow me to present a solution to this conundrum in the form of the `clamp()` function:

```
property: clamp(min, expression, max);
```

- Where:
- *`property`* is the CSS property to which you want to assign the `clamp()` result.
- *`min`* is the lowest value that can be assigned to *`property`*.
- *`expression`* is the preferred value that you want assigned to *`property`*. This can be a literal value, an expression, or a CSS function.
- *`max`* is the highest value that can be assigned to *`property`*.

*(continued)*

CSS Layout Techniques

*(continued)*

The idea behind `clamp()` is that the browser evaluates the *`expression`* parameter and then assigns a value to the property as follows:

- If the *`expression`* value is between *`min`* and *`max`*, the browser uses the *`expression`* result as the property value.
- If the *`expression`* value is less than *`min`*, the browser uses *`min`* as the property value.
- If the *`expression`* value is greater than *`max`*, the browser uses *`max`* as the property value.

Here's an example (bk03ch04/example12.html):

```
.donut-card h3 {
    font-size: clamp(1.25rem, 5cqi, 2rem);
}
```

The heading scales smoothly with the container's width (5 percent of the width) but never gets smaller than `1.25rem` or larger than `2rem`. It's like fluid typography, but based on the component's size rather than the viewport. Clever!

## Container queries versus media queries: When to use which

You might be wondering: should I use container queries or media queries? The answer is both. They solve different problems:

Use media queries for

- Overall page layout changes (such as adding or removing sidebars or changing column counts)
- Navigation that changes based on screen size (for example, a desktop menu versus a mobile hamburger)
- Typography scales that should match the viewport
- Anything that needs to know about the entire screen (such as orientation or print styles)

Use container queries for

- Reusable components that appear in different contexts (for example, cards, widgets, or modules)
- Components whose layout depends on their available space, not the page layout
- Nested components that need to adapt to their parent's size
- Design systems where components should work anywhere

For the Orbital Donuts site, you'd use media queries to switch from a single-column mobile layout to a multicolumn desktop layout. But you'd use container queries to make individual donut cards adapt whether they're in a sidebar, a grid, or a featured spotlight area. They work together to create a fully responsive design.

# Practical Layout Patterns

Now that you understand the tools, let's put them to work building the layout patterns you'll use on nearly every website you create. These patterns combine Flexbox, Grid, and media queries to solve real-world design challenges.

## Responsive headers

A responsive header — consisting of, say, a logo, a navigation menu, and a shopping cart icon — is one of the first challenges you'll face when building a website. You need it to work well on phones (where screen space is precious) and desktops (where you have room to spread out).

Here's a complete responsive header (`bk03ch04/example13.html`):

```
/* Mobile-first header: column layout */
header {
    display: flex;
    flex-direction: column;
    padding: 1rem;
    background-color: hsl(216 43% 97%);
    border-bottom: 1px solid hsl(220 14% 91%);
}
header img {
    max-height: 3rem;
}
```

```
header nav ul {
    display: flex;
    flex-direction: row;
    gap: 0.5rem;
    list-style: none;
    padding: 0;
    margin-top: 1rem;
}
/* Order Now button - hidden on mobile, shown on desktop */
.order-button {
    display: none;
}

/* Tablet and larger: Horizontal layout */
@media (min-width: 48em) {
    header {
        flex-direction: row;
        justify-content: space-between;
        align-items: center;
    }
    header nav ul {
        gap: 1rem;
        margin-top: 0;
    }
    .order-button {
        display: inline-block;
    }
}
```

On a mobile device (refer to Figure 4-4, top), the logo and shopping cart icon appear on top, and the navigation buttons are just below. (In Book 4, Chapter 3, you learn how to turn these buttons into a classic hamburger menu.) On larger screens (refer to Figure 4-4, bottom), everything appears in a single row with the logo on the left, the shopping cart icon and Order Now button on the right, and the navigation buttons in between. The `justify-content: space-between` declaration creates the nice spacing.

## Creating a floating button

In the preceding section, I talk about a responsive header, one feature of which is to hide the Order Now button on the mobile-first layout, and then use a media query to restore that button on larger displays (refer to Figure 4-4). One important rule of website ecommerce design is to always have your call-to-action button close by so your visitors can not only see it but use it when the urge strikes. Hiding the Order Now button violates that rule but restoring the button to the top row of the mobile header would likely make everything look too crowded.

**FIGURE 4-4:** A responsive header shown on a mobile screen (top) and a desktop screen (bottom).

The solution? Create a floating Order button that always appears in the bottom-right corner of the screen, even when the visitor scrolls. Here's the code (`bk03ch04/example14.html`) and Figure 4-5 shows the button.

HTML:

```
<a href="order.html" class="floating-order-button">Order</a>
```

CSS:

```
.floating-order-button {
    display: flex;
    align-items: center;
    justify-content: center;
    position: fixed;
    bottom: 1.5rem;
    right: 1.5rem;
    width: 3.5rem;
    height: 3.5rem;
    background-color: hsl(355 82% 56%);
    color: hsl(0 0% 100%);
    border-radius: 50%;
    box-shadow: 0 4px 12px hsl(225 63% 10% / 0.3);
    z-index: 100;
    font-family: 'Orbitron', sans-serif;
    font-weight: 700;
    font-size: 0.625rem;
    text-decoration: none;
    text-transform: uppercase;
}
```

**FIGURE 4-5:** A floating Order button.

## Card layouts

Cards — those rectangular containers holding an image, a title, a description, and maybe a button — are everywhere on modern websites. They're perfect for displaying products, blog posts, team members, or (in Orbital Donuts' case) delicious space-themed pastries.

Here's a responsive card grid that works beautifully at any screen size (`bk03ch04/example15.html`):

```
.card-grid {
    display: grid;
    grid-template-columns: repeat(auto-fit, minmax(300px, 1fr));
    max-width: 1400px;
    margin: 0 auto;
    gap: 1.5rem;
    padding: 2rem 1rem;
}
.card {
    background-color: hsl(0 0% 100%);
    border-radius: 0.5rem;
    box-shadow: 0 2px 8px hsl(225 63% 10% / 0.1);
    padding: 1rem;
}
```

```
.card img {
    width: 100%;
    aspect-ratio: 1 / 1;
    object-fit: cover;
    border-radius: 0.5rem;
}
```

The key here is that `grid-template-columns` line. Each card must be at least `300px` wide, but it can grow to fill the available space. The grid automatically determines how many columns fit. On a phone, you get one column. On a tablet, two or three. On a wide monitor, four. The layout adapts without you writing a single media query.

WARNING

When using `auto-fit` or `auto-fill` in grid layouts, always test with different amounts of content. A grid with two items might look great, but what happens when you have fifteen? Make sure your minimum width prevents cards from getting uncomfortably narrow.

## Multicolumn content

Sometimes you want text to flow across multiple columns, like in a newspaper or magazine. CSS has a dedicated multicolumn layout module for this (`bk03ch04/example16.html`):

```
.about-content {
    column-count: 1;
    column-gap: 2rem;
}
@media (min-width: 48em) {
    .about-content {
        column-count: 2;
    }
}
@media (min-width: 64em) {
    .about-content {
        column-count: 3;
    }
}
```

On a mobile device, the content is displayed in a single column (easiest to read on narrow screens). On tablets, it splits into two columns. On wide desktops, three columns make efficient use of the space.

You can also specify a desired column width instead of a count:

```
.about-content {
    column-width: 300px;
    column-gap: 2rem;
}
```

This code creates as many `300px`-wide columns as will fit. The browser handles the math for you. Thanks!

## Creating a sticky footer

Ever noticed how some footers awkwardly float in the middle of the page when there isn't much content? A *sticky footer* solves this by always staying at the bottom of the viewport, even when the content is short. Here's how to build one (`bk03ch04/example17.html`):

```
body {
    display: flex;
    flex-direction: column;
    min-height: 100vh;
}
main {
    flex: 1;
}
```

The `min-height: 100vh` line makes the body at least as tall as the viewport. The `flex: 1` code on the main element tells it to grow and fill any extra space, pushing the footer to the bottom. When there's lots of content, the footer sits below it. When there's little content, the footer stays at the bottom of the screen. Perfect!

# Common Layout Challenges and Solutions

As you build more layouts, you'll encounter certain challenges again and again. Here are solutions to the most common ones.

## Creating equal-height columns

Before Flexbox and Grid, getting columns to be the same height regardless of their content was a nightmare involving JavaScript or clever background image tricks. Now it's automatic with Flexbox (`bk03ch04/example18.html`):

```
.feature-cards {
    display: flex;
    gap: 2rem;
    flex-wrap: wrap;
}
.feature-card {
    flex: 1 1 300px;
    background-color: hsl(0 0% 100%);
    padding: 2rem;
    border-radius: 0.5rem;
}
```

All flex items in a row automatically stretch to match the height of the tallest item. So if one card has three paragraphs and another has just one, they'll both be the same height. The browser handles the math; you just set `display: flex`.

## Centering elements perfectly

The classic web development joke is that there are a thousand ways to center things in CSS, and somehow none of them work. (Okay, that's an exaggeration, but centering used to be genuinely tricky.) Flexbox makes centering almost trivial (`bk03ch04/example19.html`):

```
.centered-container {
    display: flex;
    justify-content: center;
    align-items: center;
    min-height: 400px;
}
```

That's it! When the flex direction is `row` (the default), the `justify-content: center` declaration centers things horizontally, and the `align-items: center` declaration centers things vertically. Whatever's inside that container will be perfectly centered both ways. This works great for loading spinners, modal dialogs, or "coming soon" pages.

With Grid, it's even simpler:

```
.centered-container {
    display: grid;
    place-items: center;
    min-height: 400px;
}
```

The `place-items` property is shorthand for both `align-items` and `justify-items`. One line, perfect centering. Beautiful.

## Preventing layout overflow

Sometimes flex items stubbornly refuse to shrink below a certain size, causing horizontal scrollbars. This usually happens with text or images. The fix is understanding the `min-width` property (`bk03ch04/example20.html`):

```
.flex-item {
    flex: 1 1 200px;
    min-width: 0;
}
```

By default, flex items won't shrink below the size of their content. Setting `min-width: 0` overrides this behavior, allowing items to shrink as much as needed. For images specifically, you'll also want:

```
.flex-item img {
    max-width: 100%;
    height: auto;
}
```

This code ensures that images scale down to fit their container while maintaining their aspect ratio.

## Reordering items visually

Sometimes you want elements to appear in a different order visually than they do in your HTML. This approach is especially useful for responsive design. For example, maybe you want the sidebar first on mobile devices but after the main content on a desktop. Flexbox and Grid both offer solutions.

With Flexbox, use the `order` property (`bk03ch04/example21.html`):

```
.main-content {
    order: 2;
}
.sidebar {
    order: 1;
}
@media (min-width: 64em) {
    .main-content {
```

```
        order: 1;
    }
    .sidebar {
        order: 2;
    }
}
```

Lower numbers appear first. On a mobile device, the sidebar (`order: 1`) comes before the main content (`order: 2`). On the desktop, we swap them. The HTML stays the same; only the visual presentation changes.

With Grid, you have multiple routes, but the most common is to use the `grid-template-areas` property (`bk03ch04/example22.html`):

```
.layout-container {
    display: grid;
    grid-template-columns: 1fr;
    grid-template-areas: 'sidebar main';
}

.main-content {
    grid-area: main;
}

.sidebar {
    grid-area: sidebar;
}


@media (min-width: 64em) {
    .layout-container {
        grid-template-columns: minmax(0, 1fr) 300px;
        grid-template-areas: 'main sidebar';
    }
}
```

On a mobile device, `grid-template-areas: 'sidebar main'` ensures that the sidebar comes before the main content. On the desktop, you swap them with `grid-template-areas: 'main sidebar'`.

WARNING

Using `order` or `grid-template-areas` to reorder elements changes only the visual order, not the tab order for keyboard navigation. Screen reader users and keyboard navigators will experience the original HTML order. Reorder only when it doesn't harm accessibility.

IN THIS CHAPTER

» Bringing your pages to life with animations and transitions

» Transforming and filtering elements

» Using pseudo-elements and pseudo-classes to enhance your designs

» Implementing dark mode

# Chapter 5
# Advanced CSS Effects

*Animation is just another way of telling a story.*

—CHRISTOPHER MILLER

CSS is a great way to beautify dishwater-dull HTML pages, but even when you've made over your page with fonts, colors, and a modern layout, it still just kind of sits there, doesn't it? This book is all about building modern websites, and the word *static* isn't part of the modern web vocabulary. No, today's web is all about *motion, interaction,* and *visual effects* that catch the eye and guide users through your content.

This chapter introduces you to some of CSS's most powerful — and fun! — features for creating dynamic, engaging web pages. You learn how to animate elements as they move across the screen, transform elements in three-dimensional space, apply Instagram-worthy filters, and even give your users the option to view your site in dark mode. It's going to be a blast, so let's dive in.

## Applying CSS Animations and Transitions

One of the most effective ways to make your website feel more professional and engaging is to add movement. Not the kind of movement that makes your users dizzy (we've all been to those websites), but subtle, purposeful animations that guide attention and provide feedback. CSS gives you two main tools for creating movement: transitions and animations. While they might sound similar, they serve different purposes and work in different ways.

## Understanding transitions: Smooth changes on demand

A CSS *transition* is a kind of smooth bridge between two states. When something on your page changes — say, a button changes color when you hover your cursor over it — a transition smoothly animates that change instead of making it happen instantly. Think of it as the difference between a light switch (instant) and a dimmer switch (gradual).

Here's a real-world example from the Orbital Donuts website. Right now, when you hover your cursor over the Order Now button, it changes background color instantly. Let's add a transition to make that change smooth (refer to `bk03ch05/example01.html` in this book's example files):

```
.order-button {
    background-color: hsl(355 82% 56%);
    /* Other styles omitted for clarity */
    transition: background-color 200ms ease-out;
}

.order-button:hover {
    background-color: hsl(355 82% 46%);
}
```

That single `transition` property does a lot of work. It tells the browser that when the `background-color` property changes, don't do it instantly. Instead, take 200 milliseconds to smoothly interpolate from the old color to the new one, and use an `ease-out` timing function to make it feel natural. (The trigger here is the `:hover` pseudo-class, which you learn about later in the "Styling with Pseudo-Elements and Pseudo-Classes" section.)

The `transition` property has four components you can specify:

- **Property:** Which CSS property should transition (`color`, `background-color`, `transform`, etc.)?
- **Duration:** How long should the transition take? Specify in milliseconds (for example, `200ms`) or seconds (`0.2s`). Keep most transitions under `300ms` to keep your site feeling snappy.

- **Timing function:** How should the speed vary during the transition? Common values include `ease-out` (starts fast, ends slow), `ease-in` (starts slow, ends fast), `ease-in-out` (slow at both ends), and `linear` (constant speed).
- **Delay:** How long to wait before starting the transition. Most of the time, you'll leave this at `0` (or omit it, which is the same thing), but delays can create interesting staggered effects.

REMEMBER

Transitions work only when a property changes from one value to another. They can't animate from nothing to something, so the element needs to have a starting value defined.

## Creating keyframe animations: Motion with personality

While transitions are perfect for reacting to user interactions, CSS *animations* enable you to create more complex, multistep movements that can run automatically when the page loads or loops continuously. Animations are defined using `@keyframes` rules that specify what should happen at different points during the animation.

Let's create a subtle floating animation for the Featured Donut of the Day card on the Orbital Donuts home page. This animation will make the card gently bob up and down, drawing attention to it without being annoying (`bk03ch05/example02.html`):

```
@keyframes float {
    0%, 100% {
        transform: translateY(0);
    }
    50% {
        transform: translateY(-0.5rem);
    }
}
.featured-donut {
    animation: float 3s ease-in-out infinite;
}
```

Let's break down what's happening here. The `@keyframes float` rule defines three *keyframes*, which are specific points in time during the animation. At `0%` (the start) and `100%` (the end), the card is in its normal position. At `50%` (halfway through), it's lifted up by half a rem. The browser automatically fills in all the positions in between, creating a smooth motion.

The animation property of the .featured-donut class applies the animation and specifies the following: use the float keyframes, take 3 seconds for one complete cycle, use an ease-in-out timing function for smooth acceleration and deceleration, and loop infinitely (otherwise it would run only once).

Here's a more complex animation that makes the floating Order Now button pulse to draw attention (bk03ch05/example03.html):

```
@keyframes pulse {
    0% {
        transform: scale(1);
        box-shadow: 0 4px 12px hsl(225 63% 10% / 0.3);
    }
    50% {
        transform: scale(1.1);
        box-shadow: 0 6px 16px hsl(225 63% 10% / 0.4);
    }
    100% {
        transform: scale(1);
        box-shadow: 0 4px 12px hsl(225 63% 10% / 0.3);
    }
}
.floating-order-button {
    animation: pulse 2s ease-in-out infinite;
}
```

This animation simultaneously changes both the button's size and its shadow, making it appear to gently pulse. By listing both transform and box-shadow in the same keyframe, the size and shadow animate together in sync.

## Respecting reduced motion preferences

WARNING

Motion can trigger discomfort or vestibular (perception of body position and movement) issues for some users. Always use the prefers-reduced-motion media query to disable or reduce animations for users who've enabled this accessibility setting in their operating system:

```
@media (prefers-reduced-motion: reduce) {
    /* Disable animations */
    * {
        animation-duration: 0.01ms !important;
        animation-iteration-count: 1 !important;
```

```
        transition-duration: 0.01ms !important;
    }
}
```

This approach preserves the structure of your animations (so nothing breaks) but makes them effectively instantaneous. Users who need reduced motion won't experience the motion effects, but all your interactive features will still work normally.

You can also take a more nuanced approach and keep certain animations while removing others. For example, you might keep color transitions but remove transforms:

```
@media (prefers-reduced-motion: reduce) {
    /* Remove transform-based animations and transitions */
    * {
        animation: none !important;
        transition: none !important;
    }
    /* Restore color-only transitions for non-motion properties */
    .floating-order-button {
        transition: background-color 200ms ease-out !important;
    }
    article:hover {
        transform: none;
    }
}
```

The key is to test your site with reduced motion enabled. On macOS, you can enable it in System Settings by choosing Accessibility ➪ Display ➪ Reduce Motion. On Windows, choose Start ➪ Settings ➪ Accessibility ➪ Visual Effects and then click the Animation Effects switch off. Now browse your site and make sure it's still usable and nothing critical is hidden by disabled animations.

REMEMBER

Respecting user preferences isn't optional; it's an accessibility requirement. Always include `prefers-reduced-motion` media queries when you use animations and transitions. Your users who need this setting will thank you.

## Animation timing and performance

When you're adding animations and transitions to your site, it's important to understand which CSS properties are cheap to animate and which ones are expensive. Some properties can be animated smoothly at 60 frames per second without breaking a sweat, while others can cause stuttering and lag.

The best properties to animate performance-wise are `transform` and `opacity`. These properties can be handled by the browsing device's *GPU* (graphics processing unit), which is designed for this kind of work. When you animate `transform` (refer to the next section), you can move, rotate, scale, and skew elements without forcing the browser to recalculate layouts or repaint other elements on the page.

Here's a comparison. This animation has poor performance because it animates the left property (`bk03ch05/example04.html`):

```
/* Poor performance - avoid */
@keyframes slide-bad {
    from {
        left: 0;
    }
    to {
        left: 300px;
    }
}
```

This version achieves the same visual effect but performs much better (also `bk03ch05/example04.html`):

```
/* Good performance - use this instead */
@keyframes slide-good {
    from {
        transform: translateX(0);
    }
    to {
        transform: translateX(300px);
    }
}
```

Both animations move an element 300 pixels to the right, but the `transform` version will be much smoother, especially on mobile devices or lower-powered computers. As a general rule: if you can accomplish something with `transform` or `opacity`, use those instead of animating properties like `top`, `left`, `width`, or `height`.

TIP

Browser developer tools include performance profilers that can show you which animations are causing problems. Chrome's DevTools, for example, has a Performance tab that enables you to record animations and see where the browser is spending its time.

# Getting Creative with Transform and Filter Effects

CSS transforms and filters are two of the most powerful visual effect tools in your CSS toolbox. Transforms enable you to manipulate elements in two-dimensional or three-dimensional space, including moving, rotating, scaling, and skewing them. Filters enable you to apply Photoshop-style effects such as blur, brightness adjustment, and color manipulation directly in CSS. Together, they open up a world of creative possibilities.

## Working with 2D transforms

The `transform` property is your gateway to moving and manipulating elements. It accepts a variety of *transform functions* that each do something different to the element. You can use them individually or combine multiple transforms together.

Let's start with *translating,* which moves an element from its normal position. We've seen this in action with `translateY()` earlier, but you can also move elements horizontally with `translateX()` or in both directions at once with the `translate()` function (refer to `bk03ch05/example05.html` for this code and the other snippets in this section):

```
.shift-element {
    /* Move 2rem right, 1rem down */
    transform: translate(2rem, 1rem);
}
```

The `rotate()` function rotates an element around its center point. You specify the angle using degrees (`deg`). Positive values rotate clockwise, and negative values rotate counterclockwise:

```
.tilt-right {
    transform: rotate(5deg);
}
.tilt-left {
    transform: rotate(-5deg);
}
```

For the Orbital Donuts site, you could add a subtle tilt to promotional badges to make them look more dynamic:

```
.promo-badge {
    background-color: hsl(16 100% 60%);
    color: hsl(0 0% 100%);
    padding: 0.5rem 1rem;
    border-radius: 0.25rem;
    transform: rotate(-3deg);
    font-weight: 700;
}
```

The `scale()` function makes elements larger or smaller. A value of `1` means no change, values greater than `1` make the element bigger, and values less than `1` make it smaller:

```
.enlarge-on-hover {
    transition: transform 200ms ease-out;
}
.enlarge-on-hover:hover {
    transform: scale(1.05);
}
```

Here's where transforms get interesting: you can combine multiple transform functions in a single declaration. Just list them separated by spaces, and they'll be applied in order from left to right:

```
.fancy-card {
    /* Rotate, then scale, then translate */
    transform: rotate(-2deg) scale(1.1) translateY(-0.5rem);
}
```

REMEMBER

The order of transform functions matters! Transform operations are applied from left to right, and changing the order can produce very different results. For example, rotating then translating gives a different result than translating then rotating.

## Understanding transform-origin

By default, transforms happen around the element's center point. But you can change this using the `transform-origin` property. This property is particularly useful for rotations and scaling.

For example, if you want a box to rotate from the center of its left edge, you'd set the transform origin to `left center` (`bk03ch05/example06.html`):

```
.rotating-box {
    transform-origin: left center;
    transition: transform 300ms ease-out;
}
.rotating-box.closed {
    transform: rotateY(-90deg);
}
```

The `transform-origin` property accepts keywords (`top`, `bottom`, `left`, `right`, `center`) or specific measurements. You can specify just one value (which sets the horizontal position with vertical centered) or two values for both horizontal and vertical positions.

## Applying CSS filters

While transforms change an element's geometry, `CSS filters` change how the element looks visually. You can blur images, adjust brightness and contrast, convert to grayscale, and apply many other effects, all without needing image-editing software.

The `filter` property accepts one or more filter functions. Let's look at the most commonly used filters (`bk03ch05/example07.html`):

```
/* Blur effect - great for backgrounds */
.background-blur {
    filter: blur(5px);
}
/* Brightness - 100% is normal, higher is brighter */
.brighten-image {
    filter: brightness(120%);
}
/* Contrast - 100% is normal */
.increase-contrast {
    filter: contrast(150%);
}
/* Grayscale - 0% is full color, 100% is black and white */
.grayscale-image {
    filter: grayscale(100%);
}
/* Saturate - increases color intensity */
.vivid-colors {
    filter: saturate(150%);
}
```

Like transforms, you can combine multiple filters. For the Orbital Donuts site, you could create an interesting hover effect on donut images that makes them slightly brighter and more saturated:

```
article img {
    transition: filter 200ms ease-out;
}
article img:hover {
    filter: brightness(110%) saturate(120%);
}
```

One particularly useful filter is `drop-shadow()`, which creates a shadow that follows the shape of the element (including transparent areas), unlike `box-shadow`, which just creates a rectangular shadow:

```
.logo-with-shadow {
    filter: drop-shadow(0 2px 4px hsl(225 63% 10% / 0.3));
}
```

TIP

Filters can be computationally expensive, especially for blur and drop shadows. Use them judiciously and test on lower-powered devices to ensure your site stays responsive.

# Styling with Pseudo-Elements and Pseudo-Classes

Before I dive into what pseudo-elements and pseudo-classes are, I need to clear up some potential confusion. Despite their similar names, these are two completely different tools that do completely different things. Pseudo-classes select elements based on their state (like `:hover` or `:focus`), while pseudo-elements enable you to style specific parts of elements or even create virtual elements in CSS.

## Styling states with pseudo-classes

You've already seen pseudo-classes in action because `:hover` is one! A *pseudo-class* is a keyword you add to a selector that specifies a special state of the selected elements. A pseudo-class always starts with a colon (`:`).

Let's look at some of the most useful pseudo-classes for interactive elements (refer to `bk03ch05/example08.html` for this code and the other snippets in this section):

```
/* :hover - when the mouse cursor is over an element */
button:hover {
    background-color: hsl(355 82% 46%);
}
/* :focus - when an element has keyboard focus */
input:focus {
    border-color: hsl(224 66% 33%);
    outline: 3px solid hsl(224 66% 33% / 0.3);
}
/* :active - when an element is being clicked */
button:active {
    transform: translateY(2px);
}
/* :disabled - when a form element is disabled */
button:disabled {
    opacity: 0.5;
    cursor: not-allowed;
}
```

Structural pseudo-classes enable you to select elements based on their position. The `:first-child` and `:last-child` pseudo-classes are particularly useful:

```
/* Style just the first article differently */
article:first-child {
    border: 2px solid hsl(16 100% 60%);
}
/* Remove bottom margin from the last paragraph in a section */
section p:last-child {
    margin-bottom: 0;
}
```

The `:nth-child()` pseudo-class is even more powerful. It lets you select elements using a formula. For example, to create alternating row colors in the Orbital Donuts menu:

```
/* Style every other article */
article:nth-child(odd) {
    background-color: hsl(0 0% 100%);
}
```

```
article:nth-child(even) {
    background-color: hsl(216 43% 97%);
}
```

You can also use `:not()` to exclude certain elements from a rule. This pseudo-class is handy when you want to style everything except one specific case:

```
/* Style all links except ones in the navigation */
a:not(nav a) {
    color: hsl(224 66% 33%);
    text-decoration: underline;
}
```

## Creating content with pseudo-elements

While pseudo-classes enable you to select elements in different states, *pseudo-elements* enable you to style specific parts of elements or even create virtual elements that don't exist in your HTML. Pseudo-elements begin with two colons (`::`) to distinguish them from pseudo-classes.

The two most commonly used pseudo-elements are `::before` and `::after`. These enable you to insert content before or after an element's content. They're incredibly versatile and can be used for decorative elements, icons, or even complex visual effects.

Here's a simple example that adds a decorative element before section headings on the Orbital Donuts site (refer to `bk03ch05/example09.html` for this code and the other snippets in this section):

```
h2::before {
    content: '🍩 ';
    margin-right: 0.5rem;
}
```

The `content` property is required when using `::before` or `::after`. It specifies what content to insert. This content can be text, an emoji, or even an empty string if you just want to create a styled box.

Here's a more practical example that adds visual indicators to external links:

```
/* Add an icon after external links */
a[href^="http"]::after {
```

```
    content: ' ↗';
    font-size: 0.75em;
    color: hsl(220 9% 46%);
}
```

You can style pseudo-elements just like regular elements. You can give them backgrounds, borders, positioning, transforms, and more. This feature makes them incredibly useful for creating decorative effects without cluttering your HTML. Here's an example that creates a colored accent bar on donut cards:

```
article {
    position: relative;
}
article::before {
    content: '';
    position: absolute;
    top: 0;
    left: 0;
    width: 4px;
    height: 100%;
    background: linear-gradient(
        to bottom,
        hsl(291 63% 42%),
        hsl(224 66% 33%)
    );
    border-radius: 0.5rem 0 0 0.5rem;
}
```

This code creates a gradient-colored bar on the left edge of each card without requiring extra HTML elements. The `content: ''` line creates an empty pseudo-element that you then position and style.

# Implementing CSS for Dark Mode

Dark mode has become a must-have feature for modern websites. Many users prefer dark interfaces for reduced eye strain, better battery life on OLED screens, or simply because they think it looks cool (and it does!). Implementing dark mode isn't just about inverting colors because it requires thoughtful design decisions to ensure that your site remains readable, accessible, and visually appealing in both light and dark themes.

## Detecting the user's preference

CSS provides a *media query* called `prefers-color-scheme` that detects whether the user has enabled dark mode in their operating system. This media query is the foundation of implementing dark mode in CSS:

```
/* Default styles (light mode) */
:root {
    --background: hsl(216 43% 97%);
    --text: hsl(218 17% 27%);
    --card-bg: hsl(0 0% 100%);
}
/* Dark mode styles */
@media (prefers-color-scheme: dark) {
    :root {
        --background: hsl(225 63% 10%);
        --text: hsl(216 43% 97%);
        --card-bg: hsl(218 17% 17%);
    }
}
body {
    background-color: var(--background);
    color: var(--text);
}
```

This approach uses CSS custom properties (variables) to store your color values. In light mode, you define one set of colors. Inside the `prefers-color-scheme` media query, you redefine those same variables with dark mode colors. Any CSS rule that uses these variables will automatically update when dark mode is enabled.

## Designing for dark mode

Dark mode isn't just light mode with inverted colors. For an effective dark theme, you should follow several important design principles.

First, pure black backgrounds — `hsl(0 0% 0%)` — can cause eye strain due to the extreme contrast with white text. Instead, use dark grays like the Space Navy color — `hsl(225 63% 10%)` — already in the Orbital Donuts design system. This color provides good contrast while being easier on the eyes.

Second, reduce the contrast of non-essential elements. In light mode, you might use pure black text, but in dark mode, pure white text can be too harsh. Use slightly dimmed whites or light grays for body text:

```
@media (prefers-color-scheme: dark) {
    :root {
        /* Don't use pure white for text */
        --text-primary: hsl(0 0% 92%);
        --text-secondary: hsl(0 0% 70%);
    }
}
```

Third, adjust your shadows. Drop shadows that work well in light mode often disappear in dark mode or look strange. In dark mode, shadows should be subtle or you might want to use lighter borders instead:

```
:root {
    --shadow-card: 0 2px 8px hsl(225 63% 10% / 0.1);
}
@media (prefers-color-scheme: dark) {
    :root {
        /* Use lighter shadows or borders in dark mode */
        --shadow-card: 0 0 0 1px hsl(0 0% 100% / 0.1);
    }
}
```

## Implementing dark mode for Orbital Donuts

Let's implement a complete dark mode for the Orbital Donuts website. The site already uses CSS custom properties for colors, which will make this implementation easier. We'll add a dark mode media query that redefines those colors (`bk03ch05/orbital-donuts/css/styles.css`):

```
/* Light mode colors (default) */
:root {
    /* Primary Colors */
    --color-rocket-red: hsl(355 82% 56%);
    --color-space-navy: hsl(225 63% 10%);
    --color-mars-orange: hsl(16 100% 60%);

    /* Secondary Colors */
    --color-galaxy-purple: hsl(291 63% 42%);
    --color-cosmic-blue: hsl(224 66% 33%);

    /* Neutrals */
    --color-moonlight: hsl(0 0% 100%);
    --color-stardust: hsl(216 43% 97%);
```

```
    --color-nebula-light: hsl(220 14% 91%);
    --color-asteroid-gray: hsl(220 9% 46%);
    --color-meteor-dark: hsl(218 17% 27%);

    /* Shadows */
    --shadow-card: 0 2px 8px hsl(225 63% 10% / 0.1);
    --shadow-hover: 0 4px 16px hsl(225 63% 10% / 0.15);

    /* Color scheme */
    color-scheme: light dark;
}

/* ============================================
   Dark Mode
   ============================================ */

@media (prefers-color-scheme: dark) {
    :root {
        /* Primary Colors - slightly adjusted for dark mode */
        --color-rocket-red: hsl(355 82% 60%);
        --color-mars-orange: hsl(16 100% 65%);

        /* Secondary Colors - brighter for dark backgrounds */
        --color-galaxy-purple: hsl(291 63% 55%);
        --color-cosmic-blue: hsl(224 66% 60%);

        /* Neutrals - inverted for dark mode */
        --color-moonlight: hsl(225 20% 12%);
        --color-stardust: hsl(225 25% 8%);
        --color-nebula-light: hsl(220 15% 20%);
        --color-asteroid-gray: hsl(220 9% 60%);
        --color-meteor-dark: hsl(216 20% 90%);

        /* Shadows - more pronounced for dark mode */
        --shadow-card: 0 2px 8px hsl(0 0% 0% / 0.3);
        --shadow-hover: 0 4px 16px hsl(0 0% 0% / 0.4);
    }

    /* Reduce image brightness slightly in dark mode */
    img {
        filter: brightness(0.75);
    }
}
```

# 4

# Adding Interactivity with JavaScript

# Contents at a Glance

IN THIS CHAPTER

» Getting to know JavaScript

» Working with variables and functions

» Controlling program flow and data

» Wielding the developer tools

# Chapter 1
# JavaScript Basics for Beginners

*Most of the good programmers do programming not because they expect to get paid or get adulation by the public, but because it is fun to program.*

—LINUS TORVALDS

HTML and CSS (which I cover in Book 3) are awesome technologies and you can use them to create pages that look amazing. But after you funnel your page through your web server and look at it a few (dozen) times, you might notice a subtle feeling of disappointment creeping in. Why? It can be hard to pin down, but that hint of dismay comes from a stark fact: Your web page just kind of sits there.

Sure, you likely have a link or three to click, but most likely those links just take you to more of your pages that also just kind of sit there. Or maybe a link takes you to another site altogether, one that feels dynamic and alive and interactive. Ah, engagement! Ooh, excitement!

What's the difference between a page that does nothing and another that seems to be always dancing? One word: JavaScript. With some notable exceptions (see my coverage of CSS animation in Book 3, Chapter 5), HTML and CSS create static pages. If you want your pages to be dynamic and interactive, you need a bit of behind-the-scenes JavaScript to make it so.

Don't worry if you've never programmed before. Over the next few chapters I take you through everything you need to know, step by step, nice and easy. As you're about to find out, it really is fun to program.

# Understanding JavaScript's Role on the Web

As I mention in Book 1, Chapter 4, every web page is built on three core technologies: HTML for structure, CSS for style, and JavaScript for interactivity. If HTML is the skeleton of your web page and CSS is the skin and clothing, JavaScript is the muscles and nervous system. It's what makes things move and respond.

## What JavaScript does

But what does *interactivity* mean in practice? Here are some common things JavaScript handles on the web:

- **Form validation:** Checking that a visitor has entered a valid email address or filled in all required fields before the form is submitted
- **Dynamic content:** Updating parts of a page — such as a shopping cart total or a notification badge — without reloading the entire page
- **User interface effects:** Opening and closing menus, showing dialogs, and creating image carousels
- **Data processing:** Sorting a table, filtering a product list, or calculating a price based on the user's selections

Essentially, anytime something on a web page changes or responds to what the user does without reloading the page, JavaScript is almost certainly behind it.

## How browsers run JavaScript

Here's something that surprises many beginners: JavaScript runs right inside the web browser. When a browser loads a page that includes JavaScript, the browser's built-in *JavaScript engine* reads and executes the code. Chrome uses an engine called V8, Firefox uses SpiderMonkey, and Safari uses JavaScriptCore. The names don't matter much, but the concept does: Your JavaScript code runs on the visitor's device, not on your web server.

This feature has a big practical benefit: JavaScript can respond instantly to user actions because it doesn't need to send a request to a server and wait for a response. When someone clicks a button, JavaScript can react immediately, right there in the browser.

JavaScript has access to the web page itself. It can read what's on the page, change it, add content, remove content, and respond to user events such as clicks, scrolls, and key presses. This capability to manipulate the page is so central to JavaScript's purpose that it gets its own chapter: Chapter 2, where I cover the Document Object Model (DOM).



WARNING

Because JavaScript runs in the browser, on the user's device, it can respond instantly to user actions — but your code is also visible to anyone who views the page source. Never put sensitive information such as passwords or API keys directly in your JavaScript code.

## Adding JavaScript to your pages

You can add JavaScript to an HTML page in two main ways, and they're similar to how you add CSS.

### Inline scripts

You can put JavaScript code directly in your HTML file using the `<script>` tag. Here's a simple example (`bk04ch01/example01.html`):

```
<!DOCTYPE html>
<html lang="en">
<head>
    <meta charset="utf-8">
    <title>inline script example</title>
</head>
<body>
    <h1>Orbital Donuts</h1>
    <p id="greeting">Welcome!</p>
    <script>
        document.getElementById('greeting').textContent =
            'Welcome to Orbital Donuts!';
    </script>
</body>
</html>
```

The `<script>` tag tells the browser, "Hey, everything between here and the closing `</script>` tag is JavaScript, not HTML." In this case, the script uses `document.getElementById` to find the element with the ID `greeting` and changes its text content. (Book 4, Chapter 2 offers more about `getElementById`.) When you open this file in a browser, you see "Welcome to Orbital Donuts!" instead of just "Welcome!" because JavaScript rewrites the text after the page loaded.

TIP

Place your `<script>` tag just before the closing `</body>` tag. This ensures that the HTML elements have already been loaded by the time JavaScript runs, which prevents errors caused by trying to access elements that don't exist yet.

## External scripts

For anything beyond a few lines of code, you're better off putting your JavaScript in a separate `.js` file and linking to it.

Here's an example JavaScript file (bk04ch01/js/main.js):

```
document.getElementById('greeting').textContent =
    'Welcome to Orbital Donuts!';
```

This code is the same as in the previous example, except you don't need the `<script>` tag because the browser already knows that anything inside a `.js` file is JavaScript code. With your JavaScript file saved, you link to it in your HTML file (`bk04ch01/example02.html`):

```
<!DOCTYPE html>
<html lang="en">
<head>
    <meta charset="UTF-8">
    <title>External script example</title>
</head>

<body>
    <h1>Orbital Donuts</h1>
    <p id="greeting">Welcome!</p>
    <script src="js/main.js"></script>
</body>
</html>
```

This new version of the `<script>` tag tells the browser to load and run the JavaScript in the `main.js` file in the `js/` subdirectory. (To help keep your code organized, it's best to create a subdirectory such as `js/` to store your JavaScript files.)

External scripts keep your HTML clean, make your JavaScript reusable across multiple pages, and allow the browser to cache the JavaScript file so it doesn't need to download it again on subsequent page views. For anything beyond a quick experiment, external scripts are the way to go.

REMEMBER

For most of the examples in this book, I use inline scripts to keep each example self-contained in a single HTML file. In a real project, you'd almost always use external script files.

# Variables, Data Types, and Operators

Every programming language needs a way to store and work with information. In JavaScript, you store information in *variables*, each of which is a named container that holds a value. Think of a variable as a labeled box: the label is the variable's name, and whatever you put inside the box is the variable's value. You can peek inside the box to read the value and, depending on how you created the variable, you might be able to swap the value for a different one.



## Declaring variables with let and const

In modern JavaScript, you create variables using one of two keywords: `let` or `const`. Here's the difference:

- **`let`:** Creates a variable whose value can change later. Use `let` for values that will be updated, such as a running total or a counter.
- **`const`:** Creates a variable whose value can't be changed after it's set. (*const* is short for *constant*.) Use `const` for values that should stay the same, such as a tax rate or a shop name.

Here are some examples:

```
let orderTotal = 0;
let customerName = "Quinn";
const taxRate = 0.08;
const shopName = "Orbital Donuts";
```

The `orderTotal` variable uses `let` because the total will change as the customer adds items. The `taxRate` variable uses `const` because the tax rate isn't going to change during a single order.

You can change a `let` variable's value after creating it:

```
let orderTotal = 0;
orderTotal = 3.50;  // Customer adds a Cosmic Cruller
orderTotal = 7.00;  // Customer adds Nebula Nuggets
```

Note that you use the `let` keyword only when you're creating — or, to use the official term, *declaring* — the variable. After that, you just use the variable's name.

What happens if you try to change a `const` variable? JavaScript throws an error:

```
const taxRate = 0.08;
taxRate = 0.10;  // TypeError: Assignment to constant variable!
```

This is actually a good thing! The error tells you immediately that you're trying to change something that shouldn't change, which helps you catch bugs before they cause problems.

TIP

When in doubt, use `const`. If you later discover you need to change the value, you can always switch to `let`. Starting with `const` helps prevent accidental changes to values that should stay the same, and it makes your code easier to follow.

You might also see the `var` keyword in older JavaScript code and tutorials. It works similarly to `let` but has some quirky behavior that can cause subtle bugs. Modern JavaScript best practice is to use `let` and `const` exclusively, and that's what I do throughout this book.

## Naming your variables

Variable names in JavaScript follow a few rules:

- » Names can contain letters, digits, underscores, or dollar signs, but they must start with a letter, an underscore, or a dollar sign (not a digit).
- » Names are case-sensitive: `orderTotal` and `OrderTotal` are two different variables.
- » Names can't be JavaScript reserved words such as `let`, `const`, `function`, or `return`.

By convention, JavaScript developers use *camelCase* for variable names, where the first word is lowercase and each subsequent word starts with an uppercase letter: `orderTotal`, `customerName`, `isOrderComplete`. This convention is so universal in JavaScript that using any other style (for example, `order_total` with an underscore separating the words) will make your code look out of place.

The best variable names are descriptive but concise. Compare these:

```
// Too vague
let x = 3.50;
```

```
let d = "Cosmic Cruller";

// Too verbose
let thePriceOfTheCurrentDonutBeingOrdered = 3.50;

// Just right
let donutPrice = 3.50;
let donutName = "Cosmic Cruller";
```

Good names make your code self-documenting. When you come back to your code a month later (or when someone else reads it), `donutPrice` tells you exactly what that variable holds. `x`? Not so much.



## Understanding data types

Variables can hold different kinds of data. JavaScript has several *data types*, but here are the ones you'll work with most often:

- **Strings** are text values. You create them by wrapping text in quotes. Single quotes ('), double quotes ("), or backticks (`) all work:

  ```
  const shopName = "Orbital Donuts";
  const tagline = 'Where every donut is out of this world!';
  const greeting = `Welcome to ${shopName}`;
  ```

  That third line uses backticks to create what's called a *template literal.* The `${shopName}` part gets automatically replaced with the value of the `shopName` variable, so `greeting` ends up containing the text `Welcome to Orbital Donuts`. Template literals are incredibly handy and you'll use them all the time.

- **Numbers** are, well, numerical values. JavaScript doesn't distinguish between integers (whole numbers) and decimals, they're all just numbers:

  ```
  const donutPrice = 3.50;
  const dozenCount = 12;
  const totalCost = donutPrice * dozenCount;  // 42
  ```

- **Booleans** represent `true` or `false` and are essential for making decisions in your code (as I show a bit later in the "Control Flow: if. . .else and Loops" section):

  ```
  const shopIsOpen = true;
  const isSoldOut = false;
  ```

JavaScript also has two special values that represent nothing:

- **undefined:** A variable that has been declared but hasn't been given a value yet.
- **null:** A variable that has been deliberately set to "no value."

```
let selectedDonut;          // undefined (no value assigned)
let couponCode = null;      // null (explicitly set to nothing)
```

## Checking data types with typeof

Sometimes you need to verify what type of data a variable holds, especially when debugging. The `typeof` operator returns a string telling you the type (`bk04ch01/example03.html`):

```
const shopName = "Orbital Donuts";
const price = 3.50;
const isOpen = true;

console.log(typeof shopName);  // "string"
console.log(typeof price);     // "number"
console.log(typeof isOpen);    // "boolean"
console.log(typeof undefined); // "undefined"
```

`console.log()` is a special function that outputs data to the browser console, which is part of the developer tools that come with every web browser. Refer to the section "Browser Developer Tools for JavaScript" for the details.

## Working with operators

Operators let you do things with values: perform calculations, compare things, and combine conditions. Here's a tour of the most important ones.

**Arithmetic operators** work the way you'd expect from basic math:

```
let subtotal = 3.50 + 4.25;     // Addition: 7.75
let change = 10 - 7.75;         // Subtraction: 2.25
let dozenPrice = 3.50 * 12;     // Multiplication: 42
let perDonut = 42 / 12;         // Division: 3.5
let leftover = 13 % 12;         // Remainder: 1
```

That last one, the % (modulo or remainder) operator, gives you the remainder after division. It's more useful than you might think — for example, you can use it to determine if a number is even (`number % 2 === 0`) or to cycle through a list of items.

*Comparison operators* compare two values and return a Boolean (`true` or `false`):

```
let price = 3.50;
price === 3.50;     // Strict equality: true
price !== 4.25;     // Not equal: true
price > 3.00;       // Greater than: true
price < 2.00;       // Less than: false
price >= 3.50;      // Greater than or equal: true
price <= 5.00;      // Less than or equal: true
```

WARNING

Always use the strict equality operator (===) with three equal signs, not the loose equality operator (==) with two. The loose version does automatic type conversion, which can lead to bizarre results. For example, `"" == 0` is `true`, but `"" === 0` is `false`. Stick with === and you'll avoid a whole category of bugs.

*Logical operators* enable you to combine multiple conditions:

```
const isWeekday = true;
const isMorning = true;

// AND (&&): Both conditions must be true
isWeekday && isMorning;        // true

// OR (||): At least one condition must be true
isWeekday || isMorning;        // true

// NOT (!): Flips true to false, and vice versa
!isWeekday;                    // false
```

## Joining strings

You can combine strings using the + operator or template literals:

```
const firstName = "Quinn";
const item = "Cosmic Cruller";

// Using the + operator
const msg1 = "Hi, " + firstName + "! Your " + item + " is ready.";
```

```
// Using a template literal (much cleaner!)
const msg2 = `Hi, ${firstName}! Your ${item} is ready.`;
```

Both produce the same result — `Hi, Quinn! Your Cosmic Cruller is ready.` — but the template literal version is far easier to read and write. Once you start using template literals, you'll never want to go back to string concatenation with the + operator. Trust me on this one.

# Functions and Scope

So far, all the code you've seen runs once, straight through from top to bottom. That works fine for simple scripts, but what happens when you need to do the same thing in multiple places? Copying and pasting code is extra work and a recipe for bugs because every time you need to change the logic, you have to find and update every copy.

The solution is a *function,* which is a reusable block of code that you name, so you can run it whenever you need it. In cooking terms, a function is like a recipe: It has a name, a list of ingredients (called *arguments* or *parameters*), a set of steps, and it produces a result.

## Creating a function

Here's the basic pattern for creating a function in JavaScript:

```
function calculateTotal(price, quantity) {
    const subtotal = price * quantity;
    return subtotal;
}
```

Let's break this down piece by piece:

- **`function`:** The `function` keyword tells JavaScript you're creating a function.
- **`calculateTotal`:** The name you choose for the function. Like variables, use descriptive camelCase names.
- **`(price, quantity)`:** The function argument, which contains placeholders for the values you'll pass in when you call the function.
- **{ and }:** These braces mark the beginning and the end of the function code.

» **`const subtotal = price * quantity:`** A function statement that (in this case) performs a calculation. You can have as many statements as you need within a function. (That said, it's a good idea for each function to perform just a single task.)

» **`return subtotal:`** The `return` statement sends a value (in this example, the value of the `subtotal` variable) back to whatever statement called the function.

To use — or *call* — the function, you write its name followed by the argument values in parentheses (`bk04ch01/example04.html`):

```
function calculateTotal(price, quantity) {
    const subtotal = price * quantity;
    return subtotal;
}

const crullerTotal = calculateTotal(3.50, 2);     // 7
const nuggetTotal = calculateTotal(4.25, 3);      // 12.75
const ringTotal = calculateTotal(3.75, 1);        // 3.75
```

See how useful a function is? You define the calculation logic once, and then you can reuse it as many times as you need with different values. If you later need to change how the calculation works — say, to include tax — you change it in only one place.

## Arrow functions

Modern JavaScript gives you a shorter way to write functions called *arrow functions.* Here's the same function written both ways:

```
// Traditional function
function calculateTotal(price, quantity) {
    return price * quantity;
}

// Arrow function
const calculateTotal = (price, quantity) => {
    return price * quantity;
};
```

The arrow function replaces the `function` keyword with a fat arrow (`=>`) between the parameters and the function body. For very short functions that just return a value, you can make them even more concise:

```
const calculateTotal = (price, quantity) => price * quantity;
```

This one-liner drops the curly braces and the `return` keyword; the result is returned automatically. Nice and tidy!

## Understanding scope

*Scope* determines where in your code a variable is accessible. JavaScript has two main types of scope:

- **Global scope:** Variables declared outside of any function or block are available everywhere in your script:

```
const shopName = "Orbital Donuts";  // Global scope

function greetCustomer() {
    // shopName is accessible here
    return `Welcome to ${shopName}!`;
}
```

- **Local (block) scope:** Variables declared inside a function or block are available only within that block:

```
function calculateTip(amount) {
    const tipRate = 0.15;    // Exists only inside this function
    return amount * tipRate;
}

calculateTip(20);       // Works fine: returns 3

// console.log(tipRate); // Error! tipRate is not defined here
```

REMEMBER

Variables declared with `let` or `const` inside a block (anything between curly braces) are accessible only within that block. This feature is called *block scoping*, and it's one of the reasons `let` and `const` are preferred over the older `var` keyword, which doesn't respect block boundaries.

# Control Flow: if. . .else and Loops

So far, your JavaScript code runs every line, one after another, from top to bottom. But real programs need to make decisions and repeat actions. That's what *control flow* is all about: directing which code runs and when.

# Making decisions with if. . .else

The `if` statement is the most basic decision-making tool in JavaScript. It checks a condition and runs a block of code only if that condition is `true` (`bk04ch01/example05.html`):

```
const donutsInStock = 5;

if (donutsInStock > 0) {
    document.querySelector('#stock-status').textContent =
        "In stock! Order now.";
}
```

You can also handle the "otherwise" case with `else`, and chain multiple conditions with `else if` (`bk04ch01/example06.html`):

```
const donutsInStock = 3;
const statusElement = document.querySelector('#stock-status');

if (donutsInStock === 0) {
    statusElement.textContent = "Sold out!";
    statusElement.style.color = "red";
} else if (donutsInStock <= 5) {
    statusElement.textContent = `Only ${donutsInStock} left!`;
    statusElement.style.color = "orange";
} else {
    statusElement.textContent = "In stock! Order now.";
    statusElement.style.color = "green";
}
```

JavaScript checks each condition in order. Only the first matching block runs — once a condition is `true`, the rest are skipped. This means the order of your conditions matters! (Furrowing your brow over the `querySelector()` method? Book 4, Chapter 2 explains all.)

# Handling multiple cases with switch

When you need to compare a value against several specific options, a `switch` statement can be cleaner than a chain of `if. . .else if` blocks (`bk04ch01/example07.html`):

HTML:

```
<h2>Featured Donut of the Day</h2>
<article class="featured-donut">
    <h3>Cosmic Cruller</h3>
    <img src="/images/cosmic-cruller.webp"
         alt="Donut of the day"
         height="256" width="256">
</article>
```

JavaScript:

```
const dayOfWeek = new Date().getDay();
let todaysSpecial;
let todaysSpecialImage;

switch (dayOfWeek) {
    case 1:
        todaysSpecial = "Meteor Munchkin";
        todaysSpecialImage = "meteor-munchkin.webp";
        break;
    case 2:
        todaysSpecial = "Asteroid Almond";
        todaysSpecialImage = "asteroid-almond.webp";
        break;
    case 3:
        todaysSpecial = "Nebula Nutella";
        todaysSpecialImage = "nebula-nutella.webp";
        break;
    case 4:
        todaysSpecial = "Vegan Vanilla Orbit";
        todaysSpecialImage = "vegan-vanilla-orbit.webp";
        break;
    case 5:
        todaysSpecial = "Rocket Red Velvet";
        todaysSpecialImage = "rocket-red-velvet.webp";
        break;
    default:
        todaysSpecial = "Starlight Sprinkle";
        todaysSpecialImage = "starlight-sprinkle.webp";
}
document.querySelector(".featured-donut h3").textContent =
    todaysSpecial;
document.querySelector(".featured-donut img").src =
    `/images/${todaysSpecialImage}`;
```

WARNING

Don't forget the `break` statement at the end of each case (except the final `default` case)! Without it, JavaScript falls through to the next case and runs that code too, which is almost never what you want.

## Repeating actions with for loops

Loops let you run the same code multiple times. The `for` loop is the most common type:

```
for (let i = 1; i <= 6; i++) {
    console.log(`Donut box #${i} is packed`);
}
```

The three parts inside the parentheses control the loop:

- **`let i = 1`:** The initializer, which creates a counter variable and sets its starting value
- **`i <= 6`:** The condition, which the loop keeps running as long as this is `true`
- **`i++`:** The update, which runs after each iteration. `i++` is shorthand for "add 1 to `i`"

## Looping through collections with for. . .of

When you need to loop through an array of items (I cover arrays in the next section), the `for. . .of` loop is the cleanest option:

```
const flavors = ["Cosmic Cruller", "Nebula Nuggets", "Saturn Ring"];

for (const flavor of flavors) {
    console.log(`Now serving: ${flavor}`);
}
```

This loop automatically steps through each item in the `flavors` list. No counter variable, no condition to manage; just clean, readable code.

# Working with Arrays and Objects

Up to this point, every variable you've created holds a single value. But real web applications often deal with collections of data. For example, a menu has multiple donuts, and an order has multiple items. To handle these situations, JavaScript gives you two powerful data structures: arrays and objects.

## Creating and using arrays

An *array* is an ordered list of values. You create one by wrapping values in square brackets (`bk04ch01/example08.html`):

```
const flavors = ["Cosmic Cruller", "Nebula Nutella", "Asteroid Almond",
                 "Meteor Munchkin", "Rocket Red Velvet"];
console.log(flavors[0]);      // "Cosmic Cruller"
console.log(flavors[2]);      // "Asteroid Almond"
console.log(flavors.length); // 5
```

Each item in the array has a position number called an *index*. Here's the crucial detail: Arrays start counting at 0, not 1. So `"Cosmic Cruller"` is at index 0, `"Nebula Nutella"` is at index 1, and so on.

## Common array methods

Arrays come with built-in methods for adding, removing, and finding items (`bk04ch01/example09.html`):

```
const cart = ["Cosmic Cruller", "Nebula Nuggets"];

// Add to the end
cart.push("Saturn Ring");

// Remove from the end
const lastItem = cart.pop();

// Check if an item exists
cart.includes("Cosmic Cruller");  // true

// Find the position of an item
cart.indexOf("Nebula Nuggets");  // 1
```

One especially useful method is `forEach`, which runs a function on every item in the array (`bk04ch01/example10.html`):

```
const prices = [3.50, 4.25, 3.75];
let total = 0;

prices.forEach(function(price) {
    total = total + price;
});

console.log(`Order total: $${total}`);  // "Order total: $11.5"
```

# Creating and using objects

Whereas an array is an ordered list, an *object* is a collection of named properties. Objects are perfect for representing things with multiple attributes (bk04ch01/example11.html):

```
const donut = {
    name: "Cosmic Cruller",
    price: 3.50,
    calories: 320,
    isVegan: false,
    description: "A glazed twist dusted with star sprinkles"
};
```

You can access object properties in two ways:

```
// Dot notation (most common)
console.log(donut.name);        // "Cosmic Cruller"
console.log(donut.price);       // 3.50

// Bracket notation (useful when the key is in a variable)
const field = "calories";
console.log(donut[field]);       // 320
```

# Combining arrays and objects

Here's where things get really powerful: you can put objects inside arrays to create structured collections of data. This pattern is the backbone of most web applications (bk04ch01/example12.html):

```
const menu = [
    { name: "Cosmic Cruller", price: 3.50, isVegan: false },
    { name: "Vegan Vanilla Orbit", price: 4.25, isVegan: true },
    { name: "Starlight Sprinkle", price: 3.75, isVegan: false }
];

const menuList = document.querySelector('#menu-list');

menu.forEach(function(item) {
    const entry = document.createElement('p');
    entry.textContent = `${item.name} — $${item.price}`;
    if (item.isVegan) {
        entry.textContent += " (Vegan)";
    }
    menuList.appendChild(entry);
});
```

REMEMBER

The pattern of an array of objects is the backbone of most web applications. Whether you have a list of products, blog posts, user comments, or donut flavors, you'll structure the data the same way. Get comfortable with this pattern and you will be well on your way to building real web features.

# Browser Developer Tools for JavaScript

As I mention in Book 3, Chapter 3, every modern browser comes with built-in developer tools. You've already seen how the Elements panel helps with HTML and CSS. Now it's time to meet the developer tools' best friend for JavaScript: the console.

## Opening the console

To open the developer tools, press F12 (or Ctrl+Shift+I on Windows/Linux, or Cmd+Option+I on Mac). Then click the Console tab. Try typing `2 + 2` and pressing Enter. You'll see `4` appear. No big deal, but you can run JavaScript commands here and you can use the *console* to output the values of your code's variables, arrays, and objects.

## Using console.log()

The `console.log()` method is your primary tool for understanding what your code is doing (`bk04ch01/example13.html`):

```
const donutName = "Cosmic Cruller";
const price = 3.50;
const quantity = 2;

console.log("Donut:", donutName);
console.log("Price:", price);
console.log("Total:", price * quantity);
```

The console also has a few other useful methods:

- **`console.error()`:** Displays messages in red, making errors easy to spot.
- **`console.warn()`:** Displays messages in yellow, useful for warnings.
- **`console.table()`:** Displays arrays and objects in a nicely formatted table, which is perfect for checking your data structures.

## Reading error messages

When your JavaScript has a problem, the console displays an error message in red. Here's a typical error:

```
Uncaught ReferenceError: donutPrice is not defined at script.js:5:1
```

This message tells you three important things: the error type (`ReferenceError` — you're using a variable that doesn't exist), the message (`donutPrice is not defined`), and the location (`script.js:5:1` — file, line, and character position). Here are the error types you'll encounter most often:

- **`ReferenceError`:** You're using a variable or function that hasn't been declared. Check your spelling and scope.
- **`TypeError`:** You're trying to do something with a value that doesn't support it, like calling a method on `null`.
- **`SyntaxError`:** Your JavaScript has a structural problem, like a missing bracket or mismatched quotes. The browser can't even run the code until you fix it.

TIP

When you get an error, don't panic. Read the error message carefully, check the line number it points to, and look for the obvious culprits: misspelled names, missing semicolons, unclosed brackets, or mismatched quotes. Most JavaScript bugs are simple typos in disguise.

## Setting breakpoints

For trickier bugs, `console.log()` might not be enough. That's where breakpoints come in. A *breakpoint* tells the browser to pause your code at a specific line so you can inspect all your variables at that exact moment.

To set a breakpoint, open the developer tools and click the Sources tab (or Debugger in Firefox). Find your JavaScript file, click the line number where you want to pause, and reload the page. The browser pauses at the breakpoint, and you can hover your cursor over any variable to see its current value. Using breakpoints is like putting your code in slow motion so you can watch exactly what happens at each step.

IN THIS CHAPTER

- » Understanding how web browsers model your page
- » Selecting and changing page elements with JavaScript
- » Responding to clicks, typing, and other user actions

# Chapter 2
# JavaScript and the DOM

*The programmer, like the poet, works only slightly removed from pure thought-stuff. He builds his castles in the air, from air, creating by exertion of the imagination.*

—FRED BROOKS

The JavaScript in Book 4, Chapter 1 was but a mere appetizer, and now it's time to sit down for the main course: programming the Document Object Model, where you take control over every aspect of the web page. Want to change some web page text on the fly? JavaScript can do that. Want to add an element to the page? JavaScript's up to the task. Want to modify an element's CSS? JavaScript's all over that.

In this chapter, you explore the fascinating world of the Document Object Model. You learn lots of powerful coding techniques that enable you to make your web pages do almost anything you want them to do. You learn, too, that this is where web coding becomes fun and maybe just a little addictive (in a good way, I promise).

# Understanding the Document Object Model (DOM)

In Chapter 1, I mention that JavaScript has access to the web page itself and can read it, change it, add new content, and remove existing content. But how? Your web page is written in HTML, and HTML is just text in a file. JavaScript doesn't work with raw text files, so the browser needs to convert that HTML text into something JavaScript can mess with. That something is the *Document Object Model,* or the *DOM* for short.

## Getting to know the DOM

When a browser loads an HTML page, it doesn't just display the text. Behind the scenes, it reads every tag, every attribute, and every bit of text content, and builds a structured representation of the entire page in memory. That structured representation is the DOM. It's a live, in-memory model of your page that JavaScript can interact with.

The DOM isn't your HTML file. It's a separate thing that the browser creates *from* your HTML. Once the DOM exists, JavaScript can manipulate it, and when the DOM changes, the browser automatically updates what you see on screen. So, the flow goes like this:

1. The browser reads your HTML file and builds the DOM.
2. The browser renders (that is, displays) the page based on the DOM.
3. JavaScript modifies the DOM.
4. The browser re-renders the page to reflect the changes.

This flow is why JavaScript feels so magical: You change something in the DOM, and the page updates right before the visitor's eyes, no page reload required.

## Viewing the DOM as a tree

The DOM organizes your page as a *tree,* a hierarchy of connected elements where each element can have child elements nested inside it. If you've ever seen a family tree, you already understand the concept: There's a root at the top (yes, it's an upside-down tree; just go with it), and branches spread outward from there.

Here's a simple HTML snippet:

```
<html>
    <head>
        <title>Orbital Donuts</title>
    </head>
    <body>
        <h1>Welcome!</h1>
        <p>Try our <strong>Cosmic Cruller</strong> today.</p>
    </body>
</html>
```

The browser turns this into a tree structure that looks something like Figure 2-1. Every item in this tree is called a *node.* The `<html>` element is *the root node*, and everything else branches off from there. There are two main types of nodes you'll work with:

- **Element nodes:** These correspond to HTML tags (`<h1>`, `<p>`, `<strong>`, and so on). Element nodes can contain other nodes.
- **Text nodes:** These are the text content inside elements (like *Welcome!* or *Cosmic Cruller*). Text nodes don't have children; they're always the endpoints of a branch.

```
html
├── head
│   └── title
│       └── "Orbital Donuts"
└── body
    ├── h1
    │   └── "Welcome!"
    └── p
        ├── "Try our "
        ├── strong
        │   └── "Cosmic Cruller"
        └── " today."
```

**FIGURE 2-1:** The tree structure that the browser creates from the HTML code.

The family-tree metaphor extends further: every node (except the root) has a *parent*, which is the element that contains it. Nodes can also have *children* (the elements nested inside them) and *siblings* (elements at the same level). In the tree in Figure 2-1, `<head>` and `<body>` are siblings, since they're both children of `<html>`. Understanding this parent-child-sibling relationship is important because it's how you navigate the DOM to find the elements you want to work with.

REMEMBER

Nodes higher in the DOM hierarchy (such as parents and the parents of those parents) are known as *ancestors,* while nodes lower in the hierarchy (such as children and the children of those children) are known as *descendants.*

## Introducing the document object

JavaScript accesses the DOM through a special built-in object called `document`. This object is your entry point to the entire page. You've already used it in Chapter 1:

```
document.getElementById('greeting').textContent =
    'Welcome to Orbital Donuts!';
```

The `document` object represents the root of the DOM tree and provides methods for finding, creating, and manipulating elements.

TIP

You can explore the DOM interactively using the browser's developer tools. Open the developer tools (press F12) and click the Elements tab, and you'll see the DOM tree for the current page. You can click elements to expand them, hover your cursor over them to highlight them on the page, and even edit them directly. It's a great way to understand how the DOM maps to what you see on screen.

# Selecting and Manipulating Elements

The first step in any DOM manipulation is finding the element you want to work with. JavaScript gives you several methods for selecting elements, each suited to different situations.

## Selecting a single element by ID

The most straightforward way to find an element is by its `id` attribute. As I mention in Book 3, Chapter 1, an ID must be unique on the page, so this method always returns exactly one element (or `null` if no element has that ID).

Here's an example (`bk04ch02/example01.html`):

HTML:

```
<p id="daily-special">Today's special: Cosmic Cruller</p>
```

JavaScript:

```
const specialElement = document.getElementById('daily-special');
console.log(specialElement.textContent);
```

The `document.getElementById()` method takes a string — the ID you're looking for — and returns the matching element. In this case, it finds the `<p>` element with the `daily-special` ID and stores it in the `specialElement` variable. You can then use that variable to read or change the element. In the example, the code uses the `textContent` property to get the element's text (refer to the "Changing text content" section for more info).

## Selecting with CSS selectors

While `getElementById` works fine for elements with IDs, you'll often need to select elements by class name, tag name, or other criteria. That's where `querySelector` and `querySelectorAll` come in. These methods accept any valid CSS selector (refer to Book 3, Chapter 3).

`querySelector` returns the *first* element that matches your selector:

```
// Select by class
const firstDonut = document.querySelector('.donut-card');

// Select by tag name
const mainHeading = document.querySelector('h1');

// Select by attribute
const emailInput = document.querySelector('input[type="email"]');

// Select a descendant (a <p> inside an element with the class "hero")
const heroText = document.querySelector('.hero p');
```

`querySelectorAll` returns *all* matching elements as a *NodeList* (which is like an array):

```
// Select all elements with the donut-card class
const allDonuts = document.querySelectorAll('.donut-card');

// Select all list items inside the nav
const navItems = document.querySelectorAll('nav li');
```

You can loop through a NodeList just like an array using `forEach` (`bk04ch02/example02.html`):

HTML:

```
<h1>Our Menu</h1>
<ul id="donut-list">
    <li class="donut-item">Galaxy Glazed – $3.49</li>
    <li class="donut-item">Cosmic Cruller – $4.99</li>
    <li class="donut-item">Starlight Sprinkle – $3.49</li>
    <li class="donut-item">Rocket Red Velvet – $3.99</li>
</ul>
```

JavaScript:

```
const donutItems = document.querySelectorAll('.donut-item');
donutItems.forEach(function(item) {
    console.log(item.textContent);
});
```

This script finds every element with the class `donut-item` and logs its text content to the console.

REMEMBER

Use `querySelector` when you want one element and `querySelectorAll` when you want many. Both accept any CSS selector, making them far more flexible than `getElementById`. In practice, `querySelector` and `querySelectorAll` are the methods you'll reach for most often.

## Changing text content

Once you've selected an element, you can change its text using the `textContent` property:

```
const heading = document.querySelector('h1');
heading.textContent = 'Welcome to Orbital Donuts!';
```

The `textContent` property replaces all the text inside the element. If the element has child elements, `textContent` replaces those too. It strips everything down to plain text. Here's an example that shows this replacement in action (`bk04ch02/example03.html`):

HTML:

```
<p id="promo">Get a <em>free donut</em> with your first order!</p>
```

JavaScript:

```
const promo = document.getElementById('promo');

// This replaces everything, including the <em> tag
promo.textContent = 'Free Starlight Sprinkle with every dozen!';
```

After the script runs, the paragraph contains only the plain text "Free Starlight Sprinkle with every dozen!" The `<em>` tag is gone.

## Changing HTML content

If you need to insert HTML (including tags) rather than plain text, use the `innerHTML` property (`bk04ch02/example04.html`):

```
const promo = document.getElementById('promo');
promo.innerHTML = 'Free <em>Starlight Sprinkle</em> with every dozen!';
```

This time, the `<em>` tag is preserved, so "Starlight Sprinkle" appears italic on the page. Use `textContent` when you're inserting plain text and `innerHTML` when you need to include HTML tags.

**WARNING**

Be cautious with `innerHTML` when inserting content that comes from user input (such as form fields). If a user types malicious HTML or JavaScript code in a form field and you insert it into the page with `innerHTML`, that code will be executed. This is called a *cross-site scripting* (XSS) attack and it's a serious security risk. When in doubt, stick with `textContent`, which always treats the content as plain text.

## Changing styles

JavaScript can change an element's CSS styles directly through the `style` property:

```
const heading = document.querySelector('h1');
heading.style.color = 'darkorchid';
heading.style.fontSize = '2.5rem';
heading.style.textAlign = 'center';
```

Note that CSS properties with hyphens (such as `font-size`) become camelCase in JavaScript (`fontSize`). JavaScript doesn't allow hyphens in these property names (in this case, it would interpret `font-size` as "font minus size"!).

Here's a practical example that changes the look of a sold-out donut (`bk04ch02/example05.html`):

HTML:

```
<article id="galaxy-glazed">
    <h4>Galaxy Glazed</h4>
    <img src="/images/galaxy-glazed.webp"
        alt="Classic glazed donut with purple and blue galaxy pattern and edible
                  glitter" height="256"
        width="256">
    <p>Our signature glaze with swirled cosmic colors and edible glitter. A
                  customer favorite since day one!</p>
    <p class="price">$3.49</p>
    <p><button type="button" disabled>Add to Cart</button></p>
    <p id="stock-status">In stock</p>
</article>
```

JavaScript:

```
const soldOut = true;

if (soldOut) {
    const card = document.getElementById('galaxy-glazed');
    card.style.opacity = '0.5';

    const status = document.getElementById('stock-status');
    status.textContent = 'Sold Out';
    status.style.color = 'red';
    status.style.fontWeight = 'bold';
}
```

When `soldOut` is `true`, the script makes the card semitransparent and changes the status text to "Sold Out" in bold red.

## Adding and removing CSS classes

While the `style` property works, it can get unwieldy if you're changing many properties at once. A better approach for bigger style changes is to toggle CSS classes. Every element has a `classList` property that gives you methods for adding, removing, and toggling classes:

- **`classList.add(`*`class1, class2. . .`*`)`**: Adds one or more classes to the element.

- **classList.remove(*class1*, *class2*. . .)**: Removes one or more classes from the element.
- **classList.toggle(*class*)**: Adds the class if it's not there; removes it if it is.
- **classList.contains(*class*)**: Returns `true` if the element has the class; `false` otherwise.

Here's an improved version of the sold-out example using CSS classes instead of inline styles (`bk04ch02/example06.html`):

CSS:

```
.sold-out {
    opacity: 0.5;
}
.status-warning {
    color: red;
    font-weight: bold;
}
```

JavaScript:

```
const soldOut = true;

if (soldOut) {
    const card = document.getElementById('galaxy-glazed');
    card.classList.add('sold-out');

    const status = document.getElementById('stock-status');
    status.textContent = 'Sold Out';
    status.classList.add('status-warning');
}
```

This version keeps the styles in CSS where they belong, and the JavaScript adds the appropriate class names. The result looks the same, but the code is cleaner and easier to maintain.

TIP

For style changes, use `classList` rather than the `style` property. Putting your styles in CSS classes keeps your JavaScript code focused on *behavior* and your CSS focused on *appearance*, which makes both easier to maintain. Save the `style` property for quick, one-off changes or for values that need to be computed dynamically (such as setting a width based on a calculation).

## Working with attributes

HTML elements have attributes (such as `href`, `src`, `alt`, and `disabled`), and JavaScript can read and change them:

- **`getAttribute(`*`attribute`*`)`**: Returns the value of an attribute
- **`setAttribute(`*`attribute, value`*`)`**: Sets an attribute to a new value
- **`removeAttribute(`*`attribute`*`)`**: Removes an attribute entirely
- **`hasAttribute(`*`attribute`*`)`**: Returns `true` if the element has the attribute

Here's an example that changes an image's source and alt text (`bk04ch02/example07.html`):

HTML:

```
<h2>Donut of the Day</h2>
<article id="galaxy-glazed">
    <h4 id="featured-name">Galaxy Glazed</h4>
    <img id="featured-donut"
        src="/images/cosmic-cruller.webp"
        alt="Twisted cruller with purple and blue galaxy glaze and
             edible stars."
        height="256" width="256">
    <p id="featured-description">A twisted masterpiece glazed with our signature
                   galaxy glaze and topped with edible stars.</p>
    <p class="price">$4.99</p>
    <p><button type="button" disabled>Add to Cart</button></p>
</article>
```

JavaScript:

```
const donutImage = document.getElementById('featured-donut');
const donutName = document.getElementById('featured-name');
const donutDescription = document.getElementById('featured-description');

// Change to a different donut
donutImage.setAttribute('src', '/images/nebula-nutella.webp');
donutImage.setAttribute('alt', 'Nebula Nutella');
donutDescription.textContent = "Cake donut filled with creamy Nutella
and topped with crushed hazelnuts.";
```

For common attributes such as `src`, `href`, and `id`, you can also access them directly as properties of the element:

```
// These two lines do the same thing
donutImage.setAttribute('src', '/images/nebula-nutella.webp');
donutImage.src = '/images/nebula-nutella.webp';
```

The direct property approach is shorter and often preferred, but `setAttribute` works with any attribute, including custom `data-` attributes (check out the next section).

## Using data attributes

Sometimes you need to store extra information in an HTML element that isn't a standard attribute. HTML5's *data attributes* are designed for exactly this purpose. Any attribute with a name that starts with `data-` is a custom data attribute (`bk04ch02/example08.html`):

```
<article class="donut-card"
    data-price="3.49"
    data-category="classic"
    data-is-vegan="false">
    <h3>Galaxy Glazed</h3>
</article>
```

In JavaScript, you access data attributes through the `dataset` property. The `data-` prefix is dropped, and hyphenated names become camelCase:

```
const card = document.querySelector('.donut-card');
console.log(card.dataset.price);        // "3.49"
console.log(card.dataset.category);     // "classic"
console.log(card.dataset.isVegan);      // "false"
```

Data attributes are incredibly useful for storing information that your JavaScript needs but that doesn't belong in a standard HTML attribute.

REMEMBER

Data attribute values are always strings. If you store a number such as `data-price="3.49"`, you get back the string `"3.49"`, not the number `3.49`. Use `parseFloat()` or `Number()` to convert the string to a number when you need to do math with it.

## Creating and adding elements

The examples I've presented so far have worked with elements that already exist on the page. But JavaScript can also create brand-new elements and add them to the DOM. Here's the basic procedure:

1. Use `document.createElement()` to create an element.
2. Set the new element's content, attributes, and classes.
3. Use `appendChild()` or `append()` to add the new element to the page.

Let's go through an example that dynamically builds donut cards and adds them to the page. First, here's some HTML (`bk04ch02/example09.html`):

```
<section>
    <h3>Classic Donuts</h3>
    <div class="donut-grid-wrapper">
        <div class="donut-grid">
        </div>
    </div>
</section>
```

The goal is to populate the `donut-grid div` with some donut cards. Here's the data:

```
const donuts = [
    {
        name: "Galaxy Glazed",
        src: "/images/galaxy-glazed.webp",
        description: "Our signature glaze with swirled cosmic colors
                      and edible glitter. A customer favorite since day one!",
        price: 3.49
    },
    {
        name: "Moonlight Maple Bar",
        src: "/images/moonlight-maple-bar.webp",
        description: "Classic maple bar topped with real maple frosting.
                      Simple, delicious, perfect.",
        price: 3.49
    },
    {
        name: "Starlight Sprinkle",
        src: "/images/starlight-sprinkle.webp",
        description: "Vanilla frosted donut covered in star-shaped sprinkles.
```

```
                  Kids love it, adults do too!",
        price: 3.49
    },
    {
        name: "Orbit Original",
        src: "/images/orbit-original.webp",
        description: "Our classic old-fashioned cake donut. No frills, just
                      pure donut perfection.",
        price: 2.99
    }
];
```

Now here's the code that creates and adds each donut card:

```
const grid = document.querySelector(".donut-grid");

donuts.forEach((donut) => {
    const article = document.createElement("article");

    const h4 = document.createElement("h4");
    h4.textContent = donut.name;

    const img = document.createElement("img");
    img.src = donut.src;
    img.alt = donut.name;
    img.height = 256;
    img.width = 256;

    const desc = document.createElement("p");
    desc.textContent = donut.description;

    const price = document.createElement("p");
    price.className = "price";
    price.textContent = `$${donut.price.toFixed(2)}`;

    const btnP = document.createElement("p");
    const btn = document.createElement("button");
    btn.type = "button";
    btn.disabled = true;
    btn.textContent = "Add to Cart";
    btnP.appendChild(btn);

    article.append(h4, img, desc, price, btnP);
    grid.appendChild(article);
});
```

This script creates four donut cards entirely from JavaScript, using data from an array of objects (a pattern you learn about in Chapter 1). Each card gets a heading, an image, a description, a price, and a button, and then gets added to the donut-display container.

### Removing elements

Sometimes you need to take elements off the page. To remove an element, call the remove() method on it:

```
const element = document.querySelector('#old-promo');
element.remove();
```

That's it! The element is gone from the DOM (and from the page).

## Event-Handling Fundamentals

In Book 4, Chapter 1 and up to this point here in Chapter 2, all the DOM manipulation code runs as soon as the page loads. That's often what you want, but one of JavaScript's most useful superpowers is responding to what the user does. When a visitor clicks a button, types in a search box, hovers the cursor over a menu item, or submits a form, the browser fires an *event*. JavaScript can listen for these events and run code in response. This process is called *event handling*, and it's the foundation of every interactive web feature.

### Understanding events

An event is the browser's way of letting you know that something just happened. Every user action generates events: clicking fires a click event, typing fires input and keydown events, moving the pointer fires pointermove events, and so on. Even the initial page load fires an event (called DOMContentLoaded).

Your job as a JavaScript developer is to write code that responds to a particular event when it happens on a particular element. That code is called an *event listener* or *event handler*.

### Adding event listeners

The modern way to respond to events is with the addEventListener method. Here's the pattern:

» *element*.addEventListener(*event*, *callback*);

» *element*: The web page element to be monitored for the event

» *event*: A string specifying the name of the event you want the browser to listen for (such as `click` or `keydown`)

» *callback*: The function that JavaScript executes when the event occurs

Here's a simple example that responds to a button click (`bk04ch02/example10.html`):

HTML:

```
<article>
    <h4>Galaxy Glazed</h4>
    <img src="/images/galaxy-glazed.webp"
        alt="Galaxy glazed"
        height="256" width="256">
    <p>
        Our signature glaze with swirled cosmic colors and edible glitter.
        A customer favorite since day one!
    </p>
    <p class="price">$3.49</p>
    <p><button id="order-button" type="button">Add to Cart</button></p>
    <p id="order-message"></p>
</article>
```

JavaScript:

```
const button = document.getElementById('order-button');
const message = document.getElementById('order-message');

button.addEventListener('click', function () {
    message.textContent = 'Donut added to cart. Thanks!';
    message.style.color = 'green';
    button.blur();
});
```

When the user clicks the button, the function runs, updating the order message's text and color. Note, too, the addition of `button.blur()`, which removes the focus from the button.

## Common event types

There are dozens of event types, but here are the ones you'll use most often:

- **click**: The user clicks an element. This event is by far the most common one you'll handle.
- **input**: The user types into or otherwise changes the value of a form field (such as an `<input>` or `<textarea>` element). This event fires on every keystroke.
- **change**: The user changes the value of a form field and then moves away from it (for text fields) or selects a new option (for `<select>` and checkbox elements).
- **submit**: The user submits a form (by clicking a submit button or pressing Enter in a form field).
- **pointerover**: The user moves the pointer over an element. (The corresponding `pointerout` event fires when the pointer leaves.)
- **keydown**: The user presses a key on the keyboard. (The corresponding `keyup` event fires when the key is released.)
- **DOMContentLoaded**: The HTML document has been loaded and parsed.

Here's an example that uses the `input` event to create an interactive search feature based on whatever the user types (`bk04ch02/example11.html`):

HTML:

```
<section>
    <h3>Search</h3>
    <input type="search" id="search-box" placeholder="Search
            donuts...">
    <div class="donut-grid-wrapper">
        <div class="donut-grid">
        </div>
    </div>
</section>
```

JavaScript:

```
const grid = document.querySelector(".donut-grid");

function createCard(donut) {
    const article = document.createElement("article");
```

```
    const h4 = document.createElement("h4");
    h4.textContent = donut.name;

    const img = document.createElement("img");
    img.src = donut.src;
    img.alt = donut.name;
    img.height = 256;
    img.width = 256;

    const desc = document.createElement("p");
    desc.textContent = donut.description;

    const price = document.createElement("p");
    price.className = "price";
    price.textContent = `$${donut.price.toFixed(2)}`;

    const btnP = document.createElement("p");
    const btn = document.createElement("button");
    btn.type = "button";
    btn.disabled = true;
    btn.textContent = "Add to Cart";
    btnP.appendChild(btn);

    article.append(h4, img, desc, price, btnP);
    return article;
}

function renderDonuts(list) {
    grid.innerHTML = "";
    list.forEach((donut) => grid.appendChild(createCard(donut)));
}

renderDonuts(donuts);

const searchBox = document.getElementById("search-box");

searchBox.addEventListener("input", function () {
    const query = searchBox.value.toLowerCase();
    const matches = donuts.filter((donut) =>
        donut.name.toLowerCase().includes(query) ||
        donut.description.toLowerCase().includes(query)
    );
    renderDonuts(matches);
});
```

As the user types, the `input` event listener looks for matching text in the `donuts` array (not shown, but similar to the `donuts` array in the "Creating and adding elements" section). For the matching donuts, the code calls the `renderDonuts()` function to display the matches to the user.

The `input` event fires on every keystroke, so the search results are always in sync with the text field. This kind of responsive interactivity makes a website feel polished and professional.

## The event object

When an event occurs, the browser automatically creates an *event object* that contains information about what happened. You can access this object by adding a parameter to your event handler function:

```
button.addEventListener('click', function(event) {
    console.log(event.type);    // "click"
    console.log(event.target);  // the element that was clicked
});
```

Here the event object is given the name `event`, but it's often abbreviated to just `e`. The event object contains different properties depending on the event type, but here are some of the most useful ones:

- **`event.target`:** The element that triggered the event. This property is hugely useful, especially when multiple elements share the same event handler.
- **`event.type`:** The type of event (for example, `"click"` or `"input"`).
- **`event.preventDefault()`:** A method that stops the browser's default behavior for this event. For example, calling `event.preventDefault()` in a form's `submit` event prevents the form from submitting. (Why? Usually because you want to process the form data in some way and then submit the form via code. Check out the example that follows.)
- **`event.key`:** For keyboard events, the key that was pressed (for example, `"Enter"`, `"a"`, or `"ArrowDown"`).

Here's a practical example that prevents a form from submitting and handles it with JavaScript instead (`bk04ch02/example12.html`):

HTML:

```
<form id="subscribe-form">
    <label for="email">Email address:</label>
    <input type="email" id="email" required>
```

```
    <button type="submit">Subscribe</button>
</form>
<p id="form-message"></p>
```

JavaScript:

```
const form = document.getElementById('subscribe-form');
const formMessage = document.getElementById('form-message');

form.addEventListener('submit', function (event) {
    event.preventDefault();

    const email = document.getElementById('email').value;
    formMessage.textContent =
        `Thanks for subscribing, ${email}!`;
    formMessage.style.color = 'green';
    form.reset();
    document.querySelector('button').blur();
});
```

Without `event.preventDefault()`, the browser would submit the form and navigate to a new page (or reload the current one). By preventing that default behavior, JavaScript handles the submission entirely on the client side.

IN THIS CHAPTER

» Validating forms

» Building a hamburger menu

» Creating modal dialog windows

# Chapter 3
# Practical JavaScript Solutions

*All great programmers learn the same way. They poke the box. They code something and see what the computer does. They change it and see what the computer does. They repeat the process again and again until they figure out how the box works.*

—SETH GODIN

In this chapter, you build three of the most common interactive patterns on the web: forms that validate as visitors type; a navigation menu that opens and closes gracefully on mobile devices; and modal popup windows that overlay the page. By the end, the Orbital Donuts site will feel like a polished, professional web experience, the kind that makes visitors feel comfortable and confident, not vaguely suspicious.

Every example in this chapter uses nothing but the plain-vanilla JavaScript you already know. No frameworks, no libraries, no magic; just clever event handling, smart DOM manipulation, and a healthy respect for the real human beings who'll use the pages you build.

# Validating Forms Like the Pros

Forms are the most important interactive element on most websites. They're how visitors contact you, place orders, sign up for your newsletter, request a catering quote, whatever. When a form works beautifully, visitors barely notice it. When a form fails — mysterious error messages after a full-page reload, no indication of which specific field has a problem, fields that forget everything you typed — visitors notice it immediately. And then they leave.

As I explain in Book 3, Chapter 2, HTML provides built-in form validation through attributes such as `required`, `minlength`, and `type="email"`. That's a genuinely useful start. But HTML validation fires only when the visitor clicks the Submit button, and the default browser error messages are famously unattractive and inconsistent from one browser to another. JavaScript lets you do something far better: validate as the visitor types, in real time, with friendly and attractive custom messages that appear right next to the field that needs attention.

## Understanding how real-time validation works

The secret to real-time validation is the `input` event (refer to Book 4, Chapter 2). Every time a user types a character, pastes text, or otherwise changes a form field, the browser fires an `input` event on that element. By listening for that event, your JavaScript can check the field's current value and update the page to reflect whether it's valid.

This type-check-update sequence creates a feedback loop that feels natural and helpful. Instead of filling out an entire form, clicking Submit, navigating back after the page reloads, and then hunting for which field has the problem, visitors know about issues the instant they make them. That's the difference between a maddening form and a satisfying one.

The second key ingredient is the `validity` object. Every input element in a form has a built-in `validity` property that tells you what's wrong with the current value. The `validity.valid` property is `true` if the value passes all the element's validation rules — including `required`, `type`, `min`, `max`, and `minlength` — and `false` if any rule is violated. Using this property means you can check whether a value is valid without having to write your own format-detection logic from scratch.

## Validating a single field

Before wiring up a full multi-field form, let's look at how validation works for a single field. The HTML structure for a validated field follows a consistent pattern: the input itself paired with a sibling `<span>` element that will hold the error message. Here's the structure for the email field on the Orbital Donuts contact page (`bk04ch03/example01.html`):

```
<label for="email">Your Email:
    <span class="field-error" id="email-error"></span>
</label>
<input type="email" id="email" name="email" required>
```

The `<span>` starts empty and hidden. A small bit of CSS handles the hiding and the error styling:

```
.field-error {
    display: none;
    color: hsl(0 79% 50%);
    font-size: 0.875rem;
    margin-top: 0.25rem;
}
```

Now for the JavaScript. Two helper functions handle showing and clearing the error message, and an event listener on the email field calls them based on the current value:

```
function showError(span, message) {
    span.textContent = message;
    span.style.display = 'inline-block';
}

function clearError(span) {
    span.textContent = '';
    span.style.display = 'none';
}

const emailField = document.querySelector('#email');
const emailError = document.querySelector('#email-error');

emailField.addEventListener('input', function() {
    const value = emailField.value.trim();

    if (value === '') {
        showError(emailError, "Please enter your email address.");
    } else if (!emailField.validity.valid) {
        showError(emailError, `That doesn't look like a valid email
```

```
            address.`);
    } else {
        clearError(emailError);
    }
});
```

When the visitor types in the email field, the input event fires and the handler runs. It trims any whitespace, and then checks whether the value is empty, fails the browser's email-format check, or is valid. The error span is updated accordingly. The moment the visitor types a properly formatted address, the error message disappears.

TIP

The trim() method strips spaces from the beginning and end of a string. Always call it before validating text input because a field containing nothing but spaces looks non-empty to JavaScript but is definitely not a valid name or email address.

## Building a full contact form validator

Now let's scale up to a complete form. Rather than writing a separate event listener for each field, you can store each field's configuration in an object and loop through them all with a single forEach call. This approach makes the code easy to extend: to add a fifth field, you add one entry to the configuration object and nothing else changes.

Assuming each contact form field (except the Phone field) has a span element to hold the field's error message, here's the complete multi-field validator for the Orbital Donuts contact form (bk04ch03/example02.html):

```
const formFields = {
    name: {
        selector: '#name',
        errorSelector: '#name-error',
        validate(val) {
            if (val === '') return 'Please enter your name.';
            if (val.length < 2) return 'Name must be at least 2 characters.';
            return '';
        }
    },
    email: {
        selector: '#email',
        errorSelector: '#email-error',
        validate(val, el) {
            if (val === '') return 'Please enter your email.';
            if (!el.validity.valid) return `That doesn't look like a
   valid email.`;
```

```
            return '';
        }
    },
    subject: {
        selector: '#subject',
        errorSelector: '#subject-error',
        validate(val) {
            if (val === '') return 'Please enter a subject.';
            return '';
        }
    },
    message: {
        selector: '#message',
        errorSelector: '#message-error',
        validate(val) {
            if (val === '') return 'Please enter your message.';
            return '';
        }
    }
};

Object.values(formFields).forEach(function (field) {
    const el = document.querySelector(field.selector);
    const errorEl = document.querySelector(field.errorSelector);

    el.addEventListener('input', function () {
        const msg = field.validate(el.value.trim(), el);
        if (msg) {
            showError(errorEl, msg);
        } else {
            clearError(errorEl);
        }
    });
});
```

The script declares a `formFields` configuration object with an entry for each required field (name, email, subject, and message), where each entry holds the field's CSS selector, its paired error `span` selector, and a `validate` function that returns an error string if the value is invalid or an empty string if it's fine. Finally, the script iterates over those field configs (using `Object.values(formFields)`, which returns an array of the fields), queries the DOM for each `input` and error `span`, and attaches an `input` event listener that runs the field's validation function on the current trimmed value and calls either `showError()` or `clearError()` (defined in the preceding section) depending on the result.

## Blocking submission when fields are invalid

Real-time feedback while typing is great, but you also need to stop the form from submitting while fields are still invalid. This matters because a visitor might click Submit without ever touching a required field, in which case no `input` events have fired and no error messages are visible yet. Listening for the form's `submit` event lets you run all the validators at once and block submission if anything fails (`bk04ch03/example03.html`):

```
document.querySelector('#contact-form').addEventListener(
    'submit', function (event) {
        let hasErrors = false;

        Object.values(formFields).forEach(function (field) {
            const el = document.querySelector(field.selector);
            const errorEl = document.querySelector(field.errorSelector);
            const msg = field.validate(el.value.trim(), el);

            if (msg) {
                showError(errorEl, msg);
                hasErrors = true;
            }
        });

        if (hasErrors) {
            event.preventDefault();
        }
    }
);
```

When `event.preventDefault()` is called inside a `submit` handler, the browser cancels the normal form-submission behavior: no page navigation, no data sent. Only when all four validators return an empty string does the form submit normally.

WARNING

JavaScript form validation runs on the visitor's device. A technically savvy person can bypass it. Never rely on client-side validation alone to protect your server from bad or malicious data. You must also implement server-side validation. Think of JavaScript validation as a courtesy to the user, not a security boundary.

## Disabling and enabling the submit button

A final form enhancement worth knowing is dynamically disabling the submit button until all required fields are valid. When the page first loads, the button is disabled. As the visitor fills in the fields correctly, one by one, the button stays disabled until every validator passes — at which point the button becomes active and clickable. This gives visitors an at-a-glance signal about the form's overall readiness.

Here's how to wire up a function that checks all the fields and updates the button's disabled state (bk04ch03/example04.html):

```
const submitButton =
    document.querySelector('#contact-form button[type="submit"]');

function updateSubmitButton() {
    const allValid = Object.values(formFields).every(function (field) {
        const el = document.querySelector(field.selector);
        const msg = field.validate(el.value.trim(), el);
        return msg === '';
    });
    submitButton.disabled = !allValid;
}

// Set the initial state when the page loads
updateSubmitButton();

// Update the state after every keystroke
Object.values(formFields).forEach(function (field) {
    const el = document.querySelector(field.selector);
    el.addEventListener('input', updateSubmitButton);
});
```

The `every()` array method returns `true` only if the callback returns `true` for every element in the array. In this example, you want all the fields to be valid. If any single validator returns a non-empty string, `every()` short-circuits and returns `false`, keeping the button disabled.



# Building a Mobile Hamburger Menu

The Orbital Donuts website navigation links — Home, Menu, Location, Catering, and About — work perfectly on a desktop-sized screen, but they barely fit on most phone-width screens. If you wanted to add a sixth navigation item, those six links on a mobile device would turn into a cramped, unusable row that either wraps awkwardly across multiple lines or overflows off the edge of the screen. Neither is a good look for a business that wants to make a sale.

The standard solution is the *hamburger menu*: a button marked with three horizontal lines (≡) that, when tapped, drops down a panel of navigation links. Tap it again and the panel closes. And because it's a vertical panel, not a horizontal line, you can add as many links as make sense (and won't overwhelm your users).

The hamburger menu is one of the most universal conventions in mobile web design, so users know what those three lines mean. As the next few sections show, building one from scratch with JavaScript is less complicated than you might think.

## How the toggle pattern works

The hamburger menu technique is built on one core idea: a CSS class that toggles the navigation panel between its hidden and visible states. Here's the mental model in three steps:

- **Default state (small screens):** The `nav` panel is hidden. The toggle button is visible.
- **Open state:** The visitor clicks the button. JavaScript adds an `is-open` class to the `nav` element. A CSS rule matches that class and makes the `nav` visible.
- **Closed state:** A second click removes the `is-open` class. CSS hides the `nav` again.

All the visual work — showing, hiding, any animation you want to add — is handled by CSS. JavaScript's only job is to add and remove that one class. This is the *separation of concerns* principle at work: CSS handles appearance and JavaScript handles behavior. Keeping these responsibilities separate makes both your stylesheets and your scripts easier to read, test, and modify without accidentally breaking the other.

## Setting up the HTML

Here's the header HTML for the Orbital Donuts site, updated to include a hamburger button (`bk04ch03/example05.html`). The button sits between the logo and the nav element:

```
<header>
    <a href="index.html" class="logo">
        <img src="/images/orbital-donuts-logo.webp"
             alt="Orbital Donuts logo" height="35" width="103">
    </a>
    <button class="nav-toggle" id="nav-toggle"
```

```
        aria-expanded="false"
        aria-controls="main-nav"
        aria-label="Open navigation menu">
      <span></span>
      <span></span>
      <span></span>
    </button>
    <nav id="main-nav">
      <ul>
        <li><a href="index.html">Home</a></li>
        <li><a href="menu.html">Menu</a></li>
        <li><a href="location.html">Location</a></li>
        <li><a href="catering.html">Catering</a></li>
        <li><a href="about.html">About</a></li>
      </ul>
    </nav>
</header>
```

The three empty `<span>` elements inside the button become the three horizontal bars of the hamburger icon, styled with CSS. The ARIA attributes on the button are doing important accessibility work: `aria-controls="main-nav"` identifies which element the button controls; `aria-expanded="false"` tells a screen reader that the panel is currently collapsed; and `aria-label` provides a spoken description for visitors who can't see the icon. Together, they turn a generic button into a properly announced, semantically meaningful control.

## Writing the CSS

The CSS does two things: it styles the hamburger icon, and it handles showing and hiding the nav panel. Orbital Donuts uses a mobile-first design, so the `nav` displays as a hamburger menu by default. Everything related to desktop behavior lives inside a media query so it applies only on wide screens, where the hamburger menu is hidden and the `nav` links are displayed in a line across the screen (`bk04ch03/css/styles.css`):

```
/* Navigation - hamburger menu on mobile */
.nav-toggle span {
    display: block;
    width: 24px;
    height: 2px;
    background-color: hsl(225 63% 10%);
    margin: 3px 0;
}

.nav-toggle {
    display: flex;
```

Practical JavaScript Solutions

```
    flex-direction: column;
    justify-content: center;
    background: none;
    border: none;
    box-shadow: none;
    cursor: pointer;
    padding: 0.5rem;
}

header nav {
    display: none;
    width: 100%;
    background-color: hsl(0 0% 100%);
    border-top: 1px solid hsl(220 14% 91%);
}

/* Revealed when JavaScript adds is-open */
header nav.is-open {
    display: block;
}

header nav ul {
    list-style: none;
    padding: 0;
    margin: 0;
}

header nav a {
    display: block;
    padding: 0.75rem 1.25rem;
    color: hsl(225 63% 10%);
    text-decoration: none;
    border-bottom: 1px solid hsl(220 14% 91%);
}

header nav a:hover {
    background-color: hsl(216 43% 97%);
}
```

The critical rule is `header nav.is-open`. That compound selector matches the `nav` only when it's a descendant of the `header` element and has the class `is-open`. On narrow screens the `nav` is hidden by default; the moment JavaScript adds `is-open`, the rule fires and reveals it. Remove the class and the `nav` hides again. The JavaScript never needs to know anything about `display` values because that's entirely the job of CSS.

## Writing the JavaScript

The JavaScript is refreshingly brief. Most of the work is done by `classList.toggle()`, which adds a class if it's absent or removes it if it's present, which is exactly the behavior a toggle button needs (`bk04ch03/example05.html`):

```
const navToggle = document.querySelector('#nav-toggle');
const mainNav   = document.querySelector('header nav');

navToggle.addEventListener('click', function() {
    const isOpen = mainNav.classList.contains('is-open');

    mainNav.classList.toggle('is-open');

    navToggle.setAttribute('aria-expanded', String(!isOpen));
    navToggle.setAttribute('aria-label',
        isOpen ? 'Open navigation menu' : 'Close navigation menu'
    );
});
```

Before toggling, the code checks the current state by calling `classList.contains('is-open')`. The result, stored in `isOpen`, is then used to keep the two ARIA attributes in sync. `aria-expanded` is updated to match the new state, and `aria-label` switches between "Open navigation menu" and "Close navigation menu" so a screen reader always announces the correct action.

## Closing the menu on link click and outside click

Two finishing touches make the hamburger menu feel properly polished. First, when a visitor taps a navigation link on a mobile device, the menu should close automatically — it looks odd if it stays open while the new page loads. Second, clicking anywhere outside the open menu should close it, which is the standard convention for any dropdown or overlay on the web (`bk04ch03/example05.html`):

```
// Close menu when a nav link is tapped
mainNav.querySelectorAll('a').forEach(function(link) {
    link.addEventListener('click', function() {
        mainNav.classList.remove('is-open');
        navToggle.setAttribute('aria-expanded', 'false');
        navToggle.setAttribute('aria-label', 'Open navigation menu');
    });
});
```

```
// Close menu when clicking anywhere outside it
document.addEventListener('click', function(event) {
    const clickedOutside =
        !mainNav.contains(event.target) &amp;&amp;
        !navToggle.contains(event.target);

    if (clickedOutside &amp;&amp; mainNav.classList.contains('is-open')) {
        mainNav.classList.remove('is-open');
        navToggle.setAttribute('aria-expanded', 'false');
        navToggle.setAttribute('aria-label', 'Open navigation menu');
    }
});
```

The outside-click detection works by asking two questions: Was the click inside the nav panel? Was it inside the toggle button? If both answers are no, the click happened somewhere else on the page, and the menu should close. The `contains()` method returns `true` if an element is the same as or a descendant of another, so `mainNav.contains(event.target)` catches clicks on the nav itself, its links, and everything nested inside it.

TIP

You can also close the menu when the visitor presses the Escape key. Add a `keydown` event listener to `document`, check whether `event.key === 'Escape'`, and call the same close logic if so. Keyboard-navigation users will thank you.

# Creating Modal Windows

A *modal* is a dialog window that opens on top of the current page, requiring the visitor to interact with it before they can continue. Modals are used to display extra info, so you encounter them constantly on the web: enlarged photos, terms-and-conditions boxes, login forms, confirmation dialogs, and quick-view panels that let you examine a product without leaving the current page.

The key word there is *extra.* A modal earns its place when it reveals something that isn't already visible on the page. For the Orbital Donuts menu, a perfect use case is allergen information. Each menu card shows the donut's name, description, and price, but there's no room on the card to list every ingredient and allergen. A visitor with a nut allergy or one ordering for guests with dietary restrictions needs that information. A modal lets them tap a button and get the full allergen details right there, without navigating away from the menu.

## The anatomy of a modal

Every modal on the web shares the same basic three-part structure:

- **The overlay:** A semitransparent layer covering the entire page behind the modal panel. It dims the background to signal that the modal demands attention, and it provides the surface that, when clicked, closes the modal (a common pattern that many visitors will expect).
- **The panel:** The visible content box that sits centered on the overlay. It holds whatever the modal is displaying, such as the allergen details for a specific donut.
- **A close button:** An explicit dismiss control, typically an X in the top corner of the panel, for visitors who don't instinctively think to click the overlay.

Like the hamburger menu I discuss in the previous section, the modal uses a CSS class to control visibility. The overlay and panel are always present in the HTML, hidden with `display: none` until JavaScript adds an `is-visible` class.

## Setting up the HTML

Here's the HTML for the allergen information modal (`bk04ch03/example06.html`). Place this markup just before the closing `</body>` tag (or just above the `<script>` tag, if you have one at the bottom of the page code) so it doesn't disrupt the normal page flow:

```
<div class="modal-overlay" id="modal-overlay"></div>

<div class="modal" id="allergen-modal"
     role="dialog"
     aria-modal="true"
     aria-labelledby="allergen-modal-title"
     tabindex="-1">
    <button class="modal-close" id="modal-close"
            aria-label="Close allergen information">&amp;#215;</button>
    <div class="modal-body">
        <h3 id="allergen-modal-title"></h3>
        <p class="modal-subtitle">Allergen Information</p>
        <ul id="allergen-list"></ul>
        <p id="allergen-note"></p>
    </div>
</div>
```

The modal's content elements start empty. JavaScript will populate them when a visitor clicks an allergen button.

The accessibility attributes each do real work. `role="dialog"` identifies this as a dialog to assistive technologies and triggers special screen-reader handling. `aria-modal="true"` signals that when the dialog is open, the rest of the page is inactive. `aria-labelledby="allergen-modal-title"` points to the heading inside the modal so a screen reader announces the dialog's name — the donut's name — when it opens. And `tabindex="-1"` makes the div programmatically focusable so you can call `focus()` on it when the modal opens, moving keyboard focus into the dialog.

## Styling the modal

The CSS uses `position: fixed` to anchor both the overlay and the panel to the viewport, so they stay centered and fully visible even when the visitor has scrolled down the page (`bk04ch03/css/styles.css`):

```
.modal-overlay {
    display: none;
    position: fixed;
    inset: 0;
    background-color: hsl(225 63% 10% / 0.65);
    z-index: 100;
}

.modal {
    display: none;
    position: fixed;
    top: 50%;
    left: 50%;
    transform: translate(-50%, -50%);
    background-color: hsl(0 0% 100%);
    border-radius: 0.5rem;
    padding: 2rem;
    width: min(90vw, 480px);
    z-index: 101;
}

.modal-overlay.is-visible,
.modal.is-visible {
    display: block;
}

.modal-close {
    position: absolute;
    top: 0.75rem;
    right: 0.75rem;
```

```
    background: none;
    border: none;
    font-size: 1.5rem;
    cursor: pointer;
    color: hsl(220 9% 46%);
    line-height: 1;
}

.modal-subtitle {
    font-size: 0.85rem;
    text-transform: uppercase;
    letter-spacing: 0.05em;
    color: hsl(220 9% 46%);
    margin-top: -0.5rem;
}
```

A few CSS details worth noting. `inset: 0` is shorthand for `top: 0; right: 0; bottom: 0; left: 0`, neatly stretching the overlay to fill the entire viewport. `width: min(90vw, 480px)` means the panel is at most 480 pixels wide on a large screen but automatically shrinks to 90% of the viewport width on smaller devices, so it never overflows on a phone. The `transform: translate(-50%, -50%)` centers the panel: `top: 50%; left: 50%` places its top-left corner at the middle of the screen, and the negative `translate` shifts it back by half its own width and height, landing it perfectly in the center.

# Triggering the modal with data attributes

Each menu card needs an Allergen Info button. The button carries all the allergen data for that donut directly in its data attributes (refer to Book 4, Chapter 2).

Here are allergen buttons for two of the Orbital Donuts menu items (`bk04ch03/example06.html`):

```
<button class="allergen-btn"
        data-name="Nebula Nutella"
        data-allergens="Wheat, Eggs, Milk, Hazelnuts, Soy"
        data-note="Made in a facility that also processes peanuts.">
    Allergen Info</button>
```

```
<button class="allergen-btn"
        data-name="Vegan Vanilla Orbit"
        data-allergens="Wheat, Soy"
        data-note="Vegan and dairy-free. No nut ingredients.">
    Allergen Info</button>
```

Storing the allergen data directly on the button like this means you don't need a separate JavaScript data structure or an extra network request. When the visitor clicks, everything the modal needs is already sitting right there on the element that was clicked.

## Opening and closing the modal

The JavaScript reads the button's data, builds a list of allergen items, populates the modal, and opens it (`bk04ch03/example06.html`):

```
const overlay      = document.querySelector('#modal-overlay');
const modal        = document.querySelector('#allergen-modal');
const closeBtn     = document.querySelector('#modal-close');
const modalTitle   = document.querySelector('#allergen-modal-title');
const allergenList = document.querySelector('#allergen-list');
const allergenNote = document.querySelector('#allergen-note');

function openModal(name, allergens, note) {
    modalTitle.textContent = name;

    // Build the allergen list from the comma-separated string
    allergenList.innerHTML = '';
    allergens.split(', ').forEach(function(item) {
        const li = document.createElement('li');
        li.textContent = item;
        allergenList.appendChild(li);
    });

    allergenNote.textContent = note;
    modal.classList.add('is-visible');
    overlay.classList.add('is-visible');
    document.body.style.overflow = 'hidden';
    modal.focus();
}

function closeModal() {
    modal.classList.remove('is-visible');
    overlay.classList.remove('is-visible');
    document.body.style.overflow = '';
}

document.querySelectorAll('.allergen-btn').forEach(function(btn) {
    btn.addEventListener('click', function() {
        openModal(
            btn.dataset.name,
```

```
            btn.dataset.allergens,
            btn.dataset.note
        );
    });
});

// Three ways to close the modal
closeBtn.addEventListener('click', closeModal);
overlay.addEventListener('click', closeModal);
document.addEventListener('keydown', function(event) {
    if (event.key === 'Escape') { closeModal(); }
});
```

Inside `openModal`, the line `allergenList.innerHTML = ''` clears the list before repopulating it, which is important because the same modal is reused for every donut. Without that reset, clicking a second button would append its allergens to the previous donut's list rather than replacing them.

Note that the modal can be closed in three different ways: clicking the X button, clicking the overlay, and pressing the Escape key. Providing all three is a small investment that makes a difference to different types of visitors. Mouse users click the button or the overlay. Keyboard users press Escape. Touch users tap the overlay. All three are covered.

REMEMBER

Always provide a keyboard way to close a modal. Many visitors — including those who use a keyboard due to a motor disability — expect the Escape key to dismiss any dialog. The feature requires only two lines of code and makes a genuine difference.

TIP

Setting `document.body.style.overflow = 'hidden'` in `openModal` prevents the page from scrolling while the modal is open; it looks jarring if the background content shifts behind the panel. Resetting it to an empty string in `closeModal` restores normal scrolling when the modal closes.

IN THIS CHAPTER

» Handling promises

» Fetching and displaying JSON data

» Working with external APIs

» Submitting form data

Chapter 4

# Asynchronous JavaScript and APIs

*The Fetch API is a game-changer for developers, giving them unparalleled flexibility . . . to easily and quickly make URL requests from your browser.*

—DANIELLE ELLIS

JavaScript does a lot of things almost instantly: updating text on the page, responding to a button click, sorting a list of items. But some tasks take longer: fetching a data file from the server, calling an API out on the internet, waiting for a form submission to go through. If JavaScript just stopped and waited for those slower jobs, the whole page would freeze solid. Visitors would stare at a motionless browser wondering if something had gone horribly wrong. Not ideal.

That problem has a name: *blocking.* And its solution, *asynchronous programming,* is what this chapter is all about. Rather than holding the page hostage while it waits, JavaScript says "go do that thing, and when it's done, run this code." The page stays alive and responsive the entire time.

In this chapter, you learn how asynchronous JavaScript works, master the `async/await` syntax that makes it approachable, and put it all to practical use.

# Understanding Asynchronous Operations

Imagine you are at a restaurant and order a bowl of soup. Blocking JavaScript code is like a waiter who stands at the kitchen door staring at the stove, doing absolutely nothing else until your soup is ready. Properly asynchronous JavaScript code is like a waiter who puts in your order and then keeps serving other tables while the kitchen staff works. When your soup is ready, the kitchen staff calls out and the waiter brings it over. Everyone gets better service.

## How JavaScript handles the wait

JavaScript solves the blocking problem through an event loop. When your code starts a slow operation, such as fetching a file, JavaScript launches that operation and then moves on to other work. The operation runs in the background. When it finishes, it places a notification in a queue. Whenever JavaScript isn't busy with anything else, the *event loop* checks that queue and, when it finds a notification, it runs the code you set aside to handle the result.

The practical upshot: your code doesn't have to stop and wait. It just needs to say, "Yo, when this finishes, do that." Figuring out the right way to express that idea is what you discover next.

## From callbacks to promises

The original way to say "do this when that finishes" is the *callback*, a function you pass into another function, to be called when the work is done. I show some callback examples earlier in this book, such as in Book 4, Chapter 2. There, the function you pass to `addEventListener` is a callback.

Callbacks work, but they can get messy fast. When one async operation depends on another, which depends on another, you end up with callbacks nested inside callbacks nested inside callbacks. The code becomes difficult to read, error handling is awkward, and debugging turns into a treasure hunt. Modern JavaScript provides a much cleaner approach: promises and `async/await`.

You don't need to master the old callback-based approach. I mention it only so you recognize it if you encounter it in older code or tutorials. From here on, `async/await` is the way to go.

# Promises and Async/Await

A *promise* is exactly what it sounds like: a commitment that a value will be available in the future. When you start an async operation, it returns a promise right away. That promise will eventually be either *fulfilled* (the operation succeeded and has a result) or *rejected* (something went wrong). While you wait, the promise is *pending*. Your code keeps running, and when the answer arrives, the promise delivers it.

You don't need to create promises yourself very often. The browser's built-in `fetch()` function returns one automatically, as do many other modern browser APIs. What you do need to know is how to work with a promise once you have one, and that's where `async/await` comes in.

## Introducing async and await

The `async` and `await` keywords arrived in JavaScript in 2017 and immediately became the preferred way to work with promises. They let you write asynchronous code that looks almost exactly like regular synchronous code, which makes it much easier to read and reason about.

The basic idea is this:

- Mark a function with the `async` keyword to signal that it contains asynchronous operations.
- Inside that function, put `await` in front of any operation that returns a promise. JavaScript pauses the function at that point until the promise resolves and then continues, while the rest of the page runs normally.

Here's a simple example that fetches a text file and logs its contents (`bk04ch04/example01.html`):

```
async function loadTextFile() {
    const response = await fetch("asynchronous-js-history.txt");
    const text = await response.text();
    console.log(text);
}
```

The function is marked `async`. The first `await` pauses until the network request completes and returns a `Response` object (refer to "The fetch() function," later in this chapter). The second `await` reads the response body as plain text. After both, the message is logged. Simple, readable, and nothing like the callback tangles of old.

## Calling an async function

An `async` function is called just like any other function. The key difference is that it returns a promise, not a plain value. In most cases — especially when calling an async function to set something up when the page loads — you can call it without worrying about the return value:

```
loadTextFile();
```

One important rule: you can use `await` only inside a function marked with `async`. The examples throughout the rest of this chapter all follow this pattern, so it will quickly become second nature.

# What Are APIs and JSON?

An API (refer to Book 1, Chapter 4 for some background) is a way for two pieces of software to communicate. For example, a weather service might say: "Send me a latitude and longitude, and I'll send you back the current temperature and conditions." You send a request; you get a response. What happens in between is their problem, not yours.

The type of API you work with in this chapter is called a REST API (again, check out Book 1, Chapter 4). REST APIs communicate over the web using the same request-and-response system your browser uses to load pages. You send an HTTP request to a specific URL, and the server responds with data, which is almost always formatted as JSON (which I describe in the next section).

You've already been using a browser API throughout this book: the DOM API. Examples such as the `document.querySelector()` method, the `addEventListener()` method, and `createElement()` are part of the browser's built-in API that lets JavaScript talk to the page. REST APIs work the same way conceptually, just across the network instead of inside the browser.

## JSON: Data in plain text

*JSON*, or JavaScript Object Notation, is a text format for representing structured data that looks almost identical to the JavaScript objects and arrays you learned about in Book 4, Chapter 1. Here's a small example:

```
{
    "name": "Cosmic Cruller",
    "price": 4.99,
```

```
    "category": "specialty",
    "available": true
}
```

JSON has a few rules that differ from regular JavaScript object syntax. Property names must be in double quotes, not single quotes, nor unquoted. String values also use double quotes. Numbers, Booleans (`true`/`false`), and `null` are written without quotes. Arrays and nested objects work as you'd expect.

When a REST API sends you data, it arrives as a JSON string, so it's just text. The browser's `fetch()` function includes a built-in `.json()` method that parses that string and turns it into a real JavaScript object you can work with in your code. And going the other direction, when you want to send data *to* an API, `JSON.stringify()` converts your JavaScript object into a JSON string for the journey.

Two more things worth noting: JSON files use the `.json` file extension, and their MIME type is `application/json`. These details matter because some servers need to know what type of content they're serving, and some APIs need to know what type of content you're sending them. You'll see JSON in action when you look at the POST example later in this chapter.

# The fetch() function

The `fetch()` function is the browser's built-in tool for making HTTP requests. You give it a URL, and it retrieves whatever is at that address and returns a promise that resolves to a `Response` object representing the server's reply.

The typical pattern for using `fetch()` with `async`/`await` looks like this:

```
async function getData() {
    const response = await fetch("https://example.com/data.json");
    const data = await response.json();
    // data is now a JavaScript object or array
}
```

The first `await` gets the `Response` object. The second `await` calls `.json()` on it, which reads the response body and parses the JSON. After both instances of `await`, `data` is a regular JavaScript object or array that you can loop through and use to build the page. You see exactly how this works in the next section.

One subtlety worth knowing: `fetch()` rejects its promise — that is, throws an error — only when the network request itself fails entirely (no internet connection, server unreachable, and so on). If the server responds with an error status such as 404 (file not found) or 500 (server error), `fetch()` still resolves successfully. The `response.ok` property is how you tell the difference: it's `true` for success status codes (200–299) and `false` for everything else. Always check `response.ok` before calling `.json()`.

# Fetching File Data

At this point in building the Orbital Donuts site, donut names, descriptions, and prices appear in at least two HTML files: `index.html` shows featured and signature donuts, and `menu.html` lists the full lineup. Every time a price changes or a new donut joins the menu, you have to track down and update every occurrence across every file. Miss one, and the site shows inconsistent information. Inconsistent websites look sloppy and, worse, erode customer trust.

The right solution is to store the donut data in one place and load it into any page that needs it. That's exactly what a JSON file lets you do. You create `donuts.json` once, keep it up to date, and `fetch()` it wherever it's needed. Change a price in the JSON file and every page that reads it reflects the change automatically.

## Creating donuts.json

The `donuts.json` file holds an array of donut objects. Each object contains the information needed to display a donut card: the name, description, price, category, and image filename. Here's part of the file showing four menu favorites (`bk04ch04/donuts.json`):

```
[
    {
        "name": "Galaxy Glazed",
        "description": "Our signature glaze with swirled cosmic colors and
        ↩edible glitter. A customer favorite since day one!",
        "price": 3.49,
        "category": "classic",
        "image": "galaxy-glazed.webp",
        "alt": "Classic glazed donut with purple and blue galaxy pattern and
        ↩edible glitter",
        "allergens": [
            "Wheat",
            "Eggs",
            "Milk",
            "Soy"
        ],
        "allergy-note": "Contains gluten. Made in a shared kitchen."
    },
```

```
    {
        "name": "Moonlight Maple Bar",
        "description": "Classic maple bar topped with real maple frosting.
        ↩Simple, delicious, perfect.",
        "price": 3.49,
        "category": "classic",
        "image": "moonlight-maple-bar.webp",
        "alt": "Long rectangular donut with creamy maple frosting",
        "allergens": [
            "Wheat",
            "Eggs",
            "Milk",
            "Soy"
        ],
        "allergy-note": "Contains gluten. Made in a shared kitchen."
    },
    {
        "name": "Cosmic Cruller",
        "description": "A twisted masterpiece glazed with our signature galaxy
        ↩glaze and topped with edible stars.",
        "price": 4.99,
        "category": "specialty",
        "image": "cosmic-cruller.webp",
        "alt": "Twisted cruller with purple and blue galaxy glaze and edible
        ↩stars",
        "allergens": [
            "Wheat",
            "Eggs",
            "Milk",
            "Soy"
        ],
        "allergy-note": "Contains gluten. Made in a shared kitchen."
    },
    {
        "name": "Vegan Vanilla Orbit",
        "description": "Delicious vegan donut with vanilla glaze. You won't
        ↩believe it's dairy-free and egg-free!",
        "price": 4.49,
        "category": "dietary",
        "image": "vegan-vanilla-orbit.webp",
        "alt": "Light golden donut with vanilla glaze",
        "allergens": [
            "Wheat",
            "Soy"
        ],
        "allergy-note": "Vegan and dairy-free. No nut ingredients."
    }
]
```

Note that the outermost brackets are `[` and `]`, so this is a JSON array. Within the array, each pair of curly braces is one donut object. The `price` values are plain numbers with no quotes, so JavaScript can do math with them (such as calling `.toFixed(2)` to format them as currency strings). The `category` field (`"classic"`, `"specialty"`, or `"dietary"`) is included because you could use it later to filter or group donuts on the page without touching the HTML. The `image` field stores just the filename, not the full path, which keeps the JSON tidy and enables you to change your image folder structure without rewriting every entry.

WARNING

Your JSON must be formatted exactly right. A missing comma between objects, a trailing comma after the last item, or a single quote instead of a double quote will cause a parse error and your data won't load. Most code editors highlight JSON syntax errors automatically. If your `fetch()` call fails with a `SyntaxError`, the JSON file is the first place to look.

## Updating the data in one place

Here's where the payoff becomes clear. Suppose the price of the Cosmic Cruller goes up to $5.49. Without `donuts.json`, you'd need to open `index.html`, find the Cosmic Cruller entry, change the price, save the file, open `menu.html`, find it again, change it again, save again. If there's an order page or a catering page that also lists it, add those to the hunt. One change, multiple files, and at least one of them will get missed eventually.

With `donuts.json` as the single source of truth, the same update takes about three seconds: open `donuts.json`, change `4.99` to `5.49`, save. Every page that fetches the file will show the new price the next time it loads. That's the whole point, and it scales beautifully. Add a new donut? Add one object to the array. Remove one from the menu? Delete its object. Rename a donut? One edit in one file. The HTML pages don't need to change at all. Sweet.

## Fetching the JSON file

With the data file in place, here's how to read it with `fetch()`. This function fetches `donuts.json` and returns the parsed array of donut objects:

```
async function getDonuts() {
    const response = await fetch("donuts.json");
    if (!response.ok) {
        throw new Error("Could not load donut data.");
    }
    const donuts = await response.json();
    return donuts;
}
```

Three jobs, six lines. The first `await` waits for the network request to complete and returns the `Response` object. The `if` check examines `response.ok`, a property that's `true` for HTTP status codes in the 200–299 range (success) and `false` for anything else, including a 404 file not found error. If the response signals failure, the code throws an `Error` (more on that in the "Handling Errors Gracefully" section). The second `await` parses the response body as JSON, and the function returns the resulting array.

## Rendering the data to the page

Fetching the data is only half the job. For the other half, here's a function that calls `getDonuts()` and then builds a grid of donut cards using the same DOM techniques you learned in Book 4, Chapter 2 (`bk04ch04/orbital-donuts/menu.html`):

```
async function buildMenu() {
    // Everything gets added here
    const menuSections = document.querySelector('#menu-sections');

    // Get the donut data
    const donuts = await getDonuts();

    // Define the display order and heading for each category
    const categories = [
        { key: 'classic', heading: 'Classic Donuts' },
        { key: 'specialty', heading: 'Specialty Donuts' },
        { key: 'dietary', heading: 'Dietary Options' }
    ];

    categories.forEach(function (cat) {
        // Filter donuts to only those belonging to this category
        const catDonuts = donuts.filter(function (d) {
            return d.category === cat.key;
        });
        if (catDonuts.length === 0) return;

        const section = document.createElement('section');

        const h3 = document.createElement('h3');
        h3.textContent = cat.heading;

        const wrapper = document.createElement('div');
        wrapper.className = 'donut-grid-wrapper';

        const grid = document.createElement('div');
        grid.className = 'donut-grid';
```

```
    // Build an article card for each donut in this category
    catDonuts.forEach(function (donut) {
        const article = document.createElement('article');

        const h4 = document.createElement('h4');
        h4.textContent = donut.name;

        const img = document.createElement('img');
        img.src = '/images/' + donut.image;
        img.alt = donut.alt;
        img.height = 256;
        img.width = 256;

        const desc = document.createElement('p');
        desc.textContent = donut.description;

        // Append an optional suffix (e.g. " (dozen)") after the formatted
           price
        const price = document.createElement('p');
        price.className = 'price';
        price.textContent = '$' + donut.price.toFixed(2) + (donut['price-
        suffix'] || '');

        const cartP = document.createElement('p');
        const cartBtn = document.createElement('button');
        cartBtn.type = 'button';
        cartBtn.disabled = true;
        cartBtn.textContent = 'Add to Cart';
        cartP.appendChild(cartBtn);

        // Wire up the allergen button to open the modal with this
           donut's data
        const allergenBtn = document.createElement('button');
        allergenBtn.className = 'allergen-btn';
        allergenBtn.dataset.name = donut.name;
        allergenBtn.dataset.allergens = donut.allergens.join(', ');
        allergenBtn.dataset.note = donut['allergy-note'];
        allergenBtn.textContent = 'Allergen Info';
        allergenBtn.addEventListener('click', function () {
            openModal(
                allergenBtn.dataset.name,
                allergenBtn.dataset.allergens,
                allergenBtn.dataset.note
            );
        });

        article.append(h4, img, desc, price, cartP, allergenBtn);
        grid.appendChild(article);
```

```
        });

        wrapper.appendChild(grid);
        section.append(h3, wrapper);
        menuSections.appendChild(section);
    });
}

buildMenu();
```

The function is marked `async` because it uses `await` to call `getDonuts()`. It then selects the menu container, creates an array of menu categories, and loops through the categories, using the `filter()` array method to get the donuts that match the category.

For each category, the code loops through the matching donut array with `forEach`. For each donut object, it creates an `<article>` element, builds the heading, description, price, image, allergy info, and other data from the object's properties, and appends the finished card to the grid.

Note that data such as `donut.name`, `donut.description`, and `donut.price` match the property names defined in `donuts.json`. That's how JavaScript knows which value to pull from each object. If you change a property name in the JSON, update the corresponding reference in the script too. Keeping the names consistent is a small habit that saves a lot of head-scratching later.

The HTML page itself needs just one container element to hold the cards:

```
<div id="menu-sections"></div>
```

That's it; there's no donut data anywhere in the HTML file. The JavaScript handles everything. When you update `donuts.json`, every page that fetches it reflects the change on the next load, an example of the power of separating data from presentation.

REMEMBER

Fetching a local JSON file with `fetch()` requires a web server. The `file://` protocol that browsers use when you open a local file directly won't work — you'll get a CORS error. (A *CORS* — Cross-Origin Resource Sharing — *error* occurs when a web application attempts to access resources from a different domain without the necessary permissions, as enforced by the browser's CORS policy.) If you're testing locally, use VS Code's Live Server extension or any similar local development server. Your live website already runs on a proper web server, so fetching a local JSON file is a concern only during development.

# Fetching Live Data from the Web

Fetching `donuts.json` is a great introduction to `fetch()`, but all the action happens locally because the JSON file lives on the same server as the page. External APIs work differently: all the action happens remotely because the URL points somewhere out on the internet. The `fetch()` call looks identical; only the URL changes.

Thousands of public APIs are available to web developers. Some require you to register for an *API key,* which is a unique identifier that lets the service track usage and prevent abuse. Others are completely open: no registration, no key, no cost. For learning, open APIs are ideal, and one of the best for weather data is Open-Meteo.

## Meeting Open-Meteo

Open-Meteo (`open-meteo.com`) provides free weather data for any location on Earth. No account, no API key, no cost. You construct a URL with the latitude and longitude of your target location, specify which data fields you want, and get back a clean JSON response.

The request URL for Springfield's current conditions looks like this:

```
https://api.open-meteo.com/v1/forecast
    ?latitude=44.04&longitude=-123.02
    &current=temperature_2m,weather_code
    &temperature_unit=fahrenheit
```

That code is really one long URL, broken across lines here for readability. The parameters after the `?` specify what you want: `latitude` and `longitude` set the location; `current` lists the real-time fields to return; and `temperature_unit` requests Fahrenheit instead of the default Celsius. Inside a property called `current` in the JSON response, you'll find `temperature_2m` (the current temperature) and `weather_code` (a number indicating sky conditions: 0 means clear, values in the 60s mean rain, and values in the 70s mean snow).

## Building the weather fetch

Here's a function that fetches the current conditions and returns a plain object with the temperature and a description (`bk04ch04/example02.html`):

```
const WEATHER_URL =
    "https://api.open-meteo.com/v1/forecast" +
    "?latitude=44.04&longitude=-123.02" +
    "&current=temperature_2m,weather_code" +
    "&temperature_unit=fahrenheit";

function describeWeather(code) {
    if (code === 0)  { return "Clear skies"; }
    if (code <= 3)   { return "Partly cloudy"; }
    if (code <= 48)  { return "Foggy"; }
    if (code <= 65)  { return "Rainy"; }
    if (code <= 77)  { return "Snowy"; }
    return "Stormy";
}

async function fetchWeather() {
    const response = await fetch(WEATHER_URL);
    if (!response.ok) {
        throw new Error("Weather data unavailable.");
    }
    const data = await response.json();
    const temp = data.current.temperature_2m;
    const code = data.current.weather_code;
    return { temp, description: describeWeather(code) };
}
```

The `WEATHER_URL` constant stores the full API URL, split across concatenated strings for readability. The `describeWeather` helper translates the numeric weather code into English. The `fetchWeather` function does the network call, awaits the response, checks `response.ok`, parses the JSON, digs into `data.current` for the temperature and code, and returns a tidy object.

# Displaying the weather on the page

With `fetchWeather()` ready, displaying the current conditions takes just a few lines (`bk04ch04/example02.html`):

```
async function showWeather() {
    const banner = document.querySelector("#weather-banner");
    const weather = await fetchWeather();
    banner.textContent =
        weather.description + " - " + weather.temp + "°F";
}

showWeather();
```

And the matching HTML:

```
<p id="weather-banner"></p>
```

On a clear afternoon in Springfield the banner might read: "Clear skies — 62°F." On a drizzly day it might show "Rainy — 49°F." Either way, the data is live, pulled from Open-Meteo every time the page loads.

What's worth appreciating here is how little the code changed compared to the `donuts.json` example. A different URL, a different property path into the JSON response (`data.current.temperature_2m` instead of just `data`), and a helper function to translate the weather code; that's it. The `fetch()`, then `.json()`, then DOM update pattern is identical. Once you know it, you can pull data from almost any public API with the same moves.

TIP

Weather codes from Open-Meteo follow the WMO (World Meteorological Organization) standard. The complete list is in the Open-Meteo documentation at `open-meteo.com/en/docs`. The `describeWeather` function uses broad groupings, so feel free to expand it with as many conditions as you like.

## Reading API documentation

Every API has documentation that tells you what requests it accepts and what responses it returns. Reading API docs is a skill that improves with practice, and Open-Meteo's documentation (`open-meteo.com/en/docs`) is an especially good place to start because it's clearly organized and includes an interactive URL builder that lets you choose variables and see the resulting request URL and sample response before you write a line of code.

When you look at an unfamiliar API response, the best approach is to log the entire object to the console first and explore it there. Add a temporary `console.log(data)` line right after the `.json()` call, load the page, open the browser's developer tools, and click through the logged object until you find the values you want. For Open-Meteo, expanding the `current` property in the console shows you every available field and its current value. Once you know the path, replace the `console.log` with the DOM-updating code.

As you get comfortable with Open-Meteo, you might find yourself wanting to try other free APIs. Some popular options that require no API key include the Open Library API for book information (`openlibrary.org/developers/api`), the REST Countries API for geographic data (`restcountries.com`), and the Open Food Facts API for ingredient information (`world.openfoodfacts.org/data`).

# Sending Form Data with fetch()

Every `fetch()` call you've made so far has been a GET request, which is the default method. GET requests are for *retrieving* data: fetch this file, get this weather reading. They're one-directional: you ask, the server responds with data.

The other major HTTP method is POST. A POST request *sends* data to the server to, say, submit a form, save a record, or trigger an action. POST requests carry a *body:* a chunk of data that travels with the request. To make a POST request with `fetch()`, you pass a second argument: an options object that specifies the `method`, `headers`, and `body`.

Think of GET and POST as two ways of communicating at a donut counter. GET is like looking at the menu board: you're retrieving information. POST is like placing your order: you're sending information to the person behind the counter, who then does something with it. Both are simple transactions, just flowing in opposite directions.

## Sending form data

For a good POST example, let's wire up the Orbital Donuts contact form, which I show you how to build in Book 3, Chapter 2. At this point, you should have a Formspree account and a form ID (again, refer to Book 3, Chapter 2), so your form endpoint will have a URL such as `https://formspree.io/f/your-form-id`. Copy that URL: it's the address you'll use in the `fetch()` call.

You also need to make sure each field in your HTML form has a `name` attribute, because `FormData` uses those names to identify the values when it bundles the submission. A contact form field without a `name` attribute is invisible to `FormData`, so it will be silently skipped. Check each `<input>`, `<textarea>`, and `<select>` in your form and confirm that the `name` attribute is present.

## Submitting the form

Traditional HTML form submission navigates to whatever the server sends back, usually a full page reload. Using `fetch()` to submit form data is much nicer: no reload, no flash of white, no lost scroll position. The visitors stay on the page, and you can show a confirmation message right where they are.

For the Orbital Donuts contact form, the HTML stays exactly as it was built in Book 3, Chapter 2. The `action` and `method` attributes on the `<form>` tag are no longer relevant because JavaScript is taking over the submission. You can leave them or remove them; either way, the `event.preventDefault()` call in the handler ensures that the browser never uses them.

For the Orbital Donuts contact form, you can use Formspree (`formspree.io`) as the backend. Formspree receives your form submissions and forwards them to your email address. When you create a free account, Formspree gives you a form endpoint URL, which is the address you POST the data to. No server-side code required on your end.

Here's the complete submit handler (`bk04ch04/orbital-donuts/contact.html`):

```
const form = document.querySelector("#contact-form");

form.addEventListener('submit', async function (event) {
    event.preventDefault();

    // Validation code from Book 4, Chapter 3 goes here

    const formData = new FormData(form);
    const response = await fetch("https://formspree.io/f/your-form-id", {
        method: "POST",
        body: formData,
        headers: { "Accept": "application/json" }
    });

    const confirmation = document.querySelector("#confirmation");
    if (response.ok) {
        confirmation.textContent =
            "Thanks for reaching out! We'll be in touch soon.";
        form.reset();
    } else {
        confirmation.textContent =
            "Something went wrong. Please try again.";
    }
});
```

The event listener is on the form's `submit` event, which fires when the visitor clicks Submit or presses Enter. The first thing the handler does is call `event.preventDefault()`, which stops the browser's default behavior of navigating away from the page. Then it creates a `FormData` object from the form, which automatically collects all the field values by name. The `fetch()` call sends a POST request to Formspree, with the form data as the body. When the response arrives, the code checks `response.ok` and displays the appropriate message in the `#confirmation` element.

The FormData object is doing a lot of quiet work here. It reads every named input, textarea, and select element in the form and bundles their current values into a format that web servers know how to receive. You don't have to query each field individually, extract its value, and assemble the data yourself. One line — new FormData(form) — handles all of it. As a bonus, FormData automatically handles special characters in the values, so names with apostrophes or messages with ampersands won't cause problems.

After a successful submission, form.reset() clears all the fields. That's a small but important touch because it signals clearly to the visitor that their message was sent and prevents the accidental double-submission that happens when someone wonders whether the first click worked and then clicks again.

The HTML needs just one extra element to hold that message:

```
<p id="confirmation"></p>
```

Replace "your-form-id" with the ID that Formspree gives you when you set up a form. The whole thing works without a single line of server-side code, which is the kind of win a small-business website builder deserves.

# Handling Errors Gracefully

Async code that reaches out to the network is inherently optimistic because it assumes the network is available, the server is running, and the data is correctly formatted. In the real world, none of those things are guaranteed. The user might be offline. The server might be temporarily down. The JSON file might have a typo. If you haven't planned for failure, the result is usually silence: nothing happens, the page doesn't update, and the visitor has no idea why. Good async code always handles errors.

## Displaying a loading message

There's also the question of what happens *while* the data is loading. On a fast connection, fetch() might complete in under a hundred milliseconds. On a slow mobile connection, it might take two or three seconds. When building a menu, for example, during that window of time the grid container is empty. A considerate page shows the visitor something, even just the message Loading. . ., so they know the page is doing something rather than broken.

Here's how to add a simple loading message that appears while the data is fetching and disappears when the cards are ready (bk04ch04/orbital-donuts/menu.html):

```
async function buildMenu() {
    // Everything gets added here
    const menuSections = document.querySelector('#menu-sections');

    // Display a loading message
    menuSections.textContent = "Loading menu...";

    // Get the donut data
    const donuts = await getDonuts();

    // Clear the loading message
    menuSections.textContent = '';

    // The rest of the menu-building code goes here
}
```

Setting menuSections.textContent to a loading message before await gives the visitor immediate feedback. Clearing it to an empty string right after getDonuts() resolves ensures that the message disappears before the donut cards appear. These two extra lines make a difference on a slow connection.

# Using try/catch with async/await

The standard JavaScript mechanism for handling errors is the try/catch block. You put the code that might fail inside try, and the code that handles the failure inside catch. If anything inside the try block throws an error — including an awaited promise that fails — execution jumps immediately to the catch block. The error doesn't crash the page; you get a chance to respond to it.

Here's the contact form fetch() code from earlier, now wrapped in a try/catch block (bk04ch04/orbital-donuts/contact.html):

```
const formData = new FormData(form);
const confirmation = document.querySelector("#confirmation");

try {
    const response = await fetch("https://formspree.io/f/your-form-id", {
        method: "POST",
        body: formData,
        headers: { "Accept": "application/json" }
    });
```

```
    if (response.ok) {
        confirmation.textContent =
            "Thanks for reaching out! We'll be in touch soon.";
        form.reset();
    } else {
        confirmation.textContent =
            "Something went wrong. Please try again.";
    }
} catch {
    confirmation.textContent = "Something went wrong. Please try again.";
}
```

The `fetch()` is now inside the `try` block. The `catch` block receives the error object that's raised by, say, a network failure. Instead of logging the error to the console and hoping nobody notices, the code puts a friendly message in the `#confirmation` container. The visitor gets an explanation; you get a gracefully degraded page instead of a broken one.

Note that the `catch` block doesn't need to know *why* it failed. Whether it was a network outage, a 404, or a malformed JSON file, the response to the visitor is the same: a calm, polite message. You can of course log the error object for debugging. Running `console.error(error)` inside the `catch` block is a reasonable addition in development. Just don't show technical error details to visitors. `SyntaxError: Unexpected token < in JSON at position 0` is not a useful message for someone who just wants to order a Cosmic Cruller.

IN THIS CHAPTER

- » Knowing when libraries are useful
- » Getting familiar with jQuery
- » Adding lightweight interactivity with Alpine.js
- » Browsing component libraries

# Chapter 5
# JavaScript Libraries

*Any fool can write code that a computer can understand. Good programmers write code that humans can understand.*

—MARTIN FOWLER

Vanilla JavaScript — the plain, no-frills kind that needs no extra downloads and no special setup — can do a remarkable amount. But spend any time reading tutorials or looking at how other sites are built, and you'll constantly run into the word *library*. You'll see references to jQuery, Alpine.js, Bootstrap, Tailwind CSS, and an entire ecosystem of tools built on top of JavaScript and CSS. What are these things? Should you use them? And if so, when?

This chapter is a broad survey rather than a deep dive. The goal is to give you enough context to know what these tools are, recognize them when you encounter them, and make an informed decision about whether any of them belong in your projects.

# Vanilla JavaScript versus Libraries: When to Use What

A *library* is a collection of prewritten JavaScript (or CSS) that someone else wrote, tested, and packaged for you to use. Think of it like a well-stocked hardware store: when you need to hang a picture, you don't forge your own nails, you grab the right size off the shelf. In a library, common, repetitive tasks have already been solved and packaged so you can just grab them and use them.

Libraries don't come preloaded in the browser. You add them to your page by linking to a downloaded file or to a copy hosted on a *content delivery network* (CDN), a network of servers around the world that delivers files quickly to visitors wherever they are. Either way, the browser downloads that extra file before your JavaScript can use what's in it.

REMEMBER

A library is something you call. Your code stays in charge, meaning that you pick up a library tool when you need it and put it down when you're done. This is different from a framework (more on that at the end of this chapter), where the framework calls your code and you work within its rules.

## The case for vanilla JavaScript

Modern browsers are remarkably capable. The features that once required a library — selecting elements, making network requests, animating things — are now built in and work consistently across all major browsers. For the kinds of websites this book focuses on, vanilla JavaScript gets you all the way there.

Before adding any library, weigh what you gain against what you give up. On the gain side: convenience and prebuilt solutions. On the give-up side: an extra file for the browser to download, a dependency to keep updated, and one more thing that can break. A good rule of thumb: if you can write it yourself in a reasonable amount of time and understand every line, you probably don't need a library for it.

## When a library makes sense

That said, there are genuinely good reasons to reach for a library:

- **You're working with inherited code.** If a project you've taken over already uses, say, the jQuery library (discussed in the next section), learning enough jQuery to maintain the code is smarter than rewriting everything from scratch.

» **You need complex UI components.** Accessible modal dialogs, date pickers, and drag-and-drop interfaces are genuinely hard to build correctly from scratch. A library that provides them is worth the trade-off.

» **The library is small and focused.** A micro-library that does one specific thing well — smooth scrolling, date formatting, charting — adds little overhead and solves a real problem.

» **Your project is growing fast.** When managing updates manually starts to feel chaotic, a well-chosen library can impose useful structure before things spiral out of control.



# Using jQuery in Legacy Projects

jQuery was released in 2006 and became the most widely used JavaScript library ever written. At its peak, it appeared on roughly 77 percent of all websites that use JavaScript libraries. Even today, a huge portion of the web still runs on jQuery, which means you *will* encounter it. Knowing how to read it is a necessity.

## Why jQuery conquered the web

To understand jQuery's rise, you have to travel back in time to the difficult years of web development — roughly 2003 to 2010 — when different browsers implemented JavaScript in wildly inconsistent ways. Selecting an element in Internet Explorer required different code than in Firefox. Making a network request involved different APIs in different browsers. Writing JavaScript that worked correctly everywhere was exhausting.

jQuery's genius was simple: write one line of jQuery, and the library handles the dirty work of figuring out how to make the code work in every browser. That promise made it indispensable almost overnight. Today, browsers have standardized enormously and most of what jQuery offered is now built directly into JavaScript. But the web is still full of jQuery code written during its dominant years, and that code isn't going away anytime soon.

## Reading jQuery code

jQuery centers on one function, written as $, that selects elements from the page and wraps them in a jQuery object loaded with methods. Here's a quick side-by-side comparison so you can map jQuery to the vanilla JavaScript you already know:

```
// Vanilla JavaScript
const el = document.querySelector("#promo");
el.textContent = "New flavors this week!";
el.classList.add("highlight");

// jQuery – same result
$("#promo")
    .text("New flavors this week!")
    .addClass("highlight");
```

Methods such as `.text()`, `.html()`, and `.addClass()` do exactly what their vanilla JavaScript equivalents — in this case, `textContent`, `innerHTML`, and `classList.add()` — do; they just look different. Chaining multiple methods on the same selection (as in the preceding jQuery example) is a hallmark of jQuery style. Once you recognize the pattern, jQuery code is straightforward to read and maintain.

One more pattern you'll see constantly in older jQuery code is `$(document).ready(function() { . . . })`, often shortened to `$(function() { . . . })`. This code is jQuery's equivalent of listening for the `DOMContentLoaded` event — it just tells the browser to run some code after the page has loaded. You'll see it wrapping virtually all jQuery code in older projects.

### jQuery today

jQuery is no longer the default choice for new projects. If you're starting fresh, vanilla JavaScript is almost certainly the right call. That said, don't feel pressured to rewrite working jQuery code just because it feels old. Libraries don't expire — if a project you inherit runs on jQuery and the site works fine, leave it alone.

WARNING

Mixing jQuery and vanilla JavaScript in the same project creates consistency problems. Code that toggles a menu with jQuery next to code that does the same thing with `classList.toggle()` is confusing to read and maintain. Pick one approach for a given project and stick with it.

## Alpine.js for Lightweight Interactivity

Alpine.js (`https://alpinejs.dev/`) is a small, modern library with a very different philosophy from jQuery. Rather than giving you functions to call in a separate JavaScript file, Alpine lets you write interactivity directly in your HTML by using special attributes. If you've ever thought "I just want this panel to open when someone clicks a button, why do I need a whole JavaScript file for that?" — Alpine was built for you.

## What makes Alpine different

Alpine's logic lives in HTML attributes rather than in a separate `.js` file, which makes it very easy to see what a piece of HTML does just by reading it. No hunting for the script that wires a button. The behavior is right there on the element. Alpine also handles the page-updating work for you: when a variable changes, Alpine automatically updates everything on the page that depends on it. This pattern, called *reactivity,* is a core concept in modern JavaScript development.

Alpine is tiny (about 15 KB) with no build step, no command-line tools, and no configuration files. You add one `<script>` tag to your page's `<head>` section pointing to Alpine's CDN file, and it's ready to go:

```
<script defer
    src="https://cdn.jsdelivr.net/npm/alpinejs@3/dist/cdn.min.js">
</script>
```

The `defer` attribute tells the browser to load Alpine in the background while the rest of the page parses, and then run it once the HTML is ready. That's important: Alpine needs to read the `x-` attributes on your HTML elements when it starts, so the page must be fully parsed first.

## Alpine's core directives

Alpine's instructions live in HTML attributes called *directives,* which all start with `x-`. Four of them handle the vast majority of everyday use:

- **`x-data`:** Declares a component and its state. This is where you define the variables Alpine tracks. Everything inside that element can read and update those variables.
- **`x-show`:** Shows or hides an element based on a `true`/`false` condition. Alpine toggles the element's display property automatically.
- **`x-on` (shorthand `@`):** Attaches an event listener. `@click` runs code when the element is clicked; `@keydown`, `@mouseover`, and other standard events work the same way.

» **`x-bind` (shorthand `:`):** Dynamically sets an HTML attribute based on a condition. Use `:class` to toggle CSS classes, `:disabled` to enable or disable a button, `:aria-expanded` to keep accessibility attributes in sync, and so on.

## Alpine in action

Here's an example of a classic web page feature: a tab interface. Clicking a tab shows one panel and hides the others (`bk04ch05/example01.html`):

```
<div class="tab-buttons">
    <button class="tab-btn active" data-target="#panel-location">Location</
   button>
    <button class="tab-btn" data-target="#panel-hours">Hours</button>
    <button class="tab-btn" data-target="#panel-parking">Parking</button>
</div>

<div id="panel-location" class="tab-panel active">
    <h3>Our Location</h3>
    <div><strong>Orbital Donuts</strong></div>
    <div>123 Space Street</div>
    <div>Springfield 98101</div>
    <div>Phone: (317) 555-3145</div>
</div>
<div id="panel-hours" class="tab-panel">
    <h3>Store Hours</h3>
    <div><strong>Monday - Friday:</strong> 6:00am - 6:00pm</div>
    <div><strong>Saturday:</strong> 7:00am - 7:00pm</div>
    <div><strong>Sunday:</strong> 7:00am - 5:00pm</div><br>
    <p><em>We're open every day except Thanksgiving and Christmas. We
        often sell out of popular flavors by mid-afternoon on weekends,
        so get here early for the best selection!</em></p>
</div>
<div id="panel-parking" class="tab-panel">
    <h3>Parking &amp;amp; Transit</h3>
    <p><strong>Parking:</strong> Street parking is available on Space Street
        and nearby side streets. We also have a small parking lot behind the
        building with 6 spaces for customer use.</p>
    <p><strong>Public Transit:</strong> We're just a 5-minute walk from the
        Springfield light rail station.
        Several bus routes stop within two blocks of our shop.</p>
    <p><strong>Bike Friendly:</strong> Bike racks are available right in front
        of our shop!</p>
</div>
```

Activating this code with vanilla JavaScript requires a fair amount of wiring: a `querySelectorAll()` call, a `forEach` loop to attach click listeners to every button, a variable to track which tab is active, and code to toggle classes on both the buttons and the panels whenever a click fires. Here's how that looks:

```
const buttons = document.querySelectorAll(".tab-btn");
const panels = document.querySelectorAll(".tab-panel");

buttons.forEach(function (btn) {
    btn.addEventListener("click", function () {
        buttons.forEach(b => b.classList.remove("active"));
        panels.forEach(p => p.classList.remove("active"));
        btn.classList.add("active");
        document.querySelector(btn.dataset.target)
            .classList.add("active");
    });
});
```

This works, but it's a lot of ceremony for a simple idea. Here's the same behavior with Alpine, written entirely in HTML (`bk04ch05/example02.html`):

```
<div x-data="{ activeTab: 'location' }">

    <div class="tab-buttons">
        <button class="tab-btn" @click="activeTab = 'location'"
            :class="{ active: activeTab === 'location' }">Location</button>
        <button class="tab-btn" @click="activeTab = 'hours'"
            :class="{ active: activeTab === 'hours' }">Hours</button>
        <button class="tab-btn" @click="activeTab = 'parking'"
            :class="{ active: activeTab === 'parking' }">Parking</button>
    </div>

    <div x-show="activeTab === 'location'">
        <h3>Our Location</h3>
        <div><strong>Orbital Donuts</strong></div>
        <div>123 Space Street</div>
        <div>Springfield 98101</div>
        <div>Phone: (317) 555-3145</div>
    </div>
    <div x-show="activeTab === 'hours'">
        <h3>Store Hours</h3>
        <div><strong>Monday - Friday:</strong> 6:00am - 6:00pm</div>
        <div><strong>Saturday:</strong> 7:00am - 7:00pm</div>
        <div><strong>Sunday:</strong> 7:00am - 5:00pm</div><br>
        <p><em>We're open every day except Thanksgiving and Christmas. We
            often sell out of popular flavors by mid-afternoon on weekends,
            so get here early for the best selection!</em></p>
    </div>
    <div x-show="activeTab === 'parking'">
        <h3>Parking &amp; Transit</h3>
```

```
        <p><strong>Parking:</strong> Street parking is available on Space
            Street and nearby side streets. We also have a small parking lot
    behind the building with 6 spaces for customer use.</p>
        <p><strong>Public Transit:</strong> We're just a 5-minute walk from
            the Springfield light rail station. Several bus routes stop
            within two blocks of our shop.</p>
        <p><strong>Bike Friendly:</strong> Bike racks are available right in
            front of our shop!</p>
    </div>
</div>
```

The `x-data` attribute declares one variable, `activeTab`, set to `'location'` so the Location tab is open by default. Each button's `@click` sets `activeTab` to that tab's name. Each panel's `x-show` checks whether `activeTab` matches its name. If it does, the panel is visible; if not, Alpine hides it automatically. The `:class` binding on each button adds the `active` CSS class when that tab is the current one, so you can style the active tab differently from the others.

No JavaScript file. No `querySelectorAll`. No `forEach`. When `activeTab` changes, Alpine updates both the button states and the panel visibility simultaneously, because everything is watching the same variable. That's reactivity in a nutshell.

TIP

Alpine also has `x-model`, which keeps a form input in two-way sync with a variable. Type into an input with `x-model="query"` and anything on the page that references `query` updates in real time, which is useful for live search filters, character counters, and similar interactive patterns.

# Component Libraries: UI in a Box

JavaScript libraries help with behavior. *Component libraries* and *CSS frameworks* address the visual side. These tools give you prebuilt, professionally designed UI components, such as buttons, navigation bars, cards, and forms. Instead of styling everything from scratch, you apply a few CSS classes and a polished component appears, just like that.

Component libraries make two promises. First, visual consistency: every element follows the same spacing, sizing, and typographic rules because they all come from the same design system. Second, the hard details are handled: hover states, focus indicators, responsive behavior, and accessibility features that would take hours to implement correctly from scratch are already built in. The trade-off is a visual style that may need customization to match your brand and a learning curve for the library's class names.

## Bootstrap: The classic choice

Bootstrap (`getbootstrap.com`) is the world's most widely used CSS framework, with a history going back to 2011. It provides a comprehensive responsive grid system, dozens of prestyled components (cards, navigation bars, alerts, modals, badges, and more), and a large set of utility classes. Adding Bootstrap to a page takes one `<link>` tag in the `<head>`; some interactive components also need Bootstrap's JavaScript file. With Bootstrap loaded, you build components entirely by applying its CSS class names:

```
<div class="card" style="max-width: 20rem;">
    <div class="card-body">
        <h5 class="card-title">Daily Special</h5>
        <p class="card-text">Today's featured item is the
            Lunar Lemon Twist. Get it before it's gone!</p>
        <a href="/menu" class="btn btn-primary">
            See the Menu</a>
    </div>
</div>
```

Classes like `card`, `card-body`, and `btn btn-primary` are all Bootstrap-defined. No custom CSS required. Bootstrap's grid system divides the page into twelve columns and lets you specify how many columns each element occupies at different screen sizes. A two-column desktop layout that stacks into a single column on a mobile device is just a matter of applying the right grid classes — Bootstrap handles the breakpoints for you.

TIP

Bootstrap 5 (the current version) dropped its jQuery dependency entirely. Earlier Bootstrap versions required jQuery, so if a tutorial tells you to include a jQuery script tag alongside Bootstrap, that tutorial is out of date.

## Tailwind CSS: A different philosophy

Tailwind CSS (`tailwindcss.com`) takes a different approach from Bootstrap. Rather than providing prebuilt component styles, Tailwind gives you hundreds of tiny *utility classes* that each do one thing: `p-4` adds padding, `text-lg` sets font size, `rounded-xl` rounds corners, `bg-blue-500` sets a background color, and so on. You build components by combining these small classes directly in HTML, which gives you granular control over every visual detail without ever writing a CSS file.

Tailwind has become enormously popular, especially among developers who work with component-based frameworks. Its class-heavy HTML can look cluttered at first, and using it properly in production requires a build step that removes unused classes from the final stylesheet. Whether the utility-class approach suits your workflow is a matter of preference — some developers find it liberating but others find it verbose. Both reactions are valid.

REMEMBER

Bootstrap and Tailwind are CSS frameworks, not JavaScript libraries. They style your pages; they don't add behavior. You can use either one alongside vanilla JavaScript, Alpine.js, jQuery, or any combination of tools.

# When You Need a Framework (Hint: Probably Not Yet)

The word *framework* gets used loosely in web development conversations, sometimes as a synonym for *library,* which causes no end of confusion. Here's the key distinction: with a *library,* your code is in charge. You call the library's functions when you need them. With a *framework,* the framework is in charge. It calls your code. You write components and functions that the framework invokes according to its own lifecycle. You don't run your code; you write code that fits the framework's structure and let the framework run it.

A useful analogy: building with vanilla JavaScript or a library is like constructing a custom house from scratch; you make every decision. Building with a framework is like buying a modular home: the structure and systems are already decided, you work within those rules, you can get a lot done quickly, but you're living by someone else's specs whether you like them or not.

## The big three: React, Vue, and Angular

When people talk about JavaScript frameworks, they almost always mean one of these three:

- **React (`react.dev`):** Created by Facebook (now Meta) and released in 2013, React organizes pages into reusable *components,* which are self-contained pieces of HTML and JavaScript. When data changes, React efficiently updates just the affected parts of the page. React is the most widely used of the three, with the largest community and job market.
- **Vue (`vuejs.org`):** Consistently recommended as the most approachable framework for developers coming from plain HTML and CSS. Vue has a gentle learning curve, excellent documentation, and a flexible design that lets you start small and add complexity only as you need it.

- **Angular (`angular.dev`):** Maintained by Google and the most opinionated and fully featured of the three. Angular uses TypeScript by default and comes with built-in tools for routing, forms, and HTTP requests. Angular is most common in large enterprise applications where its rigidity is an asset: the framework enforces consistent patterns across a large development team.

## Do you need a framework?

For a standard small-to-medium business website, you almost certainly don't need a framework. Frameworks are designed for complex, data-driven web *applications,* such as social media feeds, project management dashboards, or e-commerce systems with live updates. If your site is primarily content — pages, a menu, a contact form, a blog — a framework is solving problems you don't have.

There are signs that a framework's complexity would be worth taking on: multiple parts of the page need to stay in sync with the same data simultaneously; you're building an application with user accounts, real-time data, and complex workflows; or you're working on a large team where enforced code consistency matters. If none of these describe your project, you haven't missed anything.

The skills you've built up across Book 4 are real and practical and will work on real websites today. The web development ecosystem can look overwhelming from the outside, but the fundamentals are stable: understand HTML, CSS, and JavaScript, and you have the foundation to pick up any library or framework when you need one.

# 5

# Building with No-Code or Low-Code Platforms

# Contents at a Glance

IN THIS CHAPTER

» Discovering why WordPress rules the web

» Installing and navigating WordPress

» Customizing your site

» Adding powerful features with plugins

» Keeping your WordPress site secure

# Chapter 1

# WordPress for Small Businesses

*My life goal was to democratize publishing.*

—MATT MULLENWEG, CO-FOUNDER OF WORDPRESS

One path to building a website is to plan, design, and code it yourself, and that path has been the focus of the first four minibooks. Now it's time to explore a different path, one that lets someone — or, really, some*thing* — else do much of the heavy lifting so you can focus on running your business instead of wrestling with code.

In this chapter, that something is *WordPress,* the most widely used content management system on earth. In the pages that follow, I walk you through everything you need to get a WordPress site up and running: how to choose the right kind of hosting; how to install WordPress in about five minutes flat; how to pick and customize a theme; how to extend your site with plugins; how to build pages with WordPress's modern block editor; how to evaluate page builder tools; and, because the web is a rough neighborhood, how to keep your site secure. By the end, you'll have a fully-functioning WordPress site ready to introduce your business to the world.

# Introducing WordPress

It's hard to overstate just how dominant WordPress is. As of 2025, WordPress powers roughly 43 percent of all websites on the internet. That's not 43 percent of websites built with a particular type of tool, that's 43 percent of *everything:* News sites, blogs, restaurant pages, online stores, government portals, university sites, and on and on. When you browse the web today, there's nearly a fifty-fifty chance that whatever site you land on has WordPress purring under the hood.

Why does WordPress hold this extraordinary position? A few reasons stand out:

- It's free and open source, meaning tens of thousands of developers worldwide are constantly improving it, adding features, and fixing bugs, at no cost to you.
- Its plugin and theme ecosystem is staggeringly large, with over 60,000 free plugins and thousands of premium themes covering just about every website need imaginable.
- An enormous amount of documentation, tutorials, community forums, and professional help is available whenever you get stuck.
- It's battle-tested because it's been around so long (since 2003).

For small businesses in particular, WordPress hits a sweet spot: it's powerful enough to grow with you as your business grows, but accessible enough that a non-developer can manage day-to-day content updates without calling in a professional every time someone needs a page updated or a new blog post published.

## The two WordPresses: .com and .org

Surprisingly, there are actually *two* WordPresses, and confusing them is one of the most common mistakes new users make. The two versions are `WordPress.com` and `WordPress.org`, and they're quite different animals:

- **`WordPress.com`** is a hosted service, similar in concept to Squarespace or Wix (which I cover in Book 5, Chapter 2). You sign up, choose a plan, and

WordPress.com handles all the technical details for you, including hosting, software updates, and security. A free plan exists, but it's limited: you can't install your own plugins, your site gets a yourname.wordpress.com address rather than your own domain, and customization options are restricted. Paid plans remove some of these limitations, but costs can climb quickly and you still have less control than with the self-hosted version.

» **WordPress.org** is the free, self-hosted software that most people mean when they say "WordPress." You download it and install it on your own web-hosting account. You have complete control: you can install any plugin, use any theme, and modify any code, and own your data outright. This is the WordPress I cover throughout this chapter, and it's the version that's right for most small-business websites.

REMEMBER

Throughout this chapter, "WordPress" always means the self-hosted WordPress.org version. If I'm ever discussing the hosted WordPress.com service, I'll say so explicitly.

## WordPress versus the alternatives

Squarespace, Wix, and the other visual builders covered in Book 5, Chapter 2 are excellent tools, and I'd never talk you out of using them if they're the right fit for your situation. But self-hosted WordPress has some advantages that are worth understanding before you choose.

With a hosted builder, you're renting space in someone else's ecosystem. If the company raises its prices, changes its terms of service, or, in a worst-case scenario, shuts down, your website is at their mercy. With self-hosted WordPress, you own your content, you own your database, and you can pick up and move to a different host whenever you want. That kind of independence matters a great deal for a business whose livelihood depends on its web presence.

WordPress also wins decisively on flexibility and extensibility. Need an online booking system? There's a plugin for that. Want to add e-commerce? A free WordPress plugin called WooCommerce (wordpress.org/plugins/woocommerce/) turns your site into a full-featured online store. Need a membership area, a job board, a live chat widget, an events calendar, or a donation system? There are plugins for all of those, too. With a hosted builder, you get what the company has decided to offer. With WordPress, the answer to "Can it do X?" is almost always "Yep, and here's how."

The trade-off is that you take on more responsibility. You'll need to choose and pay for your own hosting, keep WordPress and its plugins updated, and think about security and backups. None of this is especially difficult, but it does require more attention than a fully managed hosted platform. The rest of this chapter helps you handle all of it.

# Installing and Setting Up WordPress

WordPress has famously advertised a "five-minute install" since its earliest days, and with modern hosting tools, that claim is genuinely close to accurate. The process involves three steps: picking a WordPress-friendly host, running the installation, and doing a quick first-login setup.

## Choosing a WordPress-friendly host

Not all web hosts are created equal when it comes to WordPress. You want a host that offers one-click WordPress installation (more on that in a moment), reliable uptime, and decent performance, because a slow WordPress site makes visitors click away, hurting both your reputation and your search engine rankings.

There are two main categories of WordPress-friendly hosting to consider:

- **Shared hosting:** Your site shares a server with many other websites. It's affordable — typically \$5–\$15 per month — and perfectly adequate for a new or low-traffic small-business site. Popular shared hosts with strong WordPress support include Bluehost (`bluehost.com`), SiteGround (`siteground.com`), DreamHost (`dreamhost.com`), and Hostinger (`hostinger.com`). All four offer one-click WordPress installation and are officially recommended by `WordPress.org`.
- **Managed WordPress hosting:** The host takes care of WordPress-specific chores — software updates, daily backups, security scanning, and performance optimization — so you don't have to think about them. It costs more (usually \$25–\$60 per month), but it removes a significant maintenance burden and often comes with better performance. Kinsta (`kinsta.com`), WP Engine (`wpengine.com`), and Flywheel (`getflywheel.com`) are three well-regarded managed WordPress hosts.

TIP

If this is your first WordPress site and you're watching your budget, shared hosting is a reasonable starting point. Many successful small-business sites run on shared hosting for years. You can always migrate to managed hosting later if your site grows or if you decide the maintenance work isn't worth your time.

Before settling on a host, verify that it meets WordPress's minimum technical requirements: PHP version 8.3 or higher, MySQL 8.0 or MariaDB 10.6 or higher, and HTTPS support. Every reputable host meets these requirements in 2026, but it's worth a quick check if you're considering a lesser-known provider.

## Using one-click installation

Most hosting companies offer a one-click WordPress installer through their control panel, typically powered by a tool called Softaculous or a custom installer the host has built themselves. The exact steps vary by provider, but the general process looks like this:

1. Log in to your hosting account's control panel (most hosts use a tool called cPanel; some have their own branded equivalent).
2. Find the WordPress installer. It might be labeled WordPress, Softaculous, Apps Installer, or One-Click Installs, depending on your host.
3. Click Install and fill in a few basic details: the domain where you want to install it, the name of your website, and the username and password for your WordPress admin account.
4. Click the Install or Finish button and wait roughly 60–90 seconds for the process to complete.
5. Visit the admin URL provided by the installer.



That last step takes you to `yourdomain.com/wp-admin`, where you log in with the credentials you just created. Your WordPress site now exists and is accessible on the web. Congratulations!

**WARNING**

During installation, you'll be asked to create an admin username. Do *not* use `admin` because it's the first thing automated hacking tools try when probing WordPress sites. Choose something more distinctive, like your own name or a variation of your business name, and pair it with a strong, unique password.

## Touring the WordPress dashboard

When you log in to WordPress for the first time, you land on the *dashboard,* the administrative nerve center of your site (refer to Figure 1-1). It can look a little overwhelming at first, so here's a quick orientation to help you feel at home.

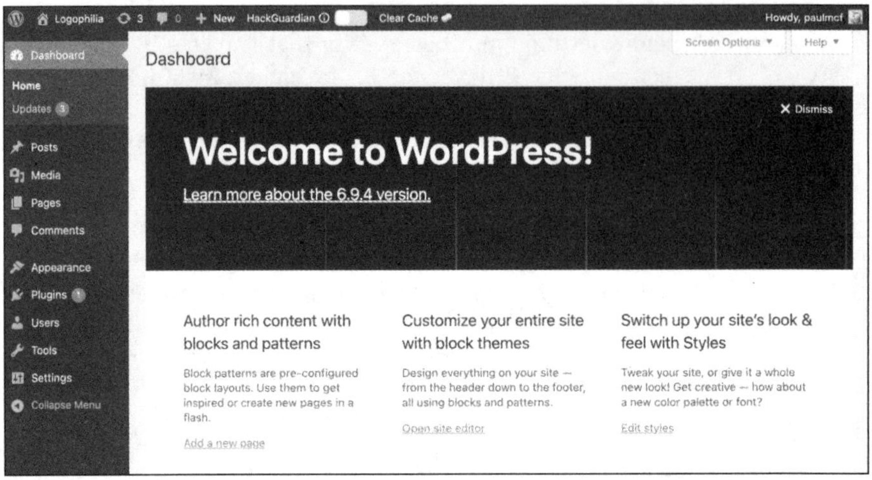


**FIGURE 1-1:** The dashboard, your WordPress administration home away from home.

The left sidebar is your primary navigation, and it stays visible no matter which section of the dashboard you're in. The menu items you'll use most often are:

- **Posts:** Write and manage blog posts. If your site doesn't have a blog, you can largely ignore this section.
- **Media:** Access your library of uploaded images, PDFs, videos, and other files. Every image you add to a page is stored here.
- **Pages:** Create and manage your site's static pages: Home, About, Services, Contact, and so on. This is where you'll spend the majority of your content-creation time.
- **Comments:** View and manage the comments folks have posted to your blog posts and pages.
- **Appearance:** Install and switch themes, manage navigation menus, and customize your site's look via Customizer or Site Editor.
- **Plugins:** Install, activate, deactivate, and delete plugins.
- **Users:** Manage user accounts, including your own admin profile. If you ever need to give a colleague or a contractor access to the dashboard, you do it here.
- **Settings:** Configure site-wide options, including your site title, tagline, time zone, reading settings, and permalink structure.

Before you do anything else, take a few minutes to complete two important initial setup tasks. First, go to Settings ➪ General and verify that your site title, tagline, and time zone are correct. The time zone setting affects when scheduled posts publish, so it's worth getting it right from the start.

Second, go to Settings ➪ Permalinks and select the Post Name option. This gives you clean, readable URLs like `yoursite.com/about-us` instead of the cryptic default format like `yoursite.com/?p=42`. Click Save Changes, and WordPress updates its URL structure automatically. This small step makes a difference for both your visitors and your search engine rankings, so don't skip it.

# Understanding Themes and Customization

WordPress neatly separates what your site *does* from how it *looks*. The looks part is handled by *themes*, which are collections of templates, stylesheets, and configuration options that control your site's visual design. Installing a new theme is like giving your website a makeover without touching a single word of content. The same pages and posts that appeared under your old theme appear under your new one but with a different visual presentation.

Every fresh WordPress installation comes with a default theme — currently called Twenty Twenty-Five — which is clean, accessible, and functional but also generic. For a business website, you'll want something that reflects your brand and your industry. The good news is that the WordPress theme ecosystem is enormous.



## Free versus premium themes

WordPress themes come in two varieties, and both have their place depending on your budget and your needs:

- **Free themes:** The official WordPress Theme Directory (`wordpress.org/themes`) offers over 14,000 free themes, all reviewed by the WordPress team for basic quality and security standards before being listed. Free themes are a respectable starting point, especially for businesses watching their budget. Many free themes are well-designed and feature-rich.
- **Premium themes:** Sold by marketplaces such as ThemeForest (`themeforest.net`) and by individual theme developers, premium themes typically cost $40–$80 as a one-time purchase. They usually include dedicated customer support, regular updates, a demo importer that sets up a sample site in one click, and more design polish than most free themes. For a business website that needs to look professional from day one, a premium theme is often worth the modest investment.

When evaluating themes, whether free or paid, look for four key things. Check when the theme was last updated: anything that hasn't been touched in a year or more may have security vulnerabilities or compatibility issues with recent versions of WordPress. Check the ratings and read recent reviews. Look for a live demo you can explore before committing. And make sure the theme is *responsive*, meaning it looks good on phones and tablets as well as desktop screens. (Any well-maintained modern theme will be responsive, but it's still worth verifying in the demo.)

WARNING

Avoid *nulled* themes, which are pirated premium themes available for free from unofficial sites. These frequently contain malicious code that creates backdoors to your site, sends spam, or harvests your visitors' data. The few dollars you save are absolutely not worth the risk.

## Finding and installing a theme

The most straightforward way to find and install a free theme is directly from the WordPress dashboard, without ever leaving the admin area:

1. **In the dashboard sidebar, choose Appearance ➪ Themes.**
2. **Click the Add Theme button near the top of the page.**
3. **Look through the directory.**

   Browse by scrolling through the Favorites or Popular tabs, use the search box to look for specific keywords (like *restaurant, consultant,* or *portfolio*), or click Feature Filter to narrow results by layout, subject, and available features.
4. **Hover your cursor over any theme thumbnail and click Preview to see a live demo of what your site would look like with that theme applied.**
5. **When you find a theme you'd like to try, click Install.**
6. **After installation completes, click Activate to make it your active theme.**

If you've purchased a premium theme from a marketplace, you'll receive a `.zip` file as your download. To install it, go to Appearance ➪ Themes, click Add Theme, click the Upload Theme button at the top, choose your `.zip` file, and click Install Now. Then click Activate.

## Customizing your theme

How you customize your WordPress theme depends on which type of theme you've installed, because WordPress currently has two distinct editing models.

Newer *block themes,* which include most themes built or significantly updated in the last few years, use Site Editor (also called Full Site Editor). Site Editor extends WordPress's block-based editing to your entire site, including the header, footer, page templates, and global styles. You can change colors, fonts, and layouts for the entire site from one centralized place. To access Site Editor, go to Appearance ➪ Editor in the dashboard.

Older *classic themes* use Customizer, a panel on the left side of the screen with options specific to that theme: color pickers, font selectors, logo uploaders, layout toggles, and so on. Customizer shows a live preview of your site as you make changes, which is useful. To access Customizer, go to Appearance ➪ Customize.

Whether you're in Site Editor or Customizer, changes are shown in a live preview before you publish them. This see-it-before-you-save-it workflow saves a lot of back-and-forth, so take advantage of it. Make a change, look at the preview, adjust, and click Publish (or Save Changes) only when you're happy with the result.

# Essential Plugins for Business Websites



If themes are the wardrobe of your WordPress site, plugins are the toolbox. *Plugins* are add-on packages that extend WordPress with new capabilities, everything from contact forms and SEO optimization to e-commerce, security scanning, and email newsletter management. With over 60,000 free plugins in the official directory alone, you can add almost any feature imaginable without writing a line of code.

Of course, 60,000 options is a lot to sort through. The good news is that you don't need most of them. Most well-functioning, small-business WordPress sites require plugins in only six key categories. The following sections cover each one with specific recommendations.

## Finding and installing plugins

Installing a plugin from the official WordPress Plugin Directory (`wordpress.org/plugins`) takes about 30 seconds and never requires leaving the dashboard:

1. **In the dashboard sidebar, click Plugins ➪ Add Plugin.**
2. **Use the search box to find a plugin by name, or browse using the Featured, Popular, or Recommended tabs.**

3. **When you find the plugin you want, click Install Now.**
4. **After installation completes, enable the plugin by clicking Activate.**

Once a plugin is activated, it typically adds a new item to your dashboard sidebar or to the Settings menu, where you can configure its options. To manage your installed plugins — for example, deactivating ones you're not using or deleting ones you don't need — go to Plugins ➪ Installed Plugins.

One important caveat: not every plugin is listed in the WordPress Plugin Directory. Some popular plugins — particularly freemium products that have a paid Pro tier — are distributed primarily through their own websites. For those, you download a `.zip` file from the developer's site, and then install it by choosing Plugins ➪ Add Plugin ➪ Upload Plugin. I note which plugins in the following list require this approach.

WARNING

Plugin quality varies considerably. Before installing any plugin, check three things: the date of the last update (anything more than a year old without recent activity is a caution sign), the number of active installations (higher generally indicates a maintained product with an engaged user community), and the average rating. Read at least a handful of recent reviews as well. A plugin with 100,000 active installations, a 4.7-star rating, and recent glowing reviews is a much safer bet than one with 300 installs and no activity in 18 months.

## The essential plugin starter pack

Here are the six plugin categories every small-business WordPress site should address, along with specific recommendations for each:

- **SEO:** Search engine optimization determines how visible your site is in Google and other search engines. Yoast SEO (`yoast.com`) is the long-established standard. It analyzes each page for SEO factors and gives you a traffic-light score with specific improvement suggestions. Rank Math (`rankmath.com`) is a newer competitor that includes many advanced features in its free version. Either is an excellent choice; install one and stick with it.
- **Security:** Wordfence Security (`wordfence.com`) provides a web application firewall, a malware scanner, and login protection in a single free plugin. Solid Security (`solidwp.com`) is another respected option with a friendly setup wizard. Either will dramatically improve your site's security compared to running WordPress without a security plugin.
- **Backups:** UpdraftPlus (`updraftplus.com`) is the most popular WordPress backup plugin, with over three million active installations. It backs up your files

and database on a schedule you set, and can automatically send copies to cloud storage services — Google Drive, Dropbox, Amazon S3, and others — so your backups are safely stored off-site. Configure it on day one, before anything goes wrong.

- **Contact forms:** WPForms (`wpforms.com`) offers a drag-and-drop form builder that's beginner-friendly, with the free Lite version sufficient for standard contact forms. Contact Form 7 (`contactform7.com`) is a powerful, free alternative with a devoted user base. WPForms is more polished to set up; Contact Form 7 is leaner and more code-friendly.
- **Performance and caching:** Without caching, WordPress regenerates each page from scratch every time a visitor arrives. A *caching plugin* saves a static copy of each page and serves that instead, making your site noticeably faster. WP Super Cache (`wordpress.org/plugins/wp-super-cache`) is a free, reliable option that works well on virtually any host. If your host uses LiteSpeed web servers, LiteSpeed Cache (`www.litespeedtech.com/products/cache-plugins/wordpress-acceleration`) is even better and also free.
- **Analytics:** Site Kit by Google (`sitekit.withgoogle.com`) is Google's official plugin for connecting your WordPress site to Google Analytics 4, Google Search Console, and other Google tools. MonsterInsights (`monsterinsights.com`) is a popular alternative that presents analytics data in a clean and readable layout in the WordPress dashboard. Both make it easy to understand where your visitors come from and which pages they visit most.



With these six categories covered, your site is findable in search, protected from common threats, recoverable from data loss, reachable via contact form, fast enough to keep visitors engaged, and connected to the analytics data you'll need to make informed decisions.

WARNING

A final note on plugin discipline: resist the temptation to install more plugins than you need. Every plugin adds overhead to your site, and every plugin is a security surface that must be kept updated. A lean, purposeful set of eight to twelve well-chosen plugins is almost always healthier than a sprawling collection of thirty. If you install a plugin to try it and it doesn't work out, deactivate and delete it rather than leaving it dormant.

# Building Pages with the Block Editor

For many years, creating content in WordPress meant using a plain-text editor that felt more like writing an email than designing a web page. In late 2018, WordPress introduced a new editing experience called the *block editor*, officially named Gutenberg, after the fifteenth-century printing pioneer. (WordPress has a fondness for naming major projects after publishing luminaries.) Today, the block editor is the default for all new WordPress installations, and it's a step forward in how pages are built.

## Thinking in blocks

The central concept is exactly what it sounds like: every piece of content on a page is a *block*. A paragraph of text is a block. An image is a block. A heading is a block. A button is a block. A video embed, a pull quote, a horizontal spacer, a data table — all blocks. You build pages by inserting, arranging, and configuring individual blocks.

Each block has its own toolbar that appears when you click it, giving you quick access to formatting options (shown a bit later in Figure 1-2). A more comprehensive settings sidebar appears on the right side of the screen when a block is selected (also shown later in Figure 1-2). A Paragraph block lets you change the font size, text color, and line height. An Image block lets you set alt text, choose a display size, and add a caption. A Button block lets you set the destination URL, the label text, the background color, and the text color. Most settings are controlled through visual interface elements, so no HTML or CSS knowledge is required.

To add a new block, click the blue plus-sign icon that appears when you hover near an empty area of the page, or at the very bottom of the existing content. A small popup shows your recently used blocks; click the search icon to browse all available blocks organized by category.

## The most useful blocks for business pages

WordPress ships with a large selection of built-in blocks. For typical small business pages, a core set of them covers the vast majority of what you'll need:

- **Paragraph:** The basic text block. The bulk of your body copy lives here.
- **Heading:** Creates H2, H3, and lower-level headings to organize your page. Your page title is automatically assigned as the H1, so start your section headings at H2.
- **Image:** Adds a photo or graphic from your media library or lets you upload a new one. You can set alignment, add a caption, and control how the image displays at different screen sizes.

- **Buttons:** Creates one or more call-to-action buttons with customizable colors, text, border radius, and link destinations. Useful for directing visitors toward a specific next step.
- **Columns:** Creates a multi-column layout. You choose the number of columns and the width distribution, then fill each column with any other blocks you like: text, images, buttons, whatever the layout calls for.
- **Cover:** Places text content over a background image or solid color. Commonly used for hero sections at the top of a page or for creating visually distinct dividers between major sections.
- **Group:** A container block that wraps multiple blocks together. You can apply a shared background color, padding, or border styling to the entire group, which is handy for creating visually distinct sections on a page.
- **List:** Creates bulleted or numbered lists. Simple and frequently useful for services, features, and step-by-step instructions.

## Building a page with the block editor

Here's how a typical page-building session goes in practice. Imagine you want to create an "About Us" page for Orbital Donuts.

In the dashboard sidebar, click Pages ➪ Add Page. If the Choose a Pattern window shows up, you can either click a starter pattern or click Close (X) to move on. The block editor appears.

At the top of the editor is a large placeholder that says "Add title." Click it and type your page title: "About Orbital Donuts." The title becomes the page's H1 heading automatically.

Below the title area, click the plus-sign button (or press /) to add your first block. Choose Paragraph and write a friendly, inviting opening paragraph about the company.

Press Enter, add an H2 Heading, "Our Story," then add a couple of paragraphs that spell out a brief history of the business. As shown in Figure 1-2, each time you add a block, you can click inside the block and then make formatting or design changes using either the toolbar or the sidebar.

Press Enter, add another H2, "What Makes Us Different," then add a List block and enter four or five compelling reasons as bullet items. Finish the page with a Buttons block: a single button labeled "Get in Touch" that links to your contact page.

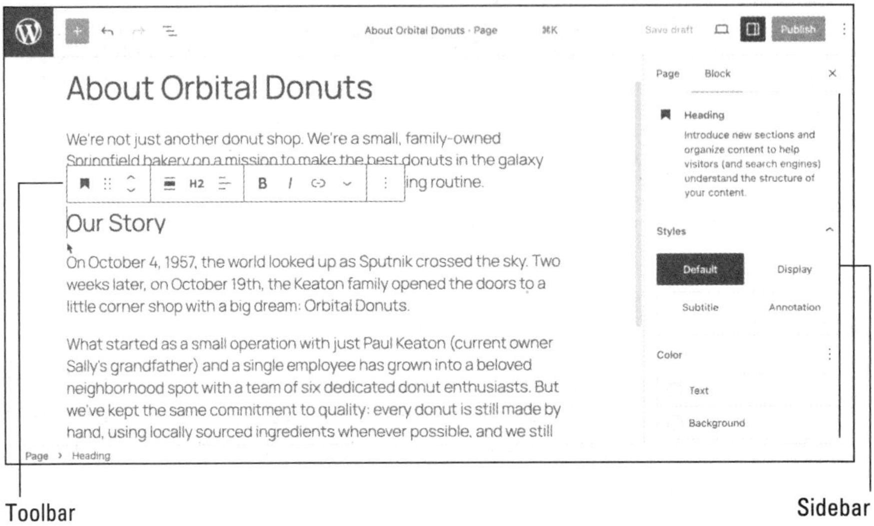


**FIGURE 1-2:** In the block editor, click a block to display its formatting options in the toolbar and sidebar.

When the page looks the way you want it, click the blue Publish button in the upper-right corner. Your page is live. To edit it in the future, select Pages ➪ All Pages in the dashboard and click the page title to reopen the editor.

TIP

Recent versions of WordPress support a feature called *Full Site Editing* (FSE), which extends the block editor beyond individual pages to your entire site's structure — headers, footers, navigation menus, and page templates. If you install a block theme built specifically for FSE, you can modify virtually every aspect of your site's appearance from the Appearance ➪ Editor screen, without touching a single theme file. It's worth exploring once you're comfortable with the basics of the block editor.

# Page Builders: Elementor and Alternatives

The block editor is capable and keeps improving with each WordPress release. But some people — particularly those who come from a graphic design background or who want more precise visual control than Gutenberg currently offers — prefer to use a dedicated *page builder* instead. A page builder is a plugin that replaces or supplements the block editor with a richer drag-and-drop design canvas, typically offering more granular control over layout, spacing, and visual styling.

Whether you'll want a page builder depends on your design goals and your comfort with the block editor. If Gutenberg gives you what you need (and for most small business sites, it does), there's no reason to add one. If you find yourself frequently frustrated by layout limitations, a page builder is worth investigating.

## What page builders bring to the table

The key advantages page builders offer over the native block editor include:

- » More precise control over spacing, margins, and padding at the element level, without writing CSS
- » Freeform positioning on some builders, allowing elements to be layered and overlapped rather than stacked strictly top-to-bottom
- » Larger libraries of pre-built section templates and full-page designs that let you assemble a polished layout in minutes
- » Specialized widgets beyond what WordPress includes natively, such as pricing tables, testimonial carousels, countdown timers, and interactive image galleries
- » Per-breakpoint responsive controls that let you specify different layouts, font sizes, or spacing for mobile, tablet, and desktop separately

The trade-offs are real. Page builders add significant weight to your pages, which can slow load times if not carefully managed. They can also create vendor lock-in: if you build your entire site in one builder and then decide to switch themes or builders later, your pages may display as jumbles of raw text rather than the polished layouts you designed. And page builders add complexity to your WordPress installation, with more settings to manage and more things that can potentially conflict with other plugins or future updates.



## Elementor: The most popular choice

Elementor (`elementor.com`) is by far the most widely used WordPress page builder, with over 22 million active installations. Its appeal is straightforward: the editing interface is intuitive, the free version is functional, and the Pro version unlocks a large additional feature set at a reasonable price.

Elementor's interface divides the screen into two sections: a widget library and settings panel on the left, and a live preview of your page on the right. You drag a widget from the left panel and drop it onto the page preview, then configure it using the settings that appear in the left panel. Changes update in the preview immediately. The experience feels closer to using a design tool like Figma or Canva than to working in a traditional content editor.

The free version of Elementor includes a solid selection of widgets — heading, text, image, button, divider, icon, video, and more — plus a useful library of section templates. Elementor Pro (starting at $5 per month, billed annually, for a single site) adds more than 50 additional widgets (including a form builder, a popup builder, and a pricing table), a theme builder for designing headers and footers visually, and a much larger template library.

For most small business sites, Elementor Free covers the basics well. If your site specifically needs custom forms, a sticky header, pop-ups triggered by user behavior, or WooCommerce customizations, Elementor Pro is likely worth the annual fee.

## Other page builders worth knowing

Elementor is the market leader, but it's not the only solid option. A couple of others are worth knowing about:

- **Beaver Builder (`wpbeaverbuilder.com`)**: A well-established page builder known for producing clean HTML output and reliable performance. It's particularly popular among WordPress developers who build sites for clients, partly because the resulting pages remain stable and readable even after updates. Less flashy than Elementor, but often more dependable. The standard license starts at $89 per year.
- **Divi (`elegantthemes.com`)**: An all-in-one product from Elegant Themes that combines a page builder with its own WordPress theme. Divi has a passionate following and an extensive library of pre-built page layouts. At $89 per year, or a one-time lifetime license for $249, it's good value if you plan to build multiple sites. Note that Divi couples the builder tightly to its theme, which is something to consider if you ever want to switch themes later.

REMEMBER

You don't need a page builder to build a great WordPress site. The block editor is capable, free, and built right in. Only reach for a page builder if you've identified a specific need it addresses that Gutenberg can't meet. The best tool is the one that gets your site finished and in front of your customers.

# WordPress Security Best Practices

WordPress's enormous popularity is, as I mention earlier in this chapter, a double-edged sword. The same ubiquity that gives you such a rich ecosystem of themes, plugins, and community support also makes WordPress the most frequently targeted content management system on the internet. Automated bots trawl millions of sites every day, probing for outdated plugins, weak passwords, and known software vulnerabilities. They don't care whether your site is a major e-commerce operation or a tiny neighborhood donut shop. Size doesn't matter to a script.

The encouraging news is that the overwhelming majority of successful WordPress attacks exploit entirely preventable mistakes. Follow the practices in this section and you'll be dramatically better protected than the average WordPress site out there.

## Why WordPress sites get hacked

Before getting into defenses, it helps to understand what attackers are actually after. The most common attack vectors are:

» **Outdated plugins and themes:** This is the single most common attack vector, by a wide margin. When a security researcher discovers a vulnerability in a plugin or theme, both the developer (who issues a patch) and attackers (who write automated scanning tools) learn about it at roughly the same time. Sites that apply the patch quickly are protected. Sites that let updates sit unapplied for weeks get added to the to-be-hacked list.

» **Weak passwords and brute-force attacks:** Automated tools systematically try common username and password combinations at the WordPress login page (`wp-login.php`). With no login-attempt limits in place, a bot can try thousands of combinations per minute. If your admin password is something predictable or your username is "admin," it's a matter of time, not chance.

» **Nulled themes and plugins:** As I mention earlier in this chapter, pirated premium software very frequently contains malicious code inserted by whoever cracked it. That code can create hidden admin accounts, redirect your visitors to harmful sites, or use your server to send spam.

» **Insecure hosting environments:** Occasionally the vulnerability isn't in WordPress itself but in the hosting environment: an outdated version of PHP, a misconfigured server, or a neighboring site on shared hosting that gets compromised and spreads the infection. This is one reason why choosing a reputable, actively maintained host matters more than just getting the cheapest possible price.

None of these are exotic attack methods. They're all straightforward to address with a bit of discipline and the right tools.

## Your security checklist

Here's the practical set of security measures every WordPress site should have in place:

- **Keep everything updated.** WordPress core, themes, and plugins all receive security updates regularly. In the dashboard, select Dashboard ➪ Updates to see everything available and apply updates promptly. Don't let a backlog of updates accumulate. For minor WordPress core releases — the kind that patch security issues without changing features — consider enabling automatic updates in Dashboard ➪ Updates.
- **Use strong, unique passwords.** Your WordPress admin password should be long, random, and used nowhere else. WordPress's built-in password generator creates strong passwords automatically when you create or update a user account. A password manager like Bitwarden (`bitwarden.com`, free) stores them for you and fills them in automatically, so you never need to memorize them.
- **Enable two-factor authentication.** Two-factor authentication (2FA) requires a second proof of identity — usually a time-sensitive code generated by an authenticator app on your phone — in addition to your password at login. Even if an attacker somehow obtains your password, they can't log in without the second factor. The WP 2FA plugin (`wp2fa.io`) makes this straightforward to configure for all your WordPress users.
- **Install a security plugin.** As I mention in the plugins section above, a plugin like Wordfence or Solid Security provides a web application firewall and malware scanning that can identify and block threats before they do damage. Both have free versions that are effective for most small business sites.
- **Limit login attempts.** Brute-force attacks depend on the ability to make unlimited login attempts without consequence. A plugin like Limit Login Attempts Reloaded (`limitloginattempts.com`) locks out an IP address after a configurable number of consecutive failed logins, making automated credential-stuffing attacks largely ineffective.
- **Maintain regular backups.** Security measures reduce the risk of something going wrong, but they don't reduce it to zero. A reliable backup strategy means that even if your site is compromised or experiences a catastrophic failure, you can restore it to a recent known-good state. Configure UpdraftPlus (or your managed host's built-in backup feature) to run daily, and store copies off-site, not just on your hosting server. Also, be sure to test restoring from a backup to make sure that crucial step works for you.

WARNING

Use caution with automatic plugin updates. While enabling auto-updates for minor WordPress core releases is generally safe and recommended, plugin updates occasionally introduce bugs or conflicts with other plugins or your theme. A common practical approach is to enable auto-updates only for your security-focused plugins, so they're patched immediately when vulnerabilities are found. Handle other plugin updates manually, reviewing the changelog first.

Security is an ongoing habit, not a one-time setup task. Make a point of checking your Updates screen at least once a week. Review your security plugin's scan results periodically and address any flagged issues promptly. Log in to the dashboard now and then just to confirm that everything looks normal and no unfamiliar admin accounts have appeared. A few minutes of regular attention is what stands between your site and the bots — and it really does make a difference.

One final thought: because the WordPress community is so large and so active, its security practices are some of the best documented in the web development world. If you run into a security issue you're not sure how to handle, the WordPress support forums at `wordpress.org/support` and the Wordfence blog at `wordfence.com/blog` are two of the most useful resources you'll find anywhere. You're not navigating this alone.

IN THIS CHAPTER

» Getting a professional site fast with Wix and Squarespace

» Designing with code-level precision using Webflow

» Creating design-forward, interactive sites with Framer

» Picking the platform that fits your project and your skills

# Chapter 2
# Visual Website Builders

*Good design is good business.*

—THOMAS WATSON JR.

Imagine dragging a headline exactly where you want it, choosing a font from a dropdown, tweaking the colors to match your brand, and clicking Publish, all without writing a single HTML tag or CSS rule. Your finished, professional website goes live before lunch. That sounds like a fantasy, but it's what visual website builders are designed to do.

In Books 3 and 4 you learn to build websites the traditional way. That knowledge is genuinely valuable because it makes you a sharper, more informed builder no matter which tools you use. But for many real-world projects, a visual builder gets you to a finished site far faster than writing every tag or declaration by hand. This chapter covers the four most capable builders available today, what each one does well, and how to choose the right one for your project.

# Wix and Squarespace: The Fast Lane to a Professional Site

Wix and Squarespace are *all-in-one hosted* platforms: they handle the server, security, backups, and software updates so you can focus on your content. Pay a monthly subscription and you get the whole package. No hosting account to manage, no FTP client, no worrying about whether your server went down at 2 a.m.

They share the same broad philosophy but express different personalities. Wix leans toward maximum flexibility and open-canvas editing. Squarespace favors design elegance and a curated, everything-fits-together approach. The right choice often comes down to which personality matches yours.

## Getting started with Wix

Wix (`wix.com`) launched in 2006 and has grown to more than 250 million users. The original Wix Website Editor (check out Figure 2-1) is a true drag-and-drop canvas: pick up any element — text, image, button, video — and drop it anywhere on the page with near-pixel precision. Nothing is locked to a grid. The newer Wix Harmony Editor is AI-based and takes a more structured, grid-based approach suited to web professionals. For most first-time builders, the original Website Editor is the better starting point.

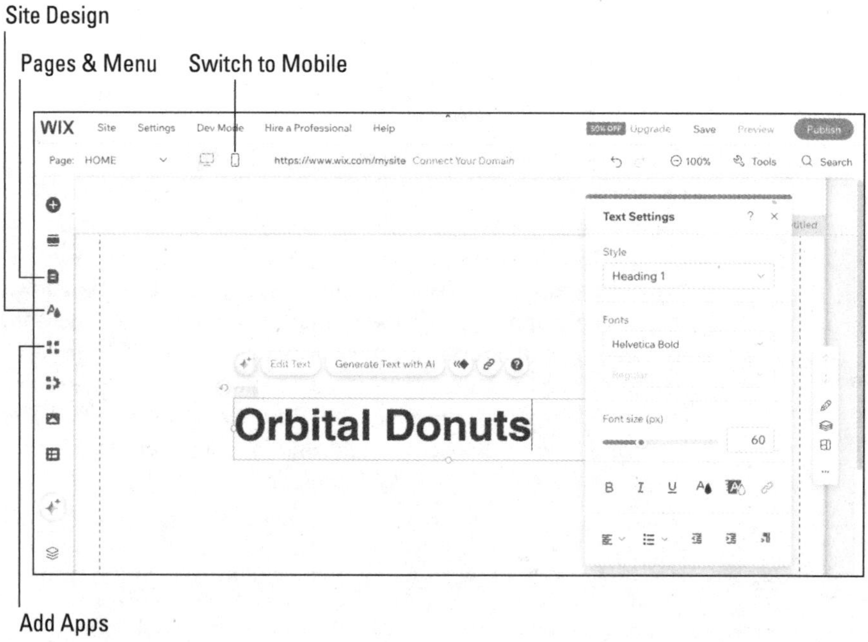


**FIGURE 2-1:** The Wix Website Editor: your drag-til-you-drop canvas.

Every element in Wix is fully customizable: background color, border, shadow, corner radius, font, and spacing are all adjustable from the panel that appears when you click something. The Site Design panel (click the icon labeled in Figure 2-1) enables you to set a global color palette and font pairing that apply across the entire site, so changing your primary color in one place updates the color everywhere it's used. Wix also includes a built-in image editor with cropping, filters, and AI background removal, so you can handle basic image adjustments without opening a separate application.

Wix's App Market (click the Add Apps icon, pointed out in Figure 2-1) is one of its greatest practical strengths. Hundreds of add-ons are available in a few clicks:

- **Wix Stores:** Full e-commerce with product pages, inventory, and checkout
- **Wix Bookings:** Appointment scheduling and payment collection
- **Wix Restaurants:** Online ordering, menu management, and table reservations
- **Wix Blog, Events, Members:** Content and community tools, all installable in one click

The flip side of Wix's drag-and-drop freedom is that it's easier to create a desktop design that becomes a confusing jumble on a phone screen. The Website Editor has a separate mobile view (click the Switch to Mobile icon pointed out in Figure 2-1) and checking it regularly as you build is highly recommended. Wix does some automatic mobile layout adjustment, but it can't anticipate every positioning decision you make. Plan for at least one round of mobile-specific adjustments once your desktop layout is settled.

Pages and navigation in Wix are managed from the Site Pages and Menu panel (click the Pages & Menu icon on the left side of the editor; refer to Figure 2-1). Adding a new page is a single click: name it and choose a blank layout or a predesigned page template, and Wix adds it to your navigation menu automatically. You can reorder pages by dragging them, set up dropdown submenus for multilevel navigation, and hide pages from the public menu while keeping them accessible by direct URL, which is useful for things like a thank-you page that should be reachable only after a form submission.

Wix also includes a solid SEO panel on every page (in the Site Pages and Menu panel, click the page, click the three dots, and then click SEO Basics) that comes with a guided SEO checklist tailored to your site type.

WARNING

One important constraint to plan for: once you choose a template and start building, you *can't* switch to a different template without starting over. The content doesn't transfer, so choose your template carefully before committing.

Pricing starts with a free tier (Wix branding, Wix subdomain). Paid plans start around $17/month for a custom domain and scale up for e-commerce and higher storage. Annual billing saves roughly 30–40 percent. The App Market apps also carry their own fees — factor those in when estimating the total monthly cost.

**TIP**

Wix AI Website Builder can generate a complete starter site — layout, colors, placeholder content — based on a few questions about your business. It's a fast way past the blank-canvas problem, even if you plan to customize heavily.

## Getting started with Squarespace

Squarespace (`squarespace.com`) has fostered its identity around design quality, and that identity is well-earned. Built on the Fluid Engine layout system, its templates are widely considered the most polished available in any website builder. If you've ever seen a small-business or portfolio site with a strikingly beautiful design, there's a good chance it was Squarespace.

The Squarespace editing experience is *block-based:* you add content blocks (text, images, galleries, buttons, forms) in structured sections. You can't position elements with pixel-level freedom the way you can in Wix, but that constraint tends to produce more consistently professional results because it prevents the layout mistakes that open-canvas editors can invite. The Site Styles panel (see Figure 2-2) sets your global color palette, font pairing, and button defaults. Because Squarespace's templates are pretuned to use those global values, a single color change can refresh the look of the entire site in seconds. A dedicated Custom CSS panel is available when the visual controls don't quite reach the result you need.

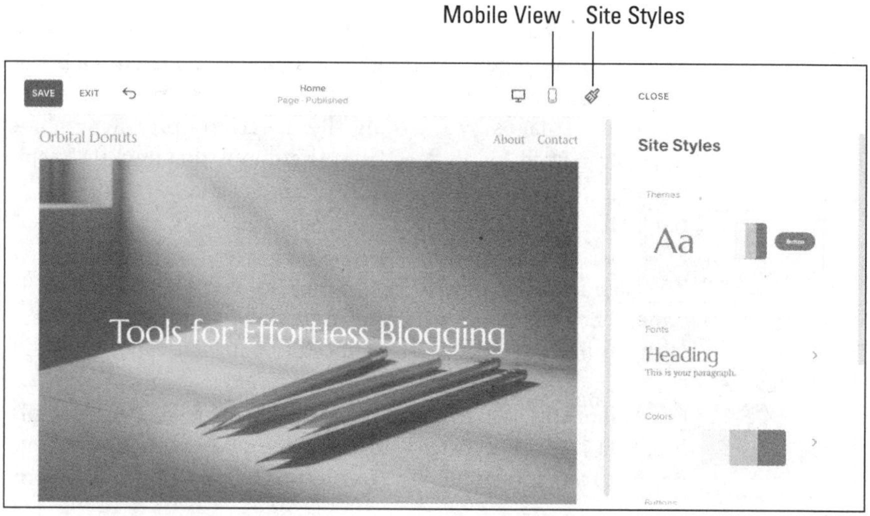


**FIGURE 2-2:** The Squarespace Site Styles panel.

Squarespace's core strengths include:

- **Design quality:** Deploy consistently polished templates with excellent typography and image handling.
- **Built-in features:** Blogging, e-commerce, appointment scheduling, email campaigns, and analytics are all included.
- **Image-heavy sites:** Photographers, restaurants, boutiques, and portfolios get outstanding results with minimal effort.
- **Custom CSS:** A dedicated panel for site-wide CSS overrides when the visual tools aren't quite enough.
- **Squarespace email campaigns:** Design and send newsletters using the same block editor as the website, keeping your look consistent.

Squarespace is especially strong for image-heavy sites. Photographers, architects, restaurant owners, and boutique retailers consistently produce attractive results with relatively little effort. The template library skews toward the creative and hospitality industries, and the image-editing tools — including built-in cropping, focal-point control, and gallery layout options — are among the best in this category. If your site's primary job is to make your visual work look great, Squarespace should be at or near the top of your shortlist.

Pricing starts at around $16 per month for a personal site and scales up for more feature-rich plans. Annual billing is significantly cheaper than monthly. Unlike Wix, Squarespace doesn't rely heavily on a third-party app marketplace to fill feature gaps. Most of what you'll need is already included in the plan, which makes the total monthly cost more predictable. The Extensions marketplace does exist for specialized integrations (shipping services, accounting tools, marketing platforms), but you're unlikely to need many.

TIP

Squarespace offers a 14-day free trial with no credit card required. You can build out much of a site before committing to a plan, so it's a commitment-free way to judge whether the platform suits you.

## Choosing between Wix and Squarespace

Both Wix and Squarespace are excellent platforms for their intended audiences. Here's the short version:

- **Choose Wix** if you want drag-and-drop freedom, you need a specific third-party app, or your project might grow in unpredictable directions that App Market can accommodate.

» **Choose Squarespace** if design quality is your overriding priority, you want as many built-in features as possible, or you're building an image-heavy site like a portfolio, restaurant, or boutique.

» **Choose either** if you want a professionally managed all-in-one platform with no server management and a workflow that stays firmly in the visual editor.

WARNING

Migrating content between Wix and Squarespace is painful since neither platform provides a clean export-and-import path. Switching means manually rebuilding your site, page by page, from scratch. Any custom design work you've done, any SEO momentum your URLs have accumulated, and any integrations you've set up all need to be recreated. Choose carefully at the outset. The time you spend picking the right platform upfront pays for itself many times over compared to switching after months of active building.

# Webflow: Visual Design with Code-Level Control

Webflow (`webflow.com`) is something different from the Wix and Squarespace platforms. When you design in Webflow's visual editor, the platform writes real, standards-compliant HTML, CSS, and JavaScript instead of a proprietary layer that runs on only Webflow's servers. The code is exportable, loads fast, and tends to score well on search-engine performance metrics because minimal runtime overhead is layered on top of it.

The trade-off is a steeper learning curve. Because Webflow exposes CSS concepts — the box model, flexbox, grid, breakpoints — through its visual controls, you need some grounding in how those work before the interface makes intuitive sense. If you worked through Books 3 and 4, you already have that grounding — Webflow will feel like a visual extension of what you learned, and the controls will map cleanly to concepts you already understand. Without that foundation, expect a longer orientation period.

The return on that investment is substantial. Webflow gives you a level of visual control that Wix and Squarespace cannot match, a CMS that handles structured content far more flexibly, and output code that a developer can work with directly if the site ever outgrows the platform. For builders who want to produce custom designs that don't look like any identifiable template, Webflow is the tool.

Webflow's hosting infrastructure also deserves a brief mention. Sites are served through a global CDN with automatic SSL certificates. Because the output is clean, static HTML and CSS with no heavy runtime framework being loaded alongside it, Webflow sites consistently score well on Google's Core Web Vitals metrics, which are the performance signals Google uses in its search-ranking algorithm. For businesses where search visibility matters, the combination of clean code and fast hosting is a meaningful practical advantage over more abstracted, heavier-weight platforms.

## Building responsive sites visually

The heart of Webflow is Designer (refer to Figure 2-3), a browser-based application with three main areas: the Navigator panel (your HTML element tree) on the left, the Style panel (every CSS property for the selected element) on the right, and the canvas in the center. Every element you add and every style you apply maps directly to HTML and CSS. Webflow is giving you visual handles for the code, not hiding it.

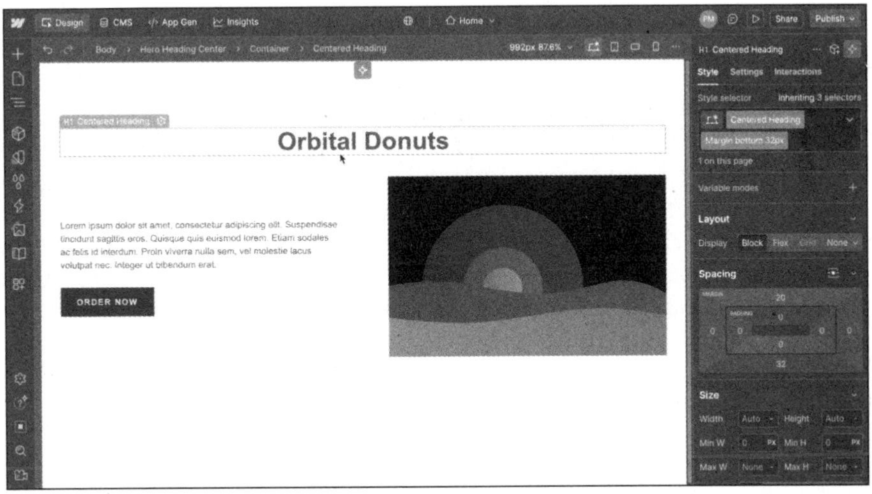


**FIGURE 2-3:** The Webflow Designer app.

Several Designer features are worth highlighting for new Webflow users:

- **Class-based styling:** Just like CSS, elements share styles through classes. Update a class and every element using it updates instantly.
- **Box model visualization:** Hover your cursor over any element to see the margin (orange), the padding (green), and the element itself (blue) rendered graphically, making the box model concrete.
- **Flexbox and grid controls:** Both layout systems are available as visual controls; no manual CSS syntax required.

» **Breakpoints:** Desktop is the base; switch to tablet, mobile landscape, and mobile portrait modes and adjust as needed. Changes cascade down to smaller sizes unless overridden, exactly as CSS media queries do.

» **Components:** Reusable components (nav, footer, cards) update everywhere when you edit the original.

The overall workflow in Webflow follows a consistent pattern: build the structure in Navigator, style each element using the Style panel, test at each breakpoint and adjust, connect any dynamic content to CMS Collections, and then publish. Internalizing this rhythm will require a few projects, but once it clicks, the workflow will be remarkably efficient for building polished, production-ready sites.

Webflow also supports global code injection in Project Settings, allowing you to add third-party scripts, analytics tags, or custom meta elements to every page without editing each one individually. And images uploaded to Webflow are stored on its CDN and automatically served in multiple sizes based on screen resolution, so you get responsive image behavior (which you'd have to implement manually in handwritten HTML) without any extra work.

# The Webflow CMS

The Webflow CMS enables you to define any content structure you need, set it up as a template, and have Webflow generate the pages automatically. The fundamental concept is the *collection:* a structured content type with fields you define, including plain text, rich text, images, numbers, dates, links, and references to other collections. A veterinary practice might have a Doctors collection with Name, Photo, Specialty, and Bio fields. Define the collection, design one template page, connect each element to its corresponding field, and Webflow builds a separate page for every doctor automatically. Add a doctor to the spreadsheet-style editor and the page appears on the live site immediately. No code, no HTML editing.

You can also place CMS content on any non-template page by using collection lists, which are dynamically generated grids, carousels, or feeds pulled from a collection. Drop a collection list on your home page, connect it to the Recipes collection, choose how many items to display, set the sort order, and style the card layout. The data lives in the collection; the visual presentation is whatever you design. This is how you build a Latest Blog Posts section, a Meet the Team grid, or a Featured Projects row without touching a line of code.

The CMS supports two distinct working modes:

» **Designer:** The full visual editor where you configure structure and style; used by builders and developers

» **Editor:** A simplified content-only overlay where clients update text and images without touching the design controls

This separation makes Webflow a strong choice for professional web work. You can hand a client a site where they can update their own content confidently without risking accidental design changes. The editor requires no Webflow account knowledge. Clients just log in to a URL, see editable fields highlighted on the live page, make their changes, and click Publish.

The CMS also handles SEO for dynamic pages automatically. Every CMS template page can connect its page title, meta description, and Open Graph image to Collection fields, so each item in the Collection gets its own properly titled, properly described search result entry without you having to set them individually. For a site with a hundred blog posts or a hundred product pages, this dynamic SEO generation saves an enormous amount of repetitive work.

## Interactions and animations

Webflow's Interactions panel lets you add animations and scroll-triggered effects without writing JavaScript. You connect an interaction to a trigger — page load, scroll into view, click, hover — and build a timeline of actions, such as set opacity to 0, move 40 px down, and then animate to opacity 1 and position 0 over 0.4 seconds. Animation speeds are configurable. Multiple animated elements can be choreographed in the same timeline.

Common uses for Webflow Interactions include:

» **Scroll animations:** Elements fade or slide in as they enter the viewport.

» **Hover effects:** Cards lift, images scale, overlays fade in when hovered over.

» **Lottie animations:** Vector animations are exported from After Effects as JSON files, for logo animations, illustrations, or loading states.

REMEMBER

Use animations with intention, not abundance. Scroll effects on every section add cognitive noise. Always test on mobile devices and respect the `prefers-reduced-motion` media query for users who find motion uncomfortable.

## Webflow pricing and the learning investment

Webflow has two pricing options: one for in-house teams and one for freelancers and designers. The latter covers your designer account (a free workspace allows two projects, which is enough to learn the platform and build a first site). In-house plans cover hosting for individual sites: free to a Webflow subdomain, paid plans from around $14/month for a custom domain, with CMS-enabled plans starting higher. See `webflow.com/pricing` for current figures, as the structure evolves.

The more significant investment is time. Expect to spend several hours in Designer to get comfortable before building confidently. The official *Webflow University* at `university.webflow.com` is one of the best free web education resources available. It includes well-produced video courses covering everything from Designer basics to advanced CMS and interactions. I strongly recommend that you work through the foundational series before creating your first real project. The few hours of investment will save many more hours of confusion.

# Framer: Where Design Meets Interactivity

Framer (`framer.com`) started as a code-based prototyping tool used by interaction designers at companies such as Google and Spotify. In 2022 it reinvented itself as a full website builder, bringing its design-forward sensibility to a much wider audience. Today Framer sits in a distinctive spot: more visually sophisticated than Wix or Squarespace, more intuitive to learn than Webflow, and particularly well-suited for landing pages, portfolios, and product marketing sites where visual quality and interactivity are the primary objectives.

The entire workflow is built around the idea that a skilled designer should be able to take an idea from first sketch to live, custom-domain website without waiting on an engineer. For solo creators and small marketing teams that need to move quickly, that premise is valuable. Framer's publishing pipeline is the fastest in this chapter: You click Publish and the site is live in seconds, with no build step, no deployment dashboard, and no FTP client.

## The Framer design canvas

Framer's canvas (see Figure 2-4) looks and feels like Figma, which is intentional since Framer deliberately modeled its interface after Figma to make it easier for designers to use the site. You work with *frames* (containers), text layers, image layers, and shape layers. If you've designed in Figma or Sketch, the gesture vocabulary will feel immediately familiar. The most important structural concept is the *component:* a reusable design element you build once and reuse throughout the site. Update the component definition and every instance updates automatically, so it's the visual equivalent of a CSS class at the element level.

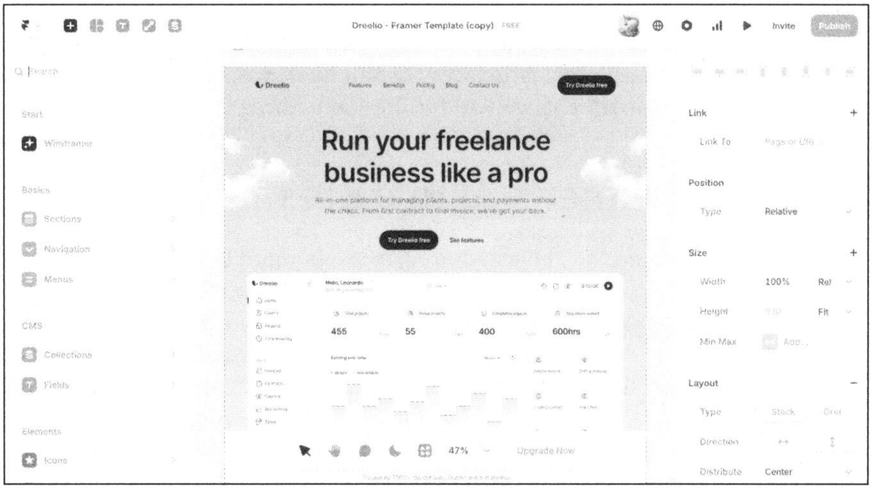


**FIGURE 2-4:** Framer's canvas.

Framer also has built-in breakpoints for responsive design: you set your desktop layout as the base, and then switch to tablet and mobile views and adjust. Changes cascade from larger to smaller breakpoints unless explicitly overridden at a smaller size. This is the same logic as CSS media queries, which should feel familiar from Book 3, Chapter 4. The combination of auto-layout and breakpoints means that well-structured Framer designs tend to hold together at multiple screen sizes with minimal manual adjustment, which is a meaningful advantage over pure drag-and-drop tools that require you to redo the layout from scratch at each breakpoint.

Key Framer concepts for new users:

- **Variants:** Alternate states of a component (Default, Hover, Active) managed at the component level without manual class juggling
- **Auto-layout:** Framer's visual flexbox; items reflow automatically as content changes, making responsive behavior predictable
- **Variables and tokens:** Named values for colors, type sizes, and spacing that update everywhere when changed in one place
- **Code components:** React components from the community marketplace that add custom interactions, charts, or 3D elements beyond what the visual tools provide

Auto-layout in particular is one of the features that most clearly separates Framer from older-generation drag-and-drop builders. Because frames reflow automatically as content changes, the responsive behavior of an auto-layout container is predictable in a way that manually positioned elements simply aren't. Once you've worked with auto-layout for an hour, manually repositioning every element after a content change will feel like something from the past.

## Framer's AI features

Framer has invested in AI features more heavily than any other platform in this chapter, and the results are practical rather than merely headline-generating. The standout is *AI page generation:* describe your site in a sentence or two — for example, "A landscape photography portfolio with a dark, dramatic aesthetic" or "A consulting firm focused on sustainable supply chain management" — and Framer generates a complete, styled, multisection starting point in seconds. The result won't be a finished site: you'll need to replace the placeholder text, swap in your images, and adjust the layout to match your brand. But the structural scaffold is surprisingly relevant to the description, and customizing an imperfect starting point is almost always faster than building from a blank canvas.

Additional AI tools are woven throughout the editor:

- **Copy assist:** Headline rewrites, shorter summary text, and call to action (CTA) suggestions as you type
- **AI image generation:** Placeholder images and section backgrounds from a text description, useful before final photography is ready
- **Smart layout suggestions:** Component and section recommendations based on the content you're working with

The cumulative effect makes Framer appealing to solo builders doing the work of designer, copywriter, and developer. The AI features don't replace expertise in any of those roles, but they do significantly reduce the friction of context-switching between them, which describes the day-to-day reality of most independent web builders.

## Publishing and the Framer CMS

Publishing in Framer is about as frictionless as website publishing gets. Click Publish, wait a few seconds, and the site is live at a Framer subdomain like `*yourname*.framer.website`. Connecting a custom domain takes about five minutes and a DNS record change at your registrar (covered in Book 1, Chapter 3). Framer handles the SSL certificate automatically. The feedback loop between making a change and seeing it live is one of the fastest in the visual website builder category.

Framer's built-in CMS manages dynamic content: blog posts, case studies, team members, product announcements. Define a collection, add content through a clean data-entry interface, and Framer generates the pages. The CMS is less structurally complex than Webflow's, but for the most common use cases — such as a blog, a portfolio, a team directory — it provides everything you need without the overhead of learning Webflow's more sophisticated collection system.

Framer integrates natively with Google Analytics, Fathom, and Plausible, and includes a built-in analytics dashboard on paid plans. Real-time team collaboration is also available on team plans. Pricing starts with a useful free plan (Framer subdomain, no credit card), with custom-domain plans from around $10 per month, which is the most affordable entry point for a custom-domain site in this chapter.

TIP

Framer's free plan lets you build and publish a complete site at no cost. The meaningful upgrade trigger is the custom domain: if you need *yourbusiness*`.com` rather than a Framer subdomain, the paid plan earns its cost.

# Choosing the Right Platform for Your Project

Four platforms, four personalities. None of them is the universally right choice because each produces professional results in the right context. The honest answer to "Which one should I use?" is almost always "It depends," and the things it depends on are worth spelling out.

One thing worth acknowledging before you dive into the decision: it's possible to overthink this. All four platforms will produce a result far better than not having a website at all. If you're stuck between options, pick the simplest one that fits your needs and start. You can always reassess once you have more experience. And building something imperfect now is almost always better than waiting for the perfect tool.

That said, your choice does have consequences. The platform shapes the editing experience for you and anyone else who maintains the site. The platform determines which integrations are available, how much the site costs each month, and — in Webflow's case — whether the underlying code can be taken elsewhere if your needs outgrow the platform. It's worth spending 20 or 30 minutes with the following questions before committing.

## Questions to ask before you choose

Before committing to a platform, run through these questions. None has a single correct answer — they're meant to surface your priorities and constraints:

- **How familiar are you with web design concepts?** If flexbox, the box model, and media queries are unfamiliar, start with Wix or Squarespace. If you worked through Books 3 and 4, Webflow will feel like a natural extension of what you already know.
- **How important is design quality?** For a site where visual sophistication is the primary measure of success, Squarespace and Framer are the strongest choices. Squarespace excels at restrained editorial elegance; Framer at modern interactive polish.
- **Do you need structured, dynamic content?** For a blog, portfolio, staff directory, or product catalog that must be easy to update, Webflow's CMS is the most powerful and flexible option. Framer's CMS handles common cases cleanly. Wix and Squarespace include blogging but are less flexible for custom content structures.
- **What's your budget, including your time?** Framer is the cheapest entry for a custom-domain site. Wix and Squarespace sit in the midrange. Webflow's CMS plans cost more. But also factor in learning time: if Webflow takes four weeks before you build confidently and Squarespace takes two days, the economics may favor Squarespace even if the monthly fee is similar.
- **Are you building for a client?** If someone else will maintain the site after you, the editing experience matters for non-technical users as much as the design tools matter for you. Webflow's editor and Squarespace's editor are both excellent for client handoff. Wix is accessible but can feel complex for first-time editors.
- **How much do you expect the site to grow?** Wix's App Market can accommodate growth in almost any direction. Webflow handles large, CMS-driven sites better than Wix or Squarespace. And only Webflow lets you export clean HTML and CSS if you ever want to move the code to a custom hosting environment.

## A quick platform guide

Here's a summary to match platform to project. Use it as a starting point, not as a final verdict — the nuances of your specific situation always matter more than any general rule of thumb:

- **Wix:** Best for small businesses that need flexibility, a broad feature ecosystem through App Market, and a drag-and-drop canvas with no structural constraints. The template-switching limitation is the one major planning concern.
- **Squarespace:** Best for creatives, restaurants, boutiques, and event businesses where design quality is the overriding goal. Built-in blogging, e-commerce, and email marketing keep the workflow consolidated.
- **Webflow:** Best for designers and technically inclined builders who need full CSS-level visual control and a serious, flexible CMS. The cleanest, fastest-loading output in this chapter. Requires a learning investment but pays it back in control and quality.
- **Framer:** Best for modern landing pages, portfolios, and product marketing sites where design sophistication and fast publishing matter most. The most AI-forward platform here, with the smoothest publishing experience and the lowest custom-domain entry price.

Whichever platform you choose, remember that the best website is one that exists. Every hour spent comparing tools is an hour you could have spent building. All four platforms in this chapter are capable of producing something professional in the hands of a builder who takes the time to learn them. Pick the one that fits your project and your skill level, and get started.

REMEMBER

None of these platforms traps you permanently, with one exception. On Wix, you can't change your template after you start building. On every other platform, migrating is painful but possible. The skills you build — clear content hierarchy, thoughtful layout, responsive thinking — travel with you regardless of which tool you use.

IN THIS CHAPTER

» Adding forms, booking, and live chat to your site

» Integrating email marketing

» Connecting tools with no-code automation

Chapter 3

# Adding Functionality without Coding

*Civilization advances by extending the number of important operations which we can perform without thinking about them.*

—ALFRED NORTH WHITEHEAD

When it comes to building a website, you can either construct things by hand (as I explain in Books 3 and 4) or use a platform to handle much of the construction for you (as I explain in Book 5, Chapters 1 and 2). This chapter takes a third path, one that's arguably the most practical of all: letting somebody else's already-built tool do the job.

Need a contact form? You could hand-code one (as I cover in Book 3, Chapter 2), wire it up to a back-end service, validate the inputs, style the error messages, handle spam prevention, and test the whole thing across browsers. Or you could sign up for a form-building service, answer a few questions, copy a snippet of code, paste it into your page, and be done before your coffee gets cold. Both approaches produce a working form. One of them leaves you with a free afternoon.

That's the idea behind *third-party tools:* specialized services that add a specific capability to your website without requiring you to build it from scratch. In this chapter, I walk you through the most useful categories — forms, scheduling, live chat, email marketing, and workflow automation — and introduce the leading tools in each. By the end, you'll have a practical toolkit for extending your website's capabilities far beyond what you'd want to build by hand.

# The Third-Party Tool Approach

Before diving into specific tools, it helps to understand how third-party services work. The mechanics are simpler than you might expect, and once you understand the pattern, you'll see that every tool in this chapter (and dozens of others you'll encounter in the wild) works essentially the same way.

## How embedding works

Almost every third-party tool follows a three-step pattern. First, you sign up for an account on the tool's website. Second, you configure whatever you need — a form, a booking calendar, a chat widget — using the tool's visual editor. Third, the service gives you a small chunk of code to paste into your site. That's it. No programming required, no server to set up, no database to manage.

The code you paste usually takes one of three forms:

- **An iframe:** A small HTML element that creates a window into the other service's content, embedded in your page. Google Forms and Calendly use this approach. The form or calendar lives on their servers and just *appears* on your page. The upside is simplicity. The downside is that iframes can look a bit like foreign objects because their styling doesn't always match the rest of your site.
- **A JavaScript snippet:** A few lines of JavaScript that load the tool's interface dynamically when the page loads. Live chat widgets almost always work this way; they inject a small floating button in the corner of your page that expands into a chat window when clicked. Because the JavaScript builds the interface on the fly, these tools tend to blend more naturally into your page than iframes do.
- **An embedded form or component:** Some services give you raw HTML — often a `form` element with hidden fields — that submits data directly to their servers. Many email marketing signup forms work like this. You get the most visual control with this approach because the HTML lives on your page and can be styled with your own CSS.

In all three cases, you're outsourcing functionality to someone else's infrastructure. The tool's servers handle the data processing, the storage, the security, and the software updates. You provide the front door on your website, and the tool provides everything behind it.

## Where to paste the code

Where you paste the embed code depends on how your site is built:

- » If you're hand-coding with HTML (as covered in Books 3 and 4), paste the snippet directly into your HTML file at the spot where you want the tool to appear.
- » In WordPress (covered in Book 5, Chapter 1), use a *custom HTML* block in the block editor. Click the plus icon, search for *Custom HTML,* and paste your code. WordPress also has dedicated plugins for many popular tools — such as a Calendly plugin and a Mailchimp plugin — that handle the embedding for you through a friendlier interface.
- » In visual builders like Wix, Squarespace, Webflow, and Framer (covered in Book 5, Chapter 2), look for an Embed or Custom Code block. Every major builder has one, though the exact name varies.

The lovely thing about embed codes is that they're platform-agnostic. A Calendly embed works the same way whether your site runs on WordPress, Squarespace, or a hand-coded HTML file sitting on a shared hosting account. Once you've learned the copy-paste-publish pattern with one tool, you've learned it for all of them.

## What to look for in a third-party tool

Not all third-party tools are created equal, and a quick evaluation before you commit can stave off headaches later. When you're considering a new tool, here are the questions worth asking:

- » **Does it have a free tier you can actually use?** Many tools advertise a free plan, but some free plans are so limited they're basically a demo. Look for plans that let you test the tool in a realistic scenario before you pay.
- » **How does it handle your data?** Can you export your data (contacts, submissions, bookings) in a standard format such as CSV? If you can't get your data out, you're locked in.
- » **What does the embed look like on a mobile device?** Some tools embed beautifully on a desktop but turn into a messy, scrollable iframe on a phone. Always test the mobile experience before committing.

- **How responsive is their support?** When something breaks (and eventually, something will), you want to know someone will answer. Check reviews for comments about support quality, especially for the pricing tier you plan to use.

One more thing: resist the temptation to sign up for every tool that catches your eye. It's easy to end up with eight overlapping services, each handling a small piece of what two or three tools could cover. Start with the tools that address your most pressing needs and add others only when you have a clear reason to.

# Gathering Information with Form Builders

Forms are the workhorses of the web. Contact forms, feedback surveys, event registrations, quote requests, job applications, newsletter signups. If your website needs to collect information from visitors, you need a form. And while you absolutely *can* build forms by hand (as I show in Book 3, Chapter 2), a dedicated form-building service handles the tedious parts: storing the responses in an organized way, sending you email notifications when someone submits, preventing spam bots from flooding your inbox, and making everything look decent on a phone.

Three services dominate this space, each with a different personality and a different idea about what a form should look like.

## Google Forms: Free and familiar

If you have a Google account — and at this point, who doesn't? — you already have access to Google Forms (`docs.google.com/forms`). It's free, it's functional, and it's genuinely hard to mess up. You create a form by adding questions (text fields, multiple choice, checkboxes, dropdowns, date pickers, even file uploads), arrange them in whatever order makes sense, and share the form via a direct link or an embed code.

Responses flow automatically into a connected Google Sheets spreadsheet, which is fantastically convenient if you already live in Google's productivity universe. You can set up email notifications so you're alerted every time someone submits a response, and basic conditional logic lets you show or hide sections based on earlier answers. (For example, if someone selects the Catering option, form fields appear for the event date and the number of guests.)

The trade-off is aesthetics. The forms look like, well, forms created by Google (see Figure 3-1). You can change the header image and the accent color, but the overall appearance is unmistakably "Google product." For an internal team survey or a quick feedback poll, that's fine. For a customer-facing form on a carefully branded business website, the visual mismatch can be jarring. You're essentially embedding Google's design language inside your own, and the seam shows.

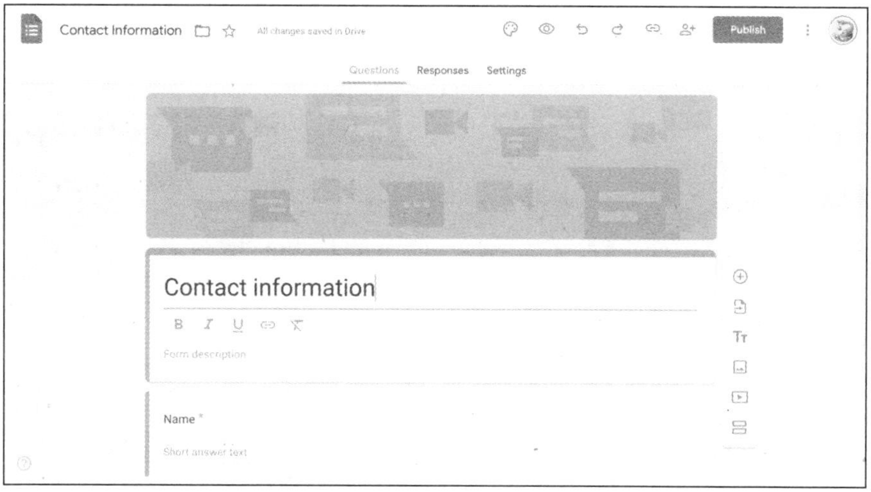


**FIGURE 3-1:** A Google Forms contact info form in the making.

Google Forms is the right choice when you need a form fast, you don't need it to look fancy, and you want the responses in a spreadsheet with zero effort. For anything more polished, read on.

## Jotform: More power, still no code

Jotform (`jotform.com`) is what Google Forms would be if it grew up, got a design degree, and learned a few tricks. It offers a full drag-and-drop form builder with hundreds of ready-made templates, over 100 integrations with other services, and — critically for business websites — extensive customization of colors, fonts, layouts, and branding. Your forms can look like they *belong* on your site rather than being borrowed from someone else's.

Where Jotform really separates itself from Google Forms is in its feature depth. Conditional logic lets you create smart forms that adapt as the user fills them out: show a Dietary restrictions field only if the customer selected a catering package, for example. Calculation fields can add up prices automatically, which is super-handy for order forms or quote calculators. Payment processing through Stripe or PayPal enables you to collect payments directly in the form. And Jotform can automatically generate PDF documents from submissions, so if a customer fills out a catering request, you can have a branded PDF summary emailed to both you and the customer without lifting a finger.

The free plan allows up to five forms with 100 monthly submissions, which is enough for many small businesses just getting started. Paid plans (starting around $34 per month) increase those limits and add features like HIPAA (Health Insurance Portability and Accountability Act, a US federal law) compliance for healthcare-related forms and larger file upload limits.

## Typeform: The conversational approach

Typeform (`typeform.com`) takes a fundamentally different approach to forms. Instead of presenting all your questions on a single page like a paper document, Typeform shows one question at a time in a full-screen, visually immersive layout. The visitor answers a question, and the next one slides or fades into view. The experience feels more like a conversation than a form.

This one-at-a-time approach tends to increase completion rates. People who start a Typeform are more likely to finish it than people who open a traditional form and see 15 fields staring them down. (That wall-of-fields feeling triggers what UX researchers politely call "form abandonment.")

The conversational format works beautifully for surveys, quizzes, and lead-generation forms where the goal is engagement. It's less suited to situations where the user needs to see all the fields at once, such as a detailed order form, or a job application where the applicant wants to jump between sections. Think of Typeform as the guided interview and traditional forms as the fill-in-the-document. Both are valid; they serve different purposes.

Typeform's free plan is limited to ten questions per form and ten responses per month, which is quite restrictive. Paid plans start at $28 per month and unlock more responses, unlimited forms, logic jumps, and integrations.

## Choosing the right form builder

If you're not sure which tool fits your situation, here's a quick guide:

- **Google Forms:** Best when you need something free, fast, and functional, and visual polish isn't a priority. Ideal for internal surveys, quick polls, and situations where the responses landing in a Google Sheet is the point.

- **Jotform:** Best for customer-facing forms that need to look professional, handle payments, or integrate with other tools. The most versatile all-around option and the one I recommend for most small-business websites.
- **Typeform:** Best for engagement-focused forms such as surveys, quizzes, and lead capture where completion rates matter more than information density. Less practical for complex multifield forms.

REMEMBER

As I cover in Book 3, Chapter 2, you can also build forms by hand with HTML and connect them to a free service like Formspree for processing. Hand-coded forms give you complete control over appearance and behavior. Third-party form builders trade some of that control for speed and convenience. Neither approach is wrong. It's a question of what matters more for your project.

# Setting Up Booking and Scheduling

If your business involves appointments — consultations, classes, demos, haircuts, tutoring sessions, whatever — you've probably experienced the soul-draining back-and-forth of scheduling by email. "How about Tuesday at 3?" "Sorry, I'm booked then. Wednesday?" "Wednesday works, but only after 2." Three days and eight emails later, you've booked a single 30-minute meeting. Ugh.

A scheduling tool eliminates this entire ritual. You define your availability, the tool shows your visitors the open slots, and they pick one. Done. No emails, no phone tag, no calendar conflicts. The tool sends automatic confirmation and reminder emails so people actually show up. For service-based businesses, a scheduling widget is often the difference between spending your evenings answering scheduling emails and spending them doing anything else.

## Calendly: The scheduling Swiss Army knife

Calendly (`calendly.com`) is the tool most people think of when they hear "online scheduling," and for good reason. It's clean, intuitive, and the free plan is useful rather than being a glorified demo designed to frustrate you into upgrading. You connect your Google, Outlook, or Apple calendar, set your available hours, create one or more *event types* (say, a 30-minute initial consultation and a 60-minute deep-dive session), and Calendly generates a booking page that shows the times when you're free. If someone books a slot, it appears on your calendar automatically and blocks that time so no one else can double-book it.

Embedding Calendly on your website is straightforward. In your Calendly dashboard, click Share, and then choose the Embed option. Calendly offers three embed styles:

- **Inline embed:** The calendar appears directly on your page as part of the content — no pop-ups or overlays. This choice is usually the best for a dedicated Book an Appointment page.
- **Pop-up widget:** A button appears on your page; clicking it opens the Calendly calendar in a centered overlay. Good when you want the booking option available but don't want it dominating the page layout.
- **Pop-up text:** A text link triggers the overlay. Useful for weaving a booking call-to-action into a paragraph of text, like "Ready to get started? Schedule a free consultation."

The free plan supports one event type and includes calendar syncing, automatic email notifications, and the capability to add your Calendly link to your email signature (which, honestly, is one of the single most useful things you can do with a scheduling tool). Paid plans (starting at $10 per month) add multiple event types, SMS reminders, payment collection through Stripe or PayPal, and team scheduling pages, where visitors can book with any available team member.

## Acuity Scheduling: For more complex needs

Acuity Scheduling (`acuityscheduling.com`), now owned by Squarespace, is aimed at businesses with more complex scheduling requirements. If you have multiple staff members each with different availability and service offerings, Acuity handles that naturally. It also supports intake forms (collect information from the client *before* the appointment), package pricing (buy five sessions, get one free), recurring appointments, and gift certificates.

Acuity doesn't offer a free plan — pricing starts at $16 per month — but it's a strong fit for service-based businesses like salons, therapy practices, fitness studios, tutoring services, or consulting firms where booking is the core interaction between business and customer. If Calendly feels too simple for your scheduling needs, Acuity is the natural step up.

One practical detail worth knowing: if you're already using Squarespace for your website, Acuity integrates natively with the platform; no embed code required. You can add scheduling directly through the Squarespace editor, which means the calendar inherits your site's styling automatically. That seamless integration is a genuine advantage over pasting an iframe from an external service.

### Use it!

Whichever scheduling tool you choose, the single most valuable thing you can do with it is put the booking link everywhere: in your email signature, on your contact page, in your social media bios, in your auto-reply emails. The fewer steps between "I want to book" and "I've booked," the more bookings you'll get. That advice sounds obvious, but you'd be surprised how many businesses bury their booking page three clicks deep on their website.

TIP

Both Calendly and Acuity connect directly with Zoom, Google Meet, and Microsoft Teams. When someone books a video meeting, the tool automatically generates the meeting link and includes it in the confirmation email. One less thing to remember, one less step to forget.

# Adding Live Chat and Chatbots

Here's a scenario that plays out on thousands of websites every day: a visitor arrives, browses for a minute, and has a quick question. It might be "Do you deliver on weekends?" or "Is the Friday morning class still available?" They hunt around for a bit, but can't find the answer. They look for a phone number, but don't see one (or don't feel like calling). They consider filling out the contact form, but a contact form feels like too much effort for a yes-or-no question. So, they leave. You've just lost a potential customer to a problem that a two-second answer would have solved.

Live chat widgets address this problem. They place (usually in the bottom-right corner of the page) a small, unobtrusive button that visitors can click to start a real-time conversation. Some tools connect the visitor to a human (you, or someone on your team). Others use an automated chatbot that can answer common questions without human involvement. And a growing number combine both: the chatbot handles routine queries, and a human steps in when the conversation needs a real person.

## Live chat tools worth knowing

Several solid live chat tools are available, and several of those have useful free tiers, where *useful* means you can run a real business on them, not just poke around a demo:

- **tawk.to (`tawk.to`):** Completely free, which sounds suspicious but isn't. The company makes its money by offering optional paid agent services for businesses that want someone else to handle the chats. The widget is customizable, supports over 45 languages, and includes canned responses for frequently asked questions. For a small business that wants live chat without a monthly bill, it's hard to beat.

- **Tidio (`tidio.com`):** Combines live chat with chatbot functionality in a single package. The free plan includes 50 live chat conversations per month and a visual chatbot builder where you can create conversation flows by dragging and connecting blocks; no coding needed. The interface is polished, setup takes about five minutes, and the mobile app lets you respond to chats from your phone.
- **Crisp (`crisp.chat`):** A more full-featured platform that bundles live chat, a shared team inbox for email, and a knowledge base (a set of help articles your visitors can search). The free plan supports two team members, which is enough for a small operation. Crisp is worth considering if you want live chat and customer support in a single tool rather than cobbling together separate services.

You install all three in the same way: sign up, customize the widget's appearance (colors, greeting message, position), copy a JavaScript snippet, and paste it into your site. If you're hand-coding, paste the snippet just before the closing `</body>` tag. In WordPress, paste it into a Custom HTML widget or use a dedicated plugin. In visual builders, use the sitewide code injection feature (in Squarespace, for example, look under Settings, then Developer Tools, then Code Injection). The widget appears automatically on every page of your site.

One practical consideration: live chat helps only if someone is there to respond. If a visitor sends a message at 10 p.m. and doesn't hear back until the next afternoon, the experience is worse than if there'd been no chat widget, because now the visitor feels ignored rather than simply uninformed. Most chat tools let you set online and offline hours. When you're offline, the widget can switch to a contact form or display a message such as "We're away right now. Leave a message and we'll get back to you by tomorrow morning." Setting those expectations makes a big difference.

If the idea of monitoring a chat window all day sounds exhausting (and for a one-person business, it genuinely can be), chatbots will earn their keep.

## AI chatbots: The new front desk

Traditional chatbots work from a script: if the visitor types *hours*, show the business hours; if they type *pricing*, link to the pricing page. These rule-based bots are fine for the most common questions but fall apart the moment someone asks something that wasn't anticipated. "Can I bring my dog?" wasn't in the script, so the bot responds with something useless like "I'm sorry, I didn't understand that. Would you like to see our FAQ?" Not exactly a stellar customer experience.

A newer generation of AI-powered chatbots changes this equation considerably. Tools like Tidio's Lyro, Intercom's Fin, and Chatbase let you feed the bot your website's content — your FAQ page, menu, policies, About Us page — and the AI can answer questions based on that content conversationally, even if the specific question was not explicitly scripted. A visitor asks, "Can I bring my dog to the Saturday workshop?" and the bot, having digested your events policy page, responds with something genuinely helpful rather than a shrug.

The catch? AI chatbots are more expensive than traditional ones. Most charge per conversation or per resolution, and costs can add up quickly for a busy site. They can also occasionally hallucinate by confidently providing an answer that sounds plausible but is flat-out wrong. (Imagine the bot cheerfully telling a customer that your store is open on Sundays when it isn't. Yikes.) For a small business, the practical approach is to start with a traditional chatbot that handles your five or ten most common questions reliably, and consider an AI upgrade once you've outgrown what scripted responses can cover.

TIP

Resist the urge to make the chat widget pop open automatically or bounce aggressively for attention every few seconds. Visitors find this about as charming as a salesperson who follows them around the store asking, "Can I help you? Can I help you? CAN I HELP YOU?" Let the widget sit quietly in the corner and be there when someone needs it.

# Integrating Email Marketing

Social media gets all the glamour, but email marketing quietly remains the highest-return channel available to most small businesses. The math is striking: for every dollar spent on email marketing, businesses see an average return of $36 to $42, depending on the study. No other channel comes close.

The reason is ownership. Your email list belongs to you. Your Instagram followers belong to Instagram, your Facebook page reach is controlled by Facebook's algorithm, and your TikTok visibility depends on whatever TikTok's algorithm happens to favor this week. If the algorithm changes tomorrow (and it will) your social reach can evaporate overnight. Your email list can't be taken away by a platform's policy change. That independence matters enormously for a business whose livelihood depends on reaching its customers.

The basic setup is simple: choose an email marketing platform, create a signup form, put that form on your website, and start sending useful content to the people who opt in. The tools in this section make all of those steps straightforward.

## Popular email platforms

Three platforms cover the vast majority of small-business needs:

- **Mailchimp (`mailchimp.com`):** The most widely recognized name in email marketing, and for many small businesses, the obvious starting point. The free plan supports up to 500 contacts and 1,000 sends per month, which is enough to get going. Mailchimp's drag-and-drop email editor makes it easy to create professional-looking emails without design skills, and its audience management tools — segmentation, tags, groups — help you organize subscribers as your list grows. The downside: Mailchimp's pricing escalates quickly once you exceed the free tier. At 2,500 contacts, you're looking at $39 per month or more.
- **Kit, formerly ConvertKit (`kit.com`):** Built specifically for creators such as bloggers, course creators, newsletter writers, podcasters, and small media businesses. Kit excels at *automation sequences* (a series of emails sent automatically based on subscriber behavior, such as sending a welcome email immediately, a tips email three days later, and a product recommendation a week after that) and tagging (organizing subscribers by interest so you can send targeted content to the right people). The free plan covers up to 10,000 subscribers with limited automation features; paid plans start at $25 per month.
- **Brevo, formerly Sendinblue (`brevo.com`):** The budget-friendly option, and one worth knowing about because it sets prices differently from most competitors. Where Mailchimp and Kit charge based on how many contacts you have, Brevo charges based on how many emails you send. This matters because many platforms charge you for every subscriber on your list, even if you email them only once a month. Brevo's free plan allows 300 emails per day with *unlimited* contacts. For a small business with a growing list and modest sending frequency, the math often works out considerably better.

## Adding signup forms to your site

Every email platform provides embeddable signup forms. The process is nearly identical across all of them: design the form in the platform's visual form builder (choose which fields to include, set the colors to match your brand, write the button text), and then copy the generated HTML or JavaScript snippet and paste it into your website using the same embed techniques I describe at the start of this chapter.

Where you place the form matters more than you might think. The most effective placements, based on what works in practice, are:

- **Header or navigation area:** A compact signup bar visible on every page works well when the ask is simple: an email field and a subscribe button, nothing more.
- **End of blog posts:** Readers who make it to the end of an article are already engaged because they liked your content enough to finish it. That's a natural moment to say, "Want more like this? Sign up."
- **Dedicated landing page:** A standalone page focused entirely on the signup is useful for linking from social media bios and ad campaigns where you want zero distractions between the visitor and the sign-up button.
- **Footer:** Less prominent but consistently visible across the site, the footer is good as a secondary placement, not your primary one, making it a steady background source of signups.

TIP

Whatever form style you choose, keep the ask small. The most effective signup forms ask for just one thing: an email address. Every additional field you add — first name, last name, company, phone number, favorite color — reduces your conversion rate. You can always collect more information later, after you've earned the subscriber's trust. For now, get the email address and get out of the way.

Finally, always offer something in return for the signup. Sorry, but "Subscribe to our newsletter" is not compelling. "Get our free guide to choosing the perfect *X*," where *X* is whatever your business sells, is. A free PDF, a discount code, early access to sales, exclusive tips — give people a reason to hand over their email address, and they'll do it much more readily.

## POP-UP FORMS: A NECESSARY EVIL?

A quick word (well, two words, actually) about pop-up signup forms: *they work.* The data on this is annoyingly clear: pop-ups consistently generate more signups than inline forms. They also consistently annoy visitors. If you use one, be respectful about it: show it once per visit (not on every page), delay it by at least 15 to 20 seconds so the visitor has time to engage with your content first, and make the close button large and obvious. Nobody in the history of the internet has ever thought, "I'm so glad that newsletter pop-up appeared before I could even read the headline."

REMEMBER

Email marketing comes up again later in this book. In Book 6, I cover content strategy for your emails, and in Book 8 I discuss email as part of e-commerce marketing. The focus here is on getting the signup form onto your website — the part that connects your site to your email platform.

# Automating Your Workflow with No-Code Tools

At this point you might have a contact form feeding responses to your email, a scheduling tool booking appointments, a live chat answering questions, and an email marketing platform collecting subscribers. That's a lot of tools. Managing them individually means a lot of browser tabs, a lot of manual copy-paste steps, and a lot of moments where you think, "Oh no, I forgot to add that person to the mailing list."

No-code automation tools solve this by connecting your services. The basic concept is beautifully simple: when something happens in one tool, automatically do something in another tool. When someone submits your contact form, add them to your Mailchimp list. When someone books a Calendly appointment, create a row in a Google Sheet. When a customer makes a purchase, send a personalized thank-you email. These connections — called *automations*, *workflows*, or *Zaps* depending on which platform you're using — run silently in the background, handling the tedious glue work that would otherwise eat into your day.

## Zapier: Connecting everything

Zapier (`zapier.com` — it rhymes with *happier*) is the most widely used no-code automation platform. It connects to over 6,000 apps and services, so whatever combination of tools you're using, Zapier almost certainly supports it.

A Zapier automation is called a Zap. Each *Zap* has two parts: a *trigger* (the event that starts the automation) and one or more *actions* (the things that happen as a result). Setting up a Zap feels a bit like giving instructions to a very literal assistant: "When you see a new form submission, take the email address and add it to this specific Mailchimp list, and then send me a Slack message saying a new lead came in."

Here are a few practical Zaps that a small business might use:

- **Form to spreadsheet:** When someone submits a Jotform contact form (trigger), add a row to a Google Sheet with their information (action) and send you a Slack notification (action).
- **Booking to CRM:** When someone books a Calendly appointment (trigger), create a contact record in your CRM (action) and send a personalized confirmation email through Gmail (action).
- **New subscriber welcome:** When someone joins your Mailchimp list (trigger), send them a welcome email with a first-time discount code (action) and tag them as a new lead in your CRM (action).
- **Review request:** Three days after an appointment is completed (trigger with a delay), send an automated email asking for a review (action). This Zap alone can transform the number of reviews a small business collects.

Zapier's free plan includes 100 tasks per month (a *task* is a single action that runs, so a two-action Zap that fires once uses two tasks) and allows 5 single-step Zaps. Paid plans start at $19.99 per month and add multistep Zaps, filters (run the actions only if certain conditions are met), and higher task limits. For a small business running a handful of straightforward automations, the free plan is often sufficient to start.

## Make: Visual automation

Make (`make.com`), formerly known as Integromat, takes a different approach to the automation-building experience. Instead of Zapier's linear trigger-then-action format, Make presents automations as visual flowcharts on a canvas. You drag circular modules onto the canvas, connect them with lines, and can build branching logic, loops, error-handling paths, and parallel actions. You do it all visually. If you're the kind of person who thinks better in diagrams than in lists, Make's interface may resonate with you immediately.

For simple two-step automations, Make and Zapier are roughly equivalent in capability and ease of use. Where Make pulls ahead is in complex workflows with branching logic, such as "Check whether the customer is new or returning, send different welcome emails based on the answer, and also update two different spreadsheets with different information." Building that kind of conditional branching in Zapier's linear format can get awkward. In Make's visual canvas, the branches are right there in front of you.

Make's free plan is notably more generous than Zapier's: 1,000 operations per month (an *operation* is Make's equivalent of a task) and two active *scenarios* (Make's term for automations). Paid plans start at $9 per month. If you're choosing between the two, my suggestion is to try both free plans with a real automation you need and see which interface clicks for you. For straightforward "when this, then that" automations, Zapier's simplicity is an advantage. For anything with branching logic, data transformations, or multiple paths, Make's visual canvas often wins.

TIP

Start with one or two automations and make sure they're running reliably before building more. Automation is powerful, but a misconfigured workflow can create a mess, such as emailing every new subscriber ten times because you accidentally set up a loop. (Don't ask me how I know this.) Always test with your own email address first.

## Which one should you choose?

If you're just getting started with automation, Zapier is the easier on-ramp. Its interface is more intuitive for beginners, its documentation is excellent, and its app directory is the largest in the space. You can set up a useful Zap in under ten minutes with no experience.

If you find yourself bumping into Zapier's limitations — such as needing more complex logic, running into task limits, or wanting more control over data transformations — that's a good signal to explore Make. The learning curve is steeper, but the ceiling is considerably higher.

And here's the thing neither platform's marketing will tell you: for many small businesses, one or two well-chosen automations provide 80 percent of the value. You don't need to automate everything. Automate the tasks that are repetitive, time-consuming, and error-prone. Leave the rest to the humans, who are, despite what the automation industry might suggest, still pretty good at quite a lot of things.

# 6

# Content Creation and Management

# Contents at a Glance

IN THIS CHAPTER

- Planning what to create and when to create it
- Writing content people will read
- Keeping your voice consistent and your content accessible

# Chapter 1
# Content Strategy for Your Website

*My four articles of faith: clarity, simplicity, brevity and humanity.*

—WILLIAM ZINSSER

Here's an uncomfortable truth about small-business websites: most of the words on them are never read. That lack of readership isn't because the people writing those words are bad writers. It's because they're writing without a strategy, cranking out pages and posts because somebody said, "We need content!," without first asking who the content is for, what it needs to do, or why anyone should care. The result is a website full of earnest, well-meaning, perfectly grammatical prose that nobody asked for and nobody will ever read.

*Content strategy* is the fix. It's the unglamorous but essential work of deciding, before you start writing, what your website needs to say, to whom, for what reason, and how often. In this chapter, I walk you through how to plan what to create, write content people will read, and keep everything sounding like it came from a single coherent human being.

# Creating a Content Plan

To begin, plan what to create. This is where a lot of small business owners get intimidated, because they picture content strategy as a 40-page document with more charts than words and enough acronyms to warm the cockles of an MBA's heart. Happily, you don't need any of that. What you need is a short document that answers four questions.

## The four questions every plan answers

Every content plan, no matter how simple or elaborate, boils down to answering these four things:

- **Who is this for?** And, no, "everyone" isn't an answer. Pick one specific audience with one specific need. If you have two audiences, that's two plans.
- **Why are you making it?** What happens after someone reads this? Do they sign up? Book a call? Understand what you do well enough to remember you next time? Every piece of content should have an intended outcome.
- **What are you going to make?** Blog posts? Service pages? Videos? A weekly newsletter? Pick a handful of content types, not all of them at once.
- **Where does it live?** On your website, obviously, but also, where on your site? A blog post? A pillar page? A resource in the footer? And does it get distributed anywhere else, such as a newsletter or on social media?

That's the whole plan. Literally one page. If you want to get fancy, add a section for metrics ("How will we know if this is working?") and another for cadence ("How often are we doing this?"). But the four questions are the core. You'd be amazed at how many businesses skip every single one.

## Content pillars: Giving your plan a shape

Once you know who and why, you need to decide what broad topics you're going to cover. These are called *content pillars*, and they're the handful of themes your content keeps circling back to. Three to five pillars are about right. Fewer and you run out of things to say. More and your site feels like it's about everything, which is another way of saying nothing.

Here's an example. Say you run a regional HVAC company. Your content pillars might be:

- **Homeowner education:** How heating and cooling systems work, what different efficiency ratings mean, when to repair versus replace
- **Energy costs and savings:** Information on how to lower your bill, rebate programs, seasonal tune-ups, smart thermostats
- **Indoor air quality:** Air purifiers, humidifiers, filters, allergies
- **Local expertise:** What's different about heating and cooling in your climate, your building stock, your utility market

Every blog post, service page, and FAQ falls under one of those four pillars. If somebody suggests a piece of content that doesn't fit a pillar, you have a decision to make: either skip it or expand your pillars to include it. Usually, the answer is skip it.

TIP

Write your pillars down and pin them somewhere visible, such as on a sticky note next to your monitor. When you're deciding whether to write about something, the first question should be "Does this fit in a pillar?" If not, the second question is "Should it?" Usually, the answer to the second question is no, and you've just saved yourself a weekend.

## What a filled-in plan looks like

Abstract descriptions get you only so far. Here's what a complete one-page content plan might look like for a small neighborhood bike shop run by two mechanics named Sam and Jordan. Note how specific everything is. There are no hedge words, no catchall audiences, no vague goals like "build brand awareness":

> **Audience:** New and returning riders in our neighborhood who want a bike they can ride, not a machine they need a degree in engineering to maintain. Budget-conscious, slightly intimidated by bike shop culture, often coming off a years-long riding break.
>
> **Why we're making content:** To be the place they trust before they walk in the door. When somebody Googles a bike question, we want ours to be the answer that feels like it was written by a human being who wants to help.
>
> **Pillars:** We have the following three content pillars:
>
> - **Getting started or starting over:** Choosing the right bike, what to expect from a tune-up, basic maintenance you can do yourself.

- **Fit and comfort:** Why your bike hurts, saddle selection, when to adjust versus replace.
- **Riding in our city:** Local routes, road conditions, weather, commuting tips, places to lock up safely.

**Content types:** Mostly blog posts and FAQ entries. One cornerstone page ("A Beginner's Guide to Buying Your First Adult Bike"). A monthly email newsletter.

**Cadence:** One post per month, one FAQ update per month, one newsletter per month. Cornerstone page gets reviewed twice a year.

**How we'll know it's working:** Phone calls or emails that reference something we wrote. Repeat visits to specific posts. People mentioning the newsletter when they come in.

This entire plan fits on one page. Anyone who writes for the shop can read it in two minutes and know exactly what fits and what doesn't, which is the whole point.

# Understanding Content Types

Content isn't just a blog post. A modern website uses a menagerie of content types, and each one does a different job. Understanding the purpose of each type helps you pick the right one for the message you're trying to get across. Let me walk you through the main ones.

## Cornerstone pages

A *cornerstone page* is a long, comprehensive page that covers a major topic in depth. If your business helps people plan destination weddings, a cornerstone page might be "The Complete Guide to Planning a Destination Wedding," a 3,000-word deep dive that links to a dozen more specific pages. Cornerstone pages are the workhorses of search engine optimization (as I discuss in Book 7), and they tend to be the pages that pull the most search traffic year after year. Every small-business site should have at least two or three.

## Blog posts

*Blog posts* are the shorter, more frequent pieces that sit between your cornerstone pages and your service pages. They're great for answering specific questions, responding to news in your industry, sharing customer stories, and generally keeping your site from feeling suspended in amber. I cover blogs in depth in Book 6, Chapter 4, so I won't belabor them here. Just know that they're a workhorse content type for most small businesses.

## Service and product pages

*Service and product pages* are the pages where you describe what you sell. That sounds straightforward, but it's where a lot of small businesses go wrong, because they write these pages as if they're describing themselves rather than helping a customer make a decision. A good service page leads with the customer's problem, explains how you solve it, and then gets into the details. A bad service page leads with "Our Commitment to Excellence" and loses the reader by the third sentence. Don't be the second type.



## FAQ pages and answer content

*Frequently asked questions* are one of the most underrated content types on the web. If you have five questions that customers ask you all the time, that's five pieces of content begging to be written. You can put them all on a single FAQ page (easy) or break them out into individual pages that go deep on each question (better for search). Either way, answering real questions is one of the fastest ways to create content that people want to read.

## Case studies and customer stories

A *case study* is a structured story about how you helped a specific customer solve a specific problem. It's one of the most persuasive content types for any business where trust matters (which is, well, all of them). A good case study includes the customer's situation, what they tried before, what you did, and what changed. Numbers help. Photos help more. Quotes from the customer help most of all.

## Landing pages

A *landing page* is a focused page built around a single goal, usually signing up, booking, or buying. Landing pages strip away the usual site navigation and distractions so the reader has one decision to make. They're especially useful for advertising campaigns, where you want to send traffic from an ad to a page that matches exactly what the ad promised.

## Newsletters

A *newsletter* isn't exactly website content, but it's close enough to belong in this list because it usually lives alongside your site and draws from the same pool of ideas. Newsletters are how you stay in touch with people who are interested but not yet ready to buy. If you're going to do one, commit to a realistic schedule (monthly is fine, weekly is a lot) and give people a genuine reason to open it.

## Video and audio

Finally, don't forget that content doesn't have to be words. Short *explainer videos, product demos, customer testimonials, and podcast episodes* are all valid content types, and they're often easier to produce than people expect. A two-minute video of you explaining a common customer question — filmed on your phone, uncut — can outperform a 1,500-word blog post on the same topic. Just remember that video content still needs a transcript for accessibility (more on that later in this chapter).

## Picking the right type for the job

With all these options on the menu, how do you know which to reach for? Here's a simple rule of thumb: match the content type to the reader's stage. Somebody who has a vague problem and doesn't even know your business exists needs different content from somebody who's about to pull out a credit card. Here are the stages to target:

- **They don't know they have a problem yet:** Blog posts, short videos, newsletters. The goal is to get on their radar by being useful, not to sell anything.
- **They know they have a problem and are researching:** Cornerstone pages, FAQ entries, comparison posts, longer videos. The goal is to be the most helpful answer they find.
- **They're deciding between options:** Case studies, customer testimonials, service pages with specifics. The goal is to build trust and make the decision feel safe.
- **They're ready to act:** Landing pages, clear calls to action, simple forms. The goal is to remove every obstacle between intent and action.

If you look at your site and realize every single page is aimed at the same stage — usually the last one — that's a content strategy problem. Most visitors arrive earlier than the "ready to buy" stage, and if you have nothing to offer them until they're ready to pull out a credit card, you're losing most of your audience before they ever become customers.

# Planning an Editorial Calendar

A content plan tells you *what* to make. An editorial calendar tells you *when*. Having a calendar is what separates people who publish content from people who merely talk about publishing content. I've seen beautiful content plans that never produced a single page, and makeshift spreadsheet-based calendars that powered years of steady output. Guess which one wins.

## Why a calendar beats a wish list

Without a calendar, content gets made whenever somebody has some free time, which for most busy small-business owners is approximately never. With a calendar, content becomes a scheduled obligation, like payroll or inventory. Nobody feels inspired to run payroll either, but it happens every two weeks because somebody put it on a calendar and made it non-negotiable.

That said, let's face facts: your calendar has to be realistic. A lot of well-meaning content plans fall apart because somebody decided they'd publish three blog posts a week but instead wrote four posts in the first two weeks and never published again. (Ah, so you *have* seen my first attempt at blogging!) One good post a month that you ship beats four planned posts that never get written.

## What to put on the calendar

At minimum, every calendar entry should include:

- **Publish date:** When it goes live. Not "sometime in Q2."
- **Title or topic:** What it's about. Draft titles are fine because they'll change.
- **Content type:** Blog post, service page, FAQ update, and so on.
- **Owner:** The one person responsible for getting it done. Emphasis on *one.* Not "the team."
- **Status:** Idea, drafting, in review, scheduled, published.
- **Pillar:** Which content pillar does this support?

That's it. You can add columns for keywords, calls to action, distribution channels, and so on, but these six are the core. If you can't fill them in, you're not ready to put the item on the calendar.

## Tools that work

You don't need fancy software to create a calendar. A Google Sheet with the six columns I just listed will take you remarkably far. Here are other options worth knowing about:

- **Trello (`trello.com`):** A free, card-based tool where each piece of content is a card that moves through columns such as Idea, Drafting, In Review, and Published. Very visual and easy to learn.
- **Notion (`notion.com`):** A more flexible workspace tool where you can build a calendar database with filters, views, and linked pages. Great if you want your content calendar, brand voice guide, and research notes all in one place.
- **Airtable (`airtable.com`):** A spreadsheet-database hybrid that's especially good if you're planning lots of content types and want to switch between list, calendar, and kanban views.
- **Asana (`asana.com`) or Todoist (`todoist.com`):** If you already use a task manager for everything else, you can use it for content too. The best tool is the one you'll actually open.

WARNING

The most common editorial calendar mistake is overcommitting in month one. You'll have a rush of enthusiasm, plan weekly posts for the next quarter, and burn out by week three. It happens, believe me. Start slower than you think you need to. You can always add more.

## A realistic schedule for a small business

For most small businesses with no dedicated content person, here's a reasonable cadence for publishing content:

- One cornerstone or evergreen blog post per month
- One FAQ update or small content refresh per month
- One newsletter per month (if you're doing one at all)
- Quarterly review of service pages to make sure they're still accurate

No, it doesn't look like much, but if you stick with this schedule, you'll end up publishing a lot more than most of your competitors.

# Writing for the Web: Scannable Content

Most people don't read web pages, at least not at first. Instead, they *scan* them: their eyes bouncing around the page, picking out headings and bold words and bullet points, looking for the specific thing they came for. If they find it, only then might they read the full page. But if they don't find it within a few seconds (yes, you read that right: *a few seconds!*), they're gone. Usability researchers have been documenting this pattern for more than two decades, and it hasn't budged.

What this means for writing is that all the habits you picked up in school — long introductions, carefully developed arguments, saving the conclusion for the end — are actively working against you on the web. If you bury the point in paragraph four, no one will ever find it, because no one will ever read paragraph four.



## The inverted pyramid

Journalists figured out something important a hundred years ago and gave it a name: the *inverted pyramid.* The idea is that you put the most important information first, then the next most important, then the details, and then the background. A reader who stops after the first sentence still gets the main point. A reader who stops after the first paragraph gets the main point plus the key supporting facts. A reader who makes it all the way to the end is a hero.

This structure works because it matches how people read on the web. The top of the page gets the most eyeballs. The bottom gets the fewest. Put the most valuable stuff where the most people will see it.

## Front-load your sentences and paragraphs

The same principle applies inside a single sentence or paragraph: put the important stuff first. Compare:

> In order to ensure that your content is accessible to the widest possible audience, it is generally considered a best practice to keep all your sentences relatively short.

Yuck. Now compare:

> Keep your sentences short. That makes your content easier to read for more people.

Same idea, but half the words. And the important takeaway — "keep your sentences short" — is the first thing the reader sees, not buried behind a pile of throat-clearing.

## Use meaningful subheads

A person scanning the page reads headings before they read anything else. If your headings are vague ("Our Approach," "More Information," "Details"), the scanner learns nothing and leaves. If your headings are specific and informative ("Why We Don't Use Chemical Treatments," "How Long the Process Usually Takes"), the scanner can find exactly what they need without reading a word of body text.

Here's a good test: if you stripped every paragraph out of your page and left only the headings, would somebody still get the gist of what the page is about? If yes, your headings are doing their job. If no, they need work.

## Keep paragraphs short

A wall of text is the fastest way to make a reader bounce. On the web, paragraphs should be two to four sentences. Sometimes one. (Sometimes even half a sentence, for emphasis.) Yes, this will offend your high-school English teacher. It's fine. Your high-school English teacher is not your audience.

TIP

Here's a quick test for any web page you've written: close your eyes, open them, and glance at the page for exactly two seconds. What did you notice? If the answer is "the main point of the page," you're in great shape. If the answer is "a big wall of text," you have work to do.

## Use lists, but don't overdo them

Bulleted — or, occasionally, numbered — lists are scanner-friendly because they visually break up the page and signal to the reader that they're looking at a discrete set of things. Use them for lists of items, steps in a process, or features and benefits. Don't use them for every paragraph on the page, because then they stop standing out and the page starts to look like a grocery list.

## Write link text that means something

When you link to another page, the link text itself should tell the reader where they're going. "Click here for more" is the classic bad example because it tells the reader nothing and is worse for screen reader users, who often navigate by jumping between links. Compare with "Click here for our pricing" or "Check out our pricing plans," both of which work well for everybody.

## A before-and-after rewrite

All this is easier to see in action than to explain in the abstract. Let me show you what a scannable rewrite looks like. Here's the opening of a service page I just made up, written in the default Small Business Website style:

> At Morgan & Taylor Accounting Services, we pride ourselves on our commitment to providing our valued clients with the highest quality professional tax preparation and bookkeeping services. With over twenty years of combined experience serving individuals and small businesses throughout the region, our dedicated team is uniquely positioned to help you navigate the complexities of today's ever-changing tax landscape. We understand that every client is different, and we take pride in offering personalized service tailored to your unique financial situation.

Oof. That's 80 words and I still have no idea what they do, who their service is for, or why I should call. Everything is hedged, generic, and focused on the firm rather than the reader. Now here's the rewrite:

> Small business taxes, done right. We handle the bookkeeping, the quarterly filings, and the messy year-end stuff so you can get back to running your business. Most of our clients are contractors, consultants, and shop owners. They're people who'd rather spend Saturday doing almost anything else than sorting receipts. If that sounds like you, let's talk.

Only 56 words. The first sentence tells you what they do. The second sentence tells you what you get. The third sentence tells you who it's for, complete with a specific, sympathetic image. The fourth sentence invites action. Same page, but a completely different experience for the reader.

# Maintaining a Consistent Brand Voice

Imagine you had coffee with a friend yesterday, and today you got an email from them, except the email is written like it came from a lawyer drafting a contract. That would be weird, right? That's what it feels like when a website's content sounds different from page to page. The home page is warm and punchy, the About page reads like a press release, and the FAQs sound like they were written by somebody's annoyed IT department. Visitors can't put their finger on what's wrong, but something feels off.

The fix is to find and maintain a *brand voice*, a consistent way of writing that makes every page on your site feel like it came from the same person, even when it didn't.

## Voice versus tone

First, a useful distinction. *Voice* is the constant. It's your underlying personality: who you are, how you think, what you sound like. Voice stays the same whether you're writing a cheerful newsletter or a sober privacy policy.

*Tone* is the variable. It's how voice adapts to a specific situation. Your voice might be friendly, direct, and a little bit playful. Your tone on a celebration post is exuberant. Your tone on an outage notification is calm and reassuring. Same voice, different tone. Think of it like a person: you're still you whether you're at a birthday party or a funeral, but you behave differently in each place.

## The "we are X but not Y" exercise

One of the easiest ways to define a voice is to fill in a grid of statements that look like this: "We are X but not Y." Here's an example for a local yoga studio:

- **We are welcoming but not saccharine.** We want people to feel invited, not hugged on sight by a stranger.
- **We are knowledgeable but not preachy.** We know our stuff, but we don't lecture.
- **We are relaxed but not sloppy.** Our posts should feel easy, not careless.
- **We are inclusive but not generic.** By *inclusive,* we mean in ways that show up in specific word choices, not in empty corporate-speak.

This exercise works because it forces you to define your voice in contrast to something. "Friendly" is too vague to act on. "Friendly but not chummy" is concrete. Now a writer who's never worked for you can read those four lines and have a fighting chance of matching the voice.

## Build a one-page voice guide

Once you've done the exercise, package it into a one-page document that anyone writing for your site can reference. The voice guide should include:

- A one-sentence summary of your voice
- Your "we are X but not Y" list (three to five items)
- A few example sentences in your voice, plus the same ideas written in a voice that's *not* yours (so people can see the contrast)

» A short list of words and phrases you use (and a shorter list of words you never use)

Keep it to one page. There's no need here for a 20-page brand guidelines document that nobody will read.

REMEMBER

Voice is a choice, not an accident. If you don't define it, every writer will default to their own voice, and your site will end up sounding like a committee. Five minutes defining the site's voice now saves hours of rewriting later.



### Keeping voice consistent across authors

If you're a solo webmaster, brand voice consistency is easier because there's just you. But if multiple people contribute content, you need a light editing process to catch voice drift. The simplest version: one person on the team has final voice approval, and nothing is published without their read-through. That person doesn't have to rewrite everything, just flag anything that sounds off and suggest a fix. Fifteen minutes per post is usually enough.

When you're flagging voice drift, it helps to have a short list of common offenders. In my experience, the things most likely to sneak into content and wreck the voice are corporate filler words (*leverage, synergy, utilize, stakeholder*), empty intensifiers (*absolutely, truly, incredibly*), and hedging phrases that kill confidence (*we believe that, it is our opinion that, generally speaking*). Every one of those can usually be cut without changing the meaning. Most of the time, cutting them makes the sentence stronger.

## Going over Some Content Accessibility Guidelines

I cover accessibility broadly in Book 2, Chapter 4, and that chapter handles the design and code side, including color contrast, keyboard navigation, and ARIA labels. This section is about the *content* side of accessibility: the word-level and structure-level decisions a writer makes that determine whether everybody can understand and make use of what you've written. Code-level accessibility gets all the attention, but content accessibility is just as important, and it's entirely in your hands as the writer.

## Write in plain language

*Plain language* means writing that a reasonable person can understand on the first read, without reaching for a dictionary. It doesn't mean dumbing things down or using baby words. It means choosing clear words over fancy ones, short sentences over long ones, and concrete nouns over abstractions.

Some practical rules of thumb:

- » Use common words instead of uncommon ones (*use*, not *utilize*; *help*, not *facilitate*).
- » Keep most sentences under 20 words.
- » Prefer active voice (*the inspector signed the form*) to passive voice (*the form was signed by the inspector*).
- » Define jargon the first time you use it or skip it.
- » Aim for around a grade 8 reading level for general audiences. Free tools such as Hemingway Editor (`hemingwayapp.com`) will tell you where you're landing.

None of this is about writing for simple people. It's about writing for busy people, for people reading on a phone in bad lighting, for people reading in their second language, for people with cognitive disabilities, and for people who are just having a bad day.

The grade-8 target might sound condescending, but it isn't. Major newspapers aim for somewhere between grade 7 and grade 10. The Associated Press style targets around grade 8. Ernest Hemingway, whose name is on the tool I mentioned a moment ago, wrote at roughly a grade-5 level and managed to win a Nobel Prize. Nobody's ever accused Hemingway of being a dumb writer. Short sentences and common words don't make your content less sophisticated. They make it more likely to reach the person you wrote it for.

## Use headings as structure, not styling

Headings aren't just big bold text. They're the scaffolding of your page, and screen readers use them to let users navigate by jumping from heading to heading. If you use an `h3` because it looks the right size, not because it represents a subsection of an `h2` above it, you're breaking the scaffolding.

The rule is straightforward: headings should nest in order, like an outline. An `h1` (one per page — your page title) can contain `h2` elements, which can contain `h3` elements, which can contain `h4` elements. Don't skip levels (no jumping from `h2` to `h4`), and don't pick headings based on font size. Use CSS for the font size. Use HTML headings for the structure.

# Captions and transcripts for media

If you publish video or audio content, provide captions (for video) and transcripts (for both). Captions help people who are deaf or hard of hearing, people in noisy environments, people in quiet environments who forgot their headphones, and non-native speakers. Transcripts help all those groups plus search engines, which can read text but can't listen to audio.

For small operations, automatic captioning from services such as YouTube or Otter (otter.ai) is usually good enough for a first pass, but always review the output. Auto-captions famously mangle proper nouns, numbers, and anything said quickly.



# Avoid ableist, exclusionary, and idiomatic language

Finally, watch out for three things that make content harder to use for more people than you'd expect:

- **Ableist language:** Uses disability as a metaphor for something negative. Examples include phrases such as *lame idea, crazy plan,* and *falling on deaf ears.* Plenty of readers find these grating. Almost any of those phrases has a clearer, punchier replacement (*bad idea, wild plan, getting ignored*).
- **Exclusionary language:** Assumes every reader can do something that not every reader can. The classic offender is *See our menu* or *View our locations,* which assumes the reader is sighted. *Listen to the latest episode* assumes the reader can hear. *Just walk over to the front desk* assumes the reader is mobile. These phrases aren't mean-spirited, but they are thoughtless. The fix is almost always a more neutral verb: *See our menu* becomes *Read our menu* or just *Our menu. Listen to the episode* becomes *Catch the latest episode. Walk over to the front desk* becomes *Head to the front desk* or *Stop by the front desk.* The replacements are not longer and not clunkier, and they don't single anybody out. Once you start noticing this pattern, you'll see it everywhere on the web. And once you start fixing it, your content quietly gets more welcoming without anyone being able to say exactly why.
- **Idiomatic language:** Uses phrases that assume native English fluency or experience. Examples such as *we're in the weeds, let's circle back,* and *ballpark figure* are rough on non-native English speakers and on people using translation tools. Use idioms sparingly, and if you're writing for an international audience, consider ditching them altogether. Your content will be clearer for everybody, not just the people who needed the help.

IN THIS CHAPTER

- » **Understanding what AI can do**
- » **Writing, editing, and polishing text with AI**
- » **Generating images and visuals with AI**
- » **Keeping your brand voice consistent**
- » **Staying on the right side of ethics**

# Chapter 2
# Using AI for Content Creation

*What is written without effort is in general read without pleasure.*

—SAMUEL JOHNSON

These days, you can't walk into a room without also sharing space with one of those proverbial elephants that people are constantly pointing out. The room of website content creation (and, it must be said, the larger room of website creation in general) contains an elephant so big it threatens to take up the entire space and all its oxygen. That pachyderm is, of course, artificial intelligence (AI), specifically the form of AI packaged as a chatbot that can, with a simple prompt, generate memos, posts, marketing copy, and realistic images with an ease that's both magical and, often, too tempting to refuse.

I could continue to ignore that elephant, but it's high time to look directly at it and see what it can do for you. That's what this chapter is all about.

# Understanding AI's Role in Web Content

Before you pour any AI-generated text into your website, you owe yourself the ten-minute version of what these tools do and how they do it. Why? Because knowing roughly how the magic trick works is the difference between using AI well and being bamboozled by it.

## What AI does

The tools I'm talking about in this chapter, including famous names such as ChatGPT, Claude, and Gemini, are called *large language models,* or *LLMs.* An LLM is, at its heart, a spectacularly well-read autocomplete tool.

Think of the autocomplete on your phone, the one that suggests *you* (or perhaps *bacon*) after you type *I love.* Now imagine that same mechanism but trained on a significant chunk of the public internet and a massive pile of books. Instead of making an educated guess about the next word in a text message, an LLM is guessing the next word in an essay, an email, or a product description. Over and over, one word at a time, each word chosen because it's statistically likely to follow the ones before it.

Yep, that's the whole enchilada. Contrary to what some people would have you believe, there's no understanding, no opinions, no little person inside the computer, no ghost in the machine. The output feels smart because the training data was written by smart people (well, mostly). The illusion is durable, and it's powerful enough to be useful. But remembering that you're talking to a digital parrot and not a real colleague will save you a lot of grief.

WARNING

When an AI sounds confident, that tells you nothing about whether it's correct. These tools are optimized to produce fluent text, not necessarily true text. Fluency and accuracy are two completely different problems.

## Where AI can help

With those caveats pinned up on the wall, let me tell you what these tools are really good at, because the list is longer than the skeptics admit. AI can help you

» **Get past the blank page:** A rough initial draft, even a bad one, is psychologically easier to edit than a blank page is to start.

- **Handle repetitive writing:** Product descriptions, meta tags, FAQ entries, social captions, and similar work that's necessary, voluminous, and not particularly creative.
- **Try out different angles:** AI is a tireless brainstorming partner, so you can ask it to rewrite something in any number of ways.
- **Summarize and translate:** Paste a long document and ask AI for a tight summary. Or you can give the chatbot an English draft and ask for first-pass versions in French and Spanish.

### Where AI cheerfully lets you down

And now the other side of the ledger. These tools have some consistent weaknesses, and your job is to know them:

- **Hallucinations:** AI happily and confidently makes things up out of whole cloth. The technical term is *hallucination,* which is a polite way of saying "lying with extreme confidence." Always check the AI's work.
- **Current events:** Most models are trained on data up to some cutoff date. Ask about last week's news and you'll get either a disclaimer or, worse, a reasonable-sounding invention. If you really want to talk about something past the model's cutoff date, tell the model you're working with new info and that it should search the web for the answer rather than relying on its training knowledge.
- **Voice:** Out of the box, every AI writes in the same mushy, inoffensive, vaguely LinkedIn-ish dialect. Getting it to sound like you takes work (which I cover later; check out "Maintaining Brand Voice with AI").
- **Judgment:** Despite the *I* (intelligence) in AI, it can't tell you what's funny, what's on-brand, or what will make your customers more likely to click the Buy button. Those calls are still yours.



## Writing with AI Tools

All right, enough context. Let's talk about the tools and how to drive them without crashing into a tree.

## The major players you'll bump into

As I write this, the AI writing landscape is dominated by a handful of products. The roster shifts every few months, but the main ones are:

- **ChatGPT (`chat.openai.com`):** OpenAI's assistant, the one that started the current boom. It's the most generalist of the big chatbots because it's equally comfortable drafting a blog post, explaining a tax concept, or writing a limerick about your cat. A good default if you have no idea where to start.
- **Claude (`claude.ai`):** Anthropic's assistant. Writers and editors tend to rate Claude highest for nuance, tone, and long-form writing. It's my pick for prose drafting, but your mileage may vary.
- **Gemini (`gemini.google.com`):** Google's entry. Notable if you already live inside Google Docs, Sheets, and Gmail, where Gemini is baked right in.
- **Copilot (`copilot.microsoft.com`):** Microsoft's assistant, deeply integrated with Windows and Microsoft 365. If your organization runs on Outlook and Word, Copilot meets you where you already work.
- **Perplexity (`perplexity.ai`):** A specialist; not a general chatbot but a research tool that combines an LLM with live web search and visible source citations. Great for fact-finding, where a regular chatbot would confidently make things up.

All five have free tiers that are more than enough for experimenting. If you end up using one daily, a paid plan (usually around $20 a month) unlocks better models, higher usage limits, and extra features.

TIP

Try at least two of these with the same prompt before you pick a favorite. Each has a subtly different personality, and the one that clicks for you might not be the one everyone else is raving about.

## Prompting 101

A *prompt* is just the instruction you type into the AI. Despite what some people on the internet will tell you, prompt engineering isn't a mystical art. It's just writing clear instructions, which you already know how to do because you've been doing it every time you've emailed a contractor.

That said, there's a pattern that works reliably. Here are four things to include in your prompts:

- **Context:** Who you are and what you're trying to accomplish.
- **Task:** What you want the AI to do.

- **Constraints:** Length, tone, audience, what to avoid, and anything else you can think of to harness the AI.
- **Format:** How you want the output structured.

Here's the "before" version of a prompt that's similar to what most people type on their first try:

```
Write a blog post about small-business marketing.
```

Here's the same request with the four ingredients added:

```
I run a three-person accounting firm serving small
businesses in the Springfield area. Write a 600-word blog
post aimed at new business owners who have never worked
with an accountant.

The tone should be friendly and reassuring, not
lecturing. Avoid jargon; when you need a technical
term, define it.

Structure the post with a short intro, three practical
tips as subheads, and a one-paragraph close. Don't
include a call to action; I'll add that myself.
```

The difference in output between those two prompts is enormous. The first gives you bland, interchangeable advice that reads like every other small-business marketing post on the internet. The second gives you something that, after a light edit, you'd be happy to use.

## Getting dramatically better results

Once you're past the basics, a few techniques consistently lift AI writing from fine to genuinely useful:

- **Give it a role.** Start your prompt with the role you want the AI to assume. For example, "You are an experienced jingle writer" or "Act as a copywriter who specializes in SaaS." This nudges the model toward a particular style and vocabulary.
- **Show, don't just tell.** If you want a specific style, paste in two or three examples of writing you like and ask the AI to match them. Describing a style in words is harder than showing samples.

» **Iterate.** The first version is almost never the keeper. Come back with "shorter," "more specific," "less corporate," or "add a concrete example in paragraph three." AI responds well to direct feedback.

» **Ask for options.** Prompting the AI with "Give me five headline choices" beats "give me a headline" almost every time.

TIP

The difference between AI as a magical productivity tool and AI as a waste of time is almost always the prompt, so keep a file of the ones that work best for you.

# Editing and Refining AI-Generated Content

Here's perhaps the most important thing to remember when working with AI-generated writing:

> AI gives you a zeroth draft, not a first draft.

Everything else flows from accepting that.

## The first-draft fallacy

Once you have 500 fluent-looking words in front of you, the temptation is to give them a quick read-through, tweak a word choice here and there, and then ship it. I've done it. You will too, at least once. Don't make a habit of it.

Unedited (or barely edited) AI prose has a distinctive smell. It's grammatically fine, factually reasonable, tonally generic, and full of filler phrases such as *in today's fast-paced digital landscape* and *it's important to note that.* And, of course, there are those infamous em dashes festooning the document, most of them used either unnecessarily or outright incorrectly. If your website is peppered with that stuff, readers can tell, even if they can't articulate why. Search engines, increasingly, can tell too.

## A practical editing pass

Here's an edit sequence you can apply to AI-generated text. Sure, it's more work than just accepting what the chatbot spits out, but it's still far less work than writing everything from scratch and far less expensive than hiring a professional to write it:

- **Fact-check everything verifiable.** Names, dates, statistics, quotations, URLs. If the AI cites a source, go find that source or ask the AI to do it for you. About a third of the time, it won't exist.
- **Cut the filler.** Search for phrases like *it's important to, in conclusion, navigate the complexities of,* and *in the ever-evolving world of.* Delete them without mercy. The paragraphs around them will usually survive just fine.
- **Inject specifics.** AI writes in generalities because it doesn't know your business. Replace *many customers* with *about 60 percent of the people we see.* Specifics enable you to turn fake writing into real writing.
- **Fix the voice.** Read a paragraph aloud. If it sounds like you wrote it, keep it. If it sounds like a LinkedIn post, rewrite it using the words and phrases you'd actually use.
- **Cut 20 percent.** AI overwrites. You can almost always delete a fifth of any AI draft and lose nothing important. Your readers will thank you.

WARNING

Never — and, yep, I do mean *never* — publish AI-generated content about legal, medical, financial, or safety-critical topics without a qualified human review. Hallucinations in those areas range from embarrassing to actively dangerous.



# Creating Images with AI Tools

Text isn't the only thing AI can generate. With startling speed, the visual side of AI has moved from a curious party trick to a surprisingly useful tool. A few minutes with a well-prompted image generator can produce a hero image, an icon set, or a social-post graphic that would have cost you hundreds of dollars and a stock-photo subscription two years ago.

## The image AI landscape

Here are the big names in image generation:

- **Nano Banana (inside Gemini; `gemini.google.com`):** Google's image-generation model. Its signature strengths are conversational editing and consistent characters across multiple images.
- **Midjourney (`midjourney.com`):** Widely considered the artistic front-runner. Produces gorgeous, stylized imagery. However, it's not as good at photorealistic faces or tightly controlled compositions. Also, it requires a paid subscription.

- **DALL-E (inside ChatGPT; `chat.openai.com`):** OpenAI's image model, available directly in ChatGPT, which is handy because you can iterate in plain English conversation (for example, "make the sky more dramatic, move the cup to the left").
- **Stable Diffusion (`https://stability.ai/`):** Open-source and free. You can run it on your own computer if you have a decent graphics card, or use one of many hosted front-ends. Infinitely customizable, but with a steeper learning curve.
- **Adobe Firefly (`firefly.adobe.com`):** Adobe's model, trained exclusively on licensed and public-domain images. Adobe offers commercial-use indemnification for Firefly output, which matters if you're worried about copyright. It's also built into Photoshop and Illustrator.

## Writing prompts to create images that don't look like stock photos

As with prompts for generating writing, a similar clarity principle applies to prompts for generating images: vague prompts produce vague images. For example:

> A coffee shop

A good image prompt describes four things: subject, style, composition, and lighting. Here's an example:

> A small independent coffee shop interior, late afternoon, shot from eye level near the counter, from the customer's side. Warm tungsten lighting and soft window light from the left. A barista in a green apron pulling an espresso shot, slight motion blur on their hands. Shallow depth of field. Style: documentary photography, natural colors, film grain.

The first prompt gives you a generic, stock-looking coffee shop. The second gives you something specific enough to feel real. Note that the good prompt reads almost like a director's shot notes.

## Where AI images fit on a website

Not every image on your site should be AI-generated, and I'd argue that some images should never be. Here's a reasonable split:

- **Good AI candidates:** Decorative hero images, background textures, illustration-style graphics, icons, social media thumbnails, concept art for pages that don't demand literal accuracy.
- **Risky AI candidates:** Anything showing your products or your actual premises. A fake photo of your store is just another way of lying to your customers.
- **Just don't use AI:** Realistic faces of people who don't exist, used as if they were real employees or customers. It's misleading, and readers are getting better at spotting it.

WARNING

AI image tools sometimes produce output that resembles copyrighted characters, real people, or specific artists' styles closely enough to cause legal trouble. If an image is going on a commercial website, consider using tools such as Adobe Firefly that offer commercial-use guarantees and steer clear of prompts that name specific living artists or brands.

# AI for Brainstorming and Optimization



Writing first (oops, I mean *zeroth*) drafts is the showy use of AI, but some of the most useful applications have nothing to do with generating final content. I've found that AI is a dramatically better brainstorming partner than it is a writer.

## Brainstorming and breaking blocks

If you find yourself stuck on what to write, here are a few prompts to try:

- "I run a small bookkeeping firm. Give me 20 blog-post ideas that would be useful to my small-business clients, ranging from beginner to intermediate."
- "Here's my home page copy. What questions might a first-time visitor have that my current copy doesn't answer?"
- "I want to write about seasonal inventory planning. Give me three different angles I could take: practical checklist, cautionary tale, and industry trend."

You're not looking for a finished idea; you're looking for a list you can riff on. The AI's job is to generate raw material; yours is to pick out the good bits.

### Outlines and structure

I've never experienced writer's block. Not once. Why not? It's not because I have some superhuman ability to crank out prose. It's because I always work from a detailed outline, so I always know what to write next.

You know who's great at creating detailed outlines? That's right: your friendly, neighborhood LLM! So, before you sit down to write a longer piece, ask your AI to create an outline for it. Here's an example prompt:

> Create an outline for a 1,200-word article aimed at small-business owners who have never hired a web designer. The article should cover what to expect a project to cost, what questions to ask, and red flags to watch for. Use H2 subheads and include a one-sentence description of what each section will cover.

You'll get a structure in seconds. Rearrange it, cut sections you don't want, add anything the AI missed, and just like that you have a writing plan. The writing itself is much easier when someone (or something) else has done the skeletal work.

### SEO and accessibility

I cover SEO (search engine optimization) in depth in Book 7 and accessibility in Book 2, Chapter 4, but a few AI-related SEO and accessibility use cases deserve a quick mention here:

- **Meta descriptions:** Paste in your page copy, ask for three different 155-character meta descriptions, and then pick the best one.
- **Headline variations:** Prompt your AI with something like, "Rewrite this headline ten different ways, each with a different emotional hook."
- **Alt text:** Describe your images in plain English, and then ask the AI to turn them into concise, descriptive alt text for accessibility.

## Using AI for Different Content Types

One prompt to rule them all is definitely not the way to go here. Different types of content need different approaches. In this section, I talk about using AI for the three main content categories you'll encounter on a typical business website.

## Short-form content

Short copy, including meta tags, social posts, button labels, and image captions, is where AI shines with the least editing required. The generation is cheap, the risk of factual error is lower because you're not asking for complex claims, and producing ten variants to pick from takes seconds.

A few other good use cases are email subject lines, form placeholders, error messages, and image alt text.

## Long-form content

Articles, guides, and how-to pieces are where the "zeroth draft" philosophy matters most. AI can get you a respectable 800-word structure in a minute, but turning it into something worth reading takes real editing work. Expect to rewrite half of any long-form AI draft and cut the filler mercilessly.

TIP

For long-form writing, try generating your piece in sections rather than all at once. Ask for the introduction, review and edit it, then ask for the first main section, and so on. You'll end up with tighter, more coherent content than if you'd asked for 1,500 words in one shot.



## Structured content

FAQs, product descriptions, comparison tables, and similar repetitive content are AI's sweet spot. You can feed the tool a template and variables and have it crank out a half-dozen variations that share a consistent structure.

Here's a prompt pattern that works well for product descriptions:

> Write a 75-word product description for the following item. Follow this format:
>
> Sentence 1: what it is and who it's for
>
> Sentences 2 and 3: two key features and why they matter
>
> Sentence 4: a concrete use case
>
> Product: [paste product info here]
>
> Tone: friendly, plain-spoken, no marketing fluff.

Paste twenty products, get twenty descriptions back with consistent voice and structure, and then edit as needed. That's a week's work reduced to an afternoon.

# Maintaining Brand Voice with AI

One consistent complaint I hear about AI writing is that it all sounds the same. And it does, out of the box. The secret to getting AI-generated content that sounds like *your* brand is a simple one: show the AI what your brand sounds like.

## Feed the AI samples

The single most effective technique is to paste two or three pieces of your existing writing into the prompt and tell the AI to match their style. Your prompt should be something along these lines:

> Here are three samples of the tone I want you to match:
>
> [Paste sample 1]
>
> [Paste sample 2]
>
> [Paste sample 3]
>
> Now, using that same tone, same sentence rhythm, same vocabulary level, same relationship with the reader, write a 300-word post about [topic].

The results will almost always be startlingly better than merely describing your voice in words ("friendly but professional, with occasional humor, not too formal"). The AI is much better at pattern-matching than it is at following adjectives.

## Build a reusable style prompt

Once you've found a prompt that reliably produces writing in your voice, save it as a template. Many AI tools let you create custom instructions, system prompts, or projects that automatically apply context to every conversation. A good style prompt includes the following:

- A one-paragraph description of your brand, audience, and goals.
- Two or three samples of the writing you want to match.
- A list of words and phrases to avoid (for example, *paradigm shift, revolutionary, game-changing*).
- Any structural or grammatical preferences (such as sentence length, use of contractions, or the Oxford comma).

# Ethical Considerations and Disclosure

I can't wrap up this chapter without a section that mentions (however briefly) some uncomfortable questions around the use of AI. The ethics of AI-generated content are still being worked out in courts, legislatures, newsrooms, and publishers as I write this, and anyone who tells you they have all the answers is selling something. But a few principles are clearly the right call today.

## The training-data question

These models were trained on enormous quantities of text and images scraped from the internet, including, in many cases, copyrighted work whose authors were not asked and not compensated. Several lawsuits are working their way through the courts on this question.

What does that mean for you? Practically, three things:

- The output of most AI tools is probably safe to use commercially, but this is not yet settled law.
- Tools such as Adobe Firefly that explicitly train only on licensed material carry less risk for commercial use.
- If an AI produces output that looks conspicuously like a specific existing work, throw it out!



## Disclosure to readers

Should you tell your readers when content was AI-assisted? My view, for whatever it's worth: yes when it matters and no when it doesn't. If you used AI to generate three headline variants and picked one, nobody needs to know. If you published an entire blog post that you barely edited, that probably belongs in a disclosure. Note, too, that depending on your profession, industry, or jurisdiction, you might be required to follow disclosure policies.

Let's run through the clearer cases:

- **Always disclose** when AI wrote content you're presenting as a human expert's opinion (for example, a CEO's letter, an author's essay).
- **Always disclose** in journalism, academic writing, and any context where authorship is the point.

- **Probably disclose** for blog posts and articles where AI did the majority of the drafting.
- **Don't need to disclose** for microcopy, meta tags, and internal-facing content nobody thinks about as authored.

### Accuracy and hallucinations

The other ethics issue isn't really about AI; it's about you. Publishing inaccurate information on your website is your problem regardless of whether the inaccuracy came from a lazy employee, a bad source, or a hallucinating chatbot. If you use AI to generate claims of fact, you're responsible for verifying them. And, no "the AI did it" isn't a defense that will satisfy an angry customer, a regulator, or a court.

REMEMBER

Anything you publish under your name or your organization's name is your responsibility. AI is a tool you used; it's not a co-author you can blame.

## Best Practices: When AI Helps (and When It Doesn't)

I'll leave you with a rough field guide to the times AI has paid off for me, and the times I've learned (often the hard way) to skip it and just write the thing.

When AI genuinely helps:

- **Initial drafts of anything structural:** Outlines, templates, skeleton pages. AI is faster than you are and your ego isn't attached to the output.
- **Repetitive content at scale:** Fifty product descriptions, thirty FAQ entries, a month of social posts. Humans get sloppy with repetition; AI doesn't.
- **Brainstorming and breaking blocks:** Even bad ideas help you clarify what the good idea is.
- **Translation and rewriting:** Turning formal copy casual, long copy short, American English into British English.
- **Editing support:** Paste in your own draft, ask for a critique, and get a useful second opinion at three in the morning.

When AI is probably the wrong tool:

- **Anything that requires lived experience:** Customer stories, case studies, your founder's origin story. Readers can smell the difference.
- **Authoritative claims in specialized fields:** Medical, legal, financial, and safety content need qualified humans, no exceptions.
- **Breaking or time-sensitive information:** AI models don't know about last week's news and will cheerfully invent plausible-sounding current events.
- **Your distinctive voice pieces:** The blog posts where your personality is the product. If it's easy for AI to write, it's easy for anyone to write, and that's not a place to compete.
- **Final copy in high-stakes contexts:** By *high stakes,* I mean important stuff such as home page hero copy, the headline on your best-performing ad, and content that will be seen by everyone who ever hears about your business. These need the human touch.

AI is a magnificent assistant and a terrible boss. Give it the right jobs — drafts, variants, summaries, the grinding repetitive work that steals your afternoons — and it'll return your time tenfold. Ask it to replace the judgment, taste, and experience that make your website uniquely yours, and you'll end up with a site that could belong to anyone. Which is to say, not much of a site at all.

IN THIS CHAPTER

» Understanding what a CMS does

» Organizing pages and media

» Setting up multi-author workflows

» Giving the headless CMS a look

# Chapter 3
# Content Management Systems

*If you can't describe what you are doing as a process, you don't know what you're doing.*

—W. EDWARDS DEMING

Nobody sets out to manage a website by hand-editing HTML files in a text editor, uploading them one at a time via FTP, and then three days later discovering that they forgot to update the navigation on six other pages. But that's exactly where you end up without a content management system.

A *content management system* (or *CMS* for short) is software that sits between you and all those raw files, handling the tedious plumbing so you can focus on the part you actually care about: the content itself. In this chapter, I walk you through how a CMS works under the hood, how to organize your pages and media files so they don't turn into digital landfill, how to set up workflows when more than one person is creating content, and when (if ever) a headless CMS makes sense for your project.

# Content Management System Basics

I introduce the idea of a CMS briefly in Book 1, Chapter 4, where I describe it as the operating system for your website. That's still a good analogy, but now it's time to open the hood and understand what's going on in there.

## The four jobs every CMS does

Whether it's WordPress, Squarespace, or something custom-built by a team of expensive developers, every CMS does four fundamental things:

- **Content creation:** Gives you an editor (usually something that looks a lot like a simplified word processor), where you write and format your content without touching any HTML. You type, you add a heading, you drop in an image, and the CMS generates the underlying code behind the scenes.
- **Content storage:** Saves your pages, posts, images, user accounts, settings, the whole shebang, in a database or other structured storage. You never have to think about where the files live on the server or how they're organized. The CMS handles all that.
- **Content organization:** Provides tools for structuring your site, such as menus, categories, tags, parent-and-child page relationships, and URL patterns. These tools keep a 10-page website from turning into a 100-page junk drawer.
- **Content delivery:** Pulls the right content from the database based on the URL requested by each visitor's browser, wraps that content in your site's design template, and sends back a finished HTML page. All that happens in a fraction of a second, invisibly.

That's it! Four jobs. Everything else a CMS does, from user management to plug-in systems to theme engines to revision history, is in service of those four things.

## The main flavors of CMS

Not all content management systems are built the same way. Here are the main categories you'll run into:

- **Traditional CMS:** This type of CMS handles both the back end (where you create content) and the front end (where visitors see your site) as one tightly connected package. WordPress, Joomla, and Drupal are the big names here.

You install them on a web server and pick a theme, and everything works together. Most small businesses use traditional CMS, and it's what I cover in detail in Book 5, Chapter 1.

- **Hosted website builders:** Platforms like Squarespace and Wix are essentially CMS products that somebody else hosts and maintains for you. You don't install anything; you sign up, pick a template, and start building. The trade-off is less flexibility for less hassle. I cover hosted website builders in Book 5, Chapter 2.
- **Headless CMS:** These handle only the back-end chores of content storage and management, and then deliver content through an API. There's no built-in front end. Developers build a separate front end (or several) that pulls content from the API. I cover headless CMS in more detail later in this chapter (check out the "Headless CMS Options" section).
- **Static site generators:** Tools such as Hugo, Jekyll, and Eleventy take your content (usually written in Markdown files), run it through templates, and produce a folder full of plain HTML files. No database, no server-side processing. Fast and secure, but not the friendliest option for beginners.
- **Flat-file CMS:** This type of CMS is a middle ground between traditional and static. Systems such as Kirby and Grav store content in files rather than a database, which makes them simpler to set up and back up, but they still generate pages dynamically when visitors arrive.

## Picking a lane

Since WordPress alone powers over 40 percent of all websites, and the hosted platforms cover a huge additional chunk, there's a good chance you'll end up using WordPress or one of the hosted builders. That's a sensible route to take because, together, they handle the needs of the vast majority of small and medium business sites.



The more specialized options — such as headless, static site generators, and flat-file — start to make sense when you have specific technical requirements that the mainstream tools can't meet. I help you figure out whether that applies to you when I get to the headless section later in this chapter.

REMEMBER

A CMS doesn't mean you never need to think about HTML, CSS, or JavaScript. As I mention in Book 1, Chapter 4, understanding these fundamentals helps you troubleshoot issues, customize your site beyond what built-in tools offer, and make better decisions about themes and plug-ins.

# Creating and Organizing Pages

Once your CMS is installed and running (or your hosted builder account is set up), your first real task is creating pages and organizing them into a structure that makes sense to your visitors. This process sounds straightforward, and it's certainly the case that creating a single page *is* usually a no-brainer. The challenge shows up when you have 20 pages, then 50, and you realize half of them are orphans that no menu links to and nobody can find.

## Pages versus posts: Pick the right tool

Most CMS platforms make a distinction between *pages* and *posts*, and choosing the wrong one for a given piece of content creates problems you'll have to untangle later.

*Pages* are for content that doesn't change very often and doesn't have a publication date that matters. Content with titles such as About Us, Contact Us, Our Services, and Privacy Policy are all pages. They live in your site's navigation and visitors expect to find them in roughly the same spot every time they visit.

*Posts* are for content that's timely and part of a stream. Content such as blog entries, news updates, announcements, and event recaps are posts. They're displayed in reverse chronological order (newest first), tagged and categorized, and they gradually scroll off the front page as newer posts replace them.

The rule of thumb: if a visitor would be confused to see a date on it, it's a page. If a visitor would be confused *not* to see a date on it, it's a post.

## Structuring your URLs

The URLs of your pages are more important than most people realize. A clean, readable URL tells visitors (and search engines) what a page is about before anyone clicks it. Compare these two URLs for the same page:

```
example.com/?p=247
example.com/services/consulting
```

The first one is the kind of default URL structure that some CMS platforms ship with out of the box. It tells you nothing. The second tells you exactly where you are in the site: you're on the Consulting page, inside the Services section. That's better for visitors, better for search engines, and better for you when you're trying to manage dozens of pages in the dashboard.

Most CMS platforms call this setting *permalinks* (that's WordPress's term) or *URL structure*. Whatever your platform calls it, change it from the default to something human-readable before you create a single page of content. As I mention in Book 5, Chapter 1, this is one of the very first things you should do after installing WordPress, and the same principle applies to any CMS.

Here are a few URL guidelines worth following:

- Use lowercase letters and hyphens, not underscores or spaces. `about-us` is correct; `About_Us` is not.
- Keep URLs short but descriptive. `example.com/services` is fine; `example.com/our-complete-range-of-professional-services` is not.
- Avoid dates in page URLs. Dates make sense for blog posts (they're time-sensitive content) but not for evergreen pages.

## Building your navigation

Your site's navigation is how visitors move around, and it deserves more thought than most people give it. A CMS typically lets you create and manage menus through a drag-and-drop interface, which makes the mechanics easy. The hard part is deciding what goes where.

Here's the rule I use: your primary navigation (the main menu across the top of the site) should have no more than seven items. Seven is about the upper limit of what a person can scan at a glance without their eyes glazing over. If you have more than seven top-level pages, group some of them under drop-down menus or move the less important ones to a secondary navigation area or the footer.

For a typical small business site, a solid primary navigation might look like this:

- Home
- About
- Products or Services (with drop-down subitems)
- Blog
- Contact

That's five items. Clean, scannable, and nobody gets lost. If you add a Shop, that's six. A Portfolio makes seven. Beyond that, start looking for things to combine or demote to a secondary menu.

Your footer navigation is the place for the pages that need to be accessible but don't deserve top billing: Privacy Policy, Terms of Service, Sitemap, Careers, and so on. Visitors who need those pages know to look in the footer. It's where they've been trained to look by every other website they've ever used.

### Categories, tags, and taxonomies

If your CMS supports blog posts (or any kind of time-based content stream), you'll have access to *categories* and *tags* for organizing that content. These two tools are related but not identical, and using them well makes a real difference in how findable your content is:

- **Categories** are broad, hierarchical groupings. Think of them as the chapters of a book: a relatively small number of them (say five to ten), each covering a major topic area. For a small business blog, your categories might be something like News, Tips, Behind the Scenes, and Industry Updates.
- **Tags** are more granular, non-hierarchical labels. Think of them as the index entries at the back of a book: more specific, more numerous, and applied to individual posts where they're relevant. A blog post in the Tips category might be tagged with `email-marketing`, `automation`, and `small-business`.

The mistake most people make is treating categories and tags as the same. They create 50 categories and no tags, or they create tags that duplicate their categories. Keep categories broad and few, tags specific and descriptive, and you'll end up with a content taxonomy that helps visitors find what they're looking for.

## Managing Media Libraries

If your page and post text is the wardrobe of your website, media files are the accessories that finish the look. Images, videos, PDFs, and downloadable documents all end up in your CMS's *media library,* which is essentially a big bucket where every file you've ever uploaded goes to live and, if you're not careful, to be forgotten.

The media library in most CMS platforms starts out organized and quickly degenerates. You upload a photo, can't remember what you named it, upload it again, and now you have two copies. Multiply that by a year of regular posting and you've got a library full of files named `IMG_4392.jpg` and `Screenshot 2027-03-15 at 2.47.12 PM.png` and no idea which ones are in use on the live site. Sound familiar? Okay, let's fix it.

## Name your files like you'll need to find them again

Before you upload a single file to your CMS, rename it on your computer. Your camera and your screenshot tool don't know what's in the image. You do. Take two seconds and give the file a name that future-you will understand (and thank past-you for):

Bad: `IMG_4392.jpg`

Good: `team-photo-annual-retreat-2026.jpg`

Bad: `download.pdf`

Good: `catering-menu-spring-2027.pdf`

Use lowercase letters and hyphens between words, and include enough context that you can identify the file six months from now without opening it. This also helps with SEO, because search engines read file names, and `team-photo-annual-retreat-2026.jpg` tells Google a lot more than `IMG_4392.jpg` does.

## Organize the library before it gets out of hand

Some CMS platforms (WordPress, for example) automatically sort uploaded media into year-and-month folders on the server, which provides a basic chronological structure but isn't terribly useful when you're trying to find a specific image from who knows when. If your CMS supports custom folders or categories for media (either natively or through a plug-in), use them. Create folders such as Photos, Documents, Logos, and Icons, and file things into them as you upload.

If your CMS doesn't support folders, use a consistent naming convention that effectively does the same thing. Prefix your file names with a category: `blog-hero-content-strategy.jpg`, `product-photo-cosmic-cruller.jpg`, `team-headshot-jordan.jpg`. When you search the library later, typing *blog-hero* will show you all your blog hero images. Alas, it's not as elegant or as efficient as real folders, but it's still miles better than scrolling through 400 files named after timestamps.

## Let the CMS do the image work

Modern CMS platforms have become impressively smart about image handling. When you upload a large photo, most will automatically generate multiple sizes — such as thumbnail, medium, and large — and serve the appropriate one depending on the context. Some will even convert your images automatically to more efficient formats like `WebP`. (As I discuss in Book 2, Chapter 2, WebP files are significantly smaller than JPEG or PNG at comparable quality, which means faster page loads.)

Take advantage of these features instead of fighting them. Upload the highest-quality version of the image you have that's suitable for web use, and let the CMS create the sizes it needs. Don't manually resize images to 400 pixels wide on your desktop and then upload the tiny version because you'll regret it the first time you need the full-size image and realize you never saved it.

TIP

Most CMS platforms let you set a maximum upload size and can auto-optimize images on upload, either natively or through a plug-in. Set this up once and forget about it. For WordPress specifically, a plug-in like Smush (`wpmudev.com`) or ShortPixel (`shortpixel.com`) handles image optimization automatically every time you upload a file. For the (very little) effort spent on a one-time setup, you get a permanent benefit.

### Write alt text in the media library, not the post

As I discuss in Book 2, Chapter 4, every image on your website needs *alt text:* a short text description that screen readers use to describe the image to visitors who can't see it. Most CMS platforms enable you to add alt text in two places: in the media library (as a property of the image file itself) and on the individual page where you insert the image.

Unless a particular image needs different alt text in different contexts, do yourself a favor and add your alt text in the media library. That way, the alt text travels with the image everywhere it's used. Every time you insert that image into a page or post, the alt text is already filled in. If you add alt text only on the individual page, you have to re-enter the text every time you reuse that image somewhere else, and (let's be honest) you probably won't or (continuing with the honesty theme) you might forget.

## Version Control for Content

If you've ever deleted a paragraph, saved the page, and then slapped your forehead when you realized you actually needed that paragraph, hard-won experience has already shown you why version control is important. *Version control* for content is your CMS's capability to save previous versions of your pages and posts so you can review what changed, compare versions side by side, and roll back the text to an earlier state when things go sideways.

This type of version control is different from the one developers use for code (which I cover in Book 10, Chapter 1). Git tracks every line of code across every file in a project, with branching, merging, and a lot of other sophisticated capabilities. CMS version control is simpler: it saves snapshots of individual pages or posts each time you click Save or Publish, and it lets you compare those snapshots. Think of it as a more sophisticated version of the Undo command's history of your recent edits.

## Drafts, revisions, and published states

Most CMS platforms organize content into a few distinct states that represent where a piece of content is in its lifecycle:

- **Draft:** The content is in progress. Only logged-in users with the correct permissions can see it. It's not live on the public site.
- **Pending review:** The content has been submitted by an author and is waiting for an editor to look it over. Not every CMS supports this state, but WordPress and many others do.
- **Scheduled:** The content has been written and approved but isn't live yet. It will automatically publish at a date and time you specified. (The "Scheduling content for later" section, coming up in just a moment, has more on scheduling.)
- **Published:** The content is live on the public site. Visitors can see it.

Every time you save a published page, most CMS platforms also save a *revision*, which is a snapshot of the page as it existed before your latest changes. WordPress, for instance, stores every revision by default, which means you can look at a complete timeline of every change ever made to a page, who made it, and when they made it.



## Reverting to an earlier version

When you need to roll back a page to a previous version, the process in most CMS platforms goes something like this:

1. Open the page in the editor.
2. Look for a revisions link or panel (in WordPress, it's in the Settings sidebar on the right).

3. Browse the timeline of saved versions.
4. Compare the current version with an earlier one side by side.
5. Restore the earlier version if that's what you want.

REMEMBER

Restoring a revision doesn't delete your current version. It creates a *new* revision that's a copy of the old one. So, you can always undo an undo. (Which, believe me, happens more often than you'd think.)

## Scheduling content for later

Most CMS platforms enable you to write content now and schedule it to publish at a future date and time that you specify. This feature is useful for a handful of common scenarios:

- You're batching a week's worth of blog posts over the weekend and want them to go live on different days.
- You're coordinating a product launch and the page needs to appear at a specific hour.
- You're going on vacation and want the blog to keep publishing while you're sipping something tropical.

The mechanics are straightforward. In most CMS editors, where you'd normally click Publish, you instead set a publication date in the future and click Schedule. The CMS handles the rest.

TIP

Before you schedule anything, make sure your CMS's time zone setting is correct. Scheduling a post for 9:00 AM is useful only if the CMS agrees with you about *which* 9:00 AM you mean. As I mention in Book 5, Chapter 1, checking the time zone is one of the first things to do after a fresh WordPress install, and the same applies to any CMS.

# Multi-Author Workflows

If you're the only person creating content for your site, feel free to skip this section and come back to it when your team grows. But the moment a second person starts contributing, whether it's a colleague, a freelance writer, or a summer intern, you need to think about who can do what and how your content progresses from first draft to published post.

## Defining roles and permissions

Every CMS that supports multiple users has a system of roles and permissions. A *role* is a label you assign to a user account, and each role comes with its own *permissions* that specify what that user is allowed to do. The role names vary by platform, but most CMS role systems look roughly like this:

- **Administrator:** Can do everything, including create content, manage other users, install plug-ins, change settings, delete the entire site if they're having a really bad day. Reserve this role for yourself and maybe one other deeply trusted person (that is, someone who *won't* delete the site when things turn sour).
- **Editor:** Can create, edit, publish, and delete any content on the site, including content created by other users. Editors are your quality gatekeepers.
- **Author:** Can create and publish their own content, but can't touch anyone else's. This role is a good fit for regular contributors who don't need editorial control over the whole site.
- **Contributor:** Can write and submit content, but can't publish it. Their posts land in a pending-review queue for an editor to approve. This role is the safest for new or occasional contributors.
- **Subscriber:** Can log in and manage their own profile, but can't create or edit content. This role is useful mostly if your site has membership or community features.

REMEMBER

Follow the *principle of least privilege:* give each user only the permissions they need to do their job. If Casey is writing guest blog posts, make Casey a contributor, not an editor. If Jordan manages the blog but shouldn't be installing plug-ins, make Jordan an editor. This is partially a trust issue, but mostly it's about reducing the number of things that can go wrong accidentally.

## The draft-review-publish workflow

Once you have roles set up, you can create a simple but effective editorial workflow. The basic version has just the three steps:

1. The author writes a post and saves it as a draft. When it's ready for review, the author changes the status to pending review (or just messages the editor that it's done).
2. The editor reviews the post, checking for accuracy, voice, formatting, and SEO basics, and then sends the writing back to the author with notes or makes edits directly or both.
3. When the piece is ready, the editor publishes it.

Write, review, publish. Next!

For most small teams, that three-step workflow is all you need. You don't need a project management tool or a Gantt chart or a twelve-person editorial board. You need one person writing, one person reviewing, and a quick way to communicate (email, Slack, a sticky note on a monitor) when something is ready for the next step.

If you need something more structured — for example, your content must pass through a legal review before publishing, or you have five writers and want to track where every piece is at any given moment — no problem. Many CMS platforms have plugins or built-in features that add approval stages, editorial comments, and status dashboards. In WordPress, a plug-in such as PublishPress Planner (`publishpress.com`) adds these capabilities without a lot of fuss.

### Tracking who changed what

When more than one person has edit access to your site, somebody will eventually change something they shouldn't have, and you'll need to figure out what happened. This is where *audit logs* come in.

An audit log records every action taken in the CMS: who logged in, who edited which page, who installed a plug-in, who changed a setting. It's the CMS equivalent of a security camera. You don't need to watch it every day, but when something goes wrong — a page looks different than it did yesterday, a menu item has vanished, a plug-in has been mysteriously deactivated — the audit log tells you who did it and when.

WordPress doesn't include an audit log by default, but the WP Activity Log plugin (`wpactivitylog.com`) adds one and is free for most use cases. If you're using a hosted platform such as Squarespace or Wix, audit-logging features vary by plan, so check what's included in yours.

## Headless CMS Options

As I mention in Book 1, Chapter 4, a traditional CMS handles both the *back end* (where you create and manage content) and the *front end* (where visitors read and navigate the pages of your site). A *headless CMS* deliberately guillotines the front end and handles only the back end. Your content lives in the headless CMS, and you build one or more separate front ends that pull content through an API.

If your immediate reaction to that is "Why would anyone want to do *that*," you're not alone. For many projects, going headless just doesn't make sense. But there are specific situations where opting for headless is a genuinely smart choice, so it's worth understanding what it is and when it applies.

## What "headless" really means

Think of a traditional CMS as a restaurant with a kitchen and a dining room. The kitchen (the back end) prepares the food (your content), and the dining room (the front end) serves it to customers (your visitors). Everything is under one roof and tightly connected.

A headless CMS is a kitchen with no dining room. It prepares the food and puts it on a counter, and then someone else — a food truck, a catering company, even three different dining rooms in three different neighborhoods — picks it up and serves it however they like. The kitchen doesn't care how the food gets served. It just makes the food available.

In technical terms, the headless CMS stores your content and exposes it through an API (as I discuss in Book 1, Chapter 4). Your website, which you build with whatever front-end technology you prefer, calls that API to fetch content and displays it however you've designed it. But so could a mobile app, a digital kiosk, a smartwatch notification, or an in-store display. Same content, multiple destinations.

## When headless is the right call

A headless CMS starts to make sense when one or more of these situations describe your project:

- **You need to deliver content to multiple front ends.** If your business has a website, a native mobile app, and digital menu boards in the store, and they all need to display the same content (product descriptions, prices, hours of operation), a headless CMS enables you to maintain that content in one place and push it to all three destinations.
- **Your development team wants front-end control.** If you have developers building a custom front end with React, Vue, or another modern JavaScript framework, a headless CMS lets them use their own tools without being constrained by the CMS's built-in templating system.
- **You need to reuse structured content across contexts.** Maybe a product description needs to appear on the product page, in search results, in an email campaign, and in a mobile push notification. A headless CMS with well-structured content models makes that kind of reuse straightforward.

- **Performance is paramount.** Because headless setups often pair with static site generators or modern front-end frameworks that pre-render pages, the resulting websites can be extremely fast. There's no database query happening on every page load — just prebuilt HTML or client-side rendering, often from cached API responses.

## When traditional is still the right call

For every use case where headless shines, there are four in which a traditional CMS is simpler, cheaper, and more practical:

- **You have one website and no plans for a mobile app or other channels.** If all your content goes to one destination, the headless architecture adds complexity you'll never benefit from.
- **Your content editors aren't developers.** One of the biggest drawbacks of headless is that the editing experience can feel abstract. Traditional CMS editors show you something close to what the finished page will look like. Headless editors often show you structured fields and raw text with no preview of the result, which can frustrate non-technical editors.
- **Budget and time are tight.** A headless setup requires building or configuring a separate front end, which means developer time and cost. A traditional CMS with a good theme is ready to go almost immediately.
- **You don't have a developer on the team.** If nobody on your team can build a front end that consumes an API, a headless CMS is a kitchen with no one to serve the food. The food just sits on the counter getting cold.

For most small- and medium-business websites, a traditional CMS such as WordPress (or a hosted builder such as Squarespace) is the right tool. Headless is a specialized solution for specialized needs, and there's nothing wrong with recognizing that your needs aren't that specialized.

## The leading headless platforms

If you've decided that headless makes sense for your project, here are the major platforms worth evaluating:

- **Contentful (`contentful.com`):** One of the most established headless CMS platforms. It offers good documentation, a generous free tier for small projects, and a polished content modeling interface. It's popular with teams that want a mature, well-supported product.

- **Sanity (`sanity.io`):** A headless CMS with a highly customizable editing interface called Sanity Studio. The free tier is generous, and the developer community is active and helpful. A strong choice if you want maximum flexibility in how the editing experience works.
- **Strapi (`strapi.io`):** An open-source, self-hosted headless CMS. You install it on your own server, which gives you complete control but also means you're responsible for hosting and maintenance. It's good for teams that want to own their infrastructure.
- **Prismic (`prismic.io`):** Focused on making the content-editing experience as pleasant as possible. Its Slice system lets editors build pages from reusable content components, which bridges the gap between headless flexibility and traditional WYSIWYG convenience.
- **Storyblok (`storyblok.com`):** A headless CMS with a built-in visual editor, which is unusual in the headless world. If your editors need to see a preview of what their content will look like on the front end, Storyblok is worth a close look.

Each of these platforms has a free tier or an open-source option, so you can experiment without spending a dime. The right choice depends on your team's technical skills, your budget, and how much control you want over the editing experience versus the front-end presentation.

IN THIS CHAPTER

» Understanding why blogging still matters for business

» Setting up your blog

» Writing posts people want to read

» Getting posts in front of the right audience

Chapter 4

# Blogging for Your Business

*The scariest moment is always just before you start.*

—STEPHEN KING

Every few years, somebody declares that blogging is dead. It happened when Twitter took off. It happened when Instagram went mainstream. It happened when TikTok ate everybody's attention span. And yet blogs are still chugging along, quietly doing the one thing none of those platforms can do: building a library of searchable, linkable content that's entirely yours on a domain you own and control.

If you run a small business and you're not blogging, you're leaving one of the most cost-effective marketing tools on the table. Sure, blogging takes work. You have to show up, you have to write, and you have to do it regularly. But the payoff in search traffic, customer engagement, and customer loyalty is hard to beat. In this chapter, I walk you through why blogging still matters, how to set up a blog, how to write posts people want to read, and how to get those posts in front of the right eyeballs.

# Why Blogging Still Matters

Okay, I hear you: When someone suggests you start a business blog, your first thought is probably something along the lines of "Who has time for *that?*" followed closely by "Does anyone even *read* blogs anymore?" The answer to the second question is: "Yep, absolutely, more people than ever." The answer to the first is: "You," once you realize how much a blog can do for your business with surprisingly little effort.

A blog gives your website a reason to change. Without one, your site is a glorified digital brochure: static, finished, and increasingly stale. With one, your site is a living thing that grows over time, answers questions from real customers, and gives search engines fresh content to index. That last point is worth emphasizing, because it's the reason most small businesses start blogging in the first place.

## Blogging versus social media

If you already post on Instagram and Facebook, isn't that the same thing? Not even close. Social media is rented land. You're building on someone else's platform, playing by someone else's rules, and subject to someone else's algorithm deciding who sees your stuff. One policy change, one algorithm tweak, one platform implosion (remember Vine?), and your audience can vanish overnight.

A blog, on the other hand, lives on your own website, under your own domain name. You own it. Nobody can throttle its reach or bury it in a feed. Every post you publish becomes a permanent, searchable page on your site that can keep bringing in visitors for years. It's not unusual for engaging blog posts from a decade ago to still generate traffic today. Try getting that kind of shelf life out of a tweet!

That said, social media and blogging aren't enemies. They're teammates. You write the blog post on your site, and then share it on social media to drive traffic back to it. The blog is the home base; social media is the megaphone. I talk more about this combination in the "Content Distribution Strategy" section, later in this chapter.

## The SEO connection

Search engines love blogs. Not because they're sentimental about the written word, but because high-quality blogs produce exactly what search engines are looking for: fresh, relevant, keyword-rich content organized around specific topics. Every targeted, relevant blog post you publish is another page that can rank in search results for a specific question or topic. Over time, those pages compound.

A site with 50 useful blog posts has 50 chances to show up in search results. A site with zero blog posts has, well, *you* do the math.

I cover search engine optimization in depth in Book 7, so I won't go deep on the mechanics here. But the short version is this: if you want your website to show up when people search for topics related to your business, a blog is one of the most effective tools you've got.

REMEMBER

Blogging isn't about publishing for the sake of publishing. Every post should serve a purpose: answer a question your customers actually ask, explain something your competitors don't bother to explain, or demonstrate your expertise in a way that builds trust. A hundred thin, pointless posts are worth less than ten good ones.

# Setting Up a Blog

If you're already running a CMS — such as WordPress, Squarespace, Wix, or any of the platforms I cover in Book 5 — adding a blog to your site is straightforward. Most of these platforms were designed with blogging in mind from the start, so the infrastructure is already there. You just need to make a few decisions about how to structure things.

## Choosing where to blog

For blog location, you have two basic options: integrate your blog into your existing website, or set up a standalone blog on a separate platform. For the vast majority of small businesses, the first option is the right one. An integrated blog lives at something like `yoursite.com/blog` and shares the same design, navigation, and domain authority as the rest of your site. That's what you want. Every visitor who lands on a blog post is already on your website, one click away from your services page, your contact form, or your online store.

A standalone blog on a separate domain or a free platform such as Medium might make sense if you're testing the waters before committing, but for a real business, keep the blog under your own roof. You want those search engine benefits going to your domain, not someone else's.

## Structuring your blog

As I mention in Book 6, Chapter 3, most CMS platforms distinguish between *pages* (static content such as About Us and Contact) and *posts* (time-stamped content that's displayed newest first). Your blog entries are posts. They get a publication date, they appear in reverse chronological order, and you can organize them with categories and tags.

The first structural decision is where your blog lives in your site's navigation. Most small business sites put a Blog link in the main navigation menu, pointing to a page that lists recent posts. That's simple, obvious, and it works. Don't overthink it.

The second decision is your permalink structure, which is the pattern your blog post URLs will use. As I discuss in Book 6, Chapter 3, clean, readable URLs matter. For blog posts, the most common (and most effective) pattern is `yoursite.com/blog/post-title`. This tells both humans and search engines what the page is about. Avoid date-heavy URL patterns like `yoursite.com/2027/04/21/post-title` unless your content is genuinely time-sensitive (like a news site). Dates in URLs make older posts look stale even when they're not.

TIP

Set your permalink structure before you publish your first post. Changing URL patterns later means every existing link to your posts breaks unless you set up redirects, and that's a headache nobody needs.

## Setting up categories

*Categories* are the broad buckets that organize your blog content. As I mention in Book 6, Chapter 3, think of categories as the chapters of a book and use a small number of them, each covering a major topic area. Five to eight categories is the sweet spot for most small business blogs. Fewer than that and categories aren't doing much work; more than that and you're slicing things too thin.

Here's a practical example. Say Jordan runs a small accounting firm. Good blog categories might be:

- **Tax Tips:** Practical advice for small business tax planning and filing
- **Bookkeeping Basics:** How-to content for business owners who handle their own books
- **Industry News:** Changes in tax law, regulatory updates, deadlines to know about
- **Small Business Finance:** Broader financial planning, cash flow, and budgeting advice
- **Behind the Scenes:** Office news, team introductions, community involvement

Every post Jordan writes should fit neatly into one of those categories. If a post idea doesn't fit any of them, it's a sign that the idea is off-topic or a new category is needed. Usually, it's the former.

# Blog Post Best Practices

Alright, your blog is set up, your categories are in place, and you're staring at a blank editor wondering what to type. This is the part where Stephen King's advice from the top of this chapter becomes relevant. The scariest moment is just before you start. So, let's take the fear out of it by breaking a blog post down into its component parts.

## The anatomy of a blog post

Every effective blog post, regardless of topic, industry, or length, follows roughly the same structure:

- **Headline:** The first thing people see and the thing that determines whether they click. I devote an entire section to headlines later in this chapter (the "Creating Engaging Headlines" section), so hold tight.
- **Hook:** The opening sentence or paragraph that pulls the reader in. A good hook makes a promise, asks a question, or states something surprising. A bad hook starts with "In today's fast-paced digital landscape . . ." (please don't).
- **Body:** The substance of the post, broken into scannable sections with subheadings. This is where you deliver on whatever the headline promised.
- **Call to action:** What do you want the reader to do next? Subscribe to your newsletter? Book a consultation? Read a related post? Don't leave them hanging.

That's it. Headline, hook, body, call to action. If you nail those four pieces, you'll have a solid blog post. Everything else is refinement.

The hook deserves a bit more attention, because it's where most business blog posts go wrong. Here's an example. Say Alex runs a landscaping company and wants to write a post about lawn care in the spring. A weak hook might be: "Spring is here and it's time to think about your lawn." True, but boring. A stronger hook would be: "If you mowed your lawn last weekend and it looked worse afterward, you probably made one of these three mistakes." The second version creates a specific, relatable scenario and a promise to solve it. That's what makes someone keep reading.

## How long should a post be?

The most frequently asked question about blogging is probably, "How long should a post be?" so you'd think I'd have a good answer for it. Alas, I don't. That's because the only possible answer is, "It depends." (I know, I know. You wanted a number!) A post needs to be long enough to fully address its topic, but it makes no sense to pad a post with filler just to meet an arbitrary word count. For most small-business blogs, heeding those two guidelines means that most posts are somewhere between 800 and 1,500 words.

Shorter posts of, say, 400 to 600 words are fine for quick tips, announcements, or news updates. Longer posts over 2,000 words work well for comprehensive guides and cornerstone content (which I discuss in Book 6, Chapter 1). But the average blog post that answers a specific question or explains a specific concept? That 800–1,500 word range will get the job done without wearing out your reader or your keyboard.

REMEMBER

If you're struggling to come up with 800 words on a topic, it might be too narrow. If you can't stop at 1,500, the topic might be too broad. As I mention in Book 6, Chapter 1, your content pillars can help you find the right scope: wide enough to be useful and narrow enough to be specific.

## How often should you post?

The second-most-frequently asked question about blogging is probably, "How often should I post?" and the answer might surprise you: "Less often than you probably think." Once a week? Great! Twice a month? That's fine. Once a month? Okay, let's call that the bare minimum if you want your blog to build and maintain some momentum. The most important thing is consistency. A blog that publishes one good post every two weeks, like clockwork, will outperform a blog that publishes five posts in January and then goes silent until June.

As I discuss in Book 6, Chapter 1, an editorial calendar is the tool that keeps you honest here. Put your blog posts on the calendar with deadlines, assign them to trustworthy people, and treat them like any other business obligation. Because that's what they are.

TIP

Perhaps the biggest obstacle to maintaining a consistent schedule is having to scramble for a topic every time a deadline rolls around. Instead, spend one morning a month brainstorming ideas and sketching outlines for your next several posts. Then, when it's time to write, you're not starting from zero because you're filling in a structure that's already there. (As I mention in Book 6, Chapter 2, AI tools are terrific at helping you generate those ideas and outlines lickety-split.)

WARNING

The most common blogging mistake is, by far, overpublishing in the first month or so. You're bursting at the seams with energy and enthusiasm, so you publish every day for a week, every second day for a couple of weeks. Woo-hoo! Ah, but then life happens and you don't post again for three months. Start with a pace you can maintain even during your busiest season. You can always publish more often if the spirit moves you.

## Formatting for scanners

It's an unfortunate fact of online reading that most people don't read blog posts word for word. They scan. They skim the headings, read the first sentence of each section, glance at any bold text, and decide whether the post is worth their time. Your job as a blogger is to make that scanning experience as productive as possible. Here are a few formatting habits that help:

- **Use subheadings generously.** Break your post into sections with clear, descriptive headings. A reader who's scanning should be able to understand the gist of your post by reading only the headings.
- **Keep paragraphs short.** Three to five sentences per paragraph is ideal. Long, dense paragraphs are intimidating on a screen, especially on a phone.
- **Use bold text for key phrases.** Bold the most important point in a paragraph so scanners catch it. But don't overdo it — if everything is bold, nothing is.
- **Include images and white space.** A wall of text with no visual breathing room sends readers running for cover. I discuss using images in more detail a bit later in the "Adding Multimedia to Posts" section.

# Creating Engaging Headlines

You can write the most brilliant, insightful, life-changing blog post in the history of the internet, but if the headline is boring, almost nobody will read it. The headline is the make-or-break moment. It's what shows up in search results, social media feeds, email subject lines, and your blog's post list. It does about 80 percent of the work of getting someone to click.

## Why headlines matter so much

When somebody sees your blog post in a list of search results, they're making a split-second decision: "Is this worth my time?" The headline is the only information they have to work with. A vague, generic headline such as "Thoughts on Marketing" gives the reader no reason to click. A specific headline like "5 Email Subject Lines That Doubled Our Open Rate" gives the reader a reason, a number, and a promise. Which one would you click?

## Headline formulas that work

You don't need to reinvent the wheel every time you write a headline. A handful of proven patterns work reliably:

- **The how-to:** Direct, practical, and promises a clear outcome: "How to Choose a Plumber Without Getting Ripped Off."
- **The numbered list:** Numbers are specific and scannable, and readers love them: "7 Mistakes First-Time Homebuyers Make (and How to Avoid Them)."
- **The question:** Questions engage curiosity and make the reader want to find out the answer: "Is Your Roof Ready for Hurricane Season?"
- **The "why" headline:** Challenges assumptions and creates urgency: "Why Your Small Business Needs a Privacy Policy (Even If You Think It Doesn't)."
- **The guide:** Signals comprehensive, trustworthy content: "The Complete Beginner's Guide to Filing Quarterly Taxes."

You can also use AI to generate headline variations quickly, as I discuss in Book 6, Chapter 2. Ask your AI tool for ten angles on the same topic and you'll often find one better (and a lot faster) than anything you'd have come up with on your own.

## Headlines to avoid

Here are a few headline anti-patterns to steer clear of:

- **The clickbait trap:** "You Won't Believe What Happened When We Changed Our Logo!" Maybe this works on a tabloid site, but for a business blog it erodes trust faster than you can say "unsubscribe."
- **The vague placeholder:** "An Update from Our Team." An update about what? Tell me before I click or I won't.
- **The jargon bomb:** "Leveraging Synergistic Omnichannel Strategies for B2B Verticals." I don't even know what that means, and I'm pretty sure the person who wrote it doesn't either.

TIP

Write three to five headline options for every post before you pick one. Your first idea is rarely your best. Read each option out loud and ask yourself: "If I saw this in a search result, would I click it?" If the answer is "Eh, maybe," keep writing.

# Adding Multimedia to Posts

A blog post doesn't have to be just text. In fact, it probably shouldn't be. Images, videos, and other visual elements break up walls of text, illustrate concepts that are hard to explain in words alone, and make your posts more shareable on social media. But there's a right way and a wrong way to use multimedia in your posts.

## Images that earn their place

The key word here is *earn.* Every image in a blog post should do at least one of these things: illustrate a concept, show a result, provide evidence, or give the reader's eyes a resting point between long sections of text. Stock photos of people in suits shaking hands do none of those.

Good blog images include screenshots of the thing you're explaining, photos of your product or workspace, simple diagrams or charts, and original graphics. If you're using stock photography, choose images that feel authentic and specific rather than generic and corporate. The less a photo looks like a stock photo, the better it works.

How many images should a blog post have? There's no magic number, but a reasonable rule of thumb is one image for every 300 to 500 words. That gives readers regular visual breaks without turning the post into a slideshow. If your post is heavy on instructions or processes, screenshots at each step are especially helpful because readers can glance at the screenshot and immediately see whether they're in the right place.

## Embedding video

Video is one of the most engaging content formats on the web, and embedding a video in a blog post is dead simple. If the video lives on YouTube or Vimeo, you copy the embed code from the video's share options and paste it into your blog editor's HTML view. Most modern CMS platforms also let you just paste the video URL directly into the editor; the embedding happens automatically. Nice.

Here are a few tips for using video in blog posts:

- **Keep videos short.** Two to five minutes is the sweet spot for most business blog content. If your video is twenty minutes long, it's a webinar, not a blog supplement.
- **Don't let the video replace the text.** Some visitors can't or won't watch video. They might be in a quiet office, on a slow connection, or using a screen reader. Summarize the key points of the video in the text of the post or, even better, provide the transcript.
- **Don't auto-play videos.** Nobody — I repeat, *nobody* — likes to navigate to a page and have a video start playing automatically. Don't do it.
- **Host the video on YouTube or Vimeo rather than uploading it directly to your website.** Video files are enormous, and self-hosting them will slow your site down and eat through your storage quota. As a bonus, folks hanging around these video sites might come across your videos and generate more traffic to your site.

## When less is more

It's vital to remember that multimedia should enhance your post, not overwhelm it. A post with one strong image and one well-placed video is better than a post stuffed with six mediocre stock photos, two animated GIFs, and an auto-playing audio clip. Every piece of media you add should earn its spot by making the post clearer, more engaging, or more useful. If it doesn't do any of those things, leave it out.

REMEMBER

As discussed in Book 6, Chapter 3, your CMS media library can get cluttered fast. Name files descriptively, organize them into folders if possible, and delete unused uploads periodically. Future-you will be grateful.

# Comment Management and Community Building

Comments used to be the beating heart of the blogosphere. (Remember that word? Blogosphere? Those were simpler times.) Readers would leave thoughtful responses, bloggers would reply, conversations would unfold, and everybody felt like part of a community. Then the spam bots arrived, and the trolls followed close behind, and a lot of bloggers started wondering whether comments were more trouble than they were worth.

## To comment or not to comment

Whether to enable comments on your blog is a legitimate question, and the answer depends on your business and your capacity to manage them. Here are the considerations.

Comments are worth enabling if you have the time (or a team member with the time) to moderate them, your audience is likely to leave constructive feedback, and your industry benefits from visible customer interaction. A local restaurant blog where regulars leave comments about their favorite dishes? That's community gold.

Comments are probably not worth the trouble if you're a solo operator with no time to moderate, your industry attracts a lot of spam or hostile commentary, or you'd rather direct conversations to social media or email. Plenty of successful business blogs, small and large, have turned off comments and haven't looked back.

## Managing comment spam

If you do enable comments, spam management is non-negotiable. Without moderation, your comment sections will fill up with links to dubious pharmaceutical websites, cryptocurrency scams, and suspiciously enthusiastic praise from accounts named BestSEOServices2026. Yuck.

Most CMS platforms have built-in spam filtering. WordPress, for instance, ships with Akismet, a spam filter that catches the majority of junk comments automatically. If you're on WordPress, activate Akismet immediately. (As I discuss in Book 5, Chapter 1, you can install and configure Akismet from the Plugins section of your WordPress dashboard.) Other platforms such as Squarespace and Wix have their own built-in comment filtering.

Beyond automated filtering, set your comments to require approval before they appear on the site. Yes, this means you must check and approve real comments manually (although check whether your blog can be set to automatically approve new comments from previously approved commenters), but it also means no spam comment ever goes live on your site. That's a trade-off worth making.

### Building community without a comment section

If you decide to turn off comments, or if you want to supplement them, there are other ways to build a community around your blog content:

- **Email responses:** End each post with "Have a question? Reply to this email" or "Drop me a line at `hello@yoursite.com`." You'd be surprised how many people prefer a private reply to a public comment.
- **Social media discussion:** Share your post on social media and invite discussion there. The comments happen on the platform where your audience is already hanging out.
- **Newsletter replies:** If you send your blog posts out as a newsletter (and you should; more on that shortly in the "Email newsletters" section), encourage subscribers to hit Reply. Newsletter replies are some of the most engaged, thoughtful feedback you'll ever get.

## Content Distribution Strategy

Publishing a blog post and hoping people find it is like printing a flyer and leaving it in your desk drawer. The writing is the first half of the job; distribution is the second half. Every post you publish should have a distribution plan, even if that plan is just a few simple steps.

### Email newsletters

Email is the most reliable distribution channel you have. Social media algorithms decide who sees your posts. Email goes straight to the inbox. If someone has given you their email address and asked to hear from you, that's permission you should use wisely.

The simplest email distribution strategy is to send your blog post to your email list when you publish it. Not the whole post, just the headline, the first paragraph or two, and a link to read the rest on your site. That link drives traffic back to your blog, where visitors can explore other content, learn about your services, and generally do all the things you built the website for in the first place.

Building that email list is a topic worthy of its own book, but the basics are simple: put a signup form on your website (your sidebar, your footer, and a dedicated landing page are all good spots), give people a clear reason to subscribe ("Get our monthly tax tips delivered to your inbox" beats "Subscribe to our newsletter" every time), and never, ever buy an email list. Bought lists are full of people who didn't ask to hear from you, and emailing them is a fast track to spam complaints and a ruined sender reputation.

As I discuss in Book 6, Chapter 1, newsletters deserve a realistic schedule. Don't promise a weekly email if you can deliver only monthly. And make sure every email gives the reader something worth opening. Nobody wants an inbox full of "Just checking in!" messages from businesses they barely remember signing up for.

## Social media sharing

Every blog post should be shared on whatever social media platforms your audience uses. That might be LinkedIn for a B2B consulting firm, Instagram for a bakery, Facebook for a local service business, or all of the above. The key is to write a caption instead of just pasting the link and walking away. Give people a reason to click. Tease the most interesting point. Ask a question. Pull out a surprising statistic.

Here's an example. Say you've published a blog post titled "5 Signs Your Water Heater Is About to Fail." A lazy social media share would be: "New blog post! 5 Signs Your Water Heater Is About to Fail." A better share would be: "Sign number three surprised us, too. If your hot water runs out faster than it used to, there might be more going on than you think." The second one gives the reader a reason to care before they click.

TIP

Don't share a post just once. A single social media post has a shelf life measured in hours. Share it the day it publishes, again a few days later with a different angle, and once more a few weeks after that. Your audience isn't sitting around waiting for your post; most of them missed it the first time.

## RSS feeds (yes, still)

If you're old enough to remember Google Reader, you might think RSS is a relic. It's not. *RSS* (which stands for *Really Simple Syndication*) is a standardized format that lets people subscribe to your blog using a feed reader app like Feedly or Feedbin. Most CMS platforms generate an RSS feed automatically, so you don't have to do anything to set it up. It's just there, quietly working in the background.

RSS won't drive huge traffic numbers, but the people who use RSS readers tend to be dedicated, tech-savvy readers who read what they subscribe to. That's a quality audience worth having, even if it's a small one.

## Repurposing your posts

A single blog post can become multiple pieces of content with little effort:

- » Pull out the key points and turn them into a series of social media posts.
- » Record yourself reading the post (or summarizing it) and you've got a podcast segment or a short video.
- » Combine several related posts into a downloadable guide or e-book.
- » Turn a list-style post into an infographic.

As I discuss in Book 6, Chapter 2, AI can help with repurposing. Paste your blog post into an AI and ask for five social media posts based on the content, or a 200-word email summary. It takes seconds, and the results are usually a solid starting point that just needs a bit of your own voice sprinkled on top.

# Measuring Blog Performance

You've written the posts, distributed them, and waited patiently. Now what? How do you know if your blog is doing anything? This is where metrics come in, and I have good news: you don't need a statistics degree to figure out whether your blog is working.

## The metrics that matter

You can measure dozens of things about a blog, but for a small business, a handful of metrics tell you most of what you need to know:

- » **Page views:** How many times each post is being viewed. Page views tell you which topics resonate with your audience and which ones fall flat.
- » **Traffic sources:** Where your visitors are coming from, such as search engines, social media, email, or direct visits. These sources tell you which distribution channels are working.
- » **Time on page:** How long visitors spend reading a post. If the average time on page is eight seconds for a 1,800-word article, people aren't reading, they're bouncing.

- **Conversion actions:** Whether readers are doing what you want them to do. Signing up for the newsletter, clicking through to a product page, filling out a contact form? This is the metric that connects your blog to actual business results.

REMEMBER

Don't check your analytics every day. Seriously. Daily fluctuations are mostly noise. Check monthly, look for trends, and make adjustments based on patterns, not individual data points. If posts about tax tips consistently outperform posts about office culture, write more about tax tips!

## Tools for tracking

The most widely used analytics tool is Google Analytics, which is free and integrates with virtually every CMS platform. Setting it up usually involves pasting a small tracking snippet into your site's header, and most CMS platforms have built-in settings or plug-ins that make the process even easier. I cover analytics setup and interpretation in detail in Book 9, Chapter 1, so I won't rehash all the how-to steps here.

If Google Analytics feels like overkill for your needs (and for a small blog, it can), simpler alternatives such as Plausible (`plausible.io`) and Fathom (`usefathom.com`) offer streamlined, privacy-focused dashboards that show you the numbers that matter without burying you in data you'll never use. Both are paid services, but the simplicity might be worth it if you'd rather spend your time writing posts than deciphering analytics dashboards.

Whatever tool you choose, the important thing is to set it up before you publish your first post. Retroactive analytics aren't a thing: you can't measure traffic that wasn't being tracked. Get the tracking in place on day one and let the data accumulate. You'll be glad you did.

# 7

# Search Engine Optimization

# Contents at a Glance

IN THIS CHAPTER

- » Understanding how search engines find, crawl, and rank your pages
- » Getting to know the signals Google cares about most
- » Making your site work for local searchers
- » Separating SEO fact from SEO fiction

# Chapter 1 Modern SEO Fundamentals

*In a busy marketplace, not standing out is the same as being invisible.*

—SETH GODIN

You've built your website. The design looks sharp, the content is solid, and you're genuinely proud of how it all came together. There's just one small problem: nobody can find it. Your site is sitting out there on the internet like a beautifully decorated shop on a street with no foot traffic. That's where *search engine optimization* — or *SEO*, as everybody calls it; "ESS-ee-oh," as everyone pronounces it — comes in.

SEO is the art and science of making your website visible to people who are actively searching for what you offer. It's not about tricking search engines or gaming some secret system. It's about understanding what search engines are looking for, and then making sure your site delivers exactly that. The good news? The fundamentals aren't complicated. The even better news? Most of your competitors aren't doing SEO well, which means a little effort goes a surprisingly long way.

In this chapter, I walk you through how search engines work (it's more interesting than it sounds, I promise), what Google's algorithm updates mean for your site, and what signals matter most for getting your pages in front of the right eyeballs. I also cover local SEO for small businesses and have a blast debunking some SEO myths that refuse to die.

# How Search Engines Work Today

Before you can optimize your site for search engines, it helps to understand what search engines *do.* Not at the PhD-in-computer-science level, but at the practical, what-happens-when-someone-types-something-into-Google level. The process boils down to three stages: *crawling*, *indexing*, and *ranking.* A good mental model is a library: someone has to go out and find all the books (crawling), catalog them so they can be looked up later (indexing), and then decide which books to recommend when a patron asks a question (ranking).

## Crawling: How search engines find your pages

Search engines use automated programs called *crawlers* (or *spiders* or *bots* — the terminology is charmingly inconsistent) to discover web pages. Google's crawler is called Googlebot, and it works by following links from one page to another, much the way you might browse the web yourself. It starts with a list of known URLs, visits each one, reads the page, finds every link on that page, and then follows those links to discover new pages. Repeat a few billion times and you're done.

This is why links matter so much on the web. If no other page links to your site, Googlebot has a hard time finding it. It's like having a store with no roads leading to it. The crawler literally can't get there from here. Conversely, the more pages that link to yours, the more paths Googlebot has to discover and revisit your content.

TIP

Submitting a *sitemap,* which is an XML file that lists all the pages on your site, is one way to help search engines find your content faster. I cover sitemaps in detail in Book 7, Chapter 4.

## Indexing: How search engines remember your pages

Once Googlebot crawls a page, Google decides whether to add it to the *index,* a massive database of all the pages Google knows about. Think of the index as the world's largest card catalog. When a page gets indexed, Google stores information about its content: what words appear on the page, what images it contains, when it was last updated, and dozens of other details.

Not every page that gets crawled ends up in the index. If a page is a near-duplicate of another page, if it's thin on content, or if it explicitly tells search engines not to index it (yes, you can do that), Google may skip it. The pages that *do* make it into the index are the ones eligible to show up in search results.

## Ranking: How search engines decide who goes first



Here's where things get interesting. When someone types a query into Google — say, "best pizza near me" or "how to fix a leaky faucet" — Google doesn't just pull up every page in its index that mentions pizza or faucets. It runs those pages through a ranking algorithm that evaluates hundreds of factors to decide which pages are the most relevant, most authoritative, and most useful for that query. The pages that score highest show up at the top of the results. The ones that don't score as well end up on page two, or worse. (And that's not good. After all, when was the last time you clicked through to the second page of a Google search result?)

The ranking factors themselves are a mix of things you can directly control — such as the quality of your content, the words on your page, and how fast your site loads — and things that are harder to influence directly, such as how many other reputable sites link to yours. The next few sections of this chapter (and the rest of the chapters here in Book 7) are all about understanding those factors and putting them to work for your site.

## What about other search engines?

I keep saying "Google" because Google handles roughly 90 percent of all web searches worldwide. But other search engines exist — Bing, DuckDuckGo, Yahoo, and others — and the good news is that the fundamentals are essentially the same across all of them. If you optimize your site for Google, you're optimizing it for Bing and everything else. The core principles of crawling, indexing, and ranking work the same everywhere. You don't need a separate SEO strategy for each search engine.

That said, Bing powers a meaningful chunk of searches, especially on Windows devices and through integrations with Microsoft products. Bing also has its own webmaster tools (`bing.com/webmasters`), and setting up your site there takes only a few minutes. It's worth doing, even if Google is your primary focus.

REMEMBER

SEO isn't about outsmarting Google. It's about aligning your site with what Google is already trying to do: connect people with the most helpful, relevant, trustworthy content for their query. If you focus on making your site genuinely useful, you're already doing SEO whether you realize it or not.

# Understanding Google's Algorithm Updates

If you've spent any time reading about SEO, you've probably come across alarming headlines about Google algorithm updates wiping out traffic overnight. And yes, that does happen, but almost exclusively to sites that were cutting corners in the first place. Understanding what these updates are and why they happen will save you a lot of unnecessary anxiety.

Google updates its search algorithm constantly. Most changes are small tweaks that nobody notices. But several times a year, Google rolls out a *core update,* a significant change to how it evaluates and ranks pages. These are the updates that make the headlines because they can cause noticeable shifts in search rankings across millions of websites.

## The updates that matter most

Over the years, a few major updates have fundamentally changed how SEO works. You don't need to memorize their names or dates (this isn't a history exam), but understanding what each one targeted will help you see the bigger picture:

- **Panda (2011):** Targeted low-quality, thin content. Sites that churned out hundreds of shallow, keyword-stuffed pages got hammered. The lesson: quality always wins over quantity.
- **Penguin (2012):** Went after manipulative link-building schemes. Sites that bought links or participated in link farms saw their rankings plummet. The lesson: earn your links naturally by creating content worth linking to.
- **Helpful Content update (2022–2024):** Rewarded content written for real people instead of content manufactured purely to rank in search results. The lesson: write for your audience first, search engines second.

- **Core updates (ongoing):** Broad changes to how Google assesses overall page quality. These roll out several times a year and can shuffle rankings significantly. The lesson: there's no single fix; just keep making your site better.

## What updates mean for you

Here's the thing about algorithm updates that most SEO articles won't tell you: if you're building a legitimate website with genuinely useful content, these updates are almost always *good* news for you. Updates exist to weed out the junk, such as spam sites, content farms, and pages that exist only to game the system. If your site isn't doing any of those things, updates tend to push you *up* in the rankings as the junk gets pushed down.



That said, it's normal to see some ranking fluctuations after a core update, even for good sites. Rankings might dip for a few days or weeks before settling into a new (often better) position. The worst thing you can do is panic and start making drastic changes to your site every time Google rolls out an update. Stay the course, keep improving your content, and let the dust settle.

If you want to keep track of when updates happen, Google publishes a list of confirmed updates on its Search Status Dashboard (`status.search.google.com`). Bookmark it if you're curious, but resist the urge to check it every time your traffic dips. Sometimes traffic dips because it's a holiday weekend, not because Google changed the algorithm.

REMEMBER

Algorithm updates reward sites that were already doing the right thing. The best SEO strategy is also the simplest: create high-quality, genuinely useful content for real people. That advice has never changed, and it probably never will.

# Core Web Vitals and Page Experience

In 2021, Google made something official that web developers had suspected for years: how your site *feels* to use matters for search rankings, not just what's on the page. Google introduced a set of metrics called Core Web Vitals that measure real-world user experience, such as how fast your page loads, how quickly it responds to clicks, and whether the layout jumps around while the page is loading. These metrics are now part of Google's ranking algorithm, which means a slow, janky site can hurt your search rankings.

## The three metrics you need to know

Core Web Vitals consist of several measurements, but three are crucial, each targeting a different aspect of user experience:

- **Largest Contentful Paint (LCP):** Measures how long it takes for the biggest visible element on your page — usually a hero image or a large block of text — to finish loading. LCP is roughly a measure of how long it takes before the page looks like it's ready. Google considers anything under 2.5 seconds to be good. Over 4 seconds? That's poor, and Google notices.
- **Interaction to Next Paint (INP):** Measures how quickly your page responds when someone interacts with it, such as clicking a button, tapping a link, typing in a form field. A noticeable lag between the interaction and the response results in a bad INP score. Google wants to see responses in under 200 milliseconds.
- **Cumulative Layout Shift (CLS):** Measures how much your page's layout moves around unexpectedly while it's loading. Have you ever been reading an article on your phone and suddenly the text jumps down because an ad loaded above it? That's layout shift, and you know from personal experience how maddening it is. The lower the number, the better. Google's threshold for good is a CLS score below 0.1.

If those numbers feel abstract, here are more concrete ways to think about things: LCP is about speed: Does the page load fast? INP is about responsiveness: Does it react when I click? CLS is about stability: Does it stay put while I'm trying to use it? A page that loads quickly, responds instantly, and doesn't jump around is a page that Google considers a good experience.

But Core Web Vitals don't just affect your search rankings; they affect whether people actually stick around once they arrive. For example, studies consistently show that even small improvements in load time lead to measurable increases in conversions, time on site, and return visits. So, don't fix your Core Web Vitals just to please Google. Fix them to please the human beings visiting your site.

## Checking your vitals

The easiest way to check your Core Web Vitals is Google's own PageSpeed Insights tool at `pagespeed.web.dev`. Paste in any URL and it gives you a detailed report with scores for each vital, along with specific suggestions for improvement. It's free, straightforward, and the tool Google itself recommends.

I cover performance optimization in much more detail in Book 9, Chapter 2, including how to improve each of these metrics. For now, just know that Core Web Vitals exist, that they affect your search rankings, and that checking them is as easy as visiting a website and pasting in your URL.

TIP

Run your site through PageSpeed Insights before you start worrying about keyword strategies and meta tags. If your site takes 7 seconds to load on a phone, no amount of SEO wizardry is going to overcome that.



# Mobile-First Indexing

Perhaps surprisingly, when Google crawls and indexes your website, it looks at the *mobile* version of your pages, not the desktop version. This is called *mobile-first indexing,* and it has been Google's default approach since 2019. If your site looks great on a desktop monitor but falls apart on a phone, Google is judging you by the version that falls apart. Yikes!

## Why this happened

The reason why Google looks at the mobile version first is simple math. More than half of all web traffic worldwide comes from mobile devices, and the percentage keeps climbing. Google's job is to deliver the best results for its users, and most of its users are searching on their phones. It makes sense for Google to evaluate pages based on the experience those users will have.

This shift didn't happen overnight. Google announced the transition gradually over several years, giving site owners plenty of time to adapt. But even now, years later, plenty of sites still serve a stripped-down or broken experience on mobile devices. If yours is one of them, fixing that should be near the top of your to-do list.

## What it means for your site

Mobile-first indexing has a few practical implications that are worth spelling out:

- **Responsive design isn't optional.** Your site needs to look good and work properly on screens of all sizes. If you followed the responsive design principles I cover in Book 2, Chapter 3, you're already in good shape. And if you didn't? Well, now you have a very good reason to go back and read that chapter!

- **Content parity matters.** Whatever content appears on your desktop site should also appear on your mobile site. If you're omitting content on mobile to save screen space, Google may not see that content at all, because it's looking only at the mobile version.
- **Test on real devices.** The responsive design preview in your browser's developer tools is useful, but it's not a substitute for pulling up your site on a phone and tapping around. You'd be amazed how many issues show up only on real hardware: buttons too small to tap, text too small to read, horizontal scrolling that shouldn't be there.

# E-E-A-T (Experience, Expertise, Authoritativeness, Trustworthiness)

If you've ever wondered what separates the pages that rank at the top of Google from the ones buried on page five, a big part of the answer is a concept Google calls *E-E-A-T*: experience, expertise, authoritativeness, and trustworthiness. It sounds like a corporate buzzword salad, I know. But it's one of the most important concepts in modern SEO, and it's surprisingly practical once you understand what it means.

E-E-A-T isn't a score or a metric that Google calculates automatically. It's a framework that Google uses to train its *quality raters*, the human beings who evaluate search results and provide feedback that helps Google refine its algorithms. Google publishes a detailed set of guidelines for these raters, and E-E-A-T is at the heart of those guidelines. Understanding what the raters are looking for gives you a clear picture of what Google values.

## Breaking down each letter

Let's take each aspect of E-E-A-T one at a time:

- **Experience:** Does the content creator have firsthand experience with the topic? A review of a hiking trail written by someone who hiked it is more valuable than one written by someone who read about it online. A product review from someone who bought and used the product is more credible than one that just summarizes the manufacturer's description. If you've done the thing you're writing about, say so.

- **Expertise:** Does the content creator have relevant knowledge or skill? This doesn't necessarily mean formal credentials (although those help). A self-taught web developer with a portfolio of successful sites has expertise, even without a computer science degree. A small-business owner who has navigated tax season for fifteen years has expertise in small business taxes, even without a CPA license. Expertise is demonstrated through the depth and accuracy of your content.
- **Authoritativeness:** Is the content creator (or the website) recognized as a go-to source on the topic? Authority is built over time through consistent, high-quality content, mentions and links from other reputable sites, and a track record of being right. A local plumber's website that has dozens of helpful plumbing articles and is linked to by the local chamber of commerce has more authority on plumbing topics than a generic directory site.
- **Trustworthiness:** Is the site trustworthy? This is the big one. In fact, Google's guidelines call trustworthiness the most important factor in E-E-A-T. Trustworthiness encompasses everything from site security (HTTPS, which I cover in Book 9, Chapter 4) to transparent business information (a real address, a real phone number, a real About page) to honest content that doesn't mislead or manipulate.



## Demonstrating E-E-A-T on your site

The good news is that demonstrating E-E-A-T doesn't require anything exotic. Most of it is stuff you should be doing anyway:

- **Create a thorough About page.** Explain who you are, what your business does, and why you're qualified to do it. Include real photos, real names, and real credentials where applicable.
- **Add author information to your content.** If you're writing blog posts or articles, include a byline and a short author bio. This signals to both readers and Google that a real person with real qualifications created the content.
- **Display contact information prominently.** A physical address, a phone number, and an email address tell visitors (and Google) that a real business is behind the website. Sites that hide their contact information look sketchy (because they usually are!).
- **Use HTTPS.** If your site isn't using HTTPS yet, fix that immediately. An insecure site undermines trustworthiness at the most basic level. (I cover HTTPS setup in Book 9, Chapter 4.)

» **Collect and display reviews and testimonials.** Social proof, where real people vouch for your business, is one of the strongest trustworthiness signals you can have.

REMEMBER

E-E-A-T is not a magic number you can check in a dashboard. It's a set of principles. If your site clearly demonstrates that real, qualified people created the content, that your information is accurate and well-sourced, and that visitors can trust you with their time and attention, you're in good shape.

# Local SEO for Small Businesses

If you run a restaurant, a law firm, a plumbing business, a yoga studio, a donut shop, or any business that serves customers in a specific geographic area, local SEO is arguably the most important type of SEO you can do. *Local SEO* is the practice of optimizing your online presence so that your business shows up when people in your area search for the products or services you offer. When someone types "coffee shop near me" or "plumber in Springfield" into Google, local SEO is what determines whether your business appears in those results.

Local search results look different from regular search results. For many local queries, Google displays a *map pack,* a map with three businesses pinned on it, along with their names, ratings, addresses, and hours. Getting into that map pack is the holy grail of local SEO, because it puts your business front and center, right at the top of the results, with a map showing people how to find you.

## Google Business Profile

The single most important step you can take for local SEO is claiming and completing your Google Business Profile. This is the free business listing that powers map pack results. If you've ever searched for a local business and seen its hours, address, phone number, and reviews displayed right in Google's search results, that information came from the business's Google business profile.

Setting up a business profile is straightforward. Head to `business.google.com`, sign in with a Google account, and follow the steps to add your business information. Google will verify that you own or operate the business, usually by mailing a postcard with a verification code to your physical address, though phone and email verification are also available for some businesses.

Once verified, fill out every single field in your profile. Yep: Every. Single. One. Your business name, address, phone number, website, hours of operation, business category, a description of what you do, and photos. Businesses with complete profiles rank higher in local results than businesses with sparse ones. It's one of the easiest wins in all of SEO.

TIP

Claim your business profile right now, before you forget. Even if you're not ready to do anything else with your SEO, this one step will make your business visible in local search results and on Google Maps. It's free, and it takes about fifteen minutes.

## Local ranking factors

Google uses three main factors to determine local search rankings:

- **Relevance:** How well does your business match what the searcher is looking for? This is where your business category, description, and the content on your website all come into play. If someone searches for "emergency plumber" and your business profile lists your category as "Plumbing Service" and your website has a page about emergency plumbing services, Google sees a strong relevance match.
- **Distance:** How close is your business to the person searching? This one you can't really control (unless you're willing to relocate, which seems extreme). But it means that local SEO rewards you for being specific about your service area rather than trying to rank everywhere.
- **Prominence:** How well-known and well-regarded is your business? Prominence is influenced by things like the number and quality of your online reviews, how many other websites mention or link to your business, and how consistent your business information is across the web.

That last point about consistency is worth underlining. Your business name, address, and phone number (often abbreviated as NAP in SEO circles) should be identical everywhere it appears online: your website, your Google business profile, your social media profiles, online directories, and anywhere else your business is listed. Even small inconsistencies — such as your address listed at 123 Main St. in one place and 123 Main Street in another — can confuse search engines and dilute your local rankings.

This sounds picky and, well, it is. But search engines can't always tell that "Quinn's Plumbing LLC" and "Quinn's Plumbing" and "Quinns Plumbing LLC" are the same business. Each inconsistency is a tiny crack in your local SEO foundation. Pick one version of your business name, one address format, and one phone number, and use them everywhere. Write them down. Tattoo them on your forearm if you have to. (Okay, maybe don't do that.)

### Reviews and reputation

Online reviews are a bona fide ranking factor for local search. Businesses with more reviews, higher-quality reviews, and (of course) higher ratings tend to rank higher in local results than businesses with few or no reviews. Google has been pretty transparent about this: reviews are one of the signals it uses to assess prominence and trustworthiness.

The best way to get reviews is embarrassingly simple: ask for them. After a successful transaction, send a follow-up email with a direct link to your Google review page. Most happy customers are willing to leave a review, they just don't think to do it unless you ask. Make it easy, make it convenient, and don't be shy about it.

Equally important: respond to your reviews. All of them. Thank people for positive reviews. Address negative reviews calmly, professionally, and constructively. Potential customers read your responses just as carefully as they read the reviews themselves, and a thoughtful response to a negative review can build trust. A defensive or dismissive response? That's a red flag that sends potential customers running.

WARNING

I suppose this goes without saying, but I'm going to say it anyway: Never, ever fake reviews or pay for them. Google is very good at detecting fake reviews, and getting caught can result in your business profile being suspended. Even if you don't get caught, fake reviews erode the trust that real reviews build. It's just not worth it.

## SEO Myths You Can Ignore

SEO has been around long enough to accumulate a thick layer of myths, misconceptions, and outdated advice that just won't die. Some of these were true once, decades ago, in the early days of search engines. Some were never true. Either way, they persist because people keep repeating them, and the internet has a long memory for bad advice. Let me save you some time and worry by setting the record straight on the most common ones:

- **"You need to submit your site to Google."** This was necessary in the late 1990s. Today? Google will find your site on its own by following links. You can submit a sitemap through Google Search Console to speed things up (and I recommend that you do; see Book 7, Chapter 4), but you don't *need* to formally submit your site for it to appear in search results.

- **"Meta keywords are important for rankings."** There's a `<meta name="keywords">` tag in HTML that lets you specify keywords for your page. Google has publicly stated — and it has done so multiple times, in no uncertain terms — that it ignores this tag and has for over a decade. You can skip it.
- **"More pages means higher rankings."** Nope. A site with 500 thin, pointless pages will get outranked by a site with 20 pages of genuinely useful content. Google cares about quality, not quantity. Publishing pages just to inflate your page count is a waste of time and possibly counterproductive, since Google's helpful content system can penalize sites with large amounts of low-quality content.
- **"Keyword density is a real thing."** The idea that your target keyword needs to appear a specific percentage of times on your page — say, 2 percent or 3 percent — is a myth that should have died years ago. Google's algorithms are sophisticated enough to understand topics and context without needing you to repeat the same phrase like a broken record. Write naturally. Use your target keyword where it makes sense. Don't force it.
- **"SEO is a one-time project."** I wish. SEO isn't something you do once and check off your list. Search engines are constantly updating their algorithms, your competitors are constantly improving their sites, and your own content needs regular updates to stay relevant. Think of SEO as ongoing maintenance, not a one-time installation. (To help you remember, consider adding SEO to the website maintenance schedule I discuss in Book 10, Chapter 4.)
- **"Social media directly affects your search rankings."** This one is complicated. Google has said that social media signals such as likes, shares, and followers are not direct ranking factors. However, social media *indirectly* helps SEO by driving traffic to your content, increasing brand awareness, and creating opportunities for other people to discover and link to your pages. So social media matters for SEO, just not in the way most people think.
- **"You need to hire an SEO expert to rank well."** For large, complex websites with thousands of pages and fierce competition, sure, a specialist might be worth the investment. But for a small-business website? You can absolutely learn and implement the fundamentals yourself. That's the entire point of this minibook, and the fact that you're reading this chapter means you're already ahead of the curve.

The common thread in all these myths is that they treat SEO as a game to be gamed, a set of tricks and shortcuts that can hack your way to the top of Google. That's not how it works. Modern SEO is fundamentally about creating a fast, well-structured, trustworthy website with genuinely useful content. Do that, and the rankings will follow. Maybe not overnight (patience is genuinely a virtue here), but they'll follow.

IN THIS CHAPTER

» Finding the right keywords for your site

» Discovering long-tail keywords

» Building a practical keyword strategy

# Chapter 2

# Keyword Research and Strategy

*If you're trying to persuade people to do something, or buy something, it seems to me you should use their language.*

—DAVID OGILVY

Even if you have solid SEO fundamentals, as I describe in Book 7, Chapter 1, your site will likely sit there collecting digital dust if your pages don't match the language people use when they search. That's what keyword research is all about: listening to the words your audience uses when they're looking for something you offer. Think of it as eavesdropping on your future customers (in the nicest possible way, of course). In this chapter, I walk you through the entire keyword research process, from understanding why someone searches for something in the first place to building a strategy that turns your research into pages on your site.

# Understanding User Intent

When someone types a query into Google, they're not just entering words. They're expressing a *need.* Maybe they want to learn something. Maybe they want to buy something. Maybe they're trying to find a specific website. The words they type are clues, and your job is to figure out what those clues are telling you.

This concept is called *user intent* (or sometimes *search intent*), and it's the foundation of everything else in this chapter. Get the intent right, and your content will naturally attract the right visitors. Get it wrong, and you'll wonder why thousands of people land on your page and immediately leave. (The answer is that they came looking for something you didn't have.)

## The categories of user intent

User intent generally falls into four categories:

- **Informational:** The searcher wants to learn something. Examples: "how to groom a poodle," "what is keyword research," "best time to plant tomatoes." These people are looking for articles, guides, tutorials, and explanations, but not products. They're in learning mode, and if you try to sell them something before they're ready, they'll leave.
- **Navigational:** The searcher is trying to reach a specific website or page. Examples: "Facebook login," "Shopify dashboard," "New York Times crossword." They already know where they want to go; they're just using Google as a shortcut to get there. Unless the person is searching for *your* brand, navigational keywords aren't usually worth targeting.
- **Commercial:** The searcher is researching options before making a decision. Examples: "best dog groomers near me," "Squarespace vs Wix," "top wireless headphones." They're shopping around but haven't pulled out their wallet yet. These searchers want comparisons, reviews, and detailed information to help them decide.
- **Transactional:** The searcher is ready to take action, usually buying something or booking a service. Examples: "buy dog nail clippers," "book pet grooming appointment," "download free invoice template." They know what they want and they're ready to do it right now. These are the keywords that most directly drive revenue.

Why does intent matter? Because when you create a page on your site, you need to match the intent behind the keywords you're targeting. If someone searches for "how to groom a poodle" and lands on a page that just says "Hire us to groom your poodle!" with a big booking button, they're going to bounce. They wanted information, not a sales pitch.

REMEMBER

Before you chase a keyword, ask yourself what someone searching for the keyword actually wants. If you don't have or can't create a page that genuinely satisfies that intent, move on to a keyword you *can* serve well. Matching intent isn't just good SEO; it's good manners.

### How intent shapes your content

Once you understand the four types of intent, you can start mapping them to the pages on your site. Here's how that looks in practice:

- **Informational keywords** map to blog posts, how-to guides, FAQ pages, and educational content. These pages build trust and demonstrate expertise (check out E-E-A-T in Book 7, Chapter 1). They're your chance to be genuinely helpful, and they often bring in visitors who later come back to buy.
- **Navigational keywords** map to your home page, your About page, and any other page people search for by name. There isn't much to optimize here. Just make sure your pages are easy to find and that your site name is clear.
- **Commercial keywords** map to comparison pages, product and service pages with detailed descriptions, case studies, and testimonials. These pages help people who are *almost* ready to buy make up their minds.
- **Transactional keywords** map to product pages, service booking pages, contact forms, and pricing pages. These should make it dead simple to take the next step, meaning no friction, no fuss.

You might notice some overlap between these categories. A single page can satisfy both informational and commercial intent if it's structured well. A detailed guide about "how to choose a dog groomer" that also includes your credentials and a booking link serves both purposes. The point isn't to create rigid categories; it's to think about what the searcher wants before you decide what goes on the page.

## Keyword Research with Modern Tools

Once you understand intent, as I describe in the preceding section, the next step is to find the keywords worth targeting. *Keyword research* is the process of discovering the words and phrases your potential visitors type into search engines, and then figuring out which of those are realistic targets for your site. It's part detective work, part data analysis, and part common sense.

The good news is that you don't need to guess. Tools (some free, some paid) can show you what people are searching for, how often they search for it, and how stiff the competition is. But before you touch any tool, start with the simplest research method of all: your own brain.

## Start with seed keywords

Grab a notebook or open a text file and brainstorm a list of *seed keywords.* These are the broad, obvious terms that describe what your business does. If you run a pet grooming shop, your seed keywords might include "pet grooming," "dog grooming," "cat grooming," and "mobile pet groomer." Don't overthink it. Just write down every word or phrase a potential customer might use to find you.

Here's a trick that helps: think beyond your own terminology. You might call what you do "pet styling" or "canine aesthetics," but your customers almost certainly search for "dog grooming." Ask your customers what they'd type into Google to find a business like yours. Their answers might surprise you. Once you have that list, you're ready to plug those terms into research tools and see what the data says.

## Google's free tools

Before you spend a dime on keyword tools, take advantage of the free resources Google itself provides. After all, if you're optimizing for Google, it makes sense to use Google's own data.

- **Google Search Console (`search.google.com/search-console`):** If your site is already live and getting some traffic, Search Console is pure gold. It shows you the queries people used to find your site, how often your pages appeared in search results, and how many people clicked through. This is real search data from real people who encountered your site. I cover setting up Search Console in Book 7, Chapter 4.
- **Google Trends (`trends.google.com`):** Shows how search interest in a topic has changed over time. It's fantastic for spotting seasonal patterns (searches for "dog grooming" spike in spring, predictably enough) and for comparing the relative popularity of different terms. Is "pet grooming" more popular than "dog grooming"? Google Trends will tell you. It won't give you exact search volume numbers, but it's great for seeing the big picture.
- **Google's autocomplete:** This one is so simple it almost feels like cheating. Go to Google, start typing one of your seed keywords, and watch what it suggests as you type. Those suggestions are based on what people *actually search for,* which makes them a surprisingly rich source of keyword ideas. Try it right now with "dog grooming" and see what pops up. I'll wait.

- **People also ask:** When you search for something on Google, you'll often see a section labeled "People also ask" with a list of related questions. These are real questions from real searchers, and each one is a potential keyword (or blog post topic) for your site. Click one of the questions and even more appear. It's like a keyword idea machine that just keeps giving.

TIP

Google's autocomplete is the fastest free keyword research tool in existence. Type a seed keyword followed by each letter of the alphabet — "dog grooming a," "dog grooming b," "dog grooming c," and so on — and you'll generate dozens of keyword ideas in minutes. It's called the *alphabet soup technique,* and yes, that's really what people call it. You can also try adding a space before your keyword to see what modifiers people put in front of it.

## Third-party keyword tools

Google's free tools are a great starting point, but if you want deeper data — search volume numbers, keyword difficulty scores, competitor analysis — you'll need a dedicated keyword research tool. Here are some solid options:

- **Ubersuggest (`neilpatel.com/ubersuggest`):** Offers a limited free tier that gives you a handful of keyword lookups per day. It's beginner-friendly, shows search volume and difficulty, and provides keyword suggestions based on your seed terms. It's a good place to start if you're not ready to commit to a paid tool.
- **Ahrefs Webmaster Tools (`ahrefs.com/webmaster-tools`):** Ahrefs is one of the most respected names in SEO, and its free Webmaster Tools gives you access to keyword data for sites you own. The paid version is extremely powerful but not cheap. Start with the free tier and upgrade if you outgrow it.
- **Google Keyword Planner (`ads.google.com`):** Originally built for advertisers running Google Ads, Keyword Planner shows search volume ranges and competition levels for any keyword. You need a Google Ads account to use it (free to create; you don't have to run any ads), and the data is a bit less precise for non-advertisers, but it's still useful.

Plenty of other tools are out there — Semrush, Moz, SE Ranking, and more — and they all do roughly the same thing: take your seed keywords and return a mountain of related keywords along with data about each one. For a small-business website, any of the tools I've listed here will do the job. Don't fall into the trap of thinking you need the most expensive tool to do good keyword research. You don't. Start with the free options, learn the ropes, and upgrade only if you find yourself needing features the free tools don't offer.

## Keeping your research organized

Here's a practical tip that will save you a lot of headaches later: as you research keywords, record them in a spreadsheet. Don't overthink it. A simple spreadsheet with columns for the keyword, its search volume, keyword difficulty, the type of intent (informational, commercial, and so on), and any notes about which page it might belong to. You'd be amazed how quickly keyword ideas pile up, and without a central place to track them, you'll end up with sticky notes, browser tabs, and text files scattered everywhere. Ask me how I know.

As your spreadsheet grows, sort it by intent type or by topic cluster (which I describe in the next section). This simple act of organizing transforms your raw research into something you can act on. You don't need a special tool for this. A Google Sheet, an Excel file, or even a plain text file will do the trick. The point is to have one place where all your keyword research lives, so you can review it, prioritize it, and update it over time.

## Reading the data

Whatever tool you use, you'll encounter a few key metrics. They might seem intimidating at first (so many numbers and scores!) but once you know what they mean, they're straightforward. Here's the plain-language version:

- **Search volume:** How many times per month people search for a keyword. Higher sounds better, but high-volume keywords are also the most competitive. A keyword with 50,000 monthly searches is great until you realize you're competing against Amazon for it.
- **Keyword difficulty (KD):** A score (usually 0 to 100, although different tools use different KD measures) estimating how hard it would be to rank on page one for that keyword. A KD of 10 is relatively easy; 80 means very stiff competition. For a new or small website, look for keywords with a KD below 30.
- **Cost per click (CPC):** How much advertisers pay per click for that keyword in Google Ads. Even if you're not running ads, a high CPC signals that the searchers behind that keyword are ready to spend money.

REMEMBER

Don't chase high-volume keywords just because the numbers look impressive. A keyword with 100 monthly searches and low competition will bring you more traffic than a keyword with 100,000 monthly searches where you'll never crack the first page. Match your keyword targets to your site's realistic chances of ranking.

# Long-Tail Keywords for Small Businesses

Here's where things get genuinely exciting for small business owners. (And I don't say that about many SEO topics, believe me.) If there's one concept in this chapter that could change the trajectory of your website's traffic, it's long-tail keywords. This is the great equalizer because it's the reason a small, scrappy website can compete with the big players and win.

A *long-tail keyword* is a longer, more specific search phrase. And by *longer* I mean typically three to five words or more. While a *short-tail* keyword such as "dog grooming" is broad and fiercely competitive, a long-tail keyword such as "mobile dog grooming for anxious dogs in Portland" is narrow, specific, and much easier to rank for. The name *long-tail* comes from a search demand curve: broad keywords sit at the fat head with massive volume, while specific keywords stretch out in a long tail with individually low volume but collectively enormous numbers.

Why should you care? Three reasons:

- **Less competition:** Fewer websites are specifically targeting "mobile dog grooming for anxious dogs in Portland" than are targeting "dog grooming." That means a small site with good content has a realistic shot at ranking on page one, which is something that's pretty much impossible for a broad head keyword.
- **Higher conversion rates:** People searching for a long-tail keyword usually know exactly what they want. They're further along in their decision-making process, which means they're more likely to take action, such as book an appointment, make a purchase, or fill out a contact form. These are the visitors you want.
- **Better intent match:** Long-tail keywords are naturally more specific, which makes it easier to create content that perfectly matches what the searcher is looking for. And as I explain earlier in this chapter, matching intent is the name of the game.

To put some rough numbers on it: a head keyword such as "dog grooming" might get 200,000 searches per month but convert at 1 percent or less. A long-tail keyword such as "affordable puppy grooming near downtown Portland" might get only 50 searches per month, but those 50 people are *exactly* the customers you want, and they might convert at 10 percent or higher. I'd take 5 highly motivated customers over 2,000 tire-kickers any day of the week.

Here's another way to think about it: there are only so many broad keywords in any niche, and the biggest sites have already claimed them. But the number of long-tail keyword combinations is practically infinite. Nobody has locked up the phrase "mobile grooming for senior golden retrievers in Northeast Portland." That's your opportunity.

So how do you find these magical long-tail keywords? A few techniques:

- **Extend your seed keywords.** Take each seed keyword and add modifiers. Add locations ("in Portland"), add qualifiers ("affordable," "mobile," "for puppies"), and add questions ("how much does," "where to find"). Each modifier narrows the search and creates a new long-tail keyword.
- **Mine the "People also ask" section.** As I mention earlier, Google's "People also ask" results are a treasure trove of long-tail keywords phrased as questions. Each question is a potential page or blog post. And here's a bonus: these questions tell you exactly what format your content should take.
- **Check your own search data.** If your site is already getting traffic, look at the queries in Google Search Console. You'll often find that people are discovering you through long-tail searches you never even considered. Build on those because they're keywords you're already ranking for, which means you have a head start.
- **Read forums and social media.** Go where your audience hangs out online — subreddits, Facebook groups, Quora threads — and pay attention to the language they use. Real people ask real questions in their own words, and those questions are keyword gold. If you don't have time for this, ask your favorite AI to handle it for you.

TIP

When brainstorming long-tail keywords, don't just think about what your business *does* — think about the problems your business *solves.* People don't search for "pet grooming services" nearly as often as they search for "my dog is matted and I don't know what to do." If you can match your content to the *problem*, you'll connect with exactly the right audience.

# Competitive Analysis

I know what you might be thinking: analyzing your competitors' keywords feels sneaky. It's not; it's *research.* The goal isn't to copy your competitors; it's to understand the landscape and find opportunities they've missed.

## Identifying your real competitors

Here's a subtle but important point: your SEO competitors and your business competitors aren't always the same people. Your business competitor is the pet-grooming shop across town. Your SEO competitor is whoever ranks on the first page of Google for the keywords you want to target, which might be a nationwide franchise, a pet care blog, or even a YouTube channel.

To find your SEO competitors, search for your target keywords with a web browser you've never used before (so Google doesn't personalize the results based on your browsing history) and note who shows up on the first page. Those are the sites you need to study. Don't be discouraged if some of them are big, well-known brands. You're not trying to outrank Amazon across the board; you're looking for specific keywords where you can realistically compete.

## Analyzing competitor keywords

Once you know who your SEO competitors are, you can peek at the keywords they're ranking for. Here's how:

- **Free approach:** Simply look at their pages. Read their page titles, headings, and body text. What topics do they cover? What words and phrases keep showing up? Also check their blog (if they have one) for topics you haven't covered yet. You'd be surprised how much you can learn just by reading a competitor's site with keyword-aware eyes.
- **Tool-assisted approach:** Most keyword research tools (Ubersuggest, Ahrefs, Semrush) let you enter a competitor's URL and see a list of keywords that site ranks for, along with their rankings and estimated traffic. This is incredibly useful because it shows you which keywords are driving visitors to your competition. And some of those keywords might be ones you never would have thought of on your own.

Pay special attention to keywords where your competitors rank on page one but aren't in the top three positions. These are keywords where the competition has proven the topic gets traffic, but the top spots are still up for grabs. If you can create a better, more thorough page on the same topic, you've got a shot at outranking them.

## Finding content gaps

A *content gap* is a keyword or topic that your competitors rank for, but you don't. Finding content gaps is one of the most effective ways to discover new pages worth creating because someone else has already proven that the topic drives traffic.

The concept is straightforward: if three of your competitors have pages about "how often should I bathe my dog" and you don't, that's a gap. Creating your own page on that topic, especially one that's better, more detailed, and more helpful than theirs, puts you in the running for that traffic.

Most keyword tools have a content gap or competitive analysis feature that automates this process. You enter your URL and a couple of competitor URLs, and the tool spits out a list of keywords they rank for that you don't. It's like having a treasure map for keywords.

One more thing about competitive analysis: don't do it just once. Your competitors are constantly publishing new content and targeting new keywords. Make competitive research a regular part of your SEO routine. Even a quick check every few months will keep you from falling behind and help you spot new opportunities as they emerge.

TIP

Search for your most important keywords in an incognito browser window at least once a month. It's the quickest way to see who's ranking above you, what their pages look like, and whether new competitors have entered the picture. Think of it as a quick health check for your keyword strategy.

# Creating a Keyword Strategy

At this point, you've probably assembled a rather impressive (and possibly overwhelming) list of keywords. Good. Now the real work begins: turning that messy pile into an organized, actionable plan. Without a strategy, keyword research is just a spreadsheet full of interesting data that sits there doing nothing. With a strategy, it becomes a roadmap for every page on your site.

## Grouping keywords by topic

Your first step is to sort your keywords into *topic clusters,* which are groups of related keywords that revolve around a single broad topic. The idea is that each cluster will eventually map to one page (or a small set of closely related pages) on your site. I know: This sounds like a bunch of organizational busywork, but it's how modern SEO gets done. Google's algorithms understand topics, not just individual keywords, so a page that thoroughly covers a topic cluster will outperform a page that targets a single keyword in isolation.

For example, if you run that pet-grooming business, you might end up with clusters like this:

- **Dog-grooming basics:** dog grooming, how to groom a dog at home, dog-grooming tips, dog grooming for beginners, what to expect at a dog-grooming appointment.
- **Pricing:** dog-grooming cost, how much does dog grooming cost, affordable dog grooming, pet-grooming prices, grooming prices by breed.
- **Breed-specific grooming:** poodle grooming, golden retriever grooming, how to groom a doodle, grooming a double-coated dog.
- **Specialty services:** mobile dog grooming, dog grooming for anxious dogs, puppy's first grooming, senior dog grooming.

Each cluster represents a distinct topic that deserves its own page, perhaps even a cornerstone page (refer to Book 6, Chapter 1). The keywords within each cluster are variations and subtopics that your page should address. This *topic clustering* approach is much more effective than the old-school method of creating a separate page for every single keyword, which just leads to a sprawling mess of thin pages that compete with each other.



## Mapping keywords to pages

Once your keywords are grouped into clusters, assign each cluster to a specific page on your site. Every page should have one *primary keyword*, the main term you're targeting, and several *secondary keywords*, the related terms that support and expand on the primary keyword.

For example, your dog grooming pricing page might look like this:

- **Primary keyword:** dog-grooming cost.
- **Secondary keywords:** pet-grooming prices, how much does dog grooming cost, affordable dog grooming near me.

The primary keyword goes in your page title, your main heading (`<h1>`), and your URL if possible. The secondary keywords appear naturally in your body text, subheadings, and image alt text. (I cover all of this in detail in Book 7, Chapter 3.) The takeaway word there is *naturally*; don't try to cram keywords in where they don't belong.

REMEMBER

One primary keyword per page. Seriously. Trying to rank a single page for multiple unrelated keywords is like trying to win three different races at the same time: you'll just exhaust yourself and finish poorly in all of them. Give each page a clear, focused target and let the secondary keywords provide supporting context. If you find yourself trying to stuff two different topics onto one page, you need two pages.

### Prioritizing your efforts

You can't optimize every page at once, so you need to decide where to start. Here's a simple framework that works well for small business websites:

- **Start with low difficulty and high relevance.** These are keywords where you can rank quickly and the traffic directly relates to what you sell. They go to the top of the list.
- **Next, tackle high-value commercial and transactional keywords.** These drive revenue because they're the keywords people search when they're ready to buy. Even if they're more competitive, the payoff is direct.
- **Then, build out informational content.** Blog posts and how-to guides targeting informational keywords are a longer play. They build authority over time and bring in visitors who may not buy today but will remember you later.

Don't treat this as a rigid formula; it's just a starting point. Adjust the framework based on what makes sense for your business and your audience. The important thing is that you have a priority order, not that you follow mine to the letter. And don't try to do everything at once. Pick your top five keyword targets, create or optimize those pages, and then move on to the next five. Steady progress beats frantic sprinting every time.

## Avoiding Keyword Stuffing and Other SEO No-Nos

I've been talking for most of this chapter about finding and using the right keywords. Now I need to talk about what happens when you use them incorrectly. Unfortunately, it's entirely possible to take all that hard-earned keyword research and use it in ways that actively hurt your site's search rankings. That's because Google doesn't merely ignore bad keyword practices. Nope, it actively penalizes them. And Google's penalties can take months to recover from.

## What natural keyword usage looks like

The most common keyword mistake is *keyword stuffing*, cramming your target keyword into every sentence, every heading, every paragraph until the text reads like it was written by a malfunctioning robot. It was a real strategy once, back in the early days of SEO when search engines were easily fooled. Those days are very, very over.

Here's what keyword stuffing looks like. Imagine your target keywords are *dog grooming Portland:*

> "Looking for dog grooming in Portland? Our dog-grooming Portland shop offers the best dog grooming Portland has to offer. For dog grooming Portland residents trust, choose our dog-grooming Portland services."

Ugh. Nobody wants to read that, and Google doesn't want to rank it. Here's the same idea written for human beings:

> "Our Portland grooming shop has been pampering local pups since 2018. Whether your dog needs a basic bath or a full breed-specific cut, our experienced groomers will have them looking and feeling their best."

See the difference? The natural version mentions the topic and the location, but it reads like a human being wrote it for other human beings. That's what Google wants. As I mention in Book 7, Chapter 1, the keyword density myth — the idea that your keyword needs to appear some specific percentage of the time — is exactly that: a myth. Write naturally, include your keyword where it fits, and stop worrying about counting.

Beyond stuffing, the following three keyword-related practices will get you into trouble:

- **Hidden text:** Making text the same color as the background, or using CSS to hide it off-screen, so that keywords are present in the code but invisible to visitors. The idea is to stuff keywords without ruining the user experience. Google's been catching this trick since roughly 2003, so it's not exactly cutting-edge deception.
- **Doorway pages:** Creating thin, nearly identical pages that each target a slightly different keyword ("dog grooming Portland," "dog grooming Beaverton," "dog grooming Lake Oswego") with the sole purpose of funneling searchers to a single destination. Google calls these *doorway pages* and will penalize or de-index them.

- **Cloaking:** Showing one version of a page to search engines and a different version to human visitors. This is one of the most serious violations in Google's book, and getting caught can result in your entire site being removed from Google's index. Don't even think about it.

WARNING

Google's penalties are real, and recovering from one can take months. If your site gets hit with a manual penalty for keyword stuffing or other manipulative practices, you'll need to fix the offending pages, submit a reconsideration request through Google Search Console, and wait for Google to review and lift the penalty. It's a slow, painful process. Much better to just do things right from the start.

## How to recover if you've been penalized

If you've inherited a site with old keyword-stuffing problems, or if you made some mistakes early on (no judgment — it happens), here's how to fix things:

- **Audit your content.** Read through your pages with fresh eyes. Does any of the text sound unnatural or repetitive? Does the same phrase appear so often that it's distracting? If so, rewrite those sections to read the way a real person would talk.
- **Check Google Search Console.** If Google has issued a manual penalty, you'll see a notification under Security & Manual Actions. The notification tells you what the problem is and which pages are affected.
- **Fix the problems.** Rewrite stuffed content, remove hidden text, consolidate doorway pages, and eliminate any other manipulative practices. Be thorough because half-measures won't cut it.
- **Submit a reconsideration request.** Once you've fixed everything, submit a reconsideration request through Search Console. Explain what was wrong, what you fixed, and what steps you've taken to prevent it from happening again. Be honest.

For algorithmic penalties where your ranking drops due to algorithm updates rather than manual action, there's no reconsideration request to submit. You just need to improve your content, fix the issues, and wait for Google's next crawl to pick up the changes. Patience is the name of the game. (Have I mentioned that patience is important in SEO? Because it really, really is.)

IN THIS CHAPTER

» Crafting page titles and meta descriptions

» Structuring headings for search

» Optimizing images, links, and URLs

» Understanding schema markup

# Chapter 3 On-Page SEO

*On-page SEO is no longer satisfied by raw keyword use. Matching keywords to searcher intent is critical.*

—RAND FISHKIN

So far, I've talked about the fundamentals of how search engines work (Book 7, Chapter 1) and the basics of keyword research (Book 7, Chapter 2). That's a great start. Now it's time to put all that knowledge to work on the pages themselves. That's what *on-page SEO* is all about: making each individual page on your site as discoverable, relevant, and click-worthy as possible.

The great thing about on-page SEO is that it's entirely within your control. You can't force other websites to link to yours, and you can't bribe Google into ranking you higher (believe me, people have tried), but you *can* control what goes on your own pages: the title tag, the meta description, how your headings are structured, whether your images have useful alt text, how your URLs read. These are all levers you can pull right now, today, without spending a dime. In this chapter, I walk you through each one.

# Optimizing Page Titles and Meta Descriptions

If there's one piece of on-page SEO that delivers the most bang for the least effort, it's your page title and meta description. These two elements are your page's first impression in search results. They are, in a sense, the headline and blurb that convince someone to click your link instead of the nine others on the page.

## What the title tag does

The `<title>` tag lives in the `<head>` section of your page (as I discuss in Book 3, Chapter 1). It doesn't appear in the body of your page, but it shows up in three important places: the browser tab, search engine results, and social media previews. Here's what it looks like:

```
<head>
    <title>Homemade Sourdough Bread: A Beginner's Guide</title>
</head>
```

One element, one line. But those few words carry enormous weight. The title tag is one of the strongest ranking signals Google uses to understand what your page is about. It's also the clickable blue link that people see in search results, which means it directly influences whether anyone visits your page.

## Writing effective title tags

A good title tag tells search engines what the page is about *and* entices humans to click. Here are the key principles:

- **Keep it under 60 characters.** Google truncates longer titles with an ellipsis (. . .), which looks sloppy and can cut off important information.
- **Put your primary keyword near the front.** People scan search results quickly, and Google gives slightly more weight to words that appear earlier. "Homemade Sourdough Bread: A Beginner's Guide" beats "A Beginner's Guide to Homemade Sourdough Bread."
- **Add your brand name at the end.** If you have room, tack on your business name separated by a pipe or dash: "Homemade Sourdough Bread | Flour & Sun Bakery."
- **Make every page title unique.** Duplicate titles confuse search engines. If 15 pages all say, "Welcome to My Website," you've got a problem.

- **Write for humans, not robots.** A title stuffed with keywords — "Sourdough Bread Homemade Bread Best Bread Buy Bread" — looks spammy to both people and search engines.

WARNING

Another good reason to follow these principles is to avoid Google coming up with its own title for your page when it's displayed in search results! That's right: if your title is too long, too keyword heavy, not unique, or not a good reflection of the page content, Google will make up a title for you.

TIP

Here's a handy title tag template: *Primary Keyword: Clarifying Detail | Brand Name.* For example: "Custom Wedding Cakes: Elegant Designs for Every Budget | Sweet Layers Bakery."

## Meta descriptions that earn clicks

Below the title in search results, you'll see a short text snippet. That snippet often comes from the page's *meta description:*

```
<meta name="description" content="Learn to bake crusty,
    tangy sourdough bread at home with this step-by-step
    guide for complete beginners.">
```

As I mention in Book 7, Chapter 1, the `<meta name="keywords">` tag is ignored by Google because meta keywords aren't a ranking factor. Google has also said publicly that meta descriptions aren't a direct ranking factor, but the difference is that meta descriptions are *not* ignored by Google because they're often used as site descriptions in search results. That usage means meta descriptions can have a huge influence on *clickthrough rate,* which is the percentage of people who see your listing and click. In other words, a well-written meta description is a kind of mini advertisement for your page.

Here are some guidelines for writing a meta description:

- **Keep it under 155 characters.** Google truncates longer descriptions.
- **Include your target keyword.** Google bolds matching words in the results, making your listing stand out visually.
- **Use an active call to action.** "Learn to bake crusty sourdough bread at home" beats "Information about sourdough bread."
- **Be specific and honest.** Describe what the page contains. If someone clicks expecting a beginner's guide and lands on a sales pitch, they'll bounce.

REMEMBER

Google sometimes ignores your meta description and generates its own snippet from your page content. This happens more often than you'd think. Write a good description anyway, just in case.

# Header Tag Hierarchy

I cover headings in detail in Book 3, Chapter 1, where I explain how the `<h1>` through `<h6>` elements create the structural outline of your page. They tell both readers and search engines how your content is organized. What I focus on here is why that structure matters for SEO.

## Why headings matter for SEO

Search engines use your heading tags as strong clues about what your page is about. When Google sees an `<h1>` tag, it treats the text inside as a primary indicator of the page's topic. The `<h2>` tags signal main subtopics, `<h3>` tags break those down further. Google can figure out your page without headings, but well-structured headings make its job easier, and making Google's job easier is never a bad strategy.

Headings also affect your chances of landing a *featured snippet*, that prominent box Google sometimes displays at the top of results with a direct answer. Google often pulls snippet content from pages with clear, well-organized headings. An `<h2>` that says "How long does sourdough take to rise?" followed by a concise answer puts you in a much better position to snag that snippet than a page that buries the answer in a wall of unstructured text.

## Building a logical heading structure

The rules for creating a heading structure are simple, but I'm constantly surprised by how many sites get them wrong:

- **Use one `<h1>` per page.** Your `<h1>` is the main heading. It should describe the page's topic and include your primary keyword. You wouldn't put two titles on a book chapter (I hope), so don't put two `<h1>` tags on a page.
- **Use `<h2>` for major sections.** Each main division of your content gets its own `<h2>`.

- **Use <h3> for subsections.** If a section needs to be broken down further, use <h3> tags. And if those need sub-subsections, use <h4>.
- **Don't skip levels.** Going from <h2> directly to <h4> creates a gap in the logical structure. It's like having Chapter 3, Section 3.1, and then jumping to Section 3.1.1.1.
- **Never use headings for visual styling.** If you want text to be big and bold, use CSS. Heading tags are for *structure*, not decoration.

Here's what a well-structured heading hierarchy looks like for a garden center's plant care page:

```
<h1>Indoor Plant Care Guide</h1>

<h2>Choosing the Right Plants</h2>
<h3>Low-light plants for apartments</h3>
<h3>Pet-safe options</h3>

<h2>Watering Basics</h2>
<h3>How often to water</h3>
<h3>Signs of overwatering</h3>

<h2>Light and Temperature</h2>
<h3>Understanding light levels</h3>
<h3>Seasonal adjustments</h3>
```

Note how you can scan that structure and immediately understand what the page covers? That's how Google reads it, too.

TIP

Your <h1> and your <title> tag don't have to be identical, but they should be closely related. A title tag of "Indoor Plant Care: Tips for Beginners | Greenleaf Garden Center" paired with an <h1> of "Indoor Plant Care Guide" is perfectly fine.

# Content Optimization Best Practices

Titles, meta descriptions, and headings are the scaffolding. The content itself is the building. You can have perfect title tags and flawless heading structure, but if the words on the page are thin, vague, or unhelpful, none of that scaffolding matters.

## Writing for people first

"Writing for people first" sounds like it belongs on an inspirational poster, but it's the most important content principle in modern SEO. Write for your readers first, search engines second. If you write a page that thoroughly, clearly, and honestly answers the question someone typed into Google, you've done 90 percent of the SEO work already.

In the early days of search engines, you could rank a page by cramming your target keyword into every other sentence and hiding white text on a white background. Those tactics seem hilariously crude in retrospect. Google's algorithms now evaluate content the way a thoughtful human editor would: Is this page helpful? Does it demonstrate real knowledge? Would you trust the advice here? The practical takeaway: before you write a page, ask what question someone is trying to answer when they search for your target keyword. Then answer it better than anyone else. That's the whole game.

## Strategic keyword placement

Writing naturally doesn't mean ignoring keywords. You still want your target keyword (the one you identified during the research I describe in Book 7, Chapter 2) to appear in a few strategic places:

- **The title tag and** <h1> **heading:** As I discuss earlier in this chapter, both should include your primary keyword.
- **The first 100 words:** Mentioning your keyword early signals relevance. If someone lands on a page about sourdough bread and *sourdough* doesn't appear until paragraph six, something has gone sideways.
- **Subheadings:** Work your keyword (or close variations) into one or two <h2> or <h3> headings where it fits naturally.
- **Throughout the body:** Use your keyword and related terms as you write. Don't force it. If a sentence sounds awkward with the keyword shoehorned in, rewrite the sentence without it.

WARNING

As I explain in Book 7, Chapter 2, trying to manipulate rankings using keyword stuffing is a penalty trigger and one that Google warns against. If your text reads like it was written by a robot with a limited vocabulary, you've gone too far.

## Content depth and freshness

There's no magic word count for SEO. Google doesn't have a rule that says pages need to be 2,000 words to rank well. What it cares about is whether your page covers the topic thoroughly enough to be useful. For some topics, 500 words is plenty. For others, you need 3,000.

A useful exercise: search for your target keyword and look at the pages currently ranking on page one. How long are they? How much detail do they provide? You don't need to match them word for word, but you should be in the same ballpark. If every top result for "how to repot a succulent" is a 1,200-word guide with photos, your 200-word paragraph probably isn't going to cut it. That said, don't pad with filler. Readers can smell filler from a mile away, and so can Google.

Google also pays attention to freshness. For queries where timeliness matters — for example, "best laptops 2026" or "current mortgage rates" — newer content ranks higher. Even for evergreen topics, periodically reviewing your pages (say, once or twice a year) to update outdated information, fix broken links, and add new details signals to Google that your content is actively maintained.

TIP

Keep a simple spreadsheet listing your key pages, when each was last reviewed, and when it's due for the next review. The hardest part of content maintenance is remembering to do it.

# Image Optimization and Alt Text

Images make your pages more engaging, but they also represent an SEO opportunity that most small-business sites completely overlook. A well-optimized image can drive traffic through Google Image Search, improve your page's ranking, and make your site more accessible. A poorly optimized image does none of those things and might even slow your page down enough to hurt your rankings.

## Writing alt text that works

The `alt` attribute on an `<img>` tag provides a text description of the image. It's what screen readers read aloud (as I discuss in Book 2, Chapter 4), what browsers display if the image fails to load, and what Google uses to understand what the image shows:

```
<img src="sourdough-loaf.jpg"
     alt="A round sourdough loaf with a deep
          golden crust, cooling on a wire rack">
```

Writing good alt text isn't complicated:

- **Be specific.** "Bread" is too vague. "A round sourdough loaf with a deep golden crust" paints a picture.
- **Include your keyword when natural.** If the image is on a page about sourdough bread and *shows* sourdough bread, mention "sourdough." But don't force it into unrelated images.
- **Don't start with "image of" or "picture of."** Screen readers already announce that it's an image.
- **Keep it concise.** A sentence or two is plenty. Aim for 125 characters or fewer.
- **Use empty alt for decorative images.** If an image is purely decorative — a divider line, a background pattern — use `alt=""`. This tells screen readers to skip it.

WARNING

Never stuff keywords into alt text. An attribute such as `alt="sourdough bread best sourdough bread buy sourdough bread homemade sourdough"` is keyword stuffing, plain and simple. It can trigger a penalty, and it makes the experience miserable for anyone using a screen reader.

## File names and image formats

Give your images descriptive file names before uploading them. A file called `sourdough-loaf-golden-crust.jpg` tells Google more than `IMG_4392.jpg`. Use lowercase letters, separate words with hyphens, and keep it short. I cover image formats in Book 2, Chapter 2, but the short version is to use WebP for photographs (better compression than JPEG with no visible quality loss) and SVG for logos and icons. Also, resize images to the dimensions at which they'll be displayed. Don't upload a 4,000-pixel-wide original for an image that displays at 600 pixels. Your page speed will thank you.

# Internal Linking Strategy

An *internal link* is a link from one page on your site to another page on the same site. You've been creating them since you built your first navigation menu (as I describe in Book 3, Chapter 1), but internal linking as an SEO strategy goes beyond the nav bar. A thoughtful linking structure helps search engines discover all your pages, distributes ranking power across your site, and guides visitors to related content.

Here's a summary of what internal links do for SEO:

- **They help crawlers find your pages.** Googlebot discovers pages by following links. If a page has no internal links pointing to it, Google may never find it.
- **They distribute link equity.** When a page earns external links from other websites, some of that ranking power flows through internal links to other pages on your site. Think of external links as water (authority) flowing into your site, and internal links as the pipes distributing it.
- **They signal importance.** The pages you link to most often are implicitly flagged as important. If every blog post links back to your "Services" page, Google takes that as a hint.

## Building a smart linking structure

The goal isn't to scatter links randomly. It's to create a deliberate structure connecting related content:

- **Link from high-authority pages to important ones.** If your home page or a popular blog post has earned lots of external links, use internal links to steer some of that authority toward pages you want to rank higher.
- **Link contextually within your content.** When you mention a topic you've covered elsewhere, link to it. These in-context links are the most valuable kind because they're surrounded by relevant text.
- **Create hub pages.** A *hub page* is a comprehensive page on a broad topic that links out to several more specific pages. A bike shop might have a "Bicycle Maintenance Guide" hub linking to pages on tire care, brake adjustment, and chain lubrication. Each page links back to the hub. Search engines love this pattern.
- **Use your blog strategically.** Every blog post is a chance to link to your core service or product pages. A post about "How to Choose the Right Mountain Bike" should link to your mountain bikes page.

## Anchor text best practices

*Anchor text* is the clickable text in a link. Google uses it as a signal about what the linked page is about, so the words you choose matter. The golden rule: make your anchor text descriptive. Compare:

- **Bad:** "To learn about our repair services, `click here`." This anchor text tells Google nothing.
- **Good:** "We offer comprehensive `bicycle repair services` for all major brands." This anchor text tells Google what that page is about.

Don't go overboard, though. Using the same anchor text for every link to a given page can look manipulative. Mix it up. Be natural.

REMEMBER

Every page on your site should have at least one internal link pointing to it. A page with no internal links is called an *orphan page* and is essentially invisible to crawlers. Use a tool such as Screaming Frog (the free version handles up to 500 URLs) to find orphan pages periodically.

# URL Structure and Permalinks

URLs might seem like a minor detail, but search engines use them as a signal for what a page is about. A clean, descriptive URL is a small but meaningful SEO advantage. A messy one is a missed opportunity.

## What makes a good URL

A good URL is short, readable, and descriptive. Compare `example.com/indoor-plant-care` (clear) with `example.com/p?id=4827&cat=7&ref=home` (not clear). Google prefers the first kind, and so do humans. The principles:

- **Use real words.** A URL should describe the page in plain language.
- **Include your target keyword.** Keep it natural: `/sourdough-bread-recipe` is great; `/best-homemade-sourdough-bread-recipe-easy-beginner-guide` is too much.
- **Use hyphens to separate words.** Google treats hyphens as word separators but treats underscores as word joiners. So `plant-care` is two words; `plant_care` is read as one. Hyphens win.

- **Keep it lowercase and short.** Some servers treat uppercase and lowercase URLs as different pages. Stick to lowercase. Trim filler words such as *the, and, of.*

## Common URL mistakes

Here are a few distressingly common URL mistakes that you should avoid at all costs:

- **Query strings for regular pages:** URLs such as `example.com/?page_id=42` are common in default WordPress installations. They work, but they're terrible for SEO. Change your permalinks to use post names (such as `example.com/my-post`; these are also known as *pretty permalinks*) by choosing Settings ➪ Permalinks and selecting the Post Name option. Do it immediately.
- **Dates in URLs:** Formats such as `example.com/2027/03/15/my-post` add clutter and make older content look stale. Use `/my-post` instead (unless your content is genuinely time-sensitive).
- **Deeply nested paths:** A URL such as `example.com/products/outdoor/furniture/chairs/folding/aluminum` has too many levels. Flatten it to `example.com/aluminum-folding-chairs`.

## Changing URLs safely

When you change a URL, the old one stops working. Anyone who bookmarked it, linked to it, or has it indexed in Google gets a 404 error. The fix is a *301 redirect*, a permanent server instruction that sends visitors and search engines from the old URL to the new one. Google transfers most of the old page's ranking power to the new URL, so you don't lose the SEO value you've built up. How you set up 301 redirects depends on your platform (WordPress has plug-ins for this; most hosts support them through configuration files), but the concept is universal.

WARNING

Never change a URL without setting up a redirect. A changed URL without a redirect is a broken link, and broken links are one of the most common and most preventable SEO problems. If you're changing many URLs at once (during a redesign, say), create a spreadsheet mapping every old URL to its new destination *before* you make any changes. Your future self will be extremely grateful.

# Schema Markup Implementation

If you've ever seen a Google search result with star ratings, recipe cooking times, FAQ dropdowns, or business hours displayed in the listing, you've seen schema markup in action. *Schema markup* is a way of adding structured information to your pages that helps search engines understand not just the *words* on your page, but the *meaning* behind them. It's the difference between Google seeing 4.8 on your page and understanding that 4.8 is a customer rating out of 5 stars.

## How schema markup affects search results

Schema markup doesn't directly improve your rankings (Google has been clear about that), but it *does* make your search listings more visually prominent. These enhanced listings are called *rich results*, and they can dramatically increase your clickthrough rate. A result with star ratings, price ranges, and availability badges stands out from the plain blue links around it. It catches the eye, builds trust, and gives searchers more reasons to click.

## Common schema types for small businesses

`Schema.org` defines hundreds of data types, but you need only a handful:

- **LocalBusiness:** Your name, address, phone number, hours, and coordinates. The big one for any business with a physical location. Reinforces your Google Business Profile (which I discuss in Book 7, Chapter 1).
- **Product:** Name, price, availability, and review ratings for individual products. Gets those price and availability badges into your search listings.
- **FAQ:** Questions and answers that Google can display as expandable dropdowns in search results, taking up more screen real estate.
- **Article:** Headline, author, date, and featured image for blog posts and guides.
- **Breadcrumb:** Your page's position in the site hierarchy. Instead of a raw URL, Google displays a clean trail such as "Home > Products > Outdoor Furniture > Chairs."

## Tools that do the work for you

You don't need to write schema markup by hand. The underlying format (*JSON-LD*) is a flavor of JSON that sits in your page's `<head>` section, but several tools generate it for you:

- **Google's Structured Data Markup Helper (`www.google.com/webmasters/markup-helper/`):** A free tool where you click elements of your page to tag them, and it generates the code.
- **WordPress SEO plugins:** Yoast SEO (`yoast.com/`) and Rank Math (`rankmath.com/`) include built-in schema generators. Fill in some fields, and the plug-in adds the code to your pages automatically.
- **Google's Rich Results Test (`search.google.com/test/rich-results`):** Paste a URL into this tool to verify that Google can read your markup and that it's eligible for rich results. Fix any errors before moving on.

The process: identify which schema types apply to your pages, use a tool to generate the markup, add it (most plug-ins handle this automatically), and validate with Google's testing tool. That's it. No new programming language required.

REMEMBER

Schema markup takes about 30 minutes to set up and then works quietly in the background forever. It won't catapult you to the top of Google overnight, but it makes your search listings more attractive and informative, so you get more clicks from the same number of impressions. For the effort involved, it's one of the best returns on investment in all of on-page SEO.

IN THIS CHAPTER

» **Making your site fast, secure, and crawlable**

» **Creating XML sitemaps and robots.txt files**

» **Finding and fixing broken links and redirects**

» **Setting up and using Google Search Console**

# Chapter 4
# Technical SEO

*Perfection is achieved, not when there is nothing more to add, but when there is nothing left to take away.*

—ANTOINE DE SAINT-EXUPÉRY

Unlike most of the user-focused SEO stuff I cover in Book 7, Chapters 1 through 3, this chapter's topic — technical SEO — deals with the infrastructure of your site: how fast it loads, whether it's secure, whether search engines can find and understand all your pages, and whether anything is broken or misconfigured behind the scenes. It's not glamorous work. Nobody has ever said, "Wow, what a beautiful robots.txt file!" (And if someone has said that to you, maybe introduce them to some new hobbies.) But if your technical foundation is shaky, all the brilliant content and perfectly researched keywords in the world won't save you. Fortunately, most technical SEO problems are straightforward to diagnose and fix, especially for a small-business site. You don't need to be a systems administrator or a networking guru. You just need to know what to look for and where to look.

# Site Speed and Performance

I cover Core Web Vitals in some detail in Book 7, Chapter 1, and I get into the nitty-gritty of performance optimization in Book 9, Chapter 2, so I won't repeat all of that here. But site speed deserves a mention in any technical SEO discussion because it's where user experience and search rankings overlap almost perfectly. A slow site frustrates your visitors *and* can hurt your rankings. A fast site does the opposite.

## Quick speed wins

If your site feels sluggish, here are a few things that tend to deliver the biggest improvements for the least effort:

- **Optimize your images.** Reducing the size of hefty image files is almost always the single biggest win. A 4MB photo that could be a 200KB compressed JPEG is dead weight. Resize images to the dimensions at which they'll display, compress them (Squoosh or TinyPNG make this trivially easy), and use modern formats such as `WebP`.
- **Enable compression.** Most web servers can compress your HTML, CSS, and JavaScript files using Gzip or Brotli compression, typically reducing file sizes by 60 to 80 percent. Many hosting providers enable this by default, but it's worth checking.
- **Use a content delivery network.** A CDN stores copies of your files on servers around the world, so visitors download from whichever server is closest. Cloudflare offers a free tier that works well for small sites.
- **Minimize redirects.** Every redirect adds a round trip between the browser and the server. One redirect is fine. A chain of three or four? That's your page speed leaking away, one hop at a time.

## Testing your speed

As I mention in Book 7, Chapter 1, Google's PageSpeed Insights tool (at `https://pagespeed.web.dev/`) is the easiest way to check your site's speed. Paste in a URL, wait a few seconds, and you get a score from 0 to 100 along with specific suggestions for improvement. Don't obsess over getting a perfect 100. A score in the 90s is excellent, 70s or 80s is solid, and below 50 is where you should start worrying. The suggestions are ranked by impact, so start at the top and work your way down. GTmetrix (at `gtmetrix.com`) is another solid option that gives you a slightly different perspective on the same data.

TIP

Test your site's speed on both desktop and mobile. PageSpeed Insights does both, and the mobile score is usually lower (sometimes significantly lower). Since Google uses mobile-first indexing, that mobile score is the one that matters most for your search rankings.

# Mobile-Friendliness

As I discuss at some length in Book 7, Chapter 1, Google uses mobile-first indexing, which means it evaluates your site based on the mobile version of your pages. If your site looks great on a 27-inch monitor but turns into a jumbled mess on a phone, Google is judging you by the jumbled mess. I also cover responsive design in detail in Book 2, Chapter 3, so I won't rehash all of that here. But a few mobile-specific things are worth checking from a technical SEO perspective.

## Testing your mobile experience

Google used to offer a standalone Mobile-Friendly Test tool, but it retired that in late 2023. The good news is that the same information is now available through Google Search Console (which I cover later in this chapter) under the Mobile Usability report. You can also use Chrome's built-in devtools to simulate different screen sizes: press F12 to open devtools, and then click the little phone-and-tablet icon in the top-left corner (or press Ctrl+Shift+M). Voilà: instant mobile preview.

## Common mobile pitfalls

Most mobile-friendliness issues boil down to a handful of recurring problems:

- **Touch targets too small:** Buttons and links need to be large enough to tap with a finger. Google recommends a minimum tap target size of 48 by 48 pixels with at least 8 pixels of spacing between targets.
- **Text too small to read:** If visitors have to zoom in to read your body text, your font size is too small. A base size of 1.25rem (20 pixels in most browsers) is a good starting point for mobile.
- **Horizontal scrolling:** If your page is wider than the screen, something in your layout isn't responding to the viewport width. Usually it's a fixed-width element (an image or a table) that refuses to shrink.

REMEMBER

Mobile-friendliness isn't just about how your site looks on a small screen. It's about how it *works:* Are the buttons tappable? Does the text reflow? Can visitors accomplish what they came to do without squinting or zooming? If yes, you're in good shape.

# HTTPS and Security Signals

Google has used HTTPS as a ranking signal since 2014. It's a relatively small signal compared to things like content quality and backlinks, but it's one of the easiest boxes to check. More importantly, browsers now actively warn visitors when a site doesn't use HTTPS. Chrome, for example, labels non-HTTPS sites as *Not secure* right there in the address bar. That's not the first impression you want to make.

## Getting HTTPS set up

HTTPS works by encrypting the connection between your visitor's browser and your web server, and it requires an *SSL certificate* (technically, these are now called *TLS certificates,* but everyone still says "SSL" because old habits die hard). The certificate proves that your site is what it says it is and that the data traveling back and forth is encrypted.

The wonderful news is that getting an SSL certificate is both free and easy for most sites. Let's Encrypt is a free certificate authority that most hosting providers support directly. Many hosts (including SiteGround, Bluehost, and Hostinger) offer one-click SSL setup right from your hosting dashboard. If your host supports Let's Encrypt, there's no reason not to enable it. I cover website security in more depth in Book 9, Chapter 4, but from a technical SEO perspective, the short version is: get HTTPS, make sure it works, and move on.

## Fixing mixed content warnings

Here's a sneaky problem that catches a lot of people. You've set up HTTPS and everything looks great. But then on certain pages, the padlock disappears or the browser shows a warning. The culprit is almost always *mixed content:* your page is loaded over HTTPS, but somewhere on that page there's a resource (an image, a script, a stylesheet) that's still being loaded over plain HTTP. The browser notices the mismatch and downgrades its security assessment.

The fix is straightforward: find every resource on your site that's still using an `http://` URL and change it to `https://`. If you're using WordPress, a plug-in like Really Simple SSL can handle this task automatically. If you're hand-coding your site, a quick search through your HTML and CSS files for `http://` will usually reveal the offenders.

WARNING

Don't ignore mixed-content warnings. A page with mixed content may not get the full HTTPS ranking benefit, and the *Not secure* warning can erode your visitors' trust, especially on pages where you're asking them to enter personal information.

# XML Sitemaps

I mention sitemaps briefly in Book 7, Chapter 1 when I talk about how search engines crawl your site. Now it's time to dig into the details. An *XML sitemap* is a file that lives on your web server and lists all the pages on your site that you want search engines to know about. Think of it as handing Google a table of contents for your site instead of making it wander around and hoping it finds everything.

To be clear: Google doesn't *need* a sitemap to find your pages. If your pages are well-linked internally (and they should be), Googlebot will eventually discover them by following those links. But *eventually* the process can be slow, especially for new sites. A sitemap speeds things up and gives you a way to tell Google about pages it might otherwise miss.

## What goes in a sitemap

An XML sitemap is, at its core, just a list of URLs. Each URL entry can include a few optional details: when the page was last modified, how often it changes, and how important it is relative to other pages on your site. The file itself is written in XML (eXtensible Markup Language), but you almost never need to write it by hand. The key thing to know is that your sitemap should include every page you want search engines to index and should *not* include pages you don't want indexed (such as admin pages, duplicate pages, or placeholder pages).

## Creating a sitemap

How you create your sitemap depends on how you built your site:

- **WordPress:** If you're using an SEO plug-in such as Yoast SEO or Rank Math (and if you're running a WordPress site, you should be using one of these), your sitemap is being generated automatically. Yoast creates it at `yoursite.com/sitemap_index.xml`. Rank Math does the same. You don't have to do anything except make sure the feature is turned on in the plug-in settings.

- **Other CMS platforms:** Most modern content management systems either generate sitemaps automatically or have plug-ins that do. Squarespace, Wix, and Shopify all create sitemaps for you with no configuration required.
- **Static or hand-coded sites:** If you built your site by hand (which is entirely possible if you followed the earlier minibooks in this book), you can use a free online generator such as `XML-Sitemaps.com`. Point it at your site, and it crawls your pages and spits out a ready-to-use sitemap file. Download the file and upload it to the root directory of your website.

## Submitting your sitemap to Google

Once your sitemap exists and is accessible on your site, you'll want to tell Google about it. The best way to do this is through Google Search Console (which I cover in detail later in this chapter in the "Using Google Search Console" section). In Search Console, navigate to the Sitemaps section in the left sidebar, enter the URL of your sitemap, and click Submit. Google will fetch it, check it for errors, and start using it to discover your pages.

You can also point crawlers to your sitemap by adding a reference to it in your `robots.txt` file (which I cover in the next section). Just add a line like this at the bottom of the file:

```
Sitemap: https://www.yoursite.com/sitemap.xml
```

That's it. Two ways to tell search engines where your sitemap lives, and both take about 30 seconds.

TIP

After you submit your sitemap, check back in a day or two. Search Console will tell you how many of the URLs in your sitemap have been indexed, how many were excluded, and why. And if you're maintaining a static sitemap (rather than one generated automatically by a plug-in), remember to regenerate it whenever you add or remove pages.

# The robots.txt File

If an XML sitemap is a table of contents you hand to search engines, then a `robots.txt` file is a set of house rules. It's a plain text file that sits in the root directory of your website (at *yoursite*`.com/robots.txt`) and tells web crawlers which parts of your site they're allowed to visit and which parts they should leave alone. Think of it as a "Staff Only" sign for search engine bots.

An important caveat: `robots.txt` is a *request*, not an enforcement mechanism. Well-behaved crawlers (like Googlebot) honor it. Poorly behaved ones ignore it entirely. If you have pages that need to be private, use proper authentication instead. But for telling legitimate search engines which pages to crawl and which to skip, `robots.txt` is the standard tool.

## Writing a robots.txt file

A `robots.txt` file is refreshingly simple. It's just plain text with a few basic directives. Here's what a typical one looks like for a small business website:

```
User-agent: *
Disallow: /admin/
Disallow: /thank-you/
Allow: /
Sitemap: https://www.example.com/sitemap.xml
```

Let me walk through that:

- **`User-agent: *`:** The asterisk is a wildcard that means what follows applies to all crawlers. You can target specific crawlers by name (such as `Googlebot`), but for most small sites the wildcard is all you need.
- **`Disallow: /admin/` and `Disallow: /thank-you/`:** These tell crawlers not to visit URLs under those paths. Use `Disallow` for admin panels, staging areas, and thank-you pages that don't belong in search results.
- **`Allow: /`:** Explicitly says that everything else is fair game. Technically, this directive is on by default, but including it makes your intentions clear.
- **Sitemap:** Points crawlers to your XML sitemap. This is a convenience line that it doesn't hurt to include.

## Common robots.txt mistakes

The most spectacular `robots.txt` mistake is also the most common: accidentally blocking your entire site. If your file contains this:

```
User-agent: *
Disallow: /
```

that single forward slash after `Disallow` means block everything. Every page, every image, every file. Google will obediently stop crawling your entire site, and your pages will gradually disappear from search results. Yikes!

This mistake happens more often than you'd think, usually because someone set up a restrictive `robots.txt` during development to keep the unfinished site out of Google and then forgot to change it after launch. Always double-check your `robots.txt` after going live.

WARNING

Another common mistake is blocking your CSS and JavaScript files. Google needs to see your CSS and JavaScript to understand how your page renders. Blocking those files can prevent Google from properly evaluating your page layout, which can hurt your rankings.

# Fixing Broken Links and Redirects

A *broken link* (sometimes called a *dead link*) points to a page that no longer exists. The visitor clicks the link, and instead of the content they expected, they get a `404 Not Found` error. It's the web equivalent of driving to a restaurant that closed six months ago: annoying, disappointing, and not exactly a vote of confidence in whoever recommended it.

## Why broken links matter

Broken links hurt you in two ways. First, they're a terrible user experience — a visitor who hits a 404 page is a visitor who's likely to leave your site. Second, broken links waste *crawl budget:* the number of pages Googlebot will crawl on your site in a given time period. For a small site, crawl budget is rarely a pressing concern, but broken links still signal to Google that your site isn't well-maintained.

There's also the issue of *link equity.* When another site links to one of your pages, that link passes some authority to you. If that page no longer exists and returns a 404, all that authority vanishes. The other site is still linking to you, but the benefit is gone.

## Finding broken links

You can't fix what you can't find, so the first step is identifying which links on your site are broken. Here are a few ways to do that:

» **Google Search Console:** The Indexing report flags pages that returned 404 errors when Googlebot tried to crawl them. This report is your best source of truth for what Google itself is seeing.

- **Broken Link Checker:** A free online tool (at `brokenlinkcheck.com`) that crawls your site and reports every link that doesn't lead somewhere valid. Simple, free, and effective.
- **Screaming Frog SEO Spider:** The free version (available from `www.screamingfrog.co.uk/seo-spider`) crawls up to 500 URLs and gives you a detailed report on broken links, redirect chains, and other technical issues. It's more powerful than an online checker, though the interface takes a bit of getting used to.

## Understanding redirects

When you remove a page or change its URL, you don't want visitors (or search engines) to hit a dead end. A *redirect* tells the browser that the page it's looking for has moved and conveys where the page lives now. The browser automatically takes the visitor to the new URL, and if everything is set up properly, the visitor barely notices.

You need to know about two types of redirects:

- **301 redirect (permanent):** This says, "This page has permanently moved to a new address." Search engines transfer most of the original page's ranking power to the new URL. Use a 301 when the change is permanent, such as when you've reorganized your site and a page's URL has changed for good.
- **302 redirect (temporary):** This says, "This page has temporarily moved, but it'll be back." Search engines keep the original URL in their index. Use a 302 for truly temporary situations, like redirecting to a maintenance page while you update your site.

REMEMBER

When in doubt, use a 301. The vast majority of redirects on a typical small business site should be 301s. A 302 is appropriate only when you genuinely intend to bring back the original URL, which is rarer than most people think.

## Setting up redirects

How you create redirects depends on your platform:

- **WordPress:** Plug-ins like Redirection or Rank Math let you set up redirects through a simple dashboard interface. Enter the old URL, enter the new URL, pick 301, and save.

- **Apache web servers:** If your site runs on Apache (which many shared hosting plans use), you can add redirect rules to your `.htaccess` file. Your hosting provider's documentation will explain how.
- **Netlify, Vercel, and similar platforms:** These modern hosting platforms support redirects through configuration files. Check your platform's documentation for the syntax.

Whatever method you use, the key is to set up the redirect *before* you delete or rename the old page. If visitors (or Googlebot) hit a 404 even briefly, you've already done some damage.

# Structured Data Testing

In Book 7, Chapter 3, I walk through schema markup in detail: what it is, which types are most useful for small businesses, and how to add it to your pages. This section is about what comes *after* you've added schema markup. Specifically, you learn how to make sure not only that it's working but that it's working correctly.

## Testing your structured data

Google provides two free tools for validating schema markup:

- **Rich Results Test (`search.google.com/test/rich-results`):** This tool checks whether your page's structured data is eligible for rich results — the enhanced search listings with star ratings, prices, FAQ dropdowns, and other eye-catching features. Enter a URL, and the tool tells you what Google sees and whether there are any errors or warnings.
- **Schema Markup Validator (`validator.schema.org`):** This one validates your markup against the full `Schema.org` specification. It's more thorough than the Rich Results Test but less focused on what Google supports. Use it as a second opinion.

## Fixing common errors

The most frequent structured data errors fall into a few predictable categories: missing required fields (for example, your LocalBusiness markup doesn't include an address), invalid values (a product price that's set to free instead of a number), and markup that doesn't match the visible page content (for example, your markup says the product costs $29.99, but the page shows $34.99). The Rich Results Test is good at identifying these. Fix whatever it flags, retest, and you're done.

TIP

Run the Rich Results Test on your most important pages — your home page, your contact page, your top product or service pages — and fix any errors it finds. You don't need to test every single page on your site; focus on the pages that are most likely to appear in search results.

# Using Google Search Console

If there's one tool in this entire chapter that I'd call essential, it's Google Search Console. It's free, it's made by Google, and it gives you a direct window into how Google sees your site: which pages are indexed, what queries bring visitors, what errors exist, and how your Core Web Vitals are doing. Not using Search Console is like driving with your eyes closed.

## Setting up Search Console

Setting up Google Search Console takes about five minutes. Go to `search.google.com/search-console` and sign in with your Google account. You'll be asked to add a property, which is Google's word for your website. There are two types of properties:

- **Domain property:** Covers your entire domain, including all subdomains. This is the option I'd recommend, but it requires verifying ownership through your DNS provider. (Your hosting provider's support team can usually walk you through the process in minutes.)
- **URL prefix property:** Covers only a specific version of your site (for example, `https://www.`*`yoursite`*`.com`). Verification is simpler — you can upload an HTML file, add a meta tag, or connect through Google Analytics — but you'll only see data for that exact prefix.

For a small-business site, either option works fine. If you're not comfortable editing DNS records, the URL prefix method is perfectly adequate. Pick the method that feels least daunting and get it done.

## The reports that matter

Search Console offers a lot of reports, and it's easy to get overwhelmed. Here are the ones I think are most useful for a small business site owner:

- **Performance report:** Shows which search queries bring visitors to your site, how many impressions and clicks each query gets, your average position, and your clickthrough rate. Pay special attention to queries with lots of impressions but few clicks because that usually means your title or meta description isn't compelling enough to earn the click.
- **Indexing report:** Tells you which pages are in Google's index, which were excluded, and why. If important pages aren't showing up in search results, this is where you'll find out what went wrong.
- **Experience report:** Surfaces your Core Web Vitals data and any mobile usability issues. This data is the same as PageSpeed Insights but aggregated across your entire site.
- **Sitemaps report:** Shows the status of any sitemaps you've submitted, including how many URLs they contain and how many have been indexed.

## Fixing what Search Console finds

Besides reporting problems, Search Console also gives you enough detail to fix them. If the Indexing report shows pages with "Crawled — currently not indexed," that often means Google found the page but didn't think it was worth indexing (thin content, duplicate content, or a `noindex` tag you forgot to remove). If, instead, the report shows "Not found (404)," you know you need to either restore the page or set up a redirect.

When you've fixed an issue, you can use the Validate Fix button in Search Console to ask Google to recheck the affected pages. Google will recrawl them over the next few days and update the report. It's not instant, but it's a satisfying feedback loop: find the problem, fix the problem, confirm the fix.

TIP

Make a habit of checking Search Console at least once a month. Set a calendar reminder if you need to. Most technical SEO problems don't announce themselves with sirens and flashing lights. Instead, they creep in quietly, and by the time you notice the drop in traffic, the damage has been accumulating for weeks.

# Common Technical SEO Problems

This final section is a quick-reference guide to technical SEO problems that tend to trip up small-business sites. Some of these I've touched on already in this chapter; others are new. Either way, knowing what to look for is half the battle.

## Duplicate content

*Duplicate content* means two or more pages on your site with the same (or very similar) content. This confuses search engines because they don't know which version to index and rank. The result? Google picks one and ignores the others, and it might not pick the one you wanted.

The most common cause of duplicate content on small sites isn't intentional copying — it's technical. Your site might be accessible at both `www.`*`yoursite`*`.com` and *`yoursite`*`.com` (without the `www`), or at both `http://` and `https://`. Each is a different URL in Google's eyes, even though they all show the same content.

The fix is a *canonical tag:* a small piece of HTML in the `<head>` section that tells search engines which version of a page is the real one. It looks like this:

```
<link rel="canonical" href="https://www.yoursite.com/page/">
```

Most CMS platforms and SEO plug-ins add canonical tags automatically, but it's worth verifying that they're present on your key pages. View the page source in your browser (right-click and choose View Page Source) and search for *canonical.* If it's there and pointing to the right URL, you're fine.

## Crawl errors and orphan pages

A *crawl error* is any problem that prevents Googlebot from accessing a page. The most common types are 404 errors (page not found), server errors (your server returned a 500 error instead of the page), and redirect loops (page A redirects to page B, which redirects back to page A, forever and ever, amen). Search Console's Indexing report is the best place to find and monitor crawl errors.

An *orphan page* is the opposite problem: a page that exists on your site but has no internal links pointing to it. Since Googlebot discovers pages by following links, an orphan page is effectively invisible to crawlers (unless it's listed in your sitemap). Orphan pages are sneakily common on sites that have been around for a while. You publish a page, link to it from a blog post, then later delete the blog post, and suddenly the page is stranded. The fix is simple: make sure every important page is linked from at least one other page. As I discuss in Book 7, Chapter 3, a solid internal linking strategy helps both your visitors and search engines navigate your site.

## Missing or duplicate meta tags

Every page on your site should have a unique `<title>` tag and a unique `<meta description>` tag. These are the elements that show up in search results (as I cover in Book 7, Chapter 3), so duplicating them across multiple pages means Google can't tell those pages apart in search results. It also means you're missing the chance to write targeted, click-worthy titles and descriptions for each page.

Search Console's Search Appearance section used to flag duplicate titles and descriptions directly. That report has been phased out, but you can catch these issues using tools like Screaming Frog (which flags duplicates automatically) or by manually reviewing your most important pages. If you're using WordPress, the Yoast SEO plug-in shows you the title and meta description for each page right in the editor, which makes duplicates easy to spot.

REMEMBER

Technical SEO isn't a one-time project. Sites change, plug-ins update, pages get added and removed, and things break quietly in the background. The best approach is a simple monthly check: open Google Search Console, scan the reports for anything new, test your site speed, and make sure your sitemap and `robots.txt` are still doing what you expect. Twenty minutes a month is enough to catch most problems before they snowball into something worse.

# 8 E-Commerce Solutions

# Contents at a Glance

IN THIS CHAPTER

» Comparing e-commerce platforms

» Setting up payment processing

» Figuring out shipping, fulfillment, and inventory

» Understanding security, compliance, and the legal stuff

# Chapter 1
# Choosing and Setting Up E-Commerce

*There is only one boss. The customer. And he can fire everybody in the company from the chairman on down, simply by spending his money somewhere else.*

—SAM WALTON, MADE IN AMERICA

E-commerce means giving your customers a complete shopping experience: browsing products, adding items to a cart, choosing shipping options, entering payment details, and getting a confirmation, all without picking up a phone or sending an email. It also means giving *you* the tools to manage inventory, process payments, handle returns, and keep track of who bought what and when.

That sounds like a lot, I know, but you don't have to build any of this from scratch. Modern e-commerce platforms handle the heavy lifting, and your job is mostly about choosing the right platform, setting it up properly, and understanding enough about payments, shipping, and legal requirements to avoid nasty surprises down the road. That's exactly what this chapter covers.

# Comparing E-Commerce Platforms

An *e-commerce platform* is software that handles the online selling side of your business. At a minimum, it gives you a product catalog, a shopping cart, a checkout process, and payment processing. Most platforms also handle inventory tracking, order management, shipping calculations, tax collection, and customer accounts. Some even throw in marketing tools, abandoned cart recovery, and built-in analytics. The idea is that you focus on your products and your customers while the platform worries about the plumbing.

The platforms I cover in this section fall into two broad camps: *hosted platforms* (where the company runs everything on their servers and you pay a monthly fee) and *self-hosted platforms* (where you install the software on your own web host and manage it yourself). Each approach has trade-offs, and the right choice depends on your technical comfort level, your budget, and how much control you want over the details.

## Shopify for beginners

If you want the fastest path from "I have products to sell" to "My online store is accepting orders," Shopify is almost certainly where you should start. It's a hosted platform, which means Shopify handles the servers, the security, the software updates, and the technical infrastructure. You sign up, pick a theme, add your products, connect a payment method, and you're selling. I'm oversimplifying a bit (okay, a lot), but the basic idea is that Shopify removes as much technical friction as possible so you can focus on running your business.

Shopify's strengths are numerous. The admin dashboard is intuitive enough that you can figure out most things without reading documentation (which is a higher compliment than it might sound). The theme store has hundreds of professionally designed templates, both free and paid. Payment processing is built right in through Shopify Payments (powered by Stripe), so you don't need to set up a separate payment gateway. And the app store has thousands of add-ons for everything from email marketing to print-on-demand products.

One thing that impresses me about Shopify is how much it handles out of the box. Abandoned cart emails? Built in. Discount codes? Built in. Gift cards? Built in. Basic SEO tools (as I discuss in Book 7)? Built in. You can get a functional, professional-looking store up and running without installing a single third-party app. That said, the app store is there when you need it, and some apps are genuinely useful; just resist the urge to install twenty of them on day one. Start lean and add functionality only when you need it.

The trade-offs? Shopify charges a monthly subscription fee (plans start around $39 per month as of this writing, though pricing can change), plus transaction fees on each sale. If you use Shopify Payments, the transaction fees are lower; if you use a third-party payment gateway, Shopify tacks on an additional fee. Also, while Shopify themes are customizable, you're working within Shopify's template system, which means you don't have the same level of control you'd get with fully custom code. For most small businesses, that's a perfectly acceptable trade-off. For a few, it's a dealbreaker.

Setting up a Shopify store is fairly straightforward. After creating an account, you pick a theme (start with a free one; you can always upgrade later), add your products with photos and descriptions, configure your shipping rates and payment settings, connect your domain name (as I discuss in Book 1, Chapter 3), and you're open for business. The entire process can take as little as an afternoon for a small product catalog, though I'd recommend spending a few days getting your product descriptions and photos right. First impressions matter, and you get only one shot at them.



TIP

Most e-commerce platforms offer free trials (Shopify's is typically three days, sometimes longer during promotions). Take advantage of these. Set up a test store, add a few products, poke around the admin dashboard, and see if the workflow feels natural to you before committing to a monthly plan.

## WooCommerce for WordPress users

If you're already running a WordPress site (or planning to, as I discuss in Book 5, Chapter 1), WooCommerce is the natural choice for adding e-commerce. WooCommerce is a free, open-source plug-in that turns any WordPress installation into a full-featured online store. *Free* is doing a lot of work in that sentence, though, because while the plug-in itself costs nothing, you'll still pay for hosting, a domain name, an SSL certificate (many hosts include this for free), and potentially some premium extensions.

The big advantage of WooCommerce is control. Because it's built on WordPress, you have access to the full WordPress ecosystem of themes and plug-ins, and you can customize virtually anything with HTML, CSS, and PHP. If you know how to code (or have been learning to code throughout this book), WooCommerce gives you the freedom to tinker with every detail of your store's look and behavior. It's also self-hosted, which means your data lives on your server, not on someone else's platform.

The downside is that with great control comes great responsibility (to paraphrase a certain fictional uncle). You're responsible for keeping WordPress, WooCommerce, and all your plug-ins updated. You're responsible for backups, security, and performance optimization. If something breaks at 2 a.m., there's no Shopify support team to call; it's just you and a search engine. For someone comfortable with WordPress, those responsibilities are manageable. For someone who just wants to sell candles online without worrying about PHP version compatibility, it might be more hassle than it's worth.

One thing I do want to mention: WooCommerce has a huge ecosystem of extensions (both free and paid) that add features that the core plug-in doesn't include. Need subscriptions? There's an extension for that. Need product bundles, booking systems, or membership gating? Extensions for all of those. The flip side is that these extensions cost money (some are one-time purchases, others are annual subscriptions), and the more extensions you add, the more complex your site becomes to maintain. I've seen WooCommerce stores with 30+ active plug-ins, and let me tell you: that's a recipe for compatibility headaches.

One more WooCommerce consideration: hosting. Because WooCommerce is self-hosted, you need web hosting that can handle the demands of an online store. A $5 per month shared-hosting plan might be fine for a personal blog, but e-commerce stores need more resources, including more memory, more processing power, and faster storage. Look for hosting providers that offer WooCommerce-optimized plans (SiteGround, Bluehost, and Cloudways all have options), and expect to pay $15–$50 per month for hosting that won't buckle when you get a spike in traffic. (Nothing kills a sale faster than a slow website.)

## Other options worth a look

Shopify and WooCommerce dominate the e-commerce landscape, but they're not the only games in town. Here are a few other platforms worth considering, depending on your situation:

- **BigCommerce (`bigcommerce.com`):** A hosted platform similar to Shopify but with more built-in features out of the box (multichannel selling, for example, is included in all plans rather than requiring an add-on). BigCommerce tends to appeal to businesses that are growing quickly and need more advanced features without relying on a stack of third-party apps.
- **Square Online (`squareonline.com`):** If you already use Square for in-person payments (at a farmers' market or a retail counter, say), Square Online lets you build a simple online store that syncs with your existing Square account. The free tier is genuinely useful for small operations, though it includes Square branding and limited customization.

- **Ecwid (`ecwid.com`):** Rather than replacing your existing website, Ecwid lets you add a store to any website by embedding a snippet of code. If you've already built a site you love (using the HTML, CSS, and JavaScript skills from Books 3 and 4, perhaps) and just want to bolt on some shopping functionality, Ecwid is worth a look. It has a free tier for up to five products.

Other platforms are out there (Wix has e-commerce features, Squarespace has a commerce plan, and industry-specific platforms exist for everything from restaurants to fitness studios), but the ones I've listed cover the most common scenarios for small-business owners. If none of these seem like the right fit, a quick search for "e-commerce platform for [*your industry*]" will usually turn up specialized options worth investigating.



## Choosing the right platform

With so many options, how do you decide? I find it helps to ask yourself four questions:

- **How technical are you?** If you're comfortable managing a WordPress site, WooCommerce gives you the most flexibility for the lowest ongoing cost. If the thought of managing plug-ins and updates makes your eye twitch, go with a hosted platform such as Shopify or BigCommerce.
- **What's your budget?** WooCommerce has lower monthly costs (just your hosting fee), but higher time costs. Shopify and BigCommerce have higher monthly fees but save you time on maintenance and troubleshooting. Factor in your time as a real cost, because it is.
- **How many products are you selling?** If you're selling up to a few dozen products, almost any platform will work. If you're selling a hundred or more, you need robust inventory management, product filtering, and search, which are features where some platforms shine and others struggle.
- **Do you already have a website?** If you've already built a site you're happy with, Ecwid or a similar embeddable solution lets you add commerce without starting over. If you're building from scratch, an all-in-one platform like Shopify is probably simpler.

## What about digital products and services?

So far, I've been talking mostly about selling physical products: things you can hold, package, and ship. But what if you're selling digital products (e-books, online courses, downloadable templates, stock photos) or services (consulting, web design, coaching sessions)? The good news is that most e-commerce platforms handle digital products just fine. You upload the file, set a price, and the platform delivers the download link after purchase. No shipping required.

Digital products have some nice advantages over physical ones. There's no inventory to manage (you never run out of downloads), no shipping costs, no packaging, and no returns in the traditional sense. The margins are typically much higher because your cost per unit is essentially zero after you've created the product. The trade-off is that digital products are easier to pirate, and customers sometimes expect them to be cheaper than physical goods.

For services, the e-commerce model looks a bit different. Instead of a product page with an Add to Cart button, you might have a booking system where customers choose a time slot and pay upfront. Platforms such as Squarespace have scheduling tools built in, and WooCommerce has booking extensions. Alternatively, you can use a standalone scheduling tool (such as Calendly or Acuity Scheduling) and integrate it with your payment provider. The key is to make it as easy as possible for customers to book and pay in one smooth flow, rather than requiring them to email you for availability and then send a separate payment.

# Setting Up Payment Processing

Here's a question that might seem obvious but is worth thinking about: When a customer enters their credit card number on your website and clicks Buy Now, what happens? Where does the money go? Who checks whether the card is valid? How does the money end up in your bank account? If your answer to all of these is "I have no idea," that's fine because most people don't. But if you're going to accept payments online, it helps to understand the basics of how the system works so you can make informed decisions about which payment services to use.

Fortunately, payment processing has become dramatically simpler over the past decade. Accepting credit cards online used to require a merchant account from a bank, a separate payment gateway, a payment processor, and probably an aspirin or two. Today, services such as Stripe and PayPal bundle all of that into a single account that you can set up in minutes, without the aspirin. But it still helps to understand what's happening behind the scenes.

## How payment processing works

When a customer makes a purchase on your site, the transaction passes through several players before the money is transferred. Here's the simplified version (and believe me, I'm simplifying):

- At checkout, **the customer** enters their payment information, such as a credit card number, expiration date, and security code.
- **The payment gateway** is the software that securely transmits the customer's payment information from your website to the payment processor. Think of the gateway as the digital equivalent of the card reader at a physical store.
- **The payment processor** communicates with the customer's bank (called the *issuing bank*) to verify that the card is valid and that the customer has sufficient funds. The processor then sends back an approved or a declined message.
- **Your merchant account** receives the funds once the transaction is approved. A *merchant account* is a special type of bank account that holds funds from card transactions before they're transferred to your regular business bank account.

Modern payment services such as Stripe and PayPal bundle all these steps. You sign up for one service, drop in a bit of configuration, and the service handles the rest. The money shows up in your bank account (usually within two business days, perhaps longer depending on the customer's location, credit history, and risk profile), minus the service's fees.

## Popular payment providers

The payment provider landscape has consolidated quite a bit over the years, and for small businesses, the choice of provider usually comes down to a handful of major players:

- **Stripe (`stripe.com`):** The developer favorite. Stripe's integration is clean, its documentation is excellent, and it supports a huge range of payment methods (credit cards, debit cards, Apple Pay, Google Pay, and more). Shopify Payments is powered by Stripe under the hood. If you're building a custom checkout or using WooCommerce, Stripe is usually the go-to choice.
- **PayPal (`paypal.com`):** The name everyone recognizes. PayPal is ubiquitous, and many customers prefer it because they can pay without entering their credit card information on an unfamiliar site. PayPal also offers PayPal Checkout, which can process regular credit card payments in addition to PayPal account payments.
- **Square (`squareup.com`):** Best known for its physical card readers for in-person transactions, Square also processes online payments. If you use Square Online for your store, payment processing is built right in. Square is particularly appealing if you sell both online and in person, because everything syncs through one dashboard.

Which one should you choose? If you're using Shopify, the answer is easy: use Shopify Payments (which uses Stripe). You'll get the lowest transaction fees and the smoothest integration. If you're using WooCommerce, I'd recommend Stripe for your primary gateway and adding PayPal as a secondary option (some customers strongly prefer PayPal, and there's no reason not to offer it). If you're already using Square for in-person sales, Square Online keeps everything under one roof.

TIP

Offer multiple payment methods at checkout if your platform supports it. Some customers prefer credit cards, others prefer PayPal, and a growing number want to use Apple Pay or Google Pay on their phones. Each payment method you add removes one more reason for a customer to abandon their cart.

## What those fees actually mean

Every payment provider charges fees, and those fees can feel confusing at first glance. Most providers use a straightforward pricing model: a small percentage of each transaction plus a fixed fee per transaction. For example, a typical rate might be 2.9 percent + $0.30 per transaction. On a $50 sale, that works out to $1.45 + $0.30 = $1.75 in fees. On a $10 sale, it's $0.29 + $0.30 = $0.59.

Notice something? The fixed fee ($0.30) hits harder on smaller transactions. If you're selling $3 stickers, that $0.30 per transaction is eating a significant chunk of your margin. That's one reason some small-item sellers set minimum order amounts or encourage customers to bundle purchases.

Let me put some real numbers on this so you can plan accordingly. Say Orbital Donuts sells an average of 50 online orders per week at an average order value of $28. At a rate of 2.9 percent + $0.30, that's about $1.11 per order in payment processing fees, or roughly $55.60 per week. Over a year, that's about $2,891 in fees. Is that a lot? It depends on your margins. But it's a cost that you need to factor into your pricing. Some store owners build the processing fee into their product prices (mark everything up by 3–4 percent) so the fee doesn't eat into their margin. Others treat it as a cost of doing business, like rent or utilities.

Beyond the standard transaction fee, watch out for a few other costs that can sneak up on you:

- **Chargeback fees:** If a customer disputes a charge with their bank, you'll typically pay a fee (often $15–$25) regardless of whether you win the dispute.
- **International transaction fees:** Some providers charge an additional 1–1.5 percent for transactions from international customers.

- **Payout fees:** Most providers offer free transfers to your bank account on a standard schedule (two business days) but charge for instant payouts.

Chargebacks deserve a special mention because they can really sting. A *chargeback* happens when a customer contacts their bank to dispute a charge on their credit card. Maybe the product never arrived. Maybe they don't recognize the charge. Maybe they're committing fraud. Whatever the reason, the bank pulls the money back from you, and your payment provider charges you a fee on top of it. You can dispute the chargeback (and you should, if you believe the charge was legitimate), but the process takes time and there's no guarantee you'll win. The best defense against chargebacks is good communication: send order confirmations, provide tracking numbers, respond to customer complaints quickly, and make sure your business name on the credit card statement is recognizable (not some cryptic abbreviation that looks like fraud).



WARNING

Never, ever store credit card numbers on your own server or in your own database. That's what payment providers are for. They handle the sensitive data so you don't have to, and they invest millions of dollars in the security infrastructure to do it safely. If you try to handle card data yourself, you're taking on enormous liability and almost certainly violating PCI compliance rules (more on that later in this chapter).

# Shipping and Fulfillment Options

If you're selling physical products (as opposed to digital downloads or services), you need to figure out how those products get from your location to your customer's doorstep. This is the part of e-commerce that people tend to underestimate. Setting up a beautiful product page? Fun. Configuring shipping zones and calculating dimensional weight? Less fun. But getting shipping right is crucial, because shipping costs and delivery speed are two of the biggest factors in whether a customer completes a purchase or abandons their cart.

WARNING

Shipping is where a lot of first-time e-commerce store owners lose money. They offer free shipping without doing the math, or they underestimate packaging costs, or they don't account for the time it takes to pack and ship orders. I'm not saying this to discourage you (quite the opposite, since forewarned is forearmed, as they say) but to encourage you to take shipping seriously from day one rather than treating it as an afterthought.

## Shipping strategies that work

There are several approaches to charging for shipping, and each one sends a different psychological signal to your customers:

- **Free shipping:** The magic words of e-commerce. Customers love free shipping, and study after study shows that unexpected shipping costs at checkout are the number one reason people abandon their carts. Of course, shipping isn't really free since you're either absorbing the cost into your product prices or eating into your margins. But the psychological impact is powerful.
- **Free shipping with a threshold:** A clever compromise. You offer free shipping on orders above a certain amount ($50, say) and charge a flat rate below that. This encourages customers to add more items to their cart to hit the threshold. You've probably done this yourself as a shopper: adding an extra item you didn't really need just to qualify for free shipping. (No judgment. I've done it too.)
- **Flat-rate shipping:** You charge the same shipping fee regardless of order size or destination. This is simple for customers to understand and simple for you to implement. The risk is that you might undercharge on heavy or distant orders and overcharge on light or local ones.
- **Real-time calculated rates:** Your checkout integrates with carriers (your local postal service — such as the United States Postal Service or Canada Post — UPS, FedEx, and so on) to calculate the actual shipping cost based on package weight, dimensions, and destination. This approach is the most accurate, but it can result in sticker shock at checkout if the customer lives far away.

Which strategy should you use? It depends on your products and your margins. If your products are small and lightweight (jewelry, stickers, small accessories), flat-rate shipping is simple and predictable. If your products vary widely in size and weight (furniture, for example), real-time calculated rates are fairer to both you and the customer. And if your margins are healthy enough to absorb shipping costs, free shipping (or free shipping with a threshold) is almost always the best choice for conversion rates.

Whatever strategy you choose, make it visible early in the shopping experience. Don't wait until the very last step of checkout to reveal the shipping cost. If a customer has spent five minutes filling out their address and payment info only to discover a $15 shipping fee they weren't expecting, they're going to feel ambushed, and ambushed customers don't complete purchases. Many successful stores display a shipping estimate on the product page itself, or at least in the cart before checkout begins.

TIP

If you offer a free shipping threshold, set it about 15–20 percent above your average order value. If your average order is $42, set the threshold at $50. This nudges customers to add one more item without setting the bar so high that it feels unreachable.

## Fulfillment: Doing it yourself versus outsourcing

*Fulfillment* is the process of receiving, packing, and shipping orders. For a small operation like Orbital Donuts (where the product is perishable and the delivery area is local), fulfillment means boxing up donuts and driving them to customers or having them picked up in-store. That's self-fulfillment, and it's the simplest model: you store the products, you pack the orders, you ship (or deliver) them yourself.

Self-fulfillment works well when you're handling a manageable volume of orders and your products don't require specialized shipping (fragile items, temperature-controlled goods, that sort of thing). It's the cheapest option in terms of fees, but it costs you time, which is time that you're not spending on marketing, product development, or, you know, sleeping.

If you go the self-fulfillment route (and most small stores start here), note the following practical tips:

- **Create a packing station.** This area is a dedicated spot with all your shipping supplies organized and within reach. You'd be amazed how much faster packing goes when you're not hunting for tape every time.
- **Batch your shipments.** Instead of running to the post office after every order, print your labels at home (most platforms let you buy and print shipping labels directly) and schedule a daily pickup or do a single drop-off.
- **Keep records of every shipment, including tracking numbers.** When a customer asks, "Where's my order?" (and they will ask), you want to be able to answer in thirty seconds, not thirty minutes.

TIP

If you're shipping with USPS, UPS, or FedEx, you can save significantly by buying and printing shipping labels through your e-commerce platform rather than paying retail rates at the counter. Shopify, for example, offers shipping discounts of up to 88 percent off retail USPS and UPS rates. That's money back in your pocket on every single order.

As your order volume grows, you might consider outsourcing fulfillment to a *third-party logistics provider* (or 3PL, because every industry needs its abbreviations). A 3PL warehouses your products, packs orders as they come in, and ships them on your behalf. Popular 3PL services include ShipBob, ShipMonk, and Amazon's Fulfillment by Amazon (FBA). The trade-off is cost: 3PLs charge storage fees, picking and packing fees, and shipping fees. But they can often negotiate lower shipping rates than you'd get on your own, and they free up your time for other parts of the business.

How do you know when it's time to switch from self-fulfillment to a 3PL? There's no magic number, but a good rule of thumb is this: if packing and shipping orders is taking so much time that it's preventing you from growing the business, it's time to outsource. For some businesses, that's 20 orders a week. For others, it's 200. It depends on how complex your products are to pack, how much you value your time, and how much a 3PL would charge compared to what you're spending now.

## Setting up shipping zones and rates

Most e-commerce platforms let you define *shipping zones,* which are geographic regions with their own shipping rules. For example, you might create one zone for domestic orders with flat-rate shipping, another zone for neighboring countries with slightly higher rates, and a third zone for the rest of the world with real-time calculated rates (or no shipping at all, if you only sell domestically and to neighboring countries).

Within each zone, you set up *shipping rates,* which are the rules that determine what a customer pays for shipping. These can be as simple as a single flat rate per zone or as complex as weight-based tiers with different rates for different product categories. My advice for getting started is to keep it simple. One or two zones with flat-rate shipping is enough for most small businesses. You can always add complexity later as you learn what your customers expect and what your margins can support.

Don't forget about local delivery and in-store pickup. If you have a physical location (like Orbital Donuts does), offering local delivery within a certain radius or free in-store pickup can reduce your shipping costs and provide a faster, more personal experience for nearby customers. Most platforms support both fulfillment options.

One more thing about shipping that often catches people off guard: packaging costs. Boxes, bubble wrap, tape, labels, tissue paper, branded stickers, it all adds up. A single corrugated shipping box might cost \$1–\$3 depending on size, and if you're shipping fragile items, the padding can cost as much as the box. Factor these costs into your shipping rates or product prices from the start. I've talked to small-business owners who didn't account for packaging costs and ended up losing money on every shipment for the first three months. Yikes.

# Managing Inventory

*Inventory management* is the system you use to track what products you have in stock, how many of each, and when you need to reorder. It sounds boring (because, well, it is), but it's one of those behind-the-scenes things that makes the difference between a smooth-running store and a customer-service nightmare.



For a small store just starting out, inventory management can be as simple as a spreadsheet or even a notebook. But once you connect an e-commerce platform, inventory tracking is built into the system, so you should use it even if your catalog is tiny. The automation alone (such as automatically hiding out-of-stock items and sending you low-stock alerts) will save you from an embarrassing oversell situation.

## Tracking stock levels

Every e-commerce platform includes some form of inventory tracking. At the most basic level, you assign a stock quantity to each product. When someone buys one, the quantity decreases by one. When the quantity hits zero, the product is automatically marked as out of stock (or, depending on your settings, hidden from the store). Simple, right?

Most platforms also let you set a *low-stock threshold,* a number that triggers a notification when a product's stock falls below it. If you set the threshold to 5, you'll get an alert when only 5 units remain, giving you time to reorder before you run out.

If you sell on multiple channels (your website plus a marketplace such as Etsy, say, or your website plus a physical storefront), inventory sync becomes critical. You don't want to sell the last unit of a product on Etsy while someone is simultaneously buying it on your website. Most platforms offer multichannel inventory sync, either built in or through an integration, but it's something you need to set up deliberately. It won't happen by itself.

As your product catalog grows, you'll want to use *SKUs* (stock keeping units) to keep track of your inventory. A SKU (pronounced "skew") is a unique code you assign to each product (or product variant). It's not the same as a barcode or a manufacturer's part number; it's your own internal code, and you can structure it however makes sense for your business.

REMEMBER

Create a consistent SKU naming convention and stick with it from the start. A common approach is to use a pattern such as category-product-variant. For Orbital Donuts, that might look like `DNT-GALAXY-6PK` for a six-pack of Galaxy Glazed donuts or `DNT-ROCKET-12PK` for a dozen Rocket Red Velvets. The format doesn't matter as much as consistency: pick a pattern and use it for everything.

## Handling product variants

Many products come in multiple variations: different sizes, colors, flavors, or configurations. A t-shirt might come in small, medium, and large, in six different colors. That's 18 variants of a single product, and each variant needs its own stock count, its own SKU, and potentially its own price.

E-commerce platforms handle variants in different ways, but the basic idea is the same: you create one product listing and then define the options (size, color, flavor) and combinations. For Orbital Donuts, a Donut Box product might have a flavor option (Galaxy Glazed, Rocket Red Velvet, Cosmic Cruller, Asteroid Almond) and a size option (half dozen, dozen, double dozen). Each combination gets its own SKU and stock level.

Some platforms handle variants more gracefully than others. Shopify, for instance, limits you to three option types per product (such as size, color, and material) with up to 100 total combinations. For most products, that's plenty. But if you sell something with many dimensions of variation (custom jewelry with five metals, eight stone types, and four chain lengths, say), you might bump up against those limits and need a workaround or a different platform.

WARNING

Don't go overboard with variants. If you offer too many options, customers get overwhelmed and *decision paralysis* sets in. If you sell handmade candles in 14 scents, 3 sizes, and 8 jar colors, that's 336 variants. Nobody needs 336 variants. Curate your options, and your customers (and your inventory spreadsheet) will thank you.

# Security and PCI Compliance

When you start accepting payments online, security stops being a nice-to-have and becomes a must-have. Your customers are trusting you with their credit card numbers, their addresses, and their personal information. If that data gets compromised because you didn't take security seriously, the consequences range from embarrassing to business-ending. I say that not to scare you (okay, maybe a little) but to emphasize that security is something you need to get right from day one.

Happily, if you're using a reputable e-commerce platform and a reputable payment provider, a huge chunk of the security burden is handled for you. You don't need to become a cybersecurity expert. You just need to understand a few key concepts, follow some common-sense practices, and let the professionals handle the really scary stuff.



## What PCI compliance means for you

You might have come across the abbreviation PCI DSS, which stands for Payment Card Industry Data Security Standard. (Try saying that three times fast.) It's a set of security requirements created by the major credit card companies (Visa, Mastercard, American Express, and others) that applies to any business that accepts, processes, stores, or transmits credit card data. In other words, if you sell stuff online, PCI DSS applies to you.

Now, before you panic: PCI compliance sounds much scarier than it is for most small online stores. The requirements are tiered based on your transaction volume, and the smallest tier (Level 4, which covers businesses processing fewer than 20,000 e-commerce transactions per year) has the lightest requirements. For most readers of this book, compliance involves filling out a self-assessment questionnaire and following some common-sense security practices.

The PCI Security Standards Council publishes several versions of the self-assessment questionnaire, and which one you need to complete depends on how you handle card data. If you use a hosted payment page (where the customer enters their card info on Stripe's or PayPal's website, not yours), you qualify for the shortest and simplest questionnaire. If the card data passes through your server at any point (even briefly), you're in a more complex category. This is yet another reason to use a hosted payment solution.

The core PCI requirements boil down to a few main ideas:

- **Don't store sensitive card data.** If you're using a payment provider such as Stripe or PayPal, your website never touches the customer's full credit card number. The payment form is either hosted by the provider or uses tokenization (replacing the card number with a random token), so the sensitive data never passes through your server.

- **Use strong encryption.** Your entire site should run on HTTPS (as I discuss in Book 1, Chapter 4), which encrypts data in transit between your customer's browser and your server.
- **Keep your software updated.** Outdated software is the single easiest way for attackers to get in. If you're using WordPress and WooCommerce, keep everything updated, including WordPress core, WooCommerce, your theme, and every plug-in.

WARNING

PCI compliance isn't optional. It's not a suggestion or a best practice. It's a contractual requirement enforced by the credit card companies. If you're found to be non-compliant after a data breach, you could face fines and increased transaction fees — or lose the ability to accept credit card payments altogether.

## Letting your platform do the work

Here's the single best thing you can do for PCI compliance: use a hosted e-commerce platform or a hosted payment solution. When you use Shopify, for example, it handles PCI compliance for the entire checkout process. They're a Level 1 PCI-compliant service provider (the highest level), which means they've undergone rigorous audits and testing. By using their platform, you inherit much of that compliance. You still need to follow basic security practices on your end (strong passwords, keeping your admin access secure), but the hard work is done for you.

The same principle applies to payment gateways such as Stripe and PayPal. Because the customer's card data goes directly to the payment provider's servers (through an embedded form or a redirect), your website never handles sensitive information. This approach dramatically reduces your PCI compliance scope and your risk.

If you're using WooCommerce (which is self-hosted), the picture is slightly more complex. WooCommerce itself doesn't handle PCI compliance; that's your responsibility. But if you use a payment gateway such as Stripe for WooCommerce (which processes card data on Stripe's servers rather than yours), you drastically reduce your compliance scope. The key is to make sure credit card data never touches your server. If it does, you're in a different compliance tier, and trust me, you do not want to be there.

I cover security in more depth in Book 9, Chapter 4, but for now, the takeaway is this: let the professionals handle the card data and focus your security efforts on keeping your own admin accounts and website software locked down.

# Legal Requirements for Online Selling

Selling products online comes with legal obligations that go beyond what a regular informational website requires. I'm not a lawyer (and nothing in this section is legal advice; please consult an attorney for anything that might land you in hot water), but I can walk you through the major areas you need to be aware of so you know what questions to ask and where to focus your attention.

The legal landscape for online selling touches on privacy, taxes, consumer protection, accessibility, and more. It can feel overwhelming, but keep in mind that millions of small businesses sell online every day without a team of lawyers on retainer. The key is to understand the basics, use tools and services that help you stay compliant, and get professional help for anything you're not sure about. Spending a few hundred dollars on a lawyer's consultation before you launch is almost always cheaper than dealing with a legal problem after the fact.



## Privacy policies and terms of service

As I mention in Book 1, Chapter 4, privacy laws such as the GDPR and CCPA require you to have a clearly written privacy policy that explains what data you collect, why you collect it, and how customers can request its deletion. For an e-commerce store, this requirement is especially important because you're collecting a lot more personal data than a typical informational website: names, email addresses, physical addresses, phone numbers, order histories, and (through your payment provider) financial information.

The stakes are higher, too. A blog that collects email addresses for a newsletter has one level of privacy obligation. A store that processes credit card payments, ships physical goods to home addresses, and sends transactional emails has a much greater responsibility to protect that data, and a much bigger target on its back if something goes wrong.

Your privacy policy should explain what data you collect, what you use it for (processing orders, sending shipping notifications, marketing emails if they opt in), who you share it with (your payment provider, your shipping carrier, your email service), and how long you retain it. If you look at the Orbital Donuts site, you'll see that `privacy.html` already covers the basics for a regular website, but adding e-commerce means updating that policy to account for the additional data you're now handling.

You also need a *terms of service* (sometimes called terms and conditions) that governs the relationship between your business and your customers. This document typically covers things like payment terms, delivery timeframes, limitation of liability, and dispute resolution. The Orbital Donuts `terms.html` page is a starting point, but an e-commerce terms of service needs to be more detailed than a basic website's.

Both of these documents should be linked from your website's footer (so they're accessible from every page) and ideally referenced during the checkout process. Some platforms let you add a checkbox at checkout that says something like "I agree to the Terms of Service and Privacy Policy," with links to both documents. That's good practice.

**TIP**

Several online services (such as Termly, Termageddon, and iubenda) generate privacy policies and terms of service based on a questionnaire about your business. These aren't a substitute for legal advice on complex matters, but they're a solid starting point for a small online store and much better than copying someone else's policy (which, yes, people actually do).

## The sales tax puzzle

If you enjoy migraines, try figuring out sales tax obligations for an online store all by yourself. I'm only half joking. In the United States, sales tax is governed at the state and local level, which means there are thousands of different tax jurisdictions with different rates, different rules about what's taxable, and different filing requirements. (Donuts are taxable in some states but not others, for example, and some states tax them only if they're sold with utensils. Really.)

If you sell only within your own state, things are relatively straightforward: you collect your state's sales tax rate on applicable products and remit it on schedule. But the moment you start selling to customers in other states (which, on the internet, is basically day one), things get complicated fast.

The key concept you need to understand is *tax nexus*, the connection between your business and a state that obligates you to collect and remit sales tax in that state. You have *physical nexus* in any state where you have a physical presence: an office, a warehouse, an employee, even a remote worker in some cases. But after a landmark 2018 Supreme Court case (South Dakota v. Wayfair, if you want to look it up), states can also establish *economic nexus* based on your sales volume or transaction count in that state, even if you have no physical presence there.

What this means in practice: if you sell enough into a given state, you might be required to collect and remit sales tax in that state, even if you've never set foot there. The thresholds vary by state (for example, $100,000 in sales or 200 transactions per year), and they can change. And once you hit that threshold, you need to register for a sales tax permit in that state, collect the correct rate on each order, and file returns on whatever schedule the state requires (monthly, quarterly, or annually, depending on your volume).

The practical solution for most small businesses is to use an automated tax calculation service. Shopify has built-in tax calculation. WooCommerce integrates with services such as TaxJar and Avalara. These services keep track of the ever-changing rates and rules across jurisdictions and automatically calculate, collect, and (in some cases) file the correct sales tax for each order. They're not free (expect to pay $10–$50 per month for a small store), but they're a lot cheaper than an audit.

If you're selling outside the United States, the rules are different but no less complex. Many countries use a value-added tax (VAT) system instead of sales tax, and the rules about when foreign sellers need to collect VAT vary by country. The European Union, for example, requires non-EU sellers to collect VAT on digital products sold to EU customers (and has different rules for physical goods). This is another area where automated tax services earn their keep.



WARNING

Don't ignore sales tax obligations, even if your store is small. States are getting increasingly aggressive about enforcing online sales tax collection, and the penalties for non-compliance can include back taxes, interest, and fines. If you're selling to customers in multiple states, set up automated tax collection from the start.

## Return and refund policies

Every online store needs a clear return and refund policy. Customers want to know: if the product isn't what I expected, can I send it back? Will I get my money back? Who pays for return shipping? The answers to these questions affect whether a customer decides to buy in the first place.

Your return policy should clearly state which products are eligible for returns (perishable goods such as donuts might not be, for obvious reasons), how long customers have to initiate a return, what condition the product needs to be in, who pays for return shipping, and whether you offer refunds, store credit, or exchanges. Make this policy easy to find (don't bury it in a footnote or behind three clicks). A prominent link in your footer and a mention during checkout are both good practices.

For what it's worth, a generous return policy tends to increase sales more than it increases returns. Customers are more willing to take a chance on a purchase when they know they can send it back. The ones who return products are a small minority, and they're often the same people who would have complained loudly (and publicly) if you hadn't offered a return option. A fair return policy is both good ethics and good business.

One more thing: be specific about your refund timeline. "Refunds will be processed" is vague. "Refunds are processed within 5 business days of receiving the returned item" is clear. Customers who know what to expect are less likely to send you anxious emails asking where their refund is. And fewer anxious emails means a better week for everyone.

## Keeping your store accessible

As I discuss in Book 2, Chapter 4, web accessibility is a legal requirement in many jurisdictions. This applies to your e-commerce store just as much as (arguably more than) a regular website. If a customer with a visual impairment can't navigate your product pages or complete your checkout process using a screen reader, you're not only losing that customer's business but also potentially exposing yourself to legal liability.

The good news is that major e-commerce platforms have made significant strides in accessibility. Shopify's default themes are generally well-coded for screen readers, and WooCommerce benefits from WordPress's long-standing commitment to accessibility. But customizations, third-party themes, and add-ons can introduce accessibility problems that weren't in the original code. If you customize your store, test it on a smartphone and with a screen reader and a keyboard (no mouse) to make sure everything works.

At a minimum, make sure your product images have descriptive alt text (not just "product photo" but something like "Galaxy Glazed donut with blue icing and edible glitter, viewed from above"). Make sure your forms are properly labeled so screen readers can announce the purpose of each field. Make sure your checkout process can be completed entirely with a keyboard. And make sure your color contrast meets WCAG guidelines, especially on buttons and links. A pale gray Add to Cart button on a white background might look elegant, but it's hard to see for customers with low vision.

There's nothing heroic about making things accessible; it's just basic professionalism. And it doesn't just help customers with disabilities. Clear labels, readable contrast, and keyboard-friendly interfaces make the shopping experience better for everyone, including customers on mobile devices, in bright sunlight, or in a hurry. Good accessibility is good usability, and good usability is good for business.

IN THIS CHAPTER

» Building great product pages

» Taking product photos that sell

» Writing descriptions that do the selling for you

» Using reviews, social proof, and smart pricing

» Testing and improving your pages

# Chapter 2

# Product Pages That Sell

*The product itself should be its own best salesman. Not the product alone, but the product plus a mental impression, an atmosphere, which you place around it.*

—CLAUDE HOPKINS, SCIENTIFIC ADVERTISING

A product page in your online store is the digital equivalent of a customer picking up a product in a physical store, turning it over, reading the label, and deciding whether to put it in the cart or back on the shelf. Except online, the customer can't touch anything, can't smell anything, can't hold it up to the light. All they have is what you show them and what you tell them.

That's a lot of pressure on a single page. But it's also an opportunity, because a great product page doesn't just display information. It persuades. It answers questions before they're asked. It makes the customer feel confident that yes, this is the right thing, and yes, this is the right place to buy it. A bad product page, on the other hand, sends people scrambling for the back button. (And once they're gone, they're almost certainly not coming back.)

This chapter is about building product pages that do the selling for you. I cover everything from photography and descriptions to pricing psychology, reviews, and testing. Whether you're selling donuts, handmade pottery, or bicycle tires, the principles are the same.

# Creating Compelling Product Pages

Before I dive into specifics such as photography and copywriting, it helps to step back and think about what a product page is supposed to do. A lot of store owners treat the product page as a formality (here's what it is, here's the price, here's the button) and then wonder why their conversion rate is dismal. The problem is that the page didn't do its job.

A product page can do a lot of things, but it has exactly one main job: convince a visitor to add the item to their cart. Everything on the page either moves the visitor closer to that decision or pushes them away from it. There is no neutral content on a product page. That blurry photo? Pushing them away. That vague description that could apply to any product in your category? Pushing them away. That wall of text with no formatting? You get the idea.

To put some numbers on this: the average e-commerce *conversion rate* (the percentage of visitors who buy something) hovers around 2–3 percent. That means for every 100 people who visit your store, 97 or 98 of them leave without buying. Sobering, right? But the good news is that improving your product pages can nudge that number meaningfully higher. Going from a 3 percent conversion rate to a 4 percent conversion rate doesn't sound dramatic, but it's a 33 percent increase in sales with the same amount of traffic. That's real money.

## The anatomy of a product page

Virtually every successful product page shares the same basic anatomy. The specifics vary by industry (a page selling running shoes looks different from one selling consulting hours), but the core elements are consistent:

- **Product title:** Clear, specific, and searchable. "Galaxy Glazed Donut" beats "Item #47."
- **Primary image:** The single most important element on the page. It's the first thing the eye goes to.
- **Price:** Visible, unambiguous, and (if applicable) showing any discounts or savings.
- **Product description:** Benefits first, features second, objections addressed throughout.
- **Call to action:** The button. Add to Cart, Buy Now, Order Online — whatever it says, it needs to be big, obvious, and impossible to miss.

- **Reviews or social proof:** Star ratings, review counts, or customer quotes that build trust.
- **Supporting details:** Shipping info, return policy, sizing or variant selectors, allergen warnings, and anything else that removes friction from the buying decision.

That's the skeleton. The rest of this chapter is about putting flesh on it.

Before I move on, one thing about the anatomy of a product page that might not be obvious: the order of these elements matters. Product pages follow a visual hierarchy, and visitors' eyes move through the page in a predictable pattern. On a desktop, the typical layout is a large image on the left and the title, price, description, and buy button stacked on the right. On a mobile device, it's all stacked vertically, with the image on top. This convention exists because it works. It matches how people scan a page, and deviating from it without a good reason just makes your visitors think harder. (And as I discuss in Book 2, Chapter 1, making visitors think is the enemy of good web design.)

## Above the fold: What customers see first

In web design, *above the fold* refers to whatever is visible on the screen before the visitor scrolls. On a product page, this area is prime real estate. If the customer has to scroll to find the price, or scroll to see a photo, or scroll to find the Add to Cart button, you've already lost some of them. Not all of them, but some, and in e-commerce, *some* adds up fast.

The goal for the above-the-fold area is to show the visitor three things as quickly as possible: what the product looks like (image), what it costs (price), and how to buy it (button). The description, reviews, and supporting details can live below the fold because interested visitors will scroll. But the image, price, and button? Those need to be right there, staring back at the customer within a second or two of the page loading.

I think of above-the-fold content as your product page's handshake. It's the first impression, and it happens in about three seconds. In those three seconds, the visitor decides whether to keep looking or leave. That's not much time, which is why clarity beats cleverness every single time. A quirky, artistic product page layout that takes 10 seconds to figure out is losing to a boring-but-clear layout where the photo, price, and button are exactly where the visitor expects them to be.

# Product Photography and Images

Here is one of those facts that's obvious once you hear it but easy to forget when you're building a store: online shoppers can't touch your product. They can't hold it, squeeze it, smell it, or try it on. The only sense available to them is sight, and that means your product photos are doing almost all the heavy lifting. A mediocre description paired with a stunning photo will outperform a brilliant description paired with a blurry snapshot taken on a kitchen counter. Every time.

I'm not saying descriptions don't matter (they absolutely do, and I cover them in the next section). I'm saying that photos are what stop the scroll, catch the eye, and create the first emotional impression. The description closes the deal. But if the photo doesn't grab the visitor's attention in the first place, they'll never read the description.

## You don't need a professional photographer (yet)

If your budget allows for professional product photography, great: hire someone. But if you're just starting out and cash is tight (and when is it not?), you can get surprisingly good results with a smartphone, a simple lighting setup, and a bit of care.

Here's the minimal setup: a table near a window for natural light, a large sheet of white poster board curved against the wall as a background (this creates a clean, seamless look called an *infinity curve*), and your phone's camera. That's it. If natural light isn't reliable (or if you're shooting in the evening), a cheap ring light or a pair of desk lamps with daylight bulbs will do the job. The total cost for this setup is under $30, and the results are night and day compared to an unlit photo snapped on a cluttered desk.

If you're selling smaller items (jewelry, candles, baked goods), a collapsible *light box* (sometimes called a photo tent) is worth the $20—$40 investment. It's a small fabric cube with built-in LED panels that diffuse the light evenly and eliminate harsh shadows. Drop your product in, snap the photo, done. For Orbital Donuts, a light box would be perfect for those individual donut glamour shots, the kind that make a Cosmic Cruller look like it belongs on the cover of a food magazine.

Here are a few practical hints that will improve your photos immediately:

- Use the back camera on your phone, not the selfie camera (the back camera has a better sensor and lens).

» Turn off the flash and rely on your lighting setup instead (camera flash creates harsh, unflattering shadows that make products look cheap).

» Hold the phone steady or, better yet, mount it on a small tabletop tripod ($10–$15).

» Clean your camera lens before you start shooting. I know that sounds obvious, but you would not believe how many product photos I've seen ruined by fingerprint smudges on the lens!

TIP

Shoot more photos than you think you need. It's much easier to choose the best shot from fifty photos than to realize later that none of your ten photos are quite right and have to set everything up again. Storage is free. Your time is not.

After shooting, spend a few minutes editing your photos before uploading them. You don't need Photoshop. Most smartphones have built-in photo editors that can adjust brightness, contrast, and white balance. The goal is to make the product look like it does in real life (not to glamorize it beyond recognition). Bump up the brightness if the shot is too dark, adjust the white balance if the background looks yellowish instead of white, and crop out any distracting edges. Five minutes of editing per photo makes a noticeable difference in the result.

## Multiple angles and context shots

A single photo of a product is better than none, but it's not enough. Shoppers want to see the product from multiple angles — front, back, side, top, close-up of important details — because they're trying to mentally reconstruct the experience of holding it in their hands. The more visual information you give them, the more confident they feel about buying.

Most e-commerce platforms let you upload multiple product images and display them in a gallery (usually with a large main image and smaller thumbnails below or beside it). Take advantage of this. For physical products, aim for at least three to five images per product. For Orbital Donuts, that might mean a top-down shot of a Galaxy Glazed, a side profile showing the glaze dripping over the edge, a close-up of the edible glitter, and a lifestyle shot of the donut on a plate with a cup of coffee.

That last one deserves special attention. A *lifestyle image* shows the product being used or enjoyed in a realistic setting. It helps the customer imagine the product in their own life, which is a surprisingly powerful motivator. A candle photographed on a white background is a product. The same candle photographed on a nightstand next to an open book, with soft lighting, is an experience. Both photos have their place, but the lifestyle shot is what creates desire.

Another category worth considering is the *scale shot:* a photo that shows your product next to a familiar object so the customer can gauge its size. This is surprisingly important for online shopping, where there's no way to pick something up and feel how big it is. A donut looks roughly the same whether it's three inches across or six inches across. But photograph it next to a coffee mug and the size becomes instantly clear. Scale shots are particularly valuable for products where size is a common question (furniture, bags, jewelry, decorative items) and can save you a pile of customer service emails.

Finally, if your product has important details that aren't visible at normal viewing distance, include at least one close-up shot. For Orbital Donuts, a tight shot of the edible glitter on a Galaxy Glazed shows the texture and sparkle that a full-product photo would miss. For a leather bag, a close-up of the stitching communicates craftsmanship. For electronics, a close-up of the ports and buttons helps customers confirm compatibility. These detail shots answer questions that descriptions alone can't.

# Writing Effective Product Descriptions

If photos are what catch the eye, descriptions are what close the sale. A well-written product description answers the customer's questions, addresses their hesitations, and gives them the confidence to click that buy button. A poorly written description (or worse, no description) leaves the customer guessing, and guessing customers don't buy.

The single biggest mistake I see in product descriptions is writing about the product instead of writing about the customer. Your description should be about what the product does *for* the person buying it, not just what the product *is.* That's the difference between features and benefits, and it's the most important concept in this section.

## Features versus benefits

A *feature* is a fact about your product: its size, material, ingredients, technical specifications. A *benefit* is what that feature means for the customer: how it solves their problem, makes their life easier, or makes them feel something positive.

Here's a quick example using Orbital Donuts' Rocket Red Velvet:

- **Feature:** Classic red velvet cake donut with cream cheese frosting
- **Benefit:** Rich, indulgent, and just sweet enough to feel like a treat without the sugar crash

See the difference? The feature tells you what it is. The benefit tells you how it feels. Both matter, but the benefit is what makes someone want it. A useful exercise is the "So what?" test: for every feature you list, ask yourself, "So what? Why should the customer care?" If you can't answer that question, the feature probably doesn't belong in the description (or it needs a benefit paired with it).

For products with many technical features (electronics, tools, sporting goods), I recommend a hybrid approach: write a benefit-driven paragraph at the top of the description, and then list the technical specs below it for the detail-oriented shoppers. This way, the casual browser gets the emotional appeal, and the researcher gets the data. Both audiences are served.

One more thing about features versus benefits: don't confuse benefits with hype. "Our most amazing donut ever!" is not a benefit. It's a superlative, and superlatives are the weakest form of persuasion because they ask the customer to take your word for it. "Rich, moist red velvet cake with a tangy cream cheese frosting that balances the sweetness" is a benefit because it tells the customer what the experience will be like. Show, don't tell. Describe, don't declare.

## Write for scanners

I talk about scannable writing in Book 6, Chapter 1, and the same principles apply here. Online shoppers don't read product descriptions word by word. They scan. They skim. They look for the bits that are relevant to them and skip the rest. Your job is to make the important bits impossible to miss.

A few techniques that work well on product pages:

- **Lead with the benefit.** The first sentence should tell the customer why they want this product. Don't bury the good stuff.
- **Use short paragraphs.** Write two to three sentences maximum. Big blocks of text are ignored.
- **Bold key phrases.** If someone is scanning for allergen information or material details, make those phrases visually distinct.
- **Use bullet points for specs.** Anything factual, such as size, weight, ingredients, or compatibility, goes in a list, not a paragraph.

Here's what a scannable description might look like for Orbital Donuts' Cosmic Cruller: a short opening sentence about the taste experience, a brief paragraph about the ingredients and what makes it special, and then a bulleted list of specs (allergens, serving size, calories). The whole thing is readable in about eight seconds, which is roughly how long the average online shopper will spend on it. (Eight seconds! I know. But that's the reality.)

One technique I've seen work well, especially for food and handmade products, is leading with sensory language. Instead of "Our classic old-fashioned cake donut," try "Crisp on the outside, pillowy-soft on the inside, with a rich, buttery flavor that takes you straight back to Saturday mornings." Sensory words (*crisp, soft, rich, buttery, warm, smooth*) help the customer imagine the experience, and imagination is the next best thing to holding the product in their hands.

Watch out for one common trap, though: don't write the same description for every product with only a few words changed. If your store has 30 products and they all start with "Handcrafted with love using only the finest ingredients," customers will notice the repetition and start tuning out. Each product should have its own distinct description, even if the format is consistent. Consistency in structure is good. Copy-and-pasted language is lazy, and customers can smell lazy from a mile away.

## Address objections before they form

Every customer who lands on your product page has questions. Some are obvious ("How much does it cost?") and some are lurking just below the surface ("Will this taste fresh after shipping?" "Is this size right for me?" "What if I don't like it?"). The best product descriptions anticipate these objections and address them before the customer has to ask.

For Orbital Donuts, a common objection might be freshness: "These are shipped donuts. Are they going to arrive stale and sad?" A smart product description addresses this directly: "Every order is baked and packed the same morning it ships, and our insulated packaging keeps your donuts fresh for up to 48 hours in transit." That's not just a description; it's objection handling disguised as information.

Think about the three or four most common hesitations for your specific product and weave the answers into your description. For clothing, it's sizing and fit. For food, it's freshness and allergens. For electronics, it's compatibility and warranty. For handmade goods, it's durability and consistency. Whatever your customers are likely to worry about, bring it up before they do.

Some stores take this a step further by adding a small FAQ section directly on the product page, below the main description. Three or four questions and answers, formatted as an accordion (click to expand), can address common objections without cluttering the page. For Orbital Donuts, the product page FAQ might include "How should I store my donuts?" "What's the shelf life?" and "Do you accommodate custom flavor requests?" Each question answered on the product page is one fewer email in your inbox and one fewer reason for a customer to leave without buying.

TIP

If you're not sure what objections your customers have, look at the questions people ask before buying (customer service emails, social media comments, live chat transcripts) and the complaints in your reviews. These are your objection list, handed to you for free.

# Pricing Strategies

Pricing is partly math and partly psychology. The math part — covering your costs, hitting your margins, accounting for fees, and so on — is something I touch on in Book 8, Chapter 1 when I talk about payment processing fees. This section is about the psychology part: how the way you present your prices affects whether people buy.

## Pricing psychology basics

Researchers have studied pricing behavior for decades, and a few findings come up again and again. You've probably experienced all of these as a shopper, even if you didn't have names for them:

- **Charm pricing** is the practice of ending prices with a 9 (or 99 or 95). A donut priced at $3.49 feels meaningfully cheaper than one priced at $3.50, even though the difference is a single penny. Rational? No. Effective? Enormously. Decades of research confirm that charm pricing increases sales in most product categories, especially for everyday purchases. You'll notice that every donut in the Orbital Donuts menu uses charm pricing: $3.49, $3.99, $4.99. That's not an accident.
- **Anchoring** is the tendency to judge a price based on the first number you see. If the first thing a customer sees on your page is a "Was $59.99" price crossed out next to a "Now $39.99" price, the $59.99 becomes the anchor. The $39.99 feels like a deal, even if the product was always going to sell for $39.99. This isn't about being deceptive (don't fake a "was" price that never existed;

that's both unethical and, in many jurisdictions, illegal). But if you genuinely mark down a product, showing the original price alongside the sale price is smart because it gives the customer a reference point.

- The **decoy effect** shows up when you offer three options and the middle one is designed to make the most expensive one look like a good deal. Classic example: a small coffee for $3, a medium for $5.50, and a large for $6. Almost nobody picks the medium, because for just 50 cents more you get the large. The medium exists to make the large look like a bargain. If you offer tiered pricing (half-dozen, dozen, double-dozen boxes of donuts, say), the decoy effect is your friend.

## Displaying your prices

How you display a price matters almost as much as what the price is. A few principles worth following:

- **Be clear.** The price should be one of the first things the customer sees. Hiding it, requiring a click to reveal it, or burying it below the fold creates friction, and friction kills conversions.
- **Include everything.** If there are additional costs (shipping, taxes, handling fees), surface them as early as possible. The number-one reason shoppers abandon their carts is unexpected costs at checkout. Don't be that store.
- **Use visual hierarchy.** The current price should be larger and bolder than any "was" price. If you're showing a discount, use strikethrough text on the original price and a different color for the sale price. The customer's eye should go to the sale price first.
- **Show savings.** If the customer is saving money, tell them. "Save $20" or "33% off" next to the price reinforces the value of the deal. People love knowing exactly how much they're saving; it makes them feel smarter about the purchase.

## Bundles and tiers

Bundling is one of the simplest and most effective pricing strategies for any store that sells products people might want in quantity. The idea is straightforward: offer a discount for buying more. Orbital Donuts, for instance, might price individual donuts at $3.49 each, a half-dozen box at $18.99 ($3.17 each), and a dozen box at $34.99 ($2.92 each). Each tier offers a better per-unit price, which encourages customers to buy more than they originally planned.

Tiered pricing works because it gives customers a sense of control (they're choosing their deal) and a sense of reward (they're getting more value at the higher tier). It also increases your average order value, which is one of the most important metrics for any e-commerce store. Pair tiered pricing with a free shipping threshold (as I discuss in Book 8, Chapter 1), and you've created two separate nudges pushing customers to spend just a little more than they intended.

You can also use bundling creatively beyond simple quantity discounts. A sampler box that includes one of each flavor is a bundle. A gift set that pairs a product with a complementary item (donuts plus a sampler bag of artisan coffee, say) is a bundle. A starter kit for a hobby or craft that includes everything a beginner needs is a bundle. Each of these feels like a curated offer rather than a bulk discount, which lets you charge a premium for the convenience of not having to choose.

REMEMBER

Display the per-unit price at each tier so customers can see exactly how much they save by buying more. Don't make them do the math. The easier you make the comparison, the more likely they are to choose the larger (and more profitable) option.

# Product Variations and Options



In Book 8, Chapter 1, I talk about product variants from the inventory side: how SKUs work, how platforms handle size/color/flavor combinations, and how many variants are too many. This section is about the other side of the same coin: how those variants appear on the product page itself, and how the way you present options affects whether people choose one.

## Presenting options clearly

When a product comes in multiple variations, the customer needs to make a selection before they can add it to their cart. The way you present that selection matters. Dropdown menus, clickable buttons, and color swatches are the three most common approaches, and each has its strengths.

- **Dropdown menus:** Compact and familiar, menus are good when you have many options (a list of 20 sizes, say) but less ideal when the options are visual (colors, patterns) because the customer can't see what they're choosing until they click.

» **Clickable buttons:** Each option is a visible, tappable button. Great for a small number of options (three to six sizes or flavors) because the customer can see all the choices at once without clicking anything. This approach is my preferred one for most products.

» **Color or image swatches:** Small colored circles or thumbnail images that represent each option. Perfect for products where color or pattern is a key differentiator (clothing, paint, phone cases).

For Orbital Donuts, a Donut Box product page might use clickable buttons for the box size (half-dozen, dozen, double-dozen) and a dropdown or swatch grid for flavor selections. The box-size buttons let the customer compare tiers at a glance (especially if the per-unit price is shown on each button), while a dropdown keeps the flavor list manageable.

Whichever approach you choose, make sure the currently selected option is visually obvious (a highlighted border, a filled button, a checkmark). And if an option is out of stock, show it as unavailable rather than hiding it. Hiding sold-out options makes customers wonder if the product comes in that size at all, while showing it grayed-out communicates both "yes, this exists" and "no, it's not available right now."

## Showing the right image for the right variant

Here's a detail that separates good product pages from great ones: when a customer selects a different variant (a different color, a different flavor, a different size), the product image should update to match. If someone clicks Rocket Red Velvet and the image still shows a Galaxy Glazed, that's confusing and feels broken.

Most e-commerce platforms support variant-specific images. In Shopify, for example, you upload images for each variant and the platform automatically swaps them when the customer makes a selection. WooCommerce has similar functionality through its variation gallery. If you're building a custom product page (using the HTML, CSS, and JavaScript skills from Books 3 and 4), a small JavaScript event listener on your variant selector can swap the `src` attribute of the main product image when the selection changes.

WARNING

If you offer variant-specific images, make sure you have photos of every variant. A product page that shows a beautiful photo for three out of five colors but a generic placeholder for the other two looks sloppy. If you can't photograph every variant, it's better to use one great universal photo than a mix of real photos and placeholders.

## Keeping it simple

I mention this in Book 8, Chapter 1 when I talk about decision paralysis, but it's worth repeating on the product page side: too many options overwhelm people. When customers are faced with 14 flavors, 3 sizes, and 4 box styles, their brain doesn't say "Wow, so many choices!" It says "I'll decide later," which is internet code for "never."

If you sell products with a lot of possible variations, consider curating. Highlight your three bestsellers. Offer a shop favorites bundle. Let the popular options be prominent and make the full catalog available through a secondary link (See all flavors). This gives the decisive customer a fast path and the browsing customer the full selection without overwhelming either one.

A related principle: don't require a variant selection before the customer can see the price or the description. I've visited product pages where the entire page below the image says "Please select options to see pricing," and nothing else is visible until you choose a size and color. That's a terrible experience. Show the base price (or a range: "$18.99–$34.99"), show the full description, and let the variant selection refine the details. The customer should never feel like they're unlocking content by making choices.

# Customer Reviews and Social Proof

If I had to pick one element that separates high-converting product pages from mediocre ones, it would be reviews. Customer reviews are the closest thing online shopping has to word-of-mouth recommendation, and word-of-mouth has been the most powerful form of advertising since before advertising existed. When a potential buyer sees that 47 other people bought this product and most of them loved it, the mental calculus shifts. It's no longer "Do I trust this company?" It's "47 people can't all be wrong."

Research backs this up. Study after study shows that products with reviews convert at significantly higher rates than products without them, and the effect is even stronger for products from brands the customer hasn't heard of. Reviews build the trust that an unknown brand hasn't earned yet.

## Getting reviews in the first place

The catch-22 of reviews is that you need sales to get reviews, but you need reviews to get sales. Here's how to break the cycle.

The simplest approach is the *post-purchase email.* A few days after a customer receives their order (give them time to use the product), send a short, friendly email asking them to leave a review. Include a direct link to the review form so they don't have to navigate there themselves. Make it easy. Friction is the enemy of reviews just as much as it's the enemy of sales.

You can also offer a small incentive: 10 percent off the next order, a loyalty point bonus, or entry into a monthly drawing. Some platforms (Shopify, for instance) have review apps that automate this entire process. Just be transparent about the incentive; asking for an honest review in exchange for a small thank-you is perfectly fine. Paying for positive reviews is not. (It's also against the terms of service of virtually every review platform and violates FTC guidelines in the US. Don't do it.)

If your store is new and you have zero reviews, consider sending your product to a few early customers, beta testers, or local community figures and asking them for honest feedback. These aren't fake reviews; they're genuine opinions from real people who used your product. Most review platforms have policies about this, so read the fine print, but the general principle is that solicited reviews are fine as long as they're genuine and uncompensated (or if compensation is disclosed). Your first five reviews are the hardest to get. After that, the flywheel starts turning.

TIP

Ask for a review at the right moment. Too early and the customer hasn't used the product yet. Too late and the purchase has faded from memory. For physical products, three to five days after delivery is the sweet spot. For digital products or services, a day or two is usually enough.

## Displaying reviews effectively

Having reviews is only half the battle. How you display them matters too. The most effective review displays combine an aggregate score (the star rating and total count) with individual featured reviews.

The star rating and review count should be visible near the top of the product page, ideally just below the product title. Something like "★★★★☆ 4.3 (47 reviews)" tells the visitor immediately that real people have bought this product and liked it. If you make the review count clickable (so it scrolls down to the full review section), even better.

For the individual reviews, display them with the reviewer's first name (or initials), a date, the star rating, and the review text. If you can include a Verified Purchase badge, do it. Verified reviews carry more weight because they confirm the reviewer bought the product rather than being someone's cousin doing a favor.

Let visitors sort reviews (most recent, highest rated, lowest rated) and filter them (only 5-star, only 1-star, or by keyword). Shoppers who are on the fence often go straight to the negative reviews to understand the worst-case scenario. Making those reviews easy to find (rather than burying them) is a trust-building move, which brings me to the next point.

If your reviews include photos from customers, feature those prominently. A customer photo of your product in the wild is worth ten studio shots because it shows the product in a context the potential buyer can relate to. A photo of Orbital Donuts on a picnic blanket, with crumbs and coffee and imperfect lighting, feels real in a way that a perfectly staged product shoot never will. If your platform supports customer photo uploads in reviews, enable it and encourage it.

# The negative review paradox

This might sound counterintuitive, but products with a few negative reviews convert better than products with nothing but five-star reviews. Why? Because a perfect rating feels fake. If every single person on earth loved this donut with no exceptions, something smells off (metaphorically speaking). A 4.3-star average with a handful of 3-star reviews feels honest and credible, which builds more trust than a suspicious 5.0.

The key is how you respond to negative reviews. Always respond, and do it publicly. Be polite, acknowledge the issue, and explain what you're doing to fix it (or offer to make it right). This shows future customers that you care about their experience and that you stand behind your products. A negative review with a thoughtful, professional response from the owner is often more persuasive than a positive review, because it demonstrates character.

What you should never do: argue, get defensive, dismiss the complaint, or ignore it. Every negative review is a conversation that future customers are watching. Act accordingly.

A practical template for responding to a negative review: start by thanking the person for their feedback (yes, even if the review is unfair). Acknowledge the specific issue they raised. Apologize if the experience fell short. Explain what you're doing about it (or offer to make it right, with a direct contact method so the conversation can move to private channels). Keep it short, professional, and empathetic. The response is not really for the reviewer. It's for the hundreds of potential customers who will read it later.

## Other forms of social proof

Reviews are the heavyweight of social proof, but they're not the only form. Other signals that build trust on a product page include:

- **Trust badges:** Logos for secure checkout, payment providers (Visa, Mastercard, PayPal), and any industry certifications your product has earned. These are especially important for stores that are new or unfamiliar to the customer.
- **Customer count or sales count:** "Over 10,000 boxes sold" or "Joined by 500+ subscribers this month." Numbers communicate popularity, and popularity signals safety.
- **Press mentions:** If your product has been featured in a publication, quote it. "As featured in `FoodNetwork.com`" carries weight, even as a small line near the product description.
- **User-generated content:** Photos or videos from real customers using your product. These are more authentic than any studio photo you could take, and they show the product in real-world conditions.

REMEMBER

Social proof is about reducing uncertainty. Every piece of evidence you can show that other real people have bought, used, and enjoyed this product makes the next customer's decision easier. Start with reviews and add other forms of social proof as they become available.

WARNING

A word of caution about trust badges: display only genuine badges. If you display a Secure Checkout badge, make sure your checkout uses HTTPS and a reputable payment provider (as I discuss in Book 8, Chapter 1). If you display an Organic Certified badge, make sure you have the certification. Fake trust badges are worse than no trust badges because they create trust that evaporates the moment a customer discovers the deception. And on the internet, deception gets discovered fast.

# A/B Testing for Conversions

Everything I've covered so far in this chapter is based on well-established best practices. But here's the thing about best practices: they're general recommendations, and your store is specific. The only way to know for certain what works best for *your* customers on *your* product pages is to test. That's where A/B testing comes in.

# What A/B testing is (and isn't)

An *A/B test* (sometimes called a *split test*) is a controlled experiment where you show two versions of a page element to different visitors and measure which version performs better. Half your visitors see version A (the current page), half see version B (the modified page), and after enough visitors have seen both versions, you compare the results.

The critical rule is this: change only one thing at a time. If you simultaneously change the product photo, the headline, and the button color, and version B converts 15 percent better, you have no idea which change caused the improvement. Maybe it was the photo. Maybe it was the button. Maybe the headline hurt conversions and the photo improvement was even bigger than 15 percent. You'll never know, because you changed too many variables at once.

One thing A/B testing is not: a silver bullet. It requires traffic. If your product page gets 20 visitors a week, you won't have a statistically meaningful result for months. A/B testing is most useful for stores that already have a decent volume of traffic and are looking to optimize an existing page, not for brand-new stores still trying to get their first hundred visitors.

That said, even if your traffic is low, the *mindset* of A/B testing is valuable from day one. The mindset is this: don't assume you know what works. Try things. Measure the results. Let the data tell you what your customers respond to, rather than going with your gut. Your gut is not your customer.



# What to test on your product pages

Almost any element on a product page can be tested, but some tests are more useful than others. Here are the elements I'd start with, roughly in order of likely impact:

- **Product images:** Try a different main image (a lifestyle shot instead of a product-only shot, or vice versa). Image changes tend to produce the biggest swings in conversion rate.
- **Call-to-action button:** Test the text (Add to Cart versus Buy Now versus Get Yours), the color (does a bright orange button outperform a subtle blue one?), and the size.
- **Price display:** Test whether showing a per-unit price alongside the total increases cart adds. Test whether a Save 15% badge next to the bundle price moves the needle.

» **Description length:** Does a short, punchy description outperform a longer, more detailed one?

» **Social proof placement:** Does moving the star rating above the price improve conversions? Does adding a Bestseller badge to the image help?

## Tools for testing

If you're using a hosted platform such as Shopify, apps in the Shopify App Store can handle A/B testing (Neat A/B Testing and Intelligems are popular options). WooCommerce users can use plug-ins or integrate with external tools. For any platform, VWO (`vwo.com`) provides a solid starting point.

If your store is small and you're not ready to commit to a dedicated testing tool, you can run a manual A/B test by changing a single element (say, your main product image) for two weeks, comparing the conversion rate to the previous two weeks, and seeing whether the change made a difference. This approach isn't as rigorous as a simultaneous split test (because you can't control for time-based variables such as holidays or promotions), but it's better than guessing.

Whatever tool you use, keep a simple log of your tests. Create a spreadsheet with columns for the date, what you tested, what the two versions were, how long the test ran, and what the result was. Over time, this log becomes an incredibly valuable reference. You'll start to see patterns (maybe your customers respond strongly to lifestyle images but don't care about button color; maybe description length matters for expensive items but not cheap ones). Those patterns inform your decisions far better than any blog post about best practices ever could, because they're based on your customers, not someone else's.

## Interpreting your results

The most important thing to understand about A/B test results is that you need enough data before you can draw conclusions. A test where version A had 12 purchases and version B had 15 doesn't tell you anything meaningful. That difference could easily be random chance. Most A/B testing tools include a *statistical significance* indicator that tells you how confident you can be that the result is real and not just noise. A common threshold is 95 percent confidence: if the tool says the result is 95 percent significant, there's only a 5 percent chance that the difference is due to randomness.

How long does that take? It depends entirely on your traffic volume. A store with 500 product page views per day might reach significance in a week. A store with 20 views per day might need two months. Be patient. Calling a test too early is worse than not testing at all, because you'll make changes based on noise instead of signal.

Remember, too, that not every test produces a winner. Sometimes version A and version B perform almost identically, which is also useful information. It means that particular element doesn't matter much for your audience, and you should test something else instead. Testing is a process of elimination as much as it is a process of discovery.

One common mistake new testers make is testing things that don't matter. Changing the button from Add to Cart to Add to Basket is unlikely to move the needle. Changing the main product image from a *flat lay* (an image shot from directly above showing the item on a horizontal surface) to a lifestyle shot? That might move it a lot. Focus your tests on the elements that carry the most weight: images, headlines, price presentation, and the position or prominence of social proof. Save the minor tweaks (font size, subtle color variations) for later, after the big wins are captured.

In addition, don't test during unusual periods. Black Friday week, a major sale, a viral social media post, a seasonal spike introduce variables that contaminate your results. Run your tests during normal, representative traffic periods so the results reflect your typical customer behavior. A test result that's valid only during a holiday sale isn't useful for the other 50 weeks of the year.



REMEMBER

A/B testing is a loop, not a one-time event. Test, measure, implement the winner, and then test the next thing. Small, steady improvements compound over time. A 5 percent improvement this month plus a 5 percent improvement next month doesn't give you 10 percent. It gives you 10.25 percent. Over a year, those small gains add up to a substantially better-performing store.

IN THIS CHAPTER

» Setting up email marketing

» Using upsells and cross-sells

» Personalizing the shopping experience

» Tracking e-commerce metrics

# Chapter 3
# E-Commerce Marketing and Optimization

*Permission marketing turns strangers into friends and friends into loyal customers. It's not just about entertainment — it's about education.*

—SETH GODIN

Having a store is not the same thing as having customers. A store without marketing is a billboard in the desert: seen by no one. Your store might be beautifully designed, but the products won't sell themselves, no matter how great they are. You need to actively bring people to your store, give them reasons to buy, and (just as importantly) give them reasons to come back.

In this chapter, I cover the major marketing levers available to you as a small e-commerce business: email marketing, abandoned cart recovery, upselling and cross-selling, discounts and promotions, personalization, customer retention, analytics, and checkout optimization. None of these require a marketing degree or a six-figure advertising budget. Most are built right into the platforms I discuss in Book 8, Chapter 1 and can meaningfully boost your sales.

# Email Marketing Automation for E-Commerce

I know what you're thinking. Email? In an age of social media, chatbots, and AI-powered everything, the humble email is still the best marketing tool for an online store? Yes. Emphatically yes. Email marketing consistently delivers the highest return on investment (ROI) of any digital marketing channel, and it's not even close. Industry estimates put the average ROI somewhere in the neighborhood of $36–$42 for every dollar spent. Social media, by comparison, is typically a fraction of that.

Why does email perform so well? Three reasons:

- **You own your email list.** You don't rent it (so to speak) from a social media platform that can change its algorithm tomorrow and crater your reach.
- **Email is personal.** Each message lands in someone's inbox, not in a feed they're scrolling past at 90 miles per hour.
- **The people on your email list have already told you they're interested.** They opted in to receive messages from you. That's a warm audience, and warm audiences buy.

## The essential automated sequences

The beauty of e-commerce email marketing is that you can set up most of it once and let it run on autopilot. These automated sequences (sometimes called *flows* or *drip campaigns*) trigger based on customer behavior, so the right message goes to the right person at the right time without you lifting a finger after the initial setup.

Here are the sequences that every e-commerce store should have:

- **Welcome sequence:** Triggered when someone signs up for your email list or creates an account. This is your chance to introduce your brand, set expectations, and maybe offer a small first-purchase incentive (10 percent off, free shipping on the first order, that kind of thing). A good welcome sequence is two to three emails spread over a week. The first email delivers the promised incentive, the second tells your brand story, and the third highlights your most popular products.

- **Post-purchase sequence:** Triggered after someone buys something. Start with an order confirmation (which is also an opportunity to suggest related products); follow up with a *Delivered* message for tracked packages, which includes links for getting started with the purchase and troubleshooting problems; then, a few days after delivery, a "How did we do?" email, which also asks for a review. As I mention in Book 8, Chapter 2, reviews are gold for your product pages.
- **Win-back sequence:** Triggered when a customer hasn't purchased in a while (60, 90, or 120 days, depending on your product cycle). The message is simple: "We miss you! Here's a reason to come back." A small discount or a "See what's new" email can reactivate customers who've drifted away.
- **Browse abandonment:** Triggered when someone looks at a product page but doesn't add anything to their cart. A gentle nudge ("Still thinking about the Galaxy Glazed?") can bring them back. This approach is less aggressive than abandoned cart emails (which I cover in the next section) and works best for higher-priced items, where customers need time to decide.

## Building your email list

Your email list is only as good as the people on it, and building a quality list takes time and a bit of strategy. The key word here is *quality.* A list of 500 people who actually want to hear from you is worth more than a list of 10,000 people who signed up for a contest and immediately forgot you existed.

Here are the most effective ways to build your list:

- **Checkout opt-in:** Add a checkbox during checkout that says something like "Keep me updated on new products and special offers." Don't pre-select it (that's annoying and may violate privacy regulations in some jurisdictions), but make it visible and appealing. This is your highest-quality signup channel because these people have already bought from you.
- **Pop-up with incentive:** A well-timed pop-up offering 10–15 percent off the first order in exchange for an email address is one of the most effective list-building tools in e-commerce. The key phrase here is *well-timed.* Display it after the visitor has been on your site for 15–20 seconds or when they scroll past 50 percent of the page, not the instant the page loads. Nobody wants to be asked for their email before they've even seen what you sell.
- **Footer signup form:** A simple, always-visible email signup in your site footer. This catches people who are interested but not ready to buy yet. Keep it short: name and email, nothing more.

WARNING

Whatever method you use to collect email addresses, make sure you're complying with privacy laws: CAN-SPAM in the United States, CASL in Canada, GDPR in Europe. The details vary, but the basics are the same: get consent before sending marketing emails, include an unsubscribe link in every message, and don't use misleading subject lines. Your email marketing platform handles most of the technical compliance for you, but you still need to understand the rules.

### Choosing an email marketing platform

You'll need a dedicated email marketing platform to manage your list, build your automated sequences, and track performance. The good news is that several excellent platforms cater specifically to e-commerce:

- **Mailchimp (`mailchimp.com`):** The most widely known email platform, with a generous free tier for small lists and a visual email builder that's genuinely easy to use. The e-commerce integrations have improved significantly over the past few years, and the automation features are solid for small to mid-sized stores.
- **Klaviyo (`klaviyo.com`):** Built specifically for e-commerce, with deep integrations into Shopify, WooCommerce, and other platforms. Klaviyo excels at segmentation and data-driven automation (such as "Send this email to customers who bought product X but not product Y"). It's pricier than Mailchimp, but many store owners consider it worth the investment once their revenue justifies the cost.
- **Omnisend (`omnisend.com`):** Another e-commerce-focused platform that combines email with SMS marketing. The prebuilt automation workflows are particularly useful if you're just getting started and don't want to build everything from scratch.

REMEMBER

Most e-commerce platforms (Shopify, WooCommerce, Squarespace) have basic built-in email tools, but dedicated email marketing platforms give you far more control over segmentation, automation, and design. Start with the built-in tools if your budget is tight, and upgrade to a dedicated platform once your list grows past a few hundred subscribers and you want to get serious about automation.

## Abandoned Cart Recovery

If there's one metric that haunts every e-commerce store owner, it's the *cart abandonment rate*, the percentage of shoppers who add items to their cart but leave without completing the purchase. The industry average sits somewhere around 70 percent. Let that number sink in for a moment. Seven out of ten people who were interested enough to put something in their cart walked away before paying for it.

That sounds terrible, but it's also an enormous opportunity. Many of those people didn't leave because they decided they didn't want the product. They got distracted. They wanted to compare prices. They were shocked by the shipping cost. Life happened. A well-crafted recovery campaign brings a significant chunk of them back, and because they've already demonstrated purchase intent, the conversion rate on these emails is much higher than on regular marketing emails.

## Why people abandon carts

Understanding why people abandon carts helps you craft better recovery messages (and, just as importantly, fix the underlying problems). The most common reasons, according to basically every study ever conducted on the topic:

- **Unexpected costs:** Shipping fees, taxes, or handling charges that weren't visible until checkout. This is the number one reason, by a wide margin. As I mention in Book 8, Chapter 1, surfacing shipping costs early is one of the most effective things you can do for your conversion rate.
- **Non-working discount offers:** When you offer a discount and that reduction fails at checkout — for example, because of conditions the customer hasn't spotted in the small print — a person can feel cheated and will abandon their cart without hesitation. Make sure the conditions on discount offers are easy to spot.
- **Required account creation:** Forcing someone to create an account before they can check out. Some people just want to buy the thing and move on with their lives. (I cover this in more detail later in this chapter in the "Optimizing the Checkout Experience" section.)
- **Complicated checkout process:** Too many form fields, too many steps, confusing navigation. Every additional click between "I want this" and "I bought this" is an opportunity for the customer to change their mind.
- **Security concerns:** If your checkout page doesn't look trustworthy — for example, no recognizable payment logos or a design that feels outdated — some customers will get cold feet about entering their credit card number.
- **Comparison shopping:** The customer isn't abandoning you specifically; they're checking whether they can find the same product cheaper somewhere else. This is normal and expected. Your recovery email is your chance to remind them why your store is the right choice.

- **Simple distraction:** The doorbell rang. The baby woke up. The meeting started. Not everything is about you. Sometimes people fully intend to come back and just forget.

## The three-email recovery sequence

The standard abandoned cart recovery sequence consists of three emails, spaced out over a few days. The timing and tone shift with each message:

- **Email 1 (1–2 hours after abandonment):** A gentle reminder. "Looks like you left something behind!" Include an image of the abandoned product, the price, and a direct link back to their cart. Keep the tone light and helpful, not pushy. No discount yet. This email alone recovers the largest share of abandoned carts, simply by reminding people who got distracted.
- **Email 2 (24 hours after abandonment):** A slightly more persuasive nudge. Address common objections: mention your free returns policy, your satisfaction guarantee, your responsive customer support. You might include a customer review or two for the abandoned product. Social proof works wonders at this stage because it reassures the customer that other people made this purchase and were happy with it.
- **Email 3 (48–72 hours after abandonment):** The last chance. This is where you might offer a small incentive to close the deal, such as a 10 percent discount or free shipping. Don't lead with the discount in the first email (if you do, you're training people to abandon their carts on purpose to get a deal), but by the third email, a nudge can tip the balance for someone who's been on the fence.

What does a good recovery email look like? Keep it short (the entire thing should fit on a phone screen without scrolling), name the specific products the customer abandoned (not just "You left items in your cart"), be friendly without being desperate, and make it trivially easy to get back to the cart with one button click. For Orbital Donuts, a first email might read: "Hi Alex, Looks like you left a Cosmic Cruller ($4.99) and a half-dozen Galaxy Glazed ($18.99) in your cart. Your items are saved and ready. Just click below to pick up where you left off." That's it. Remind, reassure, remove friction. The second email adds social proof and guarantees; the third offers a small incentive to close the deal.

TIP

Most e-commerce platforms handle abandoned cart emails natively. Shopify has a built-in abandoned checkout recovery feature you can enable with a few clicks. WooCommerce offers it through plug-ins such as AutomateWoo or through your email marketing platform's integration. If you're using Klaviyo or Omnisend, the abandoned cart flow is one of the first automations you'll set up. You don't need to build any of this from scratch.

REMEMBER

A good abandoned cart sequence can recover 5–15 percent of abandoned carts. That might not sound like much, but do the math: if your store has $10,000 in abandoned carts per month and you recover 10 percent, that's $1,000 in revenue you would have lost. Over a year, that's $12,000, which is real money for any small business.

# Upselling and Cross-Selling Strategies

If you've ever been asked "Would you like to make that a large?" at a fast-food restaurant, you've been upsold. If you've ever been asked "Would you like fries with that?" you've been cross-sold. These two techniques are the backbone of increasing your *average order value* (often abbreviated as *AOV*), the average amount a customer spends per transaction, and they work just as well online as they do at a drive-through window.

Let me be precise about the difference, because the terms get muddled constantly:

- **Upselling:** Encouraging a customer to buy a more expensive version of what they're already considering. A larger size, a premium tier, a bundle instead of a single item. The customer's intent stays the same; you're just nudging them toward a higher-value option.
- **Cross-selling:** Suggesting complementary products that go with what the customer is already buying. If someone's buying a camera, cross-sell them a memory card and a carrying case. If someone's buying donuts, cross-sell them a bag of artisan coffee.

Both techniques increase your revenue per customer without requiring you to attract additional traffic. That's important, because getting more traffic is expensive and time-consuming. Getting more revenue from the traffic you already have is comparatively cheap. A well-placed upsell or cross-sell suggestion can increase your average order value by 10–30 percent, and all it costs is a few minutes of configuration in your e-commerce platform.

It's important to note that timing matters. An upsell or cross-sell suggestion that appears at the right moment feels helpful. The same suggestion at the wrong moment feels pushy. Here are the three most effective placements:

- **On the product page:** Show a You Might Also Like or Frequently Bought Together section below the main product details. This is the most natural place for cross-sells because the customer is already in browsing mode. For upsells, a "Get more and save" message near the quantity selector or variant options works well. The key is to keep the suggestions relevant; don't recommend a product from a completely different category.
- **In the cart:** When the customer views their cart, suggest add-ons that complement what's already in there. Keep it to one or two suggestions; you don't want the cart page to feel like a bazaar. A simple Complete Your Order section with two or three relevant products is plenty.
- **After the purchase:** The order confirmation page and the post-purchase email are both excellent places for cross-sells. The customer has already committed (the transaction is done), so a suggestion feels less like pressure and more like a helpful recommendation. "Customers who bought this also loved . . ." is a classic for a reason.

WARNING

There's a fine line between helpful suggestion and aggressive selling. If every page of your store is plastered with "Buy more! Add this! Upgrade now!" the customer is going to feel like they're being hustled, not helped. Keep upsells and cross-sells relevant, limited in number (one to three per page), and useful. The goal is to increase order value by helping the customer get what they want, not by tricking them into buying things they don't.

# Discount and Promotion Strategies

Discounts are one of the most powerful tools in your marketing toolkit — and also one of the most dangerous. Used well, a discount can drive traffic, increase conversions, clear old inventory, and reward loyal customers. Used poorly, it can erode your margins, train your customers to never pay full price, and cheapen your brand. The difference between the two outcomes usually comes down to strategy.

## Types of discounts

Not all discounts are created equal, and each type sends a different signal to your customers:

- **Percentage off:** "15 percent off your order" is the most common type and the easiest for customers to understand. It works well for acquisition (enticing new customers) and re-engagement (winning back lapsed ones). The downside is that on low-priced items, the dollar savings can feel insignificant. 15 percent off a $3.49 donut is about 52 cents. Not exactly thrilling.
- **Dollar amount off:** "$5 off orders over $25" feels more concrete than a percentage, especially on midrange purchases. It also lets you set a minimum spend threshold, which protects your margins and encourages customers to add more to their cart to qualify.
- **Buy one, get one (BOGO):** "Buy a dozen, get a half-dozen free" is a classic volume driver. BOGO deals feel generous to the customer (free stuff!), even though you're essentially offering a 33 percent discount on the combined purchase. The psychology is powerful: people love getting something for nothing, even when the math works out the same as a percentage discount.
- **Free shipping:** As I discuss in Book 8, Chapter 1, free shipping is the single most effective incentive in e-commerce. If your margins allow it, a free shipping threshold ("Free shipping on orders over $35") doubles as both a discount and an upselling tool, since customers will add items to reach the threshold.

## When discounts help versus when they hurt

Here's my rule of thumb: discounts should serve a specific business objective, and you should be able to articulate what that objective is before you offer one. "I want to attract first-time buyers" is a good reason. "I want to clear out seasonal inventory before it expires" is a good reason. "I want to reward my best customers" is a good reason. "I feel like sales have been slow and I'm nervous" is not a good reason, even though it's an understandable impulse.

The danger of chronic discounting is real. If your store runs a 20 percent off sale every other week, your customers will learn the pattern and simply wait for the next sale. You've essentially lowered your prices by 20 percent permanently while giving yourself the extra administrative burden of managing constant promotions. Worse, you've trained your audience to associate your brand with discounts rather than with value. That's a hard perception to reverse.

WARNING

Be especially careful with discounting if you sell premium or handmade products. Frequent discounts signal that the product isn't worth its listed price, which undermines the craftsmanship and quality story you're trying to tell. For premium brands, limited-time promotions tied to specific events (a holiday, an anniversary, a product launch) work much better than ongoing percentage-off sales.

## Seasonal and time-limited promotions

Time-limited promotions work because they create *urgency*, the feeling that if you don't act now, you'll miss out. Black Friday is the most obvious example, but your store doesn't have to wait for major shopping holidays to run effective promotions. A Summer Launch sale, a Back-to-School promotion, or even a Tuesday Treat flash sale can all drive traffic and conversions if they're well-executed and genuinely time-limited.

The keys to a good time-limited promotion: a clear start and end date (vague urgency isn't urgency at all), a genuine reason for the sale (customers are smart and can spot manufactured urgency a mile away), and prominent placement on your site and in your emails. A countdown timer on your home page or product pages can reinforce the time pressure, but don't overdo it. If the countdown timer is on every page, all the time, for a so-called sale that suspiciously restarts every Monday, your customers will roll their eyes. (And they might even report you to the consumer watchdog agency in your jurisdiction!)

## Coupon codes versus automatic discounts

You can implement discounts in your store in two ways: using coupon codes that the customer enters at checkout, and applying automatic discounts that apply without any action from the customer. Each has trade-offs, and the right choice depends on the campaign.

Coupon codes are great for tracking. You can create unique codes for different campaigns (WELCOME15 for new customers, LOYAL10 for returning ones) and see which campaign drove which sales. They also feel like a reward because the customer has a special code, which feels exclusive. The downside is friction: customers have to remember the code, find the code entry field at checkout, and type it in correctly. Some customers will abandon their cart to go hunting for a coupon code on Google, which is the opposite of what you want.

Automatic discounts eliminate that friction. The discount appears in the cart without any action from the customer. This method is ideal for sitewide sales, free shipping thresholds, and volume discounts. The trade-off is that automatic discounts are harder to attribute to specific campaigns, and they don't have the same "special offer" feeling that a coupon code provides.

TIP

If you use coupon codes, hide or remove the promo code field for customers who already have an automatic discount applied. Nothing is more frustrating than seeing a Promo Code field at checkout, not having a code, and wondering whether you're missing out on a deal. That empty field creates anxiety, and anxious customers abandon carts.

# Personalization Techniques

When most people hear "personalization," they think of Amazon's recommendation engine or Netflix's eerily accurate "Because You Watched . . ." suggestions. Those systems are powered by machine-learning algorithms analyzing billions of data points, and replicating them is wildly impractical for a small business. The good news is that you don't need to. Effective personalization for a small e-commerce store is far simpler than what the tech giants do, but it still makes a meaningful difference in how customers experience your store.

At its core, personalization just means making the shopping experience feel relevant to the individual customer rather than generic. It can be as simple as using someone's first name in an email or as sophisticated as showing different home page content based on their browsing history. The key is that the customer feels like the experience was designed with them in mind, not for some anonymous "everyone."

Email is the easiest place to start with personalization because you already have data about your subscribers: their name, purchase history, location, and behavior on your site. At a minimum, use the customer's first name in the subject line and greeting. That alone increases open rates by a measurable amount. (Yes, everyone knows the computer did it. It still works. The human brain is funny that way.)

Beyond the name, here are some straightforward personalization tactics for your emails:

- **Purchase history recommendations:** "You loved the Galaxy Glazed last month. Have you tried the Cosmic Cruller?" Recommending products based on what a customer previously bought is far more effective than a generic best-sellers suggestion, because it tells the customer you're paying attention.

- **Location-based content:** If you know where your customers are located (and your email platform probably does, at least at the city level), you can tailor content accordingly. A customer in a cold climate might appreciate a "Warm up with our new hot chocolate donut" email in January, while a customer in a warm climate gets a different seasonal pitch.
- **Behavior-triggered messages:** Beyond the automated sequences I describe earlier in this chapter, you can send emails triggered by specific browsing actions. Did someone view the catering page three times? Send a catering-specific email with pricing details and a contact form. Did they download a menu PDF? Follow up with a first-order incentive.

TIP

Start small with personalization. Using the customer's name in emails and showing recently viewed products on your site covers 80 percent of the impact with 20 percent of the effort. Most e-commerce platforms can show personalized content to logged-in customers (recently viewed items, recommendations based on purchase history), and third-party tools such as LimeSpot and Nosto can do the same for anonymous visitors based on browsing behavior. You can add more sophisticated (but relevant; don't go all Big Brother on your customers!) personalization later as your store grows and your data improves.

# Customer Retention Strategies

There's a statistic that gets tossed around in marketing circles so often it's practically a cliché: it costs five to seven times more to acquire a new customer than to retain an existing one. Whether the exact multiple is five or seven or somewhere in between depends on who's doing the counting, but the underlying truth is solid. Customers who have already bought from you are dramatically easier and cheaper to sell to again than people who've never heard of you.

And the economics go deeper than acquisition cost. Repeat customers spend more per order, try new products more readily, leave more reviews (which, as I cover in Book 8, Chapter 2, are crucial for your product pages), and tell their friends about your store. Retention is the secret sauce that can turn a struggling store into a profitable one.

## Loyalty programs

A *loyalty program* gives customers a tangible reason to keep buying from you instead of shopping around. The simplest version is the old-fashioned punch card: buy nine donuts, get the tenth free. The digital equivalent is a points system where customers earn points on every purchase and redeem them for discounts, free products, or exclusive perks.

Loyalty programs work best when the rewards feel attainable and the mechanics are dead simple. A program where you need to spend $500 before earning a $5 reward feels like a joke. (That's a 1 percent return, which is worse than most savings accounts.) A program where you earn 1 point per dollar spent and can redeem 50 points for a free donut feels achievable and motivating. The customer can see the progress, and the next reward is always within reach.

Tiered loyalty programs add another layer of motivation. Think silver, gold, platinum or (keeping with our space theme) cadet, officer, commander. Each tier unlocks better perks: early access to new products, bigger discounts, free shipping, birthday rewards. Tiers create a sense of status and progression that keeps customers engaged. Once someone hits gold, they're not going to shop somewhere else and start over as a lowly silver.

REMEMBER

If you're on Shopify, apps such as Smile.io and LoyaltyLion can set up a points-based loyalty program in an afternoon. WooCommerce has similar plug-ins (WooCommerce Points and Rewards, for instance). The setup is straightforward; the hard part is promoting the program so customers know it exists and enroll. Feature it prominently on your site, mention it in your post-purchase emails, and include a loyalty status update in your regular marketing emails.

## Post-purchase follow-up

The moment after a purchase is a surprisingly emotional one for the customer. They've just spent money, and there's often a small pang of doubt. Your post-purchase communication can either reinforce the decision ("Great choice! Here's what happens next.") or let the doubt fester by going radio silent. Guess which one leads to more repeat purchases.

A good post-purchase flow looks like this: an immediate order confirmation with all the details (order number, items, expected delivery date), a shipping notification with tracking when the order goes out, a *Delivered* message to confirm that the shipment reached the customer, a "How was your experience?" email a few days after delivery, and a review request a day or two after that. Each touchpoint reinforces the customer's decision and demonstrates that you care about their experience, not just their wallet. And if a shipment is delayed, email the customer rather than just waiting for them to notice. Proactive communication builds trust faster than any loyalty program.

## Re-engagement campaigns

Not every customer who stops buying has left for good. Some just got busy. Others found a new favorite store. Some moved, changed jobs, or simply forgot you existed (it happens to the best of us). A *re-engagement campaign* is a targeted effort to bring inactive customers back into the fold.

The typical approach is a sequence of two or three emails, spaced a week or two apart. The first is a soft touch: "We haven't seen you in a while, here's what's new." The second offers an incentive: "We miss you! Here's 15% off your next order." The third is a last call: "Is this goodbye? We'll stop emailing if you'd prefer. Click here to stay on our list."

That last email — the breakup email — often has the highest response rate of the sequence, because nobody likes being broken up with, even by a donut shop. And for the people who don't respond, removing them from your list improves your email deliverability and open rates.

TIP

Set a clear definition of inactive before you start your re-engagement campaign. For a store selling consumable products (such as donuts or coffee), 60–90 days without a purchase might qualify. For a store selling durable goods (such as furniture or electronics), the window might be 6–12 months. Align the timing to your product's natural repurchase cycle, not to an arbitrary number.

# E-Commerce Analytics and Metrics

I'm going to let you in on a secret that most e-commerce advice glosses over: you don't need to track everything. Your e-commerce platform dashboard has dozens of metrics, Google Analytics has hundreds, and if you read enough marketing blogs, you'll come away thinking you need a dedicated data analyst just to understand how your store is performing. You don't. What you need is to understand a handful of key metrics, check them regularly, and use them to make better decisions about where to focus your time and energy. That's it.

(I cover analytics in much more depth in Book 9, including how to set up Google Analytics and how to create custom reports. This section is about the e-commerce metrics you should keep an eye on week to week and how to act on what they tell you.)

## The metrics that matter

Here are the five numbers I'd check every Monday morning if I were running an online store:

- **Conversion rate:** The percentage of visitors who complete a purchase. I introduce this metric in Book 8, Chapter 2, and it's still the most important number on your dashboard. A healthy conversion rate for a small e-commerce store is typically 2–4 percent. If yours is below 1 percent, something structural is wrong (it might be a slow site, poor product pages, or a broken checkout). If it drops suddenly, something has changed and you need to investigate.
- **Average order value:** The average dollar amount per transaction. If your AOV is $25 and you can nudge it to $30 through upselling, bundling, or a free shipping threshold, that's a 20 percent revenue increase with no additional traffic. The upselling and cross-selling strategies I describe earlier in this chapter are all aimed at moving this number up.
- **Customer lifetime value (CLV):** The total revenue (or sometimes profit) a customer generates over their entire relationship with your store. A customer who buys once and never returns has a low CLV. A customer who orders every month for two years has a high one. CLV tells you how much you can afford to spend acquiring a new customer and still make money in the long run. If your average CLV is $200, spending $50 to acquire a customer is a great deal. If your CLV is $20, that same $50 is a disaster.
- **Cart abandonment rate:** The percentage of shopping carts that get created but never converted to a purchase. I cover this earlier in the "Abandoned Cart Recovery" section. Track this metric over time to see whether your checkout improvements and recovery emails are working.
- **Return on ad spend (ROAS):** If you're running paid advertising (Google Ads, social media ads), ROAS tells you how much revenue you earned for every dollar spent on ads. A ROAS of 4:1 means you earned $4 for every $1 spent, which is generally considered strong. Anything below 2:1 for a small business is usually a sign that the campaign needs rethinking or the targeting needs refinement.

## Where to find your numbers

The good news is that you don't need to calculate most of these numbers yourself. Your e-commerce platform's built-in analytics dashboard typically shows conversion rate, AOV, and sales data out of the box. Shopify's analytics are particularly well-designed for small-business owners. WooCommerce shows similar data through its built-in analytics or through plug-ins such as Metorik. For deeper analysis such as traffic sources, user behavior, funnel drop-offs, you'll want Google Analytics 4 (GA4), which I cover in Book 9, Chapter 1. Don't wait to install it; GA4 can show you data only from the point it was installed forward.

REMEMBER

Check your key metrics weekly, not hourly. E-commerce data is noisy on a daily basis; a single bad Tuesday doesn't mean your store is failing, and a single great Saturday doesn't mean you've cracked the code. Look at weekly and monthly trends. A consistent downward slide over three or four weeks is a signal that something needs attention. A one-day dip is just noise.

## Acting on your data

Data without action is just trivia. The whole point of tracking metrics is to make better decisions, so here's a simple framework for turning your numbers into next steps:

- **Conversion rate dropping?** Check whether anything changed recently: a new design, a price increase, a broken page, a shift in traffic sources. Use GA4's landing page report to see whether the drop is sitewide or isolated to specific pages. If it's one page, fix that page. If it's sitewide, the issue is probably something systemic such as site speed or a checkout problem.
- **AOV declining?** Revisit your upselling and cross-selling strategies. Consider adding a free shipping threshold if you don't have one, or raising it slightly if you do. Check whether a recent product change or price adjustment is driving customers toward cheaper options.
- **High cart abandonment?** Walk through your own checkout process on both desktop and mobile. Is anything confusing, slow, or frustrating? Fix it. Then check whether your shipping costs are surprising people at checkout, since that's still the number-one abandonment trigger.
- **CLV lower than expected?** Your retention strategies need work. Are you sending post-purchase emails? Do you have a loyalty program? Are you running re-engagement campaigns for lapsed customers? CLV is a lagging indicator, so improvements take time to show up.

# Optimizing the Checkout Experience

If your store is a funnel (and it is), checkout is the narrowest point. Visitors enter at the top through your home page or product pages, some of them add items to their cart, and a smaller number make it all the way through checkout to complete a purchase. Every unnecessary obstacle in the checkout process costs you customers. And unlike product page improvements, which influence whether someone decides to buy, checkout improvements influence whether someone who has already decided to buy can follow through. That difference is crucial. These people have money in hand, and you're letting them slip away over form field design.

Yikes.

Let me walk you through the most effective checkout optimizations, roughly in order of how much difference they tend to make.

## Guest checkout

The single most important checkout optimization is guest checkout, and it's the hill I will die on: let people check out without creating an account. Forced account creation is consistently one of the top reasons shoppers abandon their carts, and the logic behind requiring it (wanting their data for future marketing) backfires spectacularly when the customer leaves and buys from your competitor instead. You don't get their data, you don't get their money, and you don't get a second chance.

Yes, customer accounts are useful for order history, saved addresses, and loyalty programs. But account creation should be optional. The best time to offer it is after the purchase: "Your order is confirmed! Want to save your details for faster checkout next time? Create an account in 10 seconds." At that point, the customer has already committed, and they're far more likely to say yes because you're framing the account as a convenience, not a requirement.

## Reducing form fields

Every form field is a tiny tax on your customer's patience. The fewer fields in your checkout form, the faster the checkout, the higher your completion rate. That's not a theory; it's one of the most consistently replicated findings in e-commerce usability research.

Take a critical look at what your checkout form asks for. Do you really need a phone number? (Maybe, if you deliver locally and need to coordinate delivery timing, but maybe not if you ship through a carrier.) Do you need separate billing and shipping address forms by default, or can you default to "billing same as shipping" with a checkbox to override? Can your city and state autopopulate from the ZIP or postal code? The takeaway here is to ask for only the information you need for this specific transaction.

WARNING

Test your checkout on a mobile phone. Seriously, right now. Pull up your store on your phone and try to complete a purchase. If you find yourself pinching to zoom, struggling to tap the right field, or waiting for the page to load, your mobile customers are experiencing the same frustration, and many of them are giving up. Mobile accounts for more than half of all e-commerce traffic, and its share is only growing.

## Payment options

The more ways people can pay, the fewer people you lose at the payment step. At a minimum, your checkout should accept major credit and debit cards (Visa, Mastercard, American Express). Beyond that, offering digital wallets such as PayPal, Apple Pay, Google Pay, and Shop Pay (Shopify's accelerated checkout) can significantly speed up mobile checkout because the customer doesn't have to type in their card number, address, or anything else. One tap (or one face scan) and they're done.

Buy-now-pay-later (BNPL) services such as Afterpay, Klarna, and Affirm have also become popular, especially for mid- to high-priced items. These services let the customer split the purchase into installments (typically four interest-free payments), which lowers the psychological barrier of a larger purchase. If your average order value is $50 or more, offering a BNPL option is worth considering. Most e-commerce platforms integrate with at least one BNPL provider through a simple app or plug-in.

## Trust signals at checkout

The checkout page is where the customer hands over their credit card number, which means it's where trust matters most. If anything about the checkout feels sketchy, unprofessional, or unfamiliar, the customer might bail. Here are the trust signals that belong on every checkout page:

- **SSL/security indicators:** Display a small padlock icon or Secure Checkout label near the payment fields. Most e-commerce platforms handle this automatically, but verify it's visible.

- **Recognized payment logos:** Show the logos of accepted payment methods (Visa, Mastercard, PayPal, Apple Pay, and so on). These are visual shorthand for "This is a real store that accepts real payments through real processors."
- **Return and refund policy:** A brief, visible summary of your return policy near the checkout button reduces purchase anxiety. "30-day hassle-free returns" or "Satisfaction guaranteed" is a powerful reassurance that costs you almost nothing to display.
- **Contact information:** Include a phone number, email address, or chat link on the checkout page. Even if few customers use it, its presence signals that you're a real business with real people behind it, not a fly-by-night operation.

## The one-page versus multistep debate

Should your checkout be a single long page or a multistep process with a progress indicator? Both approaches work, and the research is mixed on which converts better. My advice: go with whatever your e-commerce platform defaults to. Shopify uses a multistep checkout that's been tested through millions of transactions. WooCommerce defaults to single-page but has plug-ins for multistep. The individual optimizations I describe in this section (guest checkout, fewer fields, mobile testing, trust signals) matter far more than whether those fields are on one page or three.

TIP

Add a progress indicator to your checkout, whether it's single-page or multi-step. Even something as simple as Step 2 of 3 or a progress bar across the top of the page helps the customer understand how far along they are and reduces the "How long is this going to take?" anxiety that leads to abandonment. People are much more patient when they can see the finish line.

# 9 Website Analytics and Performance

# Contents at a Glance

IN THIS CHAPTER

» **Understanding what analytics measures**

» **Choosing the right analytics tool**

» **Decoding the metrics that mean something**

» **Tracking the actions visitors take**

» **Turning data into decisions**

# Chapter 1

# Understanding Website Analytics

*Data beats opinions.*

—AVINASH KAUSHIK

Your website is generating useful data every single day, whether you're looking at it or not. Every visitor, every page view, every click on your Contact Us button can leave a trace. That information is being generated as you read this, waiting for someone to pay attention to it.

Web analytics tools turn that raw stream of activity into reports you can read. They tell you who's visiting, where those visitors came from, what they did while they were there, and whether they did anything you wanted them to do. Your site is, right now as you read these words, producing this data. The question is whether you're taking advantage of it.

This chapter is about taking that advantage. You learn how to choose and set up an analytics tool, determine which numbers tell you something useful, track specific visitor actions, and use the data to make good decisions.

# What Analytics Can Tell You

Before setting anything up, it's helpful to understand what web analytics measures. At its core, an analytics tool answers four questions about your site:

- **Who is visiting?** How many people visited, are they new or returning, what devices are they using, and roughly where in the world are they located?
- **How did they get here?** Did they find you through a Google search, a link on another website, a social media post, or an email?
- **What do they do once they arrive?** Which pages did they read, how long did they stay, where did they enter your site and where did they leave?
- **Are they doing what you want them to do?** Did they fill out a form, click a phone number, sign up for your newsletter, or take some other action you were hoping for?

Everything else in an analytics report is a more detailed version of one of those four questions. If a number doesn't help you answer at least one of them, you can probably ignore it.

Notice what's conspicuously absent from that list: *why*. Analytics tools tell you *what* happened, not why it happened. If visitors are leaving your pricing page after six seconds, analytics tells you that, but figuring out *why* requires user testing, customer conversations, or some educated guesswork. But knowing what happened is enormously valuable on its own. Most small business owners don't even have that.

You should also know that analytics data is *sampled* and *estimated*, not perfectly precise. Cookie consent banners cause some visitors to be excluded from tracking. Ad blockers and privacy-focused browsers block some tracking scripts. Bot traffic can inflate numbers. Privacy-first tools such as Plausible and Fathom sidestep the consent banner issue by not collecting personal data, which can make their counts *more* complete than what you see in Google Analytics 4 (GA4) in certain markets.

Therefore, treat your analytics numbers as directional indicators, not precise measurements. If your user count drops from 1,200 to 850 in a week, that's a decline worth investigating; whether the exact figures are 1,200 and 850 or 1,150 and 800 doesn't really matter. Analytics is most useful when you're comparing periods and looking for trends, not when you're treating individual data points as facts.

# Choosing an Analytics Tool



Several good analytics tools exist, and they differ in three meaningful ways: how much they cost, how much data they collect and where that data goes, and how much complexity you're willing to deal with.

REMEMBER

The privacy dimension is also important to consider. When a visitor loads a page on your site with most analytics tools installed, some data about that visitor is sent to the analytics service's servers. In Europe and increasingly elsewhere, data protection laws require you to inform visitors about this and, in some cases, get their consent before collecting it — which is why you've seen (and growled at) those cookie consent banners everywhere. Privacy-first tools sidestep this issue by not collecting personal data in the first place.

Here's a quick rundown of the main analytics tools to consider:

- **Google Analytics 4 (`analytics.google.com`):** The free, industry-standard option. It's incredibly detailed, sometimes overwhelmingly so. GA4 sends visitor data to Google's servers, which means you'll need a cookie consent banner in many jurisdictions. For most people starting out, GA4 is the natural first choice: it's free, it's powerful, and it integrates with Google Search Console, Google Ads, and virtually everything else in the Google ecosystem.
- **Plausible Analytics (`plausible.io`):** A clean, privacy-first alternative that tracks visits without cookies or personal data, which means no consent banner required (yay!). The dashboard shows what you need and nothing more. Plausible is a paid service starting around $9 per month.
- **Fathom Analytics (`usefathom.com`):** Similar to Plausible in pricing and philosophy: simple, cookieless, and GDPR-compliant by design. The dashboard is minimal and intuitive.
- **Matomo (`matomo.org`):** The most full-featured privacy-focused alternative, and the closest thing to GA4 in terms of reporting depth without sending data to Google. Matomo can be self-hosted on your own server (which is free but requires technical setup) or cloud-hosted (which you pay for). If you want detailed analytics without Google involved, Matomo is the strongest option.
- **Simple Analytics (`simpleanalytics.com`):** Does exactly what the name says. No cookies, no personal data; just visit counts, top pages, and traffic sources. You can try a free version without obligation. For a small-business owner who wants a quick weekly traffic check without a learning curve, Simple Analytics is hard to beat.

For most people reading this book, GA4 is the right starting point. It's free, it's the most widely used tool in the industry, and the concepts it teaches transfer directly to any other analytics tool you might use later. The rest of this chapter uses GA4 for concrete examples, but the underlying ideas apply to all of them.

## Installing your tracking code

Every analytics tool works the same basic way. You add a short piece of JavaScript to your website — typically inside the `<head>` section of every page — and when a visitor loads a page, their browser runs that code and sends visit data back to the analytics service. The specifics of the code vary by tool, but the concept is identical.

Here's what the installation code looks like for GA4:

```
<!-- Google tag (gtag.js) -->
<script async
    src="https://www.googletagmanager.com/gtag/js?id=G-XXXXXXXXXX">
</script>
<script>
    window.dataLayer = window.dataLayer || [];
    function gtag() { dataLayer.push(arguments); }
    gtag('js', new Date());
    gtag('config', 'G-XXXXXXXXXX');
</script>
```

Replace both instances of `G-XXXXXXXXXX` with your measurement ID, the `G-AB12CD34EF`-style code you get from your GA4 property setup. If you're working with a WordPress site, most SEO plug-ins (as I discuss in Book 7, Chapter 4) include a field for your measurement ID, so you can skip touching HTML entirely.

Privacy-first tools such as Plausible and Fathom use a much simpler one-liner, which is typically a single `<script>` tag with a `data-domain` attribute pointing to your site's domain. Whichever tool you choose, its documentation will walk you through installation in a few minutes.

TIP

If your site has many pages, adding tracking code to each one manually is a slog. Google Tag Manager (`tagmanager.google.com`), a free tool separate from GA4, lets you deploy your analytics code across your entire site from a single interface without touching individual page files. It has a modest learning curve, but it's worth the effort for sites of any real size.

## Checking that it works

After installation, verify the code is firing by opening your analytics tool's real-time report. (Most tools have one. It shows visitor activity in the last minute or so.) Open your website in a second browser tab, click around, and you should see yourself appear in the real-time view within a minute. If nothing shows up after five minutes, double-check that the code is inside the `<head>` section and that any IDs or domain values match your account settings.

REMEMBER

Most analytics tools take up to 24 hours before historical data starts appearing in non-real-time reports. The real-time view updates within seconds, but your pages, acquisition, and other standard reports may show no data until the following day. This is normal. Patience is the hardest part of analytics setup.

# The Metrics That Matter

Once your analytics tool is running, you'll see more numbers than you can shake a stick at, assuming (perhaps boldly) that you're a stick-shaking type of person. In this section, you learn which of those numbers tells you something useful. Fortunately, it doesn't matter which analytics tool you're using because the same core metrics appear in every tool, using roughly the same names.

## Users, sessions, and pageviews

The following three numbers are the foundation of everything else:

- **Users (or visitors):** The number of unique people who visited your site during the selected time period. This is usually the most useful top-level number because it tells you how many real humans found your site.
- **Sessions:** The number of times your site was visited. One person visiting on three separate days generates three sessions. Sessions typically reset after 30 minutes of inactivity, so a visitor who leaves for an hour and returns counts as a new session.
- **Pageviews:** The total number of pages viewed, including repeat views of the same page. A visitor who reads your About page, then your Services page, and then goes back to About has generated three pageviews in one session.

## How your visitors found you

The acquisition or traffic sources report shows you what brought each visitor to your site. The main categories are:

- **Organic search:** Visitors who found you by searching on Google, Bing, or another search engine. Growing this number is what SEO work (Book 7) is all about.
- **Direct:** Visitors who typed your URL directly, or whose source couldn't be identified. A healthy direct share often means your brand is recognizable enough that people navigate to you without a search.
- **Referral:** Visitors who clicked a link to your site from another website, such as a local directory, a news article, or a partner's site. Referral traffic tends to be high-quality because someone else vouched for you.
- **Social:** Visitors from social media platforms. Most tools can tell you which platforms, so you can see whether your posts are driving anyone to your site. (Spoiler alert: the answer is often far less than you'd hoped. Sorry.)
- **Email:** Visitors who clicked a link in an email newsletter. Most email marketing platforms automatically tag their links so they show up correctly in this category.

Looking at your traffic sources over time tells you which of your marketing efforts are producing results. If you've been faithfully posting to a social platform for months and social traffic is flat, that's a data point to take into consideration.

## Engagement rate and bounce rate

Different tools measure visitor engagement differently. Older tools, as well as many simpler ones still in use today, report a *bounce rate:* the percentage of visitors who loaded one page and left without doing anything else. A high bounce rate was traditionally considered a warning sign.

Newer tools, including GA4, replace bounce rate with *engagement rate*, the percentage of visits where the visitor did something meaningful, such as stayed for at least ten seconds, viewed more than one page, or triggered an important event. An engaged session is one where a real human showed genuine interest. Whether your tool reports bounce rate or engagement rate, the underlying question is the same: are visitors interacting with your content, or are they arriving and immediately leaving? Look for trends over time rather than obsessing over any single day's number.

## Average time on page

Most analytics tools report how long visitors spend actively viewing your pages. Modern tools count time only when your page is the visible, active browser tab, which is way more accurate than older tools that ran the clock even when your tab was buried behind twelve others.

What counts as a good average time depends on your content. A local bakery's menu page that averages 40-second visits is perfectly fine, because 40 seconds is plenty of time to pick a croissant. A consulting firm's case study page might average 4 minutes. Compare your numbers to your own previous periods rather than some benchmark that may have nothing to do with your business.

## Using date ranges and comparisons

Raw numbers mean little without context. Most analytics tools let you create that context by comparing the current period to the previous one or to the same period last year. Comparing this month's traffic to last month's tells you whether you're trending in the right direction. Comparing this October to last October is more useful for businesses with seasonal patterns. A tax preparer's slow August doesn't mean much in isolation; compared to last August it tells you whether the business is growing. Pick a comparison that makes sense for your business and stick with it.

Most tools also let you adjust the date range you're looking at. The default view is often the last 30 days, which is reasonable for a regular check-in. But sometimes you want a longer view — say, three or six months — to see whether a trend is real and sustained, or a narrower window — such as the last seven days — to evaluate the impact of something you changed last week. Getting comfortable with the date range controls in your analytics tool is one of the most valuable skills you can develop because so many analytics questions are really questions about time.

# Understanding How Visitors Use Your Site

Beyond who's coming and where they're from, analytics can also show you what visitors *do* on your site. There's a ton of interesting data to be mined from how visitors use your site once they show up.

## Your most-visited pages

Every analytics tool has a report showing your most-visited pages, usually called something like Pages, Top Content, or Pages and Screens. It lists every page on your site sorted by the number of views, along with engagement data for each.

This report is often revealing in ways you don't expect. You might assume your home page is your most-viewed page. Sometimes that's true. But for a restaurant or food service site, the menu page often draws more views than the home page, because that's what visitors came for. If a page you thought was important is barely getting any traffic, it might mean visitors aren't finding it through your navigation or it's not appearing in search results.

Pay attention to pages with high traffic but low engagement. A page that gets a ton of visitors who leave almost immediately is a candidate for a rewrite or redesign because something about it isn't delivering what those visitors expected to find.

Also look at pages that are getting almost no traffic. If you have a Services page or a portfolio section that's essentially invisible in your analytics, two explanations are likely: visitors aren't finding their way there through your navigation, or the page doesn't rank for any search terms that your audience uses. Either problem is solvable, but you have to notice it first.

## Following visitor paths through your site

Knowing which pages are popular is useful. Knowing how visitors move *between* pages is even more useful. Most full-featured analytics tools include some form of path or flow report that shows the sequences each visitor follows: which page they visit first, where they go next, and where they eventually leave.

This kind of report can reveal interesting patterns. You might find that visitors who arrive on your menu page frequently navigate to your catering inquiry page next, suggesting those two pages are closely linked in visitors' minds, and a more prominent link between them might serve everyone better. Or you might discover that visitors consistently leave from a page you thought was a natural next step in a sequence of pages, which points to a disconnect between what you think the page offers and what visitors find there.

Path and flow reports are typically found in the more advanced parts of analytics tools. GA4 has a Path Exploration tool in its Explore section; Matomo has a visitor flow visualization. These reports can get complex quickly, but even a quick look at the most common three- or four-step sequences your visitors follow can surface insights you'd never spot in the standard page-level reports alone.

## Landing pages: First impressions in data form

A *landing page* is any page a visitor arrives on first, so it's their entry point into your site. It might be your home page, but it could equally be a blog post, a product page, your About page, or your location page. Your analytics tool's landing page report shows which pages are serving as those entry points.

Surprisingly, there's a good chance your home page isn't your top landing page. Depending on how your pages rank in search results and how other sites link to you, visitors might be entering through all kinds of doors you never consciously designed as entry points. If a page is drawing first-time visitors but has a high bounce rate or low engagement, people are arriving and leaving almost immediately. That's a signal the page isn't delivering what they expected when they clicked.

## New versus returning users

Most analytics tools report the ratio of new visitors to returning ones. An established site with mostly new visitors is drawing fresh traffic but not giving people a reason to come back. A site with a high share of returning visitors has built a loyal audience but might struggle to grow if it's not reaching new people.

For most small business sites, a split somewhere around 60–70 percent new visitors and 30–40 percent returning is healthy, but the right balance depends on what your site is trying to do. A news blog should have lots of returning readers. A local electrician's website might have mostly new visitors, since people don't typically search for an electrician twice. Neither situation is inherently good or bad; the point is understanding what the numbers mean for your particular context.

## Exit pages: Where visitors say goodbye

Exit pages are the last page a visitor viewed before leaving your site. High exits aren't automatically bad. If your Order Confirmed page has a high exit rate, well, that's great because it means your checkout is working perfectly. Visitors completed a purchase and left. Mission accomplished.

The exits you should investigate are the ones at the wrong moments: a high exit rate on the first step of your contact form, on a service page that's supposed to lead somewhere, or on a page designed to funnel visitors deeper into your site. Those exits suggest something is breaking the visitor's momentum. It might be confusing content, a missing or buried call-to-action, a broken form, or a page that loads too slowly (as I discuss in Book 9, Chapter 2).

One way to prioritize which exit pages to investigate is to cross-reference the exit rate with the page's position in your intended conversion path. A page that's supposed to lead visitors toward a goal — such as a pricing page, a services overview, or a product detail page — should have a relatively low exit rate because you want visitors to keep moving forward. If the page has a high exit rate, instead, that page is a bottleneck in your funnel that you should fix before anything else.

## Device and geographic data

Your analytics tool also shows you how visitors are accessing your site and where they're coming from. Most tools include a device breakdown (desktop, mobile, tablet) and a geographic report showing which cities, regions, or countries your traffic comes from.

The device data is particularly important to monitor. Most small-business websites now receive more than half their traffic from mobile devices. If the majority of your visitors are on mobile and your site isn't optimized for small screens (as I discuss in Book 2, Chapter 3), that's a direct line between your design decisions and your bounce numbers. For local businesses, the geographic data quickly shows whether your site is drawing traffic from people who could become customers or from places too far away to matter. (Geographic data is never all that accurate, so consider it a rough estimate rather than a pinpoint location.)

# Tracking Goals and Events

Traffic data tells you who arrived and what pages they viewed. Goal and event tracking tells you whether they did anything useful while they were there, which is often the more important measure. After all, it's better to have a few visitors who do something useful (such as sign up for your newsletter) than a ton of visitors who just browse.

Different analytics tools use different words for this concept. GA4 calls them *key events.* Older tools called them *goals* or *conversions.* Matomo and Plausible use *goals.* Whatever the name, the idea is the same: you tell your analytics tool which visitor actions represent a win for your business, and it starts counting them.

## What counts as a goal?

What counts as a goal is up to you and depends on what your site is for. Here are the most common goals for small-business websites:

- **Contact form submission:** Someone filled out and submitted your contact form, which usually means a genuine potential customer or client is reaching out.
- **Phone number click:** On a mobile device, tapping a phone number link typically triggers a call. Track these clicks; each one represents a real person who wanted to reach you.
- **Newsletter signup:** A visitor who subscribes to your email list has given you permission to stay in touch, which is a valuable asset for any small business.
- **Get Directions click:** For a local business, this type of click is a strong signal of intent to visit in person. A coffee shop, a salon, or a gym should almost certainly track this.
- **Outbound link click:** If your site links to a booking system, ticketing platform, or external store, clicks on those links mean the visitor went exactly where you sent them.

You don't need to track all of these. Start by picking the one or two that matter most for your business. Having too many goals muddies your reports and makes it harder to decide what to act on.

## What most tools track automatically

Fortunately, most analytics tools automatically record a useful set of events without any custom setup. The specifics vary by tool, but you'll typically get:

- **Page views:** Every page load. The foundation of all your traffic data.
- **Scroll depth:** When a visitor scrolls deep enough down a page, which is a rough proxy for whether they read your content rather than just landing and bouncing.

- **Outbound link clicks:** Clicks on links that leave your site entirely, so you can see which external sites you're sending your visitors to.
- **File downloads:** Clicks on links to downloadable files such as PDFs or ZIP archives.

For many small-business websites, these automatic events cover most of what you need. Custom tracking becomes necessary when you want to record something specific that your tool doesn't capture by default, such as a contact form submission or a phone number click.

## Setting up a custom event

When you want to track something specific, you add a small piece of JavaScript that fires when a visitor takes the action. The pattern is the same in every case: you attach a listener to the page element you care about, and inside that listener you call your analytics tool's tracking function.

Here's a practical example using GA4's tracking function. This code records whenever a visitor submits your contact form:

```
<script>
    document.getElementById("contact-form")
        .addEventListener("submit", function() {
            gtag("event", "contact_form_submit", {
                form_location: "contact-page"
            });
        });
</script>
```

A few things to note:

- **`contact-form`:** The `id` attribute of your form element, so make sure it matches your HTML.
- **`contact_form_submit`:** The event name you're creating. Event names use underscores instead of spaces and should be descriptive but brief.
- **`form_location`:** An example of an optional extra parameter that attaches additional data to the event on which you can filter reports later.

One practical note about the preceding code: the `<script>` block needs to appear *after* the form element in your HTML or be placed inside a `DOMContentLoaded` event listener that waits until the page has fully loaded before running. If the script tries to attach a listener to an element that doesn't exist yet, it fails silently and nothing gets tracked.

Here's another useful example: tracking clicks on your phone number link:

```
<script>
    document.getElementById("phone-link")
        .addEventListener("click", function() {
            gtag("event", "phone_number_click", {
                phone_number: "+1-555-867-5309"
            });
        });
</script>
```

This example assumes that your phone link has an `id` of `phone-link`, like this: `<a id="phone-link" href="tel:+15558675309">`. The `tel:` protocol is what makes a phone number tappable on mobile devices. Once the event appears in your analytics data, you mark it as a goal (as described in the next section) and every call your website generates shows up in your tracking.

TIP

These examples use GA4's `gtag()` function. If you're using a different analytics tool, the syntax is different but the pattern is identical: an event listener fires when the visitor takes an action, and you call your tool's tracking function inside it. Plausible uses `plausible('goal_name')`. Fathom uses `fathom.trackGoal()`. Matomo uses `_paq.push()`. Check your tool's documentation for the exact syntax.

# Marking events as goals

Once a custom event is appearing in your analytics data, you tell your tool it matters. The specifics vary by platform — in GA4 you navigate to Admin ➪ Data Display ➪ Events and toggle Mark as Key Event next to the event; in Matomo you go to Administration > Goals; Plausible and Fathom have goal-creation screens accessible from their dashboards — but the concept is universal: you're elevating a regular event into something your reports track prominently.

After marking your goals, give your analytics tool a few days to collect data before drawing any conclusions. Then look for the goal completion count alongside your traffic data. The number you really want to watch over time is your *goal completion rate,* the percentage of sessions that resulted in a goal completion. If you're getting 500 sessions per week and 12 contact form submissions, that's a 2.4 percent rate. Whether that's good depends on your industry and site type, but it gives you a baseline. If next month the rate drops to 1.2 percent without a change in traffic, something changed in the visitor experience and you should investigate it.

Once marked, your goals appear in dedicated goal reports alongside your traffic data. Now you can see not only how many people visited but also how many of them did something that matters to your business, which is a far more useful number than raw visitor counts alone.

# Building Custom Reports

The preset reports in most analytics tools are designed for the widest possible range of users, which means they're not optimized for *your* specific questions. When you want to ask something such as "Which traffic source drives the most contact form submissions?" or "Which pages do visitors typically view before they submit a form?" the standard reports often can't answer directly.

Most serious analytics tools include some kind of report builder. GA4 calls it Explore. Matomo calls it Custom Reports. The concept is the same everywhere: you choose which *dimensions* (categorical data, such as traffic source or page title) you want to see alongside which *metrics* (numbers, such as sessions or goal completions), and the tool assembles the view.

Say you want to see which of your traffic sources is driving the most goal completions. In a standard acquisition report, you can see sessions per channel. In a custom report, you can add goal completions as a second metric and immediately see both numbers side by side, which tells you not just which channel sends the most traffic but also which one sends the most *valuable* traffic.

Custom reports take a few minutes to build and can surface insights the standard views miss. Most tools let you save your custom reports for later, so you don't have to rebuild them every week. Once you've created a view you find genuinely useful — say, a breakdown of traffic sources by goal completions for the past 30 days — save it with a descriptive name. Over time, a small library of saved reports becomes a significant time-saver for your weekly check-ins.

One more useful feature in most analytics platforms: you can share reports with others who have access to your account. This feature matters when you're working with a marketing agency, a web developer, or a business partner who needs to see performance data. Most tools let you invite collaborators with limited permissions. For example, view-only access keeps your settings safe while giving collaborators the visibility they need.

# Making Data-Driven Decisions

When you first get analytics set up, you run the risk of becoming obsessed with it. Checking the numbers every hour. Watching the Realtime report. Refreshing. Refreshing again. (I'm not saying I've done this. I'm not *not* saying it either.)

Individual data points almost never mean anything on their own. One slow Tuesday is noise. One traffic spike from a single social post proves nothing. Analytics becomes useful when you look for patterns over time, and patterns take weeks, sometimes months, to become visible.

## The weekly check-in habit

The most useful analytics habit is a weekly check-in: 15 minutes, same day and time each week, looking at the same small set of metrics. Compare this week to last week, or this month to the same month last year. Consistency is what lets you distinguish signal from noise.

It also keeps you from making reactive decisions based on a single data point. If traffic dips sharply one week, the temptation is to immediately change something, such as your SEO, social posts, or page content. But before reacting, ask whether there's a simple explanation. Was last week a holiday? Did a major news event reduce overall browsing? Did you get a burst of bot traffic that inflated last week's numbers? Context matters as much as the numbers themselves, and the weekly habit is what gives you enough context to tell the difference.

Here are five questions to ask every week:

- **Are more or fewer people visiting than last period?** A consistent downtrend over several weeks is significant and should be checked into right away. A sudden spike is also something to investigate: did you get a mention somewhere, run a promotion, or publish something that got widely shared?
- **Where is my traffic coming from?** Is any channel growing or shrinking significantly? Declining organic search traffic over several weeks is often an early warning of an SEO issue that needs looking into (as I discuss in Book 7).
- **What's my top landing page?** Is it the page you *want* visitors arriving on? If your About page draws more traffic than your home page, that might be fine, or it might indicate something's amiss.

- **Are visitors completing my goals?** If traffic is steady but goal completions are dropping, something changed. A form might have broken, a page might be loading slowly, or a call-to-action might have been accidentally buried.
- **Is any page showing an unusual exit rate?** A page that's normally healthy but suddenly shows high exits often has a broken element, such as a 404 link, a missing image, or a form that stopped submitting. Catching these in your weekly check-in is much better than waiting for a customer to complain.

## Spotting patterns versus chasing noise

The hardest skill in analytics is knowing when to act on what you see and when to wait for more data. One bad week is almost never a reason to overhaul your site. A consistent downward trend over six or eight weeks usually is.

A useful test before making any change based on data: can you see the same pattern in at least three separate metrics? One week of low traffic? That's probably noise, but a quick check to make sure that a recent technical change hasn't broken something might be warranted. Three consecutive weeks of declining organic traffic, falling engagement, and rising exits on your main landing pages? That's a pattern to put on your investigation to-do list. The goal is to act on genuine trends, not react to daily fluctuations that usually correct themselves on their own.

Seasonality is also something to take into account for. Most websites have natural traffic cycles, such as lower traffic over holiday periods and higher traffic when people return to normal routines. A traffic drop in the last week of December probably says more about the calendar than about your site. Before concluding that something is wrong, check whether the same dip appeared at the same time last year. If it did, it's almost certainly seasonal, not a problem you need to fix.

## Translating data into action

Analytics data is only valuable if it leads to something. When you notice a pattern — high exits on your pricing page, for instance — form a hypothesis. "Visitors are leaving because the call-to-action is too far down the page." Make one change based on that hypothesis. Wait two or three weeks, and then check whether the numbers moved.

Change one thing at a time. If you redesign the page, rewrite the copy, *and* add a new call-to-action all at once, you won't know which change caused the result. Small, isolated changes produce cleaner data and clearer lessons. A change that doesn't help is still informative because it tells you the problem lies somewhere else.

## When to ask for help

Some analytics questions benefit from outside expertise. If you're seeing a sustained traffic decline and can't identify the cause, an SEO specialist can audit your site for technical issues (as I describe in Book 7, Chapter 4). If traffic is healthy but goal completions are mysteriously low, a UX designer can run a user testing session and watch real people interact with your site, which usually surfaces problems that no amount of analytics data would reveal on its own.

For most small-business owners, though, the approach in this chapter is enough: pick a tool, install it, check in weekly, and make small deliberate changes based on what you find. The process isn't glamorous. But that habit, maintained over months and years, is what separates websites that quietly grow from websites that stay exactly where they are.

IN THIS CHAPTER

» Understanding Core Web Vitals

» Making your images load faster

» Shrinking your code

» Checking your site performance

# Chapter 2

# Website Performance Optimization

*80–90% of the end-user response time is spent on the front-end. Start there.*

—STEVE SOUDERS

Here's a sobering statistic: 53 percent of mobile visitors will flat-out abandon a website if it takes more than three seconds to load. Three seconds! Blame social media and smartphone addiction all you want, but in roughly the time it takes you to say "loading, loading, loading" out loud, more than half your visitors are already gone. They didn't go to a competitor's site, by the way — at least, not yet. They just gave up and did something else, such as wondering why websites are so slow.

Speed, therefore, is a vital user experience issue, but remember, too, that Google uses page performance as a ranking factor. So, a slow site both frustrates visitors and slides quietly down the search results while faster sites climb past it. Speeding up your site, which is the topic of this chapter, is one of the highest-return investments you can make, and none of what you learn here requires a computer science degree to pull off.

# Understanding Core Web Vitals

I introduce Core Web Vitals in Book 7, Chapter 1 in the context of search engine optimization. Now it's time to take a closer look at these crucial metrics. If you've done the work to optimize your content and SEO (as I describe in Book 7), strong Core Web Vitals can give you the edge over a competitor with similar content but a slower site.

## LCP: The big picture loads fast

*LCP* stands for *Largest Contentful Paint*, which is a fancy-schmancy way of measuring how long it takes for the main content to appear. More precisely, it measures the time from when the page starts loading to when the largest visible element — usually a hero image, a large heading, or a banner — finishes rendering.

Why the largest element? Because that's what visitors are waiting for. A page might technically load in one second if you count the first few pixels appearing, but if the big hero image takes five seconds to show up, the visitor still feels like they're staring at a blank screen. LCP captures that experience.

The targets are:

- **Good:** 2.5 seconds or less
- **Needs improvement:** 2.5 to 4.0 seconds
- **Poor:** More than 4.0 seconds

The most common culprits for a slow LCP are large, unoptimized images and render-blocking code, both of which I cover later in this chapter.

## INP: Clicks that feel instant

*INP*, which stands for *Interaction to Next Paint*, measures how quickly your page responds to every click, tap, or keypress a visitor makes. And not just the first one, but all of them throughout the visit.

So, while LCP measures whether the page loaded fast, INP measures whether the page *feels* fast while you're using it. A dropdown menu that hesitates for half a second before opening or a button that seems to need a moment to think before reacting are INP problems.

The targets are:

- **Good:** 200 milliseconds or less
- **Needs improvement:** 200 to 500 milliseconds
- **Poor:** More than 500 milliseconds

Most beginners don't have serious INP problems unless they've loaded a lot of heavy JavaScript onto their pages. Keep your scripts lean and you'll usually be fine.



## CLS: The jumping page problem

*CLS* stands for *Cumulative Layout Shift*, and if you've ever been reading a page and had an ad or image suddenly pop in and push halfway down the screen the text you were about to click, you've experienced a CLS problem firsthand. You hate it when that happens, so you better believe your visitors will hate it if it happens on your pages.

CLS measures how much the visible page content shifts around during loading. It's scored differently from the other two metrics. Instead of seconds, it uses a unitless score calculated from how much content moved and how far it moved.

The targets are:

- **Good:** 0.1 or less
- **Needs improvement:** 0.1 to 0.25
- **Poor:** More than 0.25

The most common causes of layout shift are images without defined dimensions (so the browser doesn't know how much space to reserve); fonts that swap in after the page loads and change the text size; and third-party content such as ads, videos, and social media widgets that inject themselves into the page after it's displayed. I show you later how to address each of these.

## Checking your Core Web Vitals

The easiest way to check your scores is Google PageSpeed Insights (`pagespeed.web.dev`). Paste in any URL and click Analyze, and you'll get both lab data (simulated performance) and field data (real-world results if your page has enough traffic). The results are color-coded: green for good, orange for needs improvement, red for poor.

TIP

If your site is new or low-traffic, PageSpeed Insights may not show field data yet because Google doesn't have enough real-world measurements for your URL. That's fine, because the lab data is still useful for diagnosis.

Google Search Console (`search.google.com/search-console`) is another place to check Core Web Vitals, and it's arguably more useful for sitewide patterns. Under the Experience section, you'll find a Core Web Vitals report that shows which pages on your site are passing and which are failing, grouped by issue type. Looking at the report is a much faster way to find problems across a large site than checking each page individually.

# Image Optimization Techniques

Images are almost certainly the single biggest drag on your website's performance. A typical web page weighs somewhere between 2 and 5 megabytes, and images usually account for 60 to 70 percent of that weight. You could spend hours optimizing your CSS and JavaScript and save a few kilobytes, or you could spend 20 minutes optimizing your images and save several megabytes. Do the images first.

Happily, image optimization is one of the most approachable performance improvements you can make. No server configuration, no build tools, no command line required. (Well, mostly not. I'll warn you if something gets fancier than dragging a file into a web browser.)

## Choosing the right image format

Not all image formats are created equal, and choosing the wrong one for the job is like packing a suitcase by throwing things in randomly and then sitting on the lid to force it shut. (It works, but there's a better way.)

Here's the rundown:

- **JPEG:** Best for photographs and images with lots of colors and gradients. JPEGs compress well at the cost of some quality. Typically, a quality setting between 70 and 85 percent gives you a small file with acceptable quality. If your site has food photos, product shots, or any kind of photography, JPEG is probably your default. Even better, consider using *progressive JPEG,* which loads the image in multiple passes. The user sees a blurry image that gradually sharpens, which makes the image loading appear faster than standard JPEG's line-by-line loading.

- **PNG:** Best for images that need a transparent background, logos, icons, and anything with sharp edges or text. PNGs are lossless, meaning they don't degrade with compression, but they tend to be larger than JPEGs for photographic content. Don't use PNG for photos. Please.
- **WebP:** A modern format developed by Google that, when set to create lossy files, offers better compression than both JPEG and PNG. We're talking 25 to 35 percent smaller than an equivalent JPEG, with similar or better quality. All modern browsers support it. If you're creating new images for your site, WebP is the right choice in most cases.
- **AVIF:** Even newer than WebP, with even better compression when it's set to create lossy files. AVIF files can be 50 percent smaller than equivalent JPEGs. Browser support is now excellent (all major browsers), but encoding can be slow with some tools. Use it if your tools support it; otherwise WebP is a fine alternative.
- **SVG:** SVG is for vector graphics such as logos, icons, and illustrations. Because SVG is a text-based format that describes shapes mathematically, SVG files scale to any size without losing quality and are often tiny. If your logo is currently a PNG, converting it to an SVG is one of the best image upgrades you can make.



REMEMBER

If you're using a platform such as WordPress, Squarespace, or Shopify, check whether it already converts uploaded images to WebP automatically. Many platforms added this feature in recent years. If yours does, you're already getting this optimization for free.

## Squeezing files down with compression tools

Even after you choose the right format, there's usually more compression to be had. These tools are the simplest way to do it:

- **Squoosh (squoosh.app):** Google's free, browser-based image compression tool. Drag in an image, choose your output format (WebP, AVIF, JPEG, and others), adjust the quality slider, and compare the before-and-after side by side. It's genuinely fun to use, and you'll watch file sizes shrink dramatically in real time. For a site such as Orbital Donuts, compressing a 3MB hero photo of the Galaxy Glazed down to 280KB without any visible quality difference is entirely realistic.

- **TinyPNG (`tinypng.com`):** Despite the name, it handles both PNG and JPEG. Drag files in, download the compressed versions. It uses smart compression algorithms that reduce file size without the quality degradation you'd get from simply lowering the quality slider. The free tier handles up to 20 files at a time.
- **ImageOptim (`imageoptim.com`):** A desktop app for macOS that strips hidden metadata (GPS coordinates, camera settings, color profiles) from images and runs them through several compression algorithms. It's particularly useful for batch-processing a folder of images. Windows users have similar options in FileOptimizer and related tools.

For most beginners, Squoosh is the right starting point. It's free, requires no installation, and the visual before-and-after comparison makes it easy to find the right balance between file size and quality.

## Lazy loading: Images that wait their turn

By default, when someone loads a web page, the browser downloads *all* the images on that page, even the ones way down at the bottom that the visitor might never scroll to see. On a page with a lot of images, that's a lot of unnecessary downloading right at the moment when the visitor is most likely to give up and leave.

*Lazy loading* fixes this. It tells the browser to download an image only when it's about to scroll into view. For visitors who read the whole page, they'll see every image, but the images will be loaded progressively as they scroll. For visitors who don't scroll to the bottom (which, let's be honest, is a lot of them), those images never download.

The implementation is wonderfully simple:

```
<img src="galaxy-glazed-donut.webp"
     alt="Galaxy Glazed donut with purple and blue icing"
     width="800" height="600"
     loading="lazy">
```

That one attribute — `loading="lazy"` — is all it takes. Add it to every image on your page that isn't in the first visible section (the "above the fold" area). Don't add it to your most important images, such as a hero photo at the very top of the page, since those should load immediately.

Note that I also included the `width` and `height` attributes in the example. Those are important for CLS: by telling the browser the image's dimensions upfront, the browser can reserve the right amount of space before the image loads, preventing the layout shift problem I describe earlier in this chapter.

# Responsive images: The right size for every screen

A visitor on a phone has a screen that's maybe 390 pixels wide. If you're serving them the same 1,920-pixel-wide hero image that desktop visitors see, you're making them download about five times more data than they need. That's wasteful for your server bandwidth and painfully slow for the visitor.

HTML's `srcset` attribute solves this by letting you provide multiple versions of an image at different sizes, with instructions for the browser to pick the right one:

```
<img src="donut-hero-800.webp"
     srcset="donut-hero-400.webp 400w,
             donut-hero-800.webp 800w,
             donut-hero-1600.webp 1600w"
     sizes="(max-width: 600px) 400px,
            (max-width: 1200px) 800px,
            1600px"
     alt="Orbital Donuts signature collection"
     width="1600" height="900">
```

The `srcset` attribute lists the available image files with their widths. The `sizes` attribute tells the browser which size to use under different screen conditions. A phone gets the 400px version; a tablet gets the 800px version; a large desktop gets the 1600px version. The browser does the choosing automatically.

TIP

WordPress generates responsive image markup automatically when you upload images through the media library. Many other platforms do the same. Check your platform's documentation before spending time creating multiple versions of every image by hand.

# The picture element: Art direction for different screens

The `srcset` attribute handles serving the same image at different sizes, which is perfect for scaling a photo up or down. But sometimes a smaller screen needs more than a scaled-down version; it needs a different *composition.* A wide landscape hero shot that looks beautiful on a desktop monitor might be a confusing, hard-to-read thumbnail when squeezed onto a phone screen. That's where the `picture` element comes in.

The `picture` element lets you specify different images for different screen conditions. Designers call this *art direction:* the deliberate choice of a different crop, angle, or framing to suit the viewing context, rather than just a differently sized copy of the same shot.

Here's what it looks like in practice:

```
<picture>
  <source media="(max-width: 600px)"
          srcset="donut-hero-square-600.webp">
  <source media="(max-width: 1200px)"
          srcset="donut-hero-landscape-1200.webp">
  <img src="donut-hero-landscape-1600.webp"
       alt="Orbital Donuts storefront at night, glowing neon"
       width="1600" height="900">
</picture>
```

The browser reads the `source` elements from top to bottom and uses the first one whose `media` condition matches the visitor's screen. A phone visitor sees a square crop (better for portrait orientation), a tablet visitor sees a landscape version at 1200px, and a desktop visitor gets the full-width shot. The `<img>` tag at the end is the fallback, both for desktop visitors (no `<source>` matched) and for older browsers that don't understand `<picture>`. Always include that fallback `<img>`.

Note that there's no `loading="lazy"` or `width`/`height` on the `<source>` tags; those attributes go on the `<img>` fallback, and the browser applies them to whichever source it ends up using.

TIP

Don't reach for `<picture>` just to serve different sizes — that's what `srcset` is for and it's simpler to implement. Reserve `<picture>` for genuine art direction situations: a product shot that needs to be cropped more tightly on a mobile device, a wide banner that needs to become a square tile, or a complex infographic that needs a simplified version at small sizes.

# Minifying and Compressing Your Code

Your CSS and JavaScript files are full of things that make life easier for human readers, such as spaces for indentation, returns after each line of code, blank lines, and comments. Browsers don't need any of that. Browsers just need the instructions. All those extra spaces, newlines, and comments are bytes that get sent over the network for no functional reason.

*Minification* is the process of stripping all that human-friendly formatting out of your code files to make them as small as possible. The programming still works the same; it's just compacted into a dense agglomeration of nearly indecipherable (for humans, but not for browsers) code. Here's a quick before-and-after to make the concept concrete.

Before minification:

```
/* Navigation menu styles */
.nav-menu {
    display: flex;
    flex-direction: row;
    gap: 20px;
    background-color: navy;
    padding: 16px 24px;
}
```

After minification:

```
.nav-menu{display:flex;flex-direction:row;gap:20px;background-
   color:navy;padding:16px 24px}
```

The before code is 146 characters, while the after code is a mere 91. It's the same result for the browser, but a noticeably smaller file to download. For small chunks of code, the savings are usually modest. But for, say, a large JavaScript file, minification can cut the file size by up to 50 percent.

## Tools for minifying CSS and JavaScript

If you're using a platform such as WordPress, a caching plug-in (which I cover in the next section) typically handles minification automatically. For hand-coded sites, these tools do the job:

- **CSS Minifier (`cssminifier.com`):** Paste in your CSS, get minified CSS back. That's it. Download the result and replace your original file (keeping the original as a backup, obviously).
- **Terser (`terser.org`):** The standard tool for minifying JavaScript. There's an online playground at `terser.org/playground` where you can paste and minify JavaScript in your browser. The output will look like someone sneezed on a keyboard, but it works.
- **Build tools:** If you're working on a more complex project, tools such as Vite, Parcel, and webpack can automate minification as part of a build process. These tools are a bit beyond the scope of this chapter, but worth knowing about when your project grows.

## Server-side compression: Gzip and Brotli

Here's a separate and complementary trick: even after you've minified your files, your web server can compress them *further* before sending them to the browser. This is called HTTP compression, and the two formats are *Gzip* (the older, nearly universal standard) and *Brotli* (newer, better compression, supported by all modern browsers).

Think of it like stuffing a sweater into a vacuum bag before shipping it. The sweater is the same sweater, just compressed for transit. The browser inflates it on arrival and uses it normally.

Most web hosts and CDNs have Gzip and Brotli enabled by default. You can verify your server's compression by entering your URL at a tool such as GiftOfSpeed (`giftofspeed.com`) or by checking the Network tab in Chrome DevTools (look for `Content-Encoding: br` for Brotli or `Content-Encoding: gzip` for Gzip in the response headers).

If you're on shared hosting and need to enable Gzip manually, adding these lines to your site's `.htaccess` file (Apache servers) usually does the trick:

```
<IfModule mod_deflate.c>
    AddOutputFilterByType DEFLATE text/html text/css
    AddOutputFilterByType DEFLATE application/javascript
    AddOutputFilterByType DEFLATE image/svg+xml
</IfModule>
```

WARNING

Don't add code to your `.htaccess` file without making a backup first. A syntax error in `.htaccess` can take your entire site offline, and that's a rough afternoon. Back up the original, make your change, and test immediately.

# Caching: Making Browsers Remember

Every time a visitor loads a page on your site, their browser downloads your logo, your CSS, your JavaScript files, and all your images. Every single time. That means a visitor who comes to the Orbital Donuts site on Monday, and then again on Tuesday, downloads all those same files twice, even though nothing changed.

*Browser caching* solves this by letting the browser know that a particular file isn't going to change for a while, so it should keep a copy. That way, the next time the browser needs the file, it can use its copy instead of downloading the file all over again. The browser stores the file locally (in its *cache*), and subsequent page loads are dramatically faster because the visitor's browser doesn't have to download the same assets over and over.

From the visitor's perspective, the effect is almost magical. The first visit loads at normal speed. Every return visit loads almost instantly.

## How browser caching works

Caching is controlled by HTTP headers that your server sends along with each file. The most important one is `Cache-Control`, which tells the browser how long to keep the file before checking for a newer version.



Here's an example of what this looks like in an `.htaccess` file for an Apache server:

```
<IfModule mod_expires.c>
    ExpiresActive On
    ExpiresByType image/webp "access plus 1 year"
    ExpiresByType image/jpeg "access plus 1 year"
    ExpiresByType text/css "access plus 1 month"
    ExpiresByType application/javascript "access plus 1 month"
    ExpiresByType text/html "access plus 1 day"
</IfModule>
```

This tells browsers to cache images for a year, CSS and JavaScript for a month, and HTML pages for just a day. Why different durations? Because images and scripts change infrequently, while the HTML content (the page text) changes more often and should be refreshed more frequently.

REMEMBER

If you change a CSS or JavaScript file and your browser has it cached, visitors might keep seeing the old version until their cache expires. The solution is called *cache busting:* appending a version number or timestamp to the filename, such as `styles.css?v=2` or `styles-v2.css`. This makes the browser treat it as a new file and bypasses the cache.

## Caching plugins for WordPress

If your site runs on WordPress, you don't need to edit `.htaccess` by hand (thank goodness). A caching plug-in handles all of this (and often more) through a friendly interface:

- **W3 Total Cache (`wordpress.org/plugins/w3-total-cache`):** One of the most comprehensive WordPress caching plug-ins, with options for page caching, database caching, minification, CDN integration, and more. It has a lot of settings, which can be overwhelming, but the defaults work well for most sites.

- **WP Super Cache (`wordpress.org/plugins/wp-super-cache`):** A simpler alternative that generates static HTML files from your WordPress pages, which serve much faster than dynamically generated pages. Easier to configure than W3 Total Cache, and excellent for sites that don't update content constantly.
- **WP Rocket (`wp-rocket.me`):** A premium plug-in (not free) that many WordPress developers swear by. It combines caching, minification, lazy loading, CDN integration, and several other optimizations in one clean interface. If you'd rather pay for simplicity than fiddle with free plug-in settings, WP Rocket is worth the cost.

### What to cache (and what not to)

Not everything should be cached aggressively. A useful rule of thumb: static assets (images, CSS, JavaScript, fonts) that don't change often can be cached for a long time, such as weeks or months. HTML pages, which contain your content and might change daily, should be cached for a shorter period or not at all.

Some content should never be cached: anything personalized to the individual visitor (a logged-in user's dashboard, shopping cart contents, checkout pages), because caching those pages could mean one visitor sees another visitor's information. That would be bad. *Very* bad.

Most caching plug-ins handle this problem automatically by excluding pages such as `wp-admin`, cart, and checkout from caching. But if you're setting up caching manually, keep this in mind.

## Preloading Critical Resources

Most of the techniques in this chapter are about telling the browser what to skip or delay: lazy load this image, defer that script, cache these assets. An equally useful approach works in the opposite direction: telling the browser about important resources earlier than it would naturally find them. That's what *preloading* does. Instead of waiting for the browser to discover a critical resource while parsing HTML, you give it a heads-up in the `<head>` section so it can start downloading right away.

To understand why this matters, think about how a browser processes a page. It downloads the HTML first, and then works through it top to bottom. A CSS link near the top triggers a pause while that stylesheet downloads. The stylesheet might reference a web font, which triggers another download. By the time the browser finally discovers your hero image — maybe deep in the HTML, or referenced from CSS as a background image — it's already spent time executing a chain of sequential steps. Preloading short-circuits that chain for the resources that matter most.

## Preloading your hero image

To ensure that your page's hero image shows up early in the loading process, add a `<link rel="preload">` tag for the image in the `<head>` section of your page. This tag tells the browser to start downloading the image right away, even though it hasn't encountered the `<img>` tag in the code just yet. The browser kicks off the download immediately, in parallel with everything else, so the image is ready much sooner.

Here's what it looks like:

```
<head>
  <link rel="preload"
        href="galaxy-glazed-hero.webp"
        fetchpriority="high"
        as="image">
</head>
```

The `fetchpriority="high"` attribute tells the browser to fetch the image at a high priority relative to the page's other external resources. The `as="image"` attribute tells the browser what kind of resource this is so it can assign the right priority and apply the correct security policies. Without `as`, the preload hint is ignored by some browsers.

WARNING

Only preload the single most important image on the page, such as the hero image that directly contributes to your LCP score. Preloading multiple images doesn't help and can even hurt performance by consuming bandwidth that the browser would otherwise use for genuinely critical resources. When in doubt, leave it out.

## Preloading fonts

Fonts are another resource the browser discovers late. A web font is referenced in a CSS file, which means the browser has to download the HTML, download the CSS, parse the CSS, and *then* discover the font URL. That's three round trips before the font download even begins. In the meantime, your page is displaying text in a fallback font (or no text at all). Preloading moves the font download to happen in parallel with that CSS download, shaving off one or two of those sequential steps.

Here's an example:

```
<head>
  <link rel="preload"
        href="/fonts/orbital-regular.woff2"
        as="font"
        type="font/woff2"
        crossorigin>
</head>
```

The `crossorigin` attribute is required for font preloading, even when the font is hosted on your own server. Fonts are fetched using a CORS request, and without `crossorigin`, the browser may end up downloading the font twice: once for the preload hint and once when it encounters the actual `@font-face` rule.

Preload only the font weights and styles that appear on the page immediately. If you're using a regular weight for body text and a bold weight for headings, preload both. If you have italic or condensed variants that appear only further down the page, let those load normally.

## DNS prefetching for third-party resources

Every connection your page makes to a third-party server, such as Google Fonts, an analytics script, a social media widget, or a CDN, starts with a DNS lookup: the browser has to convert the hostname into an IP address before it can even begin the connection. On a fast network, a single DNS lookup takes 20–60 milliseconds. That might not sound like much, but if your page makes connections to five third-party servers, that's 100–300 milliseconds of pure overhead before a single byte of content is transferred.

DNS prefetching tells the browser to perform these lookups early, in the background, while the page is still loading. The syntax is minimal:

```
<head>
  <link rel="dns-prefetch" href="//fonts.googleapis.com">
  <link rel="dns-prefetch" href="//www.google-analytics.com">
  <link rel="dns-prefetch" href="//cdn.jsdelivr.net">
</head>
```

By the time the browser needs to connect to these servers, the DNS lookups are already done. The connections start immediately instead of waiting for the lookups to complete. It's free performance: one line per domain, no configuration required.

TIP

To find which third-party domains your page connects to, open Chrome DevTools, go to the Network tab, and filter by Other or look at the Domain column. Every unique domain that isn't yours is a candidate for a DNS prefetch hint. Domains you load fonts, scripts, or analytics from are the most valuable targets.



# Mobile Performance Optimization

More than half of all web traffic comes from mobile devices, and mobile users are often on cellular connections that are slower than the broadband connection you're testing on at your desk. A page that feels acceptably fast on your laptop's Wi-Fi might feel painfully slow on a phone with three bars of LTE in an area with heavy network traffic. You need to test and optimize specifically for mobile, not just assume that "it's fast on my machine" translates to fast everywhere.

## Render-blocking resources

When a browser loads a web page, it works through the HTML from top to bottom. When it encounters a `<link>` tag loading a CSS file, it stops and downloads that CSS before continuing. When it encounters a `<script>` tag loading a JavaScript file, it stops again. These are called *render-blocking resources* because they block the browser from rendering (displaying) the page while it waits for them to download.

On a fast desktop connection, this pause is barely noticeable. On a slow mobile connection, each render-blocking resource adds perceptible delay to the time before anything appears on screen.

The fix is a one-two approach. First, make sure your CSS `<link>` tags are in the `<head>` section of your HTML, which is normal best practice. Second, move your JavaScript to the bottom of the `<body>` section or add the `defer` attribute:

```
<!-- This blocks rendering while the script downloads -->
<script src="app.js"></script>

<!-- This loads the script without blocking rendering -->
<script src="app.js" defer></script>
```

The `defer` attribute tells the browser to download the script in the background while continuing to render the page, and then execute the script after the page has finished loading. For most JavaScript that isn't needed for the page's initial display, `defer` is the right choice.

### Font loading strategies

Web fonts are another common mobile performance culprit. When a browser encounters a CSS rule that references a web font, it needs to download that font file before it can display text styled with that font. Until the font arrives, the browser either shows nothing (called *FOIT*, flash of invisible text, by web developers) or shows a fallback font and then swaps in the web font once it's ready, causing a jarring flash (known in the trade as *FOUT*: flash of unstyled text).

The `font-display` CSS property gives you control over this behavior:

```
@font-face {
    font-family: 'Orbital';
    src: url('orbital-regular.woff2') format('woff2');
    font-display: swap;
}
```

The `swap` value tells the browser: show the fallback font immediately (so the visitor can start reading), and swap in the web font when it's ready. This choice is almost always the right one for body text. The font swap is usually barely noticeable and eliminates invisible text.

TIP

If you're loading fonts from Google Fonts, adding `&display=swap` to the Google Fonts URL achieves the same effect without writing your own `@font-face` rule. For example: `fonts.googleapis.com/css2?family=Open+Sans&display=swap`.

## Performance Monitoring Tools

All the optimization in the world means nothing if you don't know whether it's working. Fortunately, excellent tools for measuring site performance are available (most of them free!), and they'll tell you not just your scores but what to fix and how.

## Google PageSpeed Insights

Google PageSpeed Insights (`pagespeed.web.dev`) is the first tool to reach for. Enter any URL and it gives you performance scores for both mobile and desktop, broken down by the Core Web Vitals and a handful of other metrics. The score runs from 0 to 100:

- **90–100 (green):** Good
- **50–89 (orange):** Needs improvement
- **0–49 (red):** Poor



Scroll past the scores and you'll find two especially useful sections. The Opportunities section lists specific changes — such as optimizing images, removing unused CSS, deferring offscreen content — with estimated time savings for each one. The Diagnostics section flags issues that might not have an immediate, measurable effect but that matter for best practices and overall health.

The Opportunities section is your prioritized to-do list. Start with the items that show the largest time savings, because they'll have the biggest effect on your scores.

## Lighthouse in Chrome DevTools

Lighthouse is Google's open-source auditing tool, and it's built right into Chrome. Press F12 to open DevTools, click the Lighthouse tab, and then click Analyze Page Load. Lighthouse loads your website using your current machine's full network speed and CPU capacity. Once it records the raw load timeline (known as the *trace*), it runs a mathematical simulation to estimate how fast those same resources would load on a slower device (such as a mid-tier mobile phone on a 4G network). When the simulated dust clears, you get a report similar to PageSpeed Insights, complete with scores, opportunities, and diagnostics but based on your current browser session, which is useful for testing pages that require login or pages still in development.

Lighthouse also audits for accessibility, SEO, and best practices, not just performance. Running a Lighthouse audit on your site every few weeks is a good habit. It catches regressions — cases where something you changed made things worse — before your visitors notice.

**IN THIS CHAPTER**

- » **Checking your site in the major browsers**
- » **Testing on phones and tablets**
- » **Catching accessibility, speed, and broken-link problems**
- » **Getting honest feedback from users**
- » **Tracking and squashing bugs**

# Chapter 3

# Testing and Quality Assurance

*Testing leads to failure, and failure leads to understanding.*

—BURT RUTAN

It's a sad fact in the website-building business that the step most builders skip is the one that costs them the most. They spend weeks getting the design right, wrestling with CSS, tweaking the copy until it shines, and then they click Publish and call it done. No testing, no checking, no one-more-look. Just ship it and hope for the best.

I get it. Testing sounds like the boring part. And, yep, some of it is. But there's a significant difference between boring and unimportant. A site that looks gorgeous in your browser can look genuinely broken in someone else's. A page that loads instantly on your home Wi-Fi can take nine seconds on a phone with average cellular service. A form that works perfectly with a mouse can be an impassable obstacle for someone navigating with a keyboard.

This chapter covers the testing and quality assurance work that separates a professional website from a site that just sort of launched. Happily, none of this work requires specialized skills or expensive software. Most of the tools I cover here are straightforward to use and free. There's an investment, for sure, but it's an investment of time. The reward? Peace of mind and a good night's sleep.

# Cross-Browser Testing Strategies

You'd think that by now, every browser would display web pages identically. Alas, you'd be wrong. Browsers are crafted by competing companies — particularly Google, Apple, Mozilla, and Microsoft — using separate teams, mostly separate codebases (Chrome and Edge are both based on the Chromium open-source browser project), and separate interpretations of the web standards. They mostly agree on the basics, but they routinely diverge on newer CSS features, form element styling, font rendering, JavaScript behavior, and dozens of other details. Add different operating systems (macOS Safari renders fonts differently than Windows Chrome), and different browser versions, and you have a surprisingly wide range of ways browsers might render your site.

Those differences are trivial, though, right? Not always! Suppose you check your new navigation menu in Chrome for Windows. It looks perfect, so you ship it, but three weeks later a client emails to say the menu doesn't work on her phone. She's using Safari on an iPhone. You open Safari for the first time and — groan! — the dropdown has collapsed into a single unclickable line.

Cross-browser testing catches those problems before your clients do.

## Why browsers still disagree

Modern browsers are more compatible than they were in the chaotic early days when Internet Explorer and Netscape Navigator were locked in an arms race that gave us incompatible HTML tags and warring JavaScript engines. But compatible isn't the same as identical. A few areas still cause consistent trouble:

- **Newer CSS layout features:** While established layout tools such as CSS Grid and Flexbox work in all major modern browsers, newer layout features can have subtle rendering differences, particularly in Safari, which has historically lagged in implementing certain CSS specifications.
- **Form element styling:** Checkboxes, radio buttons, `<select>` dropdowns, and date pickers are notoriously inconsistent across browsers. Each browser has its own default visual treatment, and overriding those defaults works differently everywhere.

- **Font rendering:** macOS renders text with anti-aliasing that makes fonts appear slightly heavier than the same fonts on Windows. This usually isn't a serious problem, but it can make lightweight fonts look noticeably different.
- **JavaScript edge cases:** Most modern JavaScript is consistent across browsers, but newer browser APIs and features vary in their level of support.

## The browsers you need for testing

You need to test your site using different browsers, but fortunately you don't need to test it in every browser ever made. You just need to test in the browsers your visitors use. The breakdown, as of this writing, looks roughly like this:

- **Chrome:** The most popular browser, by far, with about 65 percent of global desktop traffic. So, if your site works in Chrome, you've covered the majority. Ah, but majority isn't everybody, so read on.
- **Safari:** The default browser on every iPhone, iPad, and Mac, which means roughly 19 percent of visitors worldwide and a significantly higher share on mobile devices. Safari is, in many developers' experience, the new Internet Explorer, meaning it's the browser most likely to behave differently from everything else. Test here carefully.
- **Edge:** Around 5 percent of global market share. Edge is built on the same Chromium engine as Chrome, so it's nearly identical in behavior. It's still worth a quick look, but Edge problems are usually Chrome problems.
- **Firefox:** Down to around 3 to 4 percent of global traffic. That's low, sure, but still worth a quick check.

REMEMBER

You can check which browsers your visitors use in your analytics tool, as I cover in Book 9, Chapter 1. If your site serves a particular audience — enterprise business software users who are largely on Windows Chrome, say — you can prioritize your testing accordingly.

## Testing without owning every device

Unless you have a collection of laptops, tablets, and phones cluttering up your home office, you'll need tools to test across browsers and devices without owning them all. Here are the most useful options:

- **Chrome DevTools (free):** The device toolbar in Chrome DevTools (press F12 and click the phone/tablet icon near the top left of the panel) lets you emulate key aspects (such as viewport size and touch input) of hundreds of devices, including iPhones, Android phones, and tablets. Not a perfect substitute for real hardware, but it catches most layout and sizing problems quickly.

- **Firefox Developer Tools (free):** Similar device emulation to Chrome DevTools. Worth using for both Firefox-specific testing and viewport testing in one session.
- **BrowserStack (`browserstack.com`):** The gold standard for multi-browser testing. BrowserStack gives you real, remote browser instances running on real hardware. You can test on a dozen browser-and-OS combinations in an afternoon without owning any of them. Paid plans start around $29 per month; even a single day of access before a major launch is money well spent.
- **TestMU AI (`testmuai.com`):** A strong competitor to BrowserStack with a similar feature set and a slightly more generous free tier. Worth comparing prices before committing to either.
- **Polypane (`polypane.app`):** A developer browser that shows multiple viewport widths side by side simultaneously. Excellent for quickly checking layout across screen sizes, though it's not a substitute for full cross-browser testing.

TIP

When testing across browsers, pay special attention to navigation menus, forms, hover states, and CSS animations. Static pages with text and images are almost always fine. Interactive elements are where browser differences live.

# Mobile Device Testing

In 2025, more than 64 percent of all web traffic came from mobile devices. That number has climbed every year since smartphones became ubiquitous, and there's no sign of a reversal. If your site doesn't work well on a phone, it doesn't work well, full stop.

## Simulating phones in your browser

Chrome DevTools is your first stop for mobile testing. Here's how to use it:

1. **Open your page in Chrome.**
2. **Press F12 (or right-click anywhere on the page and choose Inspect).**
3. **Press Ctrl+Shift+M (⌘+Shift+M on macOS) to toggle the device toolbar.**

Your page now renders as it would on a mobile device. The toolbar at the top of the simulated device lets you pick from a long list of presets — iPhones, iPads, Galaxys, and many others — or you can set a custom viewport width and height.

Things to check while you're in the simulator:

- **Navigation:** Does your desktop navigation transform into a usable mobile menu? Hamburger menus, slide-out drawers, and stacked links are all common patterns. Confirm that your navigation opens, closes, and is usable at thumb-tap scale. If you use a sticky header or footer, make sure it sticks at the correct spot when you scroll.
- **Text size:** Is body text readable without zooming in? Google recommends a minimum of 16 pixels for body text on a mobile device. Anything smaller and visitors will be pinching and squinting.
- **Tap targets:** Are buttons and links large enough to tap with a finger? Apple's Human Interface Guidelines recommend at least 44 × 44 points for interactive elements. If a button requires a pencil tip to hit accurately, it's too small.
- **Images:** Do they scale correctly? An image that's 1,200 pixels wide on desktop shouldn't cause horizontal scrolling on a 390-pixel-wide phone screen.
- **Orientation:** Use the simulator to rotate the page into both portrait and landscape modes to make sure the page is readable and well laid out in both orientations.
- **Forms:** Fill out your forms while simulating a phone. Does the keyboard pop-up obscure the fields? Do dropdowns work? Are validation error messages visible?



REMEMBER

Don't be afraid to go against guidelines to ensure that your site renders well. Sure, Google recommends a 16-pixel minimum font size, but in my opinion that's way too small on a mobile device. Try a 20-pixel body font to see how it looks.

## Testing on slow connections

Your site might load in under a second on your office Wi-Fi. On a commuter's phone with a middling cellular signal, it might take eight seconds, which is the point at which many visitors give up and do something else.

Chrome DevTools lets you throttle your network connection to simulate different speeds. In the Network tab (press F12, then click Network), use the throttling dropdown — it defaults to No Throttling — and switch to Slow 4G or even 3G, which simulates a sluggish mobile connection. Now reload your page and watch carefully.

If your home page takes 12 seconds on Slow 4G or 3G, you've just discovered why some visitors are bouncing before they even see your content. The image compression and lazy loading techniques I cover in Book 9, Chapter 2 are the fixes to reach for first.

### Why simulation isn't always enough

Chrome DevTools simulation is fast and convenient, but it's not perfect. It doesn't replicate the browser engine of an iPhone, since iOS uses a modified version of WebKit, not Blink. It doesn't simulate the quirks of Android Chrome (such as dynamic address bar resizing). And it can't show you what happens when the phone keyboard pops up and covers the bottom half of the screen while someone is filling out a form.

Before launch, test on at least one real iPhone (using Safari) and one real Android phone (using Chrome). If you don't own both, borrow them. Even 10 minutes on a borrowed device often reveals something the simulator missed entirely.

## Accessibility Testing

Web accessibility — making your site usable by people with disabilities — gets its own dedicated chapter in Book 2, Chapter 4, where I cover the principles and the HTML patterns in depth. Here, in the context of testing, I want to focus on the practical tools you use to check your site's accessibility because writing accessible HTML and pulling it off successfully are two different things. Automated tools are how you close the gap between intention and reality.

### WAVE: Seeing your errors visually

WAVE (`wave.webaim.org`) is a free online tool that analyzes a web page and overlays visual indicators directly on the page to show accessibility issues. Red icons mark errors. Yellow icons mark alerts, which are potential problems worth investigating. Green icons confirm things that are working correctly.

To use WAVE, go to `wave.webaim.org` and enter your URL, or install the free WAVE browser extension for Chrome or Firefox, which lets you run the check with one click on any page, including password-protected pages that the online tool can't reach.

WAVE is particularly good at catching the following accessibility gaffes:

- **Missing alt text:** Images without descriptive text that screen readers can announce to visually impaired visitors.
- **Empty links:** Links with no readable text. A screen reader would announce these as simply "link," which tells the visitor nothing useful.
- **Low contrast:** Text that's too light against its background to read comfortably, which is a problem that affects not only people with low vision but anyone reading outdoors on a bright screen.
- **Missing form labels:** Input fields without labels that assistive technology can announce when the field is focused.
- **Heading structure problems:** Heading levels that skip incorrectly, such as jumping from an `<h2>` straight to an `<h4>`, or that repeat at the wrong level.

The visual overlay approach makes WAVE unusually beginner-friendly. You don't have to parse a technical report because you can see the problems sitting right on top of your page content.

TIP

Run WAVE on every page of your site, not just the home page. The home page usually gets the most attention during development. The contact page, product detail pages, and blog posts are where accessibility problems tend to hide.

## axe DevTools: Digging deeper

axe DevTools (`deque.com/axe/devtools`) is a browser extension that runs a more thorough accessibility audit than WAVE. The free version catches a solid range of issues; the paid Pro version goes deeper, but for most small sites the free tier is more than enough.

To use axe DevTools, install the free extension for Chrome or Firefox, open your page, press F12 to open DevTools, click the axe DevTools tab, and click Scan. Results appear within a few seconds. axe categorizes its findings by severity: critical, serious, moderate, and minor. It maps each issue to the relevant WCAG guideline, so you know exactly what the standard says and how to fix it.

Unlike WAVE's visual overlay, axe gives you a structured list with clear guidance on what you need to do. But this isn't an either/or situation because the two tools complement each other well: WAVE is better at showing you *where* problems are on the page; axe is better at explaining *what* the problem is and *how* to fix it. Use both.

### Lighthouse: The all-in-one checkup

Lighthouse is built directly into Chrome DevTools, which means you already have it and it costs nothing. It audits your page for performance, accessibility, SEO, and best practices all at once, generating a scored report from 0 to 100 in each category.

To run a Lighthouse audit, open your page in Chrome, press F12, click the Lighthouse tab, select the categories you want to audit (Accessibility is the focus here, but running all of them adds only about 20 seconds), and click Analyze Page Load. The report appears within about 30 seconds.

Lighthouse's accessibility score is based on automated checks against a subset of WCAG criteria. A score of 100 means your page passed every check. A score below 80 is a clear signal that something needs immediate attention.

One of the most common quick fixes that Lighthouse flags is missing ARIA labels on interactive elements. If your site has an icon-only button — such as a search icon, a close button, or a shopping cart icon — with no visible text, screen readers can't tell the visitor what it does. The fix is a simple `aria-label` attribute:

```
<button aria-label="Search the site">
  <img src="search-icon.svg" alt="">
</button>
```

The `aria-label` provides the text that screen readers announce. The empty `alt=""` on the image tells screen readers to skip the image, because the button's label already covers it.

## Speed Testing Tools

I cover Core Web Vitals, Google's framework for measuring page performance, in Book 9, Chapter 2. Speed testing tools are how you measure those vitals and pinpoint what's dragging your scores down. Two tools are worth knowing well.

### Google PageSpeed Insights

PageSpeed Insights (`pagespeed.web.dev`) is Google's free performance testing tool. Enter your URL, click Analyze, and within about 30 seconds you have two types of data:

- **Lab data:** A simulated page load run on Google's servers, giving you a consistent baseline you can compare across tests and over time.
- **Field data:** Real performance data collected from visitors using Chrome over the past 28 days. If your page is new or has low traffic, field data may not yet be available, but that's fine. The lab data is still plenty useful for diagnosis.

The report breaks down your Core Web Vitals scores (Largest Contentful Paint, Interaction to Next Paint, and Cumulative Layout Shift, which are all covered in Book 9, Chapter 2) and lists specific issues to fix, ranked by their potential impact on load time.

Pay particular attention to the Opportunities section, which lists concrete changes with estimated time savings. For example, you might get "Serve images in next-gen formats" with a potential savings of 1.4 seconds. That's work worth doing this afternoon. Or you might get "Eliminate render-blocking resources" with a 0.3-second savings. Okay, sure, that's also important, but do the images first. The return on your time is much higher.

Also check the Diagnostics section, which flags best-practice violations that affect performance indirectly, including faux pas such as serving images without explicit `width` and `height` attributes (which causes layout shift) or loading unnecessarily large JavaScript files.



## GTmetrix: The extra details

GTmetrix (`gtmetrix.com`) covers much of the same ground as PageSpeed Insights but with a few extras worth running alongside it:

- **Waterfall chart:** A detailed timeline showing every single request your page makes — HTML, CSS, JavaScript, images, fonts, third-party scripts — and how long each one takes. This is where you spot the specific file that's holding everything up. If your page makes 80 HTTP requests and 15 of them are from a single advertising script, you'll see it immediately.
- **Test locations:** GTmetrix can run tests from different geographic locations, including Toronto, London, and Hong Kong on the free plan. This location data is useful if your site serves visitors in multiple regions, since server response time varies significantly based on distance.
- **Video playback and filmstrip view:** GTmetrix records a video of your page loading and gives you a frame-by-frame filmstrip view. Watching a page load in slow motion is unexpectedly illuminating because you can see the moment layout shifts occur, or when your main image finally appears, or how long the page looks like a blank screen.

# Broken Link Checking

Here's an all-too-common minor tragedy that plays out on websites everywhere: a link that worked fine at launch at some point stops working because the page it points to was deleted, the target site's URL structure was reorganized, or a file was moved without updating the references. The link is now *broken.* It leads nowhere, and the visitor who clicks it gets a 404 error page instead of what they were expecting.

Broken links are a quiet embarrassment. They suggest to visitors (and search engines!) that a site isn't being maintained. And if the broken link is in your navigation or a prominent call to action, the embarrassment becomes all the more acute.

## Why broken links happen

Three situations cause most broken links:

- **External links:** You linked to an article on another site, and that site later reorganized its URL structure, deleted the content, or went offline. You have no control over external sites, which is why ongoing monitoring matters.
- **Internal links:** You renamed or moved a page on your own site and forgot to update all the links that pointed to it. Broken internal links are preventable, but they're easy to miss when a site has dozens or hundreds of pages.
- **Missing files:** You linked to a PDF, a downloadable resource, or an image that either never got uploaded or later got deleted or moved. The link lives on in your HTML; the file, alas, does not.

## Tools for finding broken links

Manually clicking every link on your site is not a use of your time I would recommend. Use a tool instead:

- **W3C Link Checker (`validator.w3.org/checklink`):** The World Wide Web Consortium's online link checker. Enter your URL, and it crawls your pages and reports every link that returns an error. Basic, but free and effective for smaller sites.
- **Screaming Frog SEO Spider (`screamingfrog.co.uk`):** A desktop app that crawls your entire site and reports on everything, including broken links,

missing alt text, duplicate page titles, and redirect chains. The free version crawls up to 500 URLs, which is sufficient for most small sites. If you have more than 500 pages, use the paid license, which runs $279 per year.

- **Broken Link Checker (`wordpress.org/plugins/broken-link-checker`):** If your site runs on WordPress, this plug-in monitors your content continuously and flags broken links in the dashboard as it finds them. Set it up once and it watches quietly in the background.
- **Dead Link Checker (`deadlinkchecker.com`):** A simple, free, web-based tool that checks a URL or full domain and can email you the results. Good for a periodic manual check on a static site.

WARNING

Run a full link check at least once a month. External links in particular have a habit of rotting quietly in the background. A site that's been live for a year or two may have a surprising number of links leading nowhere.

# User Testing Methods

All the automated tools in the previous sections test what you built. *User testing* tests whether what you built works for the folks who are going to use it, meaning the people who aren't you, who didn't build it, and who have no idea where you hid the Contact page.

Here's the thing about your own website: you know too much. You know where everything is. You know what every button does. You've read every word of the copy so many times you've got it memorized. That familiarity makes you a genuinely terrible judge of whether your site is easy to use. You're too close to it.

User testing solves that problem by putting your site in front of people who have never seen it before and watching what happens. It's reliably humbling, occasionally hilarious, and consistently invaluable.

## Understanding user testing

User testing covers a wide range of methods, from elaborate laboratory studies with 50 participants to a 20-minute session with a single colleague. For most small site owners, the relevant question is: What's the simplest useful form of user testing I can do?

The relevant answer is just to watch someone try to accomplish a task on your site. Give them a specific goal — "find the contact form," or "figure out how much it costs to cater an event for 30 people" — and then watch without helping. Take notes on where they hesitate, get confused, or give up.

That's user testing. No lab, no special equipment, no budget required.

## The hallway test

The *hallway test* (sometimes called *guerrilla testing*) is informal user testing conducted with whoever happens to be available, including colleagues, friends, family members, the person in the next office who owes you a favor. You need about five minutes, a laptop, and a task for your tester to attempt.

According to research by usability expert Jakob Nielsen, testing with just five people uncovers around 85 percent of a site's major usability problems. You don't need a large sample to find the significant issues. You need five people to try your site.

A simple hallway test session runs like this:

1. Give the tester a brief scenario. For example, "You're planning to order donuts for a birthday party and want to find out how to place a large group order."
2. Ask the person to think out loud. You want them to narrate what they're doing and what they're looking for while they do it.
3. Say nothing while they work. When they get confused — and at some point, they probably will — every instinct will tell you to help them. Don't. The confusion is the data you came for.
4. After they finish (or give up), ask what (if anything) they found confusing, what they expected to happen, and what they'd change if they could.
5. Write down what you observed immediately afterward, while it's still fresh and before you start editing your own notes.

## The five-second test

A five-second test answers a specific and important question: When someone lands on your page for the first time, can they immediately tell what it's for?

Show your home page (or any key landing page) to a tester for exactly five seconds. Then hide it. Ask: "What is this page for? What do you remember seeing? What would you do next?"

If they answer correctly, your hero section is doing its job. If they say "Um, something about space?" when looking at the Orbital Donuts home page, your messaging needs work. Five seconds is roughly how long a new visitor spends deciding whether to stay or leave. The five-second test simulates that decision under controlled conditions.

## Remote testing options

If you want to reach testers beyond your immediate circle, online platforms let you recruit participants and observe them remotely:

- **Maze (`maze.co`):** Creates test scenarios, recruits participants, and collects results automatically. The free plan allows a limited number of responses per month, which is often enough for a focused testing round before a launch.
- **Hotjar (`hotjar.com`):** Records visitor sessions on your live site. You can watch videos of people navigating your pages, see heatmaps showing where they're clicking, and spot confusing navigation patterns. Even watching 10 to 15 visitor sessions teaches you things you'd never discover through any other testing method.
- **Lookback (`lookback.com`):** A more structured platform for live moderated sessions, where you watch and talk with a participant in real time. More involved to set up, but useful for deeper qualitative research when you want to ask follow-up questions as they happen.

TIP

If you add a session recording tool such as Hotjar to your site, make sure you disclose it in your privacy policy. Recording visitor sessions is a form of data collection, and privacy regulations in many regions require you to inform visitors that it's happening. As I cover in Book 1, Chapter 4, privacy compliance is a legal requirement, not an optional add-on.



# Bug Tracking and Resolution

Bugs are places where your site doesn't behave as intended. A bug might be a button that does nothing when clicked; a form that throws a 500 error on submission; a page that looks fine in Chrome but has a broken layout in Safari; an image that's missing; or a link that goes to the wrong page. All websites have bugs; what separates good sites from messy ones is whether those bugs get found, documented, and fixed.

Some bugs are obvious immediately. Others lurk until a visitor hits just the right combination of browser, device, and screen size. You need to deal with them all.

## Writing a bug report that makes sense

The worst bug report in the world is: "*X* is broken" (where *X* is a form, a button, a link, or whatever). The person trying to fix it — which, for small sites, is usually you or a developer you hired — can't do anything useful with that.

A useful bug report has seven parts:

- **What happened:** A specific description of the observed behavior. Not "the form is broken" but "submitting the contact form with a valid email and message returns a 500 error and shows no confirmation message."
- **Steps to reproduce:** Exactly how to make the bug happen. "Go to `contact.html`, fill all fields with valid data, click Submit."
- **Reproducibility:** Note whether the bug appears every time you run the above steps, or only sometimes.
- **Expected behavior:** What should have happened. "The form should display a thank-you message and send a confirmation email to the address entered."
- **Severity:** How serious the bug is, from minor (say, a typo in a form label) to serious (nothing happens when you click the form's Submit button).
- **Environment:** The browser, operating system, and device type. "Chrome 154 on macOS Golden Gate. Also reproducible in Safari 27 on the same machine."
- **Screenshot or recording:** A picture is worth a thousand bug reports. Attach one whenever possible because many bugs are faster to understand by seeing them than by reading about them.

Bug reports that include all seven elements get fixed faster. That's not a productivity tip so much as basic cause and effect.

## Choosing your tracking tool

How you track bugs depends on how many you have and how your site is built. Options run from low-tech to purpose-built:

- **GitHub Issues (`github.com`):** If your site's code lives in a GitHub repository — and Book 10, Chapter 1 makes a strong case that it should — GitHub Issues are the natural place to log bugs. It's free, organized, linked directly to your code, and bugs can be automatically closed when a fix is pushed.

- **Trello (`trello.com`):** A visual board system that works well for tracking bugs alongside other to-do items. A simple board with columns for Found, In Progress, and Fixed is easy to set up and easy to read at a glance. Free for personal use.
- **Linear (`linear.app`):** A faster, cleaner issue-tracking tool aimed at developers. It's overkill for a solo project but excellent if a small team is involved. Linear has a generous free tier.
- **A plain spreadsheet:** Fine for small sites. Include columns for date found, description, steps to reproduce, priority, status, and date fixed. Not glamorous. Entirely effective.

Whatever you choose, the rule is simple: write it down. A bug that exists only in your memory has a remarkable habit of never getting fixed.

# Creating a Testing Checklist



All the testing in this chapter is most useful when it happens *systematically*, meaning not as a panicked last-minute sprint the night before launch but as a planned, step-by-step process you run on a schedule. A checklist converts "I should probably test this" into "I tested this, here's what I found, and here's what I fixed."

Here's a prelaunch testing checklist that covers everything in this chapter. Not every item applies to every site, so adapt it, make it yours, and update it when you discover something new. The goal isn't rigid compliance; it's making sure you've looked at your site from every angle before you point real visitors at it.

**Cross-browser testing:**

- Tested in Chrome (latest version).
- Tested in Safari (latest version, on macOS or a real iPhone).
- Tested in Firefox (latest version).
- Tested in Edge (latest version).
- Navigation, forms, and interactive elements confirmed as working in all tested browsers.

**Mobile testing:**

- Tested using Chrome DevTools device simulator (an iPhone Pro and a common Android device at minimum).
- Tested on at least one real iPhone (Safari) and one real Android phone (Chrome).
- Mobile navigation works correctly.
- All tap targets are large enough to use accurately with a finger.
- No horizontal scrolling on phone-sized screens.
- Page loads in an acceptable time on Slow 4G and 3G throttling.

**Accessibility:**

- WAVE scan completed, all errors resolved.
- axe DevTools scan completed, all Critical and Serious issues resolved.
- Lighthouse accessibility score at 90 or above.
- All images have descriptive alt text.
- All form fields have visible labels.
- Site is fully navigable using a keyboard alone (Tab, Enter, and arrow keys).

**Performance:**

- Google PageSpeed Insights run with a mobile score at 80 or above.
- All high-impact Opportunities from PageSpeed addressed or documented with a reason for deferring.
- GTmetrix waterfall chart reviewed for unexpectedly slow or surprising requests.

**Broken links:**

- Full link check completed (W3C Checker or Screaming Frog).
- All internal broken links fixed.
- All external broken links updated or removed.

**User testing:**

- At least three people have attempted the site's core tasks without assistance.
- All observed confusion points documented and addressed (or deferred with a clear reason).
- Five-second test run on the home page.

**Bugs:**

- All known bugs documented in your tracking tool of choice.
- All Critical-severity bugs resolved before launch.
- All remaining bugs triaged with a priority level and a resolution plan.

No checklist replaces judgment. You'll find items that don't apply to your situation, and you'll encounter edge cases no checklist anticipated. The purpose isn't to follow rules; it's to make sure you've looked before you leaped.

IN THIS CHAPTER

» Understanding the threats

» Locking down a WordPress site

» Setting up SSL/HTTPS

» Keeping accounts safe

» Scanning for malware

# Chapter 4

# Website Security Essentials

*It takes 20 years to build a reputation and a few minutes of cyber-incident to ruin it.*

—STÉPHANE NAPPO

Imagine you've spent months building the perfect storefront. The sign looks great, the shelves are stocked, the register works. And then you go home and leave the front door wide open. With the lights on. And a sign that says, "Help yourself."

That's basically what happens when you launch a website without thinking about security. Your site is public by definition. It's sitting on the internet, visible to everyone, including the people who spend their days looking for easy targets. Small-business websites get attacked constantly, not because hackers have a personal grudge against donut shops or yoga studios, but because they use automated tools that scan millions of sites looking for known weaknesses. If your site has one or more of those weak spots, the bad guys will probably find it.

Fortunately, you don't need to become a cybersecurity expert to protect your site. You just need to close the doors, lock the windows, and check in regularly. This chapter covers the practical security steps that matter most for small-business websites. You learn what the threats are, how to defend against them, and how to set up a simple routine that keeps your site safe without consuming your weekends.

# Common Security Threats Explained

Before you can defend your site, it helps to know what you're defending against. Security threats sound exotic and technical — SQL injection, cross-site scripting, brute-force attacks — but the underlying ideas are straightforward once you strip away the jargon. Let me walk you through the main ones.

## The bad guys and what they want

Most attackers targeting small websites aren't sophisticated criminal masterminds. They're running automated scripts that probe thousands of sites looking for easy wins. What do they want? A few things, mostly:

- **Your visitors' data:** Attackers steal email addresses, passwords, payment details, anything they can sell or use for phishing attacks.
- **Your server resources:** Compromised servers get used to send spam, mine cryptocurrency, or launch attacks on other sites. Your hosting bill quietly goes through the roof.
- **Your visitors' browsers:** A hacked site can silently redirect visitors to malware or load malicious scripts that run on your visitors' computers.
- **Your reputation:** Competitors (or bored troublemakers) sometimes deface websites, replacing your content with something embarrassing.

None of that sounds fun. Let's talk about how these attacks work.

## The most common attacks on small sites

Here are the attack types you're most likely to encounter:

- **Brute-force login attacks:** Automated tools try thousands of username-and-password combinations against your login page, hoping to get lucky. WordPress sites are especially popular targets because the login URL is the same for every WordPress site (`wp-admin`) and millions of sites use weak passwords. I cover this more in the "Securing WordPress Sites" section below.

- **SQL injection:** An attacker enters malicious code into a form field — such as a search box or a contact form field — hoping your site will pass that code to its database and execute it. A successful attack can expose your entire database. I explain this in detail (and how to prevent it) later in the "Preventing SQL Injection and XSS Attacks" section.
- **Cross-site scripting (XSS):** The attacker tricks your site into displaying malicious JavaScript to your visitors. It's sneakier than it sounds, and I cover the defense later (also in the "Preventing SQL Injection and XSS Attacks" section).
- **Outdated software:** This is the big one for most small sites. Hackers actively scan for sites running old versions of WordPress, themes, or plug-ins with known security holes. The fix here is embarrassingly simple: keep everything updated.
- **Phishing and credential theft:** Attackers try to get your hosting or admin passwords through fake emails, fake login pages, or by guessing. Two-factor authentication (which I cover below in the "Two-factor authentication" section) closes most of this gap.

## A few less common but notable threats

Beyond the big five attacks I just described, a few other threats are worth knowing about, even if they're less universally applicable:

- **DDoS (Distributed Denial of Service) attacks:** A flood of traffic from thousands of compromised computers, designed to overwhelm your server and take your site offline. Full-scale DDoS attacks are relatively rare against small sites, but using a CDN such as Cloudflare provides meaningful protection as a side effect of its normal traffic-routing work.
- **Comment and form spam:** Not technically a security attack, but a real nuisance. Automated bots submit contact forms, comment sections, and registration fields with spam content or malicious links. CAPTCHA tools (Google reCAPTCHA at `google.com/recaptcha` is free) and *honeypot fields* — hidden form fields that real users never see but bots fill in — are the standard defenses. As I cover in Book 3, Chapter 2, honeypot fields are easy to add to any HTML form.
- **Email spoofing:** Attackers send emails that appear to come from your domain, damaging your reputation and potentially phishing your customers. The fix is to set up SPF (Sender Policy Framework), DKIM (DomainKeys Identified Mail), and DMARC (Domain-based Message Authentication, Reporting, and Conformance) DNS records for your domain, which tell email providers how to verify that the email from your domain is legitimate. Your hosting provider's documentation can walk you through the setup, which takes about 20 minutes and makes a real difference.

# Securing WordPress Sites

If your site runs on WordPress, security deserves extra attention. WordPress powers roughly 40 percent of the web, which makes it an irresistible target for automated attacks. Happily, a well-maintained WordPress site is secure. The word *maintained* is doing a lot of work in that sentence, though, so keep reading.

## Keep everything updated

Keeping everything updated is the single most important thing you can do. Most successful attacks on WordPress sites exploit known vulnerabilities in outdated versions of WordPress itself, themes, or plug-ins. These are vulnerabilities that were fixed in a newer version that the site owner never installed.

In your WordPress dashboard, go to Dashboard ➪ Updates. If you see pending updates for WordPress core, themes, or plug-ins, install them. Make this a weekly habit. WordPress can also update itself automatically for minor security releases (which it does by default), but major version updates and plug-in updates still require your attention.

WARNING

Never run WordPress with an outdated theme or a plug-in that hasn't been updated in over a year. Abandoned plug-ins are a security risk — the developer has stopped fixing bugs, which means known vulnerabilities stay unfixed indefinitely. If you can't find an actively maintained alternative, remove the plug-in rather than keep it.

## Choose your plug-ins carefully

Every plug-in you install is a potential security risk, because every plug-in has code that can contain bugs. Plug-ins are one of WordPress's great strengths, so you shouldn't avoid them, but you should be selective. Before installing a plug-in, check three things in the WordPress plug-in directory:

- **Last updated:** If the plug-in hasn't been updated in more than a year, be cautious. Two years or more is a red flag.
- **Active installations:** A plug-in with 100,000+ active installations has been widely tested and scrutinized. A plug-in with 47 installations has not.
- **Ratings and reviews:** Low ratings often include reviews that mention security or reliability problems. Read them.

And one more thing: never, ever install a *nulled* or pirated premium plug-in. These cracked versions of paid plug-ins, which are freely distributed on sketchy websites, almost always contain malware. Installing one is like inviting the burglar in and offering them a coffee.

## Change the default login URL

Every WordPress site has the same default login address: `yourdomain.com/wp-admin`. Attackers know this, and brute-force scripts go straight to it. One easy defense is to change the login URL to something less predictable, such as `yourdomain.com/staff-portal` or `yourdomain.com/manage`, for example.

The plug-in WPS Hide Login (`wordpress.org/plugins/wps-hide-login`) handles this task with a simple settings field. After you change the URL, save it somewhere safe because, of course, you'll need it to log in!

## Limit login attempts

By default, WordPress lets anyone try to log in as many times as they like. Brute-force attacks exploit this by hammering your login page with thousands of guesses. The fix is to install a plug-in that locks out a visitor after a set number of failed attempts.

Limit Login Attempts Reloaded (`wordpress.org/plugins/limit-login-attempts-reloaded`) is a free, widely trusted option. The default settings give users a maximum of four login failures, at which point they're locked out for 20 minutes, which is reasonable for most sites. (The downside is that an attacker can take advantage of this limitation to lock *you* out for 20 minutes, too!)

## Use a WordPress security plug-in

A dedicated security plug-in pulls together several protections into a single dashboard, including malware scanning, login hardening, firewall rules, and file change monitoring. Here are the best options (choose one):

- **Wordfence Security (`wordfence.com`):** The most popular WordPress security plug-in, with a free tier that includes a firewall, a malware scanner, and login protection. The paid version adds real-time threat intelligence, but the free version covers the essentials well.

» **Solid Security, formerly iThemes Security (`solidwp.com`):** Another strong option with a good free tier. Particularly strong on hardening (closing unnecessary doors) and login security.

» **Sucuri Security (`sucuri.net`):** Well-regarded for malware scanning and website firewall. The free plug-in is useful; the paid service adds a CDN-based firewall that stops attacks before they reach your server.

# SSL Certificates and HTTPS Setup

If you visit a website, click Site Controls (to the left of the URL in Chrome; other browsers have a similar icon), and see *Connection is secure*, that site is using *HTTPS* (Hypertext Transfer Protocol Secure). If, instead, you see a warning that the site is not secure, the site hasn't set up SSL. All legitimate websites should now be using HTTPS. If yours isn't, you need to fix that right now.

## What SSL does

An *SSL certificate* (technically TLS — Transport Layer Security — these days, but everyone still calls it SSL) does two things. First, it encrypts the connection between your visitor's browser and your server, so that anyone intercepting the traffic — at a coffee shop Wi-Fi, say — sees scrambled nonsense instead of readable data. Second, it proves that your site is your site, not an imposter page set up to steal login credentials.

For visitors, HTTPS provides peace of mind. For your site, it provides something more tangible: Google uses HTTPS as a ranking signal, which means a secure site has a small but real advantage in search results. And browsers such as Chrome actively label HTTP sites as *Not Secure* in the address bar, which tends to make visitors nervous. Both are good reasons to get this done.

REMEMBER

HTTPS is a confirmed Google ranking factor. It won't shoot your site to number one on its own, but not having it is a minor penalty you can easily avoid. As I cover in Book 7, every little SEO advantage adds up.

## Getting a free certificate with Let's Encrypt

SSL certificates used to cost $50–$200 per year. Then Let's Encrypt (`letsencrypt.org`) came along in 2016 and made them free. Today, almost every major hosting provider offers one-click SSL installation via Let's Encrypt.

Check your hosting control panel (cPanel, Plesk, or your host's custom dashboard) for an SSL section. Look for a button labeled something like Install SSL, Free SSL, or Let's Encrypt. Click it and select your domain; in most cases, that's the entire process. The certificate installs and renews automatically every 90 days. If your host doesn't offer this, shop for a better host, because free SSL is table stakes in the hosting industry at this point.

## Forcing HTTPS on every page

Installing the SSL certificate enables HTTPS on your site, but it doesn't automatically redirect visitors who type `http://` (without the S) to the secure version. You need to add a redirect. On Apache-based servers (which most shared hosts use), you do this in your site's `.htaccess` file in your site's root folder. Here's the redirect snippet to add near the top of that file:

```
RewriteEngine On
RewriteCond %{HTTPS} off
RewriteRule ^(.*)$ https://%{HTTP_HOST}%{REQUEST_URI} [L,R=301]
```

That code tells your server: if a request comes in over plain HTTP, send the visitor a permanent redirect (server code 301) to the same URL but with HTTPS. After adding it, test by visiting your site with `http://` and confirming you automatically land on `https://`.

If your site runs on WordPress, the Really Simple Security SSL plug-in (`wordpress.org/plugins/really-simple-ssl`) handles the redirect and a handful of other HTTPS-related fixes automatically, with no manual file editing required.

TIP

After setting up HTTPS, test your SSL configuration at SSL Labs (`ssllabs.com/ssltest`). It's a free tool that gives your certificate and server configuration a letter grade (aim for A or A+) and flags any weak settings worth fixing.

## Adding security headers for extra protection

While you've got your `.htaccess` file open, it's worth adding a few *HTTP security headers*. These are instructions your server sends to browsers along with every page, telling them how to behave in ways that reduce certain attack risks. They're invisible to your visitors, take about two minutes to add, and improve your site's security posture.

Here are the most useful ones to add, along with a brief explanation of what each one does:

```
# Prevent your site from being embedded in iframes on other sites
# (protects against clickjacking attacks)
Header always set X-Frame-Options "SAMEORIGIN"

# Stop browsers from guessing content types (reduces certain XSS risks)
Header always set X-Content-Type-Options "nosniff"

# Tell browsers to always use HTTPS for the next year
Header always set Strict-Transport-Security "max-age=31536000"

# Basic Content Security Policy: only load scripts from your own domain
Header always set Content-Security-Policy "default-src 'self'"
```

WARNING

A few caveats before you copy-and-paste these headers. The `Header` directive requires Apache's `mod_headers` module to be active on your server. Most shared hosts have it enabled, but if you get a server error after adding these lines, that's the first thing to check with your host's support. Also, the Content Security Policy (CSP) line is intentionally conservative: `default-src 'self'` means "only load resources from my own domain." If your site loads fonts from Google Fonts, analytics code from a third-party script, or video embeds from YouTube, you'll need to add those domains to the policy; otherwise the browser will block them. Test your site carefully after adding a CSP.

REMEMBER

A Content Security Policy (CSP) header is an additional layer of XSS defense that tells browsers which scripts are allowed to run on your pages. You can add one in your `.htaccess` file or server configuration. Even a basic CSP that blocks inline scripts and restricts external script sources significantly reduces XSS risk. Search *Content-Security-Policy header* to learn more.

You can check which security headers your site is sending by using the free Security Headers tool (`securityheaders.com`). Enter your URL, and it grades your headers A through F and explains what's missing and why each one matters.

# Strong Authentication Methods

Your site can have perfect code, a clean SSL certificate, and a hardened WordPress configuration, and still get compromised if someone guesses your password. *Authentication* — proving you are who you say you are — is the most human part of security, which means it's often the weakest part.

## The problem with passwords

Here's a statistic that will make you squirm: the most common password in use today is still `123456`. The second most common is `password`. Millions of accounts are protected by credentials that a ten-year-old could guess in thirty seconds.

Even people who know better tend to reuse the same password across multiple sites. That's a catastrophic habit. When one site gets breached (and, alas, breaches happen constantly), attackers immediately try those same credentials everywhere else. This is called a *credential stuffing* attack, and it's surprisingly effective because password reuse is so common.

## Building a password you can remember

Good passwords have three properties: they're long (at least 16 characters), they're random (not words or phrases you use in real life), and they're unique (never reused across sites). That sounds impossible to manage, and it is, if you're trying to memorize them all.

The solution is a *password manager:* software that generates and stores strong, unique passwords for every site, so you have to remember only one master password to unlock the vault. You'll hear no argument from me that password managers require a small investment of time to set up. But that time is nothing compared to recovering from a compromised hosting account.

TIP

The well-regarded password managers for individuals and small teams include 1Password (`1password.com`), Bitwarden (`bitwarden.com`, with a generous free tier), and Dashlane (`dashlane.com`). All of them generate strong random passwords, store them securely, and fill them automatically in your browser. Bitwarden is open source, which many security-conscious folks appreciate.

## Two-factor authentication

*Two-factor authentication* (2FA) adds a second step to your login process. Instead of just a password, you also provide something you physically have, usually a time-sensitive code from an app on your phone, or a small hardware key. Even if an attacker has your password, they can't log in without that second factor.

For WordPress, the WP 2FA plug-in (`wordpress.org/plugins/wp-2fa`) adds two-factor authentication to your WordPress login with minimal configuration. For your hosting account and domain registrar, check their account security settings since most providers now offer 2FA, and you should enable it for both. The authenticator apps most commonly recommended are Google Authenticator and Authy (`authy.com`), both free.

The mild inconvenience of the second step in two-factor authentication is dwarfed by the protection it provides. Enable it everywhere you can. That includes your hosting control panel, domain registrar, email account (this is especially important since your email is the master key to everything), and WordPress admin.

# Preventing SQL Injection and XSS Attacks

If your site has any forms — such as a contact form, an order form, or a search box — it accepts input from visitors. That's great, because forms are useful. It's also a potential security problem, because some visitors will type things into your form fields that you really don't want your server to process. The two most important attacks to understand here are SQL injection and cross-site scripting.

## Understanding SQL injection

Most dynamic websites store their data in a database. For example, a WordPress site stores posts, pages, user accounts, and settings there. Your server queries the database using a language called SQL (Structured Query Language). The problem arises when user input gets passed directly into a SQL query without being checked or sanitized first.

Here's a simplified example. Suppose your site has a search form, and your server builds a database query like this:

```
SELECT * FROM products WHERE name = 'user_input'
```

If a normal visitor types `donuts`, the query works fine. But a malicious visitor might type `' OR '1'='1`. That turns the query into:

```
SELECT * FROM products WHERE name = '' OR '1'='1'
```

The condition `'1'='1'` is always true, so the query returns every record in the database. A more targeted attack could delete tables, extract user passwords, or do worse. This is *SQL injection*, and it's been behind some of the biggest data breaches in history.

## Understanding cross-site scripting

*Cross-site scripting (XSS)* is a different attack with a similar root cause: unvalidated user input. Instead of targeting your database, XSS targets your visitors. The attacker enters a snippet of JavaScript into a form field (such as a comment box), hoping your site will display that input on a page without filtering it. If it does, any visitor who loads that page runs the attacker's script in their browser.

What can that script do? Quite a lot, potentially! It can steal the visitor's session cookies (which might let the attacker impersonate them), redirect them to a phishing page, or silently log their keystrokes. If your site has a comment section, a review system, or any user-generated content that other visitors see, XSS is a risk worth taking seriously.

## How to defend against both

The defenses against SQL injection and XSS follow the same underlying principle: never trust input from visitors and always sanitize or escape user input before using it. Here's what that means in practice:

- **Use parameterized queries:** For SQL injection, the gold-standard fix is to use *parameterized queries* (also called *prepared statements*) instead of building SQL strings by concatenating user input. Parameterized queries keep data separate from code, so there's no way for input to be interpreted as a SQL command. If you're using PHP, the PDO and MySQLi extensions both support prepared statements. If you're using WordPress, the `$wpdb->prepare()` function handles this for you.
- **Escape output:** For XSS, the key defense is escaping any user-supplied content before displaying it on a page. In PHP, the `htmlspecialchars()` function converts characters such as < and > into their HTML entity equivalents, so a script tag typed by a visitor becomes harmless text on the page rather than executable code. Here's a simple example:

```
<?php
    // Never output user input directly:
    // echo $_GET["search"];  // Dangerous!

    // Always escape it first:
    echo htmlspecialchars($_GET["search"], ENT_QUOTES, "UTF-8");
?>
```

- **Use a web application firewall (WAF):** A WAF sits between the internet and your server and filters out malicious traffic before it reaches your site. For WordPress, the Wordfence and Sucuri plug-ins both include firewall functionality. Cloudflare (`cloudflare.com`) also offers a free CDN with basic WAF features that works with any type of site.

If your site is built on WordPress and you're using well-maintained, reputable plug-ins, most of these defenses are already in place because WordPress core and quality plug-ins handle parameterized queries and output escaping automatically. The risk goes up when you write custom code or install poorly built plug-ins that skip these protections.

# Malware Scanning and Prevention

Even with good security practices in place, it's worth regularly checking that your site hasn't been compromised. Malware on websites can be subtle, for example, a small snippet of hidden code injected into a legitimate file, designed to do its damage quietly without alerting the site owner. Sometimes the first sign that a site has been hacked is a visitor email saying "Hey, your site is doing something weird." That's not a great way to find out.

## How malware gets onto websites

Malware usually arrives on a website through one of these routes:

- **Compromised credentials:** An attacker who gets your FTP, SSH, or hosting panel password can upload files directly to your server.
- **Vulnerable plug-ins or themes:** Outdated or poorly coded software with known vulnerabilities can be exploited to inject malicious code.
- **Supply chain attacks:** A legitimate plug-in or theme you trust gets compromised at the source. For example, the developer's account is hacked and an update pushes malware to every site running that plug-in. These attacks are rare but do happen.

## Scanning tools worth using

Here are the scanning tools I recommend:

- **Wordfence (`wordfence.com`):** For WordPress sites, Wordfence's built-in scanner compares your site's files against a known-clean repository and flags any that have been modified or added unexpectedly. Run a scan from Wordfence ➪ Scan in your WordPress dashboard and check the results.
- **Sucuri SiteCheck (`sitecheck.sucuri.net`):** A free external scanner that checks any public URL for known malware signatures, blacklisting status, and

outdated software. It's limited to what's visible externally, but it's a quick first check. Enter your URL and click Scan Website.

- **MalCare (`malcare.com`):** A dedicated malware scanner and removal service that offers one-click malware removal (a paid feature, but a time-saver if your site gets infected). The free plan includes scanning.

WARNING

Scanning once in a while isn't enough. Make scanning a scheduled habit, ideally automated. The WordPress security plug-ins I cover earlier in this chapter can run scheduled scans automatically and email you if they find anything. Set this up and you'll know about problems within hours of them appearing, rather than days or weeks later when a visitor or Google finally tells you something's wrong.

If a scan finds something, don't panic. (Easy for me to say, I know.) Most hosting providers have tools to restore a clean backup, and security services such as Sucuri and MalCare offer professional cleanup if the infection is serious. The most important thing is to change all your passwords immediately — hosting, WordPress, FTP, everything — once a compromise is confirmed, to prevent reinfection.

# Backup Solutions and Strategies

Every section in this chapter has been about preventing bad things from happening to your site. Backups are different. Backups are for when bad things happen anyway, even when you've done everything right: a server failure, an accidental deletion, a particularly stubborn malware infection that's faster to wipe and restore than to clean manually. Backups are your safety net, and they're useful only if they exist before you need them.

## The backup rule you should live by

In IT circles, there's a backup strategy called the *3-2-1 rule:* keep at least three copies of your data, on at least two different types of storage, with at least one copy offsite (or in the cloud, away from your server). You don't need to follow this religiously for a small website, but the underlying principle is sound: don't rely on a single backup, and don't store your only backup in the same place as the original.

If your host's backup system fails at the same time your site goes down, a backup stored only on that same server is not going to help you. Keep a copy somewhere independent.

## What to back up (and how often)

For a typical small-business website, your backup needs to cover your site's files and your database:

- **Site files:** Everything in your site's root folder, which means the HTML, CSS, JavaScript, PHP, images, uploaded media, and anything else that makes your site run.
- **Database:** If your site uses a database (WordPress does; a simple static HTML site doesn't), the database holds your content, including your posts, pages, settings, user accounts, orders. A file backup without the database backup leaves you with an empty shell.

How often should you back up? It depends on how often your content changes. A site that publishes new blog posts daily should back up daily. A mostly static site that changes a few times a month can get by with weekly backups. When in doubt, back up more often than you think you need to.

## Backup tools for WordPress and static sites

For WordPress sites, these are the tools worth knowing:

- **UpdraftPlus (`updraftplus.com`):** The most popular WordPress backup plug-in, with a free tier that covers scheduled backups of files and databases, with storage to Dropbox, Google Drive, or Amazon S3. Set it, forget it, and sleep better.
- **Jetpack Backup (`jetpack.com`):** A paid solution ($9.95 per month and up) that offers real-time backups — every change triggers an immediate backup — and one-click restore. Pricier than UpdraftPlus but excellent for sites that update frequently.
- **Your hosting provider's backup tool:** Most managed WordPress hosts and many shared hosts offer automatic daily backups from the hosting control panel. Use this option as a complement to a plug-in–based backup, not as your only option.

For static sites (plain HTML, CSS, JavaScript), the simplest backup strategy is to keep your project in a Git repository and push it to GitHub (`github.com`). Every commit is a snapshot of your site at that moment, and the entire history lives safely in the cloud. As I cover in Book 10, Chapter 1, version control is a best practice worth adopting early.

## Testing your backups: The step everyone skips

I want to spend an extra moment on backup testing because it's the most consistently neglected part of any backup strategy. It's easy to set up automated backups, see the confirmation emails roll in, and feel secure. But a backup that looks successful and a backup that restores correctly are not the same. I've seen cases where backups ran faithfully for months, only for the restore to fail when it was needed because the backup files were corrupted, incomplete, or saved to the wrong location.

Testing a backup doesn't have to be complicated. Here's a simple process for a WordPress site:

1. **Download a recent backup file** from wherever your backup plug-in stores it.
2. **Set up a local test environment** using a tool such as LocalWP (`localwp.com`), a free app that runs WordPress locally on your computer. Alternatively, many hosts offer a one-click staging environment you can use for this.
3. **Import the backup** using your backup plug-in's restore function on the local or staging install.
4. **Confirm the site works:** Log in, browse to a few pages, check that your content and settings are intact.

That's it. Do this once when you first set up your backup system and then repeat it every few months. The first time you successfully restore from a backup, you'll feel a small but genuine surge of relief, as well as a lot more confidence in the system you've built.

# Creating a Security Plan

Security is an ongoing practice, a set of habits and check-ins that keep your site healthy over time. The good news is that once you've set up the fundamentals covered in this chapter, the ongoing effort is minimal. Here's a practical monthly security routine that takes less time than watching an episode of television.

## Your monthly security checklist

Run through these steps once a month:

- **Update everything.** Log into your WordPress dashboard and install any pending updates for core, themes, and plug-ins. If your site isn't WordPress, check for updates to any CMS, framework, or server software you're using.
- **Check your backups.** Confirm that your scheduled backups ran successfully and that recent backup files exist in your backup storage location.
- **Run a malware scan.** Use Wordfence, Sucuri SiteCheck, or your chosen scanner to check for unexpected file changes or known malware signatures.
- **Review user accounts.** Check your WordPress users list (or hosting control-panel users) and remove any accounts that no longer need access. These include former employees, freelancers who finished their project, test accounts you created and forgot about.
- **Check your SSL certificate.** Make sure your certificate is still valid and not close to expiring. Let's Encrypt certificates renew automatically, but automatic processes occasionally fail.
- **Review your hosting account.** Check your hosting control panel for any unusual activity, such as unexpected email accounts, unfamiliar domains, or odd entries in your access logs. Many hosts show a resource usage summary that makes spikes (which can signal a compromise) visible at a glance.

That's it. Six checks, maybe 20 minutes, once a month. Security doesn't have to be complicated or time-consuming. It just has to be consistent. A site that gets a monthly check-in is dramatically safer than a site that was locked down once and then never looked at again.

And if something does go wrong — for example, if you spot a malware infection, a suspicious user account, or an SSL error — you'll catch it early, while it's still a manageable problem rather than a crisis. That's the real value of a security routine: not that it makes bad things impossible, but that it keeps them from going unnoticed until they're catastrophic.

## When to call in a professional

Most of the security work in this chapter is DIY-friendly. But in some situations it's worth calling in someone who does this full time. How do you know when you've crossed that line?

- **Your site is actively spreading malware.** If Google Search Console or your scanning tool tells you your site is serving malware to visitors, take it offline immediately and get professional help. Malware that reaches visitors is both a reputational emergency and a legal liability.
- **You've been compromised and can't find the source.** A clean restore followed by reinfection within a few days means the attacker has a persistent foothold you haven't found. Security professionals have tools and experience to locate and eliminate persistence mechanisms that aren't obvious to non-specialists.
- **You handle sensitive data.** If your site stores customer payment details, medical information, or other sensitive personal data, the stakes are high enough that a professional security audit is worthwhile, not just for your protection but for your customers' protection and your legal compliance.

Professional security help comes in a few forms. The security plug-ins and services I mention earlier in this chapter — Sucuri and MalCare in particular — offer paid cleanup and remediation services that are reasonably priced for small-business budgets (typically $200–$500 for a single cleanup). For more comprehensive security audits, look for a web security consultant or a firm that specializes in small-business security. Your hosting provider's support team is also worth calling. For example, many managed WordPress hosts include security incident response as part of their service.

The goal of everything in this chapter is to make your site a hard enough target that automated attacks pass you by and look for easier pickings elsewhere. The internet has no shortage of sites running three-year-old plug-ins with the default admin password still in place. Keep your site updated, backed up, and monitored, and you're already ahead of most of the crowd.

# 10
# Launching and Maintaining Your Website

# Contents at a Glance

IN THIS CHAPTER

» Understanding version control

» Learning the crucial Git commands

» Storing your project on GitHub

» Managing different environments

» Deploying your site

Chapter 1

# Version Control and Deployment

*In preparing for battle I have always found that plans are useless, but planning is indispensable.*

—DWIGHT D. EISENHOWER

Okay, you've done the hard part. You've planned your site, designed it, created it, SEO-ed it, and probably consumed more coffee than any reasonable person should. The site looks good and it works. Now what?

Now you need to get it online — and keep it online, healthy, and recoverable when something inevitably goes wrong. (And something will go wrong. That's not pessimism; it's web development.)

This chapter is about the tools and habits that turn a finished project into a properly managed, deployable website. The star of the show is *version control,* a system for tracking every change you make to your project files, so you always have a record of what changed, when, and why. The main version control tool used by web developers is called Git, and once you try it, you'll wonder how you ever worked without it. I also walk you through storing your project on GitHub, managing different versions of your site across development and production environments, and getting your site live using modern deployment tools.

# Understanding Version Control and Git

Imagine you're editing your website's home page. You move some elements around, rewrite the headline, and try a different color scheme. Then you realize the new version looks worse than the old one. You'd love to just go back, but you've been saving over the same file for the past hour. Oops.

That's the problem version control solves. A *version control system* keeps a history of every change you make to your project files. You can see what changed and when, compare old versions to new ones, and even roll back to any earlier state with a single command. It's like an infinite undo button for your entire project. Not just one file. Not just the current session. Every file, going all the way back to the first day you started the project (or, more realistically, the first day you implemented your version control system).

## Why version control matters even if you work alone

Version control is often presented as a team tool, and it's true that it's indispensable for teams. But even if you're the only person who ever touches your website, it pays back the (relatively minor) effort required to learn it in several very practical ways:

- **Safety net:** Break something? Roll back to the last working version in seconds. No more staring at broken code trying to remember what you changed.
- **Audit trail:** Every change is logged with a timestamp and a message explaining what you did and why. Future-you — the one who can't remember why they changed that CSS rule three months ago — will be deeply grateful.
- **Fearless experimentation:** Want to try a completely different layout? Rewrite the navigation from scratch? Version control means you can experiment freely, knowing you can always get back to what worked.
- **Off-site backup:** When you store your version history on a service such as GitHub, your entire project is safely backed up in the cloud. Your laptop gets stolen? Your project survives.
- **Professional habit:** Any time you hand a project to another developer — or come back to it yourself after six months away — version-controlled code with descriptive change messages is a thousand times easier to work with than a folder full of files named index-final-FINAL-v3-USE-THIS-ONE.html.

## Getting to know Git

*Git* is the world's most widely used version control system. It was created in 2005 by Linus Torvalds (who also created the Linux kernel, in case you're keeping score). Git runs on your computer as a command-line tool, inside the folder that contains your website project. You tell Git when you want to save a snapshot of your work, and it stores that snapshot — along with all the snapshots you've ever saved — in a hidden folder called a *repository* (or *repo*, if you want to sound like you've been doing this for years).

The key thing to understand about Git is that it stores the current state of your files *and* it stores every state they've ever been in, along with the capability to determine what changed between each state. That's what makes it so powerful. You're essentially building a time machine for your project.

Yes, Git has a learning curve. No, it's not as steep as people make it sound. You need about eight commands to handle 90 percent of what a solo web developer does with Git, and I walk you through all of them in the next section.

# Git Basics for Web Projects

Before you can use Git, you need it installed. Head to `git-scm.com` and download the installer for your operating system. If you're running macOS, you may already have it. To check, open a Terminal window, type `git --version`, and if you see a version number, you're good to go. If, instead, Terminal prompts you to install the command-line developer tools, follow the instruction to do that, and then run `git --version` again to confirm that all is well.

You also need to introduce yourself to Git before you start. Git uses your name and email to label your commits, so it knows who made each change. Open Terminal and run the following commands (remember to press Enter or Return after each command):

```
git config --global user.name "Your Name"
git config --global user.email "you@example.com"
```

Replace the placeholders within the quotation marks with your name and email. That's a one-time setup. Git remembers these details for all your future projects.

## Basic command-line survival skills

Everything in Git happens from the command line, which you get to via the Terminal app on both Windows and macOS. (Note that you might need to get Terminal from the Microsoft Store if you're running an older version of Windows.)

Once you have your command line open, here are a few essential commands that work on all platforms:

- **`cd` *`path`* (change directory):** Moves to the directory specified by *`path`*. In particular:
  - `cd ~` moves to your main user account directory.
  - `cd ..` moves up to the parent directory of the current directory.
  - `cd ../`*`sibling`* moves up to the parent directory of the current directory, and then into the subdirectory specified by *`sibling`*.
- **`pwd` (print working directory):** Displays the full path name of the current directory.
- **`ls` (list) on Mac or `dir` (directory) on Windows:** Displays a list of the files and subdirectories in the current directory.
- **`mkdir` *`name`* (make directory):** Creates a directory named *name*.

Don't sweat memorizing these commands now. You'll be using them a ton as you work with your Git projects, so they'll become embedded in your brain with practice.

## Initializing a repository

The first step is to turn your project folder into a Git repository. First, navigate to your project folder:

```
cd ~/path/project
```

where *`path`* is the path to the directory where your project is stored and *`project`* is the directory that contains the project files.

Then initialize a new Git repository in that folder:

```
git init
```

Git responds with something like `Initialized empty Git repository in /path/project/.git/`. That `.git` folder is where Git stores its history and configuration. You never need to touch it directly; just know it's there and don't delete it.

## Staging and committing your files

Git's workflow has two steps: staging and committing. *Staging* means telling Git which files you want to include in the next snapshot. *Committing* means saving that snapshot with a descriptive message. Here's the sequence:

First, check the current state of your project:

```
git status
```

Git displays the status, which at this early stage in your Git career will look like a bunch of gobbledygook. For now, there are two main things to look for:

- If your repo is up to date, you see one of the following messages:

  ```
  On branch main
  No commits yet
  ```

  or

  ```
  Your branch is up to date with 'origin/main'.
  nothing to commit, working tree clean
  ```

- If, more likely, you have files that are untracked or modified but not yet staged, those files appear in red.

If you have red files, the next step is to stage everything:

```
git add .
```

The dot means "everything in this folder." (If you want to stage just a particular file, run `git add filename`, where you replace *`filename`* with the name of the file you want to stage.) Run `git status` again and you see the same files now listed in green, which tells you they're staged and ready to commit. Now save the snapshot:

```
git commit -m "Initial commit: add all website files"
```

The `-m` flag is short for *message*. The message in quotes is what you'll see in the history later, so make it meaningful. After running this, Git confirms the commit with a short summary: something such as `[main (root-commit) 1c8a3d2]`

`Initial commit: add all website files`. That string of letters and numbers (`1c8a3d2`) is the commit's unique ID.

## The everyday Git rhythm

From this point on, your version control workflow is a simple three-step rhythm that you repeat every time you make a meaningful set of changes:

1. Make some changes to your files (edit HTML, update CSS, add a page, fix a bug).
2. Type `git add .` to stage all the changed files.
3. Type `git commit -m "Describe what you changed and why"` to save the snapshot.

How often should you commit? As a rule, commit after each meaningful unit of work. "Updated Galaxy Glazed donut description" is a good commit. "Fixed broken link to catering page" is a good commit. "Stuff" is not a good commit. The more granular your commits, the more precisely you can pinpoint and undo problems later.

TIP

Commit messages read best in the imperative mood: "Fix broken link in footer" rather than "Fixed broken link" or "I fixed the link." Git itself follows this convention, and a list of imperative-mood messages is much easier to scan quickly than a diary of past events. Think of each message as an instruction: If you applied this commit, what would it do to the project?

## Reading your project's history

To see a list of all your commits, type:

```
git log --oneline
```

The output looks something like this:

```
a3f92c1 Update donut prices for summer menu
7d14e88 Add catering page with inquiry form
b021f47 Fix responsive layout on mobile menu page
1c8a3d2 Initial commit: add all website files
```

The most recent commit is at the top. Each line shows a short commit ID and your message. To see what changed in any given commit, type `git show` followed by the commit ID:

```
git show b021f47
```

Git displays the full differential (or *diff*, to the cognoscenti): lines that were added are marked with a plus sign, and lines that were removed are marked with a minus sign. It's a precise, line-by-line record of what changed. Once you get used to reading it, you'll find it invaluable for understanding why the code looks the way it does.

You can also compare any two commits directly to see what changed between them:

```
git diff 1c8a3d2 a3f92c1
```

Git shows everything that changed between the initial commit and the most recent one. For a project that's been running for a few weeks, this is a surprisingly satisfying way to see how much work you've done.

## Telling Git what to ignore

In almost every web project, you'll have files that don't want Git to track. Hidden operating system files such as `.DS_Store` (a Mac thing), editor configuration folders such as `.vscode`, and any folders full of installed packages don't belong in your repository. Git has a simple, elegant solution: a file called `.gitignore`.

Create a plain text file named `.gitignore` in the root of your project folder. List any files or folders you want Git to ignore, one per line. Here's a sensible starting `.gitignore` for most web projects:

```
# Mac OS system files
.DS_Store

# Windows thumbnail files
Thumbs.db

# Editor settings folders
.vscode/
.idea/
```

Lines starting with # are comments. Once you've created `.gitignore`, commit it just like any other file. Git reads it automatically and skips the files and folders you've listed. You can also use wildcards: `*.log` ignores all log files, `temp/` ignores the entire `temp` folder. GitHub even maintains a library of ready-made `.gitignore` templates for dozens of project types at `github.com/github/gitignore`, so you're rarely starting from scratch.

# Using GitHub for Website Projects

Git by itself lives entirely on your computer. That's useful, but it has one obvious weakness: if your computer dies, your version history goes with it. GitHub (`github.com`) is a web service that hosts Git repositories in the cloud. It's free for both public and private projects, and it's where the vast majority of the world's web projects live. Think of GitHub as a combination of off-site backup, public portfolio, and collaboration hub.

WARNING

Yes, GitHub acts as a kind of off-site backup, but only for the files you've included in your commits. You still need a robust backup strategy for *all* your files, as I explain in Book 9, Chapter 4.

GitHub and Git are different things, which trips people up at first. Git is the version control tool that runs on your computer. GitHub is a website that stores Git repositories. You use Git locally, and then save (or *push*, in the vernacular) your commits to GitHub for safekeeping.

## Creating a repository on GitHub

Create a free account at `github.com` if you don't have one already. Then:

1. **Click Repositories and then click the green New button on your GitHub dashboard.**

   Alternatively, from any dashboard page, click + near the top right of the page and then click New Repository.

   The Create New Repository page shows up.

2. **In the Repository Name text box, type a name for your repo.**

   If you already have a project name for your local repo, use that name. Otherwise, something such as `orbital-donuts` or `my-portfolio-site` works fine. Lowercase letters and hyphens are the convention.

3. **(Optional) Add a description, which appears on your GitHub profile.**
4. **In the Choose Visibility list, select Private if you don't want the public to see your code, or leave Public as the default if you're fine with it being visible.**
5. **If you want GitHub to create a prepopulated `.gitignore` file for you (and you haven't already created a local `.gitignore` file), use the Add .gitignore list to select the template that best matches your code (such as WordPress).**
6. **Click Create Repository.**

GitHub presents you with a page of commands for connecting your local repository to the new GitHub one. The next section explains what those commands do.

## Connecting your local repo to GitHub

GitHub shows you two sets of commands, one for setting up your new GitHub repo locally and one for pushing an existing repo to GitHub. Assuming you already have an existing repo that you want to push to your new GitHub repo, here are the commands to use:

```
git remote add origin https://github.com/yourname/project.git
git branch -M main
git push -u origin main
```

In the first command, replace *`yourname`* with your GitHub username and replace *`project`* with your repo name. Here's what each command does:

- **`git remote`:** Tells your local Git repo where the GitHub repo lives; `origin` is a conventional nickname for the remote repository address.
- **`git branch`:** Renames your default branch to `main` (GitHub's current naming convention for the primary branch).
- **`git push`:** Pushes all your commits up to GitHub for the first time. The `-u` flag sets `origin main` as the default, so for every future push you can just run this:

  ```
  git push
  ```

Refresh your GitHub repo page and you'll see all your project files there, each one showing the commit message from when it was last changed. Just like that, your work is safely off your hard drive and living in the cloud. Sweet!

WARNING

Never put passwords, API keys, database credentials, or any other secrets directly in your project files. Once something is committed to Git, it's in the history forever, even if you delete the file in a later commit. Store secrets as *environment variables* in your hosting service's settings panel. Netlify, Vercel, and most hosting platforms have a dedicated section for this, usually called Environment Variables or Site Variables. If some sort of secret does accidentally end up committed, revoke the credential (or whatever) immediately and create a new one.

## Cloning and pulling

If you need to work on your project from a different computer — or if you've accidentally deleted your local folder (hey, it happens to the best of us) — you can *clone* the repo from GitHub to get a fresh local copy.

First use Terminal to navigate to the parent directory (that is, the directory within which you want to create the repo), and then run the following command:

```
git clone https://github.com/yourname/project.git
```

where, as usual, *yourname* is your GitHub username and *project* is your repo name. The `git clone` command creates a subdirectory named `project`, and then downloads the entire repo, including the full commit history, to that subdirectory. Everything is exactly as it was. Nothing is lost. Your sanity (or maybe your job) is saved.

If you're working on the same project from two different computers — your office desktop and your home laptop, say — you'll push from one and pull on the other to stay in sync.

After you've pushed some changes on one computer, switch to the other computer, navigate to the project directory, and then run the following command:

```
git pull
```

Git downloads any new commits from GitHub and merges them into your local copy. If you made changes in both places without syncing, Git will try to merge them automatically. Usually it succeeds. Occasionally it asks you to resolve a *merge conflict*, where two changes affect the same line and Git isn't sure which one to keep. That sounds scary, but it's straightforward because Git shows you where the conflict is and you just choose which version to keep.

# Git Workflows for Solo Developers

Git was designed for large software teams, which is why its documentation can feel overwhelming. Pull requests, rebasing, cherry-picking, upstream remotes. There's a lot in there that you don't need for a solo web project. Focus on just two things: committing well and using branches for experiments.

## Committing with intention

The single most valuable version control habit isn't any specific command; it's committing regularly and writing good messages. Compare two commit histories for the same project:

Less useful:

- Worked on site.
- More changes.
- Stuff.
- Untitled.

More useful:

- Add summer menu page with seasonal donut descriptions.
- Resize hero image to reduce load time.
- Fix contact form layout on small screens.
- Update footer with new business hours.

The second history tells a story. You can scan it in 30 seconds and know what happened and when. That matters enormously when something breaks or when you come back to a project after three months and can't remember how it works.

Here are a few commit message best practices that make the history even more useful:

- Keep the first line under 50 characters. It's the title; make it scannable.
- Use the imperative mood: *Add* not *Added, Fix* not *Fixed.*
- If the commit needs more explanation, add a blank line after the first line and write a longer description. The first line is the subject; the rest is the body.

## Branches: Your experimental playground

A *branch* is a parallel version of your project where you can make changes without affecting your main working copy. Branches are how you safely experiment with big changes — such as a new page layout, a revised navigation structure, a different color scheme — without risking the version that's currently working.

Suppose you want to try a redesigned order page for the Orbital Donuts site. Here's how to create and switch to a new branch:

```
git checkout -b order-page-redesign
```

This creates a new branch called `order-page-redesign` and switches to it immediately. Your `main` branch is untouched. Make your changes, commit them to this branch, and test everything thoroughly.

If the redesign turns out to be a disaster, you just delete the branch and your main site is completely unaffected:

```
git switch main
git branch -D order-page-redesign
```

No harm done. The experiment is gone, the main site is intact, and you're back where you started.

If, on the other hand, the redesign is a success, you can merge it back into `main`:

```
git checkout main
git merge order-page-redesign
```

Everything from the `order-page-redesign` branch is now part of `main`. Nice!

Branches make trying things genuinely low-risk, and once you get comfortable with them you'll reach for them constantly.

REMEMBER

You can see all your branches at any time with:

```
git branch
```

The current branch is marked with an asterisk. Switching between branches is always the same command: `git checkout` followed by the branch name.

# Managing Environments

When web developers talk about *environments,* they're referring to the different contexts in which a website runs at different stages of the development process. Most professional web projects use three distinct environments, each with a specific purpose:

- **Development (dev):** Your local copy, running on your own computer. This is where you write code, break things, and fix them. Nobody sees this environment but you. It's perfectly fine for it to be broken at 2 a.m. when you're in the middle of something.
- **Staging:** A copy of the site hosted somewhere online but not publicly advertised and usually behind a password or on an obscure URL. This is where you test changes in a real hosted environment before they go live. Think of staging as the dress rehearsal before opening night.
- **Production:** The live site that your visitors see. Changes land here only after they've been tested and approved in staging. This is the one you protect.

## Why the staging step matters

The classic mistake is making changes directly in production. It's tempting because it's faster, there's no setup, and the change is just a small thing. Until the small thing breaks something you didn't expect, at a moment you can't predict, in front of real visitors.

A staging environment interrupts that pattern. You deploy the change to staging, check it in a browser, make sure nothing exploded, and then — and only then! — deploy to production. The extra overhead is small, but the protection is huge.

For example, suppose you're updating the Orbital Donuts online ordering form to add a new field for special instructions. In development, you write and test the HTML. In staging, you confirm it looks right on the hosted server, that the form still submits correctly, and that the page doesn't break on mobile devices. In production, you deploy the tested, confirmed version.

## Setting up a simple staging environment

Many modern deployment platforms (which I cover in the next section) create staging environments for you automatically. Every time you push to a branch other than `main`, Netlify and Vercel generate a unique preview URL so you can see what the deployed version looks like before you merge it to production.

If you're on traditional hosting, you can set up staging manually. Create a subdomain — `staging.maplestreetbakery.com`, for example — that points to a separate folder on your server. Deploy your changes there first, test them, and then copy them to the live root folder. Add password protection to the staging subdomain through your hosting control panel so random visitors don't stumble across your half-finished work.

A staging environment doesn't need to be beautiful or fast. It just needs to work well enough for you to catch problems. The small extra effort it takes to set up will pay for itself the first time it catches a bug before a real visitor does.

# Modern Deployment Options

Getting your finished site from your computer to the web used to mean using FTP (File Transfer Protocol): connecting to your server with a dedicated app and manually uploading every changed file. FTP clients such as FileZilla still exist and still work, and I cover them in a moment. But modern deployment tools are so much better that, for any new project, it's worth knowing what's available.

## Netlify

Netlify (`netlify.com`) is one of the most popular deployment platforms for small-to-medium websites, and it's free for basic use. The core idea is simple: you connect Netlify to your GitHub repository, and from that point on, every time you push a commit to the `main` branch, Netlify automatically deploys your updated site. No FTP. No manual uploads. Just `git push` and your site is updated with your changed code within about 30 seconds.

After you create your free Netlify account, here's how to deploy a site on Netlify:

1. **From your Netlify dashboard, click Add New Project.**
2. **In the Import a Git Repository section, click GitHub.**

   The sign in to GitHub page appears in a new window.
3. **Enter your GitHub credentials, click Sign In, and then click Authorize to give your thumbs-up for Netlify to access your GitHub stuff.**
4. **When prompted to install Netlify on GitHub, select the Only Select Repositories option, and then use the Select Repositories list to choose the repository you want to use with your Netlify project.**
5. **Click Install, and then click your new project.**

6. **Leave the build settings at their defaults for a plain HTML/CSS/JS site (no build command needed).**
7. **Click Deploy *repo*, where *repo* is the name of the GitHub repo you selected in Step 4.**

   Within seconds, Netlify assigns your site a temporary URL such as `sparkling-donut-42f8a1.netlify.app`. Your site is live.

You can connect your own custom domain in Netlify's Domain Management panel. Netlify also provides free SSL certificates automatically, so your site gets HTTPS without any extra steps. As I cover in Book 1, Chapter 3, pointing your domain to Netlify is just a matter of updating two DNS records at your domain registrar.

One of Netlify's most useful features for solo developers is *deploy previews*. When you push commits to any branch other than `main`, Netlify generates a unique preview URL for that branch automatically. This feature gives you a real hosted version of your staging environment without any extra setup. You can share the URL with a client or collaborator to get feedback before the change goes live.

## Vercel

Vercel (`vercel.com`) is Netlify's closest competitor and is also free for simple web apps and personal projects. (For more advanced projects, you'll want to step up to the Pro plan, which costs $20 per month.) The workflow is nearly identical: connect your GitHub repo, and Vercel deploys automatically on every push. Vercel is particularly popular for sites built with JavaScript frameworks but also works just as well for plain HTML/CSS/JS sites.

The main practical differences between Netlify and Vercel are subtle for a beginner, and either will serve you well. If you're not sure which to choose, I suggest starting with Netlify since its dashboard is slightly more beginner-friendly and its documentation is excellent.

## GitHub Pages

If your site is entirely static — just HTML, CSS, and JavaScript with no server-side code — GitHub Pages (`pages.github.com`) is a brilliantly simple free option. You don't need a separate account or a separate service. You just enable it from the Settings tab of any GitHub repository, tell it which branch to deploy from, and GitHub automatically serves your site at *`yourname`*`.github.io/`*`your-repo-name`*.

GitHub Pages is ideal for portfolio sites, documentation, landing pages, and simple small-business sites. Its main limitation is that it doesn't support server-side processing (so contact forms need a third-party service, as I describe in Book 3, Chapter 2). For pure static sites, though, it's hard to beat because it's free, reliable, and connected to the same Git workflow you're already using.

### Traditional FTP deployment

FTP isn't dead. If your site lives on traditional shared hosting with a cPanel control panel, you'll likely deploy via FTP, which these days is best performed over its more secure variant, SFTP (Secure File Transfer Protocol). Free clients such as FileZilla (`filezilla-project.org`) handle both protocols and are straightforward to use: enter your hosting credentials, connect to your server, and drag files from your computer to the server.

The downside of FTP is that it's entirely manual. You have to remember which files changed since your last upload, transfer them one by one, and cross your fingers that you didn't miss anything or accidentally overwrite a file on the server that you intended to keep. It works, but it doesn't scale gracefully, and it's easy to introduce errors.

If you're using FTP, it's especially important to use Git alongside it. Git won't automate your deploys, but it will give you the safety net and history that FTP doesn't provide. Your deploy workflow becomes the following:

1. Make changes locally.
2. Commit to Git.
3. Push to GitHub.
4. Upload changed files via FTP.

It's an extra step, but you have a complete audit trail and rollback capability, as I describe in the next section.

## Rollback Strategies When Things Go Wrong

One of these days, you'll push a change to the live site and notice (I hope sooner rather than later) that the change broke something. Doh! Now what? Now you need to undo that change, and you need to do it fast. Fortunately, with a good version control setup at your disposal, this scenario doesn't have to be a crisis because it's a two-minute fix.

## Reverting a commit

The cleanest way to undo a specific commit is the `git revert` command. Unlike deleting a commit (which rewrites history and can cause problems if you've already pushed), `git revert` creates a new commit that undoes the changes from a previous one. The history stays intact — you can see what happened and when — but the broken change is gone.

First, find the ID of the commit you want to undo:

```
git log --oneline
```

Say the output shows:

```
f91c3a0 Restructure CSS to use new color variables
a3f92c1 Update donut prices for summer menu
7d14e88 Add catering page with inquiry form
```

The top commit (`f91c3a0`) is the one that broke something. To undo it:

```
git revert f91c3a0
```

Git opens a text editor asking you to confirm the commit message for the revert (it prefills a sensible default). Save and close the editor, and Git creates a new commit that undoes the changes. Then push it to GitHub:

```
git push
```

If you're using Netlify or Vercel, that push triggers an automatic redeployment within a minute. No muss, no fuss, no crisis. Now, with the broken change undone and the history intact, you can figure out why that particular change caused the problem.

REMEMBER

Git doesn't delete history; it only adds to it. Even after a revert, the original commit is still visible in the log. This is a feature, not a bug. It means you can always go back to any state your project has ever been in, no matter how many changes have happened since. The history is permanent.

## Rolling back with Netlify's deploy history

Netlify keeps a permanent record of every deploy it's ever done for your site. If you need to revert to an earlier version without touching Git, go to the Deploys tab in your Netlify dashboard. You'll see a list of every deployment, with timestamps and commit messages. Find the last good deploy, click it, and then click Publish Deploy. Netlify rolls the live site back to that version instantly.

This feature is particularly useful when you're managing a site for a client and need to fix a broken live site in under a minute. You can roll back in Netlify in about ten seconds while you take more time to properly diagnose and fix the problem in your local environment.

## Discarding uncommitted local changes

Sometimes the problem isn't something you've committed; it's something you've changed locally but haven't committed yet. You've spent an hour editing `styles.css` and it's a complete mess. You just want to throw away all those changes and go back to the last committed version. Here's how:

```
git restore styles.css
```

Git restores `styles.css` to the state it was in when you last committed. Your edits are gone, which is what you want.

WARNING

Note that there's no undo when you use `git restore`. Git doesn't keep uncommitted changes in a trash can. Make sure you genuinely want to discard them before running this command.

To discard all uncommitted changes across your entire project at once:

```
git restore .
```

Everything goes back to the last committed state. It's a nuclear option, but sometimes that's what you need.

# A Git Cheat Sheet

At this point, you know enough Git to handle almost everything that comes up in a web project. Here's a compact reference for the commands you'll reach for week after week:

- **`git init`:** Turn a folder into a Git repository. Run this once, in the project root folder, when you start a project.

- **`git status`:** See which files have changed since the last commit and which are staged. Run this constantly because it's the most informative command in Git.
- **`git add .`:** Stage all changed files for the next commit. To stage a single file, replace the dot with the filename (e.g., `git add menu.html`).
- **`git commit -m "`*`message`*`"`:** Save a snapshot with a descriptive *`message`*.
- **`git log --oneline`:** Show a compact history of commits, most recent first. Run `git log --oneline -10` if you only want the last ten.
- **`git push`:** Upload your local commits to GitHub. Do this regularly because it acts as a kind of cloud backup launcher.
- **`git pull`:** Download and merge commits from GitHub into your local repo. Run this when starting a session if you've worked from another machine.
- **`git checkout -b`** ***`branch-name`*:** Create a new branch and switch to it immediately. Your main branch is untouched while you experiment in here.
- **`git switch main`:** Switch back to the main branch. (Or `git switch` *`branch-name`* to switch to any branch.)
- **`git merge`** ***`branch-name`*:** Merge another branch into the current one. Run this from `main` after switching back to it.
- **`git revert`** ***`commit-id`*:** Create a commit that undoes a specific previous commit. This is the safe, history-preserving way to undo something you've already pushed.

Note that list isn't long. That's the point. Git has dozens of commands and hundreds of options, but you don't need most of them for everyday web development. Master these and you'll be in excellent shape.

IN THIS CHAPTER

» Running a final quality sweep

» Catching rogue SEO settings

» Verifying performance and analytics

» Building a launch-day plan

» Choosing between a soft launch and a full launch

# Chapter 2 Pre-Launch Preparation

*Good checklists . . . are precise. They are efficient, to the point, and easy to use even in the most difficult situations.*

—ATUL GAWANDE

Preparing to launch a website is a little bit like being a pilot getting ready for a flight. The plane is fueled, the passengers are seated, and everyone is itching to get going. But no good pilot just hurtles down the runway on vibes. They run a checklist first (a boring, methodical, slightly tedious checklist) because the alternative is discovering a problem at 30,000 feet, where problems are a great deal harder to fix. Your launch is the same, minus the beverage cart. The point of this chapter is to run that checklist while you're still safely on the ground.

I've organized the chapter as a series of pre-launch checks: testing, SEO, performance, legal, and analytics, followed by the launch plan that ties them all together. You've met most of these topics already in earlier books, so I won't reteach them from scratch. Think of this as the final walk-around before you head for the runway.

# Running a Final Quality-Assurance Sweep

As I explain in Book 9, Chapter 3, the smart move is to test as you build, squashing bugs while they're small and fresh in your mind. But testing-as-you-go has a blind spot: you test each piece in isolation, on your machine, in your browser, on your screen. Real visitors are not nearly so considerate.

A final QA sweep is different. It's a single, focused pass through the *entire* site, pretending to be a brand-new visitor who has never seen any of it before. You're not hunting for the bugs you already know about. You're hunting for the ones that show up only when all the pieces run together.

## The cross-browser and cross-device sweep

Your site might look flawless in Chrome on your laptop and fall to pieces in Safari on someone's phone. Sigh. Browsers interpret HTML and CSS with subtle differences, and screens come in every size from a phone to a 49-inch monitor that belongs on a starship.

So, open your site in more than one place. At a minimum, check it in the following:

- **Two or more browsers:** Chrome and Safari at the very least, plus Firefox or Edge if you can manage it.
- **A real phone:** Not just your desktop browser squished narrow. Borrow a friend's phone if theirs differs from yours.
- **A tablet, if your audience uses one:** The in-between sizes are where layouts love to misbehave.

On each one, scroll the full length of every important page. Does the navigation work? Do the images load? Is any text overlapping, cut off, or hiding behind something else? (For more on building layouts that flex gracefully across screen sizes, see Book 2, Chapter 3.)

## Checking every link, form, and button

The single most common thing wrong with a freshly built site is a link that goes nowhere. You typed the path incorrectly, or renamed a file, or linked to `contactus.html` when the file is `contact.html`. So check every link. Yep, every one. It won't take long if you use a link checker (refer to Book 9, Chapter 3) and will save you the special embarrassment of a customer emailing to say your menu link is broken.

Forms deserve extra attention because they're where visitors *do* something. If your site has an order form, for example, don't just look at it. Fill it out and submit it, as a customer would. Then ask the obvious questions: Did the order go somewhere? Did you get a confirmation? And what happens if someone leaves the email field blank, or types *galaxy glazed* into the quantity box where a number belongs?

TIP

Test your forms by submitting them, using both good data and deliberately bad data. A form that looks perfect but silently throws away submissions is worse than no form at all, because you won't find out until you've already lost orders.



## Testing the things that only break in public

Some parts of your site never come up while you're building, so they never get tested. The classic example is the *404 page*, which is the page a visitor lands on when they request an address that doesn't exist (a typo, an old bookmark, a search engine that hasn't caught up). Type a deliberately wrong address such as `orbitaldonuts.com/donut` and see what happens. You want a friendly, branded page that helps people find their way back, not a blank screen of despair.

A few other easy-to-miss states are worth a look:

- **Empty states:** What does your search-results page show when nothing matches?
- **Error messages:** When a form rejects bad input, is the message clear and polite, or cryptic and rude?
- **The very first load:** Clear your browser's cache and visit fresh, the way a total stranger would, with nothing helpfully preloaded.

## Proofreading the content one last time

While you're playing visitor, read the words. Typos and leftover placeholder text have a sneaky way of surviving every technical test you throw at a site, because your tools check that a page *works,* not that it makes any sense. So, search your pages for the telltale signs of an unfinished site: a stray *Lorem ipsum*, an [ADD PHOTO HERE] note you left for yourself, a price that still reads $0.00, or the classic placeholder phone number that's just a long row of fives.

Read your most important pages out loud if you can bear it. Your ear catches clumsy sentences and missing words that your eye happily skates right over after the hundredth read.

# The SEO Pre-Launch Checklist

You did the hard SEO work back in Book 7: keyword research, page titles, meta descriptions, clean URLs, the lot. This section isn't about redoing any of that. It's about confirming that the SEO you so carefully set up made it onto the live site and that nothing is quietly sabotaging it behind your back.

## The one setting that can make you invisible

Let me start with the single most important check in this entire chapter, because getting it wrong is a quiet catastrophe that nobody notices until it's far too late.

While building a site, developers routinely tell search engines and crawlers to ignore it. For example, you don't want Google indexing a half-finished site full of placeholder text and *Lorem ipsum*, after all. The two common ways to do this are a `noindex` instruction in a page's HTML (for search engines) and a `Disallow` rule in a file called `robots.txt` (for crawlers). Both are perfectly sensible during development.

Both are a disaster if you forget to remove them at launch!

I have watched a business launch a gorgeous new site, wait weeks for the Google traffic that never arrives, and slowly realize that they shipped with a giant "Do not index" sign still hanging on the door. Don't be that business. Before launch, check two things.

First, view the source of your key pages (right-click the page and then choose View Page Source) and make sure you do *not* see a line such as this one:

```
<meta name="robots" content="noindex">
```

Second, look at your `robots.txt` file, which lives at the root of your site (for example, `orbitaldonuts.com/robots.txt`). A launch-ready file should look something like this:

```
User-agent: *
Disallow:
Sitemap: https://orbitaldonuts.com/sitemap.xml
```

That empty `Disallow:` line means "don't block anything." The thing you're watching for is `Disallow: /` (with a slash), which means "block the entire site." One little character, an enormous difference.

## Titles, descriptions, and the preview test

Every page should have a unique `title` element and a `meta` description, because those two bits of text are what show up in search results. Here's the head section for a fictional yoga studio, Cedar Path Yoga:

```
<title>Cedar Path Yoga | Beginner Classes in Riverdale</title>
<meta name="description"
    content="Small-group yoga classes for beginners in Riverdale.
            Drop-ins welcome, no experience required.">
```

Now run a quick *preview test*: read each title and description as if it were the only thing in the world convincing a stranger to click. Is it clear? Does it say what the page is about? Would *you* click it? (For the full treatment of writing titles and descriptions that earn clicks, flip back to Book 7, Chapter 3.)

## Your sitemap and robots.txt

A *sitemap* is a file (usually `sitemap.xml`) that lists all the pages you want search engines to find. Most site builders and content management systems generate one for you automatically. Confirm yours exists by visiting `yoursite.com/sitemap.xml` in your browser, and make sure your real pages are listed and the leftover placeholder ones aren't. You'll submit this sitemap to Google after launch, which I cover in the next chapter.

## Confirming HTTPS and clean URLs

Two more quick checks before you move on. First, make sure your site loads over *HTTPS,* the secure version of the web, which I describe in Book 9, Chapter 4. Modern hosting almost always sets this up for you, but you should confirm it: visit your site and watch for any Not Secure warnings. Search engines quietly favor secure sites, and visitors trust them. (I cover setting up HTTPS in Book 1, Chapter 3.)

Second, take a final glance at your URLs. A clean address such as `orbitaldonuts.com/menu` is far friendlier to both humans and search engines than something cryptic such as `orbitaldonuts.com/page?id=47`. You sorted this out during the build, so this is just a last look to confirm nothing reverted on you.

# Verifying Performance

A slow site quietly bleeds visitors. People are impatient (you're impatient too, admit it), and a page that takes too long to appear gets abandoned before anyone reads a word of it. You worked on speed back in Book 9, Chapter 2. Now you verify it with a free tool and a level head.

## Running a Lighthouse report

*Lighthouse* is a free testing tool built right into the Chrome browser. It loads your page, pokes at it from every angle, and hands you a report card across four categories: performance, accessibility, best practices, and SEO. To run it, do the following:

1. **Open your site in Chrome.**
2. **Right-click anywhere on the page and choose Inspect to open the developer tools.**
3. **Click the Lighthouse tab (you may need to click the little >> arrows to find it).**
4. **Choose Mobile, click Analyze Page Load, and then wait a few seconds.**

When it finishes, you get four scores from 0 to 100. Green is good, orange is so-so, and red needs work.

## Reading the scores without panicking

Here's where people lose their minds: they see a Performance score of 78 and conclude their site is broken. It isn't! A perfect 100 is lovely but rarely necessary, and chasing the last few points can eat days of your life for almost no real-world payoff.

Aim for green (90 or above) on accessibility and SEO, because those scores reflect genuine problems that affect genuine people. For performance, treat anything in the good range as fine and dig into only the specific warnings that Lighthouse flags. Helpfully, the report tells you what to fix and roughly how much each fix would help.

## The image audit

Nine times out of ten, the thing slowing down a small-business site is images. A single photo straight off a phone camera can weigh several megabytes, which is roughly your entire page's worth of text repeated a hundred times over. On the Orbital Donuts site, the donut photos use the `.webp` format precisely because it stays sharp while keeping file sizes small.

Here's a quick win that Lighthouse loves: always tell the browser how big an image will be. When you set `width` and `height` on an image, the browser reserves the right amount of space before the file loads, so your page doesn't lurch around as things arrive. Add `loading="lazy"` and any off-screen (below the fold) images politely wait to load until the visitor scrolls near them:

```
<img src="galaxy-glazed.webp"
     width="400" height="400"
     alt="Galaxy Glazed donut with swirled cosmic glaze"
     loading="lazy">
```

That one cluster of attributes improves both raw speed and the annoying layout shift problem in a single move. (For the complete performance toolkit, including caching and minification, see Book 9, Chapter 2.)



# Reviewing Legal Compliance

Time for everyone's favorite subject: the legal stuff. I'll keep this brief and practical, with one enormous caveat up front. I am a writer, not a lawyer, and nothing here is legal advice. For a business handling customer data, a short conversation with an attorney is money well spent. With that out of the way, here are the basics every small site should have squared away before launch.

## Your privacy policy

A *privacy policy* explains what personal information you collect, why you collect it, and what you do with it once you have it. If your site has a contact form, an email signup, an analytics tool, or an online store (so, basically every site on Earth), you are collecting personal data, and most of the planet now legally requires you to disclose how.

A basic policy covers what you collect (names, email addresses, and possibly payment details if you're not using a hosted checkout), the tools that do the collecting (your analytics, your email service), how people can reach you about their data, and whether you use cookies.

WARNING

Don't just copy another company's privacy policy and swap in your own name. It'll describe data practices that aren't yours, which is arguably worse than having no policy at all. Use a reputable policy generator as a starting point, and then edit it to match what your site does.

## Terms of service in plain language

*Terms of service* (often shortened to *TOS*; sometimes called *terms and conditions*) are the rules for using your site: what people can and can't do, the limits of your liability, and how disputes get handled. For a simple brochure-style site, the terms of service can be short and sweet. For anything involving payments, accounts, or content that visitors submit themselves, it matters a great deal more.

## A quick accessibility self-check

*Accessibility* means building your site so that people with disabilities can use it, which is both the right thing to do and, increasingly, a legal expectation. I go into the accessibility details way back in Book 2, Chapter 4. Here's a fast pre-launch self-check to confirm none of it got lost along the way:

- **Images have alt text.** Every meaningful image needs an `alt` attribute describing it for screen-reader users.
- **Text has enough contrast.** Pale gray text on a white background looks terribly elegant and reads terribly, period. Make sure there's good contrast between text and background.
- **You can navigate by keyboard.** Put your mouse aside and press Tab through the page. Can you reach every link and button? Can you see where you are as you go?

None of these checks takes long, and each one matters enormously to a real person trying to use your site.

## Cookie and consent notices

If your site uses cookies, many regions require you to tell visitors about them and, in some cases, ask permission before those cookies load. That's the little banner you've now seen on approximately every website you've visited this decade. For a small site, you don't need anything fancy: a short notice explaining that you use cookies, with a link to your privacy policy, covers the basics. And since your audience almost certainly includes people in places with stricter rules (the European Union, for one), investigate a proper consent tool that delays loading analytics until the visitor agrees.

# Verifying Your Analytics Setup

You set up Google Analytics 4 back in Book 9, Chapter 1 so you could learn how people use your site. But here's the catch: analytics records data only from the moment it starts working. If your tracking is broken at launch, you permanently lose the data from your most fascinating period, the very beginning, when traffic is fresh and you're learning what works.

## Confirming the tag is on every page

Your analytics works by placing a small snippet of code (the *tag*) on every page of your site. The operative phrase there is *every page*. It's common to add the tag to the home page during setup and then forget all the others. Spot-check several pages by viewing the page source and searching for your tag, which contains your measurement ID, something in the form `G-XXXXXXXXXX`.

## Watching it work in real time

The fastest way to confirm that analytics is firing is to watch yourself visit. In Google Analytics, go to Reports and then Realtime. The Realtime report shows you activity from roughly the last 30 minutes. Now open your site in another browser tab and click around for a bit. Within a few seconds, you should see yourself pop up as an active user in the Realtime report.

See yourself show up? Your tag is working. Nothing happening after a minute or two? Then your tag is missing, mistyped, or being blocked (often by your own ad blocker, so try switching that off and reloading). Far better to discover that now than to wonder, three weeks from now, why on earth your reports are empty.

# Creating a Launch Plan

By now you've checked everything individually. The launch plan is what turns all those separate checks into a single, calm, repeatable process, so that launch day itself is gloriously boring. (Boring is the goal. Boring means nothing exploded.) At its heart, a launch plan is just a checklist with a little scheduling wrapped around it.

## Building your launch-day runbook

A *runbook* is a step-by-step list of what you'll do, in order, on launch day. Writing it down sounds like overkill right up until the moment something goes sideways and you're trying to remember Step 4 while your adrenaline does all the talking. A simple runbook for a small site might read like this:

1. Back up the current site and its database, if it has one.
2. Deploy the new files to the live server.
3. Point the domain at the new site (see Book 10, Chapter 1 for the deployment details).
4. Run a smoke test: visit five key pages and submit one form.
5. Confirm that analytics is recording in the Realtime report.
6. Tell the world (email, social, the works).

Your exact steps will depend on your setup. The point is to decide them *before* launch day, while you can still think clearly, rather than improvising under pressure with everyone watching.

## Picking a launch window

Resist the powerful urge to launch on a Friday afternoon. If something breaks, you'll either spend your weekend fixing it or leave it broken until Monday, and neither of those is anyone's idea of a good time. Launch when you have the time and energy to babysit the site for a few hours afterward. Early in the week and earlier in the day, when your traffic is naturally light, is ideal. (If your customers cluster in one time zone, aim for their quiet hours.) A bug that hits three visitors on a sleepy Tuesday morning is a far smaller crisis than the same bug hitting three hundred on a busy Friday night.

## Your rollback plan

A *rollback* is your undo button: a way to put the old site back if the new one turns out to have a serious problem. This is why I made such a fuss about version control and backups in Book 10, Chapter 1. Before you launch, come up with a set of criteria that would trigger a rollback (such as a broken login or shopping cart), know precisely how you'd revert, and figure out roughly how long it would take. If your honest answer is "I'm not entirely sure," figure it out now, while nothing is on fire.

## The post-launch watch list

Launching isn't the finish line; it's the start of a short, attentive watch period. For the first hour or two after you go live, pay attention to a few things:

- **The home page and a couple of key pages:** Load them yourself, on both your phone and your computer, just to be sure they came through intact.
- **Your analytics Realtime report:** Are visitors showing up? Are they landing on the pages you expect them to?
- **Your inbox and forms:** Submit a test through your contact or order form and confirm it lands where it's supposed to.

If everything's quiet and working after a couple of hours, congratulations: you've earned the right to stop staring at the screen. (The next chapter covers what to watch over the first 48 hours in greater detail.)



# Soft Launch versus Full Launch

Your site can go live in two broad ways, and the right one for you depends on your nerves, your audience, and how much is riding on the day.

## The soft launch

A *soft launch* opens the doors quietly. You make the site live but hold off on actively promoting it, letting a trickle of visitors find it while you keep an eye out for problems you missed. For example, if you have some newsletter subscribers, you might soft-launch by emailing them, thus inviting a friendly, forgiving crowd to kick the tires on the new site first.

The big advantage is obvious: if something's broken, a handful of loyal regulars run into it instead of the entire internet. You quietly fix it, nobody panics, and you build confidence before stepping into the real spotlight.

## The full launch

A *full launch* is the opposite approach: lights, camera, traffic. You flip the switch and promote everywhere at once, with an announcement, social posts, maybe even an ad. A coordinated full launch makes sense when timing genuinely matters, say, an outdoor retailer named Northwind Outfitters dropping a new season's gear on the same morning across email, social media, and the site. The payoff is momentum. The risk is that any problem happens in front of your largest possible audience.

## Which one fits your site

If you're new to all this or the launch is genuinely high-stakes, lean toward a soft launch. Open quietly, confirm everything works with a few visitors, and then ramp up the promotion once you're confident. Save the full launch for when you've done this a few times before or have a real reason to make a splash on one specific day. There's no prize for bravery here, and a calm launch beats a dramatic one every single time.

IN THIS CHAPTER

» Working through your launch-day sequence

» Making the switch and surviving DNS propagation

» Testing the things that only break in production

» Troubleshooting launch-day bugs

» Watching over the first 48 hours

# Chapter 3
# Going Live Successfully

*A ship in harbor is safe, but that is not what ships are built for.*

— JOHN A. SHEDD

After all the planning, designing, building, and testing (and re-testing, and that one final test just to be safe), you've reached the moment this whole book has been building toward: putting your website out into the world where people besides you and your team can find it. Exciting, isn't it? Also, if you're anything like me, a little bit terrifying. This is the point where your site stops being a private project on your computer and becomes a public place that strangers can visit, click around, and form opinions about.

Here's the reassuring part: going live isn't one heart-stopping leap off a cliff. It's a short, orderly sequence of small, manageable steps, and this chapter walks you through every one of them. By the time you're finished, your site will be live, working, and quietly getting on with its new life. Ready? Let's flip that switch.

# A Launch-Day Action Checklist

Before I dig into the tricky parts, let me hand you the entire launch in one place. Think of this as your flight checklist: a short, ordered list of everything you'll do on launch day, each with a pointer to where it's explained in full. Work through it top to bottom and you've launched. Everything after this section is really just a closer look at the steps that tend to trip people up:

1. **Back up the current site,** if you're replacing an existing one, so you have a clean copy to restore (Book 10, Chapter 1).
2. **Deploy your files to the live server,** whether that's a `git push` to Netlify or an upload over SFTP (Book 10, Chapter 1).
3. **Point your domain at the live site** by updating your DNS records, and then wait for propagation (Book 1, Chapter 3).
4. **Confirm HTTPS is working,** and you're not seeing any Not Secure warnings (Book 7, Chapter 4).
5. **Run a quick smoke test** on the live URL, loading your key pages and clicking your main navigation (Book 10, Chapter 2).
6. **Do one real end-to-end run,** placing an order or inquiry and confirming it arrives (covered later in this chapter).
7. **Confirm analytics is recording** by watching yourself show up in the Realtime report (Book 9, Chapter 1).
8. **Submit your sitemap to Google** in Google Search Console (Book 7, Chapter 4).
9. **Tell the world,** following whatever soft- or full-launch plan you settled on (Book 10, Chapter 2).
10. **Start your 48-hour watch,** keeping a light hand on the site while the first visitors arrive (covered later in this chapter).

That's the entire launch. Ten steps, most of which you already know how to do. The rest of this chapter zooms in on the handful that have a habit of going sideways.

# Making the Switch

Steps 1 through 4 of the checklist are the switch itself: back up, deploy, point the domain, confirm HTTPS. You learned how to do each one in earlier chapters, so here I want to focus on the part nobody warns you about, which is what happens in the minutes and hours right after you flip it.

## Working through your launch runbook

Back in Book 10, Chapter 2, you wrote a runbook: the exact, ordered list of steps you'd follow on launch day. Now's the moment it earns its keep. Open it and work through it one line at a time, checking off each step as you go.

Do the steps in order, and do them one at a time. If a step fails, stop and sort it out before moving on, rather than pressing ahead and hoping. A launch where you deploy, discover the domain isn't pointing anywhere, and then realize you also forgot to force HTTPS is a launch where you can no longer tell which problem is causing what. One step at a time keeps every problem isolated and easy to name. (This is why you wrote the runbook in advance: so launch day itself could be calm and mechanical instead of a frantic improvisation.)

## Pointing your domain and surviving propagation

Pointing your domain at the live site is a small technical act (as few as two DNS records, as I describe in Book 1, Chapter 3) with an outsized emotional payload, because it's the step that finally puts your site at its real, public address. Make the change, save it, and then brace yourself for the genuinely weird part: *DNS propagation.*

When you update a DNS record, the new information doesn't reach the entire world at once. Internet providers and servers around the world store copies of your old record in their temporary memory. They'll look for your update only after their specific Time to Live (TTL) countdown timers expire. Usually this process takes minutes; occasionally it takes hours. During that window you'll see things that make no sense: the new site loads on your phone but not your laptop, or a friend across town sees it while you're still staring at the old one. Nothing is broken. You're simply watching propagation happen, in real time, at different speeds in different places.

WARNING

The most important thing to do during propagation is nothing. If you entered your DNS records correctly, waiting *is* the fix. Re-editing the records every few minutes because the site isn't live yet doesn't speed anything up. Enter them once, confirm they're right, and step away.

## Confirming the switch flipped

Rather than refreshing your own browser and drawing conclusions from what one computer happens to see, check propagation properly. A free tool such as `whatsmydns.net` looks up your domain from dozens of locations around the world at once and shows you which address each one currently sees. Type in your domain, choose the record type that matches the change you made (such as A, CNAME, or MX), and you'll get a map dotted with green checkmarks (locations already seeing your new site) and red Xs (locations still catching up). As the morning goes on, you'll watch the red turn green, which is the clearest possible sign that your switch is flipping.

Once most of that map is green, your site is truly live, and it's time to work through the rest of the checklist: confirm analytics is recording, and tell the search engines you exist. You submit your sitemap in Google Search Console, which you set up back in Book 7, Chapter 4; launch day is simply when you pull the trigger.

# Testing What Breaks Only in Production

You tested your site thoroughly before launch (Book 10, Chapter 2), so why test again now? Because some things simply can't be checked until the site is live at its real address, on the real server, wired up to the real world. The technical name for your live site is *production,* and production has a way of behaving differently from the tidy version you tested on your own machine. This section covers the handful of checks that mean something only once you're live.

## Making sure you deployed the version you tested

Here's a subtle and surprisingly common launch-day problem: the version of the site sitting on the live server isn't quite the version you so carefully tested. Maybe an older set of files got uploaded, or the deploy grabbed the wrong folder, or a last-minute fix never made it across. Everything *looks* fine, because a slightly stale site still looks like a site.

So, confirm parity with a simple trick. Pick a small, recent change you know you made, something you'd remember, such as a price you updated or a headline you rewrote, and check that it's there on the live site. If your most recent change is present, you can trust that the rest of your work came along with it. If it's missing, you've deployed an older version, and it's time to redeploy before anyone notices.

## Doing one real end-to-end run

Your pre-launch testing checked your forms in isolation. This check is different because it's an end-to-end test of your site's most important workflow, which might be selling a product, booking a service, or setting up a subscription. With this test, you start at the beginning of the workflow and then walk all the way through the process, on the live site, exactly the way a paying customer would. So, become a customer for five minutes.

For Orbital Donuts, a live run-through means placing a genuine order: pick a Cosmic Cruller, go through every step of the ordering process, and submit it for real. Then check both ends of the transaction. Did the order reach you, wherever orders are supposed to land? And did you, playing the customer, get the confirmation you'd expect to see? Did the order get shipped, the service get booked, or the subscription get set up? A site where orders quietly vanish or customers never get a thank-you *feels* broken even when no error message appears, and a live run-through is the only way to catch that gap before a real customer does.

## Confirming your site's emails arrive

Websites send more email than you'd think: contact-form notifications to you, order confirmations to customers, the occasional receipt. And email is fussy. A new site sending its first messages is exactly the kind of stranger that spam filters treat with deep suspicion, so those first emails have an alarming tendency to land in a spam folder or vanish rather than in the inbox where they belong.

So, test the email paths for real. Submit your contact form and confirm the notification reaches you, checking your spam folder if it doesn't appear. If your site sends confirmations to customers, send one to an address you can check and see where it ends up. If your messages are landing in spam, that's your signal to route your site's email through a dedicated sending service, which dramatically improves the odds of reaching the inbox. Far better to discover this on launch day, with test messages, than a week from now when a customer mentions that they never got their receipt.

# When Things Go Wrong on Launch Day

Something will go a little sideways. It happens on nearly every launch, and it's not a sign that you did anything wrong; it's just what happens when a site meets the messy real world for the first time. Here are the usual launch-day suspects and how to handle each one without panicking.

## "It works for me but not for them"

A site that works for you but not someone else is the classic launch-day head-scratcher, and nine times out of ten the culprit is one of two things: DNS propagation or your browser's cache.

If a friend can't reach the site you're happily looking at, propagation is the likely cause, and the cure is simply patience while the new DNS information reaches their corner of the internet. If, instead, *you're* the one still seeing the old site after everyone else has moved on, your browser is probably showing you a saved copy. Load the site in a private window or clear your browser's cache, and the current version should appear. When you're not sure which version is real, check on your phone over cellular data — a separate network — to see what the wider world gets.

## The site loads but looks completely unstyled

Your page loads but looks like it tumbled out of 1994: plain black text on white, no colors, no layout, nothing. Don't panic. Your content is fine; the browser simply couldn't find your CSS file, so it's showing raw HTML with no styling applied on top.

The usual culprit is the path in your stylesheet link, which pointed to a spot that was correct on your computer but wrong on the live server. Open your page's HTML and find the line that links the stylesheet, something like this:

```
<link rel="stylesheet" href="styles.css">
```

Confirm that `styles.css` sits where that path says it does, relative to the page. A safe, portable fix is to start the path with a single slash (`/styles.css`), which tells the browser to look from the root of your site no matter which page is asking. Reload, and your styling should come flooding back.

## Images that work locally but vanish on the server

Your images looked perfect on your own computer, but on the live site some of them are broken, showing that sad little placeholder icon. A classic cause is capitalization. Many web servers are fussy about uppercase and lowercase letters in filenames, even though your own computer probably isn't. So, if your HTML references `Logo.webp` but the file is named `logo.webp`, your computer shrugs and shows the image anyway, while the server insists the two names are different files and comes up empty-handed.

The fix is to make your filenames and the links pointing to them match exactly, capital for capital. To dodge this headache forever, adopt one simple rule: name every file using all lowercase letters, with hyphens instead of spaces (`galaxy-glazed.webp`, never `Galaxy Glazed.webp`). Follow that convention everywhere and this whole category of bug quietly disappears.

## Forms that submit but never arrive

You fill out your own contact form, click Send, see a cheerful "Thanks, we'll be in touch!" message, and then nothing ever lands in your inbox. This one is sneaky because the visitor's side looks flawless, so you'd never suspect a problem unless you tested it yourself.

Two suspects account for most cases, and they're the same ones from the email check earlier: your spam folder and a wrong destination address. Check your spam folder first, because a new site's first emails often land there. If the message isn't there either and you're using a form-handling service, open its settings and confirm the destination email address is correct and spelled properly, because a single typo there sends every submission quietly into the void. Fix whichever it is, send one more test, and confirm it arrives.

## The page that refuses to update

You fix a typo, upload the corrected file, reload the page, and — what!? — the typo is still there, mocking you. Before you conclude that your file didn't upload (it probably did), suspect caching. Your browser, and possibly a CDN sitting in front of your site, is showing a saved copy to save time.

The first thing to try is a *hard refresh,* which forces the browser to fetch a fresh copy instead of using its saved one: hold down Shift and click your browser's Reload button, or press Ctrl+F5 on Windows or Cmd+Shift+R on a Mac. Nine times out of ten, there's your correction. If the page still won't budge and you're using a CDN or a caching plug-in, look for a Clear Cache or Purge button in its dashboard, which tells the whole system to forget its saved copies and serve the latest version.

## Making the call: Fix, wait, or roll back

Every launch-day problem eventually forces the same question: What do I *do* about this? You have three options, and picking the right one quickly is a skill worth having. Book 10, Chapter 1 covers the mechanics of each; this is about knowing which one to reach for.

- » **Fix it in place.** For small, contained problems, such as a typo, a broken link, or an image with the wrong path, just fix it and move on. The overwhelming majority of launch-day gremlins live here. They are annoying, not dangerous, and faster to correct than to agonize over.
- » **Wait it out.** Some problems aren't really problems; they're just processes in progress. DNS propagation is the classic example: the fix is patience, and doing something (like re-editing your records) only makes it worse. If you know the issue will resolve on its own, resist the urge to fight it.
- » **Roll back.** For serious, widespread breakage — the whole site is down, checkout is broken, something is actively losing orders — don't try to fix it live under pressure. Put the old, working site back first (using the rollback methods from Book 10, Chapter 1), and *then* diagnose the new one calmly, offline, where a mistake won't cost you anything.

How do you choose in the heat of the moment? Two quick questions. First, how bad is it, really: is this a cosmetic annoyance a few people might notice, or is it stopping visitors from doing the very thing your site exists to do? Second, can you fix it in a couple of minutes, with confidence? A small, well-understood problem gets fixed in place. A big or mysterious one that's actively hurting you gets a roll-back, not heroics. And when you genuinely can't tell how bad it is, roll back and investigate in peace.

REMEMBER

A boring, working old site always beats an exciting, broken new one. There's no prize for bravely fixing a serious problem live while it's costing you customers, so when in doubt, roll back, breathe, and fix it where nothing's on fire.

# The First 48 Hours

Launching isn't the finish line; it's the start of a short, attentive watch. Most problems that slipped past your testing tend to surface in the first day or two, when visitors start using your site in ways you never imagined. The goal for these 48 hours is simple: stay attentive without tipping over into obsessive, screen-refreshing panic.

## Keeping a launch-day log

One habit pays for itself the instant anything goes sideways: keep a running note of what you do on launch day, in a plain text file or a notebook. Each time you make a change, jot down the time and what you did: "9:15 — pointed the DNS," "9:40 — forced HTTPS," "10:05 — fixed the logo path." Then, if the site starts misbehaving at 10:10, your log points straight at that path change from five minutes earlier, instead of leaving you to guess which of the morning's dozen tweaks is the guilty one.

## The first few hours

Your most attentive window should be the first two or three hours. During that time, keep a light hand on the site:

- **Reload your key pages periodically.** Reload the home page and your money-makers (the menu, the order page), on both a computer and a phone.
- **Watch your analytics tool's realtime report.** As I mention in Book 10, Chapter 2, this report shows visitors as they arrive. Seeing real people land on the pages you expect is enormously reassuring.
- **Keep an eye on your inbox.** Confirm that form submissions and orders are arriving, since a silently broken form is the kind of problem that quietly costs you business.

TIP

Don't sit and refresh your analytics every thirty seconds. That way lies madness (and a strange conviction that nobody loves you because it's been four whole minutes since the last visitor). Pick a couple of check-in times, glance at things, and then step away. A watched site, like a watched pot, feels agonizingly slow.

## The rest of the 48

Once you've survived the first few hours without incident, you can relax considerably, but don't vanish. Over the next day or two, check in a few times a day rather than a few times an hour. Now you're watching for the slower-burning issues: a page loading sluggishly under real traffic, a form that works for you but not for a particular customer, a broken link on a page you rarely visit.

Check your email and contact forms for messages from visitors, too. Your first customers are often your most honest and most helpful testers, and someone kindly reporting "Hey, your Location page link seems broken" is doing you an enormous favor. Fix what they find, thank them if you can, and let the site settle into its new life.

## Knowing when the launch is truly done

So, when can you stop hovering? Some good rules of thumb: when the site has run for a full day or two without anything new breaking; when your analytics show visitors reaching the pages you expected; and when your forms and orders are reliably landing where they should. At that point, the launch is over and your site quietly graduates from "newly launched" to just "my website."

This is the moment your job shifts from *launching* to *maintaining,* which is a different rhythm entirely: slower, steadier, and measured in weeks and months rather than minutes. I cover that ongoing care, keeping your site fast, secure, current, and healthy, in Book 10, Chapter 4. For now, though, the hard part is behind you. Your site is live, it works, and people are using it. Take a breath. You've earned it.

IN THIS CHAPTER

» Setting a maintenance schedule

» Keeping your content fresh

» Monitoring uptime

» Taming comment, form, and review spam

» Updating your software safely

# Chapter 4
# Ongoing Website Maintenance

*Our England is a garden, and such gardens are not made*

*By singing: — "Oh, how beautiful!" and sitting in the shade.*

—RUDYARD KIPLING

A website isn't a painting you hang on a wall and admire for years. It's more like a garden. Leave a garden alone for six months and you don't come back to the same garden; you come back to weeds, garbage blown in on the wind, and something noxious growing out of the planter. Websites are the same. Software goes out of date, links to other sites quietly die, spam creeps into your comments, and the fresh content you were once so proud of slowly curdles into a stale collection that makes people wonder if the site is still viable.

Gardens need regular maintenance, and so does your website. This chapter shows you how to tend your site so it stays healthy, fast, and worth visiting long after launch day. None of what I talk about here is difficult and none of it takes much time. The key is to do a little bit regularly instead of a lot in a panic.

# Creating a Maintenance Schedule

Okay, when did you last confirm that every page on your site still loads? If your answer is "launch day" or "I can't remember," don't sweat it: you're in good company and you're exactly who this section is for.

The trouble with website maintenance is that almost nothing about it feels urgent until, suddenly, all of it does. A plug-in that's three versions out of date doesn't nag you. A contact form that quietly stopped emailing you doesn't send up a flare. You find out about these things the bad way: a customer mentions it or, worse, they don't. They just leave. A maintenance schedule fixes this by turning the things that you figure you should probably check sometime into things that you really do check on a specific day, which is the only version of the plan that ever happens.

## Grouping tasks by how often they're needed

The trick is to sort every maintenance task by how often it truly needs doing, so you're never facing the whole list at once. Here's a schedule that works well for a typical small-business site.

Weekly (about five minutes):

- **Skim for form submissions.** Make sure inquiries are arriving and not drowning in spam.
- **Glance at uptime and analytics.** A quick look confirms that the site is up and traffic looks normal.
- **Moderate new comments.** Approve the real ones; trash the junk.

Monthly (about half an hour):

- **Update your software.** Apply plug-in, theme, and core updates (safely; I get to that later in this chapter). For security patches, don't wait until this monthly check because they should be applied right away.
- **Run a link check.** Catch links that have rotted since last month.
- **Publish or refresh something.** Create a post, update a page, add a seasonal note, anything that shows the site is alive.

Quarterly (an hour or two):

- **Re-check performance.** Retest the pages you sped up in Book 9, Chapter 2 to make sure they haven't slowed back down.
- **Review your security basics.** Work through the security checklist from Book 9, Chapter 4.
- **Tidy the database.** Clear out the junk that piles up behind the scenes.

Yearly (an afternoon):

- **Run a full content audit.** Inventory everything and decide what to keep, update, merge, or retire.
- **Review your legal pages.** Confirm your privacy policy and terms still match what you do. Note, as well, that you should perform this review any time you make major changes to your site.
- **Renew and verify.** Check that your domain and any certificates aren't about to lapse. Your domain registrar almost certainly has tools that provide automated domain name renewal and expiration alerts, so be sure to activate those.

Note the shape of it: the frequent tasks are tiny, and the big tasks happen rarely. That's deliberate. If your weekly maintenance takes longer than the time it takes to make a coffee, you'll quietly stop doing it, and then you're back to the panic-repair cycle you're trying to escape.

## Making the schedule stick

A schedule you keep in your head is a schedule you'll forget. So, write it down somewhere it can nag you. The owner of Orbital Donuts put a recurring 15-minute "website check" on the shop calendar every Monday morning, right after the weekly supply order goes in. Because it's bolted onto something that already happens, it doesn't get skipped. That's the secret: attach your maintenance to an existing habit, and future-you will thank present-you.



REMEMBER

Maintenance is prevention, not repair. Ten quiet minutes a week keeps small problems small. The alternative is discovering all of them at once, usually during the week you're busiest.

# Content Freshness Strategies

Have you ever landed on a page that proudly announced an event from three years ago? You instantly wondered whether anyone still runs the place. That little flash of doubt is what stale content does to your visitors, and heading it off is one of the highest-value maintenance habits.

(I cover why freshness helps your search rankings in Book 7, Chapter 3, and how to plan new content on a calendar in Book 6, Chapter 1. This section is about the other half of the job: tending the content you've already published.)

## Spotting content that's gone stale

Stale content is sneaky because it usually looks fine, but just isn't true anymore. The usual suspects:

- **Dated facts:** Prices, hours, staff names, "new for 2024" banners, and anything with a year baked into it
- **Dead references:** Links to tools, partners, or articles that no longer exist
- **Old screenshots:** Software you show has since been redesigned, so your step-by-step no longer matches reality
- **Finished events:** The "Join us this Saturday!" post from a Saturday long past

## Refresh not rewrite

Here's the reassuring part: freshening content almost never means starting over. A refresh is usually a handful of small edits: update the numbers, swap the screenshot, fix the dead link, correct the date. And because you're improving a page that already exists (and has already earned whatever search ranking and links it has), a light refresh often does more good than writing something from scratch.

You certainly want to keep your most critical pages — that is, those that generate the most revenue or the most conversions, or that have legal or operational importance — refreshed. Other than those criteria, pick your battles by traffic. Your analytics (Book 9, Chapter 1) tell you which pages people visit, so refresh those first. That obscure post from 2021 that pulls four views a month can wait, or become a candidate for retirement when you run your content audit later in this chapter.

### Be honest about "updated"

WARNING

Don't fake freshness. Changing a "last updated" date without changing anything is a trick some folks try to look current, and it fools nobody for long, least of all the returning visitor who sees the same old words sitting under a shiny new date. If you say a page was updated, update it. Genuinely refreshed content builds trust; a lipstick-on-a-timestamp date quietly erodes it.

## Monitoring Uptime and Performance

Your website will go down. Notice I wrote *will,* not *might,* because all sites eventually do, at least for a little while. Servers hiccup, hosting companies have bad days, a botched update knocks a site offline. The nerve-wracking part isn't that it happens; it's that you're usually the last to know. Your site could sit dead for hours while you're asleep or busy with customers, and the only people who notice are the visitors bouncing off an error page. Not great!

### Uptime monitoring: A robot that watches while you sleep

To know when your website goes down, you can hire a robot to keep an eye on your site around the clock, a process known as *uptime monitoring.* The idea is simple: a monitoring service visits your site every few minutes from somewhere out on the internet, confirms it gets a normal response, and — this is the important part — messages you the instant it doesn't. Instead of hearing about downtime from an annoyed customer, you hear about it from your phone, often before anyone else has even noticed.

Setting up a monitoring service takes about five minutes:

- **Sign up** for a monitoring service. Several have free tiers that check every few minutes, which is plenty for a small site.
- **Enter your site's URL** and pick how often you want it checked.
- **Choose your alerts:** email, a text message, or a push notification to your phone.

That's the entire setup. From then on, the service quietly pings your site, and you hear from it only when something's wrong.

So which robot should you hire? Happily, you don't have to spend a cent to get started. Here are a few reliable services that all offer a free tier generous enough for a typical small-business site (free-plan limits do drift over time, so treat the specifics as a starting point and check the current details when you sign up):

- **HetrixTools (`hetrixtools.com`):** Also checks every minute on its free tier and tosses in a bonus you won't find elsewhere: it warns you if your domain lands on a spam blacklist, which is nice to have if you send email from your domain.
- **Pulsetic (`pulsetic.com`):** The speed demon of the bunch because its free plan checks every 30 seconds and can reach you by phone call, text, email, or Slack, no credit card required. It's a newer, less familiar name, so I wouldn't necessarily start here, but it's tough to beat when you want an alarm the instant something twitches.
- **Better Stack (`betterstack.com`):** The polished option. Its permanent free plan (again, no credit card) includes a status page you can host on your own domain, the kind you'd be proud to show customers mid-outage. The trade-off is a three-minute free check interval, which is a middle-of-the-road pace.
- **UptimeRobot (`uptimerobot.com`):** The best-known name and the quickest to set up because you can be monitoring in about 30 seconds. The free plan covers a generous 50 monitors. The catch is speed: its free checks run every five minutes, the slowest here. For a simple brochure or small-shop site that's fine (five minutes of downtime won't end the world), but if you'd rather know sooner, one of the other faster free options will serve you better.

## What "99.99 percent uptime" really means

Monitoring services also track your *uptime percentage*, which is the share of time your site was reachable. You'll see hosts brag about 99.99 percent uptime (known in the trade as *four nines*), which sounds ridiculously good until you do the math: 99.99 percent still leaves room for almost an hour of downtime a year. For a small-business site, that's pretty good. The number to worry about is a host that keeps slipping to 99.9 percent (nine hours offline per year), 99 percent (nearly four *days* offline a year), or lower. If your monitor turns up a pattern of outages, that's evidence that you might want to consider another hosting provider.

## Don't let performance creep back

Back in Book 9, Chapter 2, you did the real work of making your site fast. Unfortunately, fast sites don't stay fast on their own. Every image you upload without compressing it, every plug-in you bolt on, every marketing tag you paste in just to try it adds a little weight. On its own, none of it matters. Together, over a year, they can turn a snappy site into a sluggish one, and because the slowdown is so gradual, you never feel it happen.

The fix is easy: put a performance check on your quarterly schedule. Rerun the same speed test you used in Book 9, Chapter 2 and compare the score to last quarter. If the score has dropped, look at what you've added since the previous test. Catching a 5-point slide every few months is trivial. Discovering a 30-point collapse after a year of neglect is a project.

# Managing Comments and Spam

If you enabled comments on your blog (a decision I help you weigh in Book 6, Chapter 4), congratulations: you now own a small, unpaid inbox that fills itself with garbage. Comment spam is relentless, automated, and weirdly persistent. But comments aren't the only door spam sneaks through, and keeping on top of all of it is a routine part of ongoing maintenance.

## Know where the spam gets in

Spam isn't just those "Great post! Visit my site!!!" comments. It arrives through several doors:

- **Blog comments:** The classic gateway, where bots post links to sketchy products, usually barely related to whatever you wrote.
- **Contact forms:** Bots fill in your forms, too, so your "New inquiry!" emails start arriving stuffed with gibberish and sales pitches.
- **Fake reviews:** If you accept reviews or testimonials, expect some to be planted by bots, or occasionally by a competitor having a bad day.

## Stop most of it automatically

The good news is you don't have to fight spam by hand. An *anti-spam filter* catches the overwhelming majority before it ever reaches you. Akismet (`get.akismet.com`) is the best-known one for WordPress, and most form tools have one built in. Add an invisible trap called a *honeypot* (a hidden form field that real people never see but bots dutifully fill in, cheerfully outing themselves as robots; I cover honeypots in Book 3, Chapter 2), and you'll stop most of the rest. Between the two, the flood becomes a trickle.

### Keep a light moderation rhythm

Even with filters running, a little spam gets through, and a little more sits in your pending queue waiting for a yes or a no. Don't let it pile up. A quick weekly pass where you approve the real comments, delete the junk, and glance at the spam folder to rescue anything wrongly caught keeps things tidy in a couple of minutes.

WARNING

Don't leave spam comments sitting on your live pages while you get to them later. Visitors see them, search engines see them, and links to shady sites in your comments can drag down your reputation. If you know you can't moderate regularly, it's better to turn comments off than to leave the door propped open.

## Database Maintenance

If your site runs on WordPress or any similar system I cover in Book 5, a database is quietly doing the real work behind the friendly pages your visitors see. Picture the database as a giant, well-organized filing cabinet: every post, page, comment, setting, and user lives in there as a row in a table. Most of the time, you never think about it, and that's fine. But like any filing cabinet, it slowly fills with stuff you don't need, and an overstuffed database can make your whole site feel sluggish.

### The junk that piles up

Here's what accumulates in a database without any help from you:

- **Post revisions:** Every time you save a draft, the system may keep the old version. A single much-edited page can hoard dozens of revisions you'll never look at again.
- **Trashed and spam items:** Deleted posts and caught spam comments often linger in a trash" state, still taking up room.
- **Transients:** These are little scraps of temporary cached data that were supposed to expire but sometimes overstay their welcome.
- **Orphaned leftovers:** When you remove a plug-in, it often leaves behind its old settings and data, which of course you no longer need.

## Clean it up, but back it up first

WARNING

Always back up your database before you clean it. Database changes can't be undone with a tidy Ctrl+Z, and a careless cleanup can break your site, so back up first, every single time. I cover backups in Book 9, Chapter 4.

With a backup safely in hand, the cleanup is easy because you don't do it by hand. A maintenance plug-in (WP-Optimize is a popular, beginner-friendly one) handles the job from a checklist: remove old revisions, empty the trash, clear expired transients, and optimize the tables so they store their data more efficiently. You tick the boxes, click a button, and the plug-in does the tedious part for you.

You can also tell the system to stop hoarding revisions in the first place. Adding a single line to your `wp-config.php` file caps how many revisions each post is allowed to keep:

```
define('WP_POST_REVISIONS', 5);
```

That line keeps the five most recent versions of every post (which is plenty for a simple safety net that lets you undo your last few edits) and automatically discards the rest going forward. Set it once, and the pileup never happens again.

How often should you tidy up? For most small sites, a database cleanup once a quarter is plenty, which is why it sits on the quarterly line of the maintenance schedule from earlier in this chapter. With a backup you already have, it's a five-minute chore to make your site stay quick.

# Broken Link Management

Every link on your site is a small promise: click here and you'll get somewhere useful. *Link rot* is what happens when the internet quietly breaks those promises on your behalf. A page you linked to gets deleted, a company you recommended folds, a URL changes. Just like that, your helpful link dumps people at a dead end. You didn't do anything wrong; the web just moved on without telling you. But your visitor doesn't know that. They just see a broken promise with your name on it.

(I cover the mechanics of finding broken links and setting up redirects in Book 7, Chapter 4, in the context of SEO. Here I want to focus on why link rot is an *ongoing* problem rather than a one-time fix.)

## Two flavors of broken link

To begin, know that there are two types of broken link to manage:

- **Internal links** point to other pages on your own site. These break when you rename or delete a page, which means you control them and can fix them.
- **External links** point to other people's sites. These break whenever those sites change, which you can't control or predict. External links rot on their own mysterious schedule, which is why you have to keep checking.

## Check on a schedule, fix by decision

Because external links rot unpredictably, the only reliable defense is a periodic scan. A free *link checker* crawls your whole site and hands you a list of every link returning an error. Run one monthly (that's why it's on the maintenance schedule), and then work down the list making one of three quick calls for each:

- **Fix it.** The page just moved, so update the link to its new address.
- **Replace it.** The resource is gone for good, so point to a comparable one or link somewhere more useful.
- **Remove it.** There's no worthy replacement, so delete the link and keep the surrounding text.

So where do you find one of these link checkers? Happily, the best ones are free (or free enough for a small site) and come in a few flavors depending on how you like to work:

- **Dead Link Checker (`deadlinkchecker.com`):** The no-fuss favorite. You paste in your web address and it crawls your site right there in your browser (nothing to install), handing you a tidy list of every dead link along with the page it's hiding on. Ideal for a quick monthly scan.
- **Broken Link Check (`brokenlinkcheck.com`):** Another free, browser-based option with no sign-up required. Handy as a second opinion, or simply if you like its report better.
- **Broken Link Checker by AIOSEO:** If your site runs on WordPress (which I cover in Book 5), this free plug-in does the job from your dashboard. And better still, it lets you fix or redirect a broken link on the spot, without hunting through your pages by hand. (You'll need a free AIOSEO account to switch it on.)

» **Screaming Frog SEO Spider (`screamingfrog.co.uk`):** For the hands-on type who wants more control, this is a small program you install on your computer. It's free for up to 500 pages (far more than most small sites have) and it digs deeper than the browser-based tools.

None of these checks takes more than a few seconds. The whole job is triage: scan, decide, move on.

# Regular Content Audits

Freshening individual pages, which I describe earlier in this chapter, is like tidying your desk as you go. A *content audit* is the once-a-year deep clean, where you pull everything out, look at it honestly, and decide what deserves to stay. For a small site, it's an afternoon's work. For anyone who's inherited a sprawling site somebody else built, it's the single most useful thing you can do to get a handle on what you have.

## Start with an inventory

You can't evaluate what you can't see, so step one is making a list of every piece of content on your site, including every page and every post, gathered into one big spreadsheet. For each one, jot down a few facts:

» **The title and URL,** so you know what it is and where it lives.

» **When it was last updated,** which flags the ancient stuff at a glance.

» **How much traffic it gets,** pulled from your analytics (Book 9, Chapter 1).

» **Its purpose,** meaning what job is this page supposed to do.

Tools can generate the raw list for you (your sitemap is a decent starting point, and audit plug-ins can export one automatically), but the thinking part is yours.

TIP

A plain spreadsheet is the perfect content-audit tool. One row per page, a column for your most important metric (such as revenue, conversions, or traffic), and a keep/update/merge/ retire column you fill in as you go. Sort by your metric of choice and the decisions get a lot easier.

## Apply the ROT test

With your inventory in front of you, judge each item against a handy filter the pros call *ROT*, short for redundant, outdated, or trivial:

- **Redundant:** Does this duplicate another page? You might have three near-identical posts on the same topic, quietly competing with one another.
- **Outdated:** Is the information simply wrong now, with no easy fix?
- **Trivial:** Was this ever genuinely useful? For example, that "We're testing our shiny new blog!" post from launch week can go.

Anything that trips one of those wires is a candidate for action.

## Keep, update, merge, or retire

Every page then earns one of four fates:

- **Keep:** The page is pulling its weight, meaning it has good traffic, it's accurate, and doing its job. Leave it alone.
- **Update:** The page has good bones, but stale details. Give it the refresh I describe earlier in this chapter.
- **Merge:** Three thin posts on one topic? Combine them into a single strong page and redirect the old URLs to it (Book 7, Chapter 4 shows you how to redirect safely).
- **Retire:** No traffic, no purpose, no future. Delete it and redirect its URL somewhere sensible so you don't create a broken link on your way out.

Here's the part that feels wrong but isn't: deleting content can make your site better. A lean site where every page is relevant beats a bloated one padded with forgettable filler. The site becomes easier for visitors to navigate and easier for search engines to understand. Pruning isn't failure. It's gardening.

# Updating Plug-Ins, Themes, and Core Software

Every plug-in, theme, and piece of core software on your site gets updated regularly by the people who make it. These updates patch security holes, fix bugs, and add features, which is why keeping everything updated is the single most important security habit there is, as I stress in Book 9, Chapter 4. Skipping updates is a major way that sites get hacked.

So, updating is non-negotiable. Why, then, does everybody secretly dread it?

Because updates can also break things. A theme update might not play nicely with a plug-in you depend on. A big version change might rearrange settings you'd carefully configured. Every seasoned site owner has a story about the quick update that took a page down. The real maintenance skill is not whether to update (you must) but how to update without holding your breath.

## The safe update routine

The secret to safely updating your site is to never test an update on your live site for the first time. Here's a routine that keeps you out of trouble:

1. **Back up first.**

   Always. If an update goes sideways, your backup is the undo button (Book 9, Chapter 4).

2. **Update on staging, not live.**

   A *staging site* is a private copy of your site where you can try changes safely. I show you how to set one up in Book 10, Chapter 1. Apply the updates there first.

3. **Click around.**

   On the staging copy, load your key pages, submit your contact form, place a test order, do whatever your site does. If something broke, you'll find it here, where no customer can see it.

4. **Then update live.**

   Once staging looks good, apply the same updates to your real site with confidence.

Yes, that's more steps than clicking Update All and hoping for the best. But it's the difference between a calm five-minute chore and a frantic afternoon spent trying to remember what your homepage used to look like.

## What to automate, and what to babysit

Not every update needs the full ceremony. Software makers split their updates into minor ones (small fixes, very unlikely to break anything) and major ones (big changes, more likely to surprise you). A sensible policy:

- **Automate minor updates and security patches.** These are low-risk and time-sensitive, so you want them applied fast, and most systems can do it for you automatically.
- **Do major updates by hand, through the staging routine.** This is where the risk lives, so that's where you slow down.

## Watch for abandoned software

A plug-in that never updates isn't necessarily stable and finished; it might be *abandoned*, meaning its developer walked away and stopped patching security holes. So, while you're doing your monthly updates, glance at the date that each plug-in was last updated. If something hasn't been touched in a year or two, treat it as a liability and start shopping for a maintained alternative. (I explain why abandoned software is such a security risk in Book 9, Chapter 4; here it's simply one more thing to eyeball while you update.)

## When an update breaks something anyway

Even with staging, a live update misbehaves once in a while. Don't panic. You have two safety nets. The first is your backup: restore it and you're back to where you started. The second, for plug-ins and themes, is a simple rollback, where you deactivate the thing you just updated; if that fixes the problem, you've found your culprit. Reinstall the previous version (a rollback plug-in turns this into a one-click job) and wait for the developer to ship a fix. Either way, the site's back to normal in minutes, and nobody out in the world is any the wiser.

# Index

## Numerics



## A

# B

# D

# E

# F

# G

# H

# I

# J

# K

## L

# M

# N



# O

# P

# Q



# R

# S

# T

# U



# V

# W

# X



# Y



# Z

# About the Author

*Information appears to stew out of me naturally, like the precious ottar of roses out of the otter. —Mark Twain*

**Paul McFedries** is a technical writer who spends his days writing books just like the one you're holding in your hands. In fact, Paul has written more than 110 such books, which have sold over four million copies worldwide. Paul invites everyone to drop by his personal website at `paulmcfedries.com`.

# Dedication

To Karen, my lobster

# Author's Acknowledgments

Each time I complete a book, the publisher sends me a heavy box filled with a few so-called author copies. Opening that box, lifting out a book, feeling the satisfying weight of something that has up to now been weightlessly digital, and seeing my name printed on the cover, well, it's a genuinely fine feeling, let me tell you. That's pretty cool, but you know what's *really* cool? That I've done that over a hundred times in my writing career and seeing my name on the cover *never* gets old.

But just because mine is the only name you see on the cover, it doesn't mean this book was a one-man show. Far from it. Sure, I did write this book's text and take its screenshots, but those represent only a part of what constitutes a book. The rest of it is brought to you by the dedication and professionalism of Wiley's editing, graphics, and production teams, who toiled long and hard to turn my text and images into an actual book.

I offer my heartfelt thanks to everyone at Wiley who made this book possible, but I'd like to extend some special thank-you's to the folks I worked with directly: executive editor Steve Hayes, associate editor Alicia Sparrow, project editor and copy editor Susan Pink, and technical editor Guy Hart-Davis.

## Publisher's Acknowledgments

**Associate Editor:** Alicia Sparrow
**Managing Editor:** Ajith Kumar
**Project and Copy Editor:** Susan Pink
**Production Editor:** Magesh Elangovan
**Technical Editor:** Guy Hart-Davis
**Cover Image:** undrey/stock.adobe.com